Listen to This

SECOND EDITION

MARK EVAN BONDS

Department of Music
University of North Carolina at Chapel Hill

with contributions by Jocelyn Neal (popular music) and Joseph Kaminski and N. Scott Robinson (world music)

Prentice Hall

Boston   Columbus   Indianapolis   New York   San Francisco
Upper Saddle River   Amsterdam   Cape Town   Dubai   London   Madrid
Milan   Munich   Paris   Montréal   Toronto   Delhi   Mexico City
Saõ Paulo   Sydney   Hong Kong   Seoul   Singapore   Taipei   Tokyo

President, SSA: Yolanda de Rooy
Editorial Director: Craig Campanella
Editor-in-Chief: Sarah Touborg
Executive Editor: Richard Carlin
Editorial Assistant: Tricia Murphy
Executive Marketing Manager: Brandy Dawson
Senior Marketing Manager: Kate Mitchell
Marketing Assistant: Craig Deming
Director of Development: Rochelle Diogenes
Development Assistant: Pauline Kitele
Development Editor, MyMusicLab: Teresa Nemeth
Senior Managing Editor: Ann Marie McCarthy
Assistant Managing Editor: Melissa Feimer
Production Liaison: Joe Scordato

Full-Service Management: GEX Publishing Services
Photo Researcher: Nancy Tobin
**Senior Manufacturing and Operations Manager
    for Arts & Sciences:** Nick Sklitsis
Senior Operations Supervisor: Brian Mackey
Cover Photo: © Trinity Mirror/Mirrorpix/Alamy
Cover Design: Laura Gardner
Interior Design: Laura Gardner
Senior Digital Media Editor: David Alick
Media Project Manager: Rich Barnes
Image Permissions Coordinator: Beth Brenzel
Composition: GEX Publishing Services
Printer/Binder: Quebecor World Color
Cover Printer: Lehigh-Phoenix Color

Credits and acknowledgments borrowed from other sources and reproduced, with permission, in this textbook appear on appropriate page within text.

Library of Congress Cataloging-in-Publication Data

Bonds, Mark Evan.
  Listen to this / Mark Evan Bonds ; with contributions by Jocelyn Neal, Joseph Kaminski, and N. Scott Robinson. -- 2nd ed.
      p. cm.
  Includes bibliographical references and index.
  ISBN 978-0-205-77736-5 (pbk. : alk. paper) 1. Music appreciation. 2. Music--History and criticism. I. Neal, Jocelyn R., 1973- II. Kaminski, Joseph S. III. Robinson, N. Scott.
IV. Title.
  MT90.B63 2010
  780--dc22
                    2010033034

Prentice Hall
is an imprint of

www.pearsonhighered.com

10 9 8 7 6 5 4 3 2 1

Student Edition ISBN-10: 0-205-77736-8
Student Edition ISBN-13: 978-0-205-77736-5
Examination Copy ISBN-10: 0-205-79436-X
Examination Copy ISBN-13: 978-0-205-79436-2

To Bob

Table of Contents

Dear Reader,

This is a book that will change the way you listen to music—all kinds of music, from many different times and places, including what's already on your own personal playlist. No matter what the style or genre, all music is built on some combination of basic elements—such as melody, rhythm, harmony, texture, timbre, dynamics, and form—and if we listen for those elements we can better understand how a piece of music actually works. *Listen to This* will give you the tools needed to help you listen to the music, hear the elements, and ultimately expand your playlist.

I am very excited about the new features of *Listen to This* and MyMusicLab that will help you along the way. You now have the option of downloading the performances discussed in the text directly to your personal computer or MP3 player . . . literally expanding your playlist! And the new "Connect Your Playlist" feature makes listening a more active experience by encouraging you to apply what you've learned in each chapter to the music already on your personal playlist.

Finally, I have had the privilege to travel across the country and listen to faculty and students using *Listen to This*. This second edition reflects their input and advice, and I am grateful for the feedback and suggestions that have helped make *Listen to This* even better.

There's some great music in this book, from plainchant to Gospel, from Beethoven to Chuck Berry, and my hope is that you'll make connections here with the music you already know and love. Happy listening!

Evan Bonds

Mark Evan Bonds
Evan.Bonds@gmail.com

MARK EVAN BONDS is the Boshamer Distinguished Professor of Music at the University of North Carolina at Chapel Hill, where he has taught since 1992. He received his B.A. from Duke University and earned his Ph.D. at Harvard. He has written several books and numerous essays on music, including *Music as Thought: Listening to the Symphony in the Age of Beethoven* and *A History of Music in Western Culture,* now in its third edition. *Listen to This* reflects his experience and dedication to teaching music appreciation to undergraduates for almost twenty years.

Listen to the music. Hear the elements. Expand your playlist.

The first edition of *Listen to This* struck a chord with professors and students with its powerful message of listen to the music, hear the elements, and expand your playlist! Professors at over 160 institutions across the country selected *Listen to This* for their music appreciation students, and 70% decided to offer MyMusicLab to their students as the source for streaming audio and an interactive learning environment to improve listening skills.

What are instructors saying about *Listen to This* and MyMusicLab?

"The focus is on the music! The musical elements and historical understanding are an outgrowth of the music, rather than the music becoming examples of the elements and history."

—Janet Barnard, *Clovis Community College*

"Students expect rich Web support for their textbooks, and MyMusicLab is exquisite support, especially the guided listening feature."

—Dominic A. Aquila, *Schoolcraft College*

And what do the students think?

"MyMusicLab was essential to helping me make an A in my Music Appreciation Class. I would highly recommend this program to any and all professors and students."

—Collin College student

"I really liked how I could listen to the music that was being talked about and that I could review my test answers after I had taken a test."

—University of Utah student

"Having such a comprehensive collection of activities and practice material was beyond helpful. The many forms that the material was presented greatly facilitated learning."

—Western Washington University student

With *Listen to This*, second edition, we listened to you!

To prepare this second edition of *Listen to This,* we partnered with our current users—instructors *and* students—to hear what was working really well. Through focus groups, online surveys, and student class tests, your ideas helped shape and inform this new edition. Here is a list of the new, expanded, or improved features developed based on this market feedback:

More Historical Coverage

- **Enriched Print and Online Timelines:** Show composers in relation to each other and contemporary history.
- **Historical Context Feature:** Places the music in the context of the social history of each era (for samples, see pages 41, 271, and 408).
- **Composer Profile Sidebars:** Offer more than just birth/death dates by focusing on key moments in the composer's life and work (see pages 44, 124, and 283.)
- Over 500 composer biographies online at www.mymusiclab.com.
- **MyMusicLibrary:** Source documents for online reading or download are available on MyMusicLab.

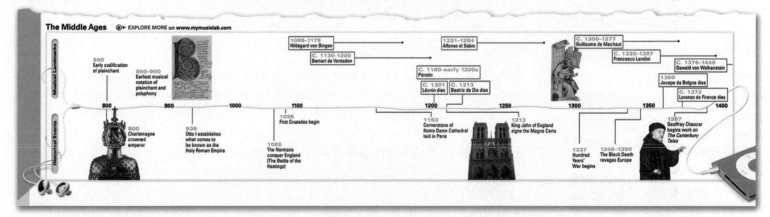

More Student Connections

- **Connect Your Playlist:** Encourages students to make their own connections to each of the book's chapters by giving an example of a work from a popular repertory that shares a basic element with the piece being studied (see pages 25, 177, and 368).
- **A Closer Look:** Annotated illustrations and maps that deepen student understanding of key historical context and music topics (see pages 52, 135, and 354).

More Repertory

- **Additions to repertory** were made based on your feedback, adding new works including Plainchant Alleluia "Caro mea" from the Mass for the Feast of Corpus Christi (web bonus chapter 1); Machaut's, "I can all too well compare my lady" (chapter 4); Billings', "Chester" (chapter 26); Bartók's, "Game of Pairs" from his Concerto for Orchestra (chapter 53), and an excerpt from Cage's *Indeterminacy* (chapter 55).

More Connections to MyMusicLab

The text is keyed to the dynamic resources on MyMusicLab, allowing instructors and students online access to additional information, music, videos, and interactive features.

LEARN MORE Expands on chapter content by providing additional information on composers, works, and musical culture, and points to self-assessment questions including needle-drop activities.

HEAR MORE Points to online streaming audio and downloadable audio, as well as links to external music services for Expand and Connect Your Playlist features.

SEE MORE Links to online video and documentaries including video clips of performance of classical, opera, and world music.

EXPLORE MORE Provides interactive versions of the print timelines, with expanded information, as well as interactive versions of the Closer Look features.

Save Time and Improve Results!

Designed to save instructors time and to improve student results, MyMusicLab is keyed specifically to the chapters of *Listen to This*. In addition, MyMusicLab's many features will encourage students to listen to the music, hear the elements, and expand their playlist. Here's how:

- The popular **Needle-Drop Activities** allow students to listen critically to key selections of each work and are now available in each area of the study plan: the pre-test, post-test and chapter exam.

- Enhanced **Automated Listening Guides** closely relate to the Listening Guides in the printed text and allow students to focus on the key listening elements.

- The **Closer Look** feature is an interactive walkthrough offering students an in-depth look at historical documents, musical instruments, and ensembles.

- A complete **e-Text**, enriched with streaming audio and dynamic multimedia links, gives students access to their book online and lets them highlight and add their own notes, just like the printed text.

- A **Gradebook** with automated grading of quizzes and assignments allows students to follow their own progress and instructors to monitor the work of the entire class.

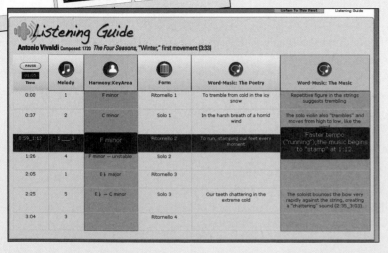

Listening Choices

Listen to This offers students quality recordings by major orchestras and performing artists. They are available as:

- **Downloadable Set:** Students can load all of the musical examples directly onto a portable music player or their own computers.

- **Five-CD Set**
  ISBN 10: 0205794386
  ISBN 13: 9780205794386

- **Free Streaming Audio** on MyMusicLab.

Whatever the format, the performances are all the same—facilitating student understanding!

Pearson Choices

Students can choose different formats of the text to meet their individual needs.

- **Books a la carte**
  ISBN 10: 0205021751 / ISBN 13: 9780205021758
  Give your students flexibility and savings with the new Books a la carte edition of *Listen to This*. This edition features exactly the same content as the traditional textbook in a convenient three-hole-punched, loose-leaf version—allowing students to take only what they need to class. The Books a la carte edition costs less than a used text—which helps students save about 35% over the cost of a used book.

- **CourseSmart** online textbooks are an exciting new choice for students looking to save money. As an alterative to purchasing the print textbook, students can subscribe to the same content online and save up to 60% off the suggested list price of the print text. With a CourseSmart eText, the student can search the text, make notes online, print out reading assignments that incorporate lecture notes, and bookmark important passages for later review. For more information, or to subscribe to CourseSmart, visit www.coursesmart.com

- **Pearson Custom Publishing:** *Listen to This* is available in a custom version specifically tailored to meet your needs. You may select the individual works that you want to study or add your own original material. The book's modular format and chapters focusing on a single work of music allows great flexibility to you to create your ideal music appreciation text. See your local publisher's representative for further information.

Resources for Teachers

- **Powerpoints:** Ready made PowerPoints® for your lectures can be accessed through your MyMusicLab instructor account. www.mymusiclab.com

- **Instructor's Manual & Test Bank:** This is an invaluable professional resource and reference for new and experienced faculty. Each chapter contains the following sections: Chapter Overview, Chapter Objectives, Key Terms, Lecture and Discussion Topics, Resources, and Writing Assignments and Projects. The test bank includes multiple choice, true/false, short answer, and essay questions, and now needle-drop questions. Available for download on www.mymusiclab.com.

- **MyTest:** This flexible, online test-generating software includes all questions found in the Test Item File. Instructors can quickly and easily create customized tests with MyTest. http://www.pearsonmytest.com

- **Clicker Response Questions:** Get instant, class-wide responses to beautifully illustrated chapter-specific questions during a lecture to gauge students' comprehension—and keep them engaged. Available for download from the instructor support section at www.mymusiclab.com.

Acknowledgments

From the very start, this book has been a collaborative effort. I am particularly grateful to my co-contributors, Jocelyn Neal, University of North Carolina at Chapel Hill; Joe Kaminski, Queens College; and Scott Robinson, Towson University, for their outstanding work on chapters dealing with popular music and non-Western music. Teresa Nemeth, my original development editor, helped improve the entire text at every stage of the process. For the second edition, several scholars assisted in updating and revising these sections. A special thank you to Nancy Guy at the University of California, San Diego, for her close reading and suggestions for improving web bonus chapter 3 on Beijing Opera. At Pearson-Prentice Hall, I am grateful to Richard Carlin, executive editor, and Christopher Johnson, my original editor; Sarah Touborg, editor-in-chief for the arts; Rochelle Diogenes, editor-in-chief of development; Ann Marie McCarthy, senior managing editor, art and music; Melissa Feimer, assistant managing editor; Joe Scordato, project manager; Laura Gardner, art director for design development services; Brandy Dawson, director of marketing; Kate Mitchell, executive marketing manager; Tricia Murphy, editorial assistant; and Kelly Morrison, senior project manager, GEX Publishing Services. For their work on MyMusicLab, thanks to David Alick, senior digital media editor, and Rich Barnes, media project manager. For his work coordinating the Instructor's Manual, IM/Test Bank, and Powerpoint slides, thanks to Dave Nitti, project manager. On the permissions front, Francelle Carapetyan (Image Research Editorial Services), Nancy Tobin, and Tom Laskey (Sony) made the extraordinary routine.

I wish also to thank the Supplement Authors: Patricia Cox, Harding University, for writing the Instructor's Manual; Karen McCall Dale, Cleveland State Community College, for the MyTest Software; Nancy Hadsell, Texas Women's University, for authoring the PowerPoint slides; and Linda Fergusson, Chair, Music Department, Valparaiso University (Indiana), for creating the Clicker Response System PowerPoint Slides.

For their assistance creating and authoring MyMusicLab, I wish to thank the following people: Anthony Paul De Ritis, PhD, Chair, Music Department, Northeastern University; Candace Bailey, North Carolina Central University; Dan Brown; Dr. Vicki Curry, James Madison University; Maureen Ton, Website Maintenance, Music Department, Northeastern University; Matt Baumer, Indiana University of Pennsylvania; Mathew E. E. Rippere, Westfield State College; Michael Condouris, Amber Digital LLC; Suzanne Stanton; Cherrie Liewellyn, Yosemite Community College; Douglas Puchowski; Ruth Spencer, CCNY/CUNY; Nan Childress-Orchard, Caldwell College; Ross Hagen, University of Colorado, Boulder; Alan Theisen; and Richard Kassel.

I am also grateful to students in my Music 141 and 142 classes at the University of North Carolina at Chapel Hill, who "test-drove" earlier versions of a number of chapters. Their feedback was invaluable. Thanks, too, to Alicia Levin, who kindly recorded several piano examples for the "Elements of Music" section of the book, and to Paul Cole, who contributed his expert skills as a recording engineer.

Developing *Listen to This, Second Edition*

The first and second editions of *Listen to This* are the result of an extensive development process involving the contributions of hundreds of instructors, as well as their students. Student reviews have sharpened the clarity of the writing style and the value of in-text learning tools, examples, and assessment features. We are grateful to all who have provided feedback on the manuscript, design, and resource package, including the following:

Alabama

Katrina Phillips, Alabama State University
Aleesa J. Naish, University of Alabama at Birmingham
Carolyn Sanders, University of Alabama in Huntsville
Alan Flowers, University of North Alabama

Nancy Kudlawiec, University of West Alabama

Arkansas

Cynthia Thompson, Carrell Harding University
Patricia Cox, Harding University
Cliff Ganus, Harding University

Steve Cooper, Northwest Arkansas Community College
Andrew Bishko, Ozarks Technical Community College
Betsy Wahl, Ozarks Technical Community College
Larisa Hart, Ozarks, Technical Community College
Milton Lites, Pulaski Technical College

Barry McVinney, Pulaski Technical College

Arizona
John T. Brobeck, University of Arizona
Patricia Cox, Harding University
Cliff Ganus, Harding University

California
Thomas W. Acord, California State University Eastbay, Hayward Campus
William Toutant, California State University, Northridge
Richard Scott Kravchak, California State University, Dominguez Hills
Timothy Howard, California State University, Northridge
Gigi Rabe, California State University, Northridge
Shulamit Hoffman, College of San Mateo
Gary McRoberts, Fullerton College
Bill Alves, Harvey Mudd College
Nedra Wheeler, Los Angeles Southwest College
David Chapman, Modesto Junior College
Gary Fair, Modesto Junior College
Laura Basini, Sacramento State
Maurice Poe, Sacramento State
Stephanie Robinson, San Diego City College
Scott Fogelsong, San Francisco Conservatory
Robert Busan, San Francisco State University
Ray Ashton, Sierra College
Cynthia McGregor, Southwestern College
Barbara Bennett, University of California, Riverside
Eric Wood, University of the Pacific
Scott Walton, Palomar College

Colorado
Tyson Alishie, Front Range Community College
Betsy Glesner, Metropolitan State College
Peter Schimpf, Metropolitan State University

Connecticut
Laura Nash, Fairfield University

District of Columbia
Emily Green, American University

Delaware
Paul K. Fessler, Wilmington University

Florida
Josh Martin, Chipola College
Matthew Shaftel, Florida State University
John Anderson, Polk Community College
Mary Macklem, University of Central Florida
Scott Warfield, University of Central Florida
Nick Curry, University of North Florida
William P. Hayden, University of South Florida
Zoe Lang, University of South Florida

Georgia
Robert L. Harris, Amstrong Atlantic State College
Sharyn Battersby, Clayton State University

Michelle Debruyn, Columbus State University
Greg McLean, Georgia Perimete College
Francisco Albo, Georgia State University
Marva Carter, Georgia State University
Gayle Melton, Gwinnett Technical College
Edward Eanes, Kennesaw State University
Tom Rule, Macon State
Andrew Kosciesza, Montgomery County Community College
Melvin Foster, Morehouse College
Robert Tanner, Morehouse College
Beth Farber, Southern Polytechnic State University
David Haas, University of Georgia
Linda C. Ferguson, Valparaiso University

Iowa
Jeanette Hinkeldey, Buena Vista University
Carol Ayres, Iowa Lakes Community College
Jonathan Sturm, Iowa State University
Elizabeth Aubrey, University of Iowa
Jonathan Chenoweth, University of Northern Iowa

Idaho
Eric Schneller, Idaho State University
Paul Moulton, The College of Idaho

Illinois
Chris Woods, Greenville College
Rudolf Zuiderveld, Illinois College
Norman Engstrom, Illinois Valley Community College
Nora Beck, Lewis & Clark Community College
Elinor Olin, National-Louis University
Rebecca Bennett, Northwestern University
Megan McFadden, Northwestern University
Peter Webster, Northwestern University
Michael Barta, Southern Illinois University
Tim Pitchford, Southern Illinois University
Meng Chun-Chi, Southern Illinois University, Carbondale
Jeanine Wagner, Southern Illinois University, Carbondale
Gail Fleming, Southwestern Illinois College
Ed Jacobs, Southwestern Illinois College
Joseph Jones, University of Illinois at Urbana-Champaign
Maria M. Chow, DePauw University

Indiana
Heather Platt, Ball State University
Linda Pohly, Ball State University
Cathy Ann Elias, DePaul University
Matthew Balensuela, DePauw University
Constance Cook Glen, Indiana University
Carole Miklos, Indiana University Northwest
Todd Guy, Indiana Wesleyan University
Valerie Meidinger, Marian College
Sr. Mary Karita Ivancic, Notre Dame College
Patricia Hales, Purdue University Calumet
William Briegel, Indiana Tech

Kansas
Steven Maxwell, Kansas State University
Bradford Blackburn, Truman State University

Kentucky
Dr. Pamela Hopton-Jones, Applachian State University
John Day, Elizabethtown Community College
Diane Earle, Kentucky Wesleyan College
Robert Reynolds, Lindsey Wilson College
Tom Jordan, Northern Kentucky University
Seow-Chin Ong, University of Louisville

Louisiana
La Wanda J. Blakeney, Louisiana State University
David Johansen, Southeastern Louisiana University
Gene Ditch, St. Charles Community College
John Walker, St. Charles Community College
Jonathan Kulp, University of Louisiana at Lafayette

Massachusetts
Janice Salvucci, Curry College
Marjorie Ness, Fitchburg State College
Vincent Cee, University of Massachusetts, Amherst
Miriam Jenkins, University of Massachusetts, Amherst
Lance Lehmberg, University of Massachusetts, Amherst
David Patterson, University of Massachusetts, Boston
Mary Brown-Bonacci, Westfield State College
Sonya Lawson, Westfield State College
Matt Rippere, Westfield State College

Maine
Dennis Harrington, Thomas College

Michigan
Keith Clifton, Central Michigan University
Margaret Skidmore, Eastern Michigan University
Richard Scott Cohen, Ferris State University
Marlen Vavrikova, Grand Valley State University
Christina Hornbach, Hope College
Beth May, Hope College
Tom Donahue, Muskegon Community College
Linda Christensen, Wayne State University

Minnesota
Gerard Aloisio, Minnesota State University

Mississippi
Jeremy Owens, Blue Mountain College
Teri Herron, Delta State University
Darcie Bishop, Jackson State University
Sandra Cox, Northwest Mississippi Community College

Missouri
Kierstin Bible, Crowder College
Robert Ensor, Crowder College
Leigh Graf, Mineral Area College
Tom Schneideer, Missouri Western State University
Karen Werner, Moberly Area Community College
Pamela Shannon, Northwest Missouri Community College
James Sifferman, Southeast Missouri State University

Montana
Fern Glass, University of Montana
James Randall, University of Montana
Jeri Bonnin, University of Montana, Western

Nebraska
Ting-Lan Chen, University of Nebraska at Kearney
Melissa Derechailo, Wayne State College

New Hampshire
Theresa Arsenault, Nashua Community College

New Jersey
Kim Hunter, Burlington Community College
James Ieraci, Burlington Community College
Michael Billingsley, Camden County Community College
Allen Cohen, Fairleigh Dickinson University
Karen Goodman, Montclair State University
James Stepleton, Stevens Institute of Technology
Peter Coll, William Paterson University
Darren Gage, William Paterson University

New York
Anne Swartz, Baruch College of the City University of New York
Andrew Tomasello, Baruch College of the City University of New York
Elizabeth Wollman, Baruch College of the City University of New York
Giuseppe Gerbino, Columbia University
Laura Silverberg, Columbia University
Carmelo Comberieti, Manhattanville College
Laura Peterson, St. Bonaventure University
Brian Campbell, St. John's University
Max Lifchitz, State University of New York at Albany

North Carolina
Stephanie Lawrence-White, Bennett College for Women
Ran Whitley, Campbell University
Jocelyn Nelson, East Carolina University
Lori Wacker, East Carolina University
Glendora Powell, Louisburg College
Michael Day, North Carolina A&T State
Candace Bailey, North Carolina Central University
Alison Arnold, North Carolina State University
Katharine Boyes, Saint Augustine's College
Anne Harley, University of North Carolina, Charlotte
James A. Grymes, University of North Carolina, Charlotte
Soo Goh, University of North Carolina, Pembroke
Emily Orr, University of North Carolina, Pembroke
Barry Salwen, University of North Carolina, Wilmington
Donna Gwyn Wiggins, Winston-Salem State University

North Dakota
Dorothy Keyser, University of North Dakota

Ohio
Karen McCall Dale, Cleveland State Community College
Will Benson, Cleveland State University
Ron Emoff, Ohio State University at Newark

Oklahoma
Mary Susan Whaley, Northeastern Oklahoma A&M College
Kristen Todd, Oklahoma Baptist University
Celeste Johnson, Oklahoma State University

Oregon
Hugh Foley, Rogers State University
Judy Cepetto Hedberg, Portland Community College
Reeves Shulstad, Salem College

Pennsylvania
Mark Jelinek, Bloomsburg University
Ann Stokes, Bloomsburg University
Barry Long, Bucknell University
Arlene Caney, Community College of Philadelphia
Bruce Kaminsky, Drexel University
Lynn Riley, Drexel University
Thomas Kittinger, Harrisburg Area Community College
Victor Vallo Jr., Immaculata University
Dr. Matthew Baumer, Indiana University of Pennsylvania
Ronald Horner, Indiana University of Pennsylvania
R. Todd Rober, Kutztown University of Pennsylvania
Mahlon Grass, Lock Haven University
Glen Hosterman, Lock Haven University
Dr. Daniel M. Heslink, Millersville University
Stephen Hopkins, Penn State University
John Packard, Penn State University
Charles Youman, Penn State University
Fred Dade, Shippensburg University
Margaret Lucia, Shippensburg University

South Carolina
Audrey L. Barksdale, Morris College
Fabio Parrini, North Greenville University

South Dakota
Christopher Hahn, Black Hills State University

Tennessee
Stephen Clark, Austin Peay State University
Francis Massinon, Austin Peay State University
Gail Robinson Oturu, Austin Peay State University
Ann L. Silverburg, Austin Peay State University
Ken Cardillo, Chattanooga State University
Amanda Hyberger, Chattanooga State University
Mark Lee, Columbia State Community College
David Bubsey, East Tennessee State University
Lee Weimer, Lambuth University
Eric Fisher, Middle Tennessee State University
Steve Shearon, Middle Tennessee State University
Laura Feo-Fernandez, University of Memphis
Julie Hill, University of Tennessee at Martin

Texas
Kimberly Harris, Collin College
Kurt Gilman, Lamar University
Charlotte Mueller, Lee College
Charles Carson, Lone Star College-Montgomery

Mandy Morrison, McLennan Community College
Norval Crews, Midwestern State University
Gary Lewis, Midwestern State University
Beth May, Northwest Vista College
Ryan Gilchrist, Sam Houston State University
Sheryl Murphy-Manley, Sam Houston State University
Karen Marston, San Jacinto College Central
Cecilia Smith, South Texas College
James Weaver, Stephen F. Austin State University
Vicky Johnson, Tarleton State University
Marianne Henry, Texas A&M University
Prudence McDaniel, Texas A&M University
Michael Berry, Texas Tech University
Eric Fried, Texas Tech University
Lynn Lamkin, University of Houston
Josef Butts, University of Texas
Ronald Noble, University of Texas at San Antonio
Drew Stephen, University of Texas at San Antonio
James Syler, University of Texas at San Antonio
Dr. Jeffrey Emge, University of Texas at Tyler
Melissa Colgin-Abeln, University of Texas, El Paso

Utah
Luke Howard, Brigham Young University
Thomas Priest, Webster State University

Virginia
Gary Evans, Ferrum College
Mary Kay Adams, James Madison University
Vicki Curry, James Madison University
Jonathan Gibson, James Madison University
Brenda Witmer, James Madison University
Lise Keiter-Brotzman, Mary Baldwin College
Louise Billaud, New River Community College
Wendy Matthews, Northern Virginia Community College
Robert C. Ford, Tidewater Community College
John Husser, Virginia Tech

Virgin Islands
Vanessa Cornett-Murtada, University of St. Thomas

Washington
Keith Ward, University of Puget Sound
Bertil van Boer, Western Washington University
Laura Stambaugh, Western Washington University

West Virginia
Lloyd Bone, Glenville State College

Wyoming
Katrina Zook, University of Wyoming

Listen to This

SECOND EDITION

THE ELEMENTS OF MUSIC: A Brief Introduction

No matter what the period or style, all music grows out of some combination of these basic elements:

Melody

Melody: The Tune. Melody is a single line of notes heard in succession as a coherent unit. A melody has shape, moving up or down in ways that capture and hold our attention over a span of time. A melody is like a story: it has a beginning, a middle, and an end.

Rhythm

Rhythm: The Time. Rhythm is the ordering of music through time. Not all music has a melody, but all music has rhythm. A drum solo, for example, makes its effect primarily through rhythm. Rhythm can operate at many levels, from a repetitive, underlying pulse or beat to rapidly changing patterns of longer and shorter sounds.

Harmony

Harmony: Supporting the Melody. Harmony is the sound created by multiple voices playing or singing together. Harmony enriches the melody by creating a fuller sound than can be produced by a single voice.

Texture

Texture: Thick and Thin. Texture is based on the number and general relationship of musical lines or voices. Every work of music has a texture from thick (many voices) to thin (a single voice). Sometimes one line or voice is more important; at other times, all the lines or voices are of equal importance.

Timbre

Timbre: The Color of Music. Timbre is the character of a sound. The same melody sounds very different when performed by a violin, a clarinet, a guitar, or a human voice. These sources can all produce the same pitch, but what makes the same melody sound different is the timbre of each one.

Dynamics

Dynamics: Loud to Soft. The same music can be performed at many degrees of volume, from very soft to very loud. Dynamics determine the volume of a given work or passage in a work of music.

Form

Form: The Architecture of Music. A single melody is usually too short to constitute a complete work of music. Typically, a melody is repeated, varied, or contrasted with a different melody. The way in which all these subunits are put together—the structure of the whole—is musical form. Form is based on repetition (**A A**), variation (**A A'**), contrast (**A B**), or some combination of these three possibilities.

Word-Music Relationships

Word-Music Relationships: How Words Shape What We Hear. If there is a text to be sung, we must consider the relationship of the words to the music. How does the music capture the meaning and spirit of its text? And even if there is not a text to be sung, many works have titles that suggest how we might hear them. Titles like *Winter*, *Rodeo*, and *The Rite of Spring* strongly influence the way in which we hear these works. Some composers have even written detailed descriptions of what a particular work is about in what we call "program music."

Genre

Genre: Great Expectations. Just as literature has its genres or categories—poems, novels, dramas, and so on—so too does music have its genres, such as symphony, opera, waltz, or cantata. A genre shapes our expectations of what we are likely to experience. Musical genres are based in part on who is playing. A symphony, for example, is normally for an orchestra of instrumentalists (though there are exceptions), while an opera is for an ensemble of singers and an orchestra. Musical genres are also based on the social function of a given work. A waltz is a dance with a certain pattern of steps that demands a certain metrical pattern in the music, while a cantata is a sacred work meant to be performed in a church.

In any given piece of music these elements all work together quite closely. By isolating and examining the nature and function of each separately, we can better appreciate their specific contributions to the music we hear.

We can best hear how each of these elements works by considering how each of them can change the nature of a single, well-known piece of music. We all know "The Star-Spangled Banner" from having heard it countless times, but how often have we actually *listened* to it? We can hear and recognize the tune easily enough, but listening demands that we focus on its various elements and the ways they work together. Let's look at each of the basic elements of music to see how it functions in this song.

Melody

Melody is a single line of notes heard in succession as a coherent unit. A **note** is the smallest unit of music, the building block out of which larger structures are created. So what makes the notes of a melody hang together? How is the melody of "The Star-Spangled Banner" organized? What are its individual units, and how do we know it's over, other than by having heard it so often? Think about how we sing this melody and where we draw a breath:

> O, say can you see (breath) by the dawn's early light (breath)
> What so proudly we hailed (breath) at the twilight's last gleaming? (breath)

These breaths correspond to the ends of **phrases** in both the poetry and the music. The first line of the text breaks down into two phrases (O, say can you see / by the dawn's early light), which together make a larger phrase (the entire line). This larger phrase constitutes a complete unit of thought, which happens to be a question. But do we feel a sense of closure when we sing "dawn's early light"? Not really. The phrase sounds as if it hasn't quite finished yet, which indeed it has not. Only when we get to the end of the second line ("twilight's last gleaming") do we feel anything approaching a sense of musical completeness. The second line is organized on the same principle as the first (two subphrases), but by the time we sing "at the twilight's last gleaming," we feel as if we have reached a goal of sorts. This is the end of a still larger phrase, a complete musical statement that covers the first two lines of text. When we hear a point of arrival like this, we are hearing what is called a **cadence**. A cadence is like a period in a sentence: it signals the end of a unit that can stand on its own. We sense a point of resolution, of closure.

LEARN MORE on
www.mymusiclab.com
Melody tutorial

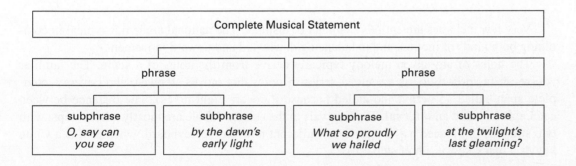

The melody of "The Star-Spangled Banner" is typical of the way melodies in general are constructed: smaller units (subphrases) combine into larger units (phrases), which in turn combine into still larger units (complete statements), which end with a cadence. These complete statements—musical sentences, in effect—combine to create an entire musical work. Sometimes it is helpful to listen to the structure of the smallest units; at other times, it is helpful to listen to the medium- and large-scale units. In the end, we can listen to how all these units operate together to form a complete and satisfying whole.

Another important component of melody is the nature of the **melodic motion**. Do the notes move smoothly in stepwise fashion (as in "land of the free")? Or do they make big leaps (as in "O, say can you see")? Smooth, stepwise motion with notes very close to each other is called **conjunct motion**; motion by leaps, especially large leaps, is called **disjunct motion**. Most melodies, including "The Star-Spangled Banner," consist of a combination of both kinds of motion. "The Star-Spangled Banner" alternates between the two, opening with disjunct motion ("O, say can you see by") followed by a brief passage of conjunct motion ("by the dawn's"), followed in turn by a large leap downward (between "dawn's" and "early"), followed by more conjunct motion. Graphically, this variety of motion can be represented in such a way that even if you cannot read music, you can see the relationship between the downward or upward movement of the notes and the distances between them.

((•● HEAR MORE on
www.mymusiclab.com
CD I • Track 1/Download
Track 1

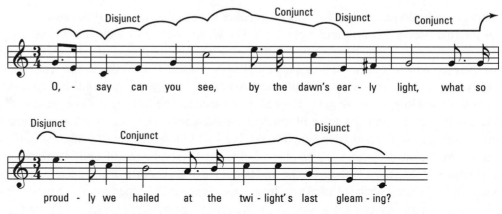

The opening of "The Star-Spangled Banner" with a line indicating steps and leaps

Very few melodies are entirely conjunct or disjunct. The national anthem is typical in combining both kinds of motion, and in balancing downward and upward movement.

The notes of any given melody typically derive from the notes of a **scale**. The familiar "do-re-mi-fa-so-la-ti-do" is a scale, a series of notes that moves stepwise and covers a complete span called an **octave** (so-called because it covers eight notes). The distance between each note is called an **interval**. The intervals in the standard scale are mostly whole steps, with two strategically placed half steps. Every adjacent note on the keyboard, whether it is a white key or a black key, is a half step apart.

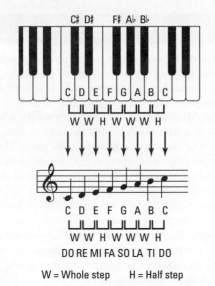

W = Whole step   H = Half step

A scale by itself is not particularly interesting as a melody, but a scale provides the notes—the essential building blocks—of a melody.

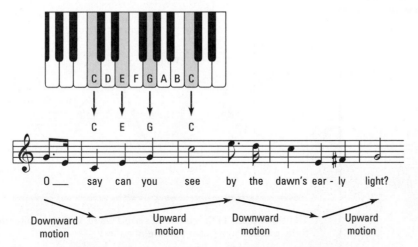

The opening of "The Star-Spangled Banner" in the key of C major

The upward or downward movement of notes is conveyed graphically in music notation. A melody that moves downward also moves downward on the staff (the system of parallel horizontal lines). Again, even if you cannot read music, you can see that higher notes appear higher on the staff than lower notes. This kind of visual aid can help reinforce what we hear.

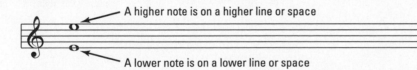

PERFORMANCE The Science of Melody

What makes the notes in a melody move up or down and sound different from one another? What makes some parts of a melody louder than others? **Acoustics** is the science of sound—how it is produced, transmitted, and perceived—and a few basic principles of acoustics help explain the most basic elements of melody.

From a technical point of view, sound is vibrating air. Musicians can cause air to vibrate in three basic ways:

- By striking a surface (drums, cymbals, xylophones, and any other percussion instrument)
- By plucking or stroking a taut string (guitar, banjo, violin, and any other plucked or bowed instrument)
- By blowing air (flute, clarinet, trumpet, and any other wind instrument, including the human voice)

The patterns of vibration set in motion by these actions determine the pitch and volume of the sound. **Pitch** is the position of a sound on a range from very low (the bass register) to very high (the soprano register). Through an oscilloscope, we can "see" the shape of the **sound wave** of any sustained pitch. In its simplest form, the sound wave of a single pitch looks like this:

The distance between the peak of each wave is known as the **wavelength**, and the number of wavelengths in one second—the **frequency**—determines the pitch of the sound. The higher the frequency, the higher the pitch. The pitch to which most North American orchestras tune their instruments is an "A" played at a frequency of 440 cycles per second (cps, also known as hertz or Hz, named after Gustav Hertz, the nineteenth-century German physicist who studied sound waves). The lowest note on the standard modern piano is also an "A," but at a frequency of only 27.5 cps; the highest note, a "C," vibrates at 4,186 cps. The normal human ear can perceive frequencies in a range from approximately 20 cps (extremely low) to 20,000 cps (extremely high). Some animals have a far wider range of hearing: dogs, for example, can respond to frequencies as high as 50,000 cps, even though the sound of the dog whistle producing this frequency is inaudible to us.

What makes sounds loud or soft? **Dynamics**—the volume of sound—is determined by the size of each wave, its **amplitude**. The same pitch—440 cps—at softer volume would look like this:

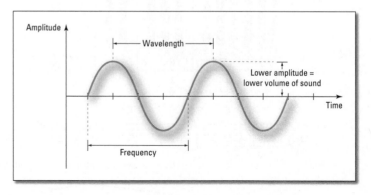

The same pitch as the previous sound wave, with a smaller amplitude, producing a lower volume of sound

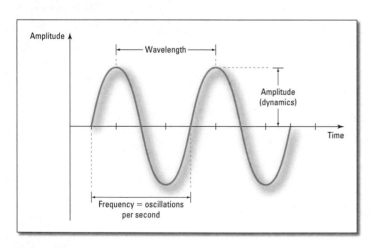

The structure of a sound wave

The frequency—the distance between the peaks of each wave—is the same, but the amplitude is smaller; thus the same pitch sounds softer. The wavelengths in a louder version of this same pitch would have the same frequency, but the amplitude would be higher.

Scales can begin and end on any pair of notes. The diagrams on page 4 show a scale that begins and ends on the note "C," and a melody that centers on this same note (on "O, *say* can you *see*"). Because C is the central note of the scale on which this melody is based, we would say that this melody is in the **key** of C. But the same melody can be played in any key. Thus "The Star-Spangled Banner" can also be performed in the key of D, or the key of A-flat, or any other key.

In the standard system in use in Western music since about 1600, there are 12 keys, one on each of the 12 half steps in any octave. An octave is an interval between two notes with the same name (a lower "C" to a higher "C," or a lower "do" to a higher "do": see the earlier scale diagram). In notation, the sharp sign (♯) indicates that a note is raised a half step, while a flat sign (♭) indicates that a note is lowered a half step. For each of these keys, whether it is E-flat or F-sharp or A, there are two modes, major and minor. The **major mode** corresponds to the scale produced by singing "do-re-mi-fa-so-la-ti-do." Melodies using these notes tend to sound brighter and somehow happier. "The Star-Spangled Banner" is in the major mode. Because it seeks to convey a mood of optimism and joy, it uses a melody derived from a major-mode scale.

The **minor mode**, by contrast, strikes most listeners as darker, more somber, and less optimistic. Most of the notes in the minor mode are also in the major. But two of the seven notes—the third ("mi") and sixth ("la")—are slightly lower, and this creates a very different kind of sound. Listen to what "The Star-Spangled Banner" would sound like in the minor mode; all the notes are the same as in the original except for "mi" and "la."

Very few national anthems begin and end in the minor mode (Israel's *Hatikva*—"The Hope"—is one notable exception). Many national anthems (and many melodies of all kinds), however, mix minor-mode phrases into the middle of melodies that begin and end in major. This creates a sense of contrasting moods that can be very effective in creating a sense of triumph over adversity, for the minor mode is especially well-suited for settings of texts that express grief or anguish or (as in the case of Israel's *Hatikva*) longing. (In fact, "mode" and "mood" come from the same root word in Latin.)

((•● **HEAR MORE** on
www.mymusiclab.com
CD I • Track 5/Download
Track 5

Rhythm

Rhythm is the ordering of music through time. The most basic framework of this temporal ordering is **meter**. In music, as in poetry, meter is an underlying pattern of beats that maintains itself consistently throughout a work. If we slowly read aloud the first line of "The Star-Spangled Banner," we can hear that it falls into a regular pattern of three-beat units: LONG-short-short, LONG-short-short, etc., with the long syllables accented (emphasized) and the short ones unaccented (´ = long; ˘ = short):

˘　　´　˘　˘　　´　˘　˘　　´　˘　˘　　´
O, | say can you | see, by the | dawn's early | light?

In poetry, this meter is known as *dactylic* (LONG-short-short). In music, this meter corresponds to what is known as **triple meter**: one accented (strong) beat followed by two unaccented (weak) beats. The rhythm of the music to "The Star-Spangled Banner" is thus organized within the framework of triple meter (**1**-2-3, **1**-2-3, **1**-2-3, etc.), following the meter of its poetry. (The

⚙ **LEARN MORE** on
www.mymusiclab.com
Rhythm tutorial

"O" at the very beginning of the text stands outside the first unit: both rhythmically and textually, its function is to get us started, without actually saying much of anything.)

3 | **1** 2 3 | **1** 2 3 | **1** 2 3 | **1**   2 3 | **1** 2 3 | **1** etc.
O, | *say* can you | *see* by the | *dawn's* early | *light* What so | *proud*-ly we | *hailed*…etc.

HEAR MORE on
www.mymusiclab.com
CD I • Track 6/Download
Track 6

In music, each of these rhythmic units is known as a **measure**. Ordinarily, the first note of each measure receives a relatively strong accent, which helps project the pattern of the meter, just as you would emphasize certain words ("say," "see," "dawn's," "light") if you were reading the text out loud without singing it.

But meter is only one aspect of rhythm. Not every note of "The Star-Spangled Banner" is simply accented or unaccented, strong or weak. Some notes are noticeably longer in duration than others ("say can you SEE," "the rockets' red GLARE"), while others are extremely brief (the word *the* in "and the rockets' red glare," for example).

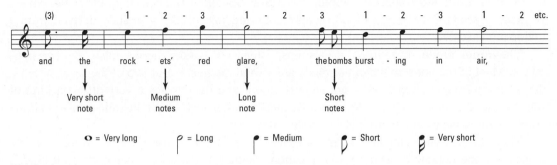

Rhythmic values

These longer and shorter notes function flexibly within the broader framework of the underlying meter. So long as the basic pattern of the rhythmic unit is maintained (**1**-2-3), the actual number and duration of the notes within each unit can vary considerably. A melody in which all the notes were exactly the same length would be quite monotonous. Here is what the beginning of "The Star-Spangled Banner" would sound like if all the notes were of equal value:

HEAR MORE on
www.mymusiclab.com
CD I • Track 7/Download
Track 7

The opening of "The Star-Spangled Banner," with notes in all the same rhythmic values

HEAR MORE on
www.mymusiclab.com
CD I • Track 8/Download
Track 8

The meter is still triple (**1**-2-3), but the individual notes have lost all rhythmic differentiation. What would "The Star-Spangled Banner" sound like in a different meter? An American composer named E. E. Bagley (1857–1922) actually worked the opening of the melody into a march he called *National Emblem*. Here, the music moves in **duple meter**, with only two beats to each measure (**1**-2 | **1**-2 | **1**-2 | etc.). This corresponds to the function of the music, to help soldiers or band members march in step (**Left**-right | **Left**-right | **Left**-right | etc.).

Notice how the pitches (the notes) are the same as the tune we know as "The Star-Spangled Banner." But the meter—the framework of the rhythm—is fundamentally different: LONG-short |

LONG-short instead of LONG-short-short | LONG-short-short. Could we march to the standard version of "The Star-Spangled Banner"? Not really, because it's in triple meter, and with two legs, it's much easier to march to duple meter.

Harmony

Harmony is the sound created by multiple notes played or sung simultaneously. Whether we realize it or not, we've all heard "The Star-Spangled Banner" performed in many different harmonizations. The melody stays the same, but the notes underneath the tune are different. The resulting harmony can change the character of the work, sometimes subtly, sometimes radically. There is no official version of the harmony of "The Star-Spangled Banner." (Indeed, there is not even an official version of the melody itself.)

If we think of music in terms of space, then melody can be said to function horizontally, harmony vertically. Just as melodies can outline selected notes of a scale through time, harmony presents notes drawn from a scale simultaneously, sounding together. When we hear three or more notes played at the same moment, we often speak of these as a **chord**. A melodic line can be accompanied by a series of chords that change as the melody progresses. A melody as rich as "The Star-Spangled Banner" would sound monotonous—and downright wrong—if it were harmonized with a single chord from beginning to end. The most common harmonization of the tune supports the melody with a variety of different chords:

E. E. Bagley's *National Emblem* sheet music
Courtesy Zach S. Henderson Library Special Collections, Georgia Southern University

HEAR MORE on
www.mymusiclab.com
CD I • Track 9/Download Track 9

LEARN MORE on
www.mymusiclab.com
Harmony tutorial

A harmonized version of "The Star-Spangled Banner," with the melody in the upper staff and the harmony in the lower staff, in red.

((• HEAR MORE on
www.mymusiclab.com
CD I • Track 10/Download
Track 10

((• HEAR MORE on
www.mymusiclab.com
CD I • Track 11/Download
Track 11

((• HEAR MORE on
www.mymusiclab.com
CD I • Track 12/Download
Track 12

We all know what a melody without harmony sounds like (just think of the early stages of contestants performing on *American Idol*). But what about harmony without melody? Here is one harmonization of "The Star-Spangled Banner" without the melody.

A single melody can always be harmonized in more than one way, and "The Star-Spangled Banner" is no exception. And some harmonizations are more unconventional than others. Consider, for example, this harmonization of the melody by the American composer Louis Moreau Gottschalk (see chapter 34), from a piece for piano entitled *Union*, written shortly after the beginning of the Civil War.

Even today, almost 150 years later, musicians are still coming up with new ways of harmonizing this same melody. South City Voices, an Atlanta-based vocal jazz ensemble, recently recorded their own version of the tune. The melody is the same as the one we hear all the time, but the harmonies are not.

Harmony works on a larger scale as well. If a melody is in the key of C major, its primary harmony also centers on C major, establishing this key at the beginning as a kind of home base and returning to it at the end to create a sense of closure. We call this primary key area the **tonic**. A piece that began in one key but ended in another would sound somehow open-ended and incomplete. "The Star-Spangled Banner" begins and ends in the same key, no matter what key is used in performance. If it begins in the key of C major, it ends in C major; if it begins in G major, it ends in G major; and so on.

HISTORICAL CONTEXT   Illegal Harmony?

The Russian-born composer Igor Stravinsky (1882–1971) immigrated to the United States in 1939 and became an American citizen in 1945. In honor of his new homeland, he made an arrangement of the national anthem that many contemporaries found offensive.

He performed the work in public only once, at the beginning of a concert by the Boston Symphony Orchestra on January 14, 1944. When word got out about the unusual harmonies in his arrangement, the police moved in and confiscated the music on the grounds of a Massachusetts state law forbidding "tampering" with state property. Threatened with arrest, Stravinsky withdrew the work from subsequent programs.

Jimi Hendrix's rendition of "The Star-Spangled Banner" on his electric guitar at the Woodstock Festival in August 1969 aroused controversy as well, but there was no suggestion that he be arrested for adding dissonances and feedback to the melody.

((• HEAR MORE on
www.mymusiclab.com
CD I • Track 13/Download Track 13
Igor Stravinsky's harmonization of
"The Star-Spangled Banner"

Igor Stravinsky leads an orchestra rehearsal at the Hollywood Bowl, ca. 1955. He lived in Los Angeles for most of the last three decades of his life. When word got out about his unconventional harmonization of "The Star-Spangled Banner" in Boston in 1944, Stravinsky was threatened with arrest.
Music Division, New York Public Library for the Performing Arts, Astor, Lenox, and Tilden Foundations

Texture

Texture is a function of the number and general relationship of musical lines to one another. Textures can range from thick (many voices) to thin (a single voice).

- When "The Star-Spangled Banner" is performed as a single melodic line, with no accompaniment at all, the texture is **monophonic** (*mono* = "single"; *phonic* = "sounding"). This may be a single soloist, or it may be a group of performers all playing or singing the same melody. When multiple performers are singing or playing a single melody together, we call this kind of monophonic texture **unison**.

- When the melody is performed with a supporting accompaniment, the texture is **homophonic** (*homo* = "same," as in "sounding at the same time"). This is the most common form of performance of this particular song whenever there is a soloist. The soloist sings the melody, while an instrumental ensemble or backup chorus provides musical support. The previous example showing the harmonized "The Star-Spangled Banner" is what homophonic texture can look like in musical notation.

- When the melody is performed against another line of equal importance, the texture is **polyphonic** (*poly* = "many"). In polyphonic texture, every line is, in effect, a melody. Think about the children's song "Row, Row, Row Your Boat," for example: every voice is singing the same music, so we can't say that one voice has the melody and others don't. And yet all the voices work together to create a satisfying sound.

Here is what the opening of "The Star-Spangled Banner" would look and sound like in a polyphonic texture:

Marvin Gaye sings "The Star-Spangled Banner." The texture is decidedly homophonic: the focus is entirely on the melody, while the accompaniment (a drum set) stays very much in the background.

HEAR MORE on
www.mymusiclab.com
CD I • Track 14/Download
Track 14

HEAR MORE on
www.mymusiclab.com
CD I • Track 15/Download
Track 15

HEAR MORE on
www.mymusiclab.com
CD I • Track 16/Download
Track 16

Opening of "The Star-Spangled Banner" in polyphonic texture

Polyphonic realizations of "The Star-Spangled Banner" in its entirety are rare, but they do exist. John Knowles Paine's *Concert Variations on "The Star-Spangled Banner,"* for organ,

LEARN MORE on
www.mymusiclab.com
Texture tutorial

Louis Armstrong playing the trumpet, 1964. Although the trumpet has its own distinctive timbre, Armstrong's style of playing creates a very different sound from that of Kevin Gaffney's rendition of "The Star-Spangled Banner," also on the trumpet.

JAN PERSSON/Lebrecht Music & Arts Photo Library

((• HEAR MORE on
www.mymusiclab.com
CD I • Track 17/Download
Track 17

((• HEAR MORE on
www.mymusiclab.com
CD I • Track 18/Download
Track 18

⚙ LEARN MORE on
www.mymusiclab.com
Timbre and Dynamics
tutorials

which he wrote at the height of the Civil War, features an extended passage in which the principal melody is played against other lines that are melodic in their own right and not mere accompaniment. Listen to the melody at the beginning in a single voice, all by itself. Then notice how the same melody enters later, in a second voice (at 0:11), later again in a third voice (at 0:34), and so on. In the end, no one voice is subordinate to any other. Polyphonic texture can also consist of melodies that are different but sound good when played or sung together.

Timbre

Timbre is the color of music, the character of sound. The same melody can sound very different depending on who is singing or what instruments are playing. At one time or another, "The Star-Spangled Banner" has been performed by probably just about every instrument or combination of instruments imaginable, from a solo kazoo to a large symphony orchestra. And even when performed on the same instrument, it can sound very different.

The range of musical timbres is enormous, extending from a single instrument or a single voice to an entire orchestra or an entire chorus—or both together. As we examine timbres in individual pieces, we will look at the instruments that create those timbres.

Dynamics

Dynamics is a term used to indicate the volume of sound, ranging from very soft to very loud. We have all heard "The Star-Spangled Banner" played at a single (loud) volume by a military band. We have also heard it performed at a level only slightly above a whisper, often by an ensemble of unaccompanied voices. And we have heard performances that move from the one extreme to the other. Dynamics can change suddenly, or they can change gradually. Volume is a relative quality: what seems loud to one listener might be barely audible to another, and vice versa.

In music, it is common to use Italian terms to refer to volume:

pianissimo (*pp*) — very soft
piano (*p*) — soft
mezzo piano (*mp*) — medium soft
mezzo forte (*mf*) — medium loud
forte (*f*) — loud
fortissimo (*ff*) — very loud

PERFORMANCE   The Acoustics of Timbre

What makes different instruments sound different? The answer to this question goes to the heart of what timbre is—the quality of a sound, apart from its pitch or volume. The pitch "A" played at 440 cps sounds quite different on an oboe than on a violin, a guitar, or a saxophone. The basic wavelength of the sound produced by these instruments on this one pitch will all be the same, but the shape of these wavelengths varies considerably.

Just as individual colors blend different light waves, any naturally produced sound is the product of a mixture of many different sound waves. The basic sound wave is known as a fundamental. When produced by a machine (as in the case of a midi file), we hear *only* the fundamental: the sound is pure, but for that very reason it is unnatural. This is what makes midi files sound so mechanical. When produced by a musical instrument like a violin, guitar, or piano, the sound wave of the fundamental is enhanced by the addition of many partials, frequencies that resonate with the fundamental to create a richer quality of sound.

You can hear an example of how some of these partials sound by doing a simple experiment on the piano. With one hand, depress the keys C and G in the octave above middle C, but do not actually play the notes: just push these keys down very slowly and hold them in place. Now, with the other hand, strike the note middle C forcefully. What you hear is mostly middle C, but if you listen carefully, you can also hear the higher notes as well. If you play middle C again, normally this time, without the additional held-down notes, you can recognize these partials in what is known as the spectral content of middle C on the piano—the full range of sounds produced in and around a given wavelength. The most prominent of the partials are known as overtones. The timbre of all acoustic instruments results from a mixture of fundamentals and partials. Instruments that create their sound digitally (such as a keyboard synthesizer) can often mimic these instruments by adding partials to the fundamentals.

| (a) flute | (b) trumpet | (c) soprano saxophone | (d) violin | (e) bassoon |

The look of different sounds: oscilloscope readings of the same pitch (A = 440 cps) played by (a) a flute, (b) a trumpet, (c) a soprano saxophone, (d) a violin, and (e) a bassoon. Notice that the wavelengths—the distance between each peak—are the same (producing the same pitch), but the shape of the vibrating air column is different in each instrument (producing contrasting timbres).

Cengage Learning—Kentucky

Form

Form is the structure of a musical work, the way in which its individual units are put together. Form is based on three and only three possible strategies: repetition, variation, and contrast. When we say something, we can then do only one of three things: say once again exactly what we have just said, word-for-word (repetition); repeat what we have just said in a slightly different manner (variation); or say something altogether different (contrast). These three strategies apply to music as well.

LEARN MORE on
www.mymusiclab.com
Form tutorial

In "The Star-Spangled Banner," the opening phrase of the music is repeated literally for the second phrase:

- Phrase 1: O, say can you see by the dawn's early light what so proudly we hailed at the twilight's last gleaming?
- Phrase 2 (same melody, repeated): Whose broad stripes and bright stars through the perilous fight, o'er the ramparts we watched were so gallantly streaming?

If we call the opening phrase of music "A," then the first half of "The Star-Spangled Banner"—the music, independent of the text—can be diagrammed as

A A

What happens next? Do we hear yet another repetition of **A**, a variation of **A**, or something completely different? "And the rockets' red glare . . ." is, of course, completely different from what we have heard before. For that reason, we can call this phrase "B." And the concluding phrase of "The Star-Spangled Banner" ("Oh, say does that star-spangled banner yet wave . . .") is different yet again ("C"). So the form of the song as a whole can be represented as

A A B C

This form happens to be extremely common in songs from many times and places (Martin Luther's famous hymn "A Mighty Fortress Is Our God," Stephen Foster's "Oh, Susanna," Radiohead's "Black Star," and even "Dixie," the unofficial anthem of the Confederate States of America during the Civil War). Forms can also be expanded (**AABCA**) or contracted (**ABA**) in an almost infinite variety of combinations.

Word-Music Relationships

LEARN MORE on
www.mymusiclab.com
Word-Music Relationships
Tutorial

Word-music relationships are many and diverse. The most obvious intersection of words and music occurs in works with a text to be sung. How do the notes relate to the words? So far, we have examined only the music of "The Star-Spangled Banner," not the words. Let's look now at the text and see how it fits the music.

Structurally, the text (or at least its first stanza) consists of three questions, interrupted by a statement. (The second, third, and fourth stanzas of the text provide answers to all these questions, but no one ever sings them, and for purposes of brevity, we will focus here on the first stanza.)

First Question

O, say can you see by the dawn's early light
What so proudly we hailed at the twilight's last gleaming?

Second Question

Whose broad stripes and bright stars through the perilous fight,
O'er the ramparts we watched were so gallantly streaming?

Statement

> And the rockets' red glare, the bombs bursting in air,
> Gave proof through the night that our flag was still there.

Third Question

> Oh, say does that star-spangled banner yet wave
> O'er the land of the free and the home of the brave?

Music	A	A	B	C
Text	Question 1	Question 2	Statement	Question 3

If we consider the overall structure of the melody—the tune—we can see how well it fits the words: The opening two questions are sung to the identical music (**A**), but the statement presents a very different melodic idea in a very different range. With the words "And the rockets' red glare...," the music moves into a different theme (**B**) and a higher range, which helps set the stage for a return to the opening range of the song (and one last question) in the concluding section (**C**).

Notice, too, how the range of the melody corresponds to the content of the text. The voice moves into a very high register at the words "And the rockets' red glare," appropriately enough. And it hits this same high note—the highest one in the entire melody—again just before the end, on "free" in "o'er the land of the free."

Genre

Genre is the category of a given work (symphony, sonata, song), determined by a combination of its performance medium and its social function. Knowing the genre of a work we are about to hear tells us a great deal about what to expect. Let's suppose you're at the Olympics, witnessing a medals ceremony. The athlete who has won the gold medal has just received her medal, but you've never heard of the country she represents, and you certainly have never heard its national anthem, which is about to play. Yet based on your knowledge of the genre of national anthem, you can actually anticipate a fair amount about this piece of music you've never heard before. You can reasonably expect a work of fairly short duration—probably between one and two minutes—that is lively in tone and has a bright sound, and that will probably be performed by a wind band (trumpets, trombones, clarinets, and the like), possibly with a drum. These expectations are based on the principal function of a national anthem: to arouse in citizens a sense of national pride. There are exceptions to this rule, of course, just as there are exceptions to generic expectations in all kinds of music, but knowing the typical nature and function of the work we are about to hear can help us relate the unknown (the new work) to its archetype (the genre, or works we know from that genre). See chart on pages 14–15.

"The Star-Spangled Banner" certainly fits the pattern of the genre of national anthem. It is short (about a minute-and-a-half to two minutes, depending on how slowly or quickly it is performed), in major mode, and is performed in its "standard" version—the one played at the Olympics, for example—by a wind band with drums.

LEARN MORE on
www.mymusiclab.com
Genre tutorial

In Review: The Elements

SEE MORE on
www.mymusiclab.com
Watch "History of
Music" video

When we listen, we normally do not think about all these elements—melody, harmony, rhythm, texture, timbre, dynamics, form, word-music relationships, and genre—separately. This is because they work together to create a satisfying whole. To isolate any one of them from the others in a particular work, we need to make a special effort to listen only to the melody, or only to the texture, or only to the form. Yet this kind of listening can help us raise our awareness of the role that these individual elements can play. For this reason we have a separate column for each significant element in the listening guides that accompany the music in this book. It may require listening a few times through to hear what is going on with each element. As we internalize these building blocks of music, we can better appreciate the complexity and beauty of the art. Do we need to be conscious of all these elements as we listen? No. But our understanding and enjoyment of a piece of music will increase the more we are aware of all that goes into music in general. The more we know, the better we can listen. And the better we listen, the more we can enjoy the experience.

Genres Represented in This Text

This table lists the genres presented in the text in the order of their first appearance.

PART 1: The Middle Ages	PART 2: The Renaissance	PART 3: The Baroque Era	PART 4: The Classical Era
Plainchant • Alleluia from the Mass for the Feast of Corpus Christi • Hildegard von Bingen: *Play of Virtues* Secular song • Landini: "Behold, Spring" • Machaut, "I can all too well compare my lady" Instrumental music • Alfonso el Sabio: Instrumental arrangement of *Songs to the Virgin Mary* no. 249	Secular song • Josquin: "The Cricket" Madrigal • Weelkes: "Since Robin Hood" Anthem • Byrd: "Sing Joyfully" Dance music • Susato: *Moorish Dance*	Opera • Monteverdi: *Orpheus* • Purcell: *Dido and Aeneas* Secular Song • Strozzi: "Revenge" Fugue • J. S. Bach: Fugue in G minor, BWV 578 Concerto • Vivaldi: *Four Seasons*, "Winter" • J. S. Bach: Brandenburg Concerto no. 2 Suite • Handel: *Water Music* Cantata • Bach: Cantata 140 Oratorio • Handel: *Messiah*	String Quartet • Haydn: String Quartet op. 76, n. 3 Symphony • Haydn: Symphony no. 102 • Mozart: Symphony no. 40 Concerto • Mozart: Piano Concerto K. 488 Opera • Mozart: *The Marriage of Figaro* Choral Music • Billings: "Chester"

PART 5: The Nineteenth Century	PART 6: The Twentieth Century	PART 7: Music Today
Symphony • Beethoven: Symphony no. 5 • Berlioz: *Symphonie fantastique* • Brahms: Symphony no. 4 Concert overture • Felix Mendelssohn: *Overture to A Midsummer Night's Dream* Chamber Music • Fanny Mendelssohn Hensel: Piano Trio, op. 11 • Dvořák: String Quartet in F Major, op. 96 ("American") Song • Schubert: "Erlkönig," D. 328 • R. Schumann: "Dedication" Choral music • C. Schumann: "Forward!" Piano music • Chopin: Mazurka in B♭, op. 7, no. 1 • Gottschalk: *Union* Opera • Verdi: *La Traviata* • Wagner: *The Valkyrie*	Piano music • Debussy: *Voiles* • Crawford: *Piano Study in Mixed Accents* Orchestral music • Ives: *The Unanswered Question* • Bartók: Concerto for Orchestra Ballet • Stravinsky: *Rite of Spring* • Copland: "Hoe-Down" from *Rodeo* Song • Schoenberg: *Pierrot lunaire* • Still: *Songs of Separation* Concerto • Tailleferre: *Concertino for Harp and Orchestra* Broadway musical • Bernstein: "Tonight" from *West Side Story* Opera • Glass: "Knee Play 1" from *Einstein on the Beach* Aleatory music • Cage: Indeterminacy Percussion ensemble music • Léon: *A la Par* Film music • Tan Dun: *Crouching Tiger, Hidden Dragon* Ragtime • Joplin: *Maple Leaf Rag* Blues • R. Johnson: "Terraplane Blues" Big band jazz • Ellington: *Cotton Tail* Bebop • Parker: *Ornithology* Rock 'n' roll/Rock • Berry: "School Day" • Beach Boys: "Good Vibrations" Gospel • Jackson: "It Don't Cost Very Much" Motown • Marvelettes: "Please, Mr. Postman" Punk • Sex Pistols, "God Save the Queen" Hip Hop • Public Enemy: "Fight the Power"	Native American chant • San Ildefonso Indians of New Mexico: *Eagle Dance* (Monophonic chant) Caribbean music • Rhyming Singers of the Bahamas: "My Lord Help Me To Pray" (Counterpoint) Central African music • Mbuti Pygmies: "Marriage Celebration Song" (ostinato) Japanese court music • Master Musicians of the Ikuta-ryu (Japan): *Cherry Blossom* (variations) Beijing Opera • Lisa Lu and the Beijing Opera Company: *The Reunion* (opera) Indian raga • Ravi Shankar (India): *Raga Bairaga* (virtuosity) Balinese gamelan • Gamelan Gong Kebyar of Belaluan (Bali): *Kebyar Ding III* (timbre)

PART 1 476 CE – Early Fifteenth Century

The Middle Ages

What we now think of as the Middle Ages, or the medieval era, covered almost a thousand years, between the fall of the Western Roman Empire in 476 CE and the beginning of the Renaissance in the early fifteenth century. The people of this time did not think of themselves as being in the "middle" or "between" anything at all, of course. Only later did historians see this span of time as a period lying between antiquity and the Renaissance.

The music of the Middle Ages reflects its many and varied social functions, both sacred and secular. The church dominated intellectual and cultural life during this period.

Music, along with all the other arts, was perceived as a means of serving God. Over the course of several hundred years, generations of anonymous composers—most of them monks or priests—developed an enormous repertory of plainchant (also known as Gregorian chant), which consisted of monophonic, unaccompanied melodies sung by a single voice or by a choir in unison. Plainchant projected the words of the sacred liturgy in a manner that was at once clear and moving. Secular courts also needed music for their ceremonies and entertainments, and composers provided a steady stream of songs, settings of poems that tell of love, pain, heroism, and

The Middle Ages ⊙→ EXPLORE MORE on www.mymusiclab.com

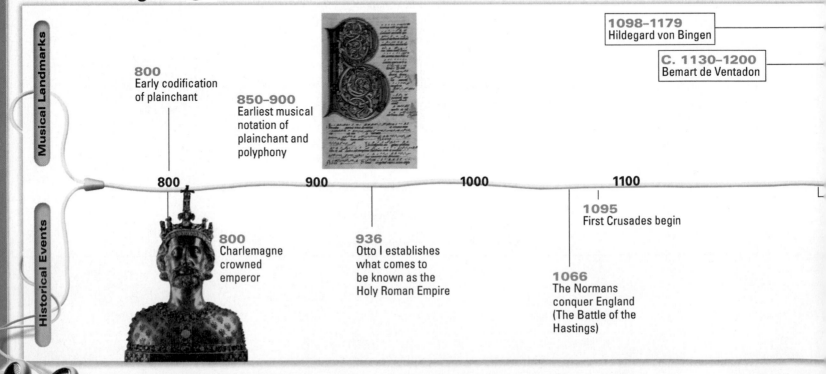

Musical Landmarks

800 Early codification of plainchant

850–900 Earliest musical notation of plainchant and polyphony

1098–1179 Hildegard von Bingen

C. 1130–1200 Bemart de Ventadon

800   900   1000   1100

Historical Events

800 Charlemagne crowned emperor

936 Otto I establishes what comes to be known as the Holy Roman Empire

1095 First Crusades begin

1066 The Normans conquer England (The Battle of the Hastings)

WARNER PACIFIC COLLEGE BOOKSTORE

9965 CASH-1   9157 0001 100

978020577736 NEW
BONDS/LISTEN TO TH   MDS 1N   60.00
                    TOTAL   60.00

                    SUBTOTAL   60.00
                    SALES TAX   .00
                    TOTAL   60.00

BRIANNE   CULBERTSON

ACCOUNT NUMBER   1220999
    Financial Aid   60.00

ast day to return books is 01-31-2011

                        1/12/11 11:56 AM

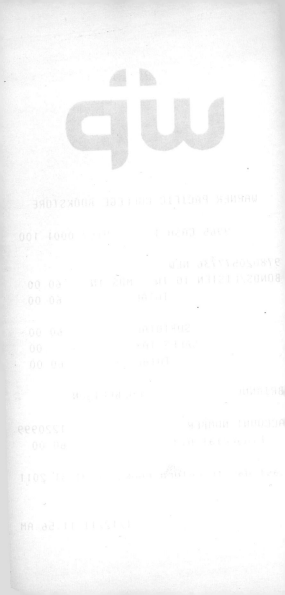

all the other emotions that make up the human condition. Polyphony—multiple independent voices sung or played together—became increasingly important for both sacred and secular music from the tenth century onward.

The sounds of medieval music, both sacred and secular, may at first seem unfamiliar to us today: the scales on which they based their melodies differ from ours, and most of their instruments are no longer in common use. But the more we listen to this music, the more we can hear in it the same basic elements we still use today. Above all, we can recognize in this music the effort of medieval composers to heighten the expressivity of the texts they set and to elevate music beyond language. This basic urge connects us with music that is a thousand years old.

Music for Sacred Spaces

By far the largest and most imposing structures of the Middle Ages were its churches, monuments to God and physical testimonies to the power of the church itself. This was the era of the great Gothic cathedrals, buildings of unprecedented size, grace, and light. These structures did more than provide a space for worship: they were meant to inspire, to lift the eye heavenward,

▲ According to legend, Pope Gregory (ca. 540–604) received the melodies of plainchant from the Holy Spirit, which appeared to him in the form of a dove. This repertory of music would later come to be known as Gregorian chant. In this 10th-century image, Pope Gregory (left) dictates the melody to a scribe.

Pope Gregory the Great (*Antiphonary of Hartker of St. Gall*, Cod. Sang. 390, p.13). Stiftsbibliothek St. Gallen.

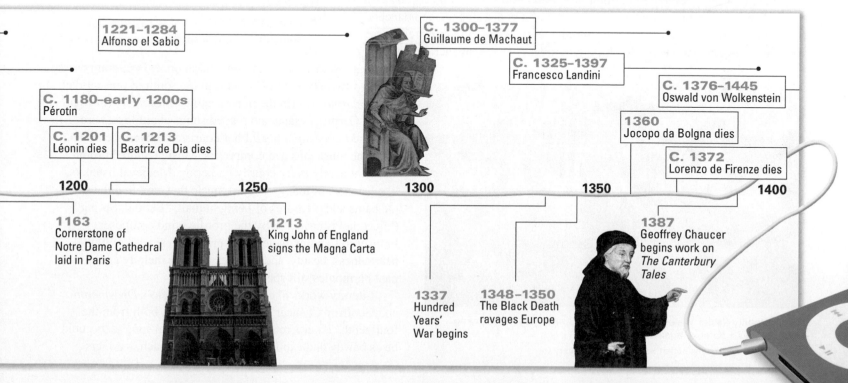

1221–1284
Alfonso el Sabio

C. 1300–1377
Guillaume de Machaut

C. 1325–1397
Francesco Landini

C. 1376–1445
Oswald von Wolkenstein

C. 1180–early 1200s
Pérotin

1360
Jocopo da Bolgna dies

C. 1201
Léonin dies

C. 1213
Beatriz de Dia dies

C. 1372
Lorenzo de Firenze dies

1200   **1250**   **1300**   **1350**   **1400**

1163
Cornerstone of Notre Dame Cathedral laid in Paris

1213
King John of England signs the Magna Carta

1337
Hundred Years' War begins

1348–1350
The Black Death ravages Europe

1387
Geoffrey Chaucer begins work on *The Canterbury Tales*

to instruct mortals about their relationship to the divine. The stained glass windows in these churches were similarly instructive, depicting biblical scenes in ways that could be understood even by those who could not read or write.

Sacred music fulfilled a similar function. Its purpose was to enhance the texts being sung and inspire worshippers with the beauty of their sound. Plainchant was the perfect vehicle for projecting sacred texts with great clarity across enormous spaces. All the services of the church were provided with their appropriate melodies. And there were many services: the typical monk or nun attended church nine times a day. Eight of these services were devoted to the reading and singing of prayers, psalms, and hymns. The most important service of each day was Mass, a ritual reenactment of Christ's Last Supper with his disciples. The anonymous composers of the early Middle Ages devoted special efforts to the many chants of the Mass. Morality plays like Hildegard von Bingen's *Play of Virtues* (*Ordo virtutum*) combined plainchant with newly composed poetry to convey the teachings of the church and help the faithful learn the differences between good and evil.

Music for Entertainment

As the great cathedrals were symbols of divine power, medieval castles were symbols of secular, worldly power. Their stone walls and moats reflect the constant threat of attack from the outside. Medieval Europe was divided into a series of kingdoms, duchies, and fiefdoms of widely varying sizes, each ruled by a lord to whom subjects paid their allegiance—and taxes. Medieval courts used the arts as a means of projecting their cultural power and impressing subjects and visitors alike. Rulers competed for the services of the best poets, singers, and dancers.

Courtly life demanded courtly entertainments. Wandering minstrels passed from town to town and castle to castle providing poetry, song, acrobatics, and

▲ The interior of Chartres Cathedral (France). By the 13th century, builders could construct high, vaulted ceilings to draw both the eye and the spirit upward, toward the heavens. Plainchant was crafted to fill these immense spaces.

Roger Moss Photography

⊙➔ **EXPLORE MORE** on **www.mymusiclab.com**
Tour Chartres Cathedral

▲ Caerphilly Castle, Wales, dates from the 13th century. Its daunting exterior was a defense against invaders.

Adina Tovy/Getty Images/Robert Harding World Imagery

juggling—sometimes combining all at once. Poet-composers known variously as *troubadours* (in the south of present-day France), *trouvères* (in the north), and *minnesingers* (in what is now Germany) sang and played songs about love, heroism, and the pastoral life. Other courts employed their own full-time musicians and composers. Music featured prominently at nearly every courtly gathering. Medieval listeners, like listeners of today, enjoyed music that captured the simple pains and pleasures of being human. "Behold, Spring" ("Ecco la Primavera"), by the prolific blind composer Francesco Landini, welcomes spring as a season of light-heartedness, beauty, and love. Its flowing melody and resonant harmonies still speak to us today.

Literary works like Giovanni Boccaccio's *Decameron* and Geoffrey Chaucer's *Canterbury Tales*, both from the fourteenth century, remind us that medieval song texts could be as bawdy and explicit as any today. In each, travelers must take turns entertaining their companions, and song plays an important role throughout. Significantly, Boccaccio (1313–1375) and Chaucer (ca. 1342–1400) both wrote in the vernacular languages of their respective regions (present-day Italy and England), rather than in Latin, the language of the church. Similarly, a good deal of medieval secular music was sung to texts in the language of the people.

Music for Dancing

In an era when relationships with the opposite sex outside of marriage were closely regulated, dance was a highly significant social activity. We have no detailed descriptions of medieval dance, but we do have images of dancing as well as actual works of dance music that have survived from this time. Most dances appear to have been group activities, somewhat similar to present-day line dancing. And almost every image of dancing comes with a drummer providing the basic beat.

When thinking about medieval art and life today, we should consider not only what it looked like, but what it sounded like. The instruments of the Middle Ages were for the most part quite different from those of today. The shawm used in Alfonso el Sabio's "He Who Gladly Serves" ("Aquel que de volontade"), for example, was an early wind instrument that would eventually be replaced by the modern oboe. Yet this work would sound very different if played on an oboe, for the shawm's more open and raspy sound belongs as much to the medieval world as the era's great churches and castles.

▲ An acrobat balances on a pair of swords, accompanied by two musicians. The one on the left plays the pipe and tabor (a small drum), while the one on the right plays a double flute.
By permission of The British Library

▲ Five couples in a line dance, accompanied by a drummer (left) and a bagpipe player (right). This image is from a medieval manuscript of the *Roman de la Rose*, an allegorical poem written in France in the 13th century. The gold paint actually contains a high percentage of finely ground gold.
Roy 20 A XVII f.9 Figures dancing to music played on tabor and bagpipes/British Library, London, UK/The Bridgeman Art Library

Information Technology 1.0

The earliest medieval music was not notated: until about the tenth century, music was transmitted orally, not in written form. (The image of the scribe writing music on page 17 was created long after the time of Pope Gregory I, who reigned in the sixth century.) The earliest chant manuscripts show simple symbols above the texts, indicating motion of the pitch up or down (*see A Closer Look: A Plainchant Manuscript* page 20).

Written music remained hard to come by, even after the development of notation. Printing did not emerge until the middle of the fifteenth century, and so music (like all other texts) had to be written out by hand, one copy at a time. Making a manuscript was a time-consuming and costly process: ink and parchment were expensive (paper did not become widely available until the Renaissance), and scribes had to work slowly and carefully. Manuscripts, moreover, are not always entirely accurate. Scribes were only human, and anyone who has ever hand-copied a text of any complexity will know how easy it is to leave out, repeat, or garble words or even whole passages of text. Even in the hands of the most-skilled medieval scribes, these manuscripts were not always entirely faithful to the original.

A CLOSER LOOK   Twelfth Century Plainchant Manuscript

⊙→ EXPLORE MORE on
www.mymusiclab.com

This 12th-century plainchant manuscript, prepared in what is now northern Germany, is a work of art in its own right. The scribes who produced documents like this were often monks of great artistic talent. Every large church or monastery had its own workshop that produced manuscripts, reminding us once again of the church's control over what could—and could not—be reproduced and distributed.

The initial letter "B," the first letter in the first word of one of the chants on this page, is oversized and elaborately illustrated with workers making wine. The images may illustrate Jesus' parable of the laborers in the vineyard (Matthew 20: 1-15).

To start the process, the worker at the top **harvests the grapes**.

To protect the harvest, this **archer** takes aim at a wild beast eating the grapes.

At the end of the **wine-making process**, this laborer mashes the grapes.

Some portions of **plainchant** are melodically simple and syllabic (see p. 25), with only one note per syllable and not very much rise or fall in the melody.

These early forms of **notes** are called **neumes**. The musical notation shows how the notes of the melody rise or fall, but it does not indicate specific pitches. The monks or nuns knew these chant melodies more or less by heart and so did not need precise notation. Newer chant melodies, such as those composed by Hildegard, called for more precise pitch-notation (see p. 24). By the time Landini was writing in the later fourteenth century, an even more precise system of notation was in place (see p. 41).

The words were written onto the parchment first, the notes added later, probably by a different scribe. Here, the **text scribe** clearly did not leave enough room for the **music scribe!**

The red lines indicate that a single syllable of text is sung to many notes. These are elaborate **melismas** (see p. 25). Here, the beauty of the music takes precedence over the intelligibility of the text.

The J. Paul Getty Museum, Los Angeles. "Inhabited Initial B" by Unknown (Illuminator). about 1170s. From the Stammheim Missal (97.MG.21, Folio 58. Tempera colors, gold leaf silver leaf, and ink on parchment bound between wood boards covered with alum tawed pigskin. Leaf: 28.2 x 18.9 cm (11 1/8" x 8 7/16").

⚙ **LEARN MORE** on **www.mymusiclab.com** MyMusicLibrary: "Words, Music, and Memory"

The Middle Ages CHAPTERS AT A GLANCE

GLOBAL CONNECTION
KEY CONCEPT
Monophonic Texture

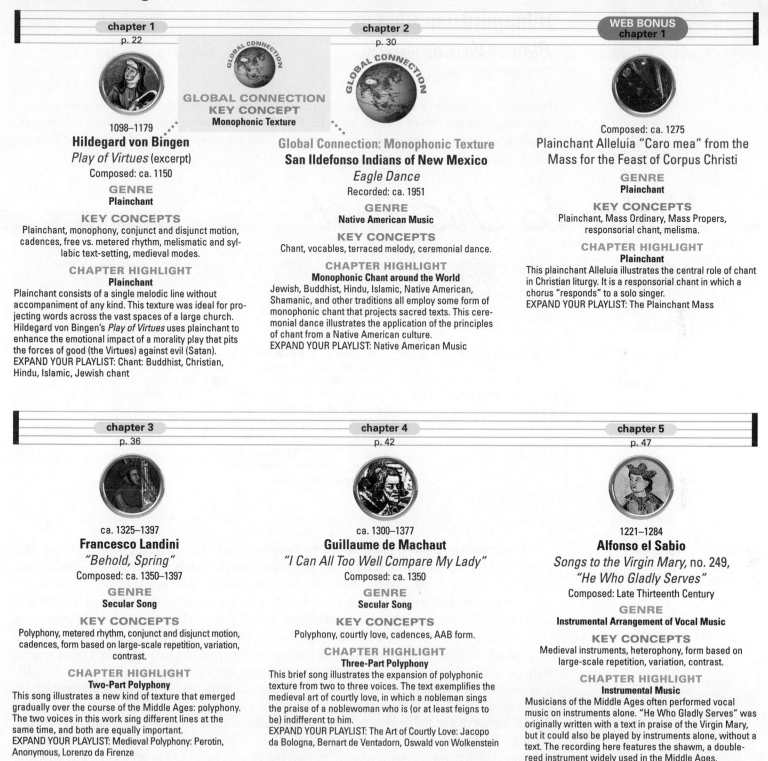

1

Hildegard von Bingen
Play of Virtues (excerpt)
Composed: ca. 1150

Hildegard von Bingen's *Play of Virtues* is a morality play, a dramatized allegory of good and evil struggling over the fate of a single soul. Each of the 16 Virtues—Charity, Obedience, Humility, Chastity, and so on—is sung by a different singer. In this excerpt we hear Humility and Victory. Satan only speaks and has no music.

Listen to this first

((• HEAR MORE on www.mymusiclab.com

 | | |

Texture	**Melody**	**Word-Music Relationships**	**Rhythm**
Listen for the sound of a single voice, or multiple voices singing together. This is **monophonic** texture.	Listen for occasional leaps in the otherwise smooth and flowing melodies. Listen, too, for the cadences—brief resting points—throughout.	Note that most characters sing their lines, but one speaks (or shouts) his. Notice how clearly the singers project the Latin words, mostly with one note per syllable, but occasionally with many notes drawn out over a single syllable. Listen also for the climax of the drama, when the pitches move into a very high range.	Listen to the way the rhythm is free for the most part, reflecting the irregular rhythms of the words being sung.

⚙ LEARN MORE on
www.mymusiclab.com
Chapter Objectives

Music exerts a powerful pull on the human spirit, and medieval composers put this power to good use. Hildegard von Bingen recognized that the words of her *Play of Virtues* (*Ordo virtutum*), while moving in their own right, could be made even more expressive set to music.

The plot of Hildegard's *Play of Virtues* centers on a series of disputes between Satan and 16 Virtues. Each of the Virtues is personified by a different singer. When the Virtues sing together as a single chorus, they all sing exactly the same melody. Satan, however, never sings at all; he simply shouts his lines. In the medieval period, music was widely perceived as a divine gift of heaven, and it seems only fitting that the devil should have no music at all. The contrast between the spoken part of Satan and the sung part of the Virtues is immediate and striking.

In setting this morality play to music, Hildegard was building on a long tradition of liturgical **plainchant**, the music used in the daily services of the church. This repertory of chant had developed slowly over many centuries. It grew out of the chants of Jewish services of worship, particularly the melodic recitation of the Psalms. Over time, many of the texts of the Christian liturgy were set to music by a series of anonymous composers, presumably monks and priests. The melodies were transmitted orally and were not put down in writing until they already had been circulating for many centuries. Hildegard's style of chant is similar to the more florid kinds of plainchant found in the services of worship. The most important service of worship—the Mass—was itself a ritual reenactment of Christ's Last Supper with his disciples, with the celebrant priest (a representative of Christ) distributing bread and wine to his followers (see Historical Context, chapter 4, page 46). The idea of a bodily reenactment of past events gradually extended to readings from scripture as well: dramatized performances of such events as the two Marys finding the empty tomb of Christ on Easter morning became increasingly common from the eleventh century onward. Hildegard's setting of a play about the struggle for an innocent soul extends this practice.

The Clarity of Monophonic Texture

The monophonic texture of this music—whether sung by one singer or by a group of singers in unison—allows the performers to project the text with great clarity. In the performance here, the musicians have taken the liberty of adding the sound of distant bells toward the end to emphasize the moment of dramatic triumph. Although the written score is for voices alone, it seems likely that performers in the Middle Ages would have added these and other instruments to give variety to the music's timbre. But these instruments are entirely independent of the words and music: in no way do they carry or even support the melodic line or affect the structure of the whole. The music remains essentially monophonic, with no instruments at all for long stretches at a time.

1098–1179
Hildegard von Bingen
Play of Virtues (excerpt)
Composed: ca. 1150

GENRE
Plainchant

KEY CONCEPTS
Plainchant, monophony, conjunct and disjunct motion, cadences, free vs. metered rhythm, melismatic and syllabic text-setting, medieval modes.

CHAPTER HIGHLIGHT
Plainchant
Plainchant consists of a single melodic line without accompaniment of any kind. This texture was ideal for projecting words across the vast spaces of a large church. Hildegard von Bingen's *Play of Virtues* uses plainchant to enhance the emotional impact of a morality play that pits the forces of good (the Virtues) against evil (Satan).

HISTORICAL CONTEXT The Morality Play

How do we learn the difference between good and evil, and how do we learn to choose between them? In the Middle Ages, morality plays like Hildegard von Bingen's *Play of Virtues* offered a way of dramatizing such questions literally. But morality plays did not end with the Middle Ages. Popular works today like the *Star Wars*, *Harry Potter*, and *Lord of the Rings* series are built on the same basic plot outline: an innocent figure struggles between the forces of good and evil.

Work	Evil	Innocent Soul	Good
Hildegard, *Play of Virtues*	Satan	The Soul, Penitent	The Virtues
Tolkien, *Lord of the Rings*	Sauron	Frodo	Gandalf
Lucas, *Star Wars*	Darth Vader	Luke Skywalker	Jedi knights
Rowling, *Harry Potter*	Voldemort	Harry Potter	Dumbledore

In each case, the embodiment of evil was once good: Sauron began as a good spirit, Darth Vader was once a Jedi knight, Voldemort was originally an innocent boy named Tom Marvolo Riddle, and Satan himself was a fallen angel.

Music plays a powerful role in the works that began as dramas (*Play of Virtues*, *Star Wars*) and in the film adaptations of the two that began as novels (*Lord of the Rings*, *Harry Potter*). Think, for example, of the difference in sound between the darkness of Darth Vader's music and the stirring march that symbolizes the Jedi knights. These aural cues reinforce the essence of the good and evil characters.

In a scene from *The Empire Strikes Back,* Luke Skywalker (Mark Hamill) and Darth Vader (David Prowse) carry out the battle between good and evil.

Lucasfilm/20th Century Fox/The Kobal Collection

The earliest preserved music from the Middle Ages was monophonic. In the church, this repertory came to be known as plainchant because of the simplicity of its texture. (Later, it would also be called **Gregorian chant** on the grounds that Pope Gregory I was said to have written the bulk of it in the late sixth century.) Plainchant fulfilled its function perfectly: it projected its text—the main focus of attention for worshippers—with wonderful clarity and a melodic beauty that enhanced the meaning of the words. It was particularly well-suited for performance in the large, resonant spaces of medieval churches. The beauty of the melodies and words together, echoing off the stone walls, must have made an enormous impact on worshippers.

Medieval Melody

Hildegard's flowing melodies move primarily by step (conjunct motion), but the occasional leaps (disjunct motion) provide variety and give each phrase of text a clear profile. Many of the melodic phrases begin with a leap upward and then descend gradually through a series of steps, cadencing on the same note with which the phrase began. This kind of melodic contour and cadencing is typical of plainchant in general and is always related to the structure of the text being sung: a sentence of text almost invariably ends with a cadence.

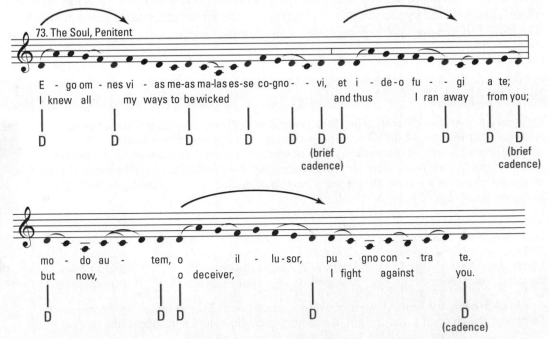

The opening of the present excerpt, represented in modern notation. The melodic phrase starts and ends on D, rising and then falling to a cadence.

Hildegard von Bingen's *Play of Virtues*, in a manuscript prepared in the scriptorium of Hildegard's own cloister in the 12th century.

Wiesbaden Hessische Landesbibliothek

What has sometimes been described as the "otherworldly" sound of plainchant—the quality that makes plainchant sound different from other kinds of music—is due in part to the scales on which these melodies are based. Whereas today we have only two modes (major and minor), medieval composers had four additional modes, each of which uses a sequence of whole steps and half steps different from the pattern found in the standard scale of today. The easiest way to imagine (and hear) the full range of medieval modes is to play a series of notes upward on the piano using only the white keys starting and ending on D, then another series on E, then another on F, and finally another on G. Each of these scales sounds slightly different from the others, and each also sounds different from the standard major and minor scales of today. (The major scale is found on the white keys from C to C, and the minor scale on the white keys from A to A.) In the Middle Ages, each of these scales (modes) was given its own Greek name, based on the mistaken belief that these corresponded to the modes of ancient Greek music. The medieval modes are Dorian (on D), Phrygian (on E), Lydian (on F), Mixolydian (on G), Aeolian (on A), and Ionian (on C). The opening of this particular excerpt is based on the Dorian mode, beginning and cadencing on the note D.

Projecting Words Through Music

A composer has two basic choices in setting words to music: she can set each syllable to a single note or she can set each syllable to multiple notes. The first style—one note per syllable—is called **syllabic**, and it ensures that the words will be heard with special clarity. The second style—more than one note per syllable—is called **melismatic**. A **melisma** is a syllable sung to many notes. This kind of setting provides variety and emphasizes key words in a text, such as the word *regina* ("queen") after 0:56 or the word *curre* ("hasten" or "run") after 1:23. An entirely melismatic setting might make it difficult for listeners to understand every word, whereas an entirely syllabic setting might not provide sufficient musical variety. By mixing syllabic and melismatic settings, Hildegard provides musical variety, even while providing for a clear projection of the text.

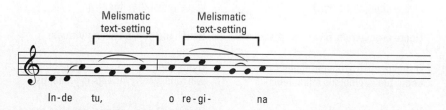

Note, too, how certain passages are sung in a very high **register**, or range. When Satan has been bound—the climactic moment of the drama (3:15 in the Listening Guide)—Victory sings in an extremely high register. The effect is thrilling.

Free Rhythm

No one is absolutely certain exactly how plainchant was performed. There are two general approaches, free or measured. The performance here presents the music in a relatively free rhythm, with the individual notes lengthened or shortened according to the length of the syllables in the words being sung. A measured performance would adhere to a consistent meter, such as **duple meter** (**1**-2-**3**-4 | **1**-2-**3**-4 | etc.).

Now listen to this excerpt again, using the Listening Guide.

CONNECT YOUR PLAYLIST

Monophony

Find a piece that contains monophonic texture.

Example: Pink, "So What" (2008) In the very opening of the song, and in each of its verses, all the instruments play the same melody as the voice, creating monophonic texture.

Listening Guide

GO TO www.mymusiclab.com
for the Automated Listening Guide
CD I • Track 19/Download Track 19

Hildegard von Bingen Composed: ca. 1150 *Play of Virtues* (excerpt) (3:51)

Time	Character	Latin Text	English Translation
0:00	The Devil (speaks, does not sing)	Que es, aut unde venis? Tu amplexata es me, et ego foras eduxi te. Sed nunc in reversione tua confundis me; Ego autem pugna mea diciam te!	Who are you, and where do you come from? You have embraced me, and I have led you forth. But now, in your turning back, you confuse me; But I will hurl you down with my assault!
0:21	The Soul, Penitent	Ego omnes vias meas malas esse cognovi et ideo fugi a te; modo autem, o illusor pugno contra te. Inde tu, o regina Humilitas, tuo medicamine adiuva me.	I knew all my ways to be evil, and therefore I ran away from you; now, however, O deceiver, I fight against you. Thence, you, O Queen Humility, help me with your medicine.
1:13	Humility (to Victory)	O Victoria, que istum in celo superasti, curre cum militibus tuis, et omnes ligate diabolum hunc.	O Victory, who conquered that one [the devil] in heaven, hasten with your knights, and all of you bind that devil.
1:40	Victory (to the Virtues)	O fortissimi et gloriosissimi milites, venite, et adiuvate me istum fallacem vincere.	O you most brave and glorious knights, come and help me to conquer that deceitful one.
2:05	The Virtues	O dulcissime bellatrix, in torrente fonte qui absorbuit, lupum rapacem! O gloriosa coronata, nos libenter militamus tecum contra illusorem hunc.	O fairest warrior, who swallowed the greedy wolf in the torrent! O glorious crowned one, we willingly fight with you against that deceiver.
2:40	Humility	Ligate ergo istrum, o virtutes preclare!	Bind him, then, o shining Virtues!
2:55	The Virtues (binding Satan here)	O regina nostra, tibi parebimus et precepta tua in omnibus adimplebimus.	O our queen, to you we will be obedient, and we will fulfill your precepts in all things.
3:15	Victory	Gaudete, o socii, quia antiquus serpens ligatus est.	Rejoice, O companions, because the old serpent has been bound.
3:38	The Virtues	Laus tibi Christe, rex angelorum!	Praise to you, O Christ, King of the Angels!

Text and translation courtesy of Hildegard Publishing Company and Theodore Presser/Carl Fischer.

Rhythm	 Word-Music Relationships	Texture
Free, corresponding to length of syllables	The devil's shouting reflects the medieval belief that hell is a place with no music	(Spoken)
	Melisma on *regina* ("queen") suggests her importance	Monophonic
	Melisma on *curre* ("run")	
	Notes in extremely high register—climax of the drama	

Student FAQs

Why are there only women's voices singing?

Two reasons: (1) During the Middle Ages, the Virtues personified in this work—Chastity, Love, Obedience, Mercy, Humility, Discretion, Patience, and so on—were almost all associated with the female gender. (2) Hildegard wrote this work to be performed in her own convent—that is, by her fellow nuns.

If it was performed by nuns, who spoke the part of the devil?

Only priests—thus only males—could celebrate the Mass, and so each convent had assigned to it a priest to administer the sacraments. In all likelihood, this priest—a monk from a nearby monastery—would have played the role of the devil.

Is plainchant still used in churches?

In some churches on some occasions, yes. Pope Benedict XVI recently announced that the Vatican choir would begin using plainchant once again on a regular basis. But chant is no longer the principal vehicle for singing texts in the Roman Catholic Church. It is still possible to hear special plainchant services from time to time, however.

PROFILE   Hildegard von Bingen (1098–1179)

Visions Through Music

We can securely attribute more compositions to Hildegard von Bingen than to any other musician, male or female, who worked before the early fourteenth century. In spite of her impressive output, Hildegard did not consider herself a professional composer or musician. Born into a noble family in what is now western Germany, she entered a Benedictine convent at the age of 7 and took vows when she was 16. In her early 30s, she began to experience visions and revelations, which she recorded in a series of books. She considered herself a channel through which the Holy Spirit transmitted its message to humankind, sometimes in the form of prose, sometimes in the form of poetry, sometimes in the form of poetry with music. Hildegard was the first woman to receive explicit permission from a pope to write on theology. She also wrote on such diverse subjects as medicine, plants, and the lives of the saints, all while directing the life of a thriving convent near Bingen, a city on the Rhine in present-day Germany. Like many medieval persons, she took her name ("of Bingen") from her place of residence.

Hildegard von Bingen shown in a contemporary manuscript. She looks heavenward for inspiration as she records what she called her "visions," which included both words and music.

Codex Lucca 1942. Biblioteca Statale, su concessione del Ministero per i Beni e le Attivita' Culturali. Photo: Studio Foto Ghilardi.

 EXPLORE MORE on **www.mymusiclab.com**

👁 **SEE MORE** on **www.mymusiclab.com**
"Life in a Medieval Monastery" documentary

⏮ EXPAND YOUR PLAYLIST: HILDEGARD VON BINGEN ⏭

Nuns and monks in Hildegard's time attended church services not just once a week, or even once a day, but usually nine times a day. Hildegard wrote many chants for these services of worship. Here are some examples:

- **"Lord, Have Mercy"** (*Kyrie eleison*) is one of five sections of the Mass, the ritual reenactment of Christ's Last Supper with his disciples. *Hildegard von Bingen: Heavenly Revelations*. Oxford Camerata, Naxos.

- **"O Blessed Infancy"** (*O beata infantia*) is an antiphon, a short piece sung before and after a psalm is sung in church. *The Complete Hildegard von Bingen, Volume Three: O Nobilissima Viriditas*. Celestial Harmonies B00005.

- **"Honor Be to the Holy Spirit"** (*Spiritui sancto honor sit*) is a responsory, a type of chant sung after the reading of scriptures in church. This type of chant takes its name from the fact that a chorus of singers responds to the singing of a soloist. *Hildegard von Bingen: 11,000 Virgins*. Anonymous 4. Harmonia Mundi Fr. B0000B003O.

- **"Hail, Generous One"** (*Ave generosa*) is a hymn, a devotional chant to a freely composed text, often with many strophes or stanzas. *Hildegard von Bingen: Heavenly Revelations*. Oxford Camerata, Naxos.

(•• **HEAR SAMPLES** on **www.mymusiclab.com**

THE COMPOSER SPEAKS   Hildegard Defends the Practice of Music

Over 850 years ago, Hildegard von Bingen was embroiled in a debate that continues today: what is the impact of music on the human mind and spirit? Does it support the religious experience, or does it serve as a sensual distraction from religion? To the present day, some religions embrace music, while some limit or even shun it.

Hildegard landed in the center of this controversy when church authorities forbade her nuns from singing in church; they were only allowed to speak the words of the services. The authorities wanted to punish Hildegard because she was alleged to have allowed excommunicated individuals—barred from receiving Communion because of a grave offense against the church—to be buried on the consecrated ground of her convent's cemetery. In a lengthy letter to the church authorities, Hildegard eloquently defended the practice of music. Church officials eventually relented and allowed Hildegard's convent to resume its singing.

In obedience to you we have until now given up the singing of the Divine Office, celebrating it only by quiet reading—and I heard a voice coming from the living light, telling of those various kinds of praise concerning which David speaks in the Psalms: "Praise him with the sound of the trumpet, praise him with the psaltery and the cithara, praise him with the tympanum and the chorus, praise him with strings and the organ, praise him with the well-sounding cymbals, praise him with the cymbals of jubilation. Let every spirit praise the Lord" [Psalm 150: 3–6]. In these words we are taught about inward concerns by external objects, how according to the makeup of material things (the properties of musical instruments) we ought best to convert and to refashion the workings of our interior man to the praise of the Creator. . . .

Thus it is just that God be praised in everything. And since man sighs and moans with considerable frequency upon hearing some song, as he recalls in his soul the quality of celestial harmony, the prophet David, considering with understanding the nature of what is spiritual (because the soul is harmonious) exhorts us in the psalm, "Let us confess the Lord on the cithara, let us play to him on the psaltery of ten strings" [Psalm 32:1], intending that the cithara, which sounds from below, pertains to the discipline of the body; that the psaltery, which sounds from above, pertains to the striving of the spirit; and that the ten strings refer to the contemplation of the Law. Thus they who without the weight of sure reason impose silence upon a church in the matter of songs in praise of God, and thereby unjustly deprive God of the honor of his praise on earth, will be deprived themselves of the participation in the angelic praises heard in Heaven, unless they make amends by true regret and humble penitence.

Source: Epistle 47: To the Prelate of Mainz. From Strunk's *Source Readings in Music History*, Leo Treitler, General Editor. Reprinted by permission of Leo Treitler.

EXPAND YOUR PLAYLIST

Chant

Christianity is only one of many faiths that use monophonic chants in sacred rituals. Jewish, Buddhist, Hindu, Islamic, Native American (see chapter 2), and other traditions employ some form of chanting.

Buddhist chant
- *Tibetan Mantras and Chants.* Buddhist Monks of Maitri Vihar. Sounds of the World B00000IXHK. A selection of Buddhist chants from a contemporary Tibetan monastery.

Christian chant
- *Chant.* The Benedictine Monks of Santo Domingo de Silos. Angel B000002. A selection of different types of plainchant sung in the Catholic Church. This recording became a triple-platinum album when it was released on CD in the mid-1990s, selling more than 3 million copies in the United States alone.

Hindu chant
- *Sacred Hindu Chants and Mantras.* Retro Music B000BS6XYS. A wide range of meditative Hindu chants.

Islamic chant
- *Music of Islam,* Vol. 10: *Qur'an Recitation.* Celestial Harmonies B0000007Z5. Selections from the *Qur'an.*

Jewish chant
- *Chants Mystique: Hidden Treasures of a Living Tradition.* Musical Heritage Society 514284Y. A wide range of chants from various branches of Judaism.

HEAR SAMPLES on **www.mymusiclab.com**

TEST YOURSELF on **www.mymusiclab.com**   Flashcards and chapter tests

2

San Ildefonso Indians of New Mexico
Eagle Dance
Traditional; recorded ca. 1951

Monophonic chant is an almost universal phenomenon, appearing in some form in a great many cultures throughout the world and across historical epochs. The *Eagle Dance* is part of an ancient Native American rain ceremony and is always accompanied by chant. This recording captures the sounds of the dance as performed by the San Ildefonso Indians of New Mexico.

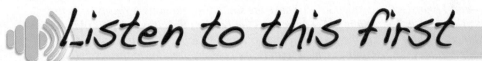 Listen to this first

((• HEAR MORE on www.mymusiclab.com

Texture	**Word-Music Relationships**	**Form**	**Melody**
Notice that all voices sing one melodic line together throughout the song.	Listen for repeated syllable groups. Notice the way the voices function like musical instruments.	How many sections can you identify? Are these sections repeated or contrasted?	Do the melodies have a generally upward or downward contour?

⚙ **LEARN MORE** on
www.mymusiclab.com
Chapter Objectives

Chant has long been—and remains—essential to sacred rituals throughout the world. Many Christians and Jews still incorporate chant in their religious services. The Hindu Vedas, Tibetan chants, Thai and Vietnamese Buddhist chants, as well as Confucian, Buddhist, Taoist, and shamanic chants in China, Korea, and Japan still occur in their cultural contexts.

Chant is the predominant form of music in Native North American Indian culture. Where it has not died out from the effects of the nineteenth-century wars with Euro-American settlers, it survives on reservations. Native American chanting can be heard today primarily at **powwows**, intertribal gatherings where Native Americans of mixed tribes express their mutual bond and identity.

The *Eagle Dance* portrays the life cycle of the eagle, a creature regarded as the connecting link between heaven and earth. Two men in eagle feathers dance movements that imitate eagles turning, flapping, and swaying in the air. The eagle's feathers bear prayers and are not allowed to touch the ground. An example of an *Eagle Dance* performed at the 202nd annual Omaha Nation Powwow in Macy, Nebraska, in 2006 can be viewed on MyMusicLab.

 **SEE MORE** on
www.mymusiclab.com
"Omaha Nation Powwow" video

Eagle Dancers from the San Juan Pueblo, New Mexico

Jack Kurtz/The Image Works

Texture: Monophony

Like the other forms of chant we have heard, the *Eagle Dance* consists of one melodic line. It is sung by male voices in unison. Even the percussion instruments are conceived as singing the chant; their sounds punctuate the rhythm of the chant rather than furnish a contrasting and independent rhythmic line. Nearly all Native American music is monophonic, and most often it is accompanied by percussion. In this case, the drumming is done with a single drumstick. If a larger drum is used, several players strike the rhythm together.

The powwow is usually organized by a committee that solicits the participants and organizes their performances. An emcee hosts the event itself, to make sure it runs smoothly.

Powwows have proven to be popular attractions for Native Americans, as well as others who are interested in learning more about Native American culture. They have also become profitable for their organizers, so they have grown in number, particularly in the western and midwestern United States. Annual listings of regional powwows can be found on the Web and in publications catering to Native Americans.

Word-Music Relationships: Beyond Language

In Native American culture, songs are believed to come from the spirit world. A song is transmitted through a person who hears it in a dream or revelation and then teaches it to others. Because songs are not about worldly matters, the words of humans have no place. Native

HISTORICAL CONTEXT   The Powwow

Originally, every Native American tribe had its own culture and traditions. However, after the European discovery of America, the Native American tribes were either eradicated or forcibly resettled, with many tribes and cultures mixed together on reservations. Eventually, individual tribal traditions gave way to a pan-Indian culture, at the heart of which is the annual pow-wow, or gathering.

The powwow is a means of celebrating Native American culture and preserving it against outside influences. Over the decades, powwows have become fairly standardized, including dancing, singing, traditional storytelling and crafts, and general socializing. Contests are held for best performances, with significant prizes to be won.

Each powwow begins with a "Grand Entry," a procession of all the participants into the arena where the event is to be held. After all have entered, flags are brought into the arena, including various tribal flags and the U.S. flag, carried by military veterans. Next to enter are the tribal elders and honored guests, followed by the dancers, men first, then women. A round dance usually ends the opening ceremonies.

Then, various groups perform dances that range from war dances to religious and ceremonial dances. Each group competes for the best performance. Singers perform the traditional songs to accompany these dances, along with other musicians, primarily drummers. Some of the traditional dances performed include the gourd dance, fancy feather or eagle dance, grass dance, and jingle dance.

At this contemporary powwow held in California, men perform the Grass Dance.
Spencer Grant/PhotoEdit Inc.

SEE MORE on **www.mymusiclab.com**
"Omaha Nation Powwow" video

American chant thus makes use of **vocables**—meaningless sung syllables, the sound of which serves like a melodic instrument. Some syllables are more accented than others, and all syllables are sung as prescribed, for they are part of the song. This requires careful memorization.

Form: ABA

The chant for the *Eagle Dance* is in three sections, **ABA**, with a brief introduction. Each section has its own melody, built of smaller, repeating units (see also "Terraced Melody"). Varied vocable order at the end of each melody group creates contrast within each section.

Terraced Melody

Although the **A** and **B** sections contrast in their rhythms and sung syllables, they are similar in the overall downward contour of their melodies. Both gradually descend the scale in what are known as **terraced** stages, eventually resolving on a low tone. This is typical of North American Indian chant melodies.

The **A** melody consists of two phrases with identical vocables:

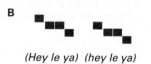

(Ya hey ya ha ye ya hey ye) (ya hey ya ha ye ya hey ye)

This melody occurs three times, on slightly different pitches, but with the same terraced downward contour. After the third time, vocables are sung in a varied order, creating a tapered ending for the **A** section.

The essential **B** melody consists of the shorter vocable set "*Hey le ya*," likewise sung twice:

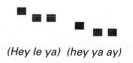

(Hey le ya) (hey le ya)

This melodic phrase is repeated. The third time, it varies slightly at the end and concludes with different vocables (*hey ya ay*):

(Hey le ya) (hey ya ay)

This is followed by a compressed version of what has been sung so far:

(Hey le ya) (hey le ya) (hey le ya)

Varied syllables bring this set of phrases to a close, and the music slows briefly. Then the entire pattern repeats, once again tapering off with a succession of varied syllables that bring the entire **B** section to a close.

Now listen to this chant again, following the Listening Guide.

Listening Guide

GO TO www.mymusiclab.com
for the Automated Listening Guide
CD I • Track 21/Download Track 21

San Ildefonso Indians of New Mexico Recorded ca. 1951 *Eagle Dance* (2:56)

Time	Form	Text (vocables)	Melody
0:00	Free introduction	*Hyo hey ya* *hyo hey ya hey ya* *hwey ye ya* *hya hey ya* *hey hey hey he* *hya hey ya* *hey hey ya*	Non-metered chant with rapid drum pulsations.
0:23	Metered part of the introduction	*Hey ye hey ya* *hey ye hey ye* *hey ya hey ye ye ye*	The chant becomes metered: slow groups of four beats.
0:31	A	*Ya hey ya ha ye ya hey ye ya hey ya ha ye ya hey ye* (three times, followed by vocables in varied order, tailing off the section)	The **A** melody is sung three times with slightly different pitches, but with the same terraced downward contour. After the third time, the vocables and melodic fragments are sung in a varied order.
1:03	B	*Hey le ya, hey le ya* (twice) *Hey le ya, hey ya ay* *Hey le ya, hey le ya, hey ya ay*	Contrasting terraced melody. Faster meter of four beats, more than double the speed of **A**.
1:16	The first half of **B** concludes	(Varied vocables)	Varied vocables and melodic fragments. The chant slows to a halt.
1:19	Resumed tempo of **B**	*Hey le ya, hey le ya* (twice) *Hey le ya, hey ya ay* *Hey le ya, hey le ya, hey ya ay*	The **B** melodic pattern repeats.
1:32	Slowing down	(Varied vocables)	The chant slows to a halt again.
1:35–end	A	*Ya hey ya ha ye ya hey ye ya hey ya ha ye ya hey ye* (three times, followed by vocables in varied order, tailing off the section)	The slow meter of the **A** unit returns with the first terraced melody.

Student FAQs

Why do traditional Native American chants often move from a higher to a lower tone?

Descending melodies are typical of many forms of traditional vocal music. The descending tone mirrors the exhalation of breath.

Why is this dance performed by men only?

Traditionally, only males were allowed to participate in the ceremonial songs and dances of Native Americans. At today's powwows, the Eagle Dance is still usually performed by men. The eagle is a strong symbol of virility to Native Americans, and in this dance it is associated with maintaining the fertility of the land and thus the survival of the tribe.

Why do Native American songs feature vocables instead of words?

There are different theories. Since many of the songs have a sacred or ceremonial meaning, the actual texts transcend ordinary language. The meaning cannot be expressed in words, so vocables stand in for them. Another theory is that because Native American tribes were combined on reservations, they needed to find a way to sing together. Using vocables allowed everyone to sing.

EXPAND YOUR PLAYLIST

Native American Music

Creation's Journey: Native American Music.
• Smithsonian Folkways Recordings SFW40410.

Anthology of North American Indian and Eskimo Music.
• Folkways Records FW04541.

Cry from the Earth: Music of the North American Indians.
• Folkways Records FW37777.
These are all good anthologies that give an overview of Native American musical styles.

Hopi Sunshield Singers.
• *Pow-Wow Songs Live!* Canyon CR-6180.
Intertribal powwow songs recorded live.

An Historical Album of Blackfoot Indian Music.
• Folkways Records FW34001.
These historic recordings are from cylinder recordings made in the 1920s and 1930s; while the sound quality is not the best, the performances are rare and interesting.

Blackfire.
• *One Nation Under.* Canyon CR-7049.
Blackfire is a group of Native American siblings who play what they describe as "fire-ball alternative punk." Joey Ramone makes a guest appearance on this disc. Political lyrics comment on the plight of Native Americans.

((•● HEAR SAMPLES on **www.mymusiclab.com**

✓ **TEST YOURSELF** on **www.mymusiclab.com**   Flashcards and chapter tests

3

Francesco Landini
"Behold, Spring"
Composed: ca. 1350–1397

This brief song illustrates an important feature in the development of medieval music: polyphony. We hear in Landini's "Behold Spring" not one voice or group of voices singing the same line, but two voices singing independent and equally important lines.

Listen to this first

((• HEAR MORE on www.mymusiclab.com

Texture	**Rhythm**	**Melody**	**Form**	**Word-Music Relationships**
Listen to how the two voices—one high, one low—relate to each other. Listen through the piece once, focusing your attention on the top voice; then listen through it again, focusing on the lower voice. Finally, listen through it a third time, noting how the two combine to create a harmonious whole.	Feel the regular pulse of three beats, the first accented (**1**-2-3 | **1**-2-3 |).	Listen for the stepwise motion in both voices. Notice the brief stopping points that subdivide the melody of each strophe into smaller units.	Listen for the repetition of large-scale units. The poetry is in three verses, with the first repeated at the end. Notice that the music for verses 1, 3, and 4 is identical; the music for verse 2 is different.	Notice the largely syllabic text setting—one note per syllable. Occasionally you will hear a melisma—multiple notes over a single syllable.

⚙ LEARN MORE on **www.mymusiclab.com** Chapter Objectives

Music was already the food of love in the Middle Ages, long before Shakespeare coined the phrase. Poets were inspired to write love poetry, and composers were inspired to set those poems to music to make them even more moving. Francesco Landini's "Behold, Spring" ("Ecco la primavera") is a setting of one such poem. It is a ballata for two voices. The ballata was one of many genres of secular song in the Middle Ages, and in the patterned rhythms of "Behold, Spring" we can hear the origins of the genre in dance (in Italian, *ballata* means "danced"). Landini's setting captures the feeling of bodies in motion.

The repertory of secular song in the Middle Ages is enormous. This was the age of courtly love, a highly stylized form of love in which a knight declares himself as the servant of the lady he is wooing. All his heroic deeds are done in her honor, and his love for her ennobles him, even if—especially if—she rejects his advances. Some songs describe the lady's beauty, others the knight's suffering (caused by her rejection of him), and still others the pleasures of love. In the *Decameron*, the poet Giovanni Boccaccio—who lived in Florence at the same time as Landini and undoubtedly knew him—describes how a small group of lords and ladies, fleeing the plague in a group, sings "Behold, Spring" and songs like it "in amorous tones" to "divert their minds with music."

Florence was—and remains—an important center of culture on the Italian peninsula. In Landini's time, it was also an important center of political power.

The Richness of Polyphonic Texture

This brief work uses a new kind of musical texture that had been emerging slowly for several centuries: **polyphony**. In polyphony, two or more voices of equal importance combine in such a way that each voice retains its own identity (*poly* = "many"; *phon* = "sound"). Here, the upper and lower voices are of equal importance, and while our ear is drawn to the upper line for acoustical reasons (higher pitches always tend to stand out more), the lower line is every bit as melodious.

Composers created the earliest polyphonic works sometime around the eighth or ninth century by adding new lines above or below existing plainchant melodies. These new melodic lines were crafted in such a way as to embellish what was already present, and church authorities sanctioned this new kind of music on the grounds that it was, in effect, a gloss or commentary on a well-known passage of text and music (the chant). Some of the earliest works of polyphony were extraordinarily long and intricate, but they were always based on an existing liturgical melody. A twelfth-century cleric named Perotin, who worked at the Cathedral of Notre Dame in Paris, wrote immensely long and intricate works known as organum (see Expand Your Playlist). These used plainchant melodies in long note values in the lowest voice, with faster-moving voices layered above the plainchant. These polyphonic works thus preserved the plainchant (in the lowest voice) even while embellishing it (in the upper voices). Gradually, composers began writing polyphony against new, original melodies, extending the technique beyond sacred music to include secular music as well. Landini's "Behold, Spring" is one of these entirely new secular compositions.

LEARN MORE on
www.mymusiclab.com
MyMusicLibrary:
"The Pope Condemns the Ars Nova"

Rhythm: The Pulse of Meter

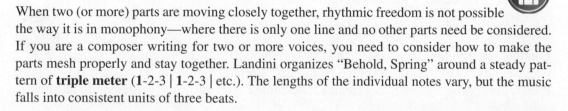

When two (or more) parts are moving closely together, rhythmic freedom is not possible the way it is in monophony—where there is only one line and no other parts need be considered. If you are a composer writing for two or more voices, you need to consider how to make the parts mesh properly and stay together. Landini organizes "Behold, Spring" around a steady pattern of **triple meter** (**1**-2-3 | **1**-2-3 | etc.). The lengths of the individual notes vary, but the music falls into consistent units of three beats.

Units of Melody

The mostly conjunct (stepwise) melodic lines are subdivided into smaller units, each of which ends with a **cadence**, a brief stopping point at which the music pauses (or, in the case of the final cadence, ends). Cadences are to music as periods are to verbal expression: when we are writing, we indicate the ends of units of thought with commas or periods, and when we speak, we make correspondingly briefer or longer pauses. By breaking our speech into units (sentences) and sub-units (clauses), we make it easier for listeners to understand what we are saying. Music operates on the same principle. Here, Landini inserts a brief cadence at the end of the second and fourth lines in each four-line strophe. In this particular work, Landini always cadences on the **unison**—that is, both voices sing exactly the same note. The rhythms of the two voices also emphasize the arrival on each cadence. At times the two voices move in the same rhythmic pattern, while at other times their rhythms diverge, but the rhythms always coincide just before each cadence.

Form: Turning Poetry into Music

In most vocal music, the form of the text shapes the form of the work. "Behold, Spring" is no exception. The poetry consists of three verses, known as **strophes** (or **stanzas**—the terms are interchangeable), with the first repeated at the end. The music of the second strophe contrasts with the others. Landini thus uses both repetition and contrast to create a musical form that can be diagrammed as **ABAA:**

Strophe   1   2   3   4 (=1, repeated)
Music   **A**   **B**   **A**   **A**

This combination of repetition, variation, and contrast is basic to all musical forms. Once an idea is presented (in this case, the text and music of the first strophe, "1/A"), only one of three things can happen:

1. It can be repeated.
2. It can be varied.
3. It can be contrasted through the introduction of a new idea.

Landini uses all three of these devices:

1. He contrasts 1/**A** by presenting both a new text and new music in 2/**B**.
2. He varies 1/**A** by presenting the same music with a new text in 3/**A**.
3. He repeats both the text and music of 1/**A** in strophe 4/**A**.

Word-Music Relationships: Syllabic vs. Melismatic

Landini sets the text in a manner that is largely syllabic. He uses melismas only occasionally, as on "temp'è" (line 3 of the first strophe) and again on "tempo" in the third line of the second strophe. This creates a welcome degree of variety: listening to an entirely

CONNECT YOUR PLAYLIST

Melismas

Find a piece that makes prominent use of melismas.

Example: Mariah Carey, "Always Be My Baby" (1995) Mariah Carey's vocal line features extended melismas.

PROFILE   Francesco Landini (ca. 1325–1397)

The Composer as Poet

Blinded by smallpox at an early age, Landini was the most famous and prolific Italian composer of the fourteenth century. He served as organist at a church in Florence for many years and also won renown as a poet. The phenomenon of the poet-composer was not unusual in the Middle Ages: many of the songs from this era are settings of poetry written by the composer himself. Landini is believed to have written more than 150 secular songs, which together represent about one-third of all Italian music that has survived from the fourteenth century.

One fourteenth-century contemporary praised Landini so lavishly as a composer, performer, and poet that he acknowledged that readers might think he was exaggerating about the abilities of any one individual in so many diverse fields. But this contemporary seemed certain that everyone would agree that

> [no one] ever played the organ so well. All musicians grant him that. And thus recently [i.e., 1364], at Venice, he was publicly crowned with laurel by His Majesty the King of Cyprus. In just this manner, once upon a time, poets were crowned by the Emperors of Rome.

Source: *The Works of Francesco Landini.* Ed. Leonard Wood. Cambridge, MA: The Medieval Academy of America, 1939, 301–303; translation modified slightly.

⊙➤ **EXPLORE MORE** on **www.mymusiclab.com**

This image of Francesco Landini is from the *Squarcialupi Codex*, a richly illuminated manuscript of polyphonic music from the 14th century. Landini is shown playing a small portative (or portable) organ.

Courtesy of Firenze, Biblioteca Medicea Laurenziana/Ministry for Cultural Affairs/Med. Palat. 87, c. 121v

---

EXPAND YOUR PLAYLIST: LANDINI

- **"I feel the flame of love"** (*Sento d'amor la fiamma*). Another ballata.

- **"My dear lady"** (*Cara mia donna*). A ballata for three voices.

- **"Farewell, farewell sweet lady"** (*Adieu, Adieu, dous dame*). A virelais (a genre of French song) that exists in two versions: one for two voices, one for three.

- **"Thus thoughtful"** (*Così pensoso*). A caccia or hunting song for three voices.

 HEAR SAMPLES on **www.mymusiclab.com**

---

syllabic setting might be a bit monotonous. But the syllabic setting allows the text to be projected quite clearly, even though the two voices are not always singing together in exactly the same rhythm.

Now listen to this ballata again, using the Listening Guide.

Listening Guide

GO TO www.mymusiclab.com
for the Automated Listening Guide
CD I • Track 22/Download Track 22

Francesco Landini Composed: ca. 1350–1397 *"Behold, Spring"* (1:13)

Time	Strophe	Italian Text	English Translation	Form	Melody
0:00	1	Ecco la primavera che 'l cor fa rallegrare; temp'è da 'nnamorare e star con lieta cera.	Behold, Spring, which makes the heart rejoice; it's the time to fall in love and to be of good cheer.	Music can be labeled as **A**.	Melisma on *primavera*. Cadence on *rallegare*. Melisma on *temp'è*. Cadence on *cera*.
0:17	2	No' vegiam l'aria e 'l tempo che pur chiama allegreza in questo vago tempo ogni cosa ha vagheza.	We see the air and weather bringing about gladness; in this lovely time every thing has loveliness.	Contrasting music (**B**)	Melisma on *tempo*. Cadence on *allegreza*. Melisma on *tempo*. Cadence on *vagheza*.
0:38	3	L'erbe con gran frescheza e fiori copron prati e gli alberi adornati sono in simil maniera.	The meadows are covered with fresh grass and with flowers; and the trees are adorned in a similar manner.	Same music as strophe 1, (**A**), different words	Melisma on *fresche*. Cadence on *prati*. Melisma on *e*. Cadence on *maniera*.
0:54	4	Ecco la primavera che 'l cor far allegrare; temp'è da 'nnamorare e star con lieta cera.	Behold, Spring, which makes the heart rejoice; it's the time to fall in love and to be of good cheer.	Text and music (**A**) of strophe 1 repeated	[Same as Strophe 1]

Excerpt modified from the translation by Giovanni Carsaniga from *I am Music: Works by Francesco Landini*. Reprinted by permission of Giovanni Carsaniga.

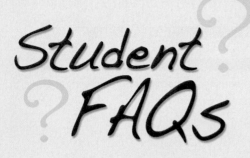

Student FAQs

The words are about spring and flowers and falling in love. Why doesn't the music sound happier?

What makes music sound "happy" differs widely according to place and time. Our notions of what makes music sound lively or optimistic today (major mode, a "bright" sound, fast rhythmic motion) are culturally conditioned and did not emerge in Western music until roughly the sixteenth century.

Was this written for women's voices?

This recording features women's voices. Women often performed together, as they do in this painting. Still, the piece could be performed just as easily by men's voices, or by men's and women's voices together.

Lebrecht Music & Arts/Lebrecht Music & Arts Photo Library

HISTORICAL CONTEXT   Producing a Manuscript

Unlike today, in the Middle Ages every musical document had to be written by hand. "Manuscript" means literally "handwritten" (*manu* = "hand"; *scriptus* = "that which is written"), so each manuscript was by its very nature unique.

These manuscripts could be extraordinarily expensive to produce. The one known today as the *Squarcialupi Codex* (a *codex* is a manuscript of many pages bound together) is an unusually elaborate example. Its material alone represented an enormous investment:

- **Parchment.**   This codex consists of more than 216 leaves of parchment, the prepared skin of a sheep or goat, cleaned, dried, and stretched to form a smooth surface for writing.

- **Gold leaf.**   Many of the painted miniatures within the codex are decorated with gold leaf, actual pieces of gold beaten very thin.

- **Miniature Portraits.**   All 146 of Landini's works in the *Squarcialupi Codex* appear in one continuous section, with his portrait at the beginning.

We know where the *Squarcialupi Codex* was made—the monastery of Santa Maria degli Angeli in Florence (present-day Italy)—but we do not know who commissioned it or paid for it. The music of the *Squarcialupi Codex* is largely secular (worldly), not sacred, and thus it was probably commissioned by an affluent individual. At some later point in the fifteenth century, this manuscript came into the possession of the Florentine organist Antonio Squarcialupi (1416–1480), after whom it is now named. There was no commercial market for a manuscript like this: it was created for, funded, and enjoyed by a single individual.

The ornamental instruments are overlaid with gold leaf.

By the 14th century, staff lines had become standard, and note-forms more closely resemble those in use today.

Francesco Landini, the composer, is shown playing a portative organ.

The Squarcialupi Codex
Courtesy of Firenze, Biblioteca Medicea Laurenziana/Ministry for Cultural Affairs/Med. Palat. 87, c. 121v

⊙→ EXPLORE MORE on **www.mymusiclab.com**
A Closer Look: Twelfth Century Plainchant Manuscript

EXPAND YOUR PLAYLIST

Medieval Polyphony

Perotin
- "All the Ends of the Earth Have Seen" ("Viderunt omnes"). The three upper voices weave in and around each other over a slow-moving fourth voice, derived from plainchant. The effect is mesmerizing.

Anonymous
- "In Paris/It Is Said / Fresh Strawberries" ("À Paris/On parole/Fraise nouvele"). One of many thirteenth-century polyphonic works with multiple texts: each of the three voices sings its own text, the upper two about the virtues of life in Paris, the third a street vendor's cry selling fresh fruit.

Anonymous
- "Summer is a-comin' in" ("Sumer is icumen in"). A round for two voices that is sung over a repeating phrase for two additional voices in the bass. This song about the arrival of summer was composed in England around 1250.

Lorenzo da Firenze
- "All in Their Places" ("A poste messe"). A fourteenth-century Italian caccia, a stylized hunting song that imitates the sounds of horns and dogs.

((•● HEAR SAMPLES on **www.mymusiclab.com**

✓ TEST YOURSELF on **www.mymusiclab.com**   Flashcards and chapter tests

4

Guillaume de Machaut
"I Can All Too Well Compare My Lady"
Composed: ca. 1350

This song by Guillaume de Machaut gives voice to the medieval art of courtly love, in which the knight praises the beauty and virtue of a noblewoman from afar. The "Pygmalion" in the text refers to the mythic sculptor of antiquity who carved a statue so realistic and beautiful that he fell in love with it and it came to life.

 Listen to this first

 HEAR MORE on www.mymusiclab.com

Texture

This work is for three voices. Listen to the way in which the uppermost voice stands out.

Melody

Listen for the cadences—points of rest in the music—within the melody.

Form

Listen for the repetition of large units of music. The music of the opening section is repeated to new words, and the closing section presents a contrasting melodic idea.

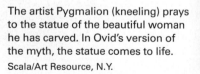 **LEARN MORE** on
www.mymusiclab.com
Chapter Objectives

The artist Pygmalion (kneeling) prays to the statue of the beautiful woman he has carved. In Ovid's version of the myth, the statue comes to life.
Scala/Art Resource, N.Y.

Love songs are as old as songs themselves. In the Middle Ages, many of these songs adopted the perspective of **courtly love**, in which a nobleman admires and literally sings the praises of a noblewoman, even if—or more to the point, *especially* if—she takes no interest in him. By forging ahead in spite of the woman's indifference, the singer could demonstrate his zeal and devotion. The words of this particular song compare the beloved lady to the statue carved by the mythic artist Pygmalion. The statue was so beautiful, according to this ancient legend, that the artist fell in love with it. In Ovid's telling of the myth, the goddess of love, Aphrodite, takes pity on Pygmalion: the statue comes alive, and the two go on to have children. In Machaut's text, the opposite occurs—the woman who is already alive remains like a statue toward the man who prays to her.

Three-Voice Texture

This work is for three voices. It has three independent lines that are completely different from one another. Medieval composers like Machaut were constantly exploring the possibilities of combining two, three, four, and even five independent voices.

The uppermost voice is the easiest to hear. Not only is it the highest voice, it is also the one that is most rhythmically active and fluid. The two lower voices move at a slower speed and sing longer (and fewer) notes. Because these two lower voices move in the same range and at a similar speed, it can be difficult to distinguish clearly between them. Probably the easiest passage in which to hear the difference between the two lower voices occurs at 0:49–1:00, at the beginning of the song's "B" section. It is at this point that the fullness of the three-voice texture also becomes most readily audible.

A Melody Punctuated by Cadences

Listen for the cadences—points of arrival, coupled with a brief pause in the forward motion of the voices—within the course of the upper voice's melody. These cadences occur at 0:15, 0:22, 0:45, 1:09, and of course at the very end (1:23). Over the span of this complete song, which runs about a minute and a half, we hear a total of five cadences. The length of the passages between each cadence varies from as little as 7 seconds to as much as 19 seconds. Think of these cadences as the equivalent of musical periods that mark off divisions between sentences in a text: each unit of the melody between the cadences presents a more or less self-contained idea, and the cadences help articulate the end and beginning of each new melodic section.

ca. 1300–1377
Guillaume de Machaut
"I Can All Too Well Compare My Lady"
Composed: ca. 1350
GENRE
Secular Song
KEY CONCEPTS
Polyphony, courtly love, cadences, AAB form.
CHAPTER HIGHLIGHT
Three-Part Polyphony
This brief song illustrates the expansion of polyphonic texture from two to three voices. The text exemplifies the medieval art of courtly love, in which a nobleman sings the praise of a noblewoman who is (or at least feigns to be) indifferent to him.

HISTORICAL CONTEXT   The Myth of Pygmalion

The story of an artist creating and then falling in love with a work that comes to life has been told and retold in many ways throughout the ages. Some examples are as follows:

- George Bernard Shaw, *Pygmalion* (1913). Professor Higgins "creates" a new person by transforming an uneducated girl (Eliza Doolittle) into a lady by teaching her how to speak and act.
- Alan Jay Lerner and Frederick Loewe, *My Fair Lady* (1956). A musical and later a film (1964) based on Shaw's *Pygmalion*.
- *Weird Science* (1985). A film directed by John Hughes in which two teenaged boys create a beautiful woman with supernatural powers.
- *She's All That* (1999). A film directed by Robert Iscove, a retelling of Shaw's *Pygmalion*, set in a California high school.

In this still from the film version of *My Fair Lady*, Eliza Doolittle (Audrey Hepburn) demonstrates at Ascot all that she has learned. Professor Henry Higgins (Rex Harrison) looks upon his "creation."
Everett Collection

PROFILE   Guillaume de Machaut (ca. 1300–1377)

Poet and Composer

Machaut was both a poet and composer, writing the words as well as music to his secular (worldly, nonsacred) songs. He spent much of his life in the service of various monarchs and traveled widely throughout northern Europe. He was appointed a canon at the Cathedral of Rheims in 1335. Toward the end of his life, he supervised the copying of what amounts to his complete works in a series of six large manuscripts called the "Machaut Manuscripts." They total more than 2,100 leaves. The image of Machaut here comes from one of those manuscripts and shows the composer still being inspired by the goddess of love, even in his old age.

Love introduces her three children, *Doux Penser* (Sweet Thoughts), *Plaisance* (Pleasure), and *Esperance* (Hope) to the elderly composer at work in his study.

Bibliotheque Nationale de France

⊙➔ **EXPLORE MORE** on **www.mymusiclab.com**

EXPAND YOUR PLAYLIST: MACHAUT

- **"Messe de Nostre Dame"** ("Mass of Our Lady"). See "The Mass" sidebar.

- **"Rose, liz, printemps verdure"** ("Rose, lily, spring, greenery"). A love song for five voices.

- **"Ma fin est mon commencement"** ("My Beginning is My End"). A song for three voices in which the two upper voices are the same melody, one sung forward, the other sung backward at the same time. The words match the structure of the music.

((•● **HEAR SAMPLES** on **www.mymusiclab.com**

CONNECT YOUR PLAYLIST

Three-Voice Texture

Find any work or extended passage for three voices.

Example: Kingston Trio, "M.T.A." (1957) This song, made popular by the Kingston Trio's recording, features three-part texture throughout.

AAB Form

Machaut's text consists of four sentences (see the Listening Guide). The music of the opening sentence (A) is repeated for the second sentence as well. In other words, we hear the same music twice, but with new words the second time. A new melodic idea (B) appears for the third and fourth sentences of the text and is not repeated. The overall form of the music can thus be represented as AAB. This is the same form as "The Star-Spangled Banner" (see page 13). As in "The Star-Spangled Banner," the "B" section is considerably longer than the "A" section. This is, as noted earlier, a common form in music of many times and places.

Now listen to the piece again, using the Listening Guide.

Listening Guide

GO TO www.mymusiclab.com
for the Automated Listening Guide
CD I • Track 23/Download Track 23

Guillaume de Machaut, Composed: ca. 1350 *"I Can All Too Well Compare My Lady"* (1:23)

Time	French Text	English Translation	Texture	Form	Melody
0:00	Je puis trop bien ma dame comparer a l'imageque fist Pymalion.	I can all too well compare my lady to the image made by Pygmalion.	Three-voice poly-phony throughout	A	Cadence at 0:15 Cadence at 0:22
0:25	D'ivoire fu, tant belle et si sans per que plu l'amaque Medée Jazon.	It was made of ivory, so beautiful and peerless that he loved it more than Jason loved Medea.		A	Cadence at 0:38 Cadence at 0:45
0:49	Li folz toudis la prioit, Mais l'image riens ne le respondoit. Einse me fait celle qui mon cuer font, Qu'ades la pri et riens ne me respont.	Foolish, he prayed to it constantly, But the image did not respond. Thus does she who melts my heart treat me, For I pray to her always and she answers me not.		B	Cadence at 1:09 Cadence at 1:23

Student FAQs

This music sounds almost modern, like something written much later. Why is that?

Medieval melodies and harmonies are based on a different system of scales (modes) than the ones we use today; many of the conventional turns of phrase we expect to hear in melodies simply did not exist at the time, which creates a feeling that the music sounds somehow strange and different, and to some ears today, "modern."

Are those men's or women's voices on the recording or both?

These are all men (three of them). The bottom two are singing in the range of a tenor, the upper end of the male register. The top voice is singing in the range of an alto, which is the lower end of the female register. The singer accomplishes this by singing in a manner known as falsetto, in which only a small portion of the singer's vocal cords vibrate; the effect is a higher-than-normal register. The Beach Boys, the Bee Gees, Michael Jackson, and Prince have all frequently used this technique.

The pronunciation of the French in this recording sounds odd. Why?

As in medieval English (think: Chaucer), some sounds in medieval French were not pronounced then as they are today. The performers are pronouncing the words in the manner of medieval French: "respondoit," for example, is pronounced re-spon-DWAY rather than re-spon-DWAH, as it would be today.

HISTORICAL CONTEXT The Mass

The Mass is the central service in many Christian denominations, including the Roman Catholic Church. It is a ritual re-enactment of Christ's Last Supper. The bread distributed to the communicants represents (or according to the doctrine of transubstantiation *becomes*) Christ's body, and the wine represents (or becomes) Christ's blood. The communion itself happens only after considerable preparation in the form of prayers and hymns. Many of these relate directly to the specific week or feast day (such as Christmas, Epiphany, or Easter): these are known as the Proper of the Mass because they are "proper" only to particular days or weeks. Other elements of the Mass never change and are spoken or sung regardless of the specific day or week. These constant elements of the Mass constitute the Ordinary ("ordinary" in the sense of "every day"). The portions of the Ordinary that are usually sung consist of the following.

- Kyrie: A prayer for mercy to God and to Christ.
- Gloria: A declaration of praise.
- Credo: A declaration of the articles of faith.
- Sanctus: The blessing of the bread and wine.
- Agnus Dei: A prayer for redemption from the Lamb of God.
- Missa ite est: A brief dismissal of the congregation ("Go, the Mass is finished.")

Guillaume de Machaut's "Messe de Nostre Dame" ("Mass of Our Lady") is the first known polyphonic setting of all the sung movements of the Mass Ordinary by one composer. The Mass had been sung as plainchant (see Web Bonus 1) for centuries before. Machaut was the first composer to write a complete set of multi-voiced movements to be sung in a service. Many centuries later other composers, including Johann Sebastian Bach, Wolfgang Amadeus Mozart, and Ludwig van Beethoven, would take up this challenge as well.

A priest (right) leads the celebration of Mass with the assistance of monks (left), who may also be singing.
Bridgeman Art Library\The Bridgeman Art Library International

LEARN MORE on **www.mymusiclab.com**
MyMusicLibrary: The Catholic Mass

EXPAND YOUR PLAYLIST

The Art of Courtly Love

Jacopo da Bologna
- "Never did Diana Please her Lover More" ("Non al suo amante"). A song for two voices by a fourteenth-century Italian composer. It ends with the words "My whole body trembled with the cold chill of love."

Bernart de Ventadorn
- "The Fool on the Bridge" ("Le fou sur le pont"). A song from the twelfth century by one of the most famous of all troubadours.

Oswald von Wolkenstein
- "Ah, Suffering and Longing" ("Ach senliches Leiden"). A song from the early fifteenth century by one of the leading *Minnesänger*, the German-language counterpart of the troubadours.

HEAR SAMPLES on **www.mymusiclab.com**

 TEST YOURSELF on **www.mymusiclab.com**   Flashcards and chapter tests

Alfonso el Sabio

Songs to the Virgin Mary, no. 249, *"He Who Gladly Serves"*
Composed: Late Thirteenth Century

The penetrating sound of the shawm, a double-reed instrument featured on this recording of "He Who Gladly Serves" ("Aquel que de volontade"), offers a good example of just how vivid and intense medieval timbres could be. This recording re-creates how drums and two wind instruments might have brought to life a work originally notated for only one voice.

 Listen to this first

((• HEAR MORE on www.mymusiclab.com

Timbre	**Form**	**Texture**
Listen for the contrast between the **percussion** instruments (two drums) and the **wind** instruments (two shawms).	Listen for the two basic units that make up the melody. They begin in the same way, but the second one moves into a higher range. Notice the way these units are repeated and varied.	Listen for three distinct textures on the shawms: 1. Both instruments play the same notes together (monophony). 2. One instrument plays the melody while the other holds a long, single note (homophony). 3. Both instruments play the same melody at the same time, but one of them plays a more elaborate and embellished form of it (**heterophony**).

Relatively little music written specifically for instruments survives from the Middle Ages. But we know from numerous accounts that composers and musicians rarely made sharp distinctions between vocal and instrumental music, and that they often performed vocal lines on instruments if not enough singers happened to be available for a performance. So while the original version of "He Who Gladly Serves" is for voices, with a text to be sung, the performance here reflects the common medieval practice of performing music with whatever was at hand. Jazz musicians still commonly arrange songs with words for instruments alone. When the great jazz saxophonist John Coltrane performed "My Favorite Things" (from *The Sound of Music*) on his saxophone, he was carrying on a tradition that had begun in the Middle Ages.

"He Who Gladly Serves" is one of the *Songs to the Virgin Mary (Cantigas de Santa Maria)* attributed to Alfonso el Sabio ("Alfonso the Wise"), who ruled the Kingdom of Castile and León on the Iberian peninsula between 1252 and 1284. The *Cantigas* is a collection of more than 400 songs

⚙ LEARN MORE on
www.mymusiclab.com
Chapter Objectives

preserved in several different manuscripts. One of these sources, now housed in the library of the monastery in Escorial, Spain, is full of miniatures showing a great variety of medieval instruments, lending further support to the idea that this music was not meant exclusively for voices.

A modern performer in medieval garb plays the shawm, the wind instrument heard in this performance of "He Who Gladly Serves." Today's musicians have revived medieval instruments, like the shawm, that fell out of use over time.

Richard E York; John A Howells Photography

The Iberian Peninsula in the Middle Ages

Timbre: The Sound of Double Reeds

The shawm is called a double-reed instrument because the player blows through the tiny space between a pair of cane strips. The vibrating air resonates down a long, open-ended tubular base made of wood and produces a reedy, slightly nasal sound. Although the shawm is still widely used in northern Africa and the Middle East, it had largely disappeared from western Europe by the end of the Renaissance. The closest relative of this instrument in the modern-day orchestra is the oboe, but the oboe's sound is more refined and not as delightfully raucous.

Form: Repetition and Contrast

The form of this piece arises out of the repetition and contrast of two fairly short melodic units. These two units (which we can label as **A** and **B**) begin in a similar manner, but **B** soon moves into a higher register. In this performance, a passage on the drums alone introduces two complete statements of the melody (that is, **ABA ABA**). The **A** section alone is repeated twice at the end to close out the work.

Three Kinds of Texture

In this piece, we hear three different textures:

1. **Monophony:**   Both instruments play the same notes together, in unison.

Monophonic texture (0:27)

CONNECT YOUR PLAYLIST

Instrumental Timbre

Find an instrumental version of a piece that originally had lyrics.

Example: John Coltrane, "My Favorite Things" (1961)
A number of jazz instrumental "standards" began as vocal music. John Coltrane borrowed the song "My Favorite Things" from the musical *The Sound of Music* (1959) by Richard Rodgers and Oscar Hammerstein.

2. **Homophony:**   One instrument plays the melody, the other a **drone bass**—that is, a long note held underneath the melodic line. The effect is very much like that of a bagpipe, another instrument widely used in medieval times.

Homophonic texture (0:54)

3. **Heterophony:**   Both instruments play the same melody at the same time, but one of them plays a more elaborate and embellished form of it. The two lines are thus similar (but not as similar as in unison texture) and at the same time different (but not as different as in homophonic texture).

Heterophonic texture (1:12)

Now listen to this work again, using the Listening Guide.

1221–1284
Alfonso el Sabio
Songs to the Virgin Mary,
no. 249, *"He Who Gladly*
Serves"
Composed: Late Thirteenth
Century
GENRE
Instrumental Arrangement
of Vocal Music

KEY CONCEPTS
Medieval instruments, heterophony, form based on large-scale repetition, variation, contrast.

CHAPTER HIGHLIGHT
Instrumental Music
Musicians of the Middle Ages often performed vocal music on instruments alone. "He Who Gladly Serves" was originally written with a text in praise of the Virgin Mary, but it could also be played by instruments alone, without a text. The recording here features the shawm, a double-reed instrument widely used in the Middle Ages.

PERFORMANCE   Reed Instruments

If you've ever created a sound by blowing on a blade of grass, you've applied the basic principle common to all reed instruments. These range from the medieval shawm (heard here) to the modern-day saxophone. By blowing into a reed instrument's mouthpiece, the player sets in motion either one or two thin strips of cane that have been specially shaped and dried. This vibrating cane, known as a *reed,* creates a resonance that produces the instrument's distinctive sound.

There are two subfamilies of reed instruments:
- **Double-reed instruments:**   The mouthpiece consists of two reeds opposed to one another. One reed thus vibrates initially against the other reed, which tends to produce the slightly "buzzy" sound heard here on the shawm. The two main double-reed instruments in use today are the oboe and the bassoon.
- **Single-reed instruments:**   The mouthpiece consists of a single reed secured to a hard surface. The principal single-reed instruments today are the clarinet and the saxophone. Finding good reeds is a challenge for musicians. More advanced players often make their own reeds, buying the raw material—strips of thin cane, specially grown and processed—and then shaving them down to just the right degree of thickness. A reed that is too thick will produce a "wooly" sound, but if it is too thin, it will break after only a short time.

👁 **SEE MORE** on **www.mymusiclab.com**
Inside the Orchestra: "Clarinet" and "Oboe"

A close-up of the mouthpiece of a shawm with its double reed
Richard E. York

Clarinet mouthpiece with reed
iStockphoto

Listening Guide

GO TO www.mymusiclab.com
for the Automated Listening Guide
CD I • Track 24/Download Track 24

Alfonso el Sabio Composed: Late Thirteenth Century *Songs to the Virgin Mary,* no. 249,
"He Who Gladly Serves" (1:48)

Time	Form	Texture	Timbre
0:00	Introduction		Drums only. Rhythm continues throughout entire work.
0:27	First statement of the melody as a whole: Section **A**	Unison	Shawms 1 and 2 in unison
0:36	Section **B**	Unison	
0:45	Section **A**	Unison	
0:54	Second statement of the melody as a whole: Section **A**	Homophonic	Shawm 1: melody Shawm 2: drone bass
1:03	Section **B**	Heterophonic	Shawm 1: melody Shawm 2: embellished version of melody played simultaneously
1:12	Section **A**	Heterophonic	Shawm 1: melody Shawm 2: embellished version of melody played simultaneously
1:22	Closing: Section **A**	Homophonic	Shawm 1: melody Shawm 2: drone bass
1:30	Section **A**	Alternates between unison and heterophonic	Shawms 1 and 2 at times in unison, at times with one of the instruments playing an embellished version of the melody

Student FAQs

Why shawms?

Why not? Perhaps the performers liked the sound of the shawm pictured here. The performers in this recording could have used almost any instrument and still been in keeping with medieval attitudes toward performing vocal music without singing.

Dorling Kindersley Media Library

Are the drum parts really that lively?

Drum parts were never notated in the Middle Ages, but we know from paintings that they were central to many instrumental ensembles, so we must assume that musicians used the notated music as a baseline, adding and embellishing as they saw fit. In this respect, medieval instrumental music was probably very much like today's jazz: a melody provides the basis of a more elaborate performance that takes liberties with the original tune.

Philip Dowell
© Dorling Kindersley

PROFILE Alfonso el Sabio (1221–1284)

The King Gets All the Credit

The manuscripts preserving the music and poetry known as the *Songs to the Virgin Mary (Cantigas de Santa Maria)* ascribe these works to Alfonso el Sabio ("Alfonso the Wise"), who ruled the Kingdom of Castile and León. Scholars now believe that if Alfonso wrote any of the words or music at all, he probably wrote only a relatively small number of them. We can be certain, however, that Alfonso was the moving force behind the creation and compilation of these songs; he commissioned many works in a wide variety of areas, including literature, philosophy, theology, and even chess.

The real composer of this particular song is in all likelihood anonymous, as is the case with so many medieval artists. After all, we often do not even know the names of the architects who designed the great Gothic cathedrals and churches being built around this same time in the thirteenth century. Many of these composers were monks, priests, or nuns; others were employed as musicians at courts; still others were troubadours, trouvères, and minnesingers, who traveled widely.

Alfonso el Sabio (center) listens to musicians performing a song in praise of the Virgin Mary (right). This image is from one of the several 13th-century manuscripts that preserve the *Songs to the Virgin Mary*.

Archivo Fotográfico Oronoz, Madrid

⊙➜ **EXPLORE MORE** on **www.mymusiclab.com**

⏪ **EXPAND YOUR PLAYLIST** ⏩

Instrumental Music of the Middle Ages

Kyrie cunctipotens genitor.
• An arrangement, for organ, of a liturgical vocal composition from the Mass, with a chant melody in the slow-moving lower voice and a free embellishment in the upper voice. Ensemble Unicorn, *Codex Faenza: Instrumental Music of the Early 15th Century.* Naxos 8.553618, Track 16.

Palästinalied.
• An arrangement of a German song from the time of the Crusades ("Palestine Song"), performed here on a recorder (a flute-like instrument) and a small drum. *The World of Early Music.* Naxos 8.554770, Track 5.

La quinte estampie real.
• The *estampie* was an energetic type of dance that involved stamping of the feet, as its name suggests. This performance is by an ensemble of wind and percussion instruments. Dufay Collective, *A Dance in the Garden of Mirth.* Chandos CHAN 9320, Track 9.

Saltarello.
• Another type of dance, this one involving leaping (*saltare* in Italian means "to jump"). This recording is for hurdy-gurdy, vielle, and drum. St. George's Canzona, *A Medieval Banquet.* ASV Living Era, Track 1.

((•• **HEAR SAMPLES** on **www.mymusiclab.com**

⊘ **TEST YOURSELF** on **www.mymusiclab.com** Flashcards and chapter tests

A CLOSER LOOK   Musical Instruments of the MIddle Ages

⊙→ EXPLORE MORE on
www.mymusiclab.com

This illustration from a fourteenth-century Italian treatise shows a variety of musical instruments. The placement of the figures is strategic, with King David, the author of the Psalms, at the top and Saint Cecilia, the patron saint of music, in the middle. The Psalms of David were meant to be sung, making frequent references to musical instruments.

The **vielle** was a forerunner of today's violin, with a wider and flatter body. Like the violin, the vielle had a penetrating sound and could be used to accompany both song and dance.

The **tambourine** is a percussion instrument. It combines the sound of a drum—the taught membrane of an animal skin—and small rattling cymbals around the edges. The tambourine, also known as the timbrel, is one of the instruments specifically mentioned in Psalm 150.

Bagpipe (left) and **shawm** (right). The bagpipe is an ancient instrument: the "bladder," which supplies the air squeezed through the pipes, was often made from an animal's stomach. The woman plays a short and therefore high-pitched shawm.

Drums, like the tambourine, are percussion instruments. They come in all shapes and sizes and can be played with the hands or (as shown here) with drumsticks. This drummer seems distracted by the volume of sound coming from the trumpets.

Scala/Art Resource, N.Y.

King David enjoys pride of place in his own special frame. Here, he plays the **psalter**, a forerunner of today's dulcimer, a plucked stringed instrument. Many of the instruments in this image are mentioned in David's Psalm 150: 3-4: "Praise him with the sound of the trumpet: praise him with the psaltery and harp. Praise him with the timbrel and dance: praise him with stringed instruments and organs."

The **lute** was one of the most popular instruments in Medieval and Renaissance times. The player here uses a plectrum or "pick" to pluck the strings.

Castanets or **"clappers."** This small percussion instrument, held in the hands, creates a very sharp sound and was used in dance music. The musician here in fact seems to be dancing.

Saint Cecilia plays the organ, one of the instruments with which she is often depicted. This type of organ is called a **portative** ("portable") **organ**. While the organ rests on the left side of her lap, she plays the keys with her right hand. With her left hand, she pumps air through the pipes with a kind of bellows mechanism not visible from this angle.

Two **straight trumpets**. These are brass instruments consisting of a single long tube, without the coiling and keys found on modern trumpets.

PART 1 Summary

 Texture Both monophonic and polyphonic

 Melody Flowing, largely conjunct, divided into sections by cadences; melodies based on scales of the medieval modes

 Rhythm Free (plainchant) and metrically structured

 Harmony A by-product of counterpoint

 Form Based on repetition, variation, and contrast

 Word-music relationships Syllabic settings to project texts clearly; melismatic settings to emphasize key words

IN REVIEW: Medieval Style

Monophony A single melodic line, whether sung by a solo voice or by a choir in unison. This was the essential texture of plainchant, the earliest music of Christian worship.
- Hildegard von Bingen, *Play of Virtues* (Chapter 1)
- San Ildefonso Indians, *Eagle Dance* (Chapter 2)
- Web Bonus Chapter 1: Plainchant Alleluia "Caro mea" from the Mass for the Feast of Corpus Christi

Polyphony Two or more different melodic lines performed simultaneously. This texture was used in both sacred and secular music.
- Francesco Landini, *"Behold, Spring"* (Chapter 3)
- Guillaume de Machaut *"I Can All Too Well Compare My Lady"* (Chapter 4)

Heterophony Two voices singing the same melody simultaneously, but with different embellishments.
- Alfonso el Sabio, *Songs to the Virgin Mary,* no. 249, *"He Who Gladly Serves"* (Chapter 5)

Syllabic and melismatic text-setting Text set to one note per syllable or multiple notes per syllable.
- Hildegard von Bingen, *Play of Virtues* (Chapter 1)
- Franceso Landini, *"Behold, Spring"* (Chapter 3)

Metered rhythm Rhythm structured around a fixed metrical pattern, allowing polyphonic voices to coordinate.
- Francesco Landini, *"Behold, Spring"* (Chapter 3)
- Guillaume de Machaut, *"I Can All Too Well Compare My Lady"* (Chapter 4)

Instrumental music Medieval performers could and did play vocal music on a variety of different instruments, such as the shawm.
- Alfonso el Sabio, *Songs to the Virgin Mary,* no. 249, *"He Who Gladly Serves"* (Chapter 5)

TEST YOURSELF on www.mymusiclab.com   Part Exam

PART 2

ca. 1425–1600

The Renaissance

During the Renaissance many of the arts and sciences from antiquity that had been lost or forgotten during the Middle Ages were recovered. "Renaissance" is the French word for "rebirth," and what was reborn in this era was the spirit of **humanism**, an intellectual and cultural movement that explored human interests and values through the pursuit of science, philosophy, literature, painting, sculpture, and music, particularly vocal music.

Renaissance composers brought the spirit of humanism to their art by setting both sacred and secular texts in ways that united words and music more directly than ever before. Composers devoted special attention to both the rhythm of the poetry and the meanings of individual words. They created a sound based on the ideal of equal-voiced parts in three, four, five, and eventually even six voices. The typical Renaissance vocal composition features a full, rich sound, intricate in both its texture and rhythm, yet always attentive to the text being sung.

Music for Catholics, Music for Protestants

As a Catholic, composer William Byrd had to watch his step in an England ruled by a Protestant monarch. While maintaining his own faith, he cultivated favor with Queen Elizabeth I in part by writing large quantities of music for Protestant church services, including the brilliant choral anthem *Sing Joyfully*

The Renaissance   ⊙→ EXPLORE MORE on www.mymusiclab.com

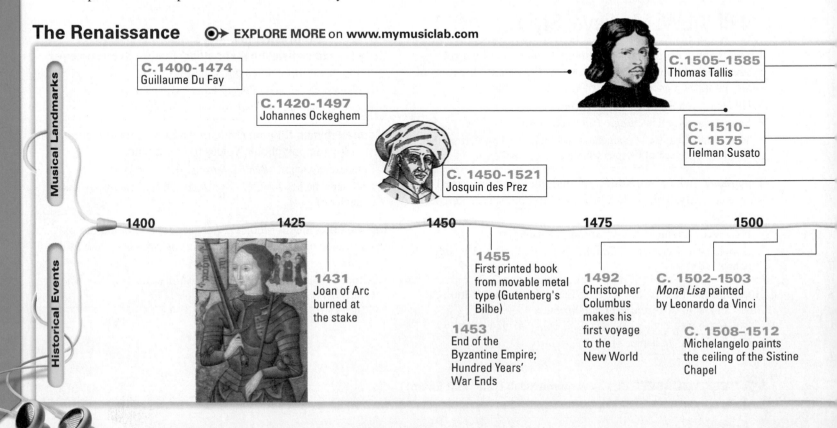

Musical Landmarks

C.1400-1474
Guillaume Du Fay

C.1420-1497
Johannes Ockeghem

C. 1450-1521
Josquin des Prez

C.1505–1585
Thomas Tallis

C. 1510–
C. 1575
Tielman Susato

1400   1425   1450   1475   1500

Historical Events

1431
Joan of Arc
burned at
the stake

1455
First printed book
from movable metal
type (Gutenberg's
Bilbe)

1453
End of the
Byzantine Empire;
Hundred Years'
War Ends

1492
Christopher
Columbus
makes his
first voyage
to the
New World

C. 1502–1503
Mona Lisa painted
by Leonardo da Vinci

C. 1508–1512
Michelangelo paints
the ceiling of the Sistine
Chapel

(see chapter 8). The rift among Christians had begun in 1517, when an obscure German monk named Martin Luther nailed a list of complaints on the doors of a church in Wittenberg. Luther was responding to what a number of people saw as growing corruption and a weakening spirituality in the church. He set in motion a revolution, known as the Reformation, that would establish Protestantism as a new branch of Christianity. From that point onward, the Western church would be divided into two main branches, Protestant and Catholic. The faith of any European monarch—Catholic or Protestant—would determine the faith and the politics of his or her realm. Composers responded to these changes by writing new music for the Protestant liturgy in languages other than Latin. Catholic composers, in what became known as the Counter-Reformation, redoubled their efforts to write music that would move the souls of the faithful.

Music for Growing Markets

Renaissance composers and musicians benefited from the enormous economic growth throughout Europe that began in the fifteenth century. The Italian peninsula and the area known as the Low Countries (present-day Belgium and the Netherlands) led the way in this new era of economic expansion. First contact with the "New World"—Christopher Columbus lived his entire life (1451–1506) in the Renaissance—swelled royal and private coffers still more. As kingdoms, duchies, and city-states expanded both in population and in wealth, the demand for music and the arts in general became greater and greater. The best composers and musicians could command high salaries.

▲ Martin Luther, 1529. Luther was a composer as well as a theologian: he wrote both the words and the music to the Protestant hymn "A Mighty Fortress Is Our God" ("Ein' feste Burg ist unser Gott"). This portrait is by the famed German artist Lucas Cranach the Elder.

Erich Lessing/Art Resource, NY

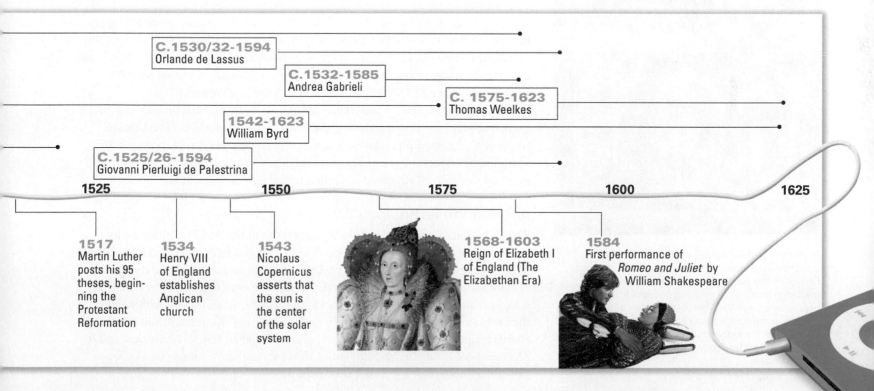

C.1530/32-1594
Orlande de Lassus

C.1532-1585
Andrea Gabrieli

C. 1575-1623
Thomas Weelkes

1542-1623
William Byrd

C.1525/26-1594
Giovanni Pierluigi de Palestrina

1525   **1550**   **1575**   **1600**   **1625**

1517
Martin Luther posts his 95 theses, beginning the Protestant Reformation

1534
Henry VIII of England establishes Anglican church

1543
Nicolaus Copernicus asserts that the sun is the center of the solar system

1568-1603
Reign of Elizabeth I of England (The Elizabethan Era)

1584
First performance of *Romeo and Juliet* by William Shakespeare

The ideal "Renaissance man" was someone who cultivated knowledge and experience in the full range of arts and sciences. In his famous handbook of behavior, *The Book of the Courtier*, the Italian nobleman and writer Baldassare Castiglione recommended that every would-be gentleman learn the basic arts of singing and playing an instrument such as the lute. Music-lovers entertained themselves and their listeners with such whimsical songs as Josquin des Prez's "The Cricket" ("El grillo") about a cricket (chapter 6), or with madrigals such as Thomas Weelkes's "Since Robin Hood" (chapter 7), using whatever instruments or voices were on hand.

A New Sense of Individuality

▲ Hans Holbein the Younger's *The Ambassadors* (1533) shows two courtly gentlemen with the symbols of their status: a globe and navigational instruments, and, on the bottom shelf of the table behind them, a lute, a set of four flutes, and an open hymnal. (The odd object in the foreground is a distorted rendering of a skull, a reminder of human mortality.)

©National Gallery, London/Art Resource, NY

The Renaissance was an age of growing confidence in the powers of human reason and the distinctiveness of every individual. Art became more personal. The contrasts between drama in the Middle Ages and in the Renaissance provide a revealing example of this new sense of individuality. Medieval drama had tended toward allegory: the Innocent Soul in Hildegard von Bingen's *Play of Virtues* (*Ordo Virtutum*) (chapter 1) is a symbolic figure torn between other symbolic figures, the Virtues and the Devil. By the end of the Renaissance, playwrights like William Shakespeare and Christopher Marlowe were writing dramas and comedies with flesh-and-blood characters. Hamlet's emotions are very human. Renaissance painting and sculpture also reflect this newfound sense of individuality. Compare, for example, the facial expressions of the figures in the Renaissance dance scene shown here with the faces in a corresponding dance scene from the Middle Ages on page 19. Each Renaissance face bears the stamp of a distinct personality.

▲ Musicians playing the drum and flute (right foreground) accompany a lord and lady in dance. Compare this painting from the 1520s with the medieval painting of dancing couples from 100 years before (see page 19). The strong sense of perspective (depth), considerable detail in the faces, and realistic portrayal of the individual figures show Renaissance art's inspiration from newly rediscovered classical Greek models.

By permission of The British Library

In a similar fashion, Renaissance composers captured human emotions in ways that seem far more personal in tone to us today. Josquin's "The Cricket" (chapter 6), for example, conveys a sense of genuinely playful humor with its imitation of cricket song, and Thomas Weelkes's "Since Robin Hood" (chapter 7) is full of unexpected rhythmic shifts that match its fanciful text at every turn.

Information Technology 2.0

The invention of printing by movable metal type in the mid-fifteenth century changed forever the way information could be transmitted. What had once circulated in scarce and enormously expensive manuscripts could now be disseminated rapidly and relatively cheaply through print. Some composers achieved international renown, thanks in no small part to the unprecedented speed with which their works could circulate across the entire continent. Tielman Susato (Web Bonus chapter 2) was both a composer and a publisher. His *Moorish Dance (La Moresca)* could be purchased in music shops throughout Europe (see *A Closer Look: A Renaissance Printing Press*, page 57).

A CLOSER LOOK   A Renaissance Printing Press   ⊙➔ EXPLORE MORE on www.mymusiclab.com

Before the invention of the printing press, the only way to reproduce a text was to copy it by hand. The end result of this laborious process was a single copy. The printing press made it possible to create hundreds and even thousands of copies of a text in a single process. Individuals could now buy music for their own use at a reasonable price. By 1500, printing had become a major enterprise, and countless presses, big and small, began to spring up across Europe.

A delivery man brings fresh paper to the shop. **Paper mills** made large sheets of paper by straining fibers, usually derived from old rags. This process was much cheaper and faster than working with animal skin to make parchment.

A workman applies ink to the set type, using two sponge-like applicators called **"ink balls."** He will then lay a sheet of clean paper over the inked type and slide both into the wooden press.

The **pressman** pulls the press: the screw mechanism (adopted from wine-making technology) exerts the enormous pressure needed to affix the ink to the paper. Printed sheets are then hung up to dry on a line nearby.

The **manuscript** of the text to be set is clipped to the wall.

Two **typesetters** set the type, pulling individual metal-cast letters one by one out of the cases before them. Each case is divided into an upper half and a lower half: the one above stores the capital letters, hence the term "upper case" for capital letters, even today.

The **owner** of the print shop supervises the operation. He pays the workers, negotiates contracts with authors, and invests the capital needed to run his small business.

This worker is one of two carrying out the **proofreading** process. His colleague, standing to his side, reads aloud the original text that has been typeset while the seated worker corrects any errors by rearranging type. The corrected typeface will go back to the press to be run off in multiple copies.

A young boy (known as the **"printer's devil"**) assists with miscellaneous tasks around the shop. If he proves himself trustworthy, he will eventually be given one of the more responsible jobs in the shop.

Art Resource/The New York Public Library for the Performing Arts

The Renaissance   CHAPTERS AT A GLANCE

| chapter 6 | chapter 7 | chapter 8 | chapter 9 | WEB BONUS chapter 2 |
| p. 59 | p. 65 | p. 71 | p. 78 | |

| ca. 1450–1521 | ca. 1575–1623 | 1542–1623 | | ca. 1510–ca. 1570 |

Josquin des Prez
"The Cricket"
Composed: ca. 1500

GENRE
Secular song

KEY CONCEPTS
Four-voice polyphonic texture, counterpoint, word painting, ternary form.

CHAPTER HIGHLIGHT
Renaissance Polyphony
This work exemplifies four-voice Renaissance polyphony, with each voice playing an equally important role. It also features word painting, in which the music replicates sounds suggested by the key words or phrases in the text, such as "cricket" or "holds a long line."
EXPAND YOUR PLAYLIST: The Music of Sounds: Clément Janequin, Kaluli of Papua New Guinea, Olivier Messiaen, Artur Honegger, Ludwig van Beethoven

Thomas Weelkes
"Since Robin Hood"
Composed: 1608

GENRE
Madrigal

KEY CONCEPTS
Three-voice texture, poetic meter and musical meter, shifting meters, syncopation, word painting.

CHAPTER HIGHLIGHT
The Madrigal
The madrigal, usually written for three to six voices, was the most important type of secular song in the Renaissance. The genre emerged in Italy and then found its way to England in the closing decades of the sixteenth century. This three-voice madrigal features extensive use of word painting, and the shifting meters of the music reflect the shifting meters of the poetry.
EXPAND YOUR PLAYLIST: The Italian Madrigal: Jacob Arcadelt, Cipriano de Rore, Luzzascho Luzzaschi, Lucca Marenzio, Claudio Monteverdi

William Byrd
"Sing Joyfully"
Composed: 1590

GENRE
Anthem

KEY CONCEPTS
Polyphony, a cappella choral music, six-voice texture, imitative counterpoint, word painting, elided cadence.

CHAPTER HIGHLIGHT
Sacred polyphony
The anthem and the motet were the two most important genres of Renaissance choral music. By the end of the sixteenth century, six-voice a cappella texture had become the norm. Imitative counterpoint and word painting brought texts alive. This anthem for six voices by William Byrd projects a Psalm text with extraordinary vigor.
EXPAND YOUR PLAYLIST: Sacred Music of the Renaissance: Giovanni Pierluigi da Palestrina, Tomás Luis de Victoria, Thomas Tallis, Martin Luther, Johann Walter

Global Connection: Polyphony
Rhyming Singers of the Bahamas
"My Lord Help Me to Pray"
Recorded: 1965

GENRE
Bahamian music

KEY CONCEPTS
Polyphony, call-and-response, syncretism, polytextuality, intonation.

CHAPTER HIGHLIGHT
Polyphony
Polyphony, the singing or intoning of many parts, is a worldwide phenomenon. In much African and African-influenced music, polyphony is created as parts overlap.
EXPAND YOUR PLAYLIST: Music of the Caribbean: Jamaica, Bahamas, Reggae, Calypso

Tielman Susato
Moorish Dance
Composed: ca. 1550

GENRE
Dance music

KEY CONCEPTS
Renaissance instruments, dance music, binary form, music publishing in the Renaissance.

CHAPTER HIGHLIGHT
Instrumental Music
Dance music is rhythmically clear and consistent to match the repeated steps of the dancers. This *Moorish Dance* consists of many small units of the same size that are joined to create a larger whole. Many of the Renaissance instruments in this recording are different from instruments in common use today.
EXPAND YOUR PLAYLIST: Renaissance Dance Music

GLOBAL CONNECTION KEY CONCEPT
Polyphony

58

Josquin des Prez
"The Cricket"
Composed: ca. 1500

"The Cricket" is a good example of Renaissance polyphony. It is for four voices, all equally important, and at times the music mimics the sound of what the text is about: a cricket.

 Listen to this first

((• HEAR MORE on **www.mymusiclab.com**

Texture

Listen for the polyphony of four distinct voices, all of equal importance. Listen for the difference between those passages in which the voices sing together in the same rhythm and those in which they go their own separate ways.

Word-Music Relationships

Listen for the examples of **word painting**, in which the music imitates the sounds suggested by the meaning of the text being sung. Listen for the long notes on the words "hold a long line" (at 0:07) and the chirping sounds (at 0:14, 0:21, and elsewhere) that imitate the sound of a cricket.

Form

Listen for the contrasting section in the middle (starting at 0:29), when the notes sound longer and more drawn out, and for the return of the opening section toward the end (at 0:55).

Why do composers write songs? Why set poetry to music? The answer, at one level, is quite simple: good music makes the meaning of a text more vivid and memorable. The poem inspires the composer, and the composer's melding of words and music inspires us as listeners. Think how much easier it is to remember verses that have been set to melody than it is to remember a poem all by itself. This was as true in the Renaissance as it is today, for composers throughout history have been drawn to the challenge of setting words to music.

When Josquin sat down to compose "The Cricket" ("El grillo"), he faced the challenge of writing music that would be as humorous as the poem itself. The text praises the singing of crickets over that of birds. It lauds the insect's versatility as a singer: he can sing long notes and stay in one place for long periods of time, unlike birds, who flit from place to place. The cricket can sing drinking songs, and when the weather turns warm in May, he sings of love. Josquin uses catchy, clever rhythms to imitate the sound of the cricket. His melodic lines enhance the spirit of the poem, and his textures bring out the meaning of key words.

Josquin's setting is typical of Renaissance song in general, in that it speaks a musical language that seems contemporary to us even today. Its melodies, rhythms, and textures certainly strike us as more familiar than those of the Middle Ages. Hildegard von Bingen (chapter 1)

⚙ **LEARN MORE** on **www.mymusiclab.com** Chapter Objectives

59

👁 **SEE MORE** on
www.mymusiclab.com
"The Renaissance in
Europe" documentary

and Francesco Landini (chapter 3) were equally inspired by the texts they set, yet their musical language is somehow less direct, more hauntingly austere. Medieval and Renaissance musical styles might be said to differ in the way that Old English differs from modern English. It is a not a matter of one language being better than the other. Medieval and Renaissance song create their own distinct kinds of beauty by using the same basic elements of music in different ways.

Medieval and Renaissance scribes often inserted humorous vignettes into otherwise very serious manuscripts. Here, the scribe seems to be commenting on the parallels between human singers and the noises animals make.

MS 127. *Chansonnier Zeghere Van Male,* 1542, f. 4r. Courtesy Mediatheque Municipale de Cambrai

Texture: Polyphony in Four Voices

The four voice parts of "The Cricket" correspond to the four registers of the human voice:

- Soprano (highest range)
- Alto (second-highest range)
- Tenor (second-lowest range)
- Bass (lowest range)

In Josquin's setting, these four voices are essentially equal, and they move together in step for most of the work. Only occasionally does Josquin differentiate among the voices rhythmically, and the words we hear at those moments stand out from the rest of the song. The most striking of these moments occur at the words *longo verso* ("long verse") at 0:07–0:13, and at *amore* ("love") at 0:50–0:54, when each voice momentarily goes its own way, setting these key words apart from all others in the text.

Equal-voice texture—**polyphony**—is the norm for Renaissance music in general, as opposed to monophony (a single melodic line) or homophony (a melodic line accompanied by other voices of lesser importance). Composers took great pride in their skill at **counterpoint**, a system of rules and procedures governing the composition of multiple melodies that are not only satisfying when played alone but that sound good when played together. "Counterpoint" takes its name from the Latin word *contrapunctum*, or "note-against-note" (the Latin word for "note" is *punctum*). Counterpoint is a demanding art and one that aspiring composers still learn today in almost exactly the same manner as in the Renaissance: by writing first one new melody against an existing one, then adding a third, and a fourth, and so on.

Word-Music Relationships: Music Imitates the Text

When the text speaks of the cricket's ability to "hold a long line" of music (*longo verso*, at 0:07), the top and bottom voices sing very long notes, while the inner voices weave around each other in the middle. Josquin is also playing on a pun in the text here: in Italian, *verso* can mean a line of verse, or it can also mean the noise an animal makes. So what we hear at this point is both a long-held note and the sound of the cricket.

When the text tells us that the cricket also sings about drinking (*dalle beve*, at 0:14), we hear a cricket-like chirping sound a little like the hiccups of someone who has had a bit too much to drink. The music then repeats these same words to a series of rapid-fire notes with all four voices singing together in exactly the same rhythm, repeating each word non-sensically ("Of of drinking drinking cricket cricket sings," at 0:21). Finally, when the cricket sings of love (*amore*, at 0:50), we hear all four voices break into an extended melisma. Here, on this one word, the music is at its most complex and intense, in keeping with the spirit of the text.

Ternary Form

As is almost always the case in vocal music, the form of the text shapes the form of the music. The text of "The Cricket" falls into two broad sections:

1. How the cricket can hold a long note and can sing of drinking
2. How the cricket is different from birds, who also sing

Josquin gives distinctive music to each of these two sections (labeled **A** and **B** in the Listening Guide). By repeating the opening section of the text and music (**A**) at the end, however, he creates what is known as **ternary form**, which consists of three parts, **ABA**. Ternary form uses the basic principles of contrast (**B** contrasts with **A**) and return (**A** comes back at the end).

Now listen to this piece again, using the Listening Guide.

ca. 1450–1521
Josquin des Prez
"The Cricket"
Composed: ca. 1500

GENRE
Secular song

KEY CONCEPTS
Four-voice polyphonic texture, counterpoint, word painting, ternary form.

CHAPTER HIGHLIGHT
Renaissance Polyphony
This work exemplifies four-voice Renaissance polyphony, with each voice playing an equally important role. It also features word painting, in which the music replicates sounds suggested by the key words or phrases in the text, such as "cricket" or "holds a long line."

CONNECT YOUR PLAYLIST

Word Painting

Find a piece that uses word painting.

Example: The Monkees, "Last Train to Clarksville" (1966)
Many "train" songs make use of word painting to replicate the sounds of a train. In this song, for example, the background singers imitate the sounds of a train whistle.

Listening Guide

GO TO www.mymusiclab.com
for the Automated Listening Guide
CD I • Track 25/Download Track 25

Josquin des Prez Composed: ca. 1500 *"The Cricket"* (1:33)

Time	Form (Musical Section)	Original Italian Text	English Translation	Word-Music Relationship	Texture
0:00	A	El grillo è buon cantore Che tienne longo verso.	The cricket is a good singer Who can hold a long line.	Word painting with long notes on *longo verso* ("long line" or "long noise").	Polyphonic (four equal voices)
0:14		Dalle beve grillo canta El grillo è buon cantore.	Of drinking the cricket sings The cricket is a good singer.	Back-and-forth between upper and lower voices imitates the chirping of the cricket.	
0:29	B	Ma non fa come gli altri uccelli, Come li han cantato un poco, Van' de fatto in altro loco Sempre el grillo sta pur saldo.	But he doesn't do what birds do: After they've sung a bit, They go somewhere else; The cricket always stays put.	Contrasting section, slightly lower in register, slightly darker in sound.	
0:43		Quando la maggior è 'l caldo Al'hor canta sol per amore.	And when the weather is hottest He sings solely for love.	Elaborate melismas make the word *amore* ("love") stand out.	
0:55	A	El grillo è buon cantore Che tienne longo verso. Dalle beve grillo canta El grillo è buon cantore.	The cricket is a good singer Who can hold a long line. Of drinking the cricket sings The cricket is a good singer.	Work ends as it began, with text and music repeated, suggesting that the cricket goes on singing just as before.	

Student FAQs

I hear only one melody here, in the top voice. How can there be more than one melody going on at the same time?

For acoustical reasons, our ear tends to be drawn to the highest-sounding voice within a group of voices. But if you listen to the lower voices—isolate them, in effect—you will hear three other well-shaped melodic lines as well.

Are the two higher voices here sung by men or women?

Normally, the soprano and alto parts are sung by women, for these ranges lie naturally within the range of the female voice. But in this recording, as in many recent recordings of earlier music (pre-1700), the two upper parts are sung by men, reflecting the performing practice of earlier times. The higher of these—the soprano part—is sung by a man singing *falsetto*, a technique by which the voice bypasses the larynx, which is the part of the throat that otherwise gives men's voices a deeper register. Many modern male groups or singers have used this technique (such as the Beach Boys, Marvin Gaye, and Coldplay). For more on this style of singing, see chapter 8.

At the very end, it doesn't sound as if the music is quite finished. Why is that?

Like most music written before 1600, the melodic lines are derived from one of the medieval modes—in this case, the mode on D (Dorian). Modal writing of this kind did not call for a work to end on what we might think of today (somewhat anachronistically) as the tonic (see page 9). So to Josquin's contemporaries, the final cadence of this work would have sounded quite normal and not incomplete at all.

PROFILE   Josquin des Prez (ca. 1450–1521)

"Master of the Notes"

Josquin was an international celebrity in his time. Even non-musicians knew who he was: the famed theologian Martin Luther declared that "Josquin is the master of the notes, which must do as he wishes, while other composers must follow what the notes dictate." And music publishers were eager to put Josquin's name on the music they wanted to sell, regardless of whether he had written it or not. Josquin knew his own worth, too. An agent of the Duke of Ferrara, who was seeking to hire a new composer for his court, reported to his master that the two best available composers were Josquin and Heinrich Isaac. "It is true that Josquin composes better," the agent wrote, "but he composes when he wants to, and not when one wants him to, and he is asking 200 ducats in salary while Isaac will come for 120." To the duke's credit, he hired Josquin anyway.

Though Josquin is generally considered the greatest composer of the early Renaissance, much of his life is shrouded in mystery. He was born and died somewhere in an area on the border between what is now France and Belgium, but he spent much of his life working in Italy, including St. Peter's in Rome. Scholars have recently discovered that there were several composers going by the name of "Josquin" in the late fifteenth and early sixteenth centuries, and it may be one of these "other" Josquins who wrote "The Cricket." For the moment though, no one can be absolutely certain.

◉➤ **EXPLORE MORE** on www.mymusiclab.com

JOSQUIN DES PREZ: STATIONS IN A CAREER

Saint-Quentin Born ca. 1450
7 Condé-sur-l'Escaut 1504–1521 (Provost of the Collegiate Church of Notre Dame)
1
Paris 1498–1503 (musician in the royal court of France) 5
Milan 1484–89 (in the service of Cardinal Ascanio Sforza)
3
6 Ferrara 1503–1504 (musician in the Mantuan court)
2 Aix-en-Provence 1475–78 (musician in the ducal chapel)
4 Rome 1489–ca. 1495 (musician in the Papal Chapel)
N

EXPAND YOUR PLAYLIST: JOSQUIN DES PREZ

- **Missa Pange Lingua.** A setting of the Ordinary of the Mass (those portions said or sung at every Mass, regardless of the occasion). The work takes its name from the medieval plainchant hymn melody that provides the basis for many of Josquin's themes.

- **Missa La Sol Fa Re Mi.** Another setting of the Mass Ordinary, this one based on a series of notes that corresponds to a scale descending from "La" (A) to "Mi" (E). Josquin challenged himself to give variety to such a basic and simple idea repeated over and over.

- **"Hail Mary . . . Serene Virgin"** (*Ave Maria . . . virgo serena*). A motet (sacred song) for four voices, one of Josquin's most famous compositions.

- **"Virgin Nurse of God, Undefiled"** (*Illibata Dei virgo nutrix*). Another motet in praise of the Virgin Mary, for five voices. The first letter of each line spells out "Josquin des Prez."

((◉ **HEAR SAMPLES** on www.mymusiclab.com

PERFORMANCE   Playing and Singing

Today's songwriters know that any big hit is likely to be performed in many different ways: with words, without words, and arranged for all kinds of instruments and instrumental ensembles. Josquin almost certainly felt the same way. Like many Renaissance composers, he wrote music in such a way that it could be either sung (with a text) or played (without a text), and played on different kinds of instruments. Indeed, a great deal of the vocal repertory from this time has come down to us in manuscripts that have no vocal texts at all. We know what words to sing only because the texts have survived in other manuscripts. Renaissance musicians were resourceful, and they used whatever combination of voices or instruments were available at any given moment. In the case of "The Cricket," listeners might lose the witty connections between the text and the music (the chirping sounds, for one), but this did not prevent them from enjoying vocal music on instruments, or allowing instruments to fill in one or more of the vocal lines.

A mixed group of instrumentalists and a vocalist perform a piece that was written as a vocal composition. The woman on the left sings; another, on the right, plays the lute; and the one in the center plays the flute. Presumably, the lutenist is also singing.

Master of Female Half Lengths (ca. 1490–ca. 1540) "The Concert"/Bridgeman Art Library

---

◀◀   EXPAND YOUR PLAYLIST   ▶▶

The Music of Sounds

All music may be sound, but are all sounds music? There are no easy answers, but sounds from the outside world have found their way into the music of almost every culture, time, and place.

Birds
- Clément Janequin's "The Song of the Birds" ("Le chant des oiseaux," early sixteenth century), imitates the songs of thrushes, robins, nightingales, and cuckoos.
- The music of the Kaluli of Papua New Guinea is modeled on the sounds of the rainforest, including frogs, insects, and birds. *Voices of the Rainforest: A Day in the Life of the Kaluli People* (Rykodisc 10173).
- The French composer Olivier Messiaen incorporated birdsong into many of his works. His "Awakening of the Birds" ("Réveil des oiseaux," 1953), consists almost entirely of imitated bird songs.

Monkeys
- The *Cecak* or *Ketjak*, also known as the "Ramayana Monkey Chant," from Bali (Indonesia) features a group of 100 or more men who imitate, through gesture and song, a group of legendary fighting monkeys. *Audio*: Nonesuch H-72028. *Video*: Video excerpts of this chant are widely available on the Internet.

Trains
- Artur Honegger named his orchestral work *Pacific 231* (1923) after a type of steam locomotive. The piece builds slowly in momentum before reaching full speed.
- Billy Strayhorn's *Take the "A" Train* (1941), made famous by Duke Ellington's big band recording, imitates the driving rhythms of the New York City subway line running from Manhattan to Harlem.

Battle
- Clément Janequin's *La bataille* (early sixteenth century) imitates battle noises, trumpet calls, cannon fire, and the cries of the wounded.
- Ludwig van Beethoven's *Wellington's Victory* (1813) imitates the firing of cannon, using bass drums.
- Pyotr Ilich Tchaikovsky's *1812 Overture* (1882) imitates cannon fire through the use of bass drums. Some orchestras, including the Boston Pops in their outdoor performances on the Fourth of July, use fireworks. Now and then, performances even use the real cannons Tchaikovsky called for in the score.

((•● **HEAR SAMPLES** on **www.mymusiclab.com**

Ø **TEST YOURSELF** on **www.mymusiclab.com**   Flashcards and chapter tests

Thomas Weelkes
"Since Robin Hood"
Composed: 1608

Thomas Weelkes's "Since Robin Hood" is a song about an actual event that took place in 1599 when William Kemp danced from London to Norwich, a distance of some 140 miles, over the course of nine days. On first listening, it strikes most people as a fairly straightforward setting of a lightweight, almost nonsensical text.

  Listen to this first

((•· HEAR MORE on www.mymusiclab.com

Texture	Rhythm	Word-Music Relationships
Listen to the three distinct voices, each of equal weight. This texture is polyphonic.	Listen for the shift in rhythm in the middle of the piece from duple to triple meter.	Listen to the descriptive nature of the music with certain words, such as "to skip" and "trip it."

What seems simple on the surface can often be quite intricate. With careful listening, we can begin to hear the many remarkable ways in which Weelkes has captured the spirit of this text.

"Since Robin Hood" is a **madrigal**, a musical setting of a text in a single strophe (stanza), and the text of this madrigal is a poem about dancing. "Kemp" is the English actor William Kemp, who was a friend of Shakespeare and an original shareholder in London's Globe Theatre. (Among his many roles, Kemp played the role of the nurse in *Romeo and Juliet* in an age when women were not allowed onstage.) What Kemp later called his "Nine-Day Wonder" was a feat of shameless self-promotion. Like any good promoter, Kemp wrote a book about his exploits.

The dance that Kemp performed over these nine days was the Morris dance, a traditional English dance of obscure origins whose name is probably a corruption of "Moorish dance." Tielman Susato's *Moorish Dance (La Moresca)* belongs to this same tradition (see Web Bonus chapter 2). It is a group dance, with stock characters that include a hobby horse (a dancer wearing the costume of a horse's body from his waist down) and Maid Marian (a male dressed in women's clothing). The dancers—all male in Kemp's time—wore small bells on their calves. The group nature of the dance made Kemp's feat all the more unusual, for as the lyrics of the song tell us, he "did dance alone," with the other figures (Robin Hood, Maid Marian, Little John, and the hobby horse) all absent ("forgot").

A famous portrayal of Kemp on his nine-day Morris dance tour, accompanied by a pipe-and-tabor player
© Dorling Kindersley

⚙ **LEARN MORE** on
www.mymusiclab.com
Chapter Objectives

👁 **SEE MORE** on
www.mymusiclab.com
"Renaissance Dance"
documentary

Texture: Polyphony in Three Voices

The texture is polyphonic throughout, which is typical of the Renaissance madrigal. No one voice predominates, and all three contribute equally to the whole. The three voices move together in more or less the same rhythm, creating a declamatory style of singing. This makes the text easier to understand, for it is as if all the voices are reciting the text together—in song.

The melody in the uppermost voice of Weelkes's setting would have been familiar to Shakespeare's contemporaries, for this was a tune already well-known by the end of the sixteenth century and one closely associated with Morris dancing. (It is even called "The Morris Tune" in various sources of the time.) But the lines in the two lower voices have their own distinctive melodic profiles as well.

Poetic Rhythm in Music

To understand the rhythm of the music, we must first consider the rhythm of the poetry. The **meter** of a poem is its basic rhythmic unit. Most metrical poems stick to a single meter from beginning to end. But "Since Robin Hood" is unusual because it keeps shifting from one meter to another.

Read the text out loud and exaggerate the rhythmic patterns of the accented (long) syllables. The pattern that emerges at the beginning is **iambic**: short-LONG, short-LONG, short-LONG, short-LONG, which can be represented by the symbols ˘ (= short) and ′ (= LONG):

Since **Robin Hood**, Maid **Marian**,

And **Little John** are **gone**,

The **hobby horse** was **quite** for**got**,

When **Kemp** did **dance** a**lone**.

But in the second section of the poem, the meter changes. Read this part out loud, again emphasizing the natural stresses within the words:

He did **labour after** the **tabor**.

For to **dance** then **into France**.

If you try to read these lines in the iambic meter of the opening (short-LONG), you'll realize at once that it just doesn't work: the accents are all wrong, because these lines are in **trochaic** meter (LONG-short, LONG-short, etc.).

In the third and final section of the poem, the meter becomes quite jumbled, moving briefly back to iambic (short-LONG) for one line:

In **hope** of **gains**

before shifting to yet another kind of meter, **anapestic** (short-short-LONG):

˘ ˘ / ˘ ˘ /

He did **trip** it on the **toe**,

Diddle **did**dle diddle **doe**.

Now that you've read the text with an eye (and ear) to its meter, listen to how these shifts in the meter of the poetry are reflected in the shifting meters of the music.

1. The opening lines (iambic) are in **duple meter**, and the note lengths are fairly even:

˘   / ˘ / ˘   / ˘ / ˘   / ˘ / ˘   /

Since | **Rob**-in **Hood**, Maid | **Mar**-i-**an**, and | **Lit**-tle **John** are | **gone**

(4) | **1**   2   3   4 | **1** 2 3   4 | **1**   2   **3**   4 | **1**

With four beats to each musical measure, beats **1** and **3** and especially

1 are the beats that are normally emphasized, and the poetry fits this scheme quite nicely.

2. The second section (trochaic) shifts to **triple meter** to accommodate the new trochaic meter of the poetry (LONG-short):

/ ˘   / ˘   / ˘   / ˘

He did | **la**- bour | **af**- ter the | **ta**- bor

1-2 3   **1**-2 3   **1**-2   3   **1**-2 3

The accented syllables on "1" are longer: they get two beats, whereas the unaccented syllables (or groups of syllables) get only one beat.

3. Even though the text remains in trochaic meter ("He took pains to skip it . . ."), Weelkes returns to duple meter, like at the beginning. But here, the notes are **syncopated**—that is, they run against the regular pulse of the musical meter, with accents on beats other than "1" and "3." This allows Weelkes to present the words "to skip" in almost graphic fashion, with the voices tossing these two words back and forth among themselves. In this way, we lose any strong sense of metrical pulse, just at that moment when the text talks about skipping.

Word Painting in the Renaissance Madrigal

As noted previously, certain words ("to skip," "did trip it") are set quite graphically, instances of **word painting**. These are among the few passages in the entire madrigal in which the voices are not singing in rhythm together. Instead of declaiming these words in a clear fashion, the voices in effect "skip" ahead of themselves. Word painting is a device that is well-suited to the Renaissance madrigal. Composers used whatever musical elements they could to enhance the meaning and pleasure of the poetry, and word painting is so common in this repertory that it is sometimes called a *madrigalism*.

Now listen to this piece again, using the Listening Guide.

ca. 1575–1623
Thomas Weelkes
"Since Robin Hood"
Composed: 1608

GENRE
Madrigal

KEY CONCEPTS
Three-voice texture, poetic meter and musical meter, shifting meters, syncopation, word painting.

CHAPTER HIGHLIGHT
The Madrigal
The madrigal, usually written for three to six voices, was the most important type of secular song in the Renaissance. The genre emerged in Italy and then found its way to England in the closing decades of the sixteenth century. This three-voice madrigal features extensive use of word painting, and the shifting meters of the music reflect the shifting meters of the poetry.

CONNECT YOUR PLAYLIST

Changing Meters

Find a piece that changes meter.

Example: The Beatles, "Lucy in the Sky with Diamonds" (1967) The opening verse is in triple meter, the chorus in duple meter.

Listening Guide

GO TO www.mymusiclab.com
for the Automated Listening Guide
CD I • Track 26/Download Track 26

Thomas Weelkes Composed: ca. 1575–1623 *"Since Robin Hood"* (1:05)

Time	Text	Poetic Meter	Musical Meter	Word-Music Relationships	Texture
0:00 (repeats at 0:09)	Since Robin Hood, Maid Marian, And Little John are gone, The hobby horse was quite forgot, When Kemp did dance alone.	Iambic (short-LONG)	Duple (1-2-**3**-4)		Polyphonic (three equal voices)
0:18 (repeats at 0:40)	He did labour after the tabor. For to dance then into France.	Trochaic (LONG-short)	Triple (**1**-2-3)	Music changes meter when the text changes meter, following— "laboring after"—the rhythm of the imaginary drum to which Kemp is dancing	
0:27 (repeats at 0:49)	He took pains to skip it	Trochaic (LONG-short)	Duple (with syncopation, that is, accents off the normally accented beats)	Syncopation reflects "skipping"	
0:31 (repeats at 0:53)	In hope of gains.	Iambic (short-LONG)	Duple (with syncopation, that is, accents off the normally accented beats)	Syncopation (in a different meter now) reflects striving, the "hope of gains"	
0:34 (repeats at 0:56)	He did trip it on the toe, Diddle diddle diddle doe.	Anapestic (short-short-LONG)	Duple (no syncopation)	"Did trip it on the toe" is an old-fashioned way of saying "danced elegantly," and a steady beat returns here, without syncopation	

Student FAQs

I can't hear the shift in meters in the music. What should I do?

Try beating time, as if you were playing a drum to back up the singers. The opening section is fairly regular (**1**-2, **1**-2, **1**-2, etc.). When you get to the shift at 0:18, shift to three beats, with the heavy beat on "1" (**1**-2-3, **1**-2-3, **1**-2-3, etc.). At 0:27, shift back to **1**-2, **1**-2, etc. This physical pattern may help you hear the shifting meters.

Philip Dowell
© Dorling Kindersley

Is that a man or a woman singing the highest voice?

As in the recording of Josquin's "The Cricket," this is a man singing *falsetto*, a technique by which a singer bypasses the voice box (larynx), thereby creating a sound in the very high range. In the 1960s, the Beach Boys (shown here) became famous for this kind of singing.

Getty Images Inc.—
Hulton Archive Photos

PROFILE   Thomas Weelkes (ca. 1575–1623)

A Shakespearean Composer

Weelkes belonged to that generation of English composers who lived during the age of Shakespeare, a period of great cultural achievements under the reigns of Elizabeth I and James I. Like Shakespeare, Weelkes and his contemporaries were fascinated by Italian poetry and music (many of Shakespeare's plays, it should be remembered, take place in Italy). The Italian madrigal came to England toward the end of the sixteenth century, and Weelkes lost no time imitating these Italian models. In an era of great poets and playwrights—Shakespeare, Ben Jonson, Christopher Marlowe, and Philip Sydney, among others—English composers had no difficulty finding new texts to set to music.

Like most composers of his day, Weelkes was a professional musician. He received a bachelor of music degree from New College, Oxford; served as organist at Chichester Cathedral; and wrote a great deal of sacred music in addition to madrigals. His career ended badly, however, when he was dismissed from his position for drunkenness and blasphemy. No likeness of him survives.

 EXPLORE MORE on **www.mymusiclab.com**

Chichester Cathedral, where Thomas Weelkes served as organist.
Tony Tree/Lebrecht Music & Arts Photo Library

EXPAND YOUR PLAYLIST: THE ENGLISH MADRIGAL

- **William Byrd,** "This Sweet and Merry Month of May"
- **John Farmer,** "Fair Phyllis I Saw Sitting All Alone"
- **Orlando Gibbons,** "The Silver Swan"
- **Thomas Morley,** "Now Is the Month of Maying"

- **Thomas Weelkes,** "As Vesta Was from Latmos Hill Descending"; "Hark, All Ye Lovely Saints"
- **John Wilbye,** "Weep, Weep, Mine Eyes"

((•● **HEAR SAMPLES** on **www.mymusiclab.com**

HISTORICAL CONTEXT Musicians as Spies

Being a musician and a spy might seem an odd combination, but in Elizabethan England at the end of the sixteenth century, playing an instrument provided the perfect cover for gathering intelligence. Over the course of the sixteenth century, England had gone back and forth between Protestant monarchs (Henry VIII) and Catholic monarchs (Mary I). Throughout the long reign of Elizabeth I (1558–1603), a Protestant, England was awash in rumors and actual plots to overthrow the monarchy and invade the country. As in today's global struggles, good intelligence about the intentions and resources of one's enemies carried a very high value. A coded message, intercepted by a spy, led to the arrest and eventual execution of Mary, Queen of Scots, in 1587.

Musicians were in an ideal position to carry secret messages between households, to eavesdrop on conversations, and to observe the comings and goings of the great households in which they were engaged. And good musicians were always in demand: no large-scale entertainment of the landed gentry was complete without dancing, and dancing required musicians, who were able to pass easily between the servants and who always knew about comings and goings, downstairs and the lords and ladies upstairs. Musicians at the royal court were routinely loaned out to loyal supporters of the queen, with the understanding that these employees would also report on any events or rumors they had witnessed; they presumably received an extra tip for particularly useful information. For an underpaid musician, then, spying provided a good source of supplementary income.

A group of musicians—or perhaps musician-spies?—playing at a masked ball in Elizabethan England
National Portrait Gallery, London

EXPAND YOUR PLAYLIST

The Italian Madrigal

The English madrigal, which blossomed at the end of the sixteenth century, was directly indebted to the Italian madrigal, which had been flourishing for more than half a century earlier. Indeed, the earliest English-language madrigals were direct translations from the Italian. Here are some of the composers that were admired (and imitated) by the English:

Jacob Arcadelt (ca. 1505–1568)
• "The White and Gentle Swan" ("Il bianco e dolce cigno"). Judging from the number of published editions, this was one of the most popular of all Italian madrigals in the sixteenth century. The text is about the swan, a bird who is mute throughout its life, yet according to legend sings just before dying.

Cipriano de Rore (1516–1565)
• "Once Again in Parting" ("Ancor che col partire"). A four-voice madrigal about the pain of parting lovers, a favorite subject of Renaissance madrigalists.

Luzzascho Luzzaschi (1545–1607)
• "I Love You, My Life" ("T'amo mia vita"). This madrigal for three women's voices was written for the celebrated Consort of Ladies ("Concerto delle donne"), a group of extraordinarily talented women musicians at the court of Ferrara, in northern Italy.

Lucca Marenzio (1553 or 1554–1599)
• "Alone and Pensive" ("Solo e pensoso"). For five voices, with lyrics by the fourteenth-century poet Petrarch, this madrigal expresses loneliness and despair.

Claudio Monteverdi (1567–1643)
• "I Love You, My Life" ("T'amo mia vita"). A setting of the same text as Luzzaschi's earlier madrigal, but in the new style of the Baroque (see part 3 of this book), with instrumental accompaniment an essential element of this five-voice work.

((•● **HEAR SAMPLES** on **www.mymusiclab.com**

⊘ **TEST YOURSELF** on **www.mymusiclab.com** Flashcards and chapter tests

William Byrd

"Sing Joyfully"

Composed: 1590

Byrd's "Sing Joyfully," a sacred work to be sung in church, exemplifies the rich sound of six-voice polyphony from the late Renaissance. The text comes from the Book of Psalms.

HEAR MORE on www.mymusiclab.com

Texture	**Form**	**Word-Music Relationships**
Try to hear the six distinct voices, all of equal weight. Listen also for passages in which one voice presents a musical idea that the other voices then imitate in quick succession.	Notice how each new section of the text receives its own new musical idea.	Listen to how Byrd captures in music the feeling of the text's key words, such as "joyfully" and "sing loud." Note the word painting on certain phrases, such as "blow the trumpet," which imitates the sound of the trumpet.

Words and music seem made for each other, but their marriage is not always a happy one. What creates verbal clarity—monophonic texture and syllabic text setting—does not always coincide with what creates musical beauty. Long, lyrical melodies, melismatic text setting, and rich polyphonic textures, although musically satisfying, run the risk of obscuring the text to be sung.

This challenge had grown particularly acute by the end of the Renaissance, when compositions for six voices, like William Byrd's "Sing Joyfully," had become the norm. The musical effect of this full-bodied sound can be irresistible. Reverberating off the high ceilings and stone walls of the large churches and cathedrals for which this work was written, Byrd's music is rich and luxuriant. Even if we did not understand the words at all, the music alone is capable of moving us, of giving us a heightened sense of spirituality. Yet Byrd and other composers of his time were deeply committed to setting music in a manner that projected the words clearly. His challenge was to do this in a way that also exploited the potentials of six-part polyphony.

Byrd's "Sing Joyfully" takes as its text the first four verses of Psalm 81. He called his setting an **anthem**, the English equivalent of what composers writing for the Roman Catholic Church called a **motet**, a sacred choral work (see Expand Your Playlist). It is an example of **a cappella choral music**: choral music because there is more than one singer to a part, and a cappella (Italian for "in the church style") because it is meant to be sung without instrumental accompaniment of any kind.

LEARN MORE on
www.mymusiclab.com
Chapter Objectives

Texture: Polyphony in Six Voices

One of the ways in which Byrd projected the text to be sung even while writing for six independent parts, was to use a technique known as **imitative counterpoint**. Counterpoint, as noted before, is basic to all polyphony, for it is a style of writing in which all voices are of equal importance. Imitative counterpoint is a particular type of counterpoint in which one voice, entirely by itself for a short time, introduces each new theme and is answered (imitated) by other voices that enter in succession shortly afterward, even as the first voice continues to sing. Imitative counterpoint, or simply **imitation**, as it is often called, has been of great importance for composers of all eras from the Renaissance onward.

At the very beginning of this work, only four voices enter in imitation, and two of them (Soprano 1 and Alto 2) enter together (at 0:03). But by the time only four voices have entered (0:07), we would be hard put to say exactly what words they are singing, for at no given point are they all singing the same word, at least not here in the opening. At the point marked with an asterisk in the preceding example, one of the voices is singing the word "God," another the "un-" syllable of the word "unto," and the third the "-to" syllable in "unto." If this were three or four different people all talking at the same time, it would be a complete jumble. Fortunately, each voice is differentiated by its range, so they do stand out from one another, even when they are singing together. And because the first voice began by itself, we are able to hear this first full statement of the opening text as a unit; when we hear the other voices enter with the same words, we know that they are singing the same text even if we cannot make out every word in every voice at all times. Finally, like other composers of his era, Byrd liberally repeats the text in all the parts several times before moving on, to help impress upon us the words being sung.

Sectional Form

The form of the music follows the form of the text. Each new line of the text receives its own melodic idea, which is shared to at least some extent by all the voices. Each line of text, in turn, ends with a cadence, marking the end of a section. Some of the cadences are **elided**—that is, a new line of text and music begins before the previous one has come to a complete stop (as between lines 1 and 2)—while other cadences bring the music to a full (if brief) stop (as at the end of line 6).

Word-Music Relationships: The Music Paints the Words

Byrd sets the opening phrase—"Sing joyfully"—to a lively, upward-moving musical motive. And at "Blow the trumpet" (1:03), we hear a clear instance of word painting, with the voices imitating the kind of fanfare-like figure associated with that instrument, complete with echoes. A more subtle instance of word painting can be found toward the end (1:50) on the words "For this is a statute for Israel." After a brief pause, all the voices sing the words "For this" in exactly the same rhythm, which creates the kind of declamatory sound fitting the public proclamation of a law or statute.

1542–1623
William Byrd
"Sing Joyfully"
Composed: 1590

GENRE
Anthem

KEY CONCEPTS
Polyphony, a cappella choral music, six-voice texture, imitative counterpoint, word painting, elided cadence.

CHAPTER HIGHLIGHT
Sacred polyphony
The anthem and the motet were the two most important genres of Renaissance choral music. By the end of the sixteenth century, six-voice a cappella texture had become the norm. Imitative counterpoint and word painting brought texts alive. This anthem for six voices by William Byrd projects a Psalm text with extraordinary vigor.

Rest (silence)

Strong cadence

"For this" all voices together in the same rhythm

CONNECT YOUR PLAYLIST

Polyphonic Texture

Find a piece of music that contains at least one passage with polyphonic texture.

Example: Jason Mraz, "I'm Yours" (2008)
In this song, the two main melodies are sung simultaneously toward the end, creating polyphonic texture.

Now listen to this piece again, using the Listening Guide.

Listening Guide

GO TO www.mymusiclab.com
for the Automated Listening Guide
CD I • Track 27/Download Track 27

William Byrd Composed: 1590 *"Sing Joyfully"* (2:46)

Time	Text	Form	Texture	Word-Music Relationships
0:00	1. Sing joyfully unto God our strength,	Musical idea **A**	Imitation among the voices	Lively, upward-moving motif for "joyfully"
0:20	2. Sing loud unto the God of Jacob.	Musical idea **B** Elided cadence: **B** music begins before **A** music ends.		Long notes on "Sing loud"
0:35	3. Take the song and bring forth the timbrel,*	Musical idea **C**	Imitation again	
0:49	4. The pleasant harp and viol.*	Musical idea **D**		Lyrical, flowing melody matches the sound of these two soft instruments
1:04	5. Blow the trumpet in the new moon,	Musical idea **E**		Fanfare-like theme on the word "trumpet"
1:23	6. Ev'n in the time appointed, and at our feast day,	Musical idea **F** Section ends with a strong cadence.		
1:50	7. For this is a statute for Israel,	Musical idea **G**		All voices sing in the same rhythm on the words "For this," as suits a public proclamation.
2:00	8. And a law of the God of Jacob.	Musical idea **H** Strongest cadence at the very end of the work.		

*A timbrel could mean either a small drum or a tambourine. A viol is a bowed string instrument.

Student FAQs

I still can't understand the words. Is that a problem?

Many listeners in Byrd's time complained about the same thing—not just for his music, but for a great many works of polyphony. Even with imitative counterpoint and the exposed declamation of certain passages, the words do tend to get lost at points. This is one of the issues that composers of the early Baroque era were keen to address (see chapters 10 and 11).

Are those boys' voices in the upper range?

No, those are women singing in a style meant to imitate boys' voices, which is what choirs in Byrd's time would have used. The sopranos and altos in this particular recording are singing with very little vibrato (vibration) in their voices, which creates a sound quality similar to that produced by boys. For an illustration of what an all-male choir sounds like, see "Performance" page 75.

PERFORMANCE   The Sound of the All-Male Choir

With few exceptions, women were not permitted to sing in church choirs until well into the eighteenth century, and in some locales even into the nineteenth. It was feared that women might create a distraction; many choruses, moreover, used students from a church or cathedral school, and the pupils at such schools were almost invariably boys. In any event, the sound of an all-male chorus, with boys singing the soprano and alto lines and men singing the tenor and bass lines, became a sound ideal that has persisted in some churches down to the present day. Listen in particular for the different quality of the upper voices.

There are some excellent albums offering examples of the all-male chorus. One that features Byrd's "Sing Joyfully" is *An English Chorister's Songbook,* by the Salisbury Cathedral Choir (Metronome MET 1016). Other all-male choirs that have recorded extensively include the Choir of King's College (Cambridge), Christ Church Cathedral Choir (Oxford), and New College Choir (Oxford).

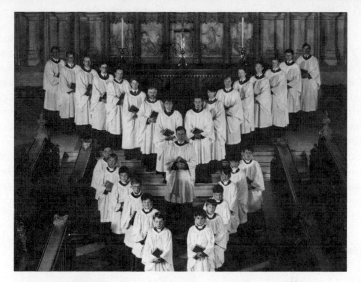

The Choir of New College, Oxford. This ensemble of 16 men and 12 boys has provided music for daily services since the 14th century.

Thomas Photos, Oxford. Courtesy New College Choir

THE COMPOSER SPEAKS   Eight Reasons for Learning How to Sing

In his *Psalmes, Sonets, & Songs* of 1588, William Byrd offered eight reasons why people should learn how to sing. Byrd was not completely objective on the matter—if more people learned to sing, more would buy his published music—but his reasons nevertheless resonate with what many others of the time said about the value of making music.

Reasons briefly set downe by th'auctor, to perswade every one to learne to sing.

1. *First it is a Knowledge easely taught, and quickly learned where there is a good Master, and an apt Scoller.*
2. *The exercise of singing is delightfull to Nature & good to preserve the health of Man.*
3. *It doth strengthen all the parts of the brest, & doth open the pipes.*
4. *It is a singular good remedie for a stuttering & stammering in the speech.*
5. *It is the best meanes to procure a perfect pronunciation & to make a good Orator.*
6. *It is the onely way to know where Nature hath bestowed the benefit of a good voyce: which gift is so rare, as there is not one among a thousand, that hath it: and in many, that excellent gift is lost, because they want Art to expresse Nature.*
7. *There is not any Musicke of Instruments whatsoever, comparable to that which is made of the voyces of Men, where the voyces are good, and the same well sorted and ordered.*
8. *The better the voyce is, the meeter it is to honour and serve God therewith: and the voyce of man is chiefly to be imployed to that ende.*

Omnis spiritus laudet Dominum *["Let every spirit praise the Lord"]*

Since singing is so good a thing,
I wish all men would learne to sing.

PROFILE   William Byrd (1542–1623)

A Catholic Composer at a Protestant Court

As a Roman Catholic in England, William Byrd had to negotiate his way carefully through the intrigues in and around the court of the Protestant queen, Elizabeth I. This was the same queen, after all, who had ordered the execution of her Catholic cousin, Mary, Queen of Scots, in 1587. Byrd was harassed at various times because of his faith: authorities searched his house on at least one occasion and kept him under varying degrees of surveillance for years on the suspicion that he was harboring "papists"—the catch-all term of the day for Catholics disloyal to the Crown. Byrd's talent as a composer seems to have provided him sufficient protection from serious persecution, however. He even managed to secure a monopoly on the printing of music in England for a short time. The fact that he also wrote large quantities of music to be performed in Anglican (Protestant) services—including the anthem "Sing Joyfully"—certainly helped Byrd avoid the fate of many other Catholics in Protestant England.

Widely regarded as the greatest English composer of the Renaissance, Byrd was also the most important English music publisher of his time.

Abigail Lebrecht/Lebrecht Music & Arts Photo Library

Queen Elizabeth I being carried through the streets of London by her courtiers.

Private Collection/The Bridgeman Art Library

⊙➔ **EXPLORE MORE** on **www.mymusiclab.com**

EXPAND YOUR PLAYLIST: BYRD

- **Mass for Four Voices.** A setting of the Mass Ordinary, in Latin.

- **O Lord, Make Thy Servant Elizabeth.** A motet for the Anglican service of worship, which included a prayer for the monarch.

- **Sadness and Anxiety (Tristitia et anxietas).** A motet with powerful settings of its key words.

- **"This Sweet and Merry Month of May."** One of Byrd's many madrigals, a secular song (see chapter 7).

((•● **HEAR SAMPLES** on **www.mymusiclab.com**

The composer Palestrina (right) presents his First Book of Masses to Pope Julius III (1554). Palestrina (see Expand Your Playlist) lived in Rome at approximately the same time that Byrd lived in London.

© Bettmann/CORBIS All Rights Reserved.

EXPAND YOUR PLAYLIST

Sacred Music of the Renaissance

In an age of spiritual strife, Catholics and Protestants alike recognized the power of music to sway the hearts and minds of the faithful. The intense spirituality of the age gave rise to some of the most moving sacred music ever written. While the Roman Catholic Church retained a liturgy entirely in Latin, Protestant denominations called for services to be conducted primarily in their native language of English.

England
- Thomas Tallis (ca. 1505–1585). "I Have Never Put My Hope in Any Other but You" ("Spem in alium"). This sacred Latin motet, for 40 different voices (eight choirs, each with five voices), is one of the monumental works of Renaissance vocal music.
- Tallis. "Verily I Say Unto You." A much more modest anthem, for four voices, written for a typical Anglican church choir.

Germany
- Martin Luther (1483–1546). "A Mighty Fortress Is Our God" ("Ein' feste Burg ist unser Gott"). Luther wrote both the words and music of what would come to be known as the anthem of the Protestant Reformation.
- Johann Walter (1496–1570). "A Mighty Fortress Is Our God" ("Ein' feste Burg ist unser Gott"). One of many elaborate settings of Luther's hymn. Walter, like many other Protestant composers, used this well-known melody as a basis for a more extended work.

Italy
- Giovanni Pierluigi da Palestrina (1525 or 1526–1594). *Mass in Honor of Pope Marcellus* (*Missa Papae Marcelli*) and *Missa brevis*. Palestrina was the leading composer of sacred music in Italy in the sixteenth century, and church leaders applauded his music for the clarity of its text settings.

Spain
- Tomás Luis de Victoria (ca. 1549–1611). "O Great Mystery" ("O magnum mysterium"). A sacred motet for six voices, written for services on Easter Monday by the greatest Spanish composer of the Renaissance.

((• HEAR SAMPLES on **www.mymusiclab.com**

✓ **TEST YOURSELF** on **www.mymusiclab.com**   Flashcards and chapter tests

Rhyming Singers of the Bahamas
"My Lord Help Me to Pray"
Recorded: 1965

Polyphony, the singing or intoning of multiple independent parts, is a worldwide phenomenon. In the Bahamas sometime during the nineteenth century, sponge fishermen passing time on their boats developed a genre known as *rhyme singing*. It features three vocalists who sing separate melodic lines.

Listen to this first

((• HEAR MORE on www.mymusiclab.com

Texture

Identify the lead part and the way the other parts respond to it. How many voices are there? In what ways do they seem dependent on each other, and in what ways independent?

Melody

Try to determine the distinctive upward, downward, or up-and-down motion of each voice.

Word-Music Relationships

Which words remain constant? Notice how the singers change and add words while maintaining the basic textual framework.

Form

Listen for the call (lead vocalist) and response (chorus) form.

⚙ **LEARN MORE** on
www.mymusiclab.com
Chapter Objectives

   This recording of the rhyme song "My Lord Help Me to Pray" is performed by Bruce Green (lead singer), his cousin Clifton Green (bass), and their friend Tweedie Gibson (treble) from Mores Island in the Bahamas. Rhyme songs, based on gospel texts, are sung in three parts, each with its own words. In this way, rhyme songs resemble Byrd's "Sing Joyfully" (chapter 8), in which the words of the individual voices often contrast with one another.

Texture: Monophony vs. Polyphony

At the beginning of "My Lord Help Me to Pray," it is easy to hear the alternation between the monophonic texture of the lead singer (known as the **rhyme singer)** and the polyphonic texture of other two parts (treble and bass) when they respond together. This alternation is known as **call-and-response**: the lead singer calls and the other parts respond. As the rhyme song progresses, the calls and responses overlap to an increasing degree, creating a thick polyphonic texture.

   Call-and-response and the overlap of parts are important structural elements of African music, as well as of African-derived music in the Americas. Rhyme singing is an African American

syncretism, which means that it combines different forms of belief and practice. The songs are mostly Christian spirituals, but they are mixed with local Bahamian religious beliefs: the rhyme part is associated with the wind, the treble part with the sky, and the bass part with the earth. In the same way, rhyme singing combines Christian gospel texts with African call-and-response.

The singers of this piece are from Mores Island in the Bahamas. Often sponge fishermen would sing when they brought their catch to Nassau.

Intoning the Melody

What we may hear as singing in "My Lord Help Me to Pray," Bahamian culture actually considers "intoning," referring more specifically to the act of "saying words in tones." While those outside Bahamian culture have come to call these pieces "songs," Bahamians call them "rhymes." Thus, the melodic lines sung by each of the three singers are called **intonations**.

Each line has its own intonation model:

- **Rhyme line.** Varied and often improvised, but always descending in motion. Each phrase ends on its lowest tone.

- **Treble line.** Consists of two halves, *a* and *b*. The *a* ascends and pauses on the highest tone of the phrase, sounding like an unresolved question. The *b* descends and resolves on the lowest tone of the phrase, giving finality.

- **Bass line.** Varied slightly, but primarily two essential tones that provide the basic harmonic support. At times, the bass line occurs under the rhyme line as additional support.

Here is a graphic representation of each:

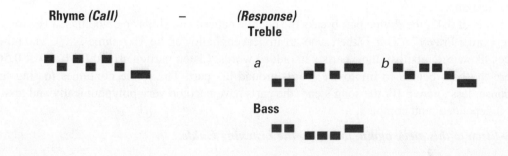

HISTORICAL CONTEXT   Bob Marley and the Birth of Reggae

Caribbean music is as rich and varied as the many islands that dot the ocean from Cuba and Haiti to Barbados and Aruba. Over the past few decades, American popular styles—particularly rock 'n' roll—have been heard throughout the Caribbean thanks to radio stations and recordings reaching the islands. Local styles have evolved that take elements of American pop and wed them with local rhythms and concerns. One of the most popular of the styles to emerge in this cultural melting pot has been reggae, and its greatest star was Bob Marley (1945–1981).

Reggae is closely associated with the Rastafarian religion. Marley was a Rasta and practiced its beliefs. The Rastafarians combine elements of Western and African religious beliefs and venerate as their leader Haile Selassie I, who led Ethiopia from the 1930s through the mid-1970s. Its emphasis on black liberation, culture, and artistic expression had strong appeal in Jamaica, the impoverished nation where Marley lived and worked.

Marley was a performer, composer, and political activist. He embodied for many the best of reggae music. Marley and his group, the Wailers, set the basic style of reggae, with its loping rhythm and topical lyrics. Among Marley's best-known songs are "I Shot the Sheriff" (popularized in a cover by Eric Clapton), "One Love" (used as a theme song on Jamaican tourism commercials), "No Woman, No Cry," and "Jammin'."

Marley died of skin cancer in 1981; however, his recordings and message continue to resonate in world popular music today.

Bob Marley, songwriter, performer, and political activist, who popularized reggae music around the world in the mid-1970s
© Michael Ochs Archives/CORBIS. All Rights Reserved.

Word-Music Relationships

The actual rhyming occurs in the couplets (pairs of metered lines) intoned by the rhyme part. After a spoken introduction of the title, the first couplet begins:

> Oh Lord, what a faithful soul
> > (My Lord, help me to pray)
> Oh Lord, what a faithful soul
> > (My Lord, help me to pray)

Subsequent couplets use different text for each line, but always with "My Lord, help me to pray" as the response.

Later, at 0:43, the rhyme part breaks the couplet pattern and sings an embellished version of "The Lord's Prayer" ("Our Father, who art in heaven, hallowed be Thy name . . ."). The other voices likewise embellish their parts with added words. Listen particularly at 0:31 and at 0:56, where the bass begins to improvise words around his part. The treble continues to sing the response, less altered. By the song's end, the parts have become very polyphonically and texturally independent and complex.

Now listen to this piece again, following the Listening Guide.

CONNECT YOUR PLAYLIST

Call and Response

Find a piece that contains a lead vocalist who states the melody ("call") and a vocal group that responds to him or her ("response").

Example: Nelly Furtado and Timbaland, "Promiscuous" (2006) Furtado sings a verse and then Timbaland responds.

Listening Guide

GO TO www.mymusiclab.com
for the Automated Listening Guide
CD I • Track 28/Download Track 28

Rhyming Singers of the Bahamas Recorded: 1965 *"My Lord Help Me to Pray"* (2:03)

Time	Form	Texture	Melody	Word-Music Relationships
0:01	Introduction	Spoken	Introduction	A singer states the title.
0:05	Call and response	Responsorial. The treble and bass are in harmony.	Phrase 1 by rhyme singer, phrase 2 by his or her partners; pause on highest note. Phrase 3 by the rhyme singer, phrase 4 by his or her partners, treble resolving on its lowest tone.	The first called rhyme, "Oh Lord what a faithful soul," followed by the response, "My Lord help me to pray." Followed by different rhymes in call and response with the treble and bass.
0:31	Metered song set by the rhythm of the treble and bass. Overlapping call and response	Polyphonic—the call and response overlap to create a thick texture.	The couplet rhyme phrases continue to alternate with the treble and bass phrases to construct complete melodies.	Rhyming becomes improvised words. The treble adds words. The bass improvises new words and rhythms.
0:43		Polyphonic overlapping maintains the sense of thick texture.	"The Lord's Prayer" melodically embellished.	The rhyme singer improvises words and rhythms around the text of "The Lord's Prayer."
0:56		Polyphonic overlapping maintains the sense of thick texture.	The bass improvises as the treble stabilizes.	The rhyme singer improvises rhymes until the end. The bass improvises more words.

Student FAQs

Why are many work songs set in call-and-response style?

Call-and-response is one way of helping a large group of people work together. The rhythm of the song and the repeated structure facilitate finishing a tough job, such as lifting heavy nets or laying railroad track. The "call" by the leader coincides with the first part of a movement (such as the lifting of hammers to lay railroad track) and the "response" with its culmination (the banging of the hammer down onto the spike).

Is rap related to Bahamian rhyme songs?

Rhyming or intoning is found in many African-influenced cultures around the world. Rap has many roots, including the African American practice of the "dozens" in which rhymed insults are traded between two or more people and the practice of mobile Jamaican deejays who traveled in sound trucks, setting up impromptu dances and using rhymed introductions to attract a crowd.

Is call-and-response heard in other religious song traditions?

Call-and-response is quite common in religious singing throughout the world. "Lining out" a hymn in American shape note singing is one form of call-and-response: a leader sings a line, and then the congregation repeats it. This is a way of learning the song. Eventually the leader may just sing a guiding word or two—between the actual lines of the hymn—to remind the congregation of what is coming next.

Cover of an early record by Lord Invader recorded in New York City in 1946.
Source: Courtesy Ben Car Archives

EXPAND YOUR PLAYLIST

Music of the Caribbean

Music of the Caribbean
- Caribbean Party. *Putamayo 132.*
  A good, short collection of representative dance recordings from throughout the Caribbean.

Jamaica
- Bongo, Backra & Coolie. *Jamaican Roots, Vol. 1,* Folkways 4231.
- Bongo, Backra & Coolie. *Jamaican Roots, Vol. 2,* Folkways 4232.
  Roots music from various different Jamaican cultural groups recorded by Kenneth Bilby in the early 1970s.

Reggae
- *Bob Marley: Natty Dread,* Tuff Gong 422-846204-2.
  Considered by many to be Marley's finest studio album.

- *Babylon by Bus,* Tuff Gong 422-846197-2.
  Influential live album recorded during Marley's European tour in 1978.

Bahamas
- *The Real Bahamas, Vols. 1 and 2,* Nonesuch Explorer 72013 and 72078.
  Recordings of various performers, including legendary guitarist Joseph Spence, made in 1965.

Calypso
- Lord Invader. *Calypsos in New York,* Smithsonian Folkways 40454.
  Calypso was very popular in the 1950s in New York, and many island musicians made their home there working at local clubs. This gathers recordings of Lord Invader, one of Calypso's major stars, made from the 1940s through the 1950s.

((• HEAR SAMPLES on www.mymusiclab.com

TEST YOURSELF on www.mymusiclab.com   Flashcards and chapter tests

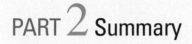

PART 2 Summary

	Middle Ages	Renaissance
Texture	Monophonic and polyphonic	Polyphonic, including imitative counterpoint
Melody	Flowing, largely conjunct, divided into sections by cadences; melodies based on scales of the medieval modes	Flowing, but with greater use of disjunct motion; divided into sections by cadences; melodies based on scales of the medieval modes
Rhythm	Free (plainchant) and metrically structured	Relatively smooth and flowing rhythms within a metrically structured framework
Timbre	No sharp distinction between instrumental and vocal music	No sharp distinction between instrumental and vocal music; a growing number and variety of instruments
Harmony	A by-product of counterpoint	A by-product of counterpoint
Form	Based on repetition, variation, and contrast	Based on repetition, variation, and contrast; primarily sectional; binary form for dance music
Word-music relationships	Syllabic settings to project texts clearly; melismatic settings to emphasize key words	Limited use of word painting

IN REVIEW: Renaissance Style

Polyphonic texture Although monophonic plainchant continued to be used in sacred services, new music is almost entirely polyphonic. Imitative counterpoint becomes increasingly important (Byrd). Four-voice texture is the norm at the beginning of the Renaissance (Josquin); six-voice texture is the norm by the end (Byrd).

• Josquin, *"The Cricket"* (Chapter 6)
• Weelkes, *"Since Robin Hood"* (Chapter 7)
• Byrd, *"Sing Joyfully"* (Chapter 8)
• Rhyming Singers of the Bahamas, *"My Lord Help Me to Pray"* (Chapter 9)
• Susato, *Moorish Dance* (Web Bonus Chapter 2)

Melody Greater use of disjunct motion; melodies still based on medieval modes.

• Josquin, *"The Cricket"* (Chapter 6)
• Weelkes, *"Since Robin Hood"* (Chapter 7)
• Byrd, *"Sing Joyfully"* (Chapter 8)
• Susato, *Moorish Dance* (Web Bonus Chapter 2)

Rhythm Metrical structure provides a framework for rhythms that are usually fluid (Josquin, Weelkes, Byrd), though in the case of dance music these rhythms are more repetitive (Susato).

• Josquin, *"The Cricket"* (Chapter 6)
• Weelkes, *"Since Robin Hood"* (Chapter 7)
• Byrd, *"Sing Joyfully"* (Chapter 8)
• Susato, *Moorish Dance* (Web Bonus Chapter 2)

Word painting Setting specific words to music that imitates the meaning of those words.

• Josquin, *"The Cricket"* (Chapter 6)
• Weelkes, *"Since Robin Hood"* (Chapter 7)
• Byrd, *"Sing Joyfully"* (Chapter 8)

Binary Form The most common form for dance movements, consisting of two sections, each repeated in performance.

• Susato, *Moorish Dance* (Web Bonus Chapter 2)

✅ **TEST YOURSELF** on **www.mymusiclab.com**   Part Exam

The Baroque Era

The period between roughly 1600 and 1750 was first called the "Baroque Era" by historians who wanted to characterize the period between the Renaissance and the Classical Era. By using the term "baroque," historians were calling attention to the extravagant and even bizarre qualities of the music and art. Indeed, music's textures, harmonies, and forms tend to be more free and unpredictable in Baroque music than in the music of the Renaissance. The standard texture of polyphony now made room for homophony in which one voice was clearly more important than the others. Putting one voice in the musical foreground meant that a solo singer could portray on stage the thoughts and actions of a single dramatic character. The new use of homophony beginning around 1600 made possible the emergence of opera. Composers extended the expressive possibilities of solo singing into sacred music as well, creating the genre of the oratorio, which was nothing less than an unstaged opera on a sacred topic. The new texture of homophony also made possible the instrumental genre of the concerto, in which a soloist or small group of soloists could stand out against the backdrop of a larger ensemble. Singers and instrumentalists alike began to display their virtuosity with pride, improvising and embellishing their parts as never before, always with exuberance and often quite elaborately.

The Baroque Era was a period of energy and motion, of ornamentation and extremes. New contrasts between light and dark appeared in painting; similarly, musical compositions exhibited bold contrasts in sounds, between high and low, soft and loud. Painting and sculpture gained a new sense of motion; music, likewise, propelled itself forward by the continuous unfolding of small groupings of notes. Architecture became increasingly ornate; musical lines, too, came to be decorated by ornamental flourishes and trills (notes next to each other that are played in alternation very rapidly). In all the arts, the expression of one particular emotion, known as an *affect*, became all-important. Baroque composers and performers were committed to representing the passions through music. These passions are not to be understood as personal self-expression, however. Like good actors, Baroque musicians could move their audiences by the artful portrayal of emotion.

▲ *A Musical Interlude*, by the Dutch painter Jan Verkolje (ca. 1674). Like a work of Baroque music, this painting uses a strong sense of movement to depict a single "affect," or emotion. The gentleman has turned, in a sudden moment of passion, and grasped the hand of his musical partner, a woman playing a viol.

▲ Louis XIV styled himself as the "Sun King," the royal center of the solar system. He even danced the part in the "Ballet of the Night," performed at his court in 1653. He spent lavish amounts of the state's money on the creation of new operas and ballets.

Lebrecht Music & Arts/Lebrecht Music & Arts Photo Library

Projecting Cultural Power through Music

One summer night in 1717, a group of festively decorated barges floated down the Thames River. Grand orchestral sounds filled the air: brass, strings, and wind instruments playing music majestic enough for a king but rhythmic enough to suggest the spirit of a dance. The king on board was an absolute monarch, a ruler who believed in his divine right to govern and in the totality of his power. He was King George I of Britain, and he wanted the world to know it. For his party on the Thames, he hired the finest musicians to play and the most accomplished composer to write and conduct. The composer was George Frideric Handel, and the work he composed was called, appropriately, *Water Music* (chapter 17). One contemporary newspaper reported that the king was so pleased with Handel's music that he had it repeated three times. Another account from that time tells us that the number of additional "boats filled with people desirous of hearing was beyond counting," [1] and that the party did not end until 4:30 in the morning.

During the Baroque Era, a nation's splendor was measured in cultural terms as well as political and economic terms. The arts were an important means of projecting power and authority. Rulers vied with one another to find and retain the best artists, poets, composers, and musicians. Across the English Channel from George I, Louis XIV, who ruled France from 1643 until his death in 1715, also insisted on the divine right of kings and the absolute nature of his power. Using state funds, he built an enormous palace at Versailles and ruled with single-handed

[1]Christopher Hogwood, *Handel: Water Music and Music for the Royal Fireworks* (Cambridge: Cambridge University Press, 2005), 12.

The Baroque Era   ◉➤ EXPLORE MORE on www.mymusiclab.com

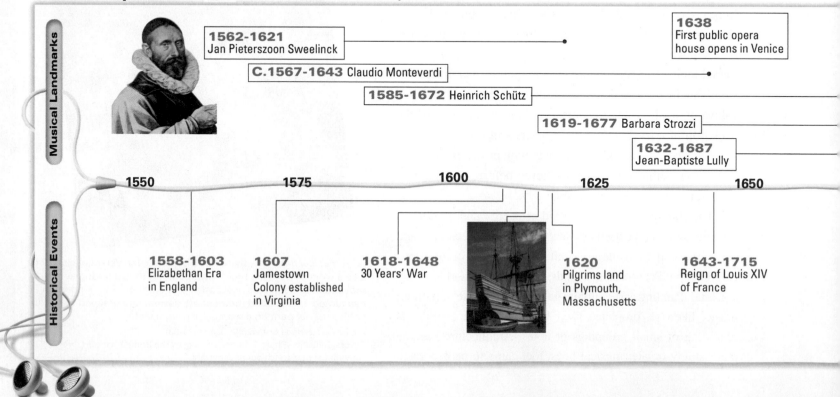

Musical Landmarks

1562-1621 Jan Pieterszoon Sweelinck

C.1567-1643 Claudio Monteverdi

1585-1672 Heinrich Schütz

1619-1677 Barbara Strozzi

1632-1687 Jean-Baptiste Lully

1638 First public opera house opens in Venice

1550   1575   1600   1625   1650

Historical Events

1558-1603 Elizabethan Era in England

1607 Jamestown Colony established in Virginia

1618-1648 30 Years' War

1620 Pilgrims land in Plymouth, Massachusetts

1643-1715 Reign of Louis XIV of France

authority. "I am the state," he is alleged to have declared. Louis XIV spared no expense on the arts and was particularly passionate about music and dance, sponsoring such composers as Jean-Baptiste Lully, Antonia Bembo, and Elisabeth Jacquet de la Guerre (see Historical Context: Female Composers in the Baroque Era, page 116).

The Splendor of the Church

The arts served also to project the power of the church. The same theatricality and intense artistic expression designed to arouse earthly passions could awaken religious passion as well. Churches spent large sums of money on lavish decoration that would both convey the church's authority and inspire religious fervor. Filling these brilliant interiors was the sound of the Baroque organ, an instrument whose powerful resonance and striking variety of timbre was unsurpassed in creating awe. Churches invested small fortunes in their organs, and organ building enjoyed its golden age in the Baroque Era. The renowned organist Johann Sebastian Bach, whose Fugue in G Minor we will hear in chapter 14, made frequent trips to towns and cities around central Germany to test the craftsmanship of newly installed instruments.

   Music also served as an important means of conveying the teachings of the church, and sacred music could be every bit as elaborate as sacred architecture. The first movement of Bach's Cantata no. 140, *Awake, A Voice Calls to Us*, (chapter 18) is based on a relatively

▲ Louis XIV's palace at Versailles, west of Paris, depicted in 1722 by Jean-Baptiste Martin. The grounds included a magnificent opera house.
Topham/The Image Works

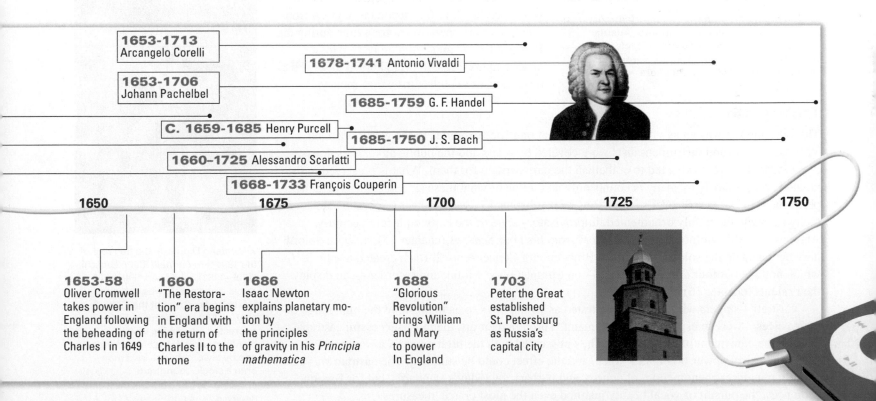

1653-1713 Arcangelo Corelli

1678-1741 Antonio Vivaldi

1653-1706 Johann Pachelbel

1685-1759 G. F. Handel

C. 1659-1685 Henry Purcell

1685-1750 J. S. Bach

1660–1725 Alessandro Scarlatti

1668-1733 François Couperin

1650   **1675**   **1700**   **1725**   **1750**

1653-58 Oliver Cromwell takes power in England following the beheading of Charles I in 1649

1660 "The Restoration" era begins in England with the return of Charles II to the throne

1686 Isaac Newton explains planetary motion by the principles of gravity in his *Principia mathematica*

1688 "Glorious Revolution" brings William and Mary to power In England

1703 Peter the Great established St. Petersburg as Russia's capital city

▲ The organ loft of the 18th-century Augustinian Monastery church in Herzogenburg, Austria. Scarcely a square inch of surface is left unadorned. In a similar manner, Baroque musicians embellished composers' works.
Hannes Sallmutter

simple and well-known hymn tune. Bach constructed an intricate and extended structure around it, while leaving the melody itself more or less intact. Listeners of all levels could thus easily follow the course of this intricate movement and be uplifted by its glorious sound.

Opera, Oratorio, and the Entrepreneurial Spirit

The earliest operas, including Claudio Monteverdi's *Orpheus* (chapter 10), were performed in private theaters at the courts of the nobility and royalty. But a growing spirit of entrepreneurship made the arts increasingly accessible to the public, most notably in Italy and England. The first public opera houses opened in Venice in 1637, and by the early eighteenth century even some theaters under the control of ruling monarchs began opening their doors to paying customers. (See A Closer Look: The Baroque Opera House, page 89.) By 1700, opera had become big business. Impresarios (producers) invested heavily in new productions and paid enormous sums to the singers who could ensure the success of a new work. When the church prohibited performances of operas during the penitential season of Lent (the period preceding Easter), these same impresarios filled their opera houses by hiring the same singers and instrumentalists to perform oratorios. The oratorio was essentially identical to opera in its musical form, but it was unstaged, and the libretto was usually based on a sacred subject. The oratorio we will hear, Handel's *Messiah* (chapter 19), moves audiences today as it did in 1742 when it was first performed.

Not all productions of opera and oratorio were successful. In fact, arson became a serious problem in the opera world for a time during the Baroque Era: in an attempt to recoup losses, unscrupulous investors were known to set fire to opera houses to collect insurance money.

▲ Stefano Dionisi in the title role of the 1994 film *Farinelli*. Carlo Broschi (1705–1782), who used "Farinelli" as his stage name, was the most celebrated castrato of the 18th century. The producers of *Farinelli* re-created his singing voice by blending two separate recordings— one by a woman, one by a man— onto a single soundtrack.
© Jean-Marie Leroy/CORBIS. All Rights Reserved.

The Virtuoso

The Baroque Era was an age of opulence, and that opulence extended to the world of sound. Virtuoso singers and instrumentalists were coveted by rulers and the public alike. As soloists, these musicians were expected to embellish the parts written for them. What is preserved in the notated score today is by many accounts only an outline of what these skilled soloists actually performed. In Barbara Strozzi's song "Revenge" (chapter 13), we will hear a soprano soloist of today re-create the highly ornamented, improvisatory style of the early eighteenth century. Antonio Vivaldi's violin concerto "Winter" from his *Four Seasons* (chapter 15), places extraordinary demands on the soloist. And in his Brandenburg Concerto no. 2, Bach created a vehicle by which not one but four different soloists—on trumpet, oboe, violin, and recorder—can display their talents (chapter 16).

Castrati—singers who had been castrated as young boys so as to preserve the high range of their voices—were in especially high demand. Through their art, the most successful castrati became the equivalent of millionaires. They possessed both the high range of a woman's voice and the physical power of a man's voice, and the effect could be stunning. The castrato was an entirely unnatural phenomenon, of course, and barbaric by today's standards, but for Baroque audiences, the pursuit of vocal beauty justified even the most drastic measures.

A CLOSER LOOK   The Baroque Opera House

EXPLORE MORE on www.mymusiclab.com
SEE MORE Documentary on *Opera in the 18th Century*

The earliest operas were performed only in private theaters of the nobility. Eventually, however, opera moved into public theaters open to paying customers. This 1740 painting shows an opera being performed at the Teatro Regio in Turin, in what is now northern Italy. The "Royal Theater" was funded by the Grand Duke of Tuscany, who could enter the hall directly from his palace without going outside. The magnificence of the staging, costumes, singing, and orchestral playing helped the duke impress visiting dignitaries and thereby enhance his standing within the cultural politics of Europe.

The more elite members of the audience sit in stalls or **"boxes"** on the theater's upper levels. Each box was rented privately for an entire season.

Stage design was a major element of the theatrical spectacle. Here, an elaborate backdrop gives the illusion of depth to a fairly small stage.

Soloists sing their parts wearing dazzling costumes, a standard feature in most Baroque operas.

Audience behavior at operas was rather relaxed. In this first row, one member of the audience gestures toward the stage, while his neighbor studies the words being sung by following the **libretto** (literally "little book"), which contains the complete text of the opera. And one of *his* neighbors is not even facing the stage!

The orchestra occupies the **"pit,"** a lowered area between the audience and the stage. Two sets of basso continuo are visible here on each side of the orchestra: one accompanies the recitatives, while the other accompanies arias and other numbers that call for a full orchestra.

A **bailiff** maintains order in the theater. Although his function is largely ceremonial, his physical presence is a reminder to all that this is a royal theater.

A **merchant** sells refreshments to members of the audience. In the Baroque Era, vendors moved up and down the aisles throughout the performance.

Pietro Domenico Oliviero, (1672–1754), "The Teatro Reale in Turin", oil on canvas/Museo Civico, Turin, Italy/The Bridgeman Art Library

The Baroque Era CHAPTERS AT A GLANCE

chapter 10
p. 92

1567–1643
Claudio Monteverdi
Orpheus, selection from Act II
Composed: 1607

GENRE
Early Baroque Opera

KEY CONCEPTS
Homophony, basso continuo, recitative, word painting.

CHAPTER HIGHLIGHT
Early Baroque Opera
The new texture of homophony—a single melodic voice with accompaniment—helped create the new genre of opera. Homophony enabled singers to portray individual characters and project texts in ways that audiences could readily grasp. Recitative, a declamatory style of singing, also helped make texts intelligible to audiences. In *Orpheus*, one of the earliest operas, Monteverdi used older polyphonic textures in the choruses, which in the manner of ancient Greek drama comment on the drama's action.
EXPAND YOUR PLAYLIST: Old and New Practices in the Seventeenth Century: Giovanni Gabrieli, Schütz, Cavalli

chapter 11
p. 98

ca. 1659–1695
Henry Purcell
Dido and Aeneas, Overture and Act I, nos. 1–4
Composed: 1689

GENRE
Baroque Opera

KEY CONCEPTS
Ostinato, overture, French overture, aria.

CHAPTER HIGHLIGHT
Baroque Opera
Purcell's *Dido and Aeneas*, the first English opera, unfolds through a series of numbers in different musical formats. It opens with an overture in two sections, the first slow, the second fast. The arias and recitatives help delineate the characters who are singing them.
EXPAND YOUR PLAYLIST: Baroque Opera: Handel, Lully, Charpentier, Rameau

chapter 12
p. 105

GLOBAL CONNECTION

Global Connection: Ostinato
Mbuti Pygmies
"Marriage Celebration Song"
Recorded: 1958

GENRE
Ostinato

KEY CONCEPTS
Ostinato, polyphony, rhythmic interlock, hocket, call-and-response, heterophony.

CHAPTER HIGHLIGHT
Ostinato
Ostinato—the repetition of one pattern of notes and rhythms—provides a unifying structure for at least some kinds of music in many different cultures. The example here is from central Africa.
EXPAND YOUR PLAYLIST: Singing in the Rain (forest): Mbuti Pygmies of the Ituri Rainforest, Baka Forest People of Southeast Cameroon, Rainforests of South America & the Caribbean

GLOBAL CONNECTION
KEY CONCEPT
Ostinato

chapter 16
p. 133

1685–1750
Johann Sebastian Bach
Brandenburg Concerto no. 2 in F Major, BWV 1047, finale
Composed: 1720

GENRE
Concerto grosso

KEY CONCEPTS
Concerto grosso, ritornello, fugal texture, harmonic basis of form.

CHAPTER HIGHLIGHT
The Baroque Concerto
The concerto highlights contrasts among instruments and performing forces, and became a vehicle for virtuosic displays. This particular concerto highlights a group of soloists—recorder, oboe, violin, and trumpet—each of whom comes to the fore at various points in this last movement of a three-movement concerto.
EXPAND YOUR PLAYLIST: The Baroque Concerto: Corelli, Vivaldi, Handel, Bach

chapter 17
p. 140

1685–1759
George Frideric Handel
Water Music, Hornpipe
Composed: 1717

GENRE
Suite

KEY CONCEPTS
Binary form, modulation, orchestration.

CHAPTER HIGHLIGHT
The Baroque Suite
Suites are collections of popular dances. The variety of dances—fast vs. slow, lively vs. stately, duple vs. triple—creates contrasting moods. In the rigaudon movement Handel establishes a regular rhythm that lends itself to dancing; the binary form allows for the kind of large-scale repetition typical of many Baroque dances.
EXPAND YOUR PLAYLIST: The Baroque Suite: Jacquet de la Guerre, Couperin, Bach, Handel

1619–1677
Barbara Strozzi
"Revenge"
Composed: 1651

GENRE
Baroque Song

KEY CONCEPTS
Embellishment, chamber music, trio-sonata
texture, contrasting timbres.

CHAPTER HIGHLIGHT
Baroque Chamber Music
Chamber music, with only one player to a
part, is intimate and just requires a few performers. In this "arietta," the solo singer is
accompanied by only two violins and a
basso continuo. The instruments and voice
engage in a kind of dialogue about the
sweetness of a lover's revenge.
EXPAND YOUR PLAYLIST: Baroque Chamber
Music: Corelli, Pachelbel, Marais

1685–1750
Johann Sebastian Bach
Fugue in G Minor, BWV 578
("Little")
Composed: 1705

GENRE
Fugue

KEY CONCEPTS
Imitative counterpoint, organ, timbre,
arrangements.

CHAPTER HIGHLIGHT
Baroque Organ Music
The fugue represents the Baroque Era's fascination with imitative polyphonic texture, and
this fugue demonstrates why the organ, with
its immense volume and range, was known in
its time as the "king of instruments."
EXPAND YOUR PLAYLIST: Baroque Organ
Music: Sweelinck, Buxtehude, Bach

1678–1741
Antonio Vivaldi
The Four Seasons, "Winter,"
first movement
Composed: 1720

GENRE
Concerto

KEY CONCEPTS
Concerto, ritornello, violin, program music.

CHAPTER HIGHLIGHT
Program Music
Program music is instrumental music explicitly connected in some way with a story, person, or idea.
This first movement of a three-movement concerto
for violin and string orchestra captures some of the
season's sounds. It follows the outline of a brief text
(probably by Vivaldi himself) that describes ice,
snow, wind, stamping feet, and chattering teeth.
EXPAND YOUR PLAYLIST: Program Music: Kuhnau,
Marais, Beethoven, Berlioz, Gershwin, Adams

1685–1750
Johann Sebastian Bach
Cantata 140: *Awake, a Voice Calls to Us,* selections
Composed: 1731

GENRE
Cantata

KEY CONCEPTS
Cantata, chorale, ritornello principle, song form (AAB).

CHAPTER HIGHLIGHT
Sacred Music of the Late Baroque
In the Protestant church, the chorale (hymn) was the basic musical element of the church
service. The entire congregation would know the words and melodies by heart and sing as a
group. In this cantata, Bach used one of the most popular of all chorale melodies as the basis
for an elaborate opening movement performed by a chorus and orchestra.
EXPAND YOUR PLAYLIST: Sacred Music of the Late Baroque: Bach, Delalande, Alessandro
Scarlatti, Carissimi, Handel

1685–1759
George Frideric Handel
Messiah, selections
Composed: 1747

GENRE
Oratorio

KEY CONCEPTS
Word-music relationships, fugue, ritornello principle.

CHAPTER HIGHLIGHT
Oratorio
An oratorio, like an opera, is a dramatic work performed by orchestra, choir, and
soloists, but it is performed as a concert work, without staging, and is usually based
on a text with a religious theme. The selection here from Handel's *Messiah* includes
a brief recitative, an aria, and the famous "Hallelujah" chorus.
EXPAND YOUR PLAYLIST: Covering the "Hallelujah" Chorus: Mozart, Johnny Mathis,
Quincy Jones, Alsop, Mannheim Steamroller

Claudio Monteverdi
Orpheus, selection from Act II
Composed: 1607

Opera was the most important new genre of the Baroque Era, and Monteverdi's *Orpheus* is one of the earliest operas. This scene presents the moment in which the legendary poet and singer Orpheus learns of the death of his wife, Euridice; the chorus, following the conventions of Greek drama, responds with an outburst of communal grief.

Listen to this first

((• HEAR MORE on www.mymusiclab.com

Texture

Listen for homophony at the beginning: the solo singer carries the melody, while a small group of instruments provides support. Toward the end, when the chorus enters, listen for the change to polyphonic texture: all voices have equal importance.

Word-Music Relationships

Listen to the way in which the music heightens the expressive emotion of what the characters are saying. Notice how the soloist's singing style differs from that of the chorus.

LEARN MORE on
www.mymusiclab.com
Chapter Objectives

While the idea of a sung drama with one performer singing the part of each character may seem perfectly obvious to us today, it was the object of heated debate in the early years of the Baroque Era. The monophonic dramas of the Middle Ages, like Hildegard von Bingen's *Play of Virtues* (chapter 1), had long since been forgotten. It was not until the decades around 1600 that a small group of philosophers, musicians, and poets began meeting in Florence (present-day Italy) to consider how they might revive the synthesis of music and drama they knew had been practiced by the ancient Greeks. The result was **opera**, a drama sung from beginning to end. For all its changes over the ensuing centuries, the genre of opera has remained devoted to its original purpose: to convey a story onstage through characters who express their thoughts and emotions by singing.

Monteverdi's *Orpheus* (*L'Orfeo*) is the most frequently performed of all early operas. The music is richly varied, with elaborate songs and choruses for the singers and lively instrumental music for the dancers. And while the story itself is based on myth, the music makes the characters seem very human, their emotions very real.

Orpheus, the legendary singer of Greek mythology, learns from a messenger that his beloved Euridice has died from the bite of a serpent. The selection here, from Act II, begins just after the messenger has delivered this terrible news. Orpheus is stunned; the chorus echoes his grief. Later in the opera, Orpheus uses the power of music to persuade the guardians and gods of the underworld (Hades) to allow him to cross the River Styx and bring Euridice back from the dead to "see the stars once more." He is allowed to do so on the condition that he not look behind him on his ascent out of the underworld. But he cannot resist the temptation to look back, and Euridice is lost to him once again. Monteverdi's setting of the myth has a bittersweet ending in which Euridice herself takes her place among the stars as a constellation.

Homophonic Texture: One Character, One Voice

The texture of homophony—a single principal voice with subordinate accompaniment (see Elements, page 10)—is essential in opera, for it allows one singer to represent a single character onstage. The group of instruments accompanying the singer here is known collectively as the **basso continuo** ("continuous bass"). This small ensemble, as its name suggests, plays more or less continuously, and it provides an underlying bass line and harmonies to the melody above. The basso continuo typically consists of two instruments: one that can sustain long notes (such as a bass viol, a cello, or a bassoon), and one that can play chords (such as a lute or a harpsichord). The organ was one of the few instruments that alone could both sustain a sound *and* play chords. In the recording here, the basso continuo part is performed by a combination of organ and lute. In practice, musicians of the Baroque Era used whatever number and combination of instruments were available.

1567–1643
Claudio Monteverdi
Orpheus, selection
from Act II
Composed: 1607
GENRE
Early Baroque Opera

KEY CONCEPTS
Homophony, basso continuo,
recitative, word painting.

CHAPTER HIGHLIGHT
Early Baroque Opera
The new texture of homophony—a single melodic voice with accompaniment—helped create the new genre of opera. Homophony enabled singers to portray individual characters and project texts in ways that audiences could readily grasp. Recitative, a declamatory style of singing, also helped make texts intelligible to audiences. In *Orpheus,* one of the earliest operas, Monteverdi used older polyphonic textures in the choruses, which in the manner of ancient Greek drama comment on the drama's action.

Voice

Tu   se' mor - ta   se' mor - ta mia vi -   ta
you   are dead   are dead   my life

Basso
continuo

Vocal line
notated by
Monteverdi

Harmonies
improvised
by performers

Bass line
notated by
Monteverdi

Homophonic texture also made it much easier for audiences to understand the text being sung. A single singer carrying the melodic line, with a subordinate accompaniment (the basso continuo), could articulate the words clearly without competition from other voices. The rich sound of polyphonic texture came at the expense of textual clarity. Listen again to William Byrd's "Sing Joyfully" (chapter 8), without following the text in the book, and see how well you can understand the words. Even the best choirs cannot project every word with equal clarity: this kind of writing for four, five, or six voices is simply too thick.

The new homophonic texture restored a greater sense of balance between text and music. Composers who used this new manner of writing argued that the text should determine the nature of the music and not vice versa—even if the expressive portrayal of certain words meant occasionally breaking long-standing musical rules about harmony and counterpoint. Composers who believed in the text as a driving force called this new way of writing the *seconda prattica* ("second practice"). This newer compositional style came to be seen in opposition to the *prima prattica* ("first practice"), the older style in which musical richness took priority over textual expression (see Expand Your Playlist).

Word-Music Relationships: Between Speech and Song

LEARN MORE on
www.mymusiclab.com
MyMusicLibrary:
The Premise of Opera

CONNECT YOUR PLAYLIST

Recitative

Find a piece that contains recitative, or is recitative-like.

Example: Usher, "Confessions Part II" (2004)
The first section of this song from Usher's 2004 album *Confessions* features a combination of speech and recitative-like singing.

The selection opens with an extended **recitative** by Orpheus. The word "recitative" derives from the same root word as "recite," and this style of singing lies somewhere between singing and speaking. It is still singing—we hear sustained pitches and definite rhythms—but the syllabic setting of the text makes it closer to speech than the more melodic, lyrical kind of singing we hear more frequently. The great advantage of recitative over more conventional styles of singing is that it allows the words to be projected with special clarity: melody is less important. In this sense, recitative is rather like plainchant (discussed in chapter 1), but with the addition of supporting instruments underneath the vocal line.

The chorus that follows is written in the older polyphonic style. As in the sung dramas of Greek antiquity, the chorus—here, the gathering of nymphs and shepherds—comments from time to time on what has just occurred. The texture is necessarily polyphonic because the chorus represents the reactions of the many characters onstage who are witnessing the drama. The textures in Monteverdi's *Orpheus* thus include both homophony and polyphony; this coexistence of old and new textures is typical of music throughout the Baroque Era.

Now listen to the excerpt again, using the Listening Guide.

GO TO www.mymusiclab.com
for the Automated Listening Guide
CD I • Track 30/Download Track 30

Listening Guide

Claudio Monteverdi Composed: 1607 *Orpheus,* selection from Act II (6:10)

Time	Singer	Italian Text	English Translation	Texture	Word-Music Relationship
0:00	Orpheus	Tu se' morta, mia vita, ed io respiro? Tu se' da me partita Per mai più non tornare, ed io rimango? No, che se i versi alcuna cosa ponno, N'andrò sicuro a' più profondi abissi; E intenerito il cor del Re dell'ombre, Meco trarrotti a riveder le stelle. O, se ciò negherammi empio destino, Rimarrò teco in compagnia di morte. Addio terra, addio cielo e sole, addio.	Thou art dead, my life, and I still breathe? Thou art departed from me, Never to return, and I remain? No, if my verses still hold any power, I shall descend to the deepest depths; And I shall soften the heart of the king of shadows And bring thee back with me to see the stars again. Or if impious fate denies me this, I shall remain there in the company of the dead. Farewell, earth, farewell, sky and sun, farewell.	Homophonic (voice and accompanying basso continuo)	Recitative (syllabic). Word painting on *abissi* ("depths"): melody descends; rises up to the word *stelle* ("stars") and sinks down again on *morte* ("the dead").
2:54	Chorus of nymphs and shepherds	Ahi caso acerbo, ahi fat'empio e crudele. Ahi stelle ingiuriose, ahi cielo avaro. No si fidi uom mortale Di ben caduco e frale, Che tosto fugge, e spesso A gran salita il precipizio è presso.(Alessandro Striggio)	Ah, bitter event! Ah, impious and cruel fate! Ah, misaligned stars! Ah, voracious heaven! Let no mortal trust in transient and frail happiness, for it soon flies away, and oftenthe great height is close to the precipice. (Transl. MEB)	Polyphonic (chorus of five parts, all equal)	Lyrical singing. Word painting on *acerbo* ("bitter), with sharp dissonance (conflicting notes). Word painting on *fugge* ("flies"), with rapid rhythms, and on *salita* ("height"), with rising melodic line.

Student FAQs

If recitative makes it so much easier to understand the words, why isn't the whole opera written in recitative?

So far as text intelligibility is concerned, recitative has definite advantages over lyrical singing. However, if an opera consisted entirely of recitative, we would likely miss the more musical elements that lyrical singing has to offer. Composers of opera typically use a combination of different singing styles and instrumental and vocal combinations to create a wide variety of timbres and textures.

Does the basso continuo play when the chorus sings?

Yes it does, though it is not as noticeable because the alto, tenor, and bass voices provide the necessary harmonic support to the upper line. Once the basso continuo took hold in the early seventeenth century, it was used for homophonic and polyphonic textures alike.

 **PROFILE   Claudio Monteverdi** (1567–1643)

Master of Old and New Styles

Claudio Monteverdi's career straddled the Renaissance and the Baroque Era, and he mastered both the old and new textures of composition. The madrigal "Luci serene e chiare," featured in the playlist, is a good example of the earlier polyphonic style. The "Lamento della ninfa," on the other hand, reflects his shift to the new homophonic way of writing. Monteverdi served for many years at the court of Mantua, where he produced *Orpheus* (1607), the first opera to win widespread acclaim. In 1613 he became director of music at St. Mark's Basilica in Venice, where he lived the rest of his life. He was constantly trying new styles and new genres. In addition to operas for an elite audience at court, he also wrote works for the new public opera houses that began to open in Venice at the end of the 1630s. His music remained a touchstone for all subsequent seventeenth-century composers.

This portrait of Monteverdi dates from around 1613, when he was appointed music director at St. Mark's in Venice, one of the most prestigious musical positions in all Italy.
Bernardo Strozzi, (1581–1644) Claudio Monteverdi, composer (1567–1643), Oil on canvas/Landesmuseum Ferdinandeum, Innsbruck, Austria/©Photograph by Erich Lessing/Art Resource, NY

 EXPLORE MORE on **www.mymusiclab.com**

EXPAND YOUR PLAYLIST: MONTEVERDI

- *Coronation of Poppea (L'incoronazione di Poppea).* This opera is based on the historical figures of the Emperor Nero (who fiddled while Rome burned) and his lover, Poppea, who schemes and plots to eliminate everyone who stands in her way of becoming empress of Rome.

- *The Return of Ulysses to His Homeland (Il ritorno d'Ulisse in Patria).* The libretto of this opera draws on the end of Homer's *Odyssey*.

- *Psalm 100 (Confitebor tibi).* Written for soloist, chorus, and orchestra, this piece is one of many sacred works Monteverdi wrote at San Marco in Venice.

- **"Serene and clear eyes"** ("Luci serene e chiare"). This madrigal is composed in the earlier polyphonic style.

- **"The Western Wind Returns"** ("Zefiro torna"). This is an Italian-language madrigal for two tenors and basso continuo, to a text by the fourteenth-century Italian poet Petrarch.

- **"Lament of the Nymph"** ("Lamento della Ninfa"). Here is an extended madrigal for vocal soloists, chorus, and basso continuo.

- *Vespers in Honor of the Blessed Virgin Mary (Vespro della Beata Vergine).* Monteverdi wrote this work when he was music director at the Basilica of San Marco in Venice. Its various movements present both old and new styles, the *prima prattica* and the *seconda prattica*.

((•● **HEAR SAMPLES** on **www.mymusiclab.com**

THE COMPOSER SPEAKS Monteverdi Turns Down a Job Offer

Noble families competed not only among themselves for the best and brightest artists and musicians, they also competed with the church. When Monteverdi became music director at St. Mark's in Venice, he received not only a higher salary than he had in Mantua (where he had first presented *Orpheus*) but also a staff of paid assistants, which allowed him the luxury of accepting commissions to write secular music—madrigals and operas—for venues outside the church. When the rulers of Mantua tried to lure Monteverdi back to their court, he declined the offer diplomatically but firmly:

I shall . . . submit for Your Lordship's consideration the fact that this Most Serene Republic [Venice] has never before given to any of my predecessors—whether it were Adriano [Willaert] or Cipriano [de Rore], or [Gioseffo] Zarlino, or anyone else—but 200 ducats in salary, whereas to me they give 400. . . . Nor, having done this for me, have they ever regretted it: on the contrary they have honored me, and honor me continually in such manner, that no singer is accepted into the choir until they ask [my] opinion . . . nor do they take on organists or an assistant director unless they have [my] opinion . . . nor is there any gentleman who does not esteem and honor me, and when I am about to perform either chamber or church music, I swear to Your Lordship that the entire city comes running.

Next, the duties are very light. . . . Moreover, [the Director of Music's] allowance is assured until his death: neither the death of a procurator nor that of a doge interferes with it, and . . . if he does not go at the appointed time to pick it up, it is brought round to his house. . . . [T]hen there is occasional income, which consists of whatever extra I can easily earn outside St. Mark's of about 200 ducats a year . . . because whoever can engage the director to look after their music—not to mention the payment of 30 ducats, and even 40, and up to 50 for two vespers and a mass—does not fail to take him on, and they also thank him afterwards with well-chosen words.

Source: Claudio Monteverdi, *The Letters of Monteverdi*. Rev. ed., ed. and trans. Denis Stevens (Oxford: Clarendon Press, 1995), pp. 190–191. Reprinted by permission of Accademia Monteverdiana.

EXPAND YOUR PLAYLIST

Old and New Practices in the Seventeenth Century

The music of the early Baroque Era encompasses both old *(prima prattica)* and new *(seconda prattica)* styles, sometimes in the same work. These composers bridged the gap between Renaissance polyphony and Baroque homophony.

Giovanni Gabrieli (ca. 1554/57–1612)
• was the most celebrated composer working in Venice in the decades before Monteverdi's arrival. His *Oh Great Mystery (O magnum mysterium)* is a sacred piece for chorus, brass ensemble, and solo vocalist, combining elements of the old and new practice in a single work.

Heinrich Schütz (1585–1672)
• was the leading German composer of the seventeenth century. He studied composition in Venice, possibly with Monteverdi.
• "Sing Unto the Lord a New Song" ("Cantate domino canticum novicum"), a setting of Psalm 96, in Latin, is written in the *prima prattica* for four-part chorus.

• "Sing Unto the Lord a New Song" ("Singet dem Herren ein neues Lied") is a version of the same psalm in German. It is written in the newer *seconda prattica*, for solo voice, two violins, and basso continuo. The vocal and instrumental parts are quite florid and virtuosic.

Pier Francesco Cavalli (1602–1676)
• was Monteverdi's successor as music director at St. Mark's in Venice. Like Monteverdi, he composed in many genres, including operas and sacred music. *Dido (La Didone)* is an opera based on the same plot as Purcell's *Dido and Aeneas* (see chapter 11), a story taken from Virgil's *Aeneid*.

((• HEAR SAMPLES on www.mymusiclab.com

✔ TEST YOURSELF on www.mymusiclab.com   Flashcards and chapter tests

11

Henry Purcell
Dido and Aeneas, Overture and Act I, nos. 1–4
Composed: 1689

Purcell's *Dido and Aeneas* is one of the first operas written in English. Its opening, heard here, consists of an instrumental overture and a series of brief numbers that are sung. The story comes from Virgil's *Aenead,* which is about the aftermath of the Trojan War and the eventual founding of Rome.

Listen to this first

((•● HEAR MORE on **www.mymusiclab.com**

Form

Listen for the variety of forms within the span of only a few minutes of action. Following the instrumental overture, we hear a vocal **recitative** answered by a **chorus**, then an aria ("song"), then another recitative, and finally another chorus.

Word-Music Relationships

Listen specifically for the difference between those passages that are recitatives (more speech-like) and those that are arias (more lyrical).

LEARN MORE on
www.mymusiclab.com
Chapter Objectives

The early performance history of *Dido and Aeneas* is shrouded in mystery. The first documented production was sometime in 1689 at a school for young ladies in Chelsea (west of London at the time, now a part of the city), but it may have been performed as early as 1685. The work seems to have disappeared from the stage shortly afterward. It was not revived until 1700, almost five years after the composer's death, in a drastically altered version. *Dido and Aeneas* may have been suppressed for political reasons, either by Purcell himself or by the Crown, on the grounds that it could have been perceived as an unflattering commentary on the dual reign of King William, a foreigner, and Queen Mary, daughter of Charles I. The opera's plot, after all, deals with a foreign prince (Aeneas) who promises to marry the Queen of Carthage (Dido) but then abandons her, driving her to suicide.

The chief characters of the opera are the following:

- Dido, the queen of Carthage (soprano; the highest vocal range)
- Aeneas, a Trojan prince (baritone; the middle-low male voice)
- Belinda, Dido's maidservant (soprano)

Aeneas is a refugee from Troy, which has just fallen to the Greeks and their Trojan Horse. Fulfilling a promise from the gods, Aeneas and his companions are now on their way from Troy to the Italian peninsula, where he is destined to establish the city of Rome. On the coast of northern

Africa (what is now Tunisia), they land at Carthage, ruled by the widowed Queen Dido. True to operatic convention, Dido and Aeneas immediately fall in love. He pledges to abandon his mission to found Rome, but when a witch disguised as Mercury, the messenger of the gods, orders him to leave, he obeys and departs. Dido dies, disconsolate, but not before singing a long lament at the very end of the opera. The excerpt here is from the very beginning of the opera.

Form by the Numbers

ca. 1659–1695
Henry Purcell
Dido and Aeneas,
Overture and Act I,
nos. 1–4
Composed: 1689
GENRE
Baroque Opera

KEY CONCEPTS
Ostinato, overture, French
overture, aria.

CHAPTER HIGHLIGHT
Baroque Opera
Purcell's *Dido and Aeneas*, the first
English opera, unfolds through a
series of numbers in different
musical formats. It opens with an
overture in two sections, the first
slow, the second fast. The arias
and recitatives help delineate the
characters who are singing them.

Purcell moves the plot forward through a series of brief, self-contained units known as "numbers," as follows:

1. **Overture.**   There had to be some way to get the audience to settle down and be quiet. Far from the well-trained classical audiences of today, who file in respectfully to hear an esteemed musical work, audiences in Purcell's time (and, indeed, for the century and a half that followed) could be quite boisterous and noisy. For one thing, the music they were about to hear was new and had not yet entered the ranks of cherished masterworks. For another, people regarded the opera as a supreme social event, as many people still do today. A purely instrumental opening, or **overture**, signaled to the audience that it was time to leave the socializing and direct attention to the stage, where the singers would soon appear.

   The form of this particular overture—a slow introduction followed by an imitative fast section—was very common in French operas of the time and for that reason is known as a **French overture**. We hear two typical characteristics of the French overture here:
   a. The slow introduction features a consistent alternation between long and short notes (a "LONG-short-LONG-short" pattern).
   b. The fast section begins with **imitation** among the voices: the same theme introduced by different instruments of the orchestra in succession.

2. **Scene and Chorus.**   An aria, sung by Belinda to Queen Dido ("Shake the cloud from off your brow"). "**Aria**" is Italian for "air" or "melody," and is used to describe any lyrical movement or piece for solo voice, usually with some kind of instrumental accompaniment. The chorus then joins in, reinforcing this same sentiment with different words ("Banish sorrow, banish care").

3. **Song.**   Another aria, this one more elaborate. Dido laments her state ("Ah! Belinda"). She sings her melody over an **ostinato** pattern in the bass, a short array of nine notes repeated over and over. ("Ostinato" comes from the same root word as "obstinate.") This kind of pattern is also known as a **ground bass** or simply a **ground**.

4. **Recitative.**   Belinda and Dido in dialogue ("Grief increases by concealing"). The recitative, as we saw in chapter 10, provided a way of delivering text quickly and clearly in a singing style similar to speech. The accompaniment is a simple basso continuo (see page 93), played by harpsichord and cello in this case.

5. **Chorus.**   In the manner of the chorus in an ancient Greek tragedy, the chorus comments on what has just happened on the stage, reinforcing Belinda's advice that Troy and Carthage join forces in the union of Dido and Aeneas ("When monarchs unite").

Michele Serrano-Möritz as Dido (left) and Elizabeth Hillebrand as Belinda in the opening scene of Purcell's *Dido and Aeneas,* from a production by the Bronx Opera Company in 2006.
Heidi Schumann

PROFILE   Henry Purcell (ca. 1659–1695)

Inspired by the Stage

Purcell was born into a family of musicians and served in his early years as a composer and organist at the English court and later at Westminster Abbey, where he is buried. He contributed songs and instrumental music to dozens of plays but wrote only one true opera, *Dido and Aeneas.* The English public was largely hostile to opera during the seventeenth century, in part because of England's strong tradition of spoken theater. Shakespeare had called for songs or instrumental music at many points in a number of his plays, but the idea of singing an entire drama from beginning to end was something most English theatergoers considered absurd. Not until the early eighteenth century would opera take hold in England, and when it did, the rage was for opera sung in Italian, not English. It would be another 50 years before audiences would begin to accept the idea of English-language opera. Purcell, in short, was far ahead of his time. When *Dido and Aeneas* was rediscovered in the late eighteenth century, it helped establish his eventual reputation as the greatest of all seventeenth-century English composers.

Purcell in the 1690s, toward the end of his brief life.
National Portrait Gallery, London

◉➨ **EXPLORE MORE** on **www.mymusiclab.com**

◀◀   EXPAND YOUR PLAYLIST: PURCELL   ▶▶

- **Chaconne in G minor, Z. 730.** A purely instrumental ground bass (ostinato) for four stringed instruments and basso continuo.

- **"Sound the Trumpet"** from *Ode for Queen Mary's Birthday.* A duet for tenors and basso continuo, with the voices imitating trumpets.

- **"One Charming Night"** from *The Faerie Queen.* An aria from a semi-opera, set to a libretto by Sir Edmund Spenser.

- **"Lord, What Is Man?"** A song for solo voice and basso continuo.

- *My Heart Is Inditing.* A full anthem (see chapter 8) in the tradition of English sacred music, for chorus and string orchestra.

((•) **HEAR SAMPLES** on **www.mymusiclab.com**

PERFORMANCE   Opera in English

Why aren't there more operas in English? Most of the works in the operatic repertory were written in other languages, particularly Italian (opera began on the Italian peninsula, after all), but also French and German. Some claim that English by its nature is not as singable as Italian with all its sustainable vowels. But the enormous repertory of English-language songs offers compelling evidence that English words lend themselves to singing just as well. In our day, many operas are being written in English, partly because it has become a language of worldwide significance—much as Italian was in the seventeenth and eighteenth centuries. Benjamin Britten's operas from the 1940s and 1950s (*Peter Grimes, The Turn of the Screw*) are staples of the repertory. More recent contributors include Thea Musgrave (*Mary, Queen of Scots*), John Adams (*Nixon in China*), and Philip Glass (*Einstein on the Beach*; see chapter 56).

Should foreign-language operas be sung in English? The advantage is obvious: audiences could easily understand what's being sung onstage. But there are drawbacks, too. It's difficult to create translations that retain the sense of the original and still mesh well with the composer's music. A composer might write a melodic phrase in such a way as to reach the highest note on one particular word, and a good translation must take that into account. Finally, English is a challenging language when it comes to rhyme: French, German, and especially Italian offer many more possibilities for rhymed words, and rhyme often plays an important role in opera texts.

Recently, opera houses have begun to address these challenges. Many use super-titles during performances. Listeners who want to follow the text can see the translations projected above the stage. A few opera houses have begun trying out personalized screens on individual seats that gives the listener the freedom to pick any language as a translation.

Word-Music Relationships: Speaking, Expressing, Commenting

LEARN MORE on
www.mymusiclab.com
MyMusicLibrary:
French vs. Italian Opera

CONNECT YOUR PLAYLIST

Ostinato

Find a piece that uses an ostinato.

Example: Pink Floyd, "Money" (1973) Popular songs based entirely on a single ground bass are rare, but "Money," by Pink Floyd, uses a single bass pattern for long stretches.

Purcell was influenced by composers of both French opera (especially Lully; see Expand Your Playlist) and Italian opera (including Alessandro Scarlatti, among others), who had begun moving more and more toward a clear division between recitative and aria.

When Purcell's characters need to talk to each other, he gives them something between speech and song: the recitative. When his characters need to convey some deeper feeling, he gives them lyrical arias in which they can linger expressively over individual words. The chorus, observing and feeling for us at closer range, punctuates these longer melodic expressions with comments communicated clearly and intelligibly, with one syllable per note. Each unit of the opera is dominated by a single *affect*, or emotion. Belinda is agitated in her opening number: she sings in uneven (dotted) rhythms, particularly on the word "shake." Dido, in turn, sings her first lament (no. 3) to a repeated bass pattern that mirrors her state of constant sorrow. The chorus "When monarchs unite," with its lively, dance-like rhythms and major mode, injects a note of optimism into the musical narrative.

Now listen to the piece again, using the Listening Guide.

GO TO www.mymusiclab.com
for the Automated Listening Guide
CD I • Track 31/Download Track 31

Listening Guide

Henry Purcell Composed: 1689 *Dido and Aeneas,* Overture and Act I, nos. 1–4 (8:11)

The Overture

Time	Number	Form: Section	Texture
0:00	1. Overture	Slow introduction (**A**)	Melody in the uppermost voice; prominent basso continuo part below
0:45		Literal repeat of slow introduction (**A**)	
1:26		Fast section (**B**)	Begins with imitative entries
1:57		Literal repeat of fast section (**B**)	

Act I

When the curtain goes up on Act I, we see the Palace of Carthage, with Queen Dido accompanied by Belinda, her maidservant and confidante, and other members of the court. Dido laments her current state: her husband has died, she has not remarried, and her kingdom, as a result, is vulnerable and unstable.

Time	Number	Character(s) Singing	Text
2:31	2. Scene and Chorus	Belinda	Shake the cloud from off your brow, Fate your wishes does allow; Empire growing, pleasures flowing, Fortune smiles and so should you.
3:04		Chorus	Banish sorrow, banish care, Grief should ne'er approach the fair.
3:30	3. Song (Aria)	Dido	Ah! Belinda, I am pressed With torment not to be confessed, Peace and I are strangers grown. I languish till my grief is known, Yet would not have it guess'd.
7:21	4. Recitative	Belinda and Dido	**Belinda:** Grief increases by concealing. **Dido:** Mine admits of no revealing. **Belinda:** Then let me speak; the Trojan guest Into your tender thoughts has pressed; The greatest blessing Fate can give Our Carthage to secure and Troy revive.
7:57	5. Chorus	Chorus	When monarchs unite, how happy their state, They triumph at once o'er their foes and their fate.

Rhythm

Dotted rhythms featured prominently.

Theme consists of notes of equal value (not dotted).

Word-Music Relationships

Rapid dotted rhythms on "shake," as if to mimic the act of shaking.

Ground bass (ostinato), a brief pattern repeated in the bass line throughout the entire number, reflecting the unceasing nature of Dido's torment.

The first part of the dialogue stands between speech and song;

Belinda's last two lines stand out because they are more lyrical and because she repeats these words.

The syllabic setting helps make the words more intelligible.

Student FAQs

Why is there so much repetition of the words?

Text repetition is common in many operas from different times and places. Repeating the words gives listeners a better chance of understanding them, and altering the music with each statement of the words allows the composer to bring out ever-deeper levels of meaning in them.

How long is this opera?

For an opera, it's very short: most performances run somewhere between 50 minutes and an hour. Most operas, by contrast, run at least two hours and often three or more, not including intermissions.

EXPAND YOUR PLAYLIST

Baroque Opera

The most important repertories of later Baroque opera were in Italian and French. Italian opera enjoyed international acclaim; French opera was limited to France. Today, both repertories are performed.

Italian Opera

- **George Frideric Handel** (1685–1759), although German by birth, wrote many Italian operas during his years in London. These operas were often based on subjects from Classical history (Roman emperors, for example) or myth.

The aria "Or la tromba" ("Now the trumpet") from *Rinaldo* is a **da capo aria**, which is very typical of **opera seria** (or "serious opera"), as Italian opera of this kind was called. A da capo aria opens with two contrasting sections, **A** and **B**; at the end of the **B** section, the singer return to the beginning of the **A** section, following the direction in the score of *da capo*—literally, "from the head," or as we would say, "from the top." When the singer performs this **A** section a second time, he or she embellishes it heavily. The typical opera seria consists of an alternation of recitatives, which move the action forward, and da capo arias, in which the singers reflect on what has just happened on the stage.

"Piangerò," a lament by Cleopatra from *Giulio Cesare*, is also a da capo aria. The **A** section is slow, the **B** section fast.

French Opera

- **Jean-Baptiste Lully** (1632–1687) was the favorite composer of King Louis XIV of France. The aria "Enfin, il est en ma puissance" from the opera *Armide*, is a stirring monologue by the sorceress Armida, who contemplates murdering the sleeping Renaud (Rinaldo) but cannot bring herself to do it because of his beauty.

- **Marc-Antoine Charpentier** (1643–1704) was another French composer who lived during the reign of Louis XIV. Charpentier's *Andromède* provides instrumental music for a play based on the Greek myth of Andromeda. In the aria "Quelle est lente, cette journée" you hear the very fluid rhythms typical of Baroque French homophony.

- **Jean-Philippe Rameau** (1683–1764) was the greatest composer of French opera in the eighteenth century. In "Rossignols amoureux" ("Amorous nightingales"), an aria from the opera *Hippolyte et Aricie*, both voice and instruments imitate the song of the nightingale.

((•● HEAR SAMPLES on **www.mymusiclab.com**

 TEST YOURSELF on **www.mymusiclab.com**   Flashcards and chapter tests

Mbuti Pygmies
"Marriage Celebration Song"
Recorded: 1958

Ostinato, such as we heard in Dido's aria "Ah! Belinda" from *Dido and Aeneas* (chapter 11), is a formal device that has been used in the music of many different times and places. In the "Marriage Celebration Song" of the Mbuti Pygmies of central Africa, the repetition of a single pattern of notes and rhythms throughout the entire song provides a unifying structure above which a variety of melodies are presented.

⚙ LEARN MORE on
www.mymusiclab.com
Chapter Objectives

Listen to this first

((• HEAR MORE on **www.mymusiclab.com**

Texture	**Rhythm**	**Form**
How many different vocal lines can you identify? Compare how they function independently and work together. How do the inner voices support each other on the same part?	Listen to how the parts are arranged rhythmically. Do the parts seem to function rhythmically as individuals, or do they work together?	Listen for the repetition of one basic unit. How would you describe the construction of this unit?

The Mbuti Pygmies from the northeastern region of the Democratic Republic of the Congo (DRC, formerly known as Zaire) use ostinatos as the basis for complex musical structures involving polyphony, interlocking rhythms, and the alternation of voices to create a melody. In recent years, the music of the Pygmies has found growing interest among Western audiences, and its influence has extended to various pop, jazz, and world beat genres.

The Mbuti Pygmies inhabit the Ituri Forest. Although they are officially citizens of the DRC, the majority of Pygmy groups maintain a semiautonomous hunting-and-gathering existence. The Mbuti Pygmies are nomads, camping for a few weeks at a time in different locations of the forest in search of game. The hunt is a communal affair in which men string nets in semicircles and women and children beat the brush to scare game into the nets. Food is shared. A political hierarchy is

The Mbuti Pygmies live in the Ituri Forest.

Mbuti Pygmies making music. The pipes they are blowing into are made of leaves; each member of the group plays a single note.

Nick Greaves/Alamy Images

absent because survival depends on cooperation and not competition. In the same way, musical parts in Pygmy songs are distributed equally and coordinated carefully. The contribution of each separate part reflects every member's contribution to food gathering in the rainforest.

Texture: Layers Upon Layers

The ostinato in this song is made of multiple layers that overlap and interlock in intriguing ways. The most obvious textural layer is the **call-and-response**, in which one group of voices sings an opening motive, and three different groups in succession sing their answers (see the top line of the following diagram).

Beneath the call-and-response structure, two heterophonic lines are stacked. **Heterophony** is the simultaneous playing or singing of two or more versions of a melody. Thus, the line marked "Heterophonic voice 1" in the following diagram actually consists of multiple voice lines all singing similar melodies but not identical pitches. (The same is true of the line marked "Heterophonic voice 2.") Heterophony is a basic way of creating harmonic support without using harmony built from chords. It gives a thicker texture to the polyphony.

The two heterophonic lines are further layered by a **hocket** construction. Hocket is a form of polyphony consisting of two or more rhythmically **interlocking** voices. When voices interlock, one voice fills the spaces left by another's rests to complete a melodic unit. In other words, the melody is distributed throughout the parts, and each part contains only its constituent notes, sounded at the precise time. Hockets were also particularly popular in medieval France (see chapter 3).

Think of a game where each player can speak only one word. Each person would then have to say this word at precisely the right moment to fit into a sentence; for example:

    Voice I: I
    Voice II: am
    Voice III: a
    Voice IV: girl.

Now imagine that each person sings just one note in a melody. The same effect would be created by having each person chime in when his or her note is needed:

    Voice I: Hap-py   Day
    Voice II: Birth-
    Voice III: to
    Voice IV: you.

In Pygmy hocketing, this is made more complicated by the fact that each singer may sing two or three different notes, but the basic challenge of fitting these notes together into a melody remains.

In the following diagram you can see the spaces left by some parts and filled by others; imagine vertical lines to make this clear. When you listen to the song, you can hear the interesting alternation of parts—identifiable by their slightly different timbres—to create one melody.

The melodic-rhythmic fragments also overlap: a singer sustains a tone over the entrance tone of the singer that follows, which fills what would otherwise be a slight gap of sound between phrases. Sounds of crickets form the background to the singing voices, adding another interesting textural element.

Here is a representation of the interlocking melodic-rhythmic fragments that create the hocket, which continues throughout the song as an ostinato:

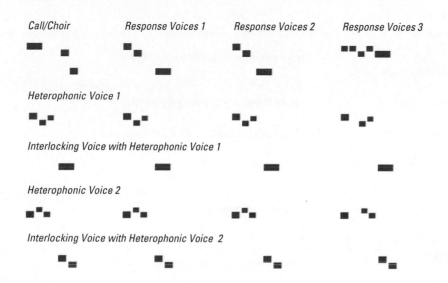

Global Connection:
Ostinato
Mbuti Pygmies
"Marriage Celebration Song"
Recorded: 1958

GENRE
Ostinato

KEY CONCEPTS
Ostinato, polyphony, rhythmic interlock, hocket, call-and-response, heterophony.

CHAPTER HIGHLIGHT
Ostinato
Ostinato—the repetition of one pattern of notes and rhythms—provides a unifying structure for at least some kinds of music in many different cultures. The example here is from central Africa.

Interlocking Rhythms

The rhythmic complexity of African hocket comes partly from the number of different parts that interlock and partly from the complexity of each individual part. No single line stands on its own. Each response in the call-and-response construction is built from interlocking sub-units. The hocket thus occurs on many levels, as shown in the diagram.

Form: A Call-and-Response Ostinato

The call-and-response may be represented as four phrases, **ABBB**, covering a total of eight beats. This essential melodic unit repeats over and over to create the ostinato. The five basic lines remain consistent. However, the pitches used to create the heterophony vary each time, as do the melody lines and vocalizations that are improvised to embellish the ostinato.

Now listen to this piece again, using the Listening Guide.

CONNECT YOUR PLAYLIST

Interlocking Rhythms

Find a piece that contains interlocking rhythms.

Example: Santana's recording of "Oye Como Va" (1970)—originally recorded by the great percussionist Tito Puente—has a complex accompaniment that uses interlocking rhythms.

GO TO www.mymusiclab.com
for the **Automated Listening Guide**
CD I • Track 32/Download Track 32

Listening Guide

Mbuti Pygmies Recorded: 1958 "Marriage Celebration Song" (1:02)

Time	Form	Texture
0:00	The song is already in progress.	Polyphonic throughout, with heterophony in each phrase subunit. The hocket is already established.
0:01	Ostinato cycle 1. **A:** the call.	Thick throughout.
0:02	**B, B, B:** the responses. One singer sets the intonation for the first response voices.	Thinner than the call. Voices overlap.
0:07	Ostinato cycle 2, beginning once again with the call.	Texture remains the same: polyphonic.
0:09	**B, B:** first two responses, sung by separate singers.	Thinner than accented call. Voices overlap.
0:12	**B:** third response; different from previous two, tapering the phrase cycle.	Voices overlap.
0:13	Ostinato cycle 3.	Polyphonic throughout.
0:20	Ostinato cycle 4. The lead singer of the call is heard over the group for the first time on this recording.	
0:26	Cycle 5	
0:32	Cycle 6	
0:38	Cycle 7	
0:44	Cycle 8	
0:51	Cycle 9	
0:57	Cycle 10	

Note: The selection begins midway through the song, and the lead singer is absent in the first three cycles but rejoins the song on the fourth cycle. Thus, in the early seconds of the excerpt, a different singer leads the response and sets the intonation.

Rhythm

Eight beats per cycle, built of four interlocking phrases. Each phrase is built from interlocking voices.

A long sung tone followed by two shorter sung tones, descending.

The first of the three interlocking responses is sung. The next two follow until up to the second cycle. All responses are constructed of interlocking subunits.

A long sung tone followed by two shorter sung tones, descending.

Interlocking responses continue after call throughout.

The same throughout.

Student FAQs

How do Pygmies learn and remember these songs if there is no written notation?

Traditional singers and musicians around the world have developed a way of learning music without using any system of notation. Often, master musicians of one generation will teach students, either formally or informally, passing on their knowledge. Of course, with no recordings or written documentation, songs may change as they are sung over time. This is called "oral transmission" by ethnomusicologists because there is nothing put in writing.

Why do Pygmies sing?

They sing for the same reason that most people do. However, many Pygmy songs have associations with specific rituals. For instance, the song featured in this chapter is linked to the wedding ceremony. Singing is a group activity in which everyone takes part, rather than one where a professional performs and others merely listen (as in many Western cultures).

How hard is it to sing in a hocketing style?

Try it with a group of friends! It's not that hard to learn your individual part, but synchronizing your singing with everyone else is very difficult if you've never tried it before. Add the idea that different melodies are occurring simultaneously (perhaps in different rhythms), and you'll get some sense of the skill of these Pygmy singers.

HISTORICAL CONTEXT   Do I Repeat Myself?

The use of an ostinato bass—a repeating bass part—onto which a melody line is overlaid is common in many different forms of music. A great example in American popular music is the doo wop vocal music of the 1950s.

How does doo wop work? In the vocal quartet, each voice has its own role. The bass singer handles the repeated foundation part, often in the form of a short phrase of nonsense syllables.

Think of the classic "Sh'Boom" by the Chords. The bass part is a simple repeated part. Above this bass line floats the melody. Between melody and bass, the other two voices fill in by also singing short melodic fragments. These four parts—fairly simple and seemingly independent—actually fit together to form one musical experience. We don't hear the individual parts as separate (although we can listen for them if we want) but instead experience the piece as a coherent whole.

How is this similar to the Pygmy music that we're hearing in this chapter?

The Chords, a 1950s doo wop group famous for their recording of "Sh'Boom."

Michael Ochs Archives Ltd./Getty Images Inc.—Los Angeles

EXPAND YOUR PLAYLIST

Singing in the Rain (Forest)

Mbuti Pygmies of the Ituri Rainforest
• Smithsonian Folkways Recordings SFW40401.
   Colin Turnbull was among the first Western anthropologists to spend considerable time studying and recording the Mbuti Pygmies in Africa. His landmark book, *The Forest People*, published in 1960, is considered a classic study of these people and helped introduce their culture to Western audiences. These recordings were made in the late 1950s and include many examples of the hocketing vocal style that we've studied in this chapter.

Heart of the Forest: The Music of the Baka Forest People of Southeast Cameroon
• Hannibal HNCD 1378.
   The Baka Forest people have their own unique form of vocal and instrumental hocketing. This recording includes a wide range of music, including performances on the single-string musical bow, and the distinctive vocal "yodeling" practiced by this tribe.

Centrafique: Anthologle de la Musique des Pygmees Aka
• Ocora C559012 13.
   Recorded by Pierre Toureille for UNESCO, this two-CD set documents the music of the Aka Forest peoples. Along with Turnbull's earlier recordings, this is considered a classic collection for those who love this musical style.

The Spirit Cries: Music from the Rainforests of South America & the Caribbean
• Rykodisc RCD 10250.
   Edited by percussionist Mickey Hart of the Grateful Dead, this collection of field recordings goes beyond Africa to trace related musical styles found across the ocean in South America and the Caribbean. The mixture of European and African influences is striking in these recordings.

((• HEAR SAMPLES on www.mymusiclab.com

✓ TEST YOURSELF on www.mymusiclab.com   Flashcards and chapter tests

Barbara Strozzi
"Revenge"
Composed: 1651

Barbara Strozzi's "Revenge" ("La Vendetta") allows the singer to display great vocal agility and makes effective use of contrasting timbres. The music requires only a small group of musicians: one singer, two violinists, and a basso continuo consisting in this performance of two instrumentalists, one playing the cello, the other playing the lute.

 Listen to this first

((• HEAR MORE on www.mymusiclab.com

Melody

Listen for the contour of the melodic lines and the way in which the singer embellishes these lines. Many of the longer notes are ornamented with shorter ones before or after.

Form

Notice the alternation of the two contrasting melodies, one in a lively duple meter, the other in a slower triple meter.

Timbre

Listen for the relationship of the two violins to the voice. The instruments echo the last phrase of each line of the text. Listen, too, for the way in which the instruments in the basso continuo (harpsichord, cello, and lute) support the vocal line.

A poetic text that expresses a jilted lover's thirst for revenge demands energetic, extroverted music, and that is exactly what Barbara Strozzi gave "Revenge." Music like this was meant to be performed for private gatherings in relatively small rooms or "chambers," hence the term **chamber music**. In chamber music, we hear only one performer on each part, in contrast to orchestral music, which features multiple players on most parts.

LEARN MORE on
www.mymusiclab.com
Chapter Objectives

Decoration of the Melody

In this performance of "Revenge," the singer adds extra notes to the notated melody line, decorating it more elaborately as the piece progresses. Listeners of the Baroque Era expected soloists to add this kind of ornamentation; the melodic lines written by the composer were only a starting point for performance. Music of the Baroque Era is in many respects like jazz today: musicians embellish a basic tune in a highly individual and often quite spontaneous manner. The opening melody returns twice (at 0:52 and at 1:45) and becomes more florid with each appearance. It is as if the jilted lover is becoming ever more agitated as she describes the revenge she will exact. Homophonic texture made this kind of improvisation possible. With two or more independent melody lines, players would have to agree in advance just how their embellishments would work together.

Form: Contrast and Repetition

Strozzi alternates the two contrasting melodies—the first in duple meter, the second in triple meter—to create a large-scale structure that can be diagrammed in this way:

A	B	A	B	A
Duple	Triple	Duple	Triple	Duple

The contours and rhythms of the two melodies differ markedly: the first moves mostly downward, with short, quick notes, while the second moves mostly upward, using longer notes. The return of each melody creates a sense of coherence for the piece. This combination of contrast and return is basic to a great deal of Baroque music. The opening melody (**A**) gives the work an anchor, while the contrasting melody provides variety.

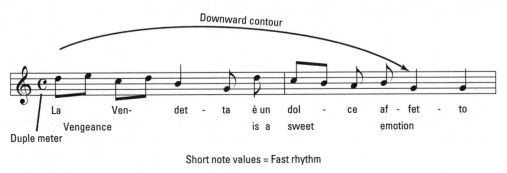

The **A** melody

The **B** melody

The words to the **A** melody do not change. This device—bringing back the same words with the same basic melody at regular intervals over the course of a work—is called a **refrain**. Refrains had been used in song since the Middle Ages, and they continue to be used today. Many popular songs rely on the use of refrains. Here are a few examples:

- "I really don't know clouds at all" (Joni Mitchell, "Both Sides Now")
- "Just another manic Monday" (The Bangles, "Manic Monday")
- "I don't even know his last name" (Carrie Underwood, "Last Name")

Timbre: Contrast and Punctuation

In addition to the basso continuo (see page 93), Strozzi uses two violins to great effect. They punctuate the end of every line in the refrain (the **A** section), each time providing an echo to what the soprano has just sung. This kind of back-and-forth between instruments and voices is another new element in Baroque music and has remained a basic compositional technique to the present day. The violins drop out entirely during the **B** sections of the work, further emphasizing the contrast between the **A** and **B** sections. The basso continuo part also participates in this interplay between instruments and voices. In the middle of the **B** section (at 0:36), you can hear the roles of voice and instruments reversed: the cello introduces the basic thematic idea before the soprano picks it up.

The sonority of the purely instrumental passages of this song—two violins and basso continuo—was a favorite in the Baroque Era. Many works of chamber music from this time feature two high instruments (violins, flutes, oboes, recorders, or any mixture of these various instruments) and basso continuo. Such a combination produced what is known as **trio-sonata texture**, with three main voices: two in the soprano and one in the bass (the basso continuo). Arcangelo Corelli, J.S. Bach, and Handel all wrote trio sonatas (see Expand Your Playlist).

Now listen to this arietta, or "little aria" as Strozzi called it, using the Listening Guide.

1619–1677
Barbara Strozzi
"Revenge"
Composed: 1651

GENRE
Baroque Song

KEY CONCEPTS
Embellishment, chamber music, trio-sonata texture, contrasting timbres.

CHAPTER HIGHLIGHT
Baroque Chamber Music
Chamber music, with only one player to a part, is intimate and just requires a few performers. In this "arietta," the solo singer is accompanied by only two violins and a basso continuo. The instruments and voice engage in a kind of dialogue about the sweetness of a lover's revenge.

CONNECT YOUR PLAYLIST

Ornamentation

Find a piece that contains both a straightforward and ornamented version of the same melody.

Example: Harold Arlen and Johnny Mercer, "Hit the Road to Dreamland" (1942)
In her 2001 recording of this song, the jazz singer Jane Monheit ornaments the melody when it returns after an instrumental solo.

GO TO www.mymusiclab.com
for the Automated Listening Guide
CD I • Track 33/Download Track 33

Listening Guide

Barbara Strozzi Composed: 1651 "Revenge" (2:14)

Time	Original Italian Text	English Translation	Timbre	Meter	Form (melodic idea)	Melody
0:00	La vendetta è un dolce affetto, il dispetto vuol dispetto, Il rifarsi è un gran diletto.	Vengeance is a sweet emotion; spite desires spite, and getting even is a great pleasure.	Soprano, basso continuo, two violins	Duple	A	Moves primarily downward in short, rapid notes
0:24	Vane son scuse e ragioni per placar donna oltraggiata, non pensar che ti perdoni! Donna mai non vendicata pace ha in bocca e guerra in petto.	Excuses and reasons are useless in placating an outraged woman; do not think that she will pardon you! A woman who has never avenged herself has peace on her lips and war in her heart.	Soprano, basso continuo	Triple	B	Moves primarily upward in longer, sustained notes
0:52	La vendetta è un dolce affetto il dispetto vuol dispetto, il rifarsi è un gran diletto.	Vengeance is a sweet emotion; spite desires spite, and getting even is a great pleasure.	Soprano, basso continuo, two violins	Duple	A'	Embellished further
1:17	Non perdona in vendicarsi all'amante più gradito che l'adora e vuol rifarsi quand'il fiero insuperbito verso lei perd'il rispetto.	She does not pardon, when taking vengeance, even the most agreeable lover who adores her and wants to make up with her when the proud and arrogant man loses respect for her.	Soprano, basso continuo	Triple	B' (embellished)	Embellished further
1:45	La vendetta è un dolce affetto il dispetto vuol dispetto Il rifarsi è un gran diletto.	Vengeance is a sweet emotion; spite desires spite, and getting even is a great pleasure.	Soprano, basso continuo, two violins	Duple	A''	Embellished still further

Student FAQs

How do performers know how to embellish this music?

At least some performance practices of the Baroque Era are documented in the books that taught musicians how to sing or play instruments. But these are really only starting points. Now, as then, musicians must use artistic judgment and embellish the music as they see fit. Opinions about what constitutes too much or too little embellishment vary widely.

If chamber music is performed by one musician to a part, is there a limit on the number of parts for it to still be considered chamber music?

A nonet—nine different parts—is generally considered to be the largest group of performers in a work of chamber music. With more than nine musicians, the "chamber" becomes rather crowded.

PROFILE   Barbara Strozzi (1619–1677)

"Secure from the Lightning Bolts of Slander"

Being a female composer—and a supremely talented one, no less—was not easy in the seventeenth century. In 1644, Barbara Strozzi dedicated her first published work, a collection of madrigals, with this note of awareness about criticism of her gender:

> To the august name of Your Highness I do reverently consecrate this first work, which I, as a woman, send forth into the light all too anxiously, so that under an oak tree of gold it may rest secure from the lightning bolts of slander prepared for it.

Her anticipation of "slander" was not without foundation. Rumors surrounded Strozzi's life. She had been adopted by the poet Giulio Strozzi and may in fact have been his natural daughter, born out of wedlock. She grew up in a family at the center of Venice's intellectual and cultural life and attended meetings of poets and philosophers that did not normally include women. Her chastity seems to have been a source of repeated satire and jest in the late 1630s as well.

Strozzi's achievements as a composer are all the more impressive in this light. By the end of her life, she had published eight volumes of music, including about 125 individual works of music, more than all but a few of her male contemporaries. What's more, she accomplished all this without benefit of a secure professional position in music and without extended support from any one patron.

⦿➔ **EXPLORE MORE** on **www.mymusiclab.com**

The Gamba Player, by Bernardo Strozzi, ca. 1640. The woman depicted here may be Barbara Strozzi.

Erich Lessing/Art Resource, NY

EXPAND YOUR PLAYLIST: STROZZI

- **"With New Bad News, I Cannot Sing"** ("Con male nuove, non si puo' cantare") is a lament for soprano and basso continuo.

- **"Proud Eyes"** ("Gl' occhi superbi") is a love song for soprano and basso continuo.

- **"Betrayal!"** ("Tradimento!") is a song from the perspective of a jilted lover for soprano and basso continuo.

- **"Between Hope and Fear"** ("Tra le spiranze e 'l timore") is a dialogue—for a single voice and basso continuo—between hope and fear.

((• **HEAR SAMPLES** on **www.mymusiclab.com**

HISTORICAL CONTEXT   Female Composers in the Baroque Era

Barbara Strozzi was one of a relatively small number of women in the Baroque Era who were able to publish their own compositions. The success of countless women composers in more recent times may make us wonder why there were so few in the past.

While many women received musical training as performers—particularly as singers or as keyboard players—very few enjoyed the benefit of instruction in composition. Francesca Caccini (1587–ca. 1641) and Elisabeth Jacquet de la Guerre (1665–1729), two accomplished composers of the Baroque period, were both daughters of musicians and learned harmony and counterpoint at home. Others, like Barbara Strozzi, grew up in highly cultured households in which musicians and composers circulated freely. But for the most part, women simply did not have access to the kind of rigorous instruction needed to learn the art of composition.

Part of the reason for this is that there were virtually no professional prospects for women composers. Of the women who published music on the Italian peninsula between 1566 and 1700, more than half were nuns. Isabella Leonarda (1620–1704) was easily the most prominent and prolific of this latter group, publishing some 20 volumes of her own compositions, mostly sacred vocal music but also some instrumental works as well. Unless they worked in convents, women could not hold positions associated with composing. Even Barbara Strozzi, with all her talents, struggled to make ends meet in the later years of her life. In spite of her prowess as a composer, she would never have been considered as a potential successor to Monteverdi as music director of St. Mark's Basilica in Venice. That honor went instead to Monteverdi's pupil (and Strozzi's teacher) Francesco Cavalli. From a strictly economic point of view, then, there was no reason for parents to encourage their daughters in this direction. Without an appointment at a church or court or some other institution, it was just not possible for a composer to earn a decent living.

These conditions would change little over the next two centuries. So while there are many examples of women performers from the Renaissance onward, including many noted virtuosos, the number of women composers in relation to men remained disproportionately small until well into the twentieth century. Only with the advent of compulsory public education and the broadening of career options to women did the phenomenon of the female composer cease to be unusual.

The first woman to write an opera in French, Elisabeth Jacquet de la Guerre was also widely admired for her abilities on the harpsichord. Here she is depicted in the act of composing at the harpsichord, with a sheet of paper in one hand and a quill pen in the other.

Francoise de Troy, "Portrait of Elisabeth-Claude Jacquet de la Guerre", (circa 1694–1695), oil on canvas, 47 3/8 in. x 36 3/4 in./Private Collection, London.

A sonata for three violins and basso continuo. The basso continuo group here consists of a harpsichordist and a cellist (right). A delineation between a leading voice or voices (the three violins) and supporting instruments (the basso continuo) marks a decisive break with the predominantly polyphonic style of the Renaissance.

Courtesy of the Cultural Affairs Bureau of the Macao S.A.R. Government

EXPAND YOUR PLAYLIST

Baroque Chamber Music

Baroque composers wrote unprecedented quantities of chamber music, both for voices and instruments and for instruments alone. One genre they cultivated with special intensity was the **sonata**, a word whose literal meaning is "that which is played" (as opposed to the **cantata**, "that which is sung"; see chapter 18). Composers wrote sonatas for many combinations of instruments; the most popular variety involved two high-ranged instruments (such as two violins, two oboes, or two flutes) and basso continuo. This combination was known as the **trio sonata**. Sonatas could be performed in the home (the **sonata da camera**, or "chamber sonata") to provide entertainment, or in the church (the **sonata da chiesa**, or "church sonata") during sacred services to provide devotional music.

Arcangelo Corelli (1653–1713)
• wrote many trio sonatas of both kinds. His Trio Sonata in A Major, op. 3, no. 12, a chamber sonata, features much interplay between the two solo violins over a basso continuo. His Trio Sonata in F Major, op. 1, no. 1, is a church sonata. His Sonata in D Major, op. 5, no. 1, is for a single violin and basso continuo and allows the violinist ample opportunity to display virtuosity on the instrument.

Johann Pachelbel (1653–1706)
• wrote the Canon and Gigue in D Major, for three violins and basso continuo, which is one of the best-known works of the entire Baroque Era. This piece features three violins that play a canon over an ostinato bass. A canon is another word for round, in which each voice sings or plays exactly the same melody with staggered entries (as in "Row, row, row your boat").

Marin Marais (1656–1728)
• composed much virtuosic music for the viola da gamba, a forerunner of today's cello. The second book of his *Pièces de violes* (*Works for Viol*) contains several suites for viol and basso continuo. Marais and his music were featured in the 1991 film *All the Mornings of the World* (*Tous les matins du monde*).

((•● HEAR SAMPLES on **www.mymusiclab.com**

✓ **TEST YOURSELF** on **www.mymusiclab.com**   Flashcards and chapter tests

14

Johann Sebastian Bach
Fugue in G Minor, BWV 578 ("Little")
Composed: 1705

This chapter presents two versions of Bach's Fugue in G minor: (1) in its original version for organ, and (2) in an arrangement for orchestra by Leopold Stokowski in 1940. The notes are exactly the same in both versions, but the timbres are very different.

Listen to this first

((• HEAR MORE on www.mymusiclab.com

Timbre

Listen for the variety of sounds in each version. The organ and orchestra are both capable of enormous timbral variety. Every "voice" (melodic line) in the work has its own distinctive sound.

Melody

There is only one real theme in this work, and we hear it many times. It appears all by itself at the very beginning. Listen to how it begins slowly and then picks up speed as it progresses.

Texture

Listen for the way in which the theme is first presented by a single voice, then imitated in a second voice, then imitated yet again with the entrances of the third and fourth voices. See how many of these iterations of the main theme your ear can pick out: in the high voice, the low voice, and (perhaps most difficult of all) the middle voices.

LEARN MORE on
www.mymusiclab.com
Chapter Objectives

A fugue is a polyphonic work based on a central theme. **Fugues** are easy to recognize: they typically begin with the theme in one voice, which is imitated by all the other voices in succession, each presenting its own statement of the theme. "Fugue" comes from the same root word as "fugitive" and refers to the tendency of voices to "chase" one another: a theme presented in one voice is "pursued," as it were, by a second (and often third or fourth) voice that brings in the same theme but slightly later. The fugue represents the continuing fascination of composers and listeners alike with the intricacies of polyphonic texture. Many composers of the Baroque regarded the fugue as the touchstone of a composer's art, for it demanded more than just the invention of a good tune. That tune also had to be capable of being played against other, independent voices derived from the tune itself.

This particular fugue for organ is an early work by Bach, written when he was only about 20 years old. He probably composed it during his years in Arnstadt, where he was the organist of the town's church. See "A Closer Look: Bach's World," page 138.

Timbres of the Organ, Timbres of the Orchestra

The organ is sometimes called the "King of Instruments" because of its size, power, and variety of tone. No other acoustic (that is, nonelectric) instrument possesses the range of volume and timbre found in the organ (see A Closer Look: The Baroque Organ, page 120). In this fugue, the variety in timbre results largely from the varying registers of the voices. High voices have a particular sound—perhaps a bit reedy—middle voices have a more rounded tone, and the lowest voices blast forth like brass instruments. The organ has a tremendous range from the lowest notes (played by the feet) to the highest notes (played on the keyboard or **manual**). The organist can choose the particular combination of pipes for any work or section of a work and give each different line its own distinctive sound. The number of possible combinations of registers on a large organ can range well into the hundreds.

In Leopold Stokowski's much later orchestral arrangement of Bach's Fugue in G minor, the timbral contrast among the various voices is even more readily audible. Taking advantage of the full range of the modern orchestra, Stokowski kept Bach's notes, but distributed the work's voices among various instruments or combinations of instruments. The opening theme, for example, is played first by the solo oboe, then by the English horn, then the bassoon, then the bass trombone. Other instruments pick up the various voices throughout the work as a whole.

Arrangements, also known as transcriptions, have been common throughout the history of music. Bach himself arranged (transcribed) a number of works by other composers. In one instance, he arranged a concerto for string orchestra and two violins by Antonio Vivaldi for solo organ.

A Distinctive Melody

The theme of this work appears many times, and its slow and stately entrance (section **A**) stands out even among a welter of fast-moving voices. After its slow beginning, the theme begins to accelerate, moving in shorter note values (section **B**). Finally, it kicks into high gear and moves very rapidly (section **C**). This rhythmic progression—slow to faster to fastest—gives the theme a strong sense of forward progression. And because this is the only real theme in the work, this sense of constant rhythmic motion extends to the work as a whole.

1685–1750
Johann Sebastian Bach
Fugue in G Minor,
BWV 578 ("Little")
Composed: 1705
GENRE
Fugue

KEY CONCEPTS
Imitative counterpoint, organ, timbre, arrangements.

CHAPTER HIGHLIGHT
Baroque Organ Music
The fugue represents the Baroque Era's fascination with imitative polyphonic texture, and this fugue demonstrates why the organ, with its immense volume and range, was known in its time as the "king of instruments."

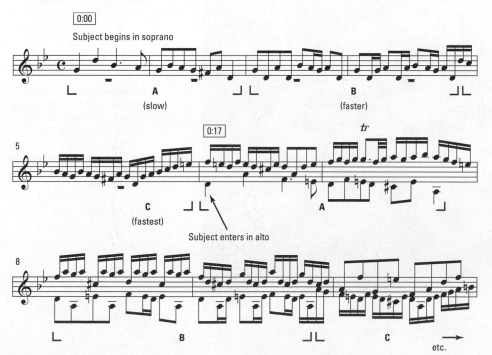

A CLOSER LOOK   The Baroque Organ

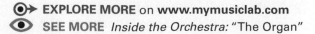
⊙→ **EXPLORE MORE** on **www.mymusiclab.com**

👁 **SEE MORE** *Inside the Orchestra:* "The Organ"

In many large churches, the organist is hidden behind pipes and casings that obscure the console, the organ's "control panel" seen here. From the console the organist determines the timbre and volume of the sound. An elaborate mechanism of knobs and pedals allows the player to control which pipes will sound at any given moment. There is no standard size or configuration for the organ: the number of keys and pipes can vary consider-ably. The largest pipes, which can be up to 16 feet high, pro-duce the lowest notes, while the smallest pipes, some as small as a pencil, produce the highest notes. While every organ is distinctive, the principal elements of the Baroque organ can be seen in this photograph of the console at Sint Jans, a large church in Gouda, The Netherlands. This organ dates from 1732 (during Bach's lifetime).

The **stops** (circular pull knobs) control which set of pipes sounds when a specific keyboard (or **manual**) is played. The organ's pipes offer a wide variety of timbres, ranging from pipes that imitate the sound of a trumpet, oboe, or even the human voice (called the "Vox Humana" from the Latin). The player controls which pipes sound by opening the related stop, which allows air to flow through its related pipes. Organists can use either one stop at a time or a combination of stops, and each keyboard can be linked to a specific stop or group of stops. The number of possible sound combinations is enormous.

The music stand displays the organist's printed or manuscript music.

Manuals are the multiple keyboards found on larger organs. Each manual is connected to particular sets of pipes, which in turn create specific kinds of sound. With multiple manuals, a player can move back and forth quickly between the different sound qualities that have been pre-set for each manual with the knob-like stops on either side of the console.

The organist can play low notes by depressing the pedals on the **pedal board** with his or her feet, even while playing the manuals by hand. Very rapid pedalwork can place great technical demands on the performer.

Photo credit: Mercator Fonds, Antwerp, from King of Instruments: A History of the Organ, transl. Stewart Spencer. NY:Rizzoli, 1985, page 167, used with permission from Rizzoli International Publications, Inc.

PERFORMANCE Changing the Sound, but Not the Notes

Leopold Stokowski (1882–1977) ranks among the most influential conductors of the twentieth century. After immigrating to the United States from his native England in 1905, he helped develop the Philadelphia Orchestra into one of the world's leading ensembles. He also played a key role in bringing classical music to Hollywood. When he appeared with Mickey Mouse in Walt Disney's *Fantasia* in 1940, Stokowski was already a celebrity himself. Musical purists looked down on Stokowski's many orchestral arrangements of works originally written for other instruments, but countless listeners have admired the way in which his arrangements illuminate the workings of the inner voices, particularly in a densely contrapuntal work like Bach's Fugue in G Minor.

Mickey Mouse congratulates Leopold Stokowski in Walt Disney's *Fantasia* (1940). The film includes a sequence in which Stokowski conducts his orchestral arrangement of another organ work by Bach, the Toccata and Fugue in D Minor.

©Walt Disney/Courtesy: Everett Collection

Fugal Texture

A fugue typically begins with its central theme, also known as a **subject**, in one voice all by itself. This subject is often quite distinctive—instantly recognizable—in its first few notes so that we can immediately recognize it upon its entrance in subsequent voices and its return later throughout the fugue. Some characteristic feature—a melodic leap, a distinctive rhythm—typically makes the subject stand out as it enters in the second voice, then the third, and so on, even as the other voices continue their independent lines. The type of polyphony used in a fugue is known as **imitative counterpoint**. The voices "imitate" one another, each sounding against ("countering") the others at the same time.

Fugue has more to do with texture—the way the voices relate to each other—than with form. Still, most fugues tend to unfold according to a conventional pattern. The opening entry of all the voices on the main subject is known as a **fugal exposition** because it "exposes" the main idea of the work. Beyond this exposition, the only formal convention is that the main theme must reappear at some point within the later course of the movement; in actual practice, it usually reappears at many points. These later entries of the subject are known as **middle entries**. Passages in which the main subject (the main theme) is absent are called **episodes**, though not every fugue has them. But the typical fugue, including this one, consists of a fugal exposition and a series of middle entries, interspersed with episodes.

Fugues—for all kinds and combinations of instruments and voices—were extremely common throughout the Baroque Era in many different genres. The finale of Bach's Brandenburg Concerto no. 2 (see chapter 16) is a fugue for solo instruments and orchestra; portions of the "Hallelujah Chorus" (see chapter 19) are, in effect, brief fugues for chorus and orchestra. In the centuries following the Baroque Era, composers continued to take up the challenge of writing fugues, both as practice exercises in composition and as works for performance. Fugal writing still turns up today in music of varying styles and genres.

Now listen to Bach's fugue again in both versions—the original for organ and the later arrangement for orchestra—using the Listening Guides.

CONNECT YOUR PLAYLIST

Arrangements

Find a piece arranged for two different kinds of ensembles.

Example: Gloria Gaynor/Cake, "I Will Survive" (1978/1996)
The alternative band Cake arranged (or "covered") Gloria Gaynor's disco-era classic "I Will Survive" by changing the instrumentation and vocal timbre of Gaynor's version, even while keeping many of the original elements.

Listening Guide

GO TO www.mymusiclab.com
for the Automated Listening Guide
CD I • Track 34/Download Track 34

Johann Sebastian Bach Composed: 1705 Fugue in G Minor, BWV 578 ("Little"),
Bach's Original Version for Organ (4:06)

Time	Form: Section	Melody: Fugue Subject
0:00	Exposition	0:00 in highest voice (soprano) 0:18 in next-highest voice (alto) 0:41 in next-lowest voice (tenor) 0:59 in lowest voice (bass)
1:14	Episode 1	(Subject is absent)
1:25	Middle Entry 1	In tenor voice
1:45	Episode 2	(Subject is absent)
1:53	Middle Entry 2	In alto voice
2:10	Episode 3	(Subject is absent)
2:22	Middle Entry 3	In bass voice
2:38	Episode 4	(Subject is absent)
2:55	Middle Entry 4	In soprano voice
3:12	Episode 5	(Subject is absent)
3:41	Final Entry	In bass voice

Student FAQs

What forces air through the organ pipes?

Nowadays, the airflow in an organ is generated by an electric pump. In Bach's day, someone—usually a small boy—had to tread on a large set of bellows that operated somewhat like a stair-climber machine in a modern-day gym. This produced a steady flow of air through the pipes. Even older organs that have been restored now use an electronically generated airflow.

So the modern organ is electronic?

Only the airflow is generated electronically. What we call the electronic organ is really a different instrument altogether. It looks and sounds like a manual organ, but it produces sound through a system of electromagnetic currents, an amplifier, and speakers. Laurens Hammond (1895–1973), an American inventor, created the first mass-market, portable electronic organ in the 1930s.

Listening Guide

GO TO **www.mymusiclab.com**
for the Automated Listening Guide
CD I • Track 35/Download Track 35

Johann Sebastian Bach Arranged: 1940 Fugue in G Minor, BWV 578 ("Little"),
Leopold Stokowski's Orchestral Arrangement (3:29)

Time	Form: Section	Melody: Fugue Subject	Orchestral Timbre
0:00	Exposition	0:00 in highest voice (soprano) 0:14 in next-highest voice (alto) 0:31 in next-lowest voice (tenor) 0:44 in lowest voice (bass)	0:00 solo oboe 0:14 English horn 0:31 bassoon 0:44 bass trombone
0:57	Episode 1	(Subject is absent)	Flutes enter
1:06	Middle Entry 1	In tenor voice	Subject = clarinets, then flutes
1:22	Episode 2	(Subject is absent)	Winds
1:29	Middle Entry 2	In alto voice	Subject = violas
1:41	Episode 3	(Subject is absent)	Violas, then various winds
1:51	Middle Entry 3	In bass voice	Subject = double basses
2:03	Episode 4	(Subject is absent)	Strings
2:17	Middle Entry 4	In soprano voice	Subject = violins
2:29	Episode 5	(Subject is absent)	Various winds, then full orchestra
2:55	Final Entry	In bass voice	Subject = trombones

PROFILE   Johann Sebastian Bach (1685–1750)

New Jobs, New Genres

Born into a family of musicians, Johann Sebastian Bach earned his living through music. He changed jobs often between the ages of 18 and 38, and with every new position, he wrote whatever music was required of him. When he was a church organist early in his career, he wrote the majority of his organ works, including the Fugue in G Minor discussed in this chapter. Later, as violinist and concertmaster at a court orchestra (Weimar) and as music director (Cöthen), he wrote the bulk of his orchestral music, including the Brandenburg Concerto no. 2 (see chapter 16). When he became cantor of St. Thomas's Church in Leipzig in 1723, he began writing new cantatas for use in the services there (see chapter 16). By the time he died, Bach had written at least one work in virtually every genre of music except for opera. Why no opera? The reason is simple: Bach never held a job that required him to write one. (See A Closer Look: Bach's World, chapter 16.)

Bach's two marriages—his first wife died in 1720—produced 20 children, 10 of whom survived into adulthood. Several of the sons became renowned composers in their own right. Carl Philipp Emanuel Bach (1714–1788) would become more famous than his father during the elder Bach's lifetime. Johann Christian Bach (1735–1782), sometimes called the "London Bach" because of his eventual home, was one of Mozart's favorite composers. Wilhelm Friedemann Bach (1710–1784), said to be perhaps the most musically gifted of all Bach's sons, met repeated misfortunes in his career and died in poverty.

⊙➔ **EXPLORE MORE** on www.mymusiclab.com

⚙ **LEARN MORE** on www.mymusiclab.com
MyMusicLibrary: "Bach the Musician"

Bach in the 1740s. Proud of his abilities as a composer, Bach chose to have himself portrayed holding a particularly complex work of imitative counterpoint of his own invention.

Lebrecht Music & Arts/Lebrecht Music & Arts Photo Library

◀◀   **EXPAND YOUR PLAYLIST: BACH**   ▶▶

- **St. Matthew Passion**, BWV 244.
  An extended work for vocalists and orchestra, with choral movements, recitatives, and arias.
  This three-hour work narrates the betrayal and crucifixion of Christ and is built around texts from the Gospel of St. Matthew.

- **Partita no. 2 for Violin**, BWV 1004: Chaconne.
  Bach's self-imposed challenge was to write a contrapuntal work for an instrument—the violin—that is essentially melodic and normally plays only one musical line at a time.

- **The Well-Tempered Clavier**, Book 1, BWV 846–69.
  Two sets of keyboard preludes and fugues in all 24 major and minor keys. Bach wrote these works for teaching purposes.

- **A Musical Offering**, BWV 1079.
  In 1747 Bach visited his son Carl Philipp Emanuel Bach, who was a musician at the court of King Frederick II of Prussia. Frederick—himself a composer and flute player—gave Bach a particularly difficult theme on which to improvise. Later, Bach composed and sent Frederick an enormous set of different works, all based on this same theme, a "musical offering" to the king.

((•)) **HEAR SAMPLES** on www.mymusiclab.com

EXPAND YOUR PLAYLIST

Baroque Organ Music

Jan Pieterszoon Sweelinck

- *"Echo" Fantasia (Ionian)* (early seventeenth century). A native of what is now the Netherlands, Sweelinck wrote a great deal of organ music. A fantasia is a freely constructed work, meant to sound improvised as if it were being thought up on the spot. This is one of several fantasias in which Sweelinck uses special echo effects.

Dietrich Buxtehude

- Praeludium in G Minor, BuxWV 149 (ca. 1675–1689). Buxtehude was the greatest organist in the generation before Bach. This prelude ("praeludium" is the Latin term) is a multisectional work: parts of it are free, parts of it are fugal.

Johann Sebastian Bach

- Toccata and Fugue in D Minor, BWV 565 (ca. 1705). Perhaps the most famous work of organ music ever written, this has been used in countless horror movies to provide "scary" music. A toccata is a "touch piece," one that calls for a light and rapid touch on the keys.
- "Jig" Fugue, BWV 577. This work may not actually be by Bach, but whoever wrote it certainly knew how to write fugues. The rhythm is so compelling that audiences have been known to clap along with it.
- *Chorale Prelude* (*Wachet auf, ruft uns die Stimme*), BWV 645. An organ version of one of the movements from the Cantata 140 (see chapter 18). Bach wrote many organ arrangements of chorale (hymn) tunes. These works are called chorale preludes because they were performed before the congregation sang the chorale.

((•● HEAR SAMPLES on **www.mymusiclab.com**

⊘ **TEST YOURSELF** on **www.mymusiclab.com**   Flashcards and chapter tests

15

Antonio Vivaldi
The Four Seasons, "Winter," first movement
Composed: 1720

This work for solo violin and string orchestra portrays, through sound alone, the season of winter. It follows the outline of a brief text (probably by Vivaldi himself) that describes ice, snow, wind, stamping feet, and chattering teeth.

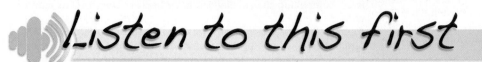 Listen to this first

((• **HEAR MORE** on www.mymusiclab.com

Timbre

Listen for the contrast in sound between the solo instrument (the violin) and the ensemble (a small orchestra of stringed instruments, plus basso continuo). Notice how the soloist plays with the orchestra at some points and not at others.

Form

Listen for the alternation of long sections with and without the soloist.

Word-Music Relationships

Vivaldi called this work "Winter." Do you hear any sounds that might suggest this season of the year?

⚙ **LEARN MORE** on
www.mymusiclab.com
Chapter Objectives

A concerto is an instrumental work for a soloist (or sometimes more than one soloist) and a larger ensemble. This particular **concerto** is for a solo violin and an orchestra of stringed instruments, plus basso continuo. It is the last of four concertos for this same combination of instruments that Vivaldi designated collectively as *The Four Seasons*. Although each of these concertos—"Spring," "Summer," "Fall," and "Winter"—stands on its own, the four together represent the cycle of the seasons, a favorite theme of painters and poets alike. "Winter," like most other concertos of its time, consists of three movements in the sequence fast-slow-fast. The movement here is the first of the three.

Contrasting Timbres

The concerto emerged as a particularly popular genre for Baroque audiences because it featured a dramatic contrast between the sound of a solo instrument and the combined sound of all the other instruments. The two forces sometimes work together and sometimes clash in opposition. Baroque audiences also thrilled to the virtuosic displays characteristic of most concertos. The solo parts in a concerto are almost always demanding and often downright flamboyant. Both as a composer and as a player, Vivaldi took the art of virtuoso violin playing to new levels. He worked in a time and a place—early eighteenth-century northern Italy—in which violin making and violin playing were at their very peak: to this day, the best violins such as those made by Antonio Stratavari or "Stradivarius" (the Latinized form of his name) are from that time. How the great violin makers produced their instruments is not entirely known to us today, but the features of the violin basically remain the same (see A Closer Look: The Violin, page 132).

The appeal of the concerto's contrasting timbres and its inherent virtuosity lasted beyond the Baroque period and into the present day. The concerto has undergone changes over the centuries but remains a popular genre among composers and audiences alike. Many modern symphony orchestra concert programs feature a concerto—from the Baroque or from a later period—and Vivaldi's masterful opposition of solo and large-group string timbres has given *The Four Seasons* lasting fame.

Form: The Ritornello Principle

This movement consists of a series of alternating sections between the orchestra (also known as the **tutti**, Italian for "all") and the soloist. Each statement and return of the full ensemble is known as the **ritornello** (Italian for "little [i.e., brief] return"). This formal design of alternating ritornello and solo sections is known as the **ritornello principle** and is basic to almost all concerto movements of the Baroque Era. The form of this movement, based on the ritornello principle, can be represented graphically in this way:

Ritornello 1	Solo 1	Ritornello 2	Solo 2	Ritornello 3	Solo 3	Ritornello 4

The form of the movement is also structured around large-scale changes of key area. A *key area* is a set of harmonies that all have a distinctive relationship to one particular note, known as the **tonic**. At the beginning and end of this movement, the tonic note is F, and because the mode is minor, this central key area is called "F minor." F minor acts as the "home" key, and it is by definition the key in which the movement begins and ends. (If it closed in a different key, the ending would not sound as conclusive.) But if the entire movement were in a single key, it would sound monotonous, and so Vivaldi moves the music to key areas other than the tonic—including some in the major mode. These other key areas provide a sense of harmonic variety.

The ritornello principle is found not only in concertos, but in almost every Baroque work that contrasts a soloist or group of soloists against a larger ensemble. Operatic arias, for example, routinely open with an instrumental ritornello (Ritornello 1), followed by the entrance of the voice (Solo 1), a brief return of the orchestra without the voice (Ritornello 2), a reentry of the voice (Solo 2), and so on. Composers and audiences of the Baroque relished the sound of contrasting forces, and the ritornello principle provided the perfect means by which to present such contrasts.

1678–1741
Antonio Vivaldi
The Four Seasons,
"Winter," first movement
Composed: 1720

GENRE
Concerto

KEY CONCEPTS
Concerto, ritornello, violin,
program music.

CHAPTER HIGHLIGHT
Program Music
Program music is instrumental music explicitly connected in some way with a story, person, or idea. This first movement of a three-movement concerto for violin and string orchestra captures some of the season's sounds. It follows the outline of a brief text (probably by Vivaldi himself) that describes ice, snow, wind, stamping feet, and chattering teeth.

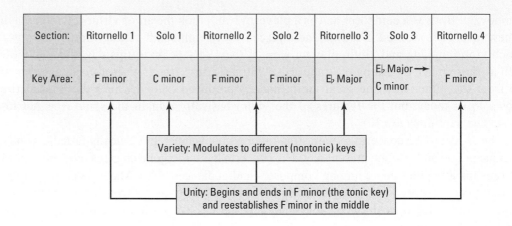

Section:	Ritornello 1	Solo 1	Ritornello 2	Solo 2	Ritornello 3	Solo 3	Ritornello 4
Key Area:	F minor	C minor	F minor	F minor	E♭ Major	E♭ Major → C minor	F minor

Variety: Modulates to different (nontonic) keys

Unity: Begins and ends in F minor (the tonic key) and reestablishes F minor in the middle

Word-Music Relationships: Program Music

The form of this particular concerto is also shaped by its relationship to a poem ("Winter") that Vivaldi appended to the first publication of the score in 1725. He indicated quite precisely which lines of the following poem corresponded to specific points of the concerto. This concerto is thus an example of program music, an instrumental work that is in some way associated with a story, event, or idea. A composer can indicate such connections by a suggestive title, a prose or poetic narrative, or both. A listener may choose to listen to the piece with the program in mind—in the case of Vivaldi's "Winter," hearing the strings shaking as if with cold in Ritornello 1, a stamping of feet in Ritornello 2, and a chattering sound in the Solo 3—or simply listen to the piece as music that does not represent anything besides itself. Indeed, some composers (for example, Berlioz—see chapter 30), have gone back and forth about whether their audiences should be aware of a program or simply be allowed to hear the music as it unfolds.

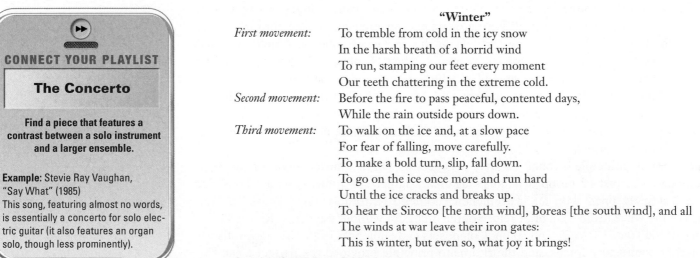

CONNECT YOUR PLAYLIST

The Concerto

Find a piece that features a contrast between a solo instrument and a larger ensemble.

Example: Stevie Ray Vaughan, "Say What" (1985)
This song, featuring almost no words, is essentially a concerto for solo electric guitar (it also features an organ solo, though less prominently).

"Winter"

First movement: To tremble from cold in the icy snow
In the harsh breath of a horrid wind
To run, stamping our feet every moment
Our teeth chattering in the extreme cold.

Second movement: Before the fire to pass peaceful, contented days,
While the rain outside pours down.

Third movement: To walk on the ice and, at a slow pace
For fear of falling, move carefully.
To make a bold turn, slip, fall down.
To go on the ice once more and run hard
Until the ice cracks and breaks up.
To hear the Sirocco [the north wind], Boreas [the south wind], and all
The winds at war leave their iron gates:
This is winter, but even so, what joy it brings!

PROFILE **Antonio Vivaldi** (1678–1741)

Composing for Orphans

Known as the "Red Priest" because he was red-haired and ordained, Antonio Vivaldi served for many years as director of music at Venice's Ospedale della Pietà ("Hospice of Compassion"), a large orphanage for girls. Being the music director of an orphanage might strike us today as a strange job for one of the most famous composers of his time, but judging from the music Vivaldi wrote for the young women at this particular institution, they must have been quite talented indeed. He actually wrote most of his concertos while in service to the orphanage.

Vivaldi was extremely prolific. He wrote almost 350 solo concertos (about two-thirds of which are for solo violin) and 45 double concertos (more than half of which are for two violins). His music was widely published and admired throughout Europe during his lifetime. J.S. Bach arranged several of Vivaldi's concertos for the organ and in the process taught himself how to write concertos "in the Italian style." Bach and Handel may have had greater facility at counterpoint, but Vivaldi was a master of melodic invention and formal novelty. Almost every one of Vivaldi's concertos contains some unusual twist that makes it different from all the rest.

Antonio Vivaldi was famous both as a composer and as a violinist during his lifetime. His red hair is covered by his wig.

Lebrecht Music & Arts/Lebrecht Music & Arts Photo Library

◉➜ **EXPLORE MORE** on www.mymusiclab.com

EXPAND YOUR PLAYLIST: VIVALDI

- **The Four Seasons:** "Spring." The opening theme (Ritornello 1) is now a popular ringtone for cell phones.

- **The Four Seasons:** "Summer." The finale depicts a violent thunderstorm.

- **The Four Seasons:** "Fall." The finale depicts a hunting scene.

- **Concerto for Mandolin**, RV 532. More typically associated with bluegrass music, the mandolin was already a popular instrument in the Baroque.

- **Gloria**, RV 589, for chorus and orchestra. A thrilling setting of the Gloria portion of the Mass Ordinary.

- **Concerto for Flute, Strings, and Basso Continuo**, op. 10, no. 1. Nicknamed "The Tempest at Sea" because of its stormy sound.

((•● **HEAR SAMPLES** on www.mymusiclab.com

Now listen again to the movement, using the Listening Guide.

Listening Guide

GO TO www.mymusiclab.com
for the Automated Listening Guide
CD II • Track 1/Download Track 36

Antonio Vivaldi Composed: 1720 *The Four Seasons,* "Winter," first movement (3:33)

Time	Timbre	Form	Harmony: Key Area	Word-Music Relationships (1): The Poetry
0:00	Orchestra	Ritornello 1	F minor	To tremble from cold in the icy snow
0:37	Solo violin and orchestra	Solo 1	C minor	In the harsh breath of a horrid wind
0:59	Orchestra	Ritornello 2	F minor	To run, stamping our feet every moment
1:26	Solo violin and orchestra	Solo 2	F minor → unstable	
2:05	Orchestra	Ritornello 3	E♭ major	
2:25	Solo violin and orchestra	Solo 3	E♭ major → C minor	Our teeth chattering in the extreme cold
3:04	Orchestra	Ritornello 4	F minor	

Translation Copyright © 1999 Dover Publications, Inc.

Student FAQs

I can't hear the difference in key areas between the sections. How can I learn to hear these changes?

With digital technology, it's easy to make side-by-side comparisons. Using the Listening Guide, start the music at 0:37. The long note to which the solo violinist keeps returning is C, the tonic of C minor. Let the music run through 1:00. Vivaldi again and again emphasizes this new key area of C minor. Now go back to the beginning, which is in F minor. Hear the difference? The main note at the beginning is F, the root of the tonic key of F minor. Now let the music run through and listen for the change of key between the opening and 0:37. This may take some time at first, but once you start listening for changes of key, it gets easier to recognize them. And even if you don't always hear the key changes consciously, you will appreciate that they affect the way the music sounds by providing both harmonic unity (the tonic) and variety (all other keys).

Lebrecht Music & Arts/Lebrecht Music & Arts Photo Library

Word-Music Relationships (2): The Music

Repetitive figure in the strings suggests trembling.

The solo violin also "trembles" and moves from high to low, like the wind.

Faster tempo ("running"); the music begins to "stamp" at 1:12.

The soloist bounces the bow very rapidly against the string, creating a "chattering" sound (2:35–3:03).

What does the violin soloist do during the tutti sections?

The soloist actually plays along with the first violin section of the orchestra. But because the sound of the solo instrument blends into the sound of the orchestra, the soloist cannot be heard as a separate, distinct voice in these sections.

Which is more important, the musical or the programmatic form?

The two work in tandem and reinforce each other. We do not know if Vivaldi began with the poem and wrote a concerto around it, or if he began with a concerto and wrote a poem around it. It's also possible that the two processes took shape simultaneously.

Private Collection/The Bridgeman Art Library

A CLOSER LOOK   The Violin

◉→ EXPLORE MORE on www.mymusiclab.com
◉ SEE MORE *Inside the Orchestra:* "The Violin"

There are more violins in an orchestra than any other instrument. The violin is also the prototype for two larger versions: the mid-range viola and the low-range cello. The basic principles of the instrument are simple: a player draws a bow perpendicularly across the strings and sets them in motion, controlling the pitch by depressing the fingers onto the individual strings. The violinist controls the volume of the instrument by pressing the bow into the strings with greater or lesser pressure, and by moving the bow at a faster or slower speed. No two instruments are identical: the slightest variations in wood quality, the size and placement of the bridge, the exact shape of the f-holes, and even the nature of the varnish can affect the quality of an instrument's sound.

The **horsehair**—from a horse's tail—is the part of the bow that sets the violin's strings in motion, creating sound.

The **tuning pegs** are turned clockwise or counterclockwise to increase or decrease tension on the strings, thereby raising or lowering the pitch of the strings as they are being tuned.

Four **strings** on the pitches G, D, A, and E. The lowest-sounding string, on the left, is the thickest; the highest string, on the right, is the thinnest.

The **fingerboard**. The violinist presses the strings onto the fingerboard, thereby shortening the length of the vibrating portion of the string. The shorter the vibrating length, the higher the pitch.

The **stick** is the wooden part of the bow that supports the horsehair.

The **bridge**, made of wood, elevates the strings and provides a fixed point at the opposite end from the top of the fingerboard. The bridge also transmits the vibration of the strings to the body of the instrument, and it is the vibration of the body's wood that amplifies the sound naturally, without any electronics.

The **f-holes** (so called because they resemble the letter "F" in italics) direct some of the vibration of the body directly out into the air.

The small metal **screw** at the end of the bow can be turned clockwise or counter-clockwise to increase or decrease the tension on the horsehair.

The **tailpiece** supports the strings. Optional small metal knobs allow for fine-tuning the strings.

The **body** of the instrument is made of specially treated and carefully carved wood covered with a varnish that both protects the wood and enhances the instrument's sound. The interior of the instrument is hollow to allow the vibrating body to resonate more fully; a **sounding post**—a small dowel of wood inside this space and not visible here—helps transmit energy from the front (top) of the instrument to its back.

The **chin rest** helps the player to hold the instrument securely under the chin.

Dorling Kindersley Media Library © Dorling Kindersley

✓ **TEST YOURSELF** on **www.mymusiclab.com**   Flashcards and chapter tests

Johann Sebastian Bach
Brandenburg Concerto no. 2 in F Major, BWV 1047, finale
Composed: 1720

Bach's Brandenburg Concerto features multiple soloists: a trumpet, oboe, violin, and recorder. The soloists function with and against a larger ensemble of stringed instruments. The movement presented here is the last one in a three-movement concerto Bach wrote for the margrave of Brandenburg.

 Listen to this first

((•◦ HEAR MORE on www.mymusiclab.com

Timbre

Form

Texture

Listen for the contrasting sounds of the four solo instruments, which enter in this order:

- The trumpet, a brass instrument, has a loud, bright sound.

- The oboe, a woodwind instrument, has a piercing, slightly nasal sound.

- The violin, a stringed instrument, has a resonant, lyrical sound.

- The recorder, another woodwind instrument, has a soft, gentle sound similar to that of a flute.

Also listen for the way in which the sound of the four solo instruments as a group contrasts with the sound of the larger ensemble, which is a small orchestra of stringed instruments (violins, violas, cellos, basses) and basso continuo.

Listen for the alternation between the soloists as a group and the orchestra as a whole. Like all concertos of the Baroque Era, this one is built around the ritornello principle, in which sections played by the soloists alone (accompanied only by the basso continuo) alternate with sections played by the full orchestra.

Listen for the way in which the melody is presented successively by each of the soloists at the beginning and then taken up by each voice in turn repeatedly over the course of the movement. This entire movement is a fugue.

Not all concertos are for only one soloist. Baroque composers also cultivated the genre of the **concerto grosso**—in Italian, this means literally "big concerto"—with multiple soloists. Bach's Brandenburg Concerto no. 2 is one of six such works dedicated to the margrave of Brandenburg (a region in what is now eastern Germany) in 1721. Bach's six Brandenburg concertos feature unique instrumental combinations and contain three or four movements each. The movement here is the last of three.

 LEARN MORE on
www.mymusiclab.com
Chapter Objectives

Extreme Timbres

Central to the solo concerto and concerto grosso is timbral contrast: soloist(s) vs. orchestra. In this particular work, the solo instruments provide unusual contrast among themselves. The trumpet is one of the loudest and most penetrating of all instruments, while the recorder is one of the softest and gentlest. The oboe and violin lie between these two extremes. Bach clearly relished the challenge of combining such a wide spectrum of solo instruments in the same concerto. It was a new and bold measure to group such different instrumental timbres together.

Form: The Ritornello Principle Returns

As in Vivaldi's concerto for solo violin and orchestra (see chapter 15), this movement is based on the **ritornello principle**: sections for the soloists (Solo 1, Solo 2, etc.) alternate with sections for the full orchestra (Ritornello 1, Ritornello 2, etc.). The soloists—or at least some of them—also play along with the full orchestra during the ritornello sections. The basso continuo instruments—harpsichord and cello—live up to their name, playing continuously throughout the movement.

Like Vivaldi in his solo concerto "Winter," Bach uses different key areas to establish a sense of a beginning, a contrasting middle, and an ending that brings harmonic closure to the whole. The movement opens and closes in the key of F major; in between, it moves through a variety of different key areas. If the movement did not **modulate**—that is, move to a different key area—the theme would not sound as fresh as it does each time it comes back (and it comes back often). If it ended in a key other than the tonic—its primary key area, the one in which it began—it would sound open-ended and inconclusive.

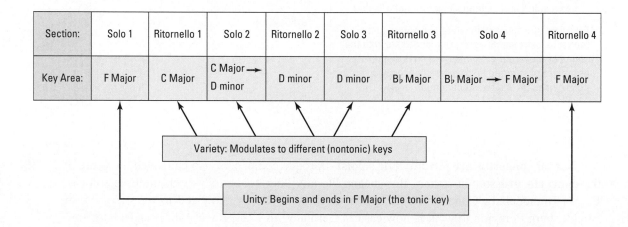

An outdoor evening instrumental concert in the town square of Jena in the 1740s. The large orchestra includes trumpets and timpani. J. S. Bach led a similar ensemble in nearby Leipzig for a time.

Museum für Kunst und Gewerbe, Hamburg, Germany

1685–1750
Johann Sebastian Bach
Brandenburg Concerto
no. 2 in F Major, BWV 1047,
finale
Composed: 1720

GENRE
Concerto grosso

KEY CONCEPTS
Concerto grosso, ritornello, fugal texture, harmonic basis of form.

CHAPTER HIGHLIGHT
The Baroque Concerto
The concerto highlights contrasts among instruments and performing forces, and became a vehicle for virtuosic displays. This particular concerto highlights a group of soloists—recorder, oboe, violin, and trumpet—each of whom comes to the fore at various points in this last movement of a three-movement concerto.

Fugal Texture

Although Bach did not label it as such, this entire movement is a fugue: a central theme is introduced and then imitated by subsequent voices. As we have seen (chapter 14), fugue is more a function of texture—imitative polyphony—than of form, but as in Bach's Fugue in G Minor, BWV 578, the fugal finale of Bach's Brandenburg Concerto no. 2 employs some of the structural features most commonly found in fugues:

- **Fugal exposition.** This section gets its name from the fact that it "exposes" the theme in each of the solo instruments in turn.

- **Middle entries.** These are passages (throughout the movement) that reintroduce the subject, often in imitation with other instruments.

- **Episodes.** Here the subject does not appear at all. In this movement, the episodes happen to coincide with the tutti sections, in which all the instruments of the orchestra play.

Now listen to this movement again, using the Listening Guide.

CONNECT YOUR PLAYLIST

Imitation

Find a piece that contains imitation between two or more voices.
Example: John Kander and Fred Ebb, "The Cell-Block Tango," from *Chicago* (1975)
Toward the end of this song, the main melody is sung in imitation: the lead singer sings a line, and the remaining singers echo it slightly later, creating an overlapping effect.

Listening Guide

GO TO www.mymusiclab.com
for the Automated Listening Guide
CD II • Track 2/Download Track 37

Johann Sebastian Bach Composed: 1720 Brandenburg Concerto no. 2 in F Major,
BWV 1047, finale (9:36)

Time	Form: Ritornello/Solo	Timbre	Texture: The Fugue	Harmony: Key Areas
0:00	Solo 1	0:00 Trumpet alone 0:08 Oboe enters 0:26 Violin enters 0:33 Recorder enters 0:51 Trumpet reenters	Fugal exposition	F major
0:59	Ritornello 1	Tutti and soloists	Episode 1	C major
1:11	Solo 2	Recorder and violin; subject in oboe at 1:23	Middle Entry 1	C major → D minor
1:31	Ritornello 2	Tutti and soloists	Episode 2	D minor
1:47	Solo 3	Oboe and violin together, then recorder, then trumpet	Middle Entry 2	D minor
2:03	Ritornello 3	Tutti and soloists	Episode 3	B♭ major
2:15	Solo 4	Trumpet and oboe together, subject in oboe; recorder at 2:23	Final Entry	B♭ major → F major
2:30	Ritornello 4	Tutti and soloists	Final Entry (cont'd.)	F major

Student FAQs

Did Bach ever write programs for his concertos the way Vivaldi did?

No. In fact, very few of Bach's instrumental works give any hint at a story or idea outside the music. He did write a work for harpsichord he called *Capriccio on the Departure of a Beloved Brother*, BWV 992, and he labeled individual sections with such titles as "Friends gather and try to dissuade him from departing," "They imagine the dangers which might befall him," and "The Friends' Lament," but on the whole, these verbal cues are the exception rather than the rule in Bach's music.

Is the basso continuo part of the ritornello or the solo group?

Both. Its function is to support whatever other instruments are playing at the moment, so it plays in both the solo and ritornello sections.

When Bach died in 1750, most of his music soon disappeared from the active repertory. Keyboard performers still knew and played some of the works that he had written for harpsichord and for organ, but the choral and orchestral music were largely forgotten. When performers began rediscovering Bach's music in the nineteenth century, they were baffled by how to perform some of it, including the very difficult trumpet part of Brandenburg Concerto no. 2.

Both trumpets and the art of trumpet playing had changed drastically over the centuries. In the nineteenth century, the instrument began to be produced with valves and keys that allowed players to produce a wider range of notes with a more uniform quality of sound. But the art of playing the "natural"—valveless—trumpet gradually disappeared. In Bach's time, and for centuries before that, trumpet playing had

⊙ **SEE MORE** on **www.mymusiclab.com**
Inside the Orchestra: "Trumpet"

been strictly regulated; the trumpet was an aural symbol of military and political power, and not just anyone could pick up the instrument. Trumpeters had to join guilds to practice their art, and the secrets of the art, as in all guilds, were transmitted largely by word of mouth. When restrictions on trumpet playing began to be lifted in the late eighteenth century, the guilds soon disappeared, and with them the knowledge of how to perform the kinds of high, rapid passagework so prevalent in Bach's Brandenburg Concerto no. 2.

In the late nineteenth century, a few trumpet players began experimenting with specially designed instruments (so-called Bach trumpets) that would allow them to play this earlier music. Over time, more and more musicians became interested in using original instruments or accurate reproductions of them. Today, the lost art of playing the high range of the Baroque trumpet has been recovered, and we can hear Bach's Brandenburg Concerto no. 2 in a manner that more closely resembles the sound of what Bach himself heard when he conducted it.

Binding
The bell and tubing sections are kept separate by a wooden block. Heavy woolen cord holds them together.

Bell
Often has an embossed rim, bearing the maker's name, the name of the town, and the date.

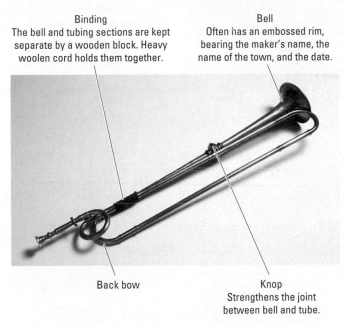

Back bow

Knop
Strengthens the joint between bell and tube.

The Baroque ("natural") trumpet. There are no keys or valves, only one long piece of coiled tubing. Bach wrote his Brandenburg Concerto no. 2 for a smaller trumpet that could reach a higher range but that similarly lacked keys or valves.
GRAHAM SALTER/Lebrecht Music & Arts Photo Library

Mouthpiece   Valves   Bell

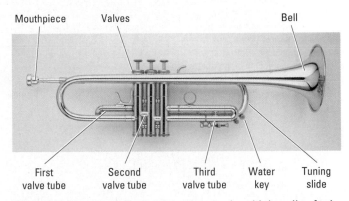

**First
valve tube**

**Second
valve tube**

**Third
valve tube**

**Water
key**

**Tuning
slide**

The modern trumpet. Notice the valves and multiple coils of tubing, both of which allow the trumpeter to lengthen or shorten the column of air, thereby making it easier to produce a wider range of notes.
© Dorling Kindersley

A CLOSER LOOK   Bach's World

⊙→ EXPLORE MORE on www.mymusiclab.com

Johann Sebastian Bach lived and worked within a relatively small area of what is now north-central Germany. Unlike Handel, his contemporary, Bach never traveled widely. The distance between Arnstadt and Cöthen, his two places of employ-ment farthest apart from each other, is only a little over 100 miles. Within this small space, however, he held a number of different kinds of positions that required him to write music in every major genre except opera.

1. Eisenach. Bach is born here on March 21, 1685, the son of a town musician. Both of his parents die when he is 10, and he is raised afterward by an older brother who is also a musician.

2. Arnstadt, 1703-1707. Bach's first full-time job is as a church organist. The congregation complains that his harmonizations of the chorales (hymns) are confusing and too elaborate. He probably writes his Fugue in G minor here (see Chapter 14).

3. Mühlhausen, 1707-1708. Again, Bach serves as organist for a church and continues to write a great deal of music for that instrument.

4. Weimar, 1708-1717. Bach is the organist and later chamber musician at the court of the Duke of Weimar. He gains a reputation as a performer and as a judge of newly built organs. Because he breaks his contract to move to Cöthen, he spends time in the duke's prison as punishment.

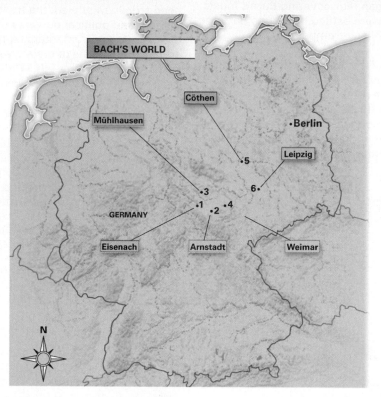

BACH'S WORLD

Cöthen

Mühlhausen

•Berlin

•5   Leipzig

•3   6•
•1   •2 •4

GERMANY

Eisenach   Arnstadt   Weimar

N

5. Cöthen, 1717-1723. Bach serves as music director ("kapellmeister") to the Prince of Anhalt. This position requires him to write a good deal of chamber music and orchestral music, including the concertos that would eventually be dedicated to the Margrave of Branden-burg (the "Brandenburg" Concertos).

6. Leizpig, 1723-1750. Bach is cantor of St. Thomas's Church and director of music for the city of Leipzig. Here he composes and supervises the per-formance of music for Leipzig's major churches, provides music for civic events, and teaches in St. Thomas's boys' school. He writes the large majori-ty of his sacred cantatas, including Cantata 140 (see Chapter 18), in Leipzig.

◀◀   ▶▶

EXPAND YOUR PLAYLIST

The Baroque Concerto

Baroque listeners responded enthusiastically to the emergence of a genre highlighting contrasts among instruments and performing forces. Here are some of the best-loved concerto composers and their works, all of which are still performed regularly today.

Arcangelo Corelli (1653–1713)

Corelli was one of the first composers to write large-scale concertos, all with two violins and basso continuo as soloists, accompanied by a string orchestra.

- Concerto Grosso in G Minor, op. 6, no. 8, known as the "Christmas Concerto" because it ends with a pastoral-like movement thought to depict the shepherds and their flocks who came to see the infant Jesus in the manger.

Antonio Vivaldi (1678–1741)

In addition to his *Four Seasons* (see chapter 15), Vivaldi wrote literally hundreds of concertos, both for solo instruments and for groups of solo instruments. Like Bach, Vivaldi seems to have been attracted to the idea of writing for unusual instruments and unusual combinations of instruments.

- Concerto in C Major for Mandolin and Strings, RV 425. The first movement of this work has been used in several movie soundtracks, including *Casanova* (2005) and *The Royal Tenenbaums* (2001), as well as for a 2005 episode of *The Sopranos*. The slow movement is a favorite for wedding ceremonies.
- Concerto in C Major for 2 Trumpets and Strings, RV 537. The two trumpets play together, often creating echo effects.

George Frideric Handel (1685–1759)

wrote many concertos, mostly during his time in England, and many imitating the style of Corelli.

- Concerto Grosso in B-flat Major for 2 Recorders, 2 Oboes, 2 Bassoons, Violin, and Strings, op. 3, no. 1. Handel gives the wind instruments unusually prominent roles in this work.

Johann Sebastian Bach

All six of his Brandenburg Concertos are well worth knowing.

- Concerto no. 1 in F Major, BWV 1046. There are no true soloists in this concerto; every instrument is treated virtuosically. Written for two horns, three oboes, bassoon, violino piccolo (a type of small violin tuned slightly higher than the standard violin), strings, and basso continuo.
- Concerto no. 3 in G Major, BWV 1048. For strings alone, with no soloists. Each of the stringed instruments (violins, violas, cellos) is subdivided into three separate parts, creating a nine-voice texture, all above the basso continuo.
- Concerto no. 4 in G Major, BWV 1049. The soloists are two recorders and violin; the orchestra consists of strings and basso continuo. The finale is a rousing fugue.
- Concerto no. 5 in D Major, BWV 1050. The soloists are a flute, violin, and—an innovation in this work—a harpsichord, which at times plays as a member of the basso continuo, at times as a true soloist.
- Concerto no. 6 in B-flat Major, BWV 1051. The scoring is limited entirely to low strings. The soloists are two violas, accompanied by viola da gambas, cellos, and basso continuo.

((•● HEAR SAMPLES on **www.mymusiclab.com**

Ⓥ **TEST YOURSELF** on **www.mymusiclab.com**   Flashcards and chapter tests

17

George Frideric Handel
Water Music, Hornpipe
Composed: 1717

This brief dance comes from a larger collection called *Water Music*, a suite of dances Handel wrote for a party on the Thames River given by King George I in 1717. A hornpipe is a small single-reed instrument that was popular in the British Isles in earlier times; the name eventually came to be associated with a lively type of dance as well.

Listen to this first

((● HEAR MORE on www.mymusiclab.com

Form

Listen for two distinct sections in each statement of the dance. Notice that each section is repeated immediately.

Timbre

Listen for the contrasting timbres among the three statements of the complete dance. The first time, we hear winds; the second time around, strings; and the third time winds and strings together.

⚙ LEARN MORE on
www.mymusiclab.com
Chapter Objectives

👁 SEE MORE on
www.mymusiclab.com
Inside the Orchestra:
"The Baroque Era"

A good party needs good music. And because eighteenth-century kings tended to have big budgets, they could hire not only the best bands but also the best composers to write the music. King George I certainly hired the best when he and his entourage traveled by boat down the River Thames from Whitehall to Chelsea and back. An orchestra of 50 musicians traveled along, and George Frideric Handel wrote parts or all of what we now know as his *Water Music* for the occasion. *Water Music* is a **suite**, a series of some two dozen individual dance movements, one of which is presented here. A suite typically consists of different types of dances, such as minuets, gavottes, and gigues. The variety of dance types—fast vs. slow, lively vs. stately, duple vs. triple—gave composers ample room to juxtapose contrasting moods. The hornpipe is a lively dance in triple meter, often associated with sailors, which certainly befits a work to be played on a boat. In his score, Handel directed that this particular dance be performed three times in succession. Whether people actually danced to this music varied from place to place and time to time. We do not know if the king and his followers actually danced at the premiere of Handel's *Water Music*, but there can be no doubt that the music was received with great enthusiasm. The music is still beloved by audiences today, and has been featured in several movie and television soundtracks, including *Dead Poets Society*, *Map of the Human Heart*, and *Moll Flanders*.

Binary Form

Like most dances of the Baroque Era, this one is in **binary form**. Binary form takes its name from the fact that any work in this form always consists of two sections, both repeated. (The symbol |: :| is used to indicate a unit of music to be repeated.)

Binary Form

|: **First Section**
Primary key (tonic) → Secondary key :||: **Second section**
Any key except tonic → Tonic :|

The pattern of the key areas helps create both unity and variety within any binary form. As shown in the diagram, the first section of a binary form begins in the primary key, or **tonic**, and often **modulates** to a secondary key area. (A **modulation** is a change of key within the course of a movement.) By the time we reach the end of the first section, we feel as if we have reached a point of arrival. But this point—this central note that is the basis of the new key area—is not the same as the point from which we began. Over the span of this first section, we have modulated, changing the sense of the harmonic "home" from one key to another. We have moved from the tonic to a new, secondary key area.

Giovanni Canaletto's *View of London and the Thames* shows a procession probably similar to the one for which Handel wrote his *Water Music*.

Bridgeman-Giraudon/Art Resource, NY.

The second section of a binary form begins in almost any key *except* the tonic and remains harmonically unstable—that is, it moves rapidly through several different key areas without settling on any particular one—before finally returning to the tonic. Without these changes, the music would sound harmonically static. If it did not end in the key in which it began, the music would sound unfinished. This basic pattern of starting and ending in the same key and moving away from it in the middle is basic to binary form and to many other musical forms as well.

Melodically, a binary form often rests on a single basic idea. Composers typically manipulate particular elements of a theme, such as its opening segment or its characteristic rhythm, but rarely do they try to create thematic contrast within a simple binary form. Binary-form movements appear in such genres as sonatas and symphonies as well as suites. Binary form eventually became the basis for sonata form, the most important instrumental form of the Classical Era (see chapter 23).

Timbre: Strings vs. Winds

Handel himself did not always specify exactly which instruments should perform which parts; instead, he left it up to the performers to create timbral variety by using a different **orchestration** each time the binary form is presented. Orchestration is the manner in which various instruments are assigned to the musical lines. In the performance here, we hear the same musical lines three times in succession, but they sound different because of the different orchestration each time:

1. The first time, we hear the dance played by strings (violins, violas, cellos, and basses) and basso continuo (harpsichord and cello).
2. The second time, we hear the winds (three oboes and, on the bottom, two bassoons) and basso continuo.
3. The third time, we hear all these instruments together: the full ensemble of strings, winds, and basso continuo. The sound thus expands both in variety and volume from beginning to end.

These contrasting timbres are in keeping with the Baroque Era's fondness for contrast and extremes. Over time, composers became more and more specific about which instruments should play which parts. By the early nineteenth century, some composers were even writing manuals of how to write for the orchestra, with special attention to the qualities of each instrument.

Now listen to this movement again, using the Listening Guide.

CONNECT YOUR PLAYLIST

Modulation

Find a song that modulates.

Example: Sonny and Cher, "I Got You Babe" (1965)
This song, made popular again by the movie *Groundhog Day*, modulates twice: once in the middle ("I got flowers in the spring") and then again with the return of the main theme shortly afterward.

Listening Guide

GO TO www.mymusiclab.com
for the Automated Listening Guide
CD II • Track 3/Download Track 38

George Frideric Handel Composed: 1717 *Water Music,* Hornpipe (6:41)

Time	Statement	Form: Section	Harmony: Key Areas	Timbre
0:00	1	First	F major → C major (0:11)	Strings and basso continuo
0:12		First (repeated)		
0:24		Second	Unstable →	
0:35		Second (repeated)	returns to F major (0:35)	
0:47	2	First	F major → C major	Winds and basso continuo
0:59		First (repeated)		
1:10		Second	Unstable → F major	
1:22		Second (repeated)		
1:33	3	First	F major → C major	Strings and winds together, with basso continuo
1:46		First (repeated)		
1:57		Second	Unstable → F major	
2:09		Second (repeated)		

Student FAQs

Why are there so many repeats in the music?

Dance music typically establishes a rhythmic pattern and then repeats it many times. While we often listen to dance music without dancing, its primary function is to make dancing easy. Consider the repetition in today's dance music. Small rhythmic and melodic units repeat, sometimes throughout the entire song, and entire sections often play several times so it's easy to focus on movement.

I don't hear the modulation? What should I do?

When you get to the end of the first section, sing the final note to yourself and hold it. Then push the "repeat" button to go back to the very beginning while you're still singing that note to yourself. You'll hear that where you landed is not the same as where you began. What happened in between was a modulation. The more of these you hear—and there will be more later in this book—the easier it will become to recognize them.

PROFILE   George Frideric Handel (1685–1759)

The Well-Traveled Composer

George Frideric Handel and J. S. Bach were born within a month of each other and less than 100 miles apart, but they never met, and their careers as composers could scarcely have been more different. Bach spent his entire life in central Germany (see A Closer Look: Bach's World, page 138), whereas Handel traveled widely throughout Europe. He moved to Italy in 1706 and soon established a name for himself as a composer of operas and oratorios. He returned to Germany as music director for the elector of Hanover in 1710, but he soon journeyed to England, where his operas won great acclaim.

When the elector of Hanover ascended the English throne as George I in 1714, Handel was still in his service and thus perfectly positioned to enjoy the new king's patronage and support. Over the course of his long career in England, Handel wrote many operas and oratorios that met with great public success. He abandoned opera altogether in 1741 and turned his attention toward the oratorio.

The music historian Charles Burney, who knew Handel personally, wrote this reminiscence:

> The figure of Handel was large, and he was somewhat corpulent, and unwieldy in his motions; but his countenance, which I remember as perfectly as that of any man I saw but yesterday, was full of fire and dignity; and such as impressed ideas of superiority and genius. He was impetuous, rough and peremptory in his manners and conversation, but totally devoid of ill-nature or malevolence; indeed, there was an original humor and pleasantry in his most lively sallies of anger or impatience, which, with his broken English, were extremely risible. His natural propensity to wit and humor, and happy manner of relating common occurrences, in an uncommon way, enabled him to throw persons and things into very ridiculous attitudes.[*]

[*]Charles Burney, *An Account of the Musical Performances in Westminster-Abbey . . . in Commemoration of Handel* (London: T. Payne, 1785), 31–32.

⊙→ **EXPLORE MORE** on www.mymusiclab.com

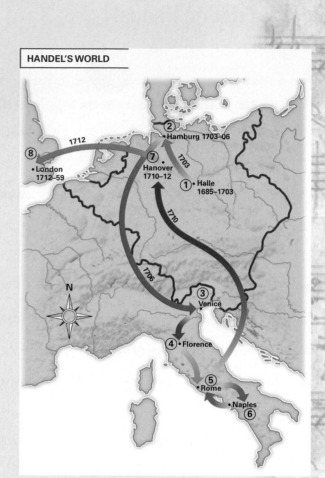

HANDEL'S WORLD

From his birthplace in Halle, Germany (1), Handel traveled extensively throughout Europe and lived for long periods in both Italy and England as well as Germany.

EXPAND YOUR PLAYLIST: HANDEL

- ***Messiah*** (oratorio). See chapter 19.

- ***Saul*** (oratorio). One of Handel's many oratorios on a story from the Old Testament. The text deals with the relationship between Saul, King of Israel, and the young David.

- ***Rinaldo*** (opera). Handel's first operatic hit premiered in London in 1711.

- ***Giulio Cesare*** (opera). One of Handel's most enduring operas, the tale of Caesar and Cleopatra in ancient Egypt.

- ***Alexander's Feast*** (ode). Set to a text by poet and playwright John Dryden, this work for soloists, chorus, and orchestra extols the power of music even over Alexander the Great, ruler of the world's greatest empire in his day.

((●• HEAR SAMPLES on www.mymusiclab.com

HISTORICAL CONTEXT   The Composer as Cultural Hero

Handel was so beloved by the English public that he was buried in Westminster Abbey, a place of special cultural importance to the nation. Westminster Abbey itself is the church in which the kings and queens of England have been crowned since 1066 and the resting place of many of those monarchs. One particular area of the church, known as "Poets' Corner," contains the graves of such literary figures as Geoffrey Chaucer, Edmund Spenser, John Dryden, Charles Dickens, Alfred Lord Tennyson, Rudyard Kipling, and Thomas Hardy. Handel is buried in that section as well.

What is Handel, a composer, doing in Poets' Corner? Other composers, like Henry Purcell, had been buried elsewhere in the abbey, but only because they had worked there. Handel was accorded this esteemed resting place by virtue of the music he had written. The court and public alike saw him as the artistic equal of England's greatest literary figures.

In 1784, a quarter century after his death, Handel was commemorated through a series of enormous concerts in Westminster Abbey organized by the monarchy with the purpose not only of honoring the composer but also of consolidating a sense of national pride. The concerts were so popular that a similar festival was held annually thereafter until 1791, with the number of participants more than doubling, from around 500 the first year to more than 1,000 in the last.

Handel was one of the first composers to become a cultural hero, a figure who was perceived to have contributed to the broader well-being of society as a whole, not merely the music-loving portion. Over the course of the nineteenth century, civic monuments would be erected to such composers as Bach, Haydn, Mozart, and Beethoven.

Handel as a young man, composing at the keyboard. Like many men of the day, he kept his head shaved to better accommodate a wig, which he always wore in public.

© Archivo Iconografico, S.A./CORBIS

EXPAND YOUR PLAYLIST

The Baroque Suite

Many Baroque composers wrote multiple series of dances that they gathered into suites that were quite successful commercially.

Elizabeth Jacquet de la Guerre
- Suite in D Minor (1707). One of several suites for harpsichord by a woman who was herself an outstanding keyboard virtuoso.

François Couperin
- Keyboard Pieces, Book IV, 25th Group (1730). Many of the movements from Couperin's suites for harpsichord bear programmatic titles, including pieces in this group with such intriguing headings as "The Visionary," "The Mysterious One," "The Victorious Muse," and "The Wandering Shadows."

Johann Sebastian Bach
- Orchestral Suite No. 3 in D Major, BWV 1068 (ca. 1730). One of four suites for orchestra by Bach, this one includes the celebrated "Air on the G String."

- Partita No. 4 in D Major, BWV 828 (1728). "Partita" is another term used in the Baroque Era for suite, and Bach wrote six partitas for harpsichord. The finale of this one is a fugue based on a theme that sounds like a jig (or gigue, to use the French form of the word).

George Frideric Handel
- *Royal Fireworks Music* (1748). Written in 1749 for a ceremony to celebrate the peace treaty that ended the War of Austrian Succession, this suite originally was scored for a large wind band. Later, it was arranged for a full orchestra.

((•● HEAR SAMPLES on **www.mymusiclab.com**

✔ **TEST YOURSELF** on **www.mymusiclab.com**   Flashcards and chapter tests

Johann Sebastian Bach
Cantata 140: *Awake, a Voice Calls to Us,* selections
Composed: 1731

The selections here are the first and last movements of a **cantata**, a work sung during a service of worship. Listen for the way in which Bach uses the melody of the same hymn tune—also known as a **chorale**—as the basis for both of these movements. To help you recognize the chorale, you may find it easier to listen to the last movement first.

Listen to this first

 HEAR MORE on www.mymusiclab.com

Melody

- *First Movement:* Listen to how the individual phrases of the chorale are separated by long passages of contrasting music.

- *Last Movement:* Listen to how the original chorale is presented in a straightforward fashion, with only brief pauses between its individual phrases.

Timbre

- *First Movement:* Listen for the contrast between the chorus and the orchestra.

- *Last Movement:* Listen for the *lack of* contrast between chorus and orchestra.

Texture

- *First Movement:* Listen for the polyphonic texture. The chorale appears in the uppermost voice, but the lower voices present contrasting, important melodic material of their own.

- *Last Movement:* Listen for the homophonic texture, with the melody in the uppermost voice and accompanying voices beneath.

Form

- *First Movement:* Listen for the orchestral ritornello that introduces the chorale and then returns between the chorale's individual phrases.

- *Last Movement:* Listen for the absence of any ritornellos in this movement.

 LEARN MORE on
www.mymusiclab.com
Chapter Objectives

When J. S. Bach became music director at St. Thomas' Church in Leipzig in 1723, he agreed to provide music for the Lutheran worship services each Sunday, and it was in this position that he wrote the vast majority of his more than 200 cantatas. The word "cantata" means simply "that which is sung," and cantatas can range from a single movement for one vocal soloist to an extended cycle of movements for soloists, chorus, and orchestra, such as Cantata 140. Had Bach written these works over the span of his 27 years in Leipzig, the accomplishment would be remarkable enough. But through detailed studies of paper, handwriting, and other evidence, scholars have discovered that Bach actually wrote about 150 cantatas within his first three years in Leipzig, at the rate of roughly one a week (see A Closer Look: Bach's World, page 138).

When one considers the time needed to compose a new work, write down the score, supervise the copying of the parts, rehearse the new work, and then perform it on Sunday—all in addition to his duties as a teacher at St. Thomas's School—Bach's achievement seems almost superhuman. What motivated him to write such elaborate music week after week, year after year? We cannot know for sure, but he clearly embraced the opportunity to express his faith through music. Just as the resident preacher would write a sermon each Sunday expounding on the biblical readings for that day, Bach would compose a cantata expressing through music the ideas or lessons gleaned from those readings.

Awake, a Voice Calls to Us (*Wachet auf, ruft uns die Stimme*) was written for the 27th Sunday after Trinity in 1731. The Gospel reading for that Sunday is Matthew 25:1–13, which is the parable of the wise and foolish virgins who attend a wedding. The wise ones are prepared for the bridegroom's arrival: they have brought extra oil for their lamps in case he is late. The foolish ones are unprepared: they must leave to buy oil, and the bridegroom arrives in their absence, at midnight. The message implicit here has to do with the second coming of Christ: who will be ready?

(1) The Chorale: Movement Seven

Awake, a Voice Calls to Us derives some of its text and a good bit of its musical material—as well as its name—from a hymn tune or chorale that was in circulation long before Bach wrote this cantata. In fact, the easiest way to approach this particular cantata is by starting with the last of its seven movements, in which Bach presents the chorale melody in its simplest form. The melody is in the uppermost voice, in a syllabic setting with a four-part harmonization.

The words here are the last stanza of the hymn, but the melody is identical to the one used in the opening movement.

Unified Timbre

The instruments of the orchestra **double** the voices—that is, the instruments play the same notes sung by the chorus: high instruments like the violin, flute, and oboe double the soprano line, while lower instruments (violas, cellos, basses) double the lower voice lines. When instruments double the voices, the contrast between chorus and orchestra is minimized, and the combined forces create a powerful sense of unity, symbolizing the unified belief of the congregation.

A Familiar Melody

The chorale melody is in the uppermost voice, and the lower voices provide a fairly simple harmonization of the tune, one that would have been familiar to every member of Bach's congregation in 1731. It is even possible that worshippers sang along with the chorus in this

1685–1750
Johann Sebastian Bach
Cantata 140: *Awake, a Voice Calls to Us,* selections
Composed: 1731

GENRE
Cantata

KEY CONCEPTS
Cantata, chorale, ritornello principle, song form (AAB).

CHAPTER HIGHLIGHT
Sacred Music of the Late Baroque
In the Protestant church, the chorale (hymn) was the basic musical element of the church service. The entire congregation would know the words and melodies by heart and sing as a group. In this cantata, Bach used one of the most popular of all chorale melodies as the basis for an elaborate opening movement performed by a chorus and orchestra.

particular movement. Lutherans, like other Protestants, placed a high importance on the personal connection of each believer to God. Chorale melodies played a role in making this connection, as they were easy to sing and the melodies were memorable, which enabled everyone to participate. Using the vernacular—in this case, German—was another way Protestants aimed to facilitate direct communication between ordinary people and God.

The melody opens with a fanfare-like figure that suits the words of the first stanza ("Sleepers, Awake!"). Notice the contour: the opening phrase (**A**) keeps moving upward before finally settling back down. The individual phrases are brief enough to be sung by untrained singers, and the space between phrases allows the congregation plenty of time to take a good breath. Phrase **A** is sung twice. The contrasting phrase (**B**) that follows has a different contour: it begins high and moves downward before making a long climb to reach the highest point of the melody.

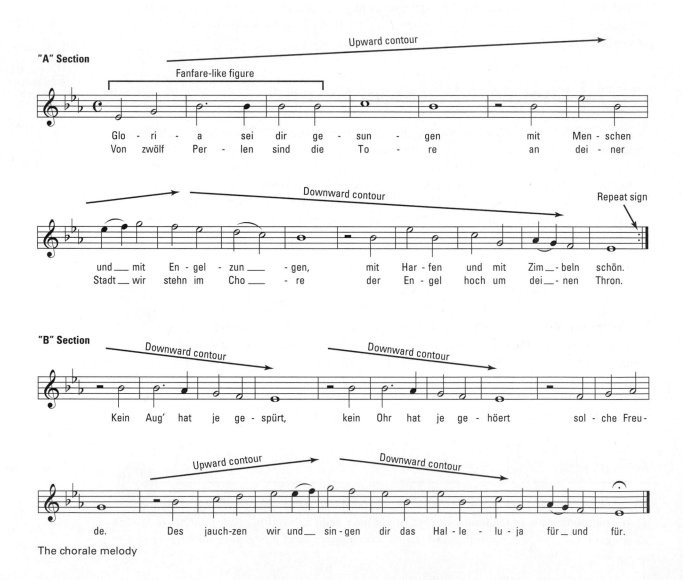

The chorale melody

Bar Form

The movement consists of one verse of the chorale melody, and so the form of the movement reflects the form of the melody: **AAB**. The opening phrase **(A)** is sung twice, and the melody concludes with a contrasting section **(B)**. This pattern is so common that it has its own name: **bar form**. It is sometimes also called song form because many popular songs from later eras—including "The Star-Spangled Banner"—follow this pattern.

Homophonic Texture: To Hear the Words

The texture is homophonic, with the melody in the uppermost voice and all four parts moving in equal or nearly equal rhythm. The bass voice, which moves at a slightly faster speed, keeps the chorale moving forward and provides rhythmic variety. But the four parts begin their articulation of nearly every word at the same time, which makes the words particularly clear to listeners.

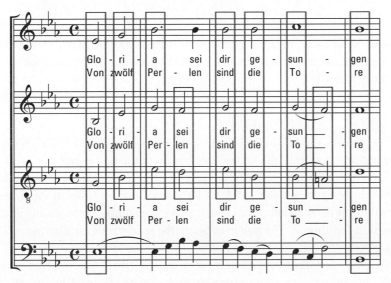

The opening of the chorale, showing all four parts

(2) The Chorus: Movement One

Bach uses this same chorale melody in a spectacular manner in the opening movement of the cantata. Dotted rhythms (LONG-short LONG-short LONG, etc.) and a steady pace suggest a march, the kind of procession described in the cantata's text. Bach's listeners would have heard these dotted rhythms as a reference to the pomp of royalty, as in the French overture (see chapter 11). As in the chorale itself (movement 7), the melody is sung from beginning to end by the soprano

THE *COMPOSER SPEAKS* Bach's Working Conditions

We have observed how churches and noble patrons competed for the best and brightest musicians, in part because of the influence and prestige the arts could confer. But Bach had a very high estimation of his self-worth, and he was not the easiest of employees. He quarreled almost constantly with his employers about his pay and working conditions no matter where he was. He even spent a month in prison for signing a contract for a new job in Cöthen against the wishes of his then-employer, the duke of Weimar (see A Closer Look: Bach's World, page 138). In 1730, about six years after moving to Leipzig, Bach wrote to a lifelong friend, venting some of his frustration about his position there:

I am still here [in Leipzig], by God's will. But as I now find that (1) this position is not nearly as agreeable as I had been led to believe; (2) many supplemental sources of income have been taken away from this position; (3) this is a very expensive place to live; and (4) the powers-that-be here are remarkably uninterested in music, I find myself in a state of such constant annoyance, envy, and persecution that I am now compelled to seek my fortune elsewhere.

My current salary is approximately 700 thalers, and when there are more funerals than usual, the supplemental income rises accordingly. But when the air is wholesome, this income declines accordingly, as it did last year, when I had to forego more than 100 thalers from funerals. In Thuringia I can do more with 400 thalers than in this place with double that amount, due to the extremely high cost of living here in Leipzig.

Source: Letter to Georg Erdmann, 28 October 1730, trans. MEB.

voices. But instead of a straightforward harmonization, Bach weaves elaborate lines of counterpoint underneath the melody with the other voices and with the instruments of the orchestra.

Melody Interrupted

The melody is sung in the soprano voices, as in the finale, but in this opening chorus, Bach creates substantial pauses after each line and even longer pauses between the main sections (**A | A | B**). These interruptions in the uppermost voices are filled in by the orchestra (which plays constantly throughout) and by the other voices in the chorus. The music between the sections of the chorale melody thus provides both contrast and commentary.

Like other Protestant composers of his time, Bach often worked chorale melodies into larger, more complex movements. In his Cantata 80, for example, Bach wove the well-known chorale "A Mighty Fortress Is Our God," or some variation of it, into three of the work's eight movements (see Expand Your Playlist). His Cantata 78 (also in the playlist) follows a similar pattern.

Form: The Ritornello Principle

St. Thomas's Church in Leipzig, where Cantata 140 (*Awake, a Voice Calls to Us*) received its premiere in 1731. Bach is buried inside this church.
AKG-Images

The first movement presents the chorale melody in its entirety in very long note values (in the soprano line), with an instrumental ritornello on each end as well as between major text sections. In this way, the ritornello provides a "frame" for the chorale melody on multiple levels, introducing and concluding the movement, and also introducing and concluding the individual melodic subunits. The ritornello principle here is very similar to the one Vivaldi used in the first movement of "Winter" from *The Four Seasons* (see chapter 15).

Section:	Ritornello 1	Chorale A	Ritornello 2	Chorale A	Ritornello 3	Chorale B	Ritornello 4
Timbre:	Orchestra	Orchestra & Chorus	Orchestra	Orchestra & Chorus	Orchestra	Orchestra & Chorus	Orchestra

Now listen to the movements again, using the Listening Guide. As suggested earlier, you may find it easier to listen to the last movement first in order to hear the chorale in its simplest, most straightforward form.

CONNECT YOUR PLAYLIST

Re-Using the Familiar

Find a song that uses pre-existing musical material.

Example: Kid Rock, "All Summer Long" (2008)
This song combines new lyrics with elements of two pre-existing songs: Warren Zevon's "Werewolves of London" and Lynyrd Skynyrd's "Sweet Home Alabama."

◀◀   **EXPAND YOUR PLAYLIST**   ▶▶

Sacred Music of the Late Baroque

Baroque composers wrote vast quantities of music for services of different faiths, including Catholicism and the various Protestant sects. The cantata was used in both Catholic and Protestant services, but it was more important in the latter and more closely connected to the traditions of the chorale. J. S. Bach wrote more than 300 cantatas, of which about 200 survive, including the following:

- *A Mighty Fortress Is Our God*
  (*Ein' feste Burg ist unser Gott*), BWV 80, is based on the words and melody of the well-known hymn by Martin Luther. One of Bach's sons later added trumpets and timpani to the score; this version is most often performed today.

- *Praise God in All Lands*
  (*Jauchzet Gott in allen Landen*), BWV 51, for soprano solo, trumpet solo, strings, and basso continuo. The two solo parts (one vocal, one instrumental) are spectacular—and spectacularly difficult.

The **motet**, similar to the cantata, was used widely in both Protestant and Catholic services. Here are some examples:

- *Sing Unto God*
  (*Cantate Domino*) by **Michel-Richard Delalande** (1657–1726) is a good example of the French motet, for tenor soloist, chorus, and orchestra. The text is in Latin, and the tenor part is highly virtuosic.

- *Sing Unto the Lord a New Song*
  (*Singet dem Herrn ein neues Lied*), BWV 225, is a motet for chorus alone, without soloists or instruments.

The **Mass** is the central liturgical service of the Catholic church, recreating, in symbolic fashion, Christ's Last Supper with his disciples. Although retained in the Protestant service to some extent (usually in the language of the people), the Mass in Latin was associated primarily with the Catholic Church.

- The *Saint Cecilia Mass* (*Missa Santa Cecilia*) by **Alessandro Scarlatti** (1660–1725) is an elaborate setting of the Mass text, with spectacularly florid parts for the vocalists.
- Though a Lutheran himself, Bach also wrote an important Mass for the Catholic court at Dresden, near Leipzig. The B-Minor Mass, BWV 232, is for chorus, soloists, and orchestra, and it is widely considered the greatest of all Baroque Masses.

The **oratorio** (see chapter 19) is musically very similar to an opera—usually for soloists, chorus, and orchestra—but it is unstaged and often based on a sacred topic:

- Giacomo Carissimi's *Jephthe* depicts the story of an Israelite caught between his duty to God and love of his family.
- George Frideric Handel (1685–1759) was the most celebrated composer of oratorios in the Baroque Era. Audiences responded enthusiastically to his *Messiah* (see chapter 19), *Samson*, and other oratorios.

((•• **HEAR SAMPLES** on **www.mymusiclab.com**

Listening Guide

GO TO www.mymusiclab.com
for the Automated Listening Guide
CD II • Track 4/Download Track 39

Johann Sebastian Bach Composed: 1731 Cantata 140: *Awake, a Voice Calls to Us,*

Movement I: Chorus (6:06)

Time	Form	Original German Text	English Translation
0:00	Ritornello 1		
0:28	Chorale A	Wachet auf, ruft uns die Stimme, der Wächter sehr hoch auf der Zinne, wach auf, du Stadt Jerusalem.	"Awake," a voice calls to us, the watchman high in the tower: "Awake, thou city of Jerusalem."
1:32	Ritornello 2		
2:00	Chorale A	Mitternacht heißt diese Stunde, sie rufen uns mit hellem Munde, wo seid ihr klugen Jungfrauen?	Midnight the hour is called; they call to us with bright voices: "Where are you, wise virgins?"
3:04	Ritornello 3		
3:24	Chorale B	Wohlauf, der Bräut'gam kömmt, steht auf, die Lampen nehmt, Alleluia! Alleluia! Macht euch bereit zu der Hochzeit, ihr müsset ihm entgegengehn.	Behold, the bridegroom comes; rise up and take your lamps, Alleluia! Alleluia! Prepare yourselves for the wedding, you must go to meet Him.
5:32	Ritornello 4		

GO TO www.mymusiclab.com
for the Automated Listening Guide
CD II • Track 5/Download Track 40

Movement VII: Chorale (1:25)

Time	Form	Original German Text	English Translation
0:00	A	Gloria sei dir gesungen, mit Menschen- und englischen Zungen, mit Harfen und mit Zimbeln schon.	Let Gloria be sung to You with mortal and angelic tongues, with harps and even cymbals.
0:24	A	Von zwölf Perlen sind die Pforten, an deiner Stadt sind wir Konsorten der Engel hoch um deinen Thron.	Of twelve pearls the portals are made, in your city we are consorts to the angels high around your throne.
0:47	B	Kein Aug' hat je gespürt, kein Ohr hat je gehört solche Freude, des sind wir froh, io, io, ewig in dulci jubilo.	No eye has ever glimpsed, no ear has ever heard such joy which makes us glad, io, io eternally, with sweet rejoicing!

Melody

Texture

Melody	Texture
Dotted rhythms, march-like feeling	Polyphonic
Chorale melody in the highest (soprano) voice, which enters first. "Wachet auf" ("Awake") set to fanfare-like figure (using skips), rather like a trumpet that would awaken a sleeper.	
Dotted rhythms; same melody as in Ritornello 1.	
Same melodic phrase as Chorale A.	
Same melody as in previous ritornellos.	
Chorale melody enters after the other voices, at 3:26.	
Same melody as in previous ritornellos.	

Melody

Texture

Melody	Texture
Fanfare-like opening (disjunct, upward). Leaps upward again on "mit Menschen" and again on "mit Harfen." Otherwise conjunct motion or repeated notes.	Homophonic
Same music as above, with upward motion at the beginning and leaps upward again on "an deiner Stadt" and "der Engel hoch."	
First two lines: Descending conjunct motion. Next line ("solche Freude"): ascends and descends by conjunct motion. "Des sind wir froh" ("which makes us glad"): ascends by conjunct motion to highest pitch of the chorale.	

Student FAQs

What are the other movements of this cantata like?

The second movement is a recitative for tenor and basso continuo; the third movement is a duet for soprano and bass, with a solo violin and basso continuo accompaniment; the fourth movement presents the chorale melody as sung by the tenors of the chorus, with a contrapuntal line weaving around it, played by the violins and violas; the fifth movement is a recitative for bass; and the sixth movement is another duet for soprano and bass, with an oboe solo.

How large was Bach's chorus?

This has been a matter of heated debate among scholars in recent years. Documentary evidence has come to light that indicates that for at least some performances there was only one singer to a part. But there is no consensus on whether this represented standard practice or an exception. Conductors today must take into account the quality of the singers in their ensemble and the size of the space in which they are performing. There is no one "right" size for a chorus when performing this work.

This satirical depiction of a chorus, by the English artist William Hogarth (1697–1764), shows a conductor who has gotten so caught up in the moment that he has literally flipped his wig. Only one of the singers seems to notice.
William Hogarth (1697–1764), "The Chorus". 1833 Lithograph. From 'The Works of William Hogarth'. ©Private Collection/Ken Welsh/The Bridgeman Art Library

19

George Frideric Handel
Messiah, selections
Composed: 1747

The "Hallelujah Chorus" is one of the most famous works of music ever written. What many people do not realize is that it is only one movement out of a much larger work called *Messiah.* In addition to the "Hallelujah Chorus," the selection here includes the recitative and aria that immediately precede it.

Listen to this first

((• HEAR MORE on www.mymusiclab.com

Timbre	**Melody**	**Word-Music Relationships**	**Form**	**Texture**
Listen to the expanding variety of timbres, from (1) solo voice and basso continuo in the recitative; to (2) solo voice, basso continuo, and violins in the aria; to (3) a large group of singers and a large orchestra in the chorus.	Notice that the aria has just one distinctive melody from beginning to end, in keeping with the single-mindedness of the text. By contrast, listen to the multiple melodies in the chorus, which reflect its more varied text.	Try to identify specific ways the music supports and describes the words being sung.	Listen to the different style of singing in each of the three formal types: recitative, aria, and chorus. Consider how each allows its text to be projected in a different way and how the three work together to form a dramatic unit.	Listen to the variety of textures, from homophony in the recitative and aria, to a full array in the chorus: homophony, monophony, and polyphony.

⚙ LEARN MORE on
www.mymusiclab.com
Chapter Objectives

⚙ LEARN MORE on
www.mymusiclab.com
MyMusicLibrary:
"The Oratorio in Rome"

Throughout the Baroque Era, the church remained deeply ambivalent toward opera. On the one hand, authorities recognized the power of music to move the spirits of the faithful, and a number of composers in the seventeenth century even wrote operas on sacred subjects, such as the lives of particular saints. On the other hand, opera had become a spectacle—both visual and aural—by the end of the seventeenth century, and the church could not sanction such elaborate productions during the penitential seasons of Lent (40 days in early spring before Easter) and Advent (30 days in the fall before Christmas), when the faithful were supposed to give up worldly pleasures and devote themselves to inward contemplation. Fortunately, the new genre of the **oratorio** offered a way out of this dilemma that satisfied both the church and music lovers alike.

Musically, an oratorio is virtually identical to an opera: it includes recitatives, arias, and choruses, and the singing can be quite elaborate. The key differences are that an oratorio is not staged—there are no costumes, no sets—and is usually based on a sacred topic. The word "oratorio" is the Italian word for "prayer hall," which is where these works were performed in the seventeenth century. The genre soon spread across Europe and became a standard substitute for opera during the penitential seasons.

Most oratorios have characters and a plot, just as in an opera. Handel's *Messiah*, the most popular of all oratorios, is actually somewhat unusual in this regard. There are no characters and no plot, save a general trajectory from prophecy and the birth of Christ (Part 1) to the crucifixion and resurrection (Part 2) to meditations on the eternal life of the soul (Part 3). The text is drawn from various biblical passages, including both Old and New Testaments. Musically, however, *Messiah* is typical in that it uses the basic conventions of opera. The movements presented here include a recitative, an aria, and a chorus.

1685–1759
George Frideric Handel
Messiah, selections
Composed: 1747

GENRE
Oratorio

KEY CONCEPTS
Word-music relationships, fugue, ritornello principle.

CHAPTER HIGHLIGHT
Oratorio
An oratorio, like an opera, is a dramatic work performed by orchestra, choir, and soloists, but it is performed as a concert work, without staging, and is usually based on a text with a religious theme. The selection here from Handel's *Messiah* includes a brief recitative, an aria, and the famous "Hallelujah" chorus.

(1) Recitative ("He That Dwelleth in Heaven") and Aria ("Thou Shalt Break Them")

This pair of joined movements, both for tenor soloist, forms a sequence of recitative and aria that would have been familiar to Handel's original audiences from opera. The brief recitative ("He that dwelleth in heaven"), for tenor and basso continuo alone, introduces the more extended aria, for tenor and a reduced orchestra of violins and basso continuo.

Form: Paired Movements

The declamatory recitative sets up the more musically elaborate aria that follows. The aria is built on the ritornello principle, in which the ensemble (the orchestra) and the soloist (the tenor) alternate. The text of the aria is also quite brief, but Handel, like a great many composers of his time, spins a few short phrases into an extended aria by repeating the words several times and by writing long melismas on certain key words.

> Thou shalt break them with a rod of iron,
> Thou shalt dash them to pieces like a potter's vessel.
> *(Psalm 2:9, King James Version)*

Word-Music Relationships: Virtuosic Word Painting

Those being "broken" and "dashed" in the text are the heathen, the unbelievers who scorn God. Handel captures the violence of this text from the very start with a back-and-forth shaking figure in the violins, two rapidly alternating notes repeated several times. And he sets the words "dash them" at several points to a large downward leap, a moment of word painting that suggests an object being thrown from a great height. The words "potter's vessel"—that is, a clay pot—receive elaborate melismatic settings at several points: the many notes sung to these words can be heard to represent the many pieces into which these objects will be broken. The elaborate melodic line of the aria interprets the text and allows the singer to display his virtuosity as a musician. It also gave audiences the kind of florid singing they would not otherwise have been able to hear during the periods of the year when operatic performances were banned.

The theme of the aria

A Single Melody

The brief text of the aria speaks of one thing and one thing only: destruction. The first half of Psalm 2:9 is about the tool of destruction ("a rod of iron"), and the second half is about the nature of that destruction ("dash them to pieces like a potter's vessel"). Handel responds to this text with a single melodic idea. He does not use any kind of melodic contrast in his music because there is no real contrast within the text itself.

Homophonic Texture

The homophonic texture in both the recitative and aria allows the solo singer to project his words with great clarity. In the aria, the instruments present the "shaking" melody repeatedly so that it is not merely subordinate to the voice. But the voice stands out, particularly in those passages of the aria in which it is accompanied only by the basso continuo.

A Stark Timbre

The recitative is accompanied only by the basso continuo, following standard practice. But when the tenor's aria begins, only the violins join in. This not only falls well short of the full orchestra—Handel is saving that larger sound for the chorus to follow—but it does not even include all the stringed instruments. Moreover, both sections of violins (Violin 1 and Violin 2) play exactly the same notes, which creates a strong single line that contrasts markedly with both the basso continuo and the solo tenor voice. The result is a stark timbre of only three lines: the voice, the violins, and the basso continuo.

(2) Chorus ("Hallelujah")

Just as the recitative introduces the aria, the aria introduces the chorus, the celebrated "Hallelujah." The text now jumps from the Old Testament to the New. The words of this chorus are a compilation of different verses from the Book of Revelations:

> Hallelujah, for the Lord God Omnipotent reigneth, Hallelujah! (*Revelation 19:6*)
> The Kingdom of this world is become the Kingdom of our Lord, and of His Christ;
>   and He shall reign for ever and ever, Hallelujah! (*Revelation 11:15*)
> King of Kings, and Lord of Lords, and He shall reign for ever and ever, Hallelujah!
>   (*Revelation 19:16*)

Sectional Form

Handel allows the form of the text to shape the form of the music. Each verse or half-verse receives its own melodic material so that there are four large sections within the chorus as a whole (labeled **A**, **B**, **C**, and **D** in the Listening Guide). After the introductory, narrative singing style of the recitative and the highly ornamented, reflective style of the aria, the clear and mostly syllabic singing style of the culminating "Hallelujah" chorus makes it easy to understand the jubilant and victorious text. It also enhances these joyous words, which provide the conclusion to Part 2 of *Messiah*.

The Same Melody for the Same Words

Even though the text draws on three different biblical verses, they contain a good bit of repetition. All three end with the opening word of the entire chorus ("Hallelujah"), and the phrase "And He shall reign for ever and ever" appears in two of the three verses. Handel, accordingly, uses the same melodic ideas when these words return later in the text.

Melody 1 consists of short notes that repeat or move in mainly conjunct motion.

Melody 2 is a unison line that rises and falls.

Melody 3 is a long, descending line with a dramatic leap up at "the Kingdom of our Lord."

The Kingdom of this world   is be - come   the Kingdom of our Lord and of His Christ, and of His Christ,

Melody 4 is a disjunct line, with several leaps up and down but a generally downward contour.

and He shall   reign for ev - er and ev - er,

Melody 5 consists of very long notes in a unison line that rises quite slowly.

King of   Kings, _____   and Lord of   Lords, _____

Sometimes, different melodies appear at the same time. At 0:45, melodies 1 and 2 appear together; at 1:48, we hear both 1 and 5; and at 2:29, melodies 1, 4, and 5 join for a grand polyphonic climax.

Varied Textures

This movement features all three basic textures of music: monophony, homophony, and polyphony. The textures are driven in large part by the text. We hear homophony at the beginning ("Hallelujah"), monophony on the line that emphasizes God's power ("For the Lord God Omnipotent reigneth"), and polyphony whenever these texts are combined with other texts. All this contributes to a sense of variety reinforced by the new words, new melodies, and new timbres in each section of the chorus.

Varied Timbres

In the aria immediately preceding this chorus ("Thou shalt break them"), Handel had used a reduced orchestra of only violins and basso continuo. As a result, the full orchestra in this chorus of exaltation ("Hallelujah") sounds even fuller. The timbre also varies within the movement itself. It begins with strings and basso continuo (0:00), which are soon joined by the full chorus and oboes (0:06), and later still by trumpets and timpani (0:29). As the movement progresses, instruments drop out and reenter, building to a climax at the end on the final word, "Hallelujah."

Now listen to these movements again, using the Listening Guide.

CONNECT YOUR PLAYLIST

Varied Textures

Find a song with at least two distinctly varied textures (monophony, homophony, or polyphony).

Example: Whitney Houston, "I Will Always Love You" (1992)
This song begins monophonically, with only the voice. Instruments later provide support, creating a homophonic texture.

Listening Guide

GO TO www.mymusiclab.com
for the **Automated Listening Guide**
CD II • Track 6/Download Track 41

George Frideric Handel Composed: 1747 *Messiah,* selections

(1) Recitative: "He that dwelleth in heaven" (2:20)

Time	Text	Texture	Timbre	Word-Music Relationships	Melody
0:00	He that dwelleth in heaven shall laugh them to scorn; the Lord shall have them in derision.	Homophonic	Tenor (voice) and basso continuo (in this performance, harpsichord and cello)	Line goes up to word "heaven," descends on "laugh"	Recitative

Aria: "Thou shalt break them"

Time	Form: Ritornello/Solo	Text	Timbre	Word-Music Relationships	Melody
0:17	Ritornello 1		Sharp contrast between the violins above and the basso continuo below.	Minor mode and melody establish the violent mood of the text	Theme 1 here and throughout; there is no contrasting melody
0:33	Solo 1	Thou shalt break them with a rod of iron;	The tenor soloist enters.	Downward leap on "break them"	
0:43		Thou shalt dash them in pieces like a potter's vessel.		Downward leaps on "dash them" and "in pieces." Long melisma on "potter's," evoking the many pieces of a smashed clay pot	
1:06	Ritornello 2		Violins and basso continuo alone.		
1:13	Solo 2	Thou shalt break them with a rod of iron;	The tenor solo returns. Violins recede or drop out entirely on melismas in this section, exposing the emphasized words still further.	Long melisma on "rod"	
1:28		Thou shalt dash them in pieces like a potter's vessel.		Long melisma on "potter's"	
2:04	Ritornello 3				

Listening Guide

GO TO www.mymusiclab.com
for the Automated Listening Guide
CD II • Track 7/Download Track 42

George Frideric Handel Composed: 1747 *Messiah,* selections

(2) Chorus: "Hallelujah" (3:33)

Time	Form: Section	Melody	Text	Texture
0:00	Introduction			Homophonic
0:06	A	Melody 1	Hallelujah,	Homophonic
0:23		Melody 2	for the Lord God Omnipotent reigneth,	Monophonic
0:29		Melody 1	Hallelujah!	Homophonic
0:34		Melody 2	for the Lord God Omnipotent reigneth,	Monophonic
0:45		Melodies 1 & 2 together	Hallelujah, for the Lord God Omnipotent reigneth, Hallelujah!	Polyphonic
1:09	B	Melody 3	The Kingdom of this world is become the Kingdom of our Lord, and of His Christ;	Homophonic
1:26	C	Melody 4	and He shall reign for ever and ever,	Polyphonic (imitative)
1:48	D	Melodies 5 & 1 together	King of Kings, and Lord of Lords, and He shall reign for ever and ever, Hallelujah!	Polyphonic
2:29		Melodies 1, 4, & 5 together	And He shall reign for ever and ever, King of Kings and Lord of Lords, Hallelujah!	Polyphonic

Word-Music Relationships	Timbre
	Strings and basso continuo.
Melody 1: Rhythm of music matches two different ways of saying "Hallelujah," either with a long first syllable (HA-le-lu-jah), or with a long third syllable (Ha-le-LU-jah)	The full chorus and oboes join in.
Melody 2: Large leap down and up on "omnipotent," as if to show the range of God's power	
	Trumpets and timpani join in.
	Chorus, strings, bassoons, and basso continuo only.
Melodies 1 and 2 together when their texts are combined	Trumpets and timpani join in at 0:51.
Melody 3: Notes moving from high to low suggest the "Kingdom of our Lord" descending to "the Kingdom of this world," that is, Earth. The leap upward suggests that Earth and heaven are now connected.	Chorus, strings, oboes, bassoons, and basso continuo only.
Imitative entries give the impression that this section might continue indefinitely ("for ever and ever").	
"King of Kings" in uppermost (soprano) line, literally above all the other notes, perhaps to parallel God's position in relation to Earth. The melodic line reaches its highest point at 2:21.	Trumpets and timpani join in at 1:50.
Melodies 4, 5, and 1 together. Movement ends with the same melodic idea with which it began (1), suggesting the idea of God's eternal power.	Chorus, strings, oboes, bassoon, and basso continuo only. Trumpets and timpani join in at 2:39.

Student FAQs

Is the title of this work The Messiah *or* Messiah?

Handel called it simply *Messiah*, though the definite article started creeping into accounts of the work almost at once. Everyone would know what you mean if you called the work *The Messiah*, but *Messiah* is the correct title.

Annie Griffiths Belt/CORBIS—NY

Why is this work performed so often around Christmas?

Part 1 has a definite Christmas theme to it: the prophecy and birth of Christ. But Parts 2 and 3 belong more appropriately to Easter, as they deal with the Crucifixion and Resurrection. But like the tradition of standing for the "Hallelujah" chorus (see Historical Context, page 162), any tradition, once started, can take on a life of its own. And as shown here, choruses attract people of all ages.

Cleve Bryant/PhotoEdit Inc.

So the "Hallelujah" is not the end of the work?

No. It's the end of Part 2, and if the work is performed in its entirety, all of Part 3 follows. *Messiah* concludes with an enormous chorus on the word "Amen" that in its own way is as impressive as the "Hallelujah" chorus.

©Ellen B. Senisi/Ellen Senisi

HISTORICAL CONTEXT   Why Stand?

If you have ever attended a live performance of Handel's *Messiah*, chances are good that the entire audience stood up for the singing of the "Hallelujah" chorus. It is widely believed that this replicates the actions of King George II, who, during the London premiere of the work in 1743, was moved to rise because of the sheer beauty and majesty of the music. And when the king stands, everyone else stands, too—so the audience rose.

It is a good story, and it may even be true, but the fact is that we have no record of the king having attended any performance of any of Handel's oratorios after 1739. Newspapers and diarists of the time routinely took note of the king's comings and goings, especially to public events, so it seems likely that someone would have recorded this event had George II in fact attended *Messiah* at some point. The first report of the king's response comes to us from 1780, long after the death of not only Handel but of George II (1683–1760) as well.

Yet who is to say whether this actually happened or not? Proving a negative ("King George II never attended a performance of *Messiah*") is virtually impossible. Whatever its origin, the tradition of rising for the "Hallelujah" chorus has grown over time and today symbolizes the emotional connection listeners feel with this music.

A performance of Handel's *Messiah* in Westminster Abbey in 1784, with a massive chorus and orchestra.
Lebrecht Music & Arts/Lebrecht Music & Arts Photo Library

A *Messiah* sing-in at the University of Virginia. Many communities around the country organize public performances of *Messiah* around Christmas in which anyone—singers and instrumentalists, professional and amateur alike—can participate.
Courtesy of University of Virginia/McIntire Department of Music

EXPAND YOUR PLAYLIST

Covering the "Hallelujah Chorus"

When an artist interprets a song made famous by another artist, we call the new version a "cover." Musicians have been covering the celebrated "Hallelujah" from Handel's *Messiah* since the late eighteenth century, altering the orchestration, the tempo, and even the notes themselves. Here are some examples:

Wolfgang Amadeus Mozart
• *Der Messias* (1789). Mozart arranged several of Handel's oratorios for performance in Vienna, using a German translation of the text, lengthening and shortening some numbers, and adding new instruments—flutes, clarinets, bassoons, horns, and trombones.

Johnny Mathis
• "Hallelujah Chorus" (1972). A relatively standard version with orchestra and chorus, but with Mathis alone singing the tenor part.

The Roches
• "Hallelujah Chorus" (1982). An a cappella version—three voices, no instruments—by an ensemble of three women.

Quincy Jones (producer)
• *Handel's Messiah: A Soulful Celebration* (1992). A gospel-style rendition of *Messiah* performed by a variety of different artists, this album won the Grammy Award for Best Contemporary Soul Gospel Album in 1992.

Marin Alsop
• *Too Hot to Handel* (1993). A gospel-jazz-rock-funk version by a noted conductor who now directs the Baltimore Symphony Orchestra.

Mannheim Steamroller
• "Hallelujah" (2004). A purely instrumental version of the chorus, on rock instruments and synthesizers.

Relient K
• "Handel's Messiah: The Hallelujah Chorus" (2006). A rock interpretation that adds some counterpoint to the original in places and subtracts it in others.

((⦁ **HEAR SAMPLES** on **www.mymusiclab.com**

TEST YOURSELF on **www.mymusiclab.com**   Flashcards and chapter tests

PART 3 Summary

	Renaissance	Baroque
Texture	Polyphonic	Polyphonic and homophonic coexist
Melody	Lyrical, rarely virtuosic	Lyrical and declamatory (recitative) coexist; often virtuosic
Rhythm	Relatively smooth and flowing	Wider range of extremes, from smooth and flowing to choppy and irregular
Timbre	No sharp distinction between instrumental and vocal music	Sharp distinction between vocal and instrumental parts
Harmony	Harmony as a by-product of the relationship among polyphonic voices	Harmony as an underlying basis for melody
Form	Primarily sectional	Greater variety of formal principles: sectional form, binary form, theme and variations, ostinato
Word-music relationships	Limited use of word painting	Even greater use of word painting. Texture and musical affect strongly support text.

IN REVIEW: Baroque Style

Homophonic Texture A texture in which one voice predominates and the others support it.
- Monteverdi, *Orpheus* (Chapter 10)
- Purcell, *Dido and Aeneas* (Chapter 11)
- Strozzi, "Revenge" (Chapter 13)

Basso Continuo The group of instruments accompanying the lead voice in homophonic texture, playing the bass line ("basso") continuously, thereby allowing the solo voice to pursue its own melody, drop out, and return.
- Almost all the works in this part fall into this category except Bach's Fugue in G Minor, a purely polyphonic work for organ.

Recitative A style of singing midway between lyrical song and speech, usually syllabic (one note per syllable).
- Monteverdi, *Orpheus* (Chapter 10)
- Purcell, *Dido and Aeneas* (Chapter 11)
- Handel, *Messiah* (Chapter 19)

Word Painting While not an entirely new development, word painting—the depiction of specific words through music that imitates the meaning of those words—becomes particularly important in the Baroque Era.
- Monteverdi, *Orpheus* (Chapter 10)
- Purcell, *Dido and Aeneas* (Chapter 11)

- Strozzi, "Revenge" (Chapter 13)
- Bach, Cantata 140 (Chapter 18)
- Handel, *Messiah* (Chapter 19)

Ritornello Structure The regular alternation between sections for contrasting ensembles (soloist vs. orchestra; voices vs. instruments).
- Vivaldi, *The Four Seasons*, "Winter" (Chapter 15)
- Bach, Brandenburg Concerto no. 2 (Chapter 16)
- Bach, Cantata 140 (Chapter 18)

Program Music Instrumental music that is in some way associated with a story, event, or idea.
- Vivaldi, *The Four Seasons*, "Winter" (Chapter 15)

Binary Form The most common form for dance movements, consisting of two sections, each repeated in performance.
- Handel, *Water Music* (Chapter 17)

Ostinato A short repeated pattern of notes.
- Purcell, *Dido and Aeneas* (Chapter 11)

Counterpoint Two independent melodies, played simultaneously.
- Bach, Fugue in G Minor (Chapter 14)

☑ **TEST YOURSELF** on **www.mymusiclab.com**   Part Exam

PART 4 (1750–1800)
The Classical Era

A classic is something that endures. The music of what we now call the Classical Era was the first to thrive without interruption long after its time. Joseph Haydn (1732–1809) (chapters 20 and 22) and Wolfgang Amadeus Mozart (1756–1791) (chapters 23–25), the two leading composers of this era, wrote music that has never really gone out of fashion. The term "classical" also refers to Greek and Roman antiquity, which strongly influenced the arts and architecture of this period. As a new kind of thinking took hold, the Baroque love of ornamentation, virtuosity, and expressive extremes gave way to more classical ideals of balance, clarity, and naturalness.

The eighteenth century as a whole, but particularly the period between about 1720 and 1790, is known as the Age of Enlightenment. Enlightenment thought held that reason could bring humankind to a new age of splendor, freed from the dark superstitions of the past (hence "en*light*enment"). Science became more important during the Enlightenment. For Enlightenment artists and thinkers, the power to convince lay not in overwhelming displays of opulence or in larger-than-life drama aimed to influence the emotions, but rather in critical thinking and reasoned discussion, which persuaded the mind.

The music of the Classical Era reflects these principles of clarity, proportion, and what critics of the day called

The Classical Era ⊙→ EXPLORE MORE on www.mymusiclab.com

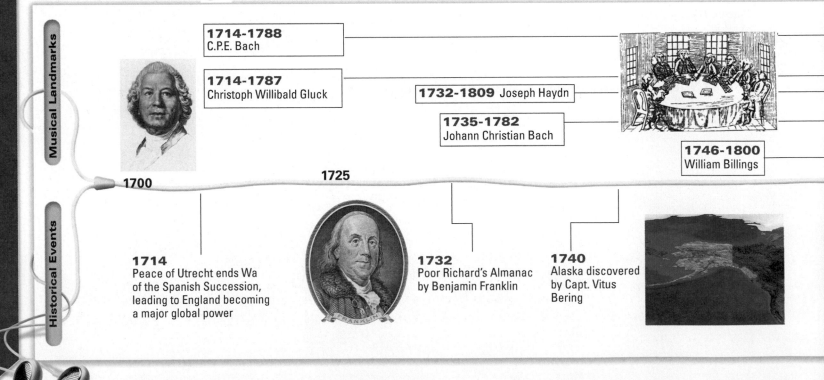

Musical Landmarks

1714-1788
C.P.E. Bach

1714-1787
Christoph Willibald Gluck

1732-1809 Joseph Haydn

1735-1782
Johann Christian Bach

1746-1800
William Billings

1700   1725

Historical Events

1714
Peace of Utrecht ends Wa of the Spanish Succession, leading to England becoming a major global power

1732
Poor Richard's Almanac by Benjamin Franklin

1740
Alaska discovered by Capt. Vitus Bering

"naturalness." Classical Era melodies are on the whole more tuneful, less complicated, and more balanced than those of the Baroque Era. More symmetrical melodic phrasing, based on the rhythms of dance music, extended itself across all genres, both vocal and instrumental. Critics of the day praised homophonic texture for its clarity and grace, and the dense textures of counterpoint became the exception rather than the rule. But this does not mean that music of the Classical Era is somehow simpler, for a typical movement of music from this period features more internal contrasts than its Baroque counterpart. A movement in sonata form, the most important new structural innovation of the Classical era—one used in Mozart's Symphony no. 40 in G Minor (chapter 23)—juxtaposes multiple themes that differ markedly in their melody, rhythm, harmony, dynamics, and timbre.

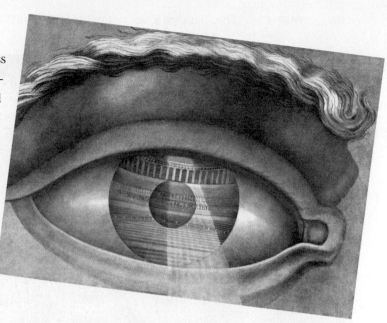

Music as the Language of the Heart

The string quartet—a work for two violins, viola, and cello—was another innovation of the Classical Era, and it is no coincidence that critics of the time spoke of works like Joseph Haydn's String Quartet in C Major, op. 76, no. 3 (chapter 20), as a rational conversation among four intelligent individuals. In the second movement, each of the

▲ This intriguing image captures the Enlightenment's ideal of the mind—the seat of reason—as the focal point of all perception.
Claude Nicolas Ledoux (1736–1806), "Eye enclosing the theatre at Besancon, France" 1847. Engraving.
© Bibliothèque des Arts Décoratifs, Paris, France. Archives Charmet/The Bridgeman Art Library. Out of copyright.

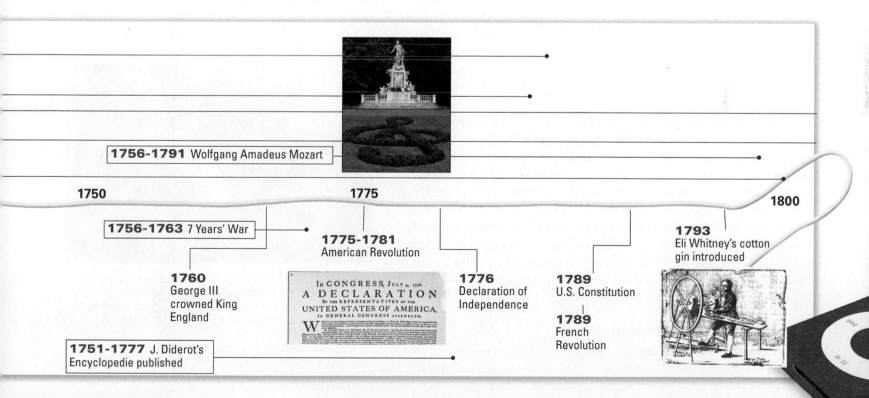

1756-1791 Wolfgang Amadeus Mozart

1750   1775   1800

1756-1763 7 Years' War

1775-1781 American Revolution

1793 Eli Whitney's cotton gin introduced

1760 George III crowned King England

IN CONGRESS, JULY 4, 1776.
A DECLARATION
BY THE REPRESENTATIVES OF THE
UNITED STATES OF AMERICA,
IN GENERAL CONGRESS ASSEMBLED.

1776 Declaration of Independence

1789 U.S. Constitution

1789 French Revolution

1751-1777 J. Diderot's Encyclopedie published

▲ Joseph Wright, *An Experiment on a Bird in the Air-Pump,* 1768. A scientist demonstrates the effect of a vacuum jar on a small bird. The young boy at the right lowers the cage for the bird, which will be revived when air is reintroduced to the bowl. Empirical science and the application of reason dominated Enlightenment thought.

© National Gallery, London/Art Resource, NY

instruments presents the theme in succession while the other three weave an ever-changing commentary around that theme. The melody itself, like many Classical melodies, consists of an opening (antecedent) and closing (consequent) phrase. Writers of the Enlightenment recognized the structural parallels with language and began to call instrumental music the "language of the heart." Instrumental music lacked the specificity of words (the "language of the mind") but the perception of it as a language of any kind helped raise the prestige of such genres as the string quartet, the symphony, and the concerto.

Music and Revolution

The plot of Wolfgang Amadeus Mozart's comic opera *The Marriage of Figaro* (1786) (chapter 25) would have been unthinkable only a generation before. Count Almaviva, a nobleman, is outwitted by his servants. This opera captures the growing mood of discontent with the established order of society in the decades leading up to the French Revolution. Basic ideas about human rights ("life, liberty, and the pursuit of happiness," to quote the U.S. Declaration of Independence) won growing acceptance during this time. Enlightenment social critics such as Voltaire (1694–1778) and Jean-Jacques Rousseau (1712–1778) argued for the innate goodness of human beings and for the rational pursuit of personal and societal betterment. The U.S. Declaration of Independence is a quintessential document of the Enlightenment, for it recognizes the inherent dignity of the individual. Its principal author, Thomas Jefferson, established the University of Virginia (see image) on the premise that the institution would be "based on the illimitable freedom of the human mind. For here we are not afraid to follow truth wherever it may lead, nor to tolerate any error so long as reason is left free to combat it."

The American Revolution (1775–1781) established the independence of the United States from Great Britain, and the French Revolution (1789) overthrew the power of what until that point had been the world's most powerful monarchy. The results affected not just the countries immediately involved, but ultimately every nation in the Western world. National independence and democracy, if not always realized in practice, became new ideals of social order. These new ideals, in turn, paved the way for new approaches to education, including the establishment of the first state-run conservatory of music, in Paris, in 1795. The leaders of the new French Republic and the monarchy they had just overthrown agreed on at least one point: that music was an important means of projecting cultural power.

▲ George Washington accepts the surrender of British troops at Yorktown in 1781, marking the end of the Revolutionary War. The military band present at the occasion played "Yankee Doodle" and a tune called "The World Turned Upside Down."

John Trumbull (American 1756–1843), "The Surrender of Lord Cornwallis at Yorktown, 19 October 1781", 1787–c. 1828. Oil on canvas, 53.3 x 77.8 x 1.9 cm (21 x 30 5/8 x 3/4 in.), 1832.4. Yale University Art Gallery/Art Resource, NY

Music and the New Economy

The second half of the eighteenth century witnessed the beginnings of an even more powerful revolution, one that would change everyday life throughout the Western world. Rapid advances in technology—the

◀ Thomas Jefferson's University of Virginia, shown in an early engraving. Jefferson designed the Rotunda after the Pantheon of ancient Rome. Symmetry is important in Classical architecture as well as in the music of the Classical Era, though on closer inspection very few structures—or melodies—prove entirely symmetrical. Each of the large houses for faculty in this "academical village" is slightly different from the others.

Tracy W. McGregor Library of American History, Special Collections, University of Virginia Library

steam engine, the cotton gin, and the principle of manufacturing based on interchangeable parts, to cite just a few examples—made it possible to produce goods on a far greater scale than ever before. Many national and local economies based on agriculture began to shift toward industry. Cities grew rapidly and this growth in urban populations in turn created new demands for cultural institutions of all kinds, including music.

While the churches and royal courts remained important centers of culture, theaters and concert halls open to the paying public began to flourish for the first time on a widespread scale. We see these changes in the careers of both Haydn and Mozart. Haydn worked almost all his adult life in the service of one aristocratic family, composing symphonies, sonatas, and operas according to the desires of his employers. By the 1790s, however, Haydn was lured away to England to write symphonies, including the Symphony no. 102 in B♭ Major (chapter 22), for a series of public concerts organized by a musical entrepreneur. Mozart left his native Salzburg at the age of 25 to seek his fortune in Vienna. He tried unsuccessfully to land a secure job at the imperial court there, but he managed to support himself reasonably well (for a time, at least) by giving public concerts, by writing operas, and by composing works that could be published and sold to music-loving amateurs. Composers had to write in ways that would appeal to this expanded audience even while maintaining the high standards of their craft. Works like the Piano Concerto in A Major, K. 488, (chapter 24) were the perfect lure for audiences intrigued by Mozart's virtuosity both as a composer and as a performer.

The Art of the Natural

Throughout the Classical Era, artists in every field looked to nature as a model. The ideal work of art, according to this view, was one that hid its artifice, that concealed its mechanical elements, and that appeared to be the product of effortless—natural—genius. Composers still had to learn technique and to study such topics as harmony and counterpoint with great diligence. The goal of all this study was not to show off one's art, but rather to touch the hearts of listeners in a manner that was direct and (seemingly) spontaneous.

This new aesthetic manifested itself in music in many ways. Melodies and ornamentation became less ornate. Textures on the whole tended more toward homophony than polyphony, homophony being the more "natural" of the two textures because it allowed the ear to focus on a single melody. In opera, plots and characters became more realistic. Mozart and others devoted great energies to the new genre of **opera buffa** or "comic opera," which portrayed real-life characters and situations, as opposed to the mythological and historical figures that populate so much of Baroque opera. In Mozart's *The Marriage of Figaro* (chapter 25), we can immediately identify with the emotions and actions of the characters because they are presented in a manner that is true to life, in a manner that is, in a word, natural.

▲ A family making music together in late 18th-century England.

Johann Zoffany (1733–1810), "George, 3rd Earl Cowper, with the Family of Charles Gore". 1775. Oil on Canvas.

Yale Center for British Art/Paul Mellon Collection. The Bridgeman Art Library, NY

The Classical Era CHAPTERS AT A GLANCE

1732–1809
Joseph Haydn
String Quartet in C Major,
op. 76, no. 3, second movement
Composed: 1797

GENRE
String Quartet

KEY CONCEPTS
Theme and variations form, periodic phrase structure, musical appropriation.

CHAPTER HIGHLIGHT
The Language of Instrumental Music
The string quartet embodies the idea of instrumental music as a language, a "conversation" among four intelligent individuals—two violins, a viola, and a cello—who use music rather than words to express themselves. The second movement of this quartet is a series of variations on a single theme; each instrument comes to the fore at some point to present its interpretation of this melody.
EXPAND YOUR PLAYLIST: Chamber Music and Solo Keyboard Music of the Classical Era: Haydn, Mozart, C. P. E. Bach, J. C. Bach

Master Musicians of the Ikuta-ryu
Cherry Blossom
Recorded: ca. 1965

GENRE
Japanese music

KEY CONCEPTS
Theme and variations form, pentatonic scale, tremolo, extramusical content.

CHAPTER HIGHLIGHT
Theme and Variations Form
A theme followed by a series of varied versions is a basic form in musical cultures throughout the world. In this piece for koto, a plucked stringed instrument from Japan, a Japanese folk melody provides the basis for a series of six variations.
EXPAND YOUR PLAYLIST: Zither-Dee-Dee: Zither music from Japan, China, Austria, and the United States

1732–1809
Joseph Haydn
Symphony no. 102 in B♭ Major, third and fourth movements
Composed: 1795

GENRE
Symphony

KEY CONCEPTS
Minuet form, rounded binary form, rondo form, finale, concert manners, concert programs.

CHAPTER HIGHLIGHT
Minuet Form; Rondo Form
The symphony was the largest, loudest, and most prestigious of all instrumental genres in the Classical Era. By the end of the eighteenth century, most symphonies included a minuet (a dance-inspired movement) and a finale, which often followed the conventions of rondo form.
EXPAND YOUR PLAYLIST: Haydn's Symphonies

1756–1791
Wolfgang Amadeus Mozart
Symphony no. 40 in G Minor, K. 550, first movement
Composed: 1788

GENRE
Symphony

KEY CONCEPTS
Sonata form, exposition, development, recapitulation, coda, modulation, contrasting themes and harmonic areas.

CHAPTER HIGHLIGHT
Sonata Form
Sonata form was the most important structural convention to emerge from the Classical Era. It provided the structural basis for the first movement of many symphonies, sonatas, and string quartets. It is a flexible format in which contrasting themes and harmonic areas are juxtaposed, transformed, and ultimately reconciled.
EXPAND YOUR PLAYLIST: Mozart's Symphonies

GLOBAL CONNECTION
KEY CONCEPT
Theme and Variations Form

1756–1791

Wolfgang Amadeus Mozart
Piano Concerto in A Major, K. 488, first movement
Composed: 1786

GENRE
Concerto

KEY CONCEPTS
Double-exposition concerto form, the cadenza.

CHAPTER HIGHLIGHT
The Classical Concerto
The concertos of the Classical Era combine the ritornello principle of the Baroque Era with the newer sonata form. A cadenza lets the soloist improvise.
EXPAND YOUR PLAYLIST: The Classical Concerto: C. P. E. Bach, J. C. Bach, Mozart, Haydn, Marianne Martinez

1756–1791

Wolfgang Amadeus Mozart
The Marriage of Figaro, Act I, "Cosa sento"
Composed: 1786

GENRE
Comic opera

KEY CONCEPTS
Opera, drama through music, relationship of dramatic and musical structures, accompanied recitative.

CHAPTER HIGHLIGHT
Comic Opera
Opera remained the most prestigious and lucrative genre throughout the Classical Era and inspired some of its greatest music. In addition to providing entertainment, the opera also served as a kind of pressure-release valve on social tensions: in Mozart's *Marriage of Figaro*, the servants outwit their master. In this scene, the musical form and singing styles reflect and reinforce the events on the stage.
EXPAND YOUR PLAYLIST: Opera in the Classical Era: Mozart and Christoph Willibald Gluck

GLOBAL CONNECTION

Jingju
The Reunion
Recorded: ca. 1970

GENRE
Chinese opera

KEY CONCEPTS
Opera, language tones, stock characters, pentatonic scale, metabole.

CHAPTER HIGHLIGHT
Recitative and Aria
In opera of both the West and the East, recitative or heightened speech often narrates dramatic action, while arias express the lyrical sentiments of the characters.
EXPAND YOUR PLAYLIST: Traditional Chinese Music

1746–1800

William Billings
"Chester"
Composed: 1770

GENRE
Song

KEY CONCEPTS
Hymn, periodic phrase structure, four-part harmony, melodic contour.

CHAPTER HIGHLIGHT
This song, the unofficial anthem of the American Revolution, follows the musical conventions of hymnody, with four voices moving in rhythm together.
EXPAND YOUR PLAYLIST: Music of the American Revolution

GLOBAL CONNECTION

GLOBAL CONNECTION
KEY CONCEPT
Opera

20 Joseph Haydn
String Quartet in C Major, op. 76, no. 3, second movement
Composed: 1797

The string quartet is often compared to a conversation among four friends. In the second movement of Joseph Haydn's String Quartet in C Major, op. 76, no. 3 each of the instruments—two violins, a viola, and a cello—presents the melody in succession while the other three weave their own "commentary" around it.

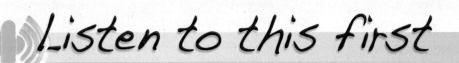

((• HEAR MORE on www.mymusiclab.com

Timbre

Listen to how the sounds of the four instruments blend together and stand apart. The registers of these instruments range from high (the two violins) to medium (the viola) to low (the cello), but their sound quality is similar.

Texture

Notice how the melody always appears in one of the instruments while the other three move around it. Is the texture homophonic or polyphonic? Also listen for the passages in which not all of the instruments are playing.

Melody

Listen for the pauses that break the melody into sections known as phrases. Which phrases sound like endings? Which demand a continuation of the music? Which phrases are repeated?

Form

Listen to the way the melody is first presented by one of the violins and then repeated with very little change by each of the other instruments across the course of the movement.

⚙ LEARN MORE on
www.mymusiclab.com
Chapter Objectives

A good melody is worth hearing again and again. But at some point, we also want to hear something different, either a different version of the melody or a different melody altogether. Composers use a combination of repetition, variation, and contrast to satisfy and sustain our interest as listeners. The second movement of Haydn's String Quartet in C Major, op. 76, no. 3, offers a good example of how music can deliver repetition, variation, and contrast all at the same time. The melody is from a song Haydn himself had written a few months earlier for the birthday of Holy Roman Emperor Franz II, who resided in Vienna. The song, set to the words "God save Franz, the Emperor," was an immediate hit with the public and soon became Austria's unofficial national anthem.

The melody was so closely associated with the emperor that Haydn faced a dilemma in writing variations on it. He decided he could not alter the melody itself, for the ideal emperor is steadfast and not subject to change. So he created an ingenious solution to this problem by repeating the emperor's theme more or less unchanged four times in succession, varying only the instrument that played it and writing contrasting musical lines to surround the theme each time. Thus, though the theme remains essentially the same throughout, it stays fresh because the voices surrounding it are constantly changing.

In setting this theme with variations for four instruments of similar timbre, Haydn imposed an additional challenge on himself. Without the full orchestra at his disposal, he could not rely on winds, brass, or timpani to create varieties of sound. This makes his accomplishment—a movement that sustains interest while repeating a melody four times—all the more remarkable.

Haydn was not the first to write string quartets, but he did more than any other composer to establish this new genre's significance from the middle of the eighteenth century onward. Not in spite of its timbral constraints but *because* of them, Haydn, Mozart, and later Beethoven all took up the challenge of writing for the string quartet repeatedly throughout their careers. By the end of the eighteenth century, the string quartet had acquired the reputation of being the most demanding of all musical genres, one that allowed composers to demonstrate their talents more fully.

The quartet is a decidedly intimate genre. In Haydn's time, it was usually performed in the home and only rarely in public concerts. Unlike the concerto, no soloist or small group of soloists stands out; instead, all four instrumentalists operate on an equal footing. Commentators since Haydn's day have repeatedly likened the string quartet to a conversation among four equal participants. The conversational aspect of the genre reinforced the sense that these works were written primarily for the pleasure of the performers. Listeners in private settings sometimes even compared themselves to eavesdroppers.

The typical string quartet of the Classical Era consisted of four contrasting movements:

1. The first movement, usually in a fast tempo, is most often written in what came to be known as "sonata form," the most significant new form to come out of the Classical Era. We will take up the sonata form in chapter 23 of this book, with Mozart's Symphony no. 40.

2. The second movement is usually in a slow tempo and a contrasting key. Slow movements could assume many different forms: sonata form, theme and variations, and **ABA** are the most common. (The movement that we are listening to here is a set of variations on a theme.)

3. The third movement is usually a minuet, a lively, stylized dance in triple meter, in the tonic key. We will take up the minuet in chapter 22 of this book, with Haydn's Symphony no. 102.

4. The fourth movement, also known as the finale, is a somewhat lighter and usually very fast movement. The most common forms used in finales are sonata form and rondo. We will take up the rondo in chapter 22 of this book, with Haydn's Symphony no. 102.

The Timbre of the String Quartet

The string quartet creates an unusually homogeneous timbre, for its instruments are all variants of the same basic instrument. The viola and cello are essentially larger and therefore deeper versions of the violin. Together, these four instruments correspond to the four standard ranges of the singing voice:

HIGHEST	Soprano:	Violin 1
	Alto:	Violin 2
	Tenor:	Viola
LOWEST	Bass:	Cello

Like any good vocal ensemble, the instruments of a string quartet can blend together to sound almost like a single instrument or emphasize their differences. The violin has a sweet, piercing sound, while the cello has a more resonant, richer tone. The viola creates a sound somewhere

1732–1809
Joseph Haydn
String Quartet in C Major,
op. 76, no. 3, second
movement
Composed: 1797

GENRE
String Quartet

KEY CONCEPTS
Theme and variations form,
periodic phrase structure, musical
appropriation.

CHAPTER HIGHLIGHT
**The Language of Instrumental
Music**
The string quartet embodies the
idea of instrumental music as a language, a "conversation" among
four intelligent individuals—two
violins, a viola, and a cello—who
use music rather than words to
express themselves. The second
movement of this quartet is a series
of variations on a single theme;
each instrument comes to the fore
at some point to present its interpretation of this melody.

SEE MORE on
www.mymusiclab.com
Inside the Orchestra:
"Violin", "Viola", "Cello"

A string quartet in performance. From left to right: violin 1, violin 2, viola, and cello.
Zdenek CHRAPEK/Lebrecht Music & Arts Photo Library

between these two extremes of high and low. It is particularly easy to compare the differences between the sounds of the individual instruments in this movement because Haydn gives the main theme to each at some point.

Changing Textures

Haydn expands the timbral variety of this movement by changing textures throughout. The theme is first presented in a hymn-like fashion, with the melody in the top voice (Violin 1) and the other instruments supporting it, moving at the same pace, rather like the chorale in the last movement of Bach's Cantata no. 140 (see chapter 18). The texture is homophonic. In Variation 1, Violin 2 carries the theme while Violin 1 weaves an intricate accompanimental figure around it: this is two-part homophony. In Variation 2, the cello carries the theme, with the three other voices weaving around it. Variation 3 begins with only three voices, with the melody in the viola and the cello silent; when the cello enters, Violin 1 drops out. Only later in this variation do we hear all four voices together. Variation 4 features four-part polyphony from beginning to end.

Melody: Periodic Phrase Structure

The melody of this movement is made of five phrases, each marked at the end by a cadence, a brief resting point:

- The first two phrases (labeled **A**) are the same.
- They are followed by a phrase that is not repeated (**B**).
- This is followed by two final phrases (**C**) that are the same.

Neither the **A** phrase nor the **B** phrase sounds complete at the end: with each, we expect the music to continue. Not until the end of the **C** phrase do we feel a sense of conclusion.

The structure of these units (**A**, **B**, and **C**) can be compared to the elements that make up a sentence. The opening **A** and **B** sections act as **antecedent** phrases (*ante* = before), while **C** functions as a **consequent** phrase (*sequent* = following). As in a sentence, an antecedent phrase sets up a consequent phrase and the two together make a complete sentence.

Antecedent phrase 1	Antecedent phrase 2	Consequent phrase
If I'm still here tomorrow,	and if you're back,	I'll stop by your place.
comma	*comma*	*period*

Neither of the antecedent phrases here is complete: we expect each to continue. In Haydn's melody, neither the **A** nor the **B** phrase of the melody sounds complete because neither finishes on the tonic (home) note of the key. Phrases **A** and **B** both end on the note D, which creates a certain sense of arrival but not closure. These points of arrival are called **half cadences**: they create a moment of punctuation more like a comma than a period. But the melody of the **C** phrase ends on the main note of the tonic key (G), and for that reason, we call it a **full cadence**, and we hear its arrival as a moment of closure.

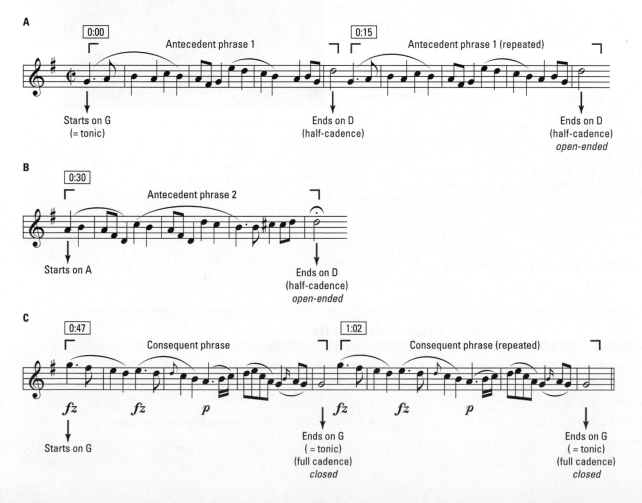

PROFILE   Joseph Haydn (1732–1809)

Writing to Order

It is hard to imagine any individual having his or her own orchestra at home nowadays, but that's exactly what Prince Nicholas Esterházy had in the second half of the eighteenth century in Vienna.

For almost three decades, Joseph Haydn was the prince's music director, responsible for writing new music, conducting the orchestra, and keeping order among the musicians, who could be a rowdy bunch at times. Fortunately for Haydn, Prince Nicholas (known far and wide as "The Magnificent") was willing to spend huge amounts of money on music, and Haydn was thus in charge of one of the best orchestras in all of Europe.

"My Prince was satisfied with all of my works," Haydn told one of his biographers late in life, "and I received applause. As the director of an orchestra, I could make experiments, observe what elicited or weakened an impression, and thus correct, add, delete, take risks. I was cut off from the world, no one in my vicinity could cause me to doubt myself or pester me, and so I had to become original." Haydn wrote whatever works the prince requested: string quartets, operas, sonatas. In fact, his original contract required him to appear in uniform every morning before the prince and receive instructions as to what kinds of works he was to compose.

The death of Prince Nicholas in 1790 opened a new chapter in Haydn's life. He made two extended tours to England, where he composed symphonies, songs, and a number of works for piano. After returning to Vienna for good in 1795, he produced two highly successful oratorios (*The Creation* and *The Seasons*), a handful of Masses, and several of his finest string quartets. The young Ludwig van Beethoven was one of his last composition pupils.

Joseph Haydn, in a portrait done during his years in London in the 1790s.

Thomas Hardy "Joseph Haydn (Franz Joseph) Composer" 1792. Painting London, (active 1778–1801). London, Royal College of Music. AKG London.

◉➔ **EXPLORE MORE** on **www.mymusiclab.com**

EXPAND YOUR PLAYLIST: HAYDN

- String Quartet in E♭, op. 33, no. 2 . Nicknamed "The Joke" because of its comical ending.

- String Quartet in D Major, op. 76, no. 5

- Piano Sonata in E♭ Major, Hob. XVI: 53

- *The Creation*. An oratorio based on the book of Genesis; the opening is a purely instrumental representation of Chaos.

((•● **HEAR SAMPLES** on **www.mymusiclab.com**

HISTORICAL CONTEXT   Musical Appropriation

Music is often used in ways its composers could never imagine. **Musical appropriation** is the use or adaptation of a work to serve something other than its original purpose. The melody Haydn wrote in honor of Emperor Franz II became so popular that many different poets set new words to it:

- One text praised the people of Hamburg.
- Several praised rulers other than Franz II.
- Another text (in Latin) came from the Book of Psalms.
- Several other texts praised God.

   The most famous of all the new texts, though, was "Germany Above All Else" ("Deutschland über alles"), written in 1841 by the German poet August Heinrich Hoffmann von Fallersleben. This song would eventually become the German national anthem, though only the third strophe is used today.

   A work setting new words to an established melody is known as a **contrafactum**. Nothing prevents any person or institution—a political party, a nation, a church—from appropriating an existing melody, often in ways that are quite different from the purpose of the original. Often new lyrics turn the original song on its head. The British national anthem, "God Save the King," provided the melody for "My Country, 'tis of Thee," one of the most popular of all patriotic songs in the breakaway colonies of North America. The tune now known as "The Star-Spangled Banner" first accompanied a text that was originally a drinking song.

This kind of phrase structure, with antecedent and consequent units that together make a larger whole, is called **periodic phrase structure**. The term "periodic" comes from the Latin word for sentence—*periodus*, the same word for the mark of punctuation that indicates the end of a sentence—emphasizing the link between musical and linguistic structures. Periodic phrase structure provides the basis for many melodies from different eras of music, but it is particularly associated with music of the Classical Era.

The Theme and Variations Form

The **theme and variations form** was an extremely popular form throughout the Classical Era. It is a basically simple structure: a theme is presented and then altered in some way—through harmony, melody, texture, dynamics, or some combination of these—in a succession of individual variations.

   Composers often used well-known themes as the basis of new variations. Mozart, for example, wrote a set of variations on the French song "Ah, vous dirai-je, maman" (better known as "Twinkle, Twinkle, Little Star"; see Expand Your Playlist), and Beethoven later wrote a set on the melody to "God Save the King" (better known in the United States as "My Country 'tis of Thee").

   Haydn's unusual move—to keep the theme almost completely intact in each variation, altering only its register (the instrument) and changing the other three voices around the theme—takes on symbolic significance when one considers that the theme began as a birthday melody celebrating his emperor. The constancy of the melody can be heard as a portrait of the constancy of Emperor Franz. Circumstances around him may change, the music seems to say, but the emperor himself remains unchanged.

Now listen to this movement again, using the Listening Guide.

CONNECT YOUR PLAYLIST

Musical Appropriation

Find a work that has been appropriated for a purpose quite different from that for which it was originally created.

Example: Of Montreal, "Wraith Pinned to the Mist (and Other Games)" (2005) This song by the indie band Of Montreal appeared with altered lyrics in a series of commercials for the restaurant chain Outback Steakhouse.

GO TO www.mymusiclab.com
for the Automated Listening Guide
CD II •Track 8/Download Track 43

Listening Guide

Joseph Haydn Composed 1797 String Quartet in C Major, op. 76, no. 3, second movement (6:46)

Time	Formal Section	Melodic Phrases	Timbre
0:00	Theme	A (0:00) A (0:15) B (0:30) C (0:47) C (1:02)	Theme in the first violin
1:18	Variation 1	A (1:18) A (1:32) B (1:45) C (1:59) C (2:12)	Theme in the second violin
2:27	Variation 2	A (2:27) A (2:42) B (2:57) C (3:13) C (3:29)	Theme in the cello
3:45	Variation 3	A (3:45) A (3:59) B (4:14) C (4:28) C (4:42)	Theme in the viola
4:58	Variation 4	A (4:58) A (5:14) B (5:30) C (5:46) Now moved to a very high range, the highest in the entire movement C (6:01) In a very high range again	Theme in the first violin
6:15	Coda	Cadential passage	Cadential material in first violin

Texture

Homophonic. Hymn-like, with all four voices moving at the same speed.

Homophonic. The first violin plays a rapid accompanimental figure, while the lower voices (viola and cello) are silent.

Polyphonic. The other three voices are playing lines that have distinctive profiles of their own and are not merely accompanimental.

Polyphonic. As in Variation 2, the other three instruments play lines that have distinctive profiles of their own and are not merely accompanimental.

Polyphonic. Same as in Variations 2 and 3.

Student FAQs

I can't always tell the difference among the four instruments. The cello in Variation 2 and the viola in Variation 3 sound almost the same. Is this a problem?

The three kinds of instruments used in a string quartet all overlap to some degree. So a cello, like the one pictured here, playing in a high range is in fact playing some of the same pitches as a viola, and a viola in its high range covers many of the notes available on the lower end of the violin's range. There is a difference in the quality of sound of the instruments, however, and it is worth listening closely for this difference. If you are able to experience a live performance of this work, or at least watch a video of a live performance, the visual cues will help reinforce the individual qualities of the instruments. Photos.com

Without a conductor, who leads the quartet in performance?

As any string player will tell you, playing in a quartet is very different from playing in an orchestra. A quartet is a collaborative enterprise: the players discuss and agree among themselves in rehearsal about such matters as tempo, phrasing, and dynamics. In performance, the first violinist, such as the one pictured here, gives subtle indications to lead the other players, often through a glance, a raised eyebrow, or a slight gesture of the head. But at times other players might give such signals, depending on which instrument leads at any given moment. The longer a group has performed together, the better the individual members know one another's manner of playing, and the more subtle the gestures.

Photos.com

Chamber Music and Solo Keyboard Music of the Classical Era

The second half of the eighteenth century witnessed a tremendous growth in amateur music making at home. New printing technologies had reduced the cost of sheet music, and the fortepiano (a new instrument, the forerunner of the modern-day piano) was less expensive than the harpsichord (the principal domestic keyboard instrument of the Baroque Era). The string quartet was one of several genres intended primarily for use in the home.

Joseph Haydn

- String Quartet in E♭ Major, op. 76, no. 6. The first movement is a set of variations on a theme.

- Piano Trio in G Major, Hob. XV: 25. The piano trio is an ensemble consisting of a piano, a violin, and a cello. The finale of this particular trio is a rondo "in the Hungarian Style," often called the "Gypsy Rondo."

Wolfgang Amadeus Mozart

- String Quartet in C Major, K. 456. The slow introduction to the first movement has so many clashing sounds that the entire quartet is known as the "Dissonance" Quartet.

- String Quartet in D Major, K. 575. One of three quartets Mozart wrote for the king of Prussia, who was a cellist, this work includes an unusually prominent cello part.

- Variations on "Ah vous dirai-je, maman," K. 265. A set of variations for piano on the tune known as "Twinkle, Twinkle, Little Star."

- Piano Sonata in A Major, K. 331. The finale is a rondo "alla Turca" ("in the Turkish style"), imitating what Mozart thought music from the Ottoman Empire sounded like.

Carl Philipp Emanuel Bach

- Fantasia in C Minor, H. 75. A fantasia is a work that follows no formal conventions, guided only by the composer's fantasy. A writer set the words of Hamlet's celebrated monologue "To be or not to be . . ." to this fantasia. C. P. E. Bach (1714–1788) was one of several of Johann Sebastian Bach's sons who had distinguished musical careers.

Johann Christian Bach

- Keyboard Sonata in D Major, op. 5, no. 2. The young Mozart liked this solo sonata (which could be played on harpsichord or piano) so well that he rearranged it as a piano concerto. J. C. Bach (1735–1782), another son of J. S. Bach, was known as the "London Bach" because he lived there for so long.

((•● **HEAR SAMPLES** on **www.mymusiclab.com**

✓ **TEST YOURSELF** on **www.mymusiclab.com**   Flashcards and chapter tests

Master Musicians of the Ikuta-ryu
Cherry Blossom
Recorded: ca. 1965

A theme followed by a series of variations is a basic form used in musical cultures throughout the world. In *Cherry Blossom* the koto, a plucked stringed instrument from Japan, plays a Japanese folk melody that provides the basis for a series of six variations.

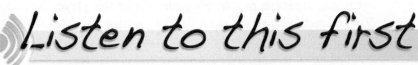 *Listen to this first*

((∙ HEAR MORE on www.mymusiclab.com

Timbre	Melody	Form	Texture
Listen for the variety of sounds produced by different plucking and strumming techniques.	Listen to the three different sections of the melody and to the direction in which each moves.	Identify the melody when it enters, then listen for the ways it is varied throughout the piece.	Listen to the way the texture changes from homophonic to polyphonic in the middle of the piece, and then back again to homophonic. How many players are there?

The koto is a plucked zither with 13 silk strings stretched over its wooden board. The strings of the koto are tightly stretched across the board and are supported by 13 moveable bridges that are adjusted during tuning. The player wears three ivory *plectra* (picks) on the right thumb and first two fingers for plucking the strings. Traditionally, players used the left hand to the left of the bridge to press a string to raise its pitch, and, conversely, to pull a string to lower its pitch. In the modern technique used in this performance of *Cherry Blossom*, the player's left hand plucks in alternation with the right hand to execute rapid passages.

Koto music originated in the Japanese court as early as the eighth century, when a variety of instruments were brought from the Korean Paekche kingdom to the Japanese Fujiwara regent. Early koto music does not survive because it was an oral tradition; that is, it was learned and transmitted without the aid of written notation. The koto was used for the private entertainment of the nobles, and it was also integrated with other court instruments for ceremonies.

During Japan's Edo Period and the reign of the Tokugawa Shoguns (Japanese rulers), from 1603 to 1867, the theme and variations form became well developed in this part of the world. This period happens to coincide in part with the era in which Joseph Haydn wrote his String Quartet in C Major, op. 76, no. 3 (which we discussed in chapter 20), though there is no evidence of influence in either direction. Cultural and commercial contacts between Japan and

⚙ **LEARN MORE** on
www.mymusiclab.com
Chapter Objectives

👁 **SEE MORE** on
www.mymusiclab.com
Ishigure Masayo performs the piece "Torino yo-ni" on the koto.

The koto originated in the region that includes what is now Japan and Korea.

the Western world were extremely limited at this time. What this similarity of musical forms demonstrates, instead, is the ways in which different cultures have applied similar means to achieve very different musical ends.

Popular koto playing is believed to date back to the early seventeenth century, when a blind musician named Yatsuhashi Kengyo learned the art of koto playing from a palace musician. A number of methods for learning koto technique and improvisation developed later. With these schools of playing, known as *ryu*, a notation system developed that uses *kanji* (Chinese-Japanese pictographs) that direct the player but allow for some creativity. This education method is still in use today, and it takes up most of a musician's adolescent and young adult life. Students learn the *ryu* in private institutions and universities throughout Japan, and graduation confers upon the player the title of master.

Through the centuries, koto masters have often been women, many of them geisha—"geisha" translates literally as "arts person" (see Historical Context, page 186). The koto is now used in ensembles and for vocal accompaniment as well as for solo works such as *Cherry Blossom*. Modern Japanese composers still compose for it.

The Timbre of the Koto

The focused, penetrating sound of the koto comes from the tension of its strings, which produce few overtone partials. As we saw in the Elements section under "Timbre" (page 1), partials are frequencies that resonate with the fundamental sound wave to create a richer quality of sound. Western violins and acoustic guitars, for example, produce more partials than the koto and have a correspondingly fuller tone. The characteristically tense timbre of the koto is highly

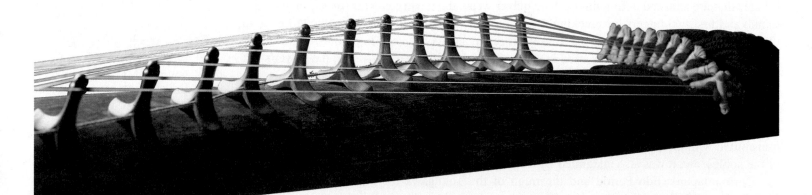

This closeup of a koto shows the strings stretched across its soundboard. They are held by 13 footed bridges that can be moved to change the tuning of the instrument.

Photos.com

valued within traditional Japanese musical culture, and a similar tone may also be heard in Japanese vocal music.

Melody: The Wilt of Sorrow

The word *sakura* means "cherry blossom." The melody is a popular Japanese folk tune with a sad sentiment; cherry blossoms are beautiful but short lived, and the Japanese perceive this as sorrowful. The variations on *Cherry Blossom* portray a cherry blossom's various stages of blossoming and wilting. In a broader sense, they symbolize the human life cycle. Like the *Cherry Blossom* variations, many Japanese melodies have **extramusical** connotations, which means that the music refers to ideas (such as a dying flower) outside of the sound. This is in some ways the equivalent of program music in Western music (see chapter 15). The piece is shaped by its relationship to the title, and a title may be associated with an idea, story, or event. A listener may choose to listen to the piece with the extramusical idea in mind or just listen to the music as it unfolds.

On this recorded example of *Cherry Blossom*, the master musician first plucks through a short section devoted to testing and tuning the instrument's strings. This tuning is considered part of the performance, and it serves as a prelude. After this short prelude, the musician introduces the *Cherry Blossom* melody. It is in the *in* mode, a particularly sorrowful-sounding Japanese tonal sequence similar to the European minor mode. The *in* mode consists of five tones. Five-tone modes, also known as **pentatonic scales**, have long appeared in Asian music and in the folk music of Europe and the Americas, but were not taken up by Western classical music until the nineteenth century.

Form: Theme and Variations

After the theme is played, the master koto musician then performs six variations on it, all with different plucking and strumming techniques that create rhythmic and timbral variety. Before the final variation, the koto master performs an improvisation around the theme's phrases, **A**, **B**, and **C**. The variations are learned by rote as part of the *ryu*, but the improvised section is freely played from the musician's inner creativity, which is part of being a master.

Textural Variety on the Koto

Although this work is performed by only one musician, the technique of right- and left-hand alternation results in the performance sounding as though it were played by two musicians, sometimes homophonic and other times polyphonic. The right hand steadily plays the theme's phrases each time they occur, while the left hand creates variations around them.

Now listen to this piece again, using the Listening Guide.

Master Musicians of the Ikuta-ryu
Cherry Blossom
Recorded: ca. 1965
GENRE
Japanese music
KEY CONCEPTS
Theme and variations form, pentatonic scale, tremolo, extramusical content.
CHAPTER HIGHLIGHT
Theme and Variations Form
A theme followed by a series of varied versions is a basic form in musical cultures throughout the world. In this piece for koto, a plucked stringed instrument from Japan, a Japanese folk melody provides the basis for a series of six variations.

CONNECT YOUR PLAYLIST
Theme and Variation

Find a piece that contains a melodic theme followed by a series of variations

Example: Jerry Lee Lewis, "Good Golly, Miss Molly" (1964) Each successive statement of the theme is varied.

Listening Guide

GO TO www.mymusiclab.com
for the Automated Listening Guide
CD II • Track 9/Download Track 44

Master Musicians of the Ikuta-ryu Recorded: ca. 1965 *Cherry Blossom* (3:08)

Time	Form: Section	Melody	Timbre
0:00	Tuning Prelude	Introduction	Penetrating and focused tones plucked melodically throughout the instrument's range.
0:19	Theme	A (0:19) B (0:23) C (0:28) B (0:32) C (0:37) A (0:41) Ending (0:46)	Theme plucked by the right hand with a full timbre. The accompaniment is plucked by the left hand; the tense, higher-register strings create a piercing sound.
0:52	Variation 1	A (0:52) B (0:57) C (1:01)	The right hand plucks the theme in three-note rhythmic groupings. The tones are more connected but accented, creating a stronger timbre.
1:06	Variation 2	A (1:06) B (1:11) C (1:15)	Rapid left-hand variation in four-note rhythmic groupings. The timbre becomes smooth and fuller.
1:20	Variation 3	B (1:20) C (1:24) Slight pause before next variation (1:28)	The tense higher-register strings now sound detached and penetrating.
1:30	Variation 4	A (1:30) B (1:37) C (1:44)	Theme played slowly, with right hand tremolo. The tremolo creates a "shivering" effect (mood).
1:50	Variation 5	A (1:50) B (1:57) Ending (2:01)	Theme with more rapid tremolo, further intensifying the "shivering" effect. There is then an adjusted tuning, giving a different timbre to those changed tones.
2:08	Improvisation	Through-composed variations on phrase fragments.	Rapid, penetrating, and focused tones, as the musician plucks with extreme speed.
2:33	Variation 6	A (2:33) B (2:36) C (2:39) A (2:42) B (2:45) C (2:49) A (2:52) B (2:54) Ending (2:27–3:06)	Theme played with extreme speed and set by the tempo of the improvisation. Each repetition of the theme is faster.

Texture

Monophonic. Strings are individually tested and tuned by both hands in alternation.

Homophonic. The left hand plays an accompanimental figure around the phrases, increasing in speed around the B and C phrases.

Homophonic. The left-hand variation accompanies the theme in rhythm.

Polyphonic. The left-hand variation is independent and moves much faster than before, like flowing water.

Polyphonic. The left-hand variation is in triplets, like raindrops falling.

Homophonic. The left hand strums an accompaniment in rhythm and then plucks a pattern.

Homophonic. The left hand continues to strum in accompaniment to the theme.

Homophonic. The left hand accompanies the right hand improvisation.

Homophonic. The left hand accompanies the theme.

Student FAQs

How does the koto player create the wide vibrato that I hear on this recording?

There is considerable play in the strings of the koto; unlike a guitar string, which is kept at a fairly high tension, the koto string can be moved up and down easily by pressing on it with the fretting hand as you can see these players doing. As the player presses down on the string, the pitch is raised. A talented player can create everything from a slight to a very wide vibrato using this method.

iStockphoto.com

Why does Japanese music sound foreign to me?

Like other forms of world music, Japanese music uses a "gapped" scale; instead of having seven notes, typically Japanese scales have only five notes. (These are also called pentatonic scales.) Western ears are used to hearing melodies based on seven tones, and so these missing notes—or gaps—can make the music sound odd or foreign to us.

Why is the koto so soft compared to Western string instruments?

The koto's strings are made of silk, while the strings on many modern violins are made of a synthetic material such as nylon or steel. The silk strings are also at a lower tension than violin strings, so they don't vibrate as efficiently. The koto soundboard is a simple, slightly arched board, which does little to amplify the vibrations of the strings, whereas the violin's sound chamber—the inside of the instrument's body—is very efficient at amplifying the sound of its strings (see A Closer Look: The Violin, page 132). All these factors combine to make the sound produced by the koto very soft. Because the koto was designed to be played in small rooms or with only a few other instruments, there was no need for it to be louder. In modern concert halls, the koto's sound is usually amplified by a microphone.

HISTORICAL CONTEXT Geisha in Japanese Life

The stereotyped image of the geisha as a paid companion who caters to the whims of her male patrons is—like many stereotypes—only partially true. In fact, geisha are more like paid performers than they are servants or—as commonly believed—prostitutes. Geisha are paid for their accomplishments as musicians, dancers, and experts in the tea ceremonies and other ceremonial practices enjoyed by their clients.

To become geisha, young girls were often sold into a kind of indentured service by their parents. They went through rigorous training that took years to complete. The final part of this training focused on the traditional arts, and many geisha became renowned for their talents at playing traditional instruments, including the koto or *shamisen* (a kind of plucked lute), and singing and dancing.

Geisha must be single. They often have a sole patron who supports them by underwriting their education, clothing, and other expenses. However, the relationship is never sexual. A geisha must retire if she marries. Many also retire to become music and dance teachers. Arthur Golden's *Memoirs of a Geisha*, published in 2005, provides a sensitive, realistic portrait of a geisha.

Yuki Yamada playing the Japanese koto. The long-bodied zither is placed on a table or directly on the floor. Notice how the individual bridges are placed at various places to tune the strings to the correct pitches.

Photograph © 2003 Jack Vartoogian/FrontRowPhotos. ALL RIGHTS RESERVED.

EXPAND YOUR PLAYLIST

Zither-Dee-Dee

The koto is one type of zither; various other types are found around the world.

Japan
• Nanae Yoshimura. *The Art of the Koto, Vol. 1*. Celestial Harmonies B00004X0T4.
This is the first of five CDs showing the development of koto music from the seventeenth century to today.

• Satomi Saeki, koto, and Alcvin Takegawa Ramos, shakuhaci. *Japanese Traditional Koto and Shakuhachi Music*. Oliver Sudden Productions B000CQNIHY.
Traditional pieces played on the low-voiced Japanese flute (shakuhachi) and koto.

China
• Zhiming Han on yangqin and Hsinmei (Cynthia) Hsiang on zheng (Chinese zither). *Celestial Echo: Live Performance on Yangqin—Chinese Butterfly Harp and Zheng*. Plectrum Recordings B000W1MJV0.

Duets on the Chinese hammer dulcimer (or yangqin) and the zheng (a long zither, similar to the Japanese koto).

Austria
• *Anton Karas: First Man of the Zither*. Jasmine Music B00006J9M2. Played on the Austrian zither, Karas's famous theme for the 1949 thriller *The Third Man*, starring Joseph Cotton and Orson Welles, was a top pop hit in its day.

United States
• *Dulcimer World: Kevin Roth*. Star Gazer Productions B000CAKC3I. A selection of popular and traditional melodies played on a range of Appalachian dulcimers.

((• HEAR SAMPLES on **www.mymusiclab.com**

✓ **TEST YOURSELF** on **www.mymusiclab.com** Flashcards and chapter tests

Joseph Haydn

Symphony no. 102 in B♭ Major, third and fourth movements

Composed: 1795

The third and fourth movements of Haydn's Symphony no. 102 are part of a four-movement symphony written for a concert series in London in 1795. The third movement is a minuet, a stylized dance movement, while the fourth movement is a rondo, a rollicking finale to the symphony as a whole.

 Listen to this first

((• HEAR MORE on www.mymusiclab.com

Timbre	**Dynamics**	**Form**
Listen for the breadth of sound from the full orchestra: many strings (first and second violins, violas, cellos, double basses), winds (flutes, oboes, bassoons), brass (horns and trumpets), and percussion (timpani, also known as "kettledrums").	Listen for the frequent changes in dynamics between very loud and very soft.	Listen for the return of the opening idea in each movement.

Listeners hear music against the backdrop of their times. In the middle of World War II, audiences in the United States rejected Igor Stravinsky's unusual harmonization of "The Star-Spangled Banner" for orchestra (see page 9). Twenty-five years later, during the Vietnam War, listeners at Woodstock embraced Jimi Hendrix's jarring, distorted rendition of the melody on the electric guitar.

The backdrop in London 1795 was revolution and its aftermath. Among the audience at the premiere of Haydn's Symphony no. 102 in B♭ Major were French aristocrats who had only recently fled the bloody Reign of Terror that followed the French Revolution. The English press and public were now debating at length how to reconcile the three goals of the French Revolution: "liberty and equality"—personal freedom and democracy—with "fraternity," the need for social order.

Some in Haydn's audience heard this social ideal realized in the sound of this symphony. A large number of varied instruments—strings, winds, percussion—contributed uniquely and in equal measure to an all-encompassing harmony. It was a mirror of the ideal society. And unlike chamber music works such as the string quartet, played in small spaces and private homes, the symphony brought large numbers of the public together to hear music give voice to their personal and collective aspirations.

LEARN MORE on www.mymusiclab.com
Chapter Objectives

Haydn was already well known when he came to London from Austria (see The Composer Speaks, page 190).

Haydn's London audiences could not get enough of his symphonies. By the time he had finished his two extended visits to the English capital (1791–1792, 1794–1795), he had written 12 altogether. Each of these "London" symphonies follows a standard pattern of four movements, along the lines of the typical string quartet (see chapter 20).

1. First movement: A substantial movement in a fast tempo, usually in what is known as *sonata form* (we will discuss this form on page 198).

2. Second movement: Another substantial movement, but in a slow tempo and in a contrasting key. Slow movements assume many different forms: sonata form, theme and variations, and **ABA** are the most common.

3. Third movement: A minuet, a lively, stylized dance in triple meter, in the tonic key. Minuets are always in ternary form (**ABA**), with the **A** and **B** sections each consisting of a binary form. The third movement we are listening to follows this form.

4. Fourth movement: A somewhat lighter and usually very fast movement. The most common forms used in the finale are sonata form and rondo. The finale of Haydn's Symphony no. 102 is a rondo.

The Timbre of the Full Orchestra

The size of an orchestra performing a symphony can vary widely, depending on the composer's instructions, the availability of players, and the size of the concert hall. In Haydn's time, a large orchestra would have consisted of strings (about 8–10 first violins, 6–8 second violins, 4–6 violas, 3–4 cellos, and 2 double basses), winds (2 flutes, 2 oboes, 2 bassoons, 2 trumpets, and 2 horns), and percussion (timpani, also known as "kettledrums"). Listen to the ways in which these various instruments and groups of instruments combine and contrast with one another. Haydn uses the full orchestra judiciously. We hear all the instruments playing together at times, but more often we hear smaller groups of instruments: just the strings, or just the winds, or just the winds and percussion. The variety of sound available from the possible combinations is enormous.

The Dynamics of Surprise

Changes in dynamics can help guide our listening. The entire middle section ("trio") of the third movement of Symphony no. 102, for example, is played softly, which helps set it off against the two mostly loud outer sections. Whether we realize it or not, we also have certain expectations about dynamics. When we hear a very soft passage for a long stretch, we begin to anticipate the music getting loud again. Haydn always obliges, but not always in the ways we expect. Sometimes the music stays unusually soft for much longer than we think it will, such as at the very beginning of the finale (the fourth movement). When the full orchestra comes in, after almost a whole minute, we feel a sense that what we have long anticipated has at last arrived.

While the full orchestra often plays at a very loud volume, as might be expected, dynamics operate independently of the number or combination of the instruments that happen to be playing. Even a large number of instruments playing together can create a soft sound.

(1) Third Movement: Minuet

The minuet is a courtly, elegant dance, although it often assumes a playful character in Haydn's hands. Like all minuets, this one is in triple meter, with an accent on the first beat of each measure (**1**-2-3, **1**-2-3, etc.).

Minuet Form

In **minuet form**, the opening section, known as the minuet proper (**A**), is followed by a contrasting trio (**B**), which is followed by a repeat of the minuet proper, thus creating the pattern **ABA**. This is called **ternary form**.

A: The minuet proper

- Is in **binary form** (see page 141), with two sections, each of which is repeated in performance.
- About halfway through the second section, the opening idea returns in the tonic key, "rounding out" the form. This creates what is known as **rounded binary form**.

B: The trio

- Is also in binary form (two sections).
- The trio provides a contrasting theme and mood to the minuet proper.
- At the end of the trio stands the Italian phrase *da capo*, meaning literally "from the head," or as we would say more colloquially in English, "from the top" or "from the beginning." This indicates that the orchestra is to play the minuet proper again.

A: The return of the minuet proper

- The performers return to the beginning, and the movement as a whole ends with the end of the minuet proper (the **A** section).
- Many modern-day ensembles omit the repetition of these sections the second time around.

This structural pattern—**ABA**—was used frequently in the Classical Era. Composers continued to use it on occasion throughout the nineteenth century and into the twentieth.

(2) Fourth Movement: Finale

The last movement of Haydn's Symphony no. 102—its **finale**—is lighter in tone than the other movements, a "happy ending" to the cycle of the work's four movements. In this respect, it is very typical of the symphonic finale in the Classical Era. Haydn, Mozart, and other composers of the time liked to use the rondo form in the finale of symphonies and other multi-movement works (sonatas, string quartets, etc.) because rondos are jaunty and bright, and their principal melodies are often quite catchy.

1732–1809
Joseph Haydn
Symphony no. 102 in
B♭ Major, third and
fourth movements
Composed: 1795

GENRE
Symphony

KEY CONCEPTS
Minuet form, rounded binary form, rondo form, finale, concert manners, concert programs.

CHAPTER HIGHLIGHT
Minuet Form; Rondo Form
The symphony was the largest, loudest, and most prestigious of all instrumental genres in the Classical Era. By the end of the eighteenth century, most symphonies included a minuet (a dance-inspired movement) and a finale, which often followed the conventions of rondo form.

THE COMPOSER SPEAKS Haydn in London

Written a week after Haydn arrived in England, this fascinating letter was addressed to Maria Anna von Genzinger, a talented pianist who lived in Vienna. It reminds us of the physical and emotional distance the composer had traveled from his native Austria. When Haydn arrived in London, he was already a celebrity. He granted interviews to three newspapers and received invitations to dine at the highest levels of English society. Only a few months before, he had been going about his daily routine in remote Esterháza, his patrons' palace in the Hungarian countryside.

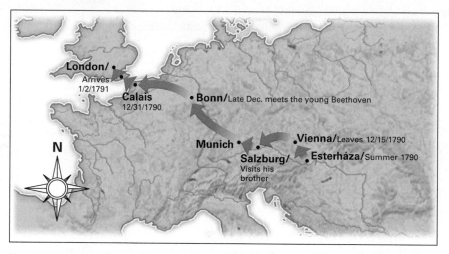

Haydn's trip to London began in Esterhaza, Hungary.

My arrival caused a great sensation throughout the whole city, and I went the round of all the newspapers for 3 successive days. Everyone wants to know me. I had to dine out 6 times up to now, and if I wished, I could dine out every day; but first I must consider my health, and 2nd my work. . . . I have nice and comfortable, but expensive, lodgings. My landlord is Italian, and also a cook, and serves me 4 very respectable meals; we each pay 1 fl. 30 kr. a day excluding wine and beer, but everything is terribly expensive here. Yesterday I was invited to a grand amateur concert, but I arrived a bit late, and when I showed my ticket they wouldn't let me in but led me to an antechamber, where I had to wait till the piece which was then being played in the hall was over. Then they opened the door, and I was conducted, on the arm of the entrepreneur, up the center of the hall to the front of the orchestra, amid universal applause, and there I was stared at and greeted by a great number of English compliments. I was assured that such honors had not been conferred on anyone for 50 years. After the concert I was taken to a handsome adjoining room, where a table for 200 persons, with many places set, was prepared for all the amateurs; I was supposed to be seated at the head of the table, but since I had dined out on that day and had eaten more than usual, I declined this honor, with the excuse that I was not feeling very well, but despite this I had to drink the harmonious health, in Burgundy, of all the gentlemen present; they all returned the toast, and then allowed me to be taken home.

Source: *The Collected Correspondence and London Notebooks of Joseph Haydn*, ed. and trans. H. C. Robbins Landon (London: Barrie and Rockliff, 1959), pp. 111–113.

Concerts in Haydn's time were far longer than today, with many of them lasting four hours or more. On the other hand, audience members were not expected to sit as still and silent as statues through the entire performance. As in the Baroque era (see A Closer Look: Baroque Opera, page 89) sizeable portions of the audience socialized during concerts and felt free to converse even while the music was being played.

Audiences were also much more open about expressing their reactions to performances, both favorable and unfavorable. Composers could always tell which portion of a particular symphony or concerto an audience liked best, because listeners clapped immediately. Sometimes a movement would even be encored in its entirety.

Contemporary accounts tell us that eighteenth-century audiences could burst into applause even *while* the music was playing—much as what occurs today after a jazz solo, for example. Mozart once described in a letter to his father how he had counted on this custom while composing the finale of one of his symphonies:

> Having observed that all finales as well as opening Allegros begin here [in Paris] with all the instruments playing together and generally in unison, I began mine with two violins only, *piano* [softly] for the first eight measures, followed instantly by a *forte* [loud outburst]. The audience, as I expected, said "hush" at the soft beginning, and when they heard the *forte*, began at once to clap their hands. [Letter of 3 July 1778]

In short, concert manners in the late eighteenth century were rather more like concert manners at a rock or jazz concert today. The gap between "serious" art and "popular" entertainment was not nearly as wide in Haydn's time as it is today.

Rondo Form

In **rondo form**, an opening theme (**A**) returns repeatedly over the course of the movement, interspersed with contrasting ideas (**B**, **C**, etc.). In this instance, the pattern is **ABACADACA**. In Italian, *rondo* means "round dance," in which any one dancer in a circle of dancers repeatedly moves away from his or her starting point and then returns to it. In a similar fashion, the musical form of the rondo keeps moving away from and returning to its opening idea (**A**).

The main theme (**A**) of a rondo is typically brief and simple, which makes it that much easier to recognize when it returns. The main theme of this particular rondo is almost instantly recognizable because of the distinctive rhythm of its opening (da-da-DUM).

From the listener's perspective, rondos are easy to follow—no matter how intricate the music might be at any given point, even the most casual listener can anticipate and recognize the return of the opening theme. But rondos are not always so simple underneath the surface. Haydn (and later, Beethoven) liked to play with listeners' expectations of the form. In the finale of Symphony no. 102, Haydn repeatedly teases the listener into thinking that the opening theme is about to return, only to deflect (or delay, at least temporarily) this return. The net result is a movement that is at once simple and sophisticated.

Now listen to the third and fourth movements of this symphony again, using the Listening Guide.

CONNECT YOUR PLAYLIST

Dynamics

Find a piece that makes use of sharply contrasting dynamics.

Example: Bonnie Tyler, "Total Eclipse of the Heart" (1983) This song uses sudden contrasts between soft and loud dynamics to excellent dramatic effect.

Listening Guide

GO TO www.mymusiclab.com
for the Automated Listening Guide
CD II • Track 11/Download Track 46

Joseph Haydn Composed: 1795 Symphony no. 102 in B♭ Major, (1) third movement: Minuet (4:46)

Time	Formal Section	Subsection	Timbre	Dynamics
0:00	A (minuet proper)	First section: melody is very disjunct.	Full orchestra: the melody is primarily in the first violins.	Frequent alternations between loud and soft.
0:20		Repeat of first section.		
0:39		Second section: begins with three low notes, tossed from cellos and basses to violas, up to the violins; opening idea of minuet returns at 0:56.		
1:27		Repeat of second section; opening idea of minuet returns at 1:44.		
2:16	B ("trio")	First section: melody more lyrical, mostly conjunct.	Reduced orchestra: trumpets and timpani are silent throughout. The melody is carried primarily by the winds (oboes and bassoons).	Entirely soft.
2:32		Repeat of first section.		
2:48		Second section, with return of the B section's opening idea at 2:56.		
3:12		Repeat of second section, with return of the B section's opening idea at 3:20. Section ends with the instruction "da capo," indicating that the orchestra returns to the beginning of the minuet.		
3:36	A (return of the minuet proper)	Return of first section of minuet proper (this recording does not repeat the first section here).	Full orchestra; the melody is primarily in first violins.	Frequent alternations between loud and soft.
3:55		Return of the second section of the minuet proper; opening idea returns at 4:12 (this recording does not repeat the second section here).		

Listening Guide

GO TO www.mymusiclab.com
for the Automated Listening Guide
CD II • Track 12/Download Track 47

Joseph Haydn Composed: 1795 Symphony no. 102 in B♭ Major, (2) fourth movement: Rondo (4:53)

Time	Section	Melody	Timbre	Dynamics	Harmony: Key Area
0:00	A (main theme)	Rapid stepwise motion.	Reduced orchestra (strings and woodwinds alone).	Soft	Tonic (B♭ major)
1:00	B	Wide leaps, dotted rhythms.	Full orchestra: horns, trumpets, and timpani join in.	Loud	
1:26	A	Rapid stepwise motion.	Strings alone.	Soft	Not tonic (F major)
1:33	C	Meandering melody over a drone bass—a single note repeated over and over.	Full orchestra.	Loud/soft/loud; much contrast of dynamics within this section	
2:16	A	Rapid stepwise motion.	Strings and flute, then full orchestra (but softly, starting at 2:25), with back-and-forth between winds and timpani (high) and strings (low).	Soft	Tonic (B♭ major)
2:46	D	Leaping melody striding upward.	Full orchestra.	Loud	Tonic (but in minor mode—B♭ minor), then unstable (moves through various key areas)
3:25	A	Rapid stepwise motion; note how the theme is interrupted at 3:32.	Strings, alone, then winds join in.	Soft	Tonic (B♭ major)
3:40	C	Meandering melody over a drone bass.	Full orchestra.	Loud/soft/loud	
4:04	A	Rapid stepwise motion; note how Haydn plays with our expectations of how a piece should end.	Winds, then strings, then full orchestra.	Soft/loud	

Student FAQs

Why is there no basso continuo in the orchestra?

Most performances of Haydn's later symphonies dispense with the basso continuo for the simple reason that it's not necessary: the voices are sufficiently full without it. Some ensembles do use a basso continuo, however, for there is evidence that Haydn himself conducted from the keyboard in London. Whether he actually played while sitting at the harpsichord or piano is not clear, but he did write a surprise solo passage for himself into the finale of his Symphony no. 98.

Why does the recording omit the repeats when playing the da capo portion of the minuet proper?

Listeners today tend to be less tolerant of literal repetition than their eighteenth-century counterparts. When all the repeats are observed, the minuet proper (that is, the opening two sections of the minuet movement, excluding the trio) is heard altogether four times. But repetition was basic to dance music, and Haydn's audiences would not have considered so many repeats unusual in any way.

A CLOSER LOOK   The Chamber Orchestra

What counted for a large orchestra in Joseph Haydn's time is relatively small by modern standards. Today we call an ensemble that would have been used to perform a work like Haydn's Symphony No. 102 a **chamber orchestra.** There are no standard numbers of instruments or players for a chamber orchestra: four of the twelve symphonies Haydn wrote call for clarinets, for example, while eight of them (including Symphony No. 102) do not. The Chamber Orchestra of Philadelphia pictured here reflects the approximate size and makeup of the orchestra that first performed Haydn's Symphony No. 102 in 1795.

Timpani (1) The **timpani** ("kettledrum") was often the only percussion instrument in the orchestras of Haydn's time. The pitch of each drum is controlled by tightening or loosening the pressure on the surface of the drum-head. In earlier times, the drum-head surface was made of dried animal skin. It is now made of a synthetic material.

Trumpets (2) The brightest and most penetrating of the brass instruments, the **trumpet** began as a valveless instrument but later acquired a mechanism so performers could play a wider range of notes more readily.

Horns (2) Sometimes called "French" horns, these instruments evolved out of the early hunting horn. In Haydn's time, the natural (valveless) horn was the norm. The musicians here hold valved instruments, which emerged during the first half of the nineteenth century and made it easier for players to negotiate a wider range of notes.

Alan Kolc, Courtesy The Chamber Orchestra of Philadelphia

First violins (6) Violins are divided into two sections, first and second. The **first violins** are usually larger in number because they carry the principal melodic line most often. The leader of this section, called the concertmaster or concertmistress, is the "lead player" not only within this group, but for the orchestra as a whole. In some ensembles the concertmaster doubles as the conductor, leading the performance from his or her seat while playing.

Violas (4) In orchestral music of the Classic Era, the **violas** rarely came to the fore with an independent melodic line of their own. Instead, they supplied the important inner lines between the higher violins and the lower cellos and double basses.

Flutes (2) The highest of the woodwinds, **flutes** were made of wood in Haydn's time but have more recently been constructed from metal, as shown here. The timbre of the metal is slightly different, but the range is the same.

EXPLORE MORE on **www.mymusiclab.com**

SEE MORE *Inside the Orchestra:* "The Classical Era"

Oboes (2) A double-reed instrument, the **oboe** is often regarded as the woodwind instrument that most closely resembles the human voice. It is particularly adept at projecting a lyrical, "singing" line that can stand out through the orchestra as a whole.

Bassoons (2) The **bassoon** is the lowest of the woodwinds. This double-reed instrument often doubles or plays the same notes a the cellos or double basses, though it can also carry the principal melody on its own.

Double basses (2) The largest of the string instruments, the **double basses** sound exactly one octave lower than the cellos. In Haydn's time, they usually doubled the line being played by the cellos, giving additional richness and color to the bottom end of the orchestral register.

Conductor

Cellos (3) The **cellos** typically provide the harmonic underpinning for other melodic instruments (such as the violins or woodwinds), but they can carry the principal melody on their own as well.

Second violins (5) The **second violins** sometimes double the first violins—playing exactly the same line—but more often complement them, enriching the harmony or adding a different contrapuntal line.

Haydn's Symphonies

Haydn wrote 106 symphonies, and each is distinctive. Here are some of the more famous:

Symphony no. 8 in G Major

- ("Evening/Le soir")

  The third of three programmatic symphonies depicting the times of day (no. 6 is Morning/Le matin; no. 7 is Noon/Le midi). Haydn wrote these works shortly after arriving at the Esterházy court, and he ingratiated himself with the leading members of the orchestra by giving them important solo passages. The evening concludes with a tempest, complete with lightning.

Symphony no. 45 in F# Minor

- ("Farewell")

  While the Esterházy castle was still under construction, the musicians had to live some distance away from their families for the whole of the summer. When the prince kept delaying his return to Eisenstadt, Haydn wrote a finale to remind him that the musicians longed to go home. In the finale of this symphony the players stop playing, one by one, and exit the stage so that at the end only two violinists are left. They, too, extinguish their candles and leave the stage.

Symphony no. 94 in G Major

- ("Surprise")

  "I wanted to create a sensation" was Haydn's explanation for the wholly unprepared and—yes—surprisingly loud chord near the beginning of the slow movement. Everyone remembered this effect, and the symphony received the nickname of "Surprise," which has stuck ever since.

Symphony no. 101 in D Major

- ("Clock")

  This work takes its nickname from the persistent tick-tock rhythm of the slow movement. It is one of the 12 (nos. 93–104) Haydn wrote for London audiences.

((•● **HEAR SAMPLES** on **www.mymusiclab.com**

⊘ **TEST YOURSELF** on **www.mymusiclab.com**   Flashcards and chapter tests

Wolfgang Amadeus Mozart
Symphony no. 40 in G Minor, K. 550, first movement
Composed: 1788

Mozart's Symphony no. 40 in G Minor is one of three symphonies that he wrote in Vienna in 1788, probably for a concert he organized himself, although no record of the event survives. The first movement, presented here, is full of dramatic contrasts.

 **Listen to this first**

((• HEAR MORE on www.mymusiclab.com

Form

Listen for the repeated return of various themes over the course of this movement. Notice, too, the sharp contrast between the character of the themes. The opening is quietly agitated, but within less than a minute, we hear themes that are louder and brighter and still others that are softer and calmer.

Harmony

Listen for the contrast between key areas early in this movement. The change in keys coincides with a change in mode: the opening theme is in the minor mode, the next main theme is in major. Which sounds darker? Which sounds brighter? Which mode predominates in this movement?

Melody

How would you characterize the themes of this movement? What makes them different from each other?

If we think of this piece's various themes as characters, this movement features all the essential elements of a good drama: memorable personalities (melodies), conflict (the juxtaposition and transformation of those melodies), and resolution (the restoration of these melodies in their more-or-less original form). The events of this musical drama without words unfold in the same kind of logical sequence that we see in a three-act play presented on the stage:

⚙ **LEARN MORE** on
www.mymusiclab.com
Chapter Objectives

- We meet the main character and the supporting characters (Act 1).

- We witness their interaction and transformation: they fall in and/or out of love, they fight, they search or struggle for something (Act 2).

- We experience some kind of resolution in the end: it may be a happy or an unhappy ending, or something in between, but we recognize it as an ending because all the strands of the plot are resolved (Act 3).

How does Mozart present this drama in purely musical terms? He organizes the first movement of this symphony around a musical structure known as **sonata form**, a form that was new in the Classical Era and that allowed for the presentation, development, and resolution of multiple themes within a single movement. From roughly 1750 to the present day, composers have written literally thousands of movements in sonata form, for it provides a versatile framework for creating a drama without words.

Sonata Form

The three acts of a drama outlined previously correspond to the three parts of sonata form:

Act 1: The **exposition** introduces us to—*exposes* us to—all the movement's thematic ideas. By the end of the exposition, we have met all the musical "characters."

Act 2: The **development** is the middle part of a sonata-form movement, in which the thematic ideas are most intensively *developed*, both thematically and harmonically. Themes are taken apart, combined in different ways, and tried in different keys.

Act 3: The **recapitulation** comes in the last third of the movement. The themes we heard in the exposition are *recapitulated* or *recapped*. This provides a resolution to all we have heard before.

Sonata form emerged around the middle of the eighteenth century as an expansion of a form already well-established, **rounded binary form** (see page 189). Rounded binary form consists of two sections in which the opening idea and the tonic key return simultaneously about a third of the way through the movement. (We saw this structure in the minuet of Haydn's Symphony no. 102, discussed in chapter 22.) In sonata form, two important new elements are added:

1. The first section—the exposition—always modulates, presenting themes in a new, contrasting key area.
2. The theme(s) presented in the new key area in the exposition are repeated in the recapitulation *in the tonic*—that is, in the original key of the movement. This is what helps give a sense of resolution to any sonata-form movement.

Sonata form thus consists of three sections—exposition, development, and recapitulation—that are superimposed on a binary form. The exposition takes up the whole of the first binary section. The development and recapitulation both fall within the second binary section. Almost by definition, the second binary section is longer than the first, because it develops the themes *and* recapitulates them. Graphically, this form can be represented as follows:

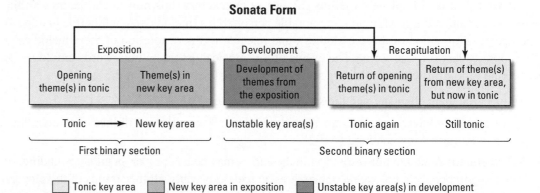

In practice, no two sonata-form movements are entirely alike. Sonata form is a broad and flexible scheme, and composers were extremely adept at manipulating it. There are, however, several predictable features that a listener can recognize:

- There is always a modulation from a primary to a secondary key area in the exposition.
- The first binary section is always repeated; the second binary section may or may not be repeated.

- There is always a departure from these harmonic areas in the development.
- The development moves through various keys and rarely settles on any one of them for very long. This section features bits and pieces of one or more earlier themes, transformed and combined in different ways.
- There is always a return to the primary key area in the recapitulation, and it almost always coincides with the return to the opening idea in its original form. This is the onset of the recapitulation, and it is often a dramatic moment in a sonata-form movement. After the unpredictability and instability of the development, we are now finally back on familiar ground, both thematically (the opening idea) and harmonically (the tonic key).
- The sequence of themes in the recapitulation usually follows the sequence of themes as presented in the exposition.
- The recapitulation always stays in the tonic throughout.

The first movement of Mozart's Symphony no. 40 in G Minor follows the conventions of sonata form fairly closely:

- It opens with an exposition that modulates from the tonic of G Minor to the contrasting key area of B♭ major. The contrast of mode between the minor mode (the tonic) and the major mode (the new key area) helps make the contrast between the two key areas more audible.
- The development is quite unstable harmonically, and it features an intense manipulation of the movement's opening theme.
- The onset of the recapitulation provides a strong and dramatic sense of return: the music comes back to the tonic, and the opening theme reappears more or less in its original guise.
- Later in the recapitulation, what had been heard outside the tonic in the exposition is now presented in the tonic: again, the contrast of mode (B♭ major in the exposition, G minor in the recapitulation) makes the resolution easier to hear. What we heard in B♭ major in the exposition now returns in G Minor, and the difference is striking.

The movement concludes with a brief **coda**. "Coda" is the Italian word for "tail," and it brings the movement to a close after the recapitulation. Codas stand outside of the sonata-form structure itself and may or may not be present in a sonata-form movement.

1756–1791
Wolfgang Amadeus Mozart
Symphony no. 40 in G Minor, K. 550, first movement
Composed: 1788

GENRE
Symphony

KEY CONCEPTS
Sonata form, exposition, development, recapitulation, coda, modulation, contrasting themes and harmonic areas.

CHAPTER HIGHLIGHT
Sonata Form
Sonata form was the most important structural convention to emerge from the Classical Era. It provided the structural basis for the first movement of many symphonies, sonatas, and string quartets. It is a flexible format in which contrasting themes and harmonic areas are juxtaposed, transformed, and ultimately reconciled.

Harmony: Minor to Major

Harmony plays an important role in the sonata-form structure, as we have seen, and to sustain a musical argument across such a long span of time, Mozart uses different key areas to create variety. The modulation in this movement from the tonic to the new key area is particularly clear because it coincides with a change in mode. The first key area is G minor; the mood is dark and brooding. The new key area is B♭ major; here, the music sounds brighter and more optimistic. But when the themes presented in this new key area return in the recapitulation, they are played in G Minor (the tonic), and now they, too, sound dark and brooding. It is as if all the melodies—all the "characters"—have finally come under the spell of the tonic, thereby creating a sense of resolution and closure.

HISTORICAL CONTEXT   The Drama of Sonata Form

If sonata form can be thought of as a drama in three acts, perhaps there are dramas that can be thought of in terms of sonata form. The original movie version of *The Wizard of Oz*, for example, bears striking parallels. The chart below shows how scenes in the movie correspond to sections of sonata form. Think of the characters as themes and the places where the action occurs as the key areas. The black-and-white scenes at the beginning and end of the movie function as the exposition and recapitulation, respectively. We meet all the main characters of the story in two different places: first at home, and then later as Dorothy is running away from home. In the "development"—the bulk of the movie, which takes us through many different places (from Munchkinland, along the Yellow Brick Road, to Oz itself)—those same characters are transformed. At the end, even Professor Marvel, whom Dorothy had met away from home, drops by her house. He is the same person, but now he is in a different place, in Dorothy's home—in musical terms, her tonic key. It is a satisfying conclusion to the whole, in which the characters have all covered a great deal of ground but all return home.

Dorothy wakes up in her room toward the end of *The Wizard of Oz*. The characters from the black-and-white "exposition" (Professor Marvel and the three farmhands) who were transformed in the color "development" (into the Wizard of Oz, the Scarecrow, the Tin Woodsman, and the Cowardly Lion) are now reunited in the black-and-white "recapitulation" in their original form on Dorothy's home ground (the tonic or "home key" of the film).
MGM/The Kobal Collection/Picture Desk

Sonata Form Section	Musical Drama	The Wizard of Oz
Exposition	The themes of the movement are "exposed" to us.	In the opening black-and-white section, we meet all the major characters of the story.
Tonic	Theme(s) are presented in the tonic, the "home" key.	Dorothy at home on her farm; we meet the farmhands and the dreaded Miss Gulch.
→ modulates to	→ modulates to	→ runs away from home
Secondary key area	A new theme or themes are presented in a key area that is not the tonic, away from the "home" key.	Away from home, Dorothy meets a new character, Professor Marvel.
Development	Harmonically unstable. Themes are transformed so that they are different from how we first heard them, yet are recognizably the same.	The film turns to color, and all the characters are transformed: Miss Gulch has become the Wicked Witch of the West; the farmhands are now the Scarecrow, the Tin Woodsman, and the Lion; and Professor Marvel has turned into the Wizard of Oz.
Recapitulation	Return to the "home" key of the tonic. All themes heard in the exposition are now presented in the tonic.	Dorothy returns to Kansas and the film returns to black-and-white. The characters of the opening scene (even Professor Marvel, whom Dorothy had met away from home) all reappear in their original form and visit at her bedside.

Contrasting Principal Melodies

The dramatic interest of this movement depends not just on forms and harmonies but also on the compelling and contrasting nature of the principal melodies. The music begins with an accompanimental figure in the low strings that sets both a mood (quietly agitated) and a mode (minor). When the first theme enters in the violin soon after, we hear many repetitions of a brief downward step. The melodic line sounds almost like a series of short sighs.

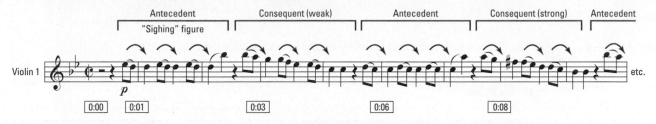

The second principal theme, by contrast, consists of much longer notes, and the agitated accompanimental figure is no longer present. The effect is a mood that is much calmer.

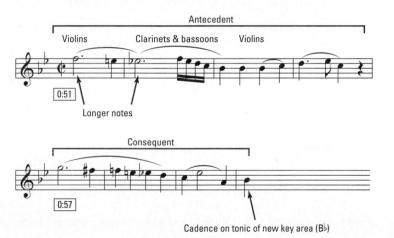

Both themes are constructed around a series of antecedent (opening) and consequent (closing) phrases. But the opening theme (first example, shown previously; Theme 1 in the Listening Guide) stretches out over a much longer span of time: the first consequent phrase gives a sense of only partial resolution, and even the second (stronger) consequent seems to demand a sense of continuation. Even though it establishes the tonic key, the restlessness of this theme gives it a sense of constant forward motion. The first theme in the new key area, by contrast (second example, shown previously; Theme 3 in the Listening Guide), moves in a slower rhythm and is much more regular and compact.

Throughout this movement, Mozart dismantles and puts back together these two principal melodies, particularly the opening theme and a portion of the transitional theme that connects the two (Theme 2 in the Listening Guide). He varies them in multiple ways by presenting them in different keys and by giving them to different instruments or combinations of instruments. In this way, even though Mozart adheres to the conventions of sonata form, he manipulates its content in surprising and unusual ways.

Now listen to this movement again, using the Listening Guide.

CONNECT YOUR PLAYLIST

Modulation

Find a song that modulates.

Example: Taylor Swift, "Love Story" (2008)
Like many songs, "Love Story" modulates near its end for dramatic effect. The type of modulation heard here, which occurs suddenly and obviously, is called a "direct modulation."

Listening Guide

GO TO www.mymusiclab.com
for the Automated Listening Guide
CD II • Track 12/Download Track 47

Wolfgang Amadeus Mozart Composed: 1788 Symphony no. 40 in G Minor, K. 550, first movement (8:10)

Time	Sonata Form	Melody
0:00	Exposition	1 = "Sighing" theme, repeated and then interrupted by the transitional theme.
0:33		2 = Transitional theme, sudden shift in dynamics (loud) and mode (major); ends with a rapid upward-moving, scale-like figure.
0:51		3 = Calm theme, divided between strings and winds.
1:28		4 = Very similar to opening theme, but now in the new key area and thus conveying a different mood.
2:02	Exposition Repeat	1 = "Sighing" theme.
2:35		2 = Transitional theme.
2:53		3 = Calm theme.
3:30		4 = Similar to opening theme, but in the new key area.
4:07	Development	1 = Opening theme, fragmented and harmonically unstable.
4:21		1 = Fragment of opening theme; highly contrapuntal passage, combining 1 with the rapid upward-moving scale-like figure from theme 2. Winds, high strings, and low strings present different ideas simultaneously.
4:49		3 = Opening theme fragmented and transformed still further. Beginning of a long passage leading back to the recapitulation.
5:23	Recapitulation	1 = Return of the opening theme in the tonic key, with slight alterations in the orchestration (notice the added bassoon part here).
5:54		2 = Transitional theme, but altered here in the recapitulation so as not to modulate.
6:36		3 = Same as theme 3 in exposition, but now in tonic (G minor).
7:19		4 = Same as theme 4 in exposition, but now in the tonic (G minor).
7:43	Coda	1 = Sudden intensification, return of opening theme in tonic, with a full cadence to end the movement.

Harmony: Key Area

Tonic (G minor)

Modulating to

New key area (B♭ major)

Tonic (G minor)

Modulating to

New key area (B♭ major)

Unstable: moves through many different key areas, avoids tonic

Tonic (G minor)

Student FAQs

I don't hear the modulations within the sonata form. Is that a problem?

Everyone hears differently, but digital technology makes it easier to improve your ability to perceive changes in key. For this particular movement, try listening up to the point just before the recapitulation begins (at 5:25), then hit the button that takes you back to the very beginning of the entire movement and listen through the end of the exposition. What you will have heard, in effect, is a recapitulation that modulates and does not end in the tonic; the effect is quite different from the actual recapitulation, which stays in the tonic throughout.

What are some other examples of modulation?

Modulation—moving from one key to another—is a very common device in music. Here are some other examples that may already be familiar to you, even if you've never thought about them in these terms:

- Hymns with many stanzas. Organists will often modulate up a step for the last stanza to give the music renewed freshness.
- The "Final Jeopardy" theme song of the well-known game show. Listen carefully next time you watch this show. The theme is stated once in the tonic; the second time around, it is presented in a new key.
- Most popular songs. Almost every popular song that lasts more than a couple of minutes will modulate for the sake of variety, usually in the middle or toward the end of the song.

Sony Pictures Entertainment

PROFILE   Wolfgang Amadeus Mozart (1756–1791)

The Composer as Chameleon

Mozart once observed that he could "write in any style I choose." This wasn't bragging: it was simply the truth. This extraordinary flexibility was due to Mozart's innate genius and his education. His father, Leopold Mozart, a composer of some renown, quickly recognized the musical talent of his young son and took him on a number of extended journeys throughout Europe to perform and learn from others (see A Closer Look: Mozart's World, page 205).

Like many child stars today, Mozart had difficulty in making the transition to adulthood. He found his native Salzburg increasingly provincial, but a series of job searches across Europe proved fruitless. Against his father's wishes, Mozart left Salzburg in 1781 for Vienna hoping to land a position at the imperial court there. Unfortunately, the vicious world of Viennese musical politics did not embrace Mozart. He was rather eccentric and rarely said anything nice about contemporary composers (Haydn was the exception). It must have been painful for Mozart to see court appointments go to lesser composers like Antonio Salieri. Although fictionalized to some degree, Peter Shaffer's play *Amadeus* (1980) brilliantly captures the sense of mutual frustration between the competent Salieri and the genius Mozart.

While waiting for an appointment, Mozart supported himself and his new wife, Constanze, by giving public performances on the piano, selling his published compositions, and giving lessons in piano and composition. He did fairly well for a time but for reasons that remain obscure—the fickleness of Viennese tastes, hard economic times, or perhaps compulsive gambling—he was in serious debt by the early

The Mozart family, ca. 1780. Leopold Mozart (right) was an accomplished violinist and a composer; Nannerl, the composer's sister, excelled as a keyboard player. Mozart's mother, whose portrait hangs on the wall, had died a few years earlier.

Della Croce, Johann Nepomuk. The Mozart Family: at the piano, Wolfgang and his sister "Nannerl"; father Leopold Mozart with violin; mother Anna Maria, dead by the time the painting was made, present in her portrait. (1780–1781). Oil on canvas. 140 x 168 cm. Mozart House, Salzburg, Austria. Erich Lessing/Art Resource, NY

1790s and had to borrow money from friends. He died at the age of 35, just when his popularity (and income) seemed to be on the rise again.

⊙ **EXPLORE MORE** on **www.mymusiclab.com**

⚙ **LEARN MORE** on **www.mymusiclab.com**
    MyMusicLibrary: "Genius as Technique"

⏪ EXPAND YOUR PLAYLIST: MOZART ⏩

- **Mass in C Minor**, K. 427. Unfinished, but a magnificent setting for soloists, chorus, and orchestra, with unusually demanding parts for the vocal soloists.

- *A Musical Joke* (*Ein musikalischer Spaß*), K. 522. A chamber work for string quartet and two horns, this piece is full of intentional mistakes and pokes fun at bad composers.

- *A Little Serenade* (*Eine kleine Nachtmusik*), K. 525. A suite for strings, among Mozart's most popular works.

- **String Quintet in G Minor**, K. 516. Similar in mood to the Symphony in G Minor (the same key), this work is scored for string quartet plus an additional viola.

- **Requiem**, K. 626. Mozart's last work, a funeral Mass commissioned by a mysterious stranger, a count (not Salieri!) who later tried to pass it off as his own composition.

((• **HEAR SAMPLES** on **www.mymusiclab.com**

A CLOSER LOOK   Mozart's World

◉➤ **EXPLORE MORE** on **www.mymusiclab.com**
◉ **SEE MORE** Documentary on *Vienna in the 18th Century*

Before he turned 18, Mozart had met more famous musicians and heard more kinds of music in more cities than probably any other composer in all of Europe. His father, Leopold, a talented composer and violinist in his own right, took his son from Salzburg on tours across the continent from the time Wolfgang was seven. Some of these trips lasted more than a year. At each stop, the Mozarts would meet the local composers, perform in public, and absorb different styles of composition and performance. Mozart continued traveling on his own from Vienna after 1781, often in search of a full-time position.

Berlin: Mozart visits the Prussian capital in hopes of securing a position at the court of the new king, who is an avid cellist. He writes some string quartets with prominent parts for the cello, but otherwise comes away empty-handed.

London: The young boy astonishes the English public with his keyboard skills, at one point dazzling his audience by playing on a keyboard covered with a cloth.

Paris: Mozart makes three extended visits to Paris. On the last of these, he seeks a position at the court, but without success.

Italy: With its long tradition of music-making, Italy attracts performers and composers from all over Europe. The Mozarts make the arduous trek across the Alps three times in five years, visiting all the major cities, including Milan, Bologna, Mantua, Florence, Rome, Naples, and Venice. In Rome, Pope Clement XIV makes the 16-year-old Wolfgang a Knight of the Golden Spur.

Prague: Mozart is a huge favorite in Prague, more so than in Vienna. The theater there commissions his *Don Giovanni,* which premieres in 1787.

Vienna: At 25, Wolfgang moves to Vienna and continues his travels from there. He establishes himself as a composer and keyboard virtuoso, but dies 10 years later before securing a major position at the imperial court. (See Profile, p. 204)

Salzburg: Mozart is born here on January 26, 1756. His father has just published his *Method of Playing the Violin,* soon to become a standard in the field. From Salzburg, Leopold and Wolfgang set out on many trips to London, Paris and Italy.

MOZART'S TRAVELS

London 1764–65

England: 1 trip 1764–65

• The Hague 1765–66

Frankfurt 1763, 1790

• Berlin 1789

Berlin: 1 trip 1789

Prague 1787

Prague: 4 trips 1787 (2x) 1789 1791

• Paris

Paris: 3 trips 1763–64 1766 1778

• Dijon 1766

• Lyons 1766

Milan 1770, 1772–73 •

Verona 1769 •

★ Vienna (resides 1781–91)

★ Salzburg (resides 1756–81)

• Venice 1770

• Bologna

Italy: 3 trips 1769–71 1771 1772–73

• Florence

• Rome 1770

• Naples

N

HISTORICAL CONTEXT Mozart's Sister

Maria Anna ("Nannerl") Mozart (1751–1829) was as much a child prodigy on the keyboard as her younger brother. A notice in a German newspaper of the time described her as "a young girl of eleven" who "played with the greatest clarity and an effortlessness scarcely to be believed" the "most difficult sonatas and concertos of the great masters on the harpsichord or on the piano, all with the greatest taste." Their father, Leopold, took both children on concert tours across Europe, and gave her, not Wolfgang, top billing when the family visited London in 1765.

But for reasons that remain unclear, Nannerl eventually stopped traveling with her father and brother. She did not accompany them on two extended tours of Italy in the late 1760s and early 1770s. This may have been by her own choice, her father's choice, or some combination of the two. In any case, Leopold seems to have made a conscious decision to invest his primary energies in the promotion of Wolfgang's career, affording him extensive training in composition as well as performance. All that survives of Nannerl's compositions are a few brief exercises. Professional outlets for women composers were virtually nonexistent in that place and time.

On the other hand, women could and did enjoy successful careers as performers, especially in Vienna. Wolfgang tried to persuade his sister to join him there in 1781: "Believe me, you could earn a great deal of money in Vienna . . . by playing at private concerts and by giving piano lessons. You would be very much in demand—and you would be well paid." Nannerl chose not to pursue a career as a performer, however. Her father arranged for her to marry a baron in 1784, and she bore three children by him—one of whom she named Wolfgang—but she apparently did not perform in public again. After her husband died in 1821, Nannerl returned to Salzburg and gave piano lessons for the rest of her life.

A portrait of Maria Anna ("Nannerl") Mozart. Notice her unusually long fingers, which undoubtedly served her well as a pianist.

Dagli Orti (A)/Picture Desk, Inc./Kobal Collection

◀◀   **EXPAND YOUR PLAYLIST**   ▶▶

Mozart's Symphonies

Mozart, like Haydn, seems to have relished the challenge of writing for a large ensemble. Here are some of his better-known symphonies:

Symphony no. 1 in E♭ Major, K. 16.
• A small-scale work, but nevertheless an impressive accomplishment for an eight-year-old composer.

Symphony no. 25 in G Minor, K. 185.
• Known as the "Little" G Minor symphony, this work is featured prominently in Milos Forman's film version of Peter Schafer's play *Amadeus*.

Symphony no. 38 in D Major, K. 504.
• Known as the "Prague" symphony because of its popularity there during Mozart's lifetime. The first movement opens with an extended slow introduction, and the symphony lacks a minuet movement, unlike Mozart's other late symphonies.

Symphony no. 41 in C Major, K. 551.
• Nicknamed the "Jupiter" symphony sometime after Mozart's death because of its size and exuberant nature. The finale is a remarkable synthesis of fugue and sonata form.

((• HEAR SAMPLES on www.mymusiclab.com

✓ **TEST YOURSELF** on www.mymusiclab.com   Flashcards and chapter tests

Wolfgang Amadeus Mozart
Piano Concerto in A Major, K. 488, first movement
Composed: 1786

In his Piano Concerto in A Major, K. 488, Mozart explores a variety of moods across three movements, from the serene but passionate first movement to the dark, contemplative second movement to the rousing, exuberant finale. Here, we are listening to the first movement alone.

 Listen to this first

((• HEAR MORE on www.mymusiclab.com

Timbre

Listen to the fluid relationship between the solo instrument—the piano—and the ensemble, an orchestra of strings and winds. Like characters in a drama, they cooperate at times, oppose each other at times, and appear by themselves, without the other at times.

Melody

Listen to the number and variety of the melodies, each with its own distinct character. Notice, too, how these melodies rarely appear in exactly the same guise twice.

Form

Listen for the entrance of the soloist and then later on for the return of the opening idea about two-thirds of the way through the movement, which marks the onset of the recapitulation.

When Mozart moved to Vienna in 1781, he was determined to make an impression on the Imperial Court and the public, both as a pianist and as a composer. His piano concertos provided him with the ideal vehicle for achieving this dual goal: audiences marveled at the young man's virtuosity at the keyboard and his ingenuity as a composer. Over the span of less than 10 years, Mozart composed 17 piano concertos, including this one from 1786. Like so many of Mozart's works, the Piano Concerto in A Major, K. 488, seems effortless and natural, clear and unforced. On closer listening, however, we can hear that what sounds effortless is in no way simple.

⚙ LEARN MORE on
www.mymusiclab.com
Chapter Objectives

Timbre: The Drama of Contrast

The driving force behind any concerto lies in the inherently dramatic tension between the soloist and the orchestra. The two forces collaborate at times and compete at others; on still other occasions, each appears alone. There are five basic scenarios:

1. Orchestra alone
2. Soloist alone

3. Orchestra supporting the soloist
4. Soloist supporting the orchestra
5. Soloist and orchestra on an equal footing

Listen once through this movement to identify these five different combinations. Here are a just a few examples:

0:00 The orchestra plays by itself for an extended time at the beginning (1).

2:04 When the piano enters for the first time, it plays alone briefly (2).

2:12 When the orchestra reenters, it supports the piano (3).

3:18 The orchestra carries the melody while the piano supports it (4).

3:33 The orchestra and piano engage in dialogue, tossing the theme back and forth between each other (5).

By varying the timbre so frequently and by using so many different combinations, Mozart is able to sustain our interest across a relatively long movement.

Melodic Generosity

One feature that sets Mozart's music apart from that of almost all his contemporaries is the sheer number and variety of musical ideas within a given movement. Indeed, some critics of the time complained that Mozart's music presented them with too many ideas, and that his melodies moved from one to the next faster than audiences could follow. Where another composer might be satisfied with two different melodies, for example, Mozart provides his listeners with three or four or five. This first movement of this concerto offers a good example of Mozart's melodic generosity, as well as the way in which he alters the combination of dynamics, texture, and rhythm to create a sense of variety.

Theme 1

The opening idea is serene and balanced, a statement that sets the mood for the movement as a whole. The texture is homophonic, the dynamics soft. The melodic motion is a mixture of conjunct and disjunct, and the contour moves down, then up, ending where it began.

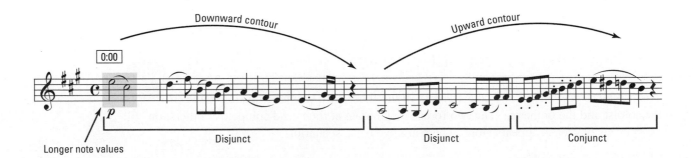

Theme 2

The second idea is more agitated, more propulsive: it moves in a faster rhythm (with shorter note values). The texture is homophonic, the dynamics loud. The melodic motion is marked by prominent upward leaps, and the contour moves largely upward.

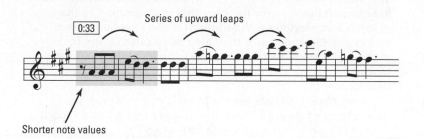

Series of upward leaps

0:33

Shorter note values

1756–1791

Wolfgang Amadeus Mozart

Piano Concerto in A Major, K. 488, first movement
Composed: 1786

GENRE
Concerto

KEY CONCEPTS
Double-exposition concerto form, the cadenza.

CHAPTER HIGHLIGHT
The Classical Concerto
The concertos of the Classical Era combine the ritornello principle of the Baroque Era with the newer sonata form. A cadenza lets the soloist improvise.

Theme 3

This theme also uses shorter note values, but it restores a sense of calm because its many repeated notes help create an impression of not hurrying anywhere. The texture is homophonic, the dynamics soft. The melodic motion is primarily conjunct, and the contour moves largely downward.

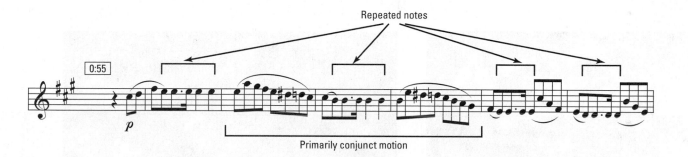

Repeated notes

0:55

𝑝

Primarily conjunct motion

Theme 4

This theme is also calm, but the effect comes from the longer note values that make it move more slowly. The texture this time is polyphonic, with some imitation between the voices. The dynamics are soft, and the melodic motion is marked by an initial down contour followed by upward leaps.

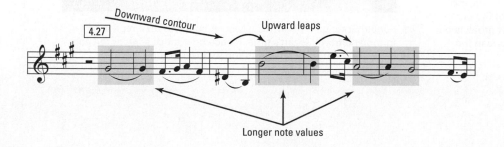

Downward contour

4.27

Upward leaps

Longer note values

PERFORMANCE Mozart on Modern Instruments

The recording here presents Mozart's music played on the kinds of instruments he would have known in his lifetime. These differ in subtle but noticeable ways from modern instruments. The violins, violas, cellos, and basses of the eighteenth century, for example, all used strings made from catgut, not wire as they are today; this made their sound warmer, softer, and less penetrating than the sound of modern instruments.

The piano, in particular, has changed considerably since Mozart's day. It is a much longer, heavier, and louder instrument. In Mozart's time, the hammers that struck the strings were covered with leather, not felt, producing a lighter, more percussive sound. The fortepiano, as it was known back then, is a more delicate and intimate instrument than today's grand piano. It produces far less volume, but this was not a drawback, as concert halls in Mozart's time were much smaller. Many musicians and listeners today prefer the sound of Mozart's music on the fortepiano than on the modern piano.

Which is better? That is entirely a matter of taste. Advocates of the fortepiano argue that we should try to re-create the sound that Mozart had in mind when he wrote his music. Advocates of the modern piano make the case that in proportion to the size of today's concert halls, the modern piano alone creates a sound that fills the space; they also point out that the fortepiano had already begun to grow in size and volume during Mozart's lifetime, and that Mozart himself embraced these developments.

Fortunately, as listeners in today's music world, we have plenty of choices. The following are some good recordings of Mozart's Piano Concerto in A Major, K. 488 on modern instruments:

- Alfred Brendel, piano. Academy of St. Martin in the Fields, Neville Marriner, conductor. Philips 000552102.

- Murray Perahia, piano. English Chamber Orchestra, Murray Perahia, conductor. Sony 87230.

- Ingrid Haebler, piano. London Symphony Orchestra, Witold Rowicki, conductor. Eloquence 468171.

Christian Zacharias plays and conducts a Mozart piano concerto from the keyboard on a modern grand piano. The lid of the piano has been removed to reduce the volume of sound that projects out to the audience. This also improves the sight lines between the soloist-conductor and the members of the orchestra.

Richard Termine/Richard Termine Photography

Ronald Brautigam performs a Mozart concerto on a replica of a fortepiano from Mozart's time. Notice how much smaller the earlier instrument is compared to the modern grand piano.

Courtesy of Ronald Brautigam

Form: Double-Exposition Concerto Form

Like other composers of his time, Mozart adapted sonata form—which was new in the middle of the eighteenth century—to the concerto. But he also retained elements of the contrast between ritornello and solo that was so basic to the Baroque concerto (see chapters 15, 16). Mozart organized the melodic and harmonic structure of the first movement of the Piano Concerto in A Major, K. 488, around a form known as the **double exposition concerto form**. Although based on the same principles as sonata form, double-exposition concerto form differs in several important respects:

Standard Sonata Form	Double-Exposition Concerto Form
• One exposition, repeated literally.	• Two different expositions: one for the orchestra, and one for the soloist and orchestra together.
• Exposition modulates from tonic.	• The first exposition (for the orchestra alone) stays in the tonic. Only the second exposition (for soloist and orchestra together) modulates to new key area.
• Development avoids the tonic.	• Same.
• Recapitulation.	• Same.
• No cadenza.	• At the end of the recapitulation, the soloist plays a *cadenza*—an elaborate improvisation on themes heard earlier in the movement, with no accompaniment at all from the orchestra.

The only entirely new element here is the **cadenza**, a moment when the soloist can display his or her virtuosity to the fullest. Mozart actually wrote down cadenzas for many of his own concertos, but in performance, improvisation was the order of the day. A long trill from the soloist was the standard signal to the orchestra that the cadenza was about to end, and with a gesture from the soloist, the orchestra resumed playing its written parts. Mozart conducted his music from the keyboard; conductors did not arrive on the scene until the early nineteenth century.

Graphically, the double-exposition concerto structure can be represented in this manner:

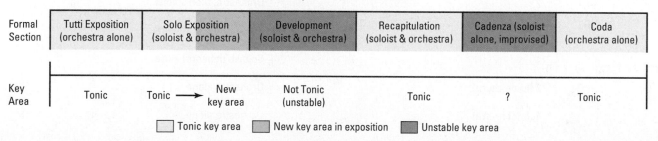

Now listen to the first movement of this piano concerto again, using the Listening Guide.

GO TO www.mymusiclab.com
for the Automated Listening Guide
CD II • Track 13/Download Track 48

Listening Guide

Wolfgang Amadeus Mozart Composed: 1786 Piano Concerto in A Major, K. 488, first movement (10:54)

Time	Form: Section	Melody	Timbre
0:00	Tutti exposition (orchestra alone)	1 = lyrical, begins with long notes, downward contour	Strings alone present the theme, which is then repeated by the winds alone.
0:32		2 = more energetic theme, begins with repeated notes but then has several upward leaps and a generally upward contour	Full orchestra
0:56		3 = another lyrical theme, largely conjunct, downward contour	Strings alone at first, winds join in later
2:04	Solo exposition (soloist and orchestra together)	1 = a more elaborate presentation of the theme	Soloist alone, joined gradually by orchestra
2:32		2 = begins as above, but continues differently so that it modulates, taking the music to a new key area	Orchestra alone, joined by soloist
3:03		3 = as above, but now in the new key area	Soloist alone, joined by the orchestra (at 3:15)
4:27		4 = a new theme, not heard in the tutti exposition; long notes, disjunct motion, generally downward contour	Orchestra (strings alone), joined by soloist (at 4:48)
4:52	Development (soloist and orchestra together)	4 = dialogue between soloist and orchestra on fragments of this theme	Winds alone at first, joined by soloist and strings
6:12	Recapitulation (soloist and orchestra together)	1	Orchestra (with winds now), soloist joins in (at 6:27)
6:40		2	Orchestra, then soloist
7:10		3	Soloist, then orchestra
8:12		4	Soloist, then orchestra
8:55		2 (brief return)	Orchestra alone
9:07		4 (brief return)	Orchestra alone
9:20	Cadenza	Improvisation on themes heard earlier in the movement	Soloist alone
10:20	Coda (orchestra alone)	3 (fragment)	Orchestra alone

Harmony: Key Areas

Tonic (A major)

Tonic

→ (modulating to) . . .

New key area (E major)

Unstable: the music moves quickly through many key areas

Tonic: a strong sense of arrival at the beginning of the recapitulation, both to the opening theme and to the opening key

Does not modulate; stays in the tonic

Tonic

Unstable, returns to tonic

Tonic

Student FAQs

Isn't the piano soloist playing very softly with the orchestra in the tutti exposition?

Yes, and you have an extremely good ear if you can hear this. The piano's very discreet (almost inaudible) part here represents a holdover from the days when the keyboard soloist would perform double duty as both a soloist and as a member of the basso continuo. In modern performances that strive to replicate eighteenth-century performance practice (as in the recording here), the soloist helps support the basso continuo in the tutti exposition and at the end, in the coda, fills out harmonies here and there without really calling attention to him- or herself.

How could Mozart have conducted from the keyboard while playing? Didn't he need his arms to conduct?

Yes, but playing the lead on the piano created a basic beat for the musicians to follow. Also, Mozart could use his head and eyes to gesture to the musicians while playing. In those passages in which the orchestra took the lead (as in the tutti exposition), Mozart probably did conduct with one or both arms.

Did Mozart really improvise his cadenzas on the spot?

It's hard to say for sure—even if we could ask him, would we believe his answer? It seems likely, though, that Mozart would have given at least some advance thought to how he might improvise on the themes of a concerto movement, combining those premeditated strategies with genuine improvisation at the moment of performance. Jazz musicians today often do the same thing: to varying degrees, their solo riffs represent a combination of both the planned and the spontaneous.

Della Croce, Johann Nepomuk. The Mozart Family: at the piano, Wolfgang and his sister "Nannerl"; father Leopold Mozart with violin; mother Anna Maria, dead by the time the painting was made, present in her portrait. (1780–1781). Oil on canvas. 140 x 168 cm. Mozart House, Salzburg, Austria. Erich Lessing/Art Resource, NY

213

HISTORICAL CONTEXT   Mozart's Concerts: The Bottom Line

When Mozart moved to Vienna from Salzburg in 1781, he was taking a calculated risk, believing that he could secure a steady position at the Imperial Court or, failing that, earn enough money from concerts, opera commissions, publications, and teaching to support himself (and, after he married, his family).

For a time, at least, Mozart's gamble paid off. His concert series in the years 1783–1786 were a great success and attracted many subscribers, including wealthy aristocrats whose opinions could make or break the career of any new musician who had just arrived in Vienna. Mozart kept his expenses down in part by doing almost everything himself.

The actor Tom Hulce in the role of Mozart in *Amadeus* (1984). Mozart was in fact fascinated with the game of billiards, and the image of him composing on a billiard table is entirely plausible.
© Saul Zaentz Company/Courtesy Everett Collection

He wrote the music for his concerts (symphonies and, above all, piano concertos), performed the music himself as soloist and conductor (sometimes filling both functions simultaneously), hired the musicians, and even sold the tickets from his own apartment. (Mozart was affluent enough to afford a servant, and it was presumably the servant, rather than Mozart himself, who actually sold the tickets.)

One reliable recent estimate of Mozart's balance sheet for his 1785 subscription concert series shows that he in fact made a healthy profit on his venture:

Income:

150 subscribers @ 13.5 Gulden ea. for 6 concerts =	2,025 Gulden

Expenses:

Orchestra musicians (estimated):	420 Gulden
Concert hall rental	80
Lighting, printing, and other miscellaneous expenses:	100
Total Expenses:	600 Gulden
Net Profit:	1,425 Gulden

To give some sense of what this meant in terms of purchasing power, the rent for Mozart's apartment at this time was 460 Gulden per year. His subscription series of six concerts thus generated more than three times his annual housing costs. Beyond the subscription concerts, of course, Mozart was also free to give special additional concerts as well.

Source: Mary Sue Morrow, *Concert Life in Haydn's Vienna: Aspects of a Developing Musical and Social Institution*, Pendragon Press, 1988.

EXPAND YOUR PLAYLIST

The Classical Concerto

Carl Philipp Emanuel Bach (1714–1788) one of J. S. Bach's sons, wrote more than 50 keyboard concertos. The Concerto in G Minor, H. 442, is from the mid-1750s.

Johann Christian Bach (1735–1782), like his much older half-brother, Carl Philipp Emanuel Bach, wrote dozens of keyboard concertos. J. C. Bach's Concerto in B♭ Major, op. 7, no. 4 (1770) is written in a more modern style, closer to that of W. A. Mozart.

W. A. Mozart wrote concertos for a variety of different instruments, including not only piano (27 of them) but also violin (5), horn (4), bassoon (1), and flute and harp (1), among others. Some recommendations for further exploration:
• Piano Concerto in D Minor, K. 466. This is one of the darker and more turbulent of the 27 piano concertos Mozart wrote for himself.

• Concerto for Two Pianos in E♭, K. 365. Mozart wrote this to be performed jointly with his sister Nannerl, an accomplished pianist in her own right.
• Sinfonia Concertante in E♭, K. 364. A "concerto-like symphony," grand in scale and sound, for solo violin and viola, with orchestra.
• Clarinet Concerto in A Major, K. 622. Mozart's last concerto for any instrument, written for a friend of his, the clarinetist Anton Stadler.

Joseph Haydn's most celebrated concertos are the Cello Concerto in D Major, Hob. XIIb: 2 and the Trumpet Concerto in E♭, Hob. VIIe:1.

Marianne Martinez (1744–1812), who in her youth studied composition with Haydn, wrote three concertos for piano.

((•● HEAR SAMPLES on **www.mymusiclab.com**

✓ **TEST YOURSELF** on **www.mymusiclab.com**   Flashcards and chapter tests

Wolfgang Amadeus Mozart
The Marriage of Figaro, Act I, "Cosa sento"
Composed: 1786

The dramatic contrasts, modulations, and sudden changes so characteristic of instrumental music in the Classical Era provided composers with the means by which to enhance dramatic action on the stage. In this excerpt from Mozart's *Marriage of Figaro*, the music gives added depth to the words and actions of the characters on stage.

 Listen to this first

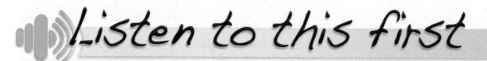

((•● HEAR MORE on www.mymusiclab.com

Word-Music Relationships	Form	Melody
Listen to the contrasting singing styles of Susanna (soprano), Basilio (tenor), and the Count (bass). The three personalities are shaped not only by the words, but by the way each character sings them.	Much of the drama is in the music itself. Listen to the increasing and decreasing tension of the music over the course of this one selection. These three characters are singing to one another, not just to the audience.	Listen for the return of the opening melody at various points. In the middle of the scene, notice the sudden change in the Count's singing style from lyrical to declamatory.

In this trio from Mozart's opera *The Marriage of Figaro* (*Le nozze di Figaro*), words and music combine to create a moment of intense confrontation full of both suspense and humor. The text enriches the music, and the music enriches the text. The scene occurs toward the end of the opera's first act. The three characters singing in this selection are the following:

- Count Almaviva (bass), who is married to the Countess but has his eyes on Susanna.
- Susanna, the Countess's maidservant. Susanna is engaged to be married to Figaro, the Count's manservant.
- Basilio, the music teacher at the court. He is meddlesome and loves to gossip.

There is actually a fourth character on stage as well, but Cherubino (a page boy) is silent in this scene because he is hiding. When he is discovered, about midway through the selection, he is too mortified to sing.

How did we get into this situation? Cherubino is infatuated with women in general and the Countess in particular. In the scene just prior to this one, Cherubino has been asking Susanna's help in calming the anger of the Count, who the day before has caught him making advances on

LEARN MORE on
www.mymusiclab.com
Chapter Objectives

◉ **SEE MORE** on
www.mymusiclab.com
Documentary:
Opera in the 18th Century

Barbarina, the young daughter of the gardener. But while Cherubino and Susanna are discussing the matter, the Count arrives unexpectedly, and Cherubino must hide behind a large chair. (The audience, of course, can see everyone on the stage.) In the process of trying to seduce Susanna, the Count is in turn interrupted by the impending arrival of the music teacher, Basilio. So now the *Count* must hide, and he goes to conceal himself behind the very same chair where Cherubino is crouching. Using her quick wits, Susanna steps between the Count and the chair and directs Cherubino to slip onto the seat itself and conceal himself underneath one of the Countess's dresses that happens to be lying there. Just as the Count assumes his position behind the chair, Basilio enters the room. He is a meddlesome creature, and he teases Susanna about the Count's interest in her. He then goes on to tell her about Cherubino's interest in the Countess, which by now has become common knowledge at the court. At this moment an indignant Count bursts out from his hiding place. "I heard that!" he roars ("Cosa sento!"). And with that, our scene begins.

Mozart's *The Marriage of Figaro* is a **comic opera** or *opera buffa*, to use its Italian name. *Buffa* comes from the same root word as "buffoon." The genre uses many of the same conventions as serious opera—arias, recitatives, ensembles, choruses—but the plots do not revolve around mythical or historical figures. Instead, comic operas tend to deal with very believable characters who behave as individuals, not as symbols, and we can relate to all of them to varying degrees. Mozart's music makes them even more believable.

Word-Music Relationships: The Character of Each Voice

Even without music, this is a highly dramatic scene. The witty libretto, by the Italian poet Lorenzo da Ponte (1749–1838), is based on a stage play of the same name by the French dramatist Pierre Augustin Caron de Beaumarchais (1732–1799). A great deal happens here within a short span of time. As soon as the Count emerges from his hiding place ("Cosa sento!"—"I heard that!"—he exclaims), Basilio backtracks and apologizes, claiming that what he had just been saying about Cherubino and the Countess was merely a suspicion rather than a fact. But the Count is all the more determined now to banish Cherubino from his court. He tells Susanna and Basilio about his encounter with the page the day before and describes exactly how he had discovered Cherubino under the table by lifting the tablecloth. He illustrates his discovery of the previous day by lifting the dress off the chair—only to find Cherubino cringing before him, hiding yet again.

The duplicity and irony of it all is hilarious, for the Count himself had been hiding behind this very same chair only moments before. The Count had come to seduce Susanna (on the day of her wedding!) and yet when he overhears Basilio talking about Cherubino's infatuation with the Countess, he becomes outraged. And just what was the Count doing at Barbarina's house the day before, when he discovered Cherubino there? She was "more flustered than usual," the Count observes; this clearly was not the first time the Count had visited Barbarina.

This scene illustrates Mozart's uncanny ability to capture the essence of individual characters and at the same time move a plot forward through the music. What Mozart's music portrays so convincingly in this brief trio is the fluidity of each character's emotions. We witness the following changes:

1. The Count moves from outrage (on hearing of Basilio's suspicions about Cherubino and the Countess) to astonishment at discovering Cherubino in hiding once again, for the second time in two days.
2. Basilio moves from embarrassment (on realizing that the Count has overheard his gossip about the Countess) to triumph when Cherubino's presence in the Countess's chamber bears out what Basilio had at first called "mere suspicions."
3. Susanna moves through states of increasing humiliation that her reputation has been compromised by the presence of all three male visitors, none of whom should really be where they are and certainly should not be alone with her on the day of her own wedding.

These contrasting and evolving emotional states are reflected in the contrasting melodies Mozart gives to each character.

Contrasting Melodies

Mozart associates distinctly different melodies with each of the emotional states of the three characters. The Count's opening theme (Theme 1 in the Listening Guide, later in this chapter)—a slow, rising line—reflects his determination to banish Cherubino from the court. Basilio's whiny and slightly hesitant descending line (Theme 2) matches his embarrassment at having been overheard repeating malicious gossip about the Countess. Susanna's agitated melody (Theme 3) sounds like it is shaking: it moves up and down, back and forth with a very narrow register, reflecting her personal agitation: at this point, she alone knows that Cherubino, who is the object of all this gossip, is still hiding in the room.

Later on (at 2:12), when the Count tells about his encounter with Cherubino the day before, he suddenly shifts to a more syllabic, declamatory style of singing. This is **accompanied recitative**—recitative accompanied by the orchestra, as opposed to the more standard recitative accompaniment of basso continuo alone. This passage stands in marked contrast to the rest of the scene, for it is a narration of something that has already happened.

Dramatic Form, Musical Form

As in any opera, the form of this selection is built around its text. Mozart structures the music around a recurring musical theme that reflects the scene's recurring dramatic theme: the Count's resolve to send Cherubino away from the court. We hear some variation of this theme ("1" in the Listening Guide) three times:

• At the very beginning, when the Count reacts to Basilio telling Susanna about Cherubino's interest in the Countess

• After Susanna's "fainting" spell, when Basilio apologizes for what he has said about Cherubino and the Countess

• After the Count discovers Cherubino hiding under a dress on the chair

1756–1791
Wolfgang Amadeus Mozart
The Marriage of Figaro,
Act I, "Cosa sento"
Composed: 1786

GENRE
Comic opera

KEY CONCEPTS
Opera, drama through music, relationship of dramatic and musical structures, accompanied recitative.

CHAPTER HIGHLIGHT
Comic Opera
Opera remained the most prestigious and lucrative genre throughout the Classical Era and inspired some of its greatest music. In addition to providing entertainment, the opera also served as a kind of pressure-release valve on social tensions: in Mozart's *Marriage of Figaro,* the servants outwit their master. In this scene, the musical form and singing styles reflect and reinforce the events on the stage.

Count Almaviva, outraged, uncovers the young page, Cherubino, hiding beneath a dress draped over a chair. Basilio (left) is delighted; Susanna (right) is horrified. The character of the young man Cherubino, who is silent throughout the trio "Cosa sento," is always performed by a woman dressed as a man.
Photo by Susan E. Picinich

CONNECT YOUR PLAYLIST

Simultaneous Contrasting Melodies

Find a song that features two different voices singing different musical lines and different words at the same time.

Example: Sleater-Kinney, "Burn, Don't Freeze" (1999)
For most of this song by the indie rock group Sleater-Kinney, the two singers sing different words with simultaneous complementary melodies.

These moments are separated by two dramatic interruptions. Susanna pretends to faint to draw attention away from Cherubino. But she has to "revive" quickly so as not to be placed on top of him, for the two men are trying to help her sit down on the very chair where he is hiding. The second interruption comes from the Count himself when he narrates the events of the day before, describing how, while visiting Barbarina (another young girl he is pursuing), he had discovered Cherubino hiding under the table. He demonstrates to Susanna and Basilio how he had lifted the tablecloth, using the dress on the chair as a prop to demonstrate his actions of the previous day—only to find Cherubino once again.

This sequence of dramatic events suggests a musical form rather like the rondo (see page 191). In a rondo, an opening melodic idea returns repeatedly over the course of a movement, and these points of return are separated by a series of contrasting melodic ideas. Mozart seems to have recognized a parallel between rondo form and the dramatic situation in this particular scene, and he set the action to music following the conventions of rondo form, with the moments of musical and dramatic return and interruption closely coordinated.

EXPAND YOUR PLAYLIST

Opera in the Classical Era

Opera remained the most prestigious (and lucrative) genre in the Classical Era and inspired some of its greatest music. Mozart and

Wolfgang Amadeus Mozart

- *Don Giovanni*, K. 527. The story of Don Juan ("Don Giovanni" in Italian) and his many amorous conquests. The libretto is by Lorenzo da Ponte, who also wrote the text for *The Marriage of Figaro*.
- *Così fan tutte*, K. 588. "All women act that way" is a loose translation of the title. The libretto, again by da Ponte, traces the fate of two couples and a bet by the men that their fiancées will not be unfaithful. The men lose their bets.
- *The Magic Flute (Die Zauberflöte)*, K. 620. A fairy-tale *Singspiel*—a play combining spoken text with music—about a prince and his birdlike companion and their search for knowledge (and a princess).

Christoph Willibald Gluck are generally considered the two principal composers of opera in this period. A sampling of their works follows:

Christoph Willibald Gluck (1714–1787)

Gluck was born in what is now Germany but spent much of his life in Italy, England, France, and Austria. He worked to bring a sense of naturalness to opera, avoiding excessive displays of virtuosity.

- *Orfeo ed Euridice*. Another setting of the legend of Orpheus and his use of music to bring his beloved Eurydice back from Hades to the land of the living. Gluck also produced a French-language version of this same opera (*Orphée et Eurydice*).
- *Alceste*. Based on the Greek legend of Queen Alceste, who offers to sacrifice her own life to save that of her husband, King Admetus. The music includes extensive choral numbers and accompanied recitatives as well as arias.

((• **HEAR SAMPLES** on **www.mymusiclab.com**

THE COMPOSER SPEAKS   Gluck on Opera

Christoph Willibald Gluck (1714–1787) was one of the most successful and prolific composers of operas of the classical era. His preface to his opera *Alceste* is a manifesto of his artistic beliefs, setting out the principles by which he sought to make the music serve the plot of the opera and curb the abuse of singers who sought to show off their technique rather than serve the music.

"When I began to write the music for Alceste, *I resolved to free it from all the abuses which have crept in either through ill-advised vanity on the part of the singers or through excessive complaisance on the part of composers. . . . I sought to restrict the music to its true purpose of serving to give expression to the poetry and to strengthen the dramatic situations, without interrupting the action or hampering it with unnecessary and superfluous ornamentations. . . . So I have tried to avoid interrupting an actor in the warmth of dialogue with a boring intermezzo or stopping him in the midst of his discourse, merely so that the flexibility of his voice might show to advantage in a long passage, or that the orchestra might give him time to collect his breath for a cadenza. I did not think I should hurry quickly through the second part of an air, which is perhaps the most passionate and most important, in order to have room to repeat the words of the first part regularly four times or to end the aria quite regardless of its meaning, in order to give the singer an opportunity of showing how he can render a passage with so-and-so many variations at will; in short, I have sought to eliminate all these abuses, against which sound common sense and reason have so long protested in vain.*

"I imagined that the overture should prepare the spectators for the action, which is to be presented, and give an indication of its subject; that the instrumental music should vary according to the interest and passion aroused, and that between the aria and the recitative there should not be too great a disparity, lest the flow of the period be spoiled and rendered meaningless, the movement be interrupted inopportunely, or the warmth of the action be dissipated. I believed further that I should devote my greatest effort to seeking to achieve a noble simplicity; and I have avoided parading difficulties at the expense of clarity. I have not placed any value on novelty, if it did not emerge naturally from the situation and the expression; and there is no rule I would not have felt in duty bound to break in order to achieve the desired effect.

"These are my principles. . . . My maxims have been vindicated by success, and the universal approval expressed in such an enlightened city [Vienna] has convinced me that simplicity, truth and lack of affectation are the sole principles of beauty in all artistic creations."

Source: Hedwig and E. H. Mueller von Asow, eds., *The Collected Correspondence and Papers of C. W. Gluck* (London: Barrie and Rockliff, 1962), pp. 22–4.

Now listen to the **Marriage of Figaro** *excerpt again, using the Listening Guide.*

Listening Guide

GO TO www.mymusiclab.com
for the Automated Listening Guide
CD III • Track 1/Download Track 49

Wolfgang Amadeus Mozart Composed: 1786 *The Marriage of Figaro,*
Act I, "Cosa sento" (4:07)

Time	Character(s) Singing	Original Italian	English Translation
0:00	Count	Cosa sento! Tosto andate, e scacciate il seduttor!	I heard it all! Go at once and throw the seducer out!
0:16	Basilio	In mal punto son qui giunto; perdonate, o mio signor.	I have arrived at an unfortunate moment; forgive me, my lord.
0:25	Susanna (*as if fainting*)	Che ruina! me meschina! Son' oppressa dal dolor!	What a catastrophe! I am ruined! I am oppressed with sadness!
0:47	Basilio and Count (*supporting Susanna*)	Ah, già svien la poverina, Come, oh Dio, le batte il cor!	The poor child has fainted! My Lord, how her heart is beating!
		(*Basilio and the Count draw Susanna toward the chair to set her down in it—the chair on which Cherubino is hiding under a dress.*)	
1:05	Basilio	Pian pianin: su questo seggio.	Gently, gently, to this chair.
1:09	Susanna (*reviving*)	Dove sono? cosa veggio? Che insolenza, andate fuor.	Where am I? What do I see? What insolence, get away.
		(*She frees herself from both of them.*)	
1:17	Count and Basilio	Siamo qui per aiutarti, [Count]: Non turbarti, o mio tesor. [Basilio]: è sicuro il vostro onor.	We're here to help you, [Count]: Don't be alarmed, my dear. [Basilio]: Your honor is safe.
1:34	Basilio (*to the Count*)	Ah del paggio quel ch'ho detto Era solo un mio sospetto!	What I was saying about the page Was merely a suspicion I had!
1:43	Susanna	È un'insidia, una perfidia, Non credete all'impostor.	It's a snare, a lie; Don't believe this impostor.
1:53	Count	Parta, parta il damerino!	The young girly-boy must go!

Form: Parallels to Rondo Form	Melody	Word-Music Relationships
A	(1) Rising contour	This theme recurs whenever the Count reacts to news about Cherubino's amorous advances.
	(2) Falling contour	This theme recurs whenever a character refers to his suspicions about Cherubino's attempted seductions.
	(3) Narrow range, static motion: the melody winds around on itself	The rapid, fluttering notes of this theme reflect Susanna's agitation.
B	(4) New melody, rising contour	This theme recurs whenever the Count and Basilio try to assist Susanna.
		"Faints" in a low register but suddenly starts singing in a high one when she realizes she is about to be put on the same seat where Cherubino is hiding.
	(4) Same as 0:47	Again, the two men assist Susanna.
	(2) Same as 0:16	Basilio apologizes for having suggested that the Countess and Cherubino have been meeting in secret.
	(3) Variant of earlier melody (at 0:24)	Susanna is agitated again; she has barely managed to conceal Cherubino's presence.
A	(1) Return to opening theme	Varied return of the opening theme emphasizes the Count's resolve to banish Cherubino from the court.

Student FAQs

Why are they singing in Italian? Wasn't German the language that was spoken in Vienna?

Yes, but Italian was the international language of opera throughout Europe at this time, even in England. Most of the leading singers of Mozart's day were Italian by birth, as was Mozart's librettist, Lorenzo da Ponte. *Don Giovanni* and *Così fan tutte*, two other librettos he wrote for Mozart, are also in Italian. And although German was the standard language in Mozart's Vienna, many audience members also spoke and understood Italian; those who did not could buy a copy of the libretto—a word whose literal meaning in Italian is "little book"—with parallel texts in Italian and German.

Why is there so much repetition of the text in the singing?

This is standard practice in operas. Music gives added emotional depth to the words, but it can also make those words more difficult to understand. Repetition helps audiences grasp the actual words being sung. This is especially important when two or more characters are singing at the same time. When the Count narrates his discovery of Cherubino from the day before, on the other hand, he does so in recitative, which allows him to present quite a large quantity of text in a short time: because recitative stands halfway between speech and song, it is easier to comprehend its words.

Time	Character(s) Singing	Original Italian	English Translation
1:56	Susanna and Basilio	Poverino!	Poor boy!
2:02	Count	Poverino! Ma da me sorpreso ancor.	Poor boy! But I have found him out yet again.
2:07	Susanna	Come?	How's that?
2:08	Basilio	Che?	What?
2:12	Count	Da tua cugina L'uscio ier trovai rinchiuso, Picchio, m'apre Barbarina, Paurosa fuor dell'uso. Io dal muso insospettito, Guardo, cerco in ogni sito,	At your cousin's yesterday I found the door locked; I knocked, and Barbarina opened it, more flustered than usual. My suspicions aroused, I looked in every corner,
2:31		Ed alzando piano pianino Il tappeto al tavolino, Vedo il paggio!	And lifted, ever so quietly, The tablecloth on the table, And there I saw the page!
2:40	(*He illustrates his action of the day before by raising the dress draped over the chair, only to discover Cherubino once again.*)		
2:47	Count	Ah, cosa veggio!	Ah! What do I see?
2:50	Susanna	Ah, crude stelle!	Ah, cruel fate!
2:52	Basilio (*laughing*)	Ah, meglio ancora!	Ah, it's getting even better!
2:56	Count	Onestissima signora! Or capsico come va.	O madame of highest virtue, Now I see how things are.
2:58	Susanna	Accader non può di peggio; Giusti Dei! che mai sarà?	Nothing worse could happen now; Ye gods of justice! What will happen?
3:03	Basilio	Così fan tutte le belle Non c'è alcuna novità.	All beautiful women act the same! There's nothing new about this.
3:21	Basilio (*to the Count*)	Ah del paggio quel ch'ho detto Era solo un mio sospetto!	What I was saying about the page Was merely a suspicion I had!
3:29	Count, Susana, Basilio	(All three repeat their texts from 2:56–3:20)	(All three repeat their texts from 2:56–3:20)

Form: Parallels to Rondo Form	Melody	Word-Music Relationships
		Susanna and Basilio sing a continuation of the Count's theme (1). For the first time, the two agree on something.
C	(5) Declamatory	Accompanied recitative, not very melodic, as the Count narrates yesterday's events.
	(2)	The "suspicion" theme returns.
A	(1) Opening theme again	The Count reacts again to news of Cherubino. Susanna is mortified, the Count feels vindicated, and Basilio gloats over the misfortunes of others.
B	(2)	Basilio repeats his earlier apology, but this time it sounds triumphant: the "suspicion" has turned out to be true.
A	(1)	The Count and Basilio feel vindicated, Susanna feels humiliated. (But she will get her revenge in Act 4!)

Student FAQs

Why do characters sing different texts at the same time? They seem to cancel each other out.

In a play, when two or more characters are talking at the same time, it's almost impossible to understand either one. In opera, however, each character sings in a distinctive vocal range (soprano, tenor, and baritone in this case), which allows listeners to distinguish among the lines more easily. The repetition of texts also helps us understand what is being sung.

Cherubino is silent in this scene. What does he sound like when he's singing?

Cherubino is a young teenager whose voice has not yet broken, and the role is always sung by a woman dressed as a man. This kind of role—a woman playing the part of a young man as you can see here—is known as a "trousers role."

26

William Billings
"Chester"
Composed: 1770

"Chester" was the unofficial anthem of the American Revolution. Composed by William Billings of Boston, a tanner by trade, its melody and words stirred the hearts of colonists fighting for their freedom from Great Britain.

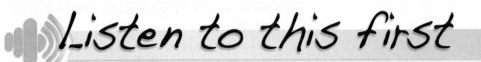

Listen to this first

((•● HEAR MORE on www.mymusiclab.com

Melody

The melody in each of the five verses is sung by the tenor voice. Listen for the antecedent-consequent structure of the melody's four phrases.

Texture

In this recording, the tenors and basses sing the first verse, with the melody in the tenor, the higher of the two voices. Listen for the growing texture as the sopranos enter in the third verse, the altos in the fourth.

Harmony

Listen for the growing richness of the harmony with each verse as new voices come in.

⚙ LEARN MORE on
www.mymusiclab.com
Chapter Objectives

Virtually every war and every revolution has fostered its own songs, and among the colonists fighting for their independence in the American Revolution the most popular song by far was "Chester." Unlike many songs of the time, it had not been imported from Great Britain; both the words and music had been written by William Billings, a native of Boston. Billings embodied the ideals of Yankee independence and self-reliance: a tanner by trade, he had taught himself how to write music, and his first publication, *The New-England Psalm-Singer* (1770), enjoyed great commercial success.

"Chester" is a song that follows the musical conventions of a hymn, with four voices moving for the most part in rhythm together. The musical style is very similar to that found in the chorale that ends Bach's Cantata 140 (see chapter 18). The text-setting is largely syllabic, with a few melismas that give added emphasis to key words. Groups singing this work could have sung the melody alone (in the tenor voice), or they could have sung all four independent parts. Unlike most hymns, however, "Chester" has a text that is largely secular. It begins and ends with praises of God but devotes itself largely to a description of the struggle for American independence. Only the first verse of text ("Let tyrants shake . . .") appeared initially in 1770; over time Billings added new verses that reflected events and personages of the war. The second verse even singles out a series of British generals—Howe, Burgoyne, Clinton, Prescott, and Cornwallis—by name.

A Structured Melody

The melody of "Chester" is built on the same principles of **periodic phrase structure** common in other works of the Classical Era. The structure of the tune reflects the structure of the text, which consists of two antecedent and two consequent phrases:

1746–1800
William Billings
"Chester"
Composed: 1770

GENRE
Song

KEY CONCEPTS
Hymn, periodic phrase structure, four-part harmony, melodic contour.

CHAPTER HIGHLIGHT
This song, the unofficial anthem of the American Revolution, follows the musical conventions of hymnody, with four voices moving in rhythm together.

Phrase	Text	Grammatical structure	Melodic structure	Melodic contour
1	Let tyrants shake their iron rod,	Antecedent phrase: the thought is incomplete and ends with a comma.	Ends on nontonic note (C): antecedent	Arching: the melody begins and ends on the same note and moves up and down in between.
2	And Slav'ry clank her galling chains,	Completes the antecedent phrase, but the two lines together do not constitute a satisfying whole; again, this line ends with a comma.	Ends on nontonic note (G): antecedent	Downward
3	We fear them not, we trust in God,	Completes the thought, although the comma indicates that this is not in fact the end of the text.	Ends on tonic note (F), but in a high register; weak consequent	Upward
4	New England's God forever reigns.	Completes the thought conclusively by providing reasons why "we fear them not" and why "we trust in God."	Ends on tonic note (F) in lower register, the lowest note in the entire melody; strong consequent	Downward

Billings uses the melodic contour of each phrase to reinforce its antecedent or consequent function:

- The first phrase ("Let tyrants shake . . .") begins and ends on the same note: it arches upward in the middle but in the end does not "go" anywhere. In terms of contour, it provides a neutral opening.

- The second phrase ("And Slav'ry. . . .") begins on this same note but moves decidedly lower in a downward contour. We have the sense now of having "gone" somewhere. We also have a sense that we need to return to the tonic.

- The third phrase ("We fear them not . . .") begins on the same opening note as phrases 1 and 2 but moves upward now, and ends on the tonic. To some extent, this sounds like an ending—we have, after all, returned to the tonic—but our voices are high, and when we make an assertion in speech, we usually lower the pitch. (We raise the pitch, by contrast, to ask a question.)

- The fourth phrase ("New England's God . . .") moves from the pitch we landed on at the end of the third phrase—the high tonic note, "F"—and descends rapidly, with shorter, faster notes, to the lower "F." This is in fact the lowest note of the melody, and it reinforces the sense of an ending.

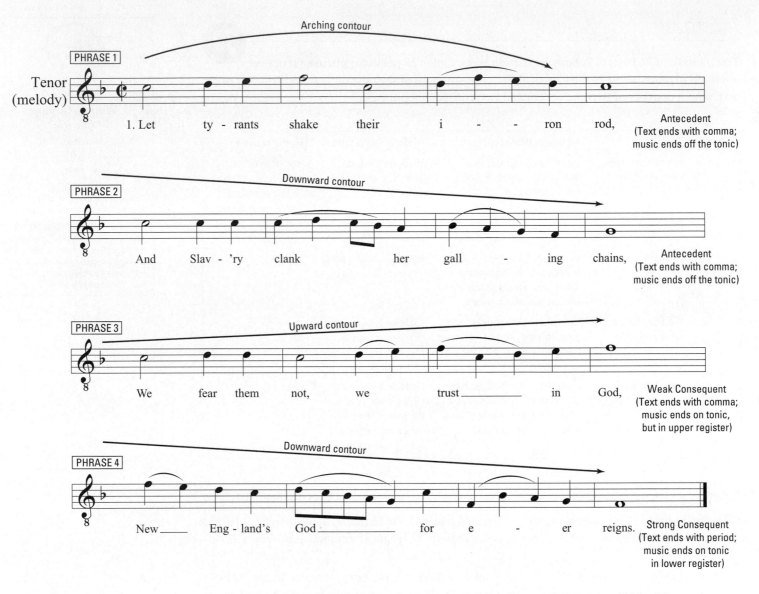

Schematically, then, the phrase structure of the music can be represented in this way:

<table>
<tr><td></td><td>Antecedent</td><td></td><td>Consequent</td><td></td></tr>
<tr><td>Antecedent 1</td><td>Antecedent 2</td><td></td><td>Consequent 1</td><td>Consequent 2</td></tr>
<tr><td>Let tyrants . . .</td><td>And Slav'ry . . .</td><td></td><td>We fear them not . . .</td><td>New England's God . . .</td></tr>
</table>

Changing Textures

When Billings published this work, he wrote out the full parts for all four voices (soprano, alto, tenor, bass), with the melody always in the tenor. In this recording, however, the group sings the first verse with only two voices (tenor and bass), then adds the soprano in the second verse (doubling the tenor an octave above) and the alto (with a new line) in the third verse. In the fourth verse, all four voices continue, but now the sopranos switch to the independent line notated in Billings' original score. The fifth stanza retains the texture of the fourth.

A re-creation of a Revolutionary-era marching band celebrates Patriots Day in Concord, Massachusetts. During the Revolutionary War, an instrumental arrangement of Billings' "Chester" would have been a staple of the group's repertory.
Matthew M. Lug/Middlesex County Volunteers

Changing Harmonies

The changing textures allow us to hear with special clarity the changing harmonies of the various verses. The first verse is in two-part harmony (tenor and bass). This two-part harmony continues in the second verse even though a third voice (soprano) has joined in. Because the soprano is doubling the tenor line (the melody), we hear a richer texture but not a richer harmony. In harmonic terms, the sopranos and tenors are singing the same line, even though they are an octave apart, with one of them higher than the other.

True three-part harmony begins with the third verse, when the altos join in with their own independent line. And four-part harmony begins with the fourth verse when the sopranos stop singing the melody and switch instead to their own distinctive line, different from all the others. Only now do we hear true four-part harmony, with each voice singing its own distinctive line. The fifth verse is also in true four-part harmony, with the same music but different words as the fourth verse.

With these points in mind, listen again to "Chester," using the Listening Guide.

> **CONNECT YOUR PLAYLIST**
>
> **Periodic Phrase Structure**
>
> **Find a song with a melody based on the principle of periodic phrase structure.**
>
> **Example:** Johnny Cash, "Daddy Sang Bass" (1969)
> The song opens with a clear antecedent-consequent phrase structure.

Listening Guide

GO TO **www.mymusiclab.com**
for the Automated Listening Guide
CD III • Track 2/Download Track 50

William Billings Composed: 1770 "Chester" (2:15)

Time	Verse	Text	Texture	Harmony	Melody
0:00	1	Let tyrants shake their iron rod, And Slav'ry clank her galling chains, We fear them not, we trust in God, New England's God forever reigns.	Tenor and Bass	Two parts	In the Tenor here and in all five verses
0:25	2	Howe and Burgoyne and Clinton too, With Prescott and Cornwallis join'd, Together plot our Overthrow, In one Infernal league combin'd.	Tenor and Bass, with Soprano doubling the melody an octave above the Tenor: still two-part harmony	Two parts	
0:51	3	When God inspir'd us for the fight, Their ranks were broke, their lines were forc'd, Their ships were Shatter'd in our sight, Or swiftly driven from our Coast.	New Alto part joins in with its own independent line	Three parts	
1:17	4	The Foe comes on with haughty Stride; Our troops advance with martial noise, Their Vet'rans flee before our Youth, And Gen'rals yield to beardless Boys.	As in Verse 3, but now the Soprano part sings its own independent line	Four parts	
1:42	5	What grateful Off'ring shall we bring? What shall we render to the Lord? Loud Halleluiahs let us Sing, And praise his name on ev'ry Chord.	As in Verse 4	Four parts	

Student FAQs

Why is it called "Chester"?

It was customary in Billings' time to give song and hymn tunes a distinctive name, because these tunes could be (and often were) sung to different texts. Many of Billings' tune names appear to have been arbitrary: one of his finest hymns is called "Africa," but it has no connection with that continent any more than do the tunes he called "Asia" and "Europe." "Chester" is a town in western Massachusetts; Billings named a series of other tunes after cities and towns in the Bay State, such as "Lexington," "Medford," and "Waltham."

The last chord sounds strange. Why is that?

Even when there are four independent lines (as in verses 4–5 in this recording), the last chord contains only two different notes, an F and a C, which together make up the interval of a fifth. A fifth all by itself, without a third (which in this case would be the note "A") sounds "empty" or "hollow" to our ears.

PROFILE   **William Billings** (1746–1800)

Independent Composer

Born in Boston, Billings trained as a tanner and was largely self-taught as a composer. He was an enthusiastic supporter of the Revolution and counted Paul Revere among his friends. Billings' *The New-England Psalm Singer* (1770) remains a landmark in the history of American music: it was the first published collection of musical works by an individual native-born composer.

Billings would go on to publish another five major collections of his works—more than 300 compositions in all, almost all for four-part chorus—and would establish or help set up several different schools in Massachusetts and Rhode Island. But without copyright laws, he could not support himself financially as a composer. He died in poverty and was buried in an unmarked grave, presumably in the old Central Burying Ground in on the edge of the Boston Common. In a fitting if posthumous tribute, Billings was inducted into the Songwriters Hall of Fame in 1970. He was in many respects the first great American songwriter.

⊙➤ **EXPLORE MORE** on **www.mymusiclab.com**

The frontispiece to Billings' *New-England Psalm-Singer* shows a group of men seated at a round table singing a round ("Wake ev'ry breath"), in which all voices sing the same tune, but each enters at a different point (in the manner of "Row, row, row your boat"). The melody itself encircles the musicians. This engraving was done by one of Billings' Boston friends and fellow patriots, the silversmith Paul Revere, better known for his ride from Boston to Lexington to warn the people of advancing British troops.

The Granger Collection, New York

EXPAND YOUR PLAYLIST: BILLINGS

- **Wake Ev'ry Breath.** This canon (round) for six voices over a contrasting bass line is depicted in the illustration above.

- **Lamentation Over Boston.** An anthem written after American troops had evacuated Boston following the battle of Bunker Hill in 1775. The text ("By the Rivers of Watertown we sat down and wept, / we wept when we remember'd, O Boston . . .") is a variant on Psalm 137, sung by the exiled Israelites ("By the rivers of Babylon there we sat down / yea, we wept, when we remembered Zion").

- **I am the Rose of Sharon.** An anthem on a text from the Song of Solomon, 2:1–11.

- **Africa.** A stirring hymn to words by the great English hymnodist Isaac Watts.

((•• **HEAR SAMPLES** on **www.mymusiclab.com**

THE COMPOSER SPEAKS

Billings seems to have been quite proud to have taught himself composition. In the introduction to his *New-England Psalm Singer*, he argued that nature was the true source of all art. The excerpt here preserves Billings' idiosyncratic spelling and syntax.

Perhaps it may be expected that I should say something concerning Rules for Composition; to those I answer that Nature is the best dictator, *for all the hard, dry, studied Rules that ever was prescribed, will not enable any Person to form an Air [i.e., melody] any more than the bare Knowledge of the four and twenty Letters, and strict Grammatical Rules will qualify a Scholar for composing a Piece of Poetry, or properly adjusting a Tragedy, without a Genius. It must be Nature, Nature who must lay the foundation. Nature must inspire the Thought . . . For my own part, as I don't think myself confin'd to any Rules for* Composition, *laid down by any that went before me, neither should I think (were I to pretend to lay down Rules) that any one who came after me were in any ways obligated to adhere to them, any further than they should think proper: So in fact I think it best for every* Composer *to be his own* Carver. *Therefore, upon this Consideration, for me to dictate, or pretend to prescribe Rules of the Nature for others, would not only be very unnecessary, but also a great Piece of Vanity.*

Source: William Billings, Introduction to *The New-Engalnd Psalm Singer* (Boston, 1770).

EXPAND YOUR PLAYLIST

Music of the American Revolution

"The Liberty Song"
• Set to an old English tune, the lyrics, by John Dickinson, of Pennsylvania, begin, "Come, join hand in hand, brave Americans all, / And rouse your bold hearts at fair Liberty's call."

"Yankee Doodle"
• This popular tune served literally hundreds of different texts, including "Yankee Doodle's Expedition to Rhode Island."

"The World Turned Upside Down"
• An old English ballad supposed to have been played when Cornwallis surrendered to Washington at Yorktown, Virginia. (Coldplay would record an entirely different song of the same name more than 225 years later.)

"The British Grenadiers"
• A popular song among the British forces at the time.

HEAR SAMPLES on **www.mymusiclab.com**

TEST YOURSELF on **www.mymusiclab.com**   Flashcards and chapter tests

PART 4 Summary

	Baroque	**Classical**
Texture	Polyphonic and homophonic coexist.	Both polyphonic and homophonic, but on the whole more homophonic.
Melody	Lyrical and declamatory (recitative) coexist; often virtuosic.	Growing importance of periodic phrase structure in all genres of music, not just in dance.
Rhythm	Wider range of extremes, from smooth and flowing to choppy and irregular.	More smoothly flowing melodies.
Timbre	Sharp distinction between vocal and instrumental parts.	Establishment of the modern orchestra (strings, winds, percussion).
Harmony	Harmony as an underlying basis for melody.	Harmony becomes increasingly important as a large-scale structural element (tonic/nontonic/tonic).
Form	Greater variety of formal principles: sectional form, binary form, theme and variations, ostinato.	Theme and variations, minuet (**ABA**), rondo, sonata form, double-exposition concerto form.
Word-music relationships	Even greater use of word painting. Texture and musical strongly support text.	Word painting still present, but not as prevalent and often more subtle.

IN REVIEW: Classical Style

Periodic phrase structure Melodies are constructed of antecedent (opening) and consequent (closing) phrases.
- Haydn, String Quartet in C Major, op. 76, no. 3, second movement (Chapter 20)
- Haydn, Symphony no. 102 in B♭ Major, third and fourth movements (Chapter 22)
- Mozart, Symphony no. 40 in G minor, K. 550, first movement (Chapter 23)
- Billings, "Chester" (Chapter 26)

Theme and variations A modular form, with a theme followed by a series of discrete units, each of which presents a varied restatement of the theme.
- Haydn, String Quartet in C Major, op. 76, no. 3, second movement (Chapter 20)
- Master Musicians of the Ikuta-ryu (Japan): *Cherry Blossom* (Chapter 21)

Binary form A structure consisting of two sections, each of which is repeated in performance (**AABB**).
- Haydn, Symphony no. 102 in B♭ Major, third movement (Chapter 22)

Minuet form A **ternary form** (**ABA**) with a strong sense of contrast between the **A** and **B** sections, each of which is itself a binary form.
- Haydn, Symphony no. 102 in B♭ Major, third movement (Chapter 22)

Rondo form A structure in which the opening idea (**A**) returns repeatedly after the presentation of contrasting ideas (**B, C, D**, etc.), creating the pattern **ABACADA**.
- Haydn, Symphony no. 102 in B♭ Major, fourth movement (Chapter 22)

Sonata form An expanded type of binary form in which the music modulates to a secondary key area in the first section and then returns to the tonic about midway through the second section. A sonata form movement consists of an exposition, a development, and a recapitulation.
- Mozart, Symphony no. 40 in G minor, K. 550, first movement (Chapter 23)

Double-exposition concerto form A type of sonata form often used in concertos of the Classical Era, with two separate expositions, the first for the orchestra (which does not modulate) and the second for the soloist and orchestra together (in which the music does modulate). The development and recapitulation follow the standard pattern of sonata form.
- Mozart, Piano Concerto in A Major, K. 488, first movement (Chapter 24)

The orchestra An ensemble of strings, winds, and percussion. The orchestra would expand in size and range later in the nineteenth and twentieth centuries, but its nucleus established itself in the second half of the eighteenth century.
- Haydn, Symphony no. 102 in B♭ Major, third and fourth movements (Chapter 22)
- Mozart, Symphony no. 40 in G minor, K. 550, first movement (Chapter 23)
- Mozart, Piano Concerto in A Major, K. 488, first movement (Chapter 24)

Accompanied recitative A type of recitative in which the orchestra (and not merely the basso continuo) accompanies the singer.
- Mozart, *The Marriage of Figaro*, Act I, "Cosa sento" (Chapter 25)

⊘ TEST YOURSELF on **www.mymusiclab.com**   Part Exam

5

The Nineteenth Century

In the nineteenth century, the rationality of the Enlightenment gave way to a new fascination with imagination, individual emotion, and longing. "Romanticism," as this movement was called, does not refer to a kind of love; it derives its name from a literary genre—the "romance," forerunner of today's novel—that was largely free of structural or narrative conventions. For the Romantic, dreams were as important as the intellect, and art—particularly music, which did not rely on words or the representation of objects—offered access to a realm of ideals beyond the limitations of human reason and the physical world. It was less a new style of art than a new way of thinking about art.

The music of the nineteenth century reflects this increased sense of freedom from convention. Composers felt obligated to develop their own distinctive voices. To make their music original, they explored musical extremes of all kinds. They wrote for orchestras that were bigger and louder than ever before. They emphasized extreme contrasts of texture between the simple and the complex. They wrote music that ranged from the disarmingly simple to the fiendishly difficult, often within the course of the same work. They gave growing importance to program music, sometimes exploring the darker side of the human psyche in what many of the time considered shocking detail: the "March to the Scaffold" of Berlioz's *Symphonie fantastique* (chapter 30) depicts an artist being led to his execution, with music so graphic that we hear the sound his head makes when it falls into the bucket at the base of the guillotine. In short, the range of each musical element available to composers—melody, rhythm, harmony, dynamics, timbre, texture, form—grew exponentially in the nineteenth century.

▲ Caspar David Friedrich's *The Wanderer* (1818) captures the Romantic fascination with dream, contemplation, and the infinite.
Caspar David Friedrich (1774–1840), "The Wanderer above the Sea of Clouds". 1818. Oil on Canvas. Hamburg Kunsthalle, Hamburg, Germany. Bridgeman Art Library

"Most Romantic of All the Arts"

The way audiences listened to music—especially instrumental music—also changed in the nineteenth century. Because it lacked words, instrumental music had long been perceived as somewhat vague, not "about" anything in particular. Romanticism changed all that. Precisely *because* it lacked words, instrumental music could engage the imagination of listeners more directly and evoke ideas and emotions that could not be captured by nouns, verbs, and adjectives. This new way of listening is captured in a review of Beethoven's

Fifth Symphony by E. T. A. Hoffmann (best known as the author of *The Nutcracker* and other fantastical tales) in 1810. "Beethoven's music sets in motion the machinery of awe, of fear, of terror, of pain," Hoffmann declared, "and awakens that infinite yearning which is the essence of Romanticism." For Hoffmann music was "the most Romantic of all the arts," for it "opens to mankind an unknown realm, a world that has nothing in common with the outer sensual world that surrounds him." This was particularly true of instrumental music, he felt, because it was unencumbered by words. Hoffmann's review won widespread praise because it articulated a fundamental shift from eighteenth-century thinking, which had held that the verbal arts gave form to the highest expressions of thought.

Composers, once seen as artisans providing musical goods made to order, were now perceived to have a window on the infinite and the spiritual, and their social status rose accordingly. They received invitations to gatherings at the highest levels of society and commanded enormous fees for their performances. They joined the pantheon of painters and poets who gave voice to that which could not be expressed in ordinary language.

▲ An American piano factory in the late 19th century. The scale of production reduced costs and made it possible for most middle-class households to own an instrument.

Photograph courtesy of the Hagley Museum and Library, Wilmington, Delaware

A Piano in Every Home

Today, one is most likely to hear a song like Schubert's "Erlkönig" (chapter 28) in the concert hall, with a highly trained singer and a skilled pianist performing from the stage for a quiet audience. The song was composed, however, to meet the growing nineteenth-century demand for

Nineteenth Century ⊙➔ EXPLORE MORE on www.mymusiclab.com

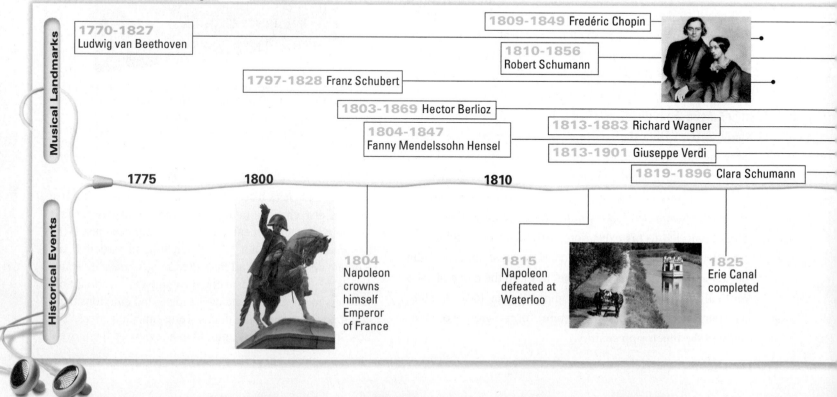

Musical Landmarks

1770-1827 Ludwig van Beethoven

1797-1828 Franz Schubert

1803-1869 Hector Berlioz

1804-1847 Fanny Mendelssohn Hensel

1809-1849 Frédéric Chopin

1810-1856 Robert Schumann

1813-1883 Richard Wagner

1813-1901 Giuseppe Verdi

1819-1896 Clara Schumann

1775   1800   1810

Historical Events

1804 Napoleon crowns himself Emperor of France

1815 Napoleon defeated at Waterloo

1825 Erie Canal completed

music that could be played at home, because in the nineteenth century pianos became a common fixture of middle-class households. The Industrial Revolution, which had begun toward the end of the eighteenth century, made it possible to manufacture goods on a scale never before imagined, which in turn made them cheaper to produce and sell. In Mozart's time, a piano maker built instruments one at a time, and only the wealthy could afford them. By the middle of the nineteenth century, pianos and other instruments could be produced in mass quantities in large factories. Having a piano in one's home was as much a social as a musical statement. Demand grew steadily through the century for piano compositions, songs, and chamber music, and composers wrote works to meet this demand. See A Closer Look: The Power of Music, p. 236.

Music as Political Force

"Leave the dreaming and hesitation behind/Without fatigue, go forward!" With these words, set to music in 1848 by Clara Schumann in her song "Vorwärts!" (chapter 32), the Dresden Choral Society exhorted listeners to work—and fight, if necessary—for a united and democratic Germany. This push was part of a broader impulse throughout Europe to achieve the goals set out by the French Revolution of 1789: freedom in the form of representative government, equality through the abolition of hereditary class privilege, and fraternity through rights of assembly and association. A series of uprisings in 1848–1849 throughout continental Europe was largely unsuccessful at the time but helped pave the way for later political reforms.

▲ Street fighting in Berlin, 1848. Barricades were constructed by ordinary citizens to block the movement of the royal armies.
Art Resource/Bildarchiv Preussischer Kulturbesitz

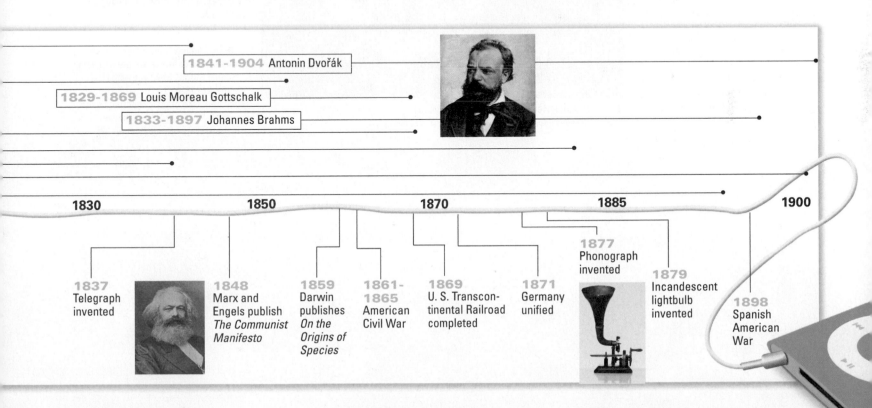

1841-1904 Antonin Dvořák

1829-1869 Louis Moreau Gottschalk

1833-1897 Johannes Brahms

1830   1850   1870   1885   1900

1837
Telegraph
invented

1848
Marx and
Engels publish
*The Communist
Manifesto*

1859
Darwin
publishes
*On the
Origins of
Species*

1861-
1865
American
Civil War

1869
U. S. Transcon-
tinental Railroad
completed

1871
Germany
unified

1877
Phonograph
invented

1879
Incandescent
lightbulb
invented

1898
Spanish
American
War

A CLOSER LOOK   The Power of Music

◉➤ EXPLORE MORE on www.mymusiclab.com

Josef Danhauser's *Franz Liszt at the Piano* (1840) shows the composer and pianist Franz Liszt surrounded by a gathering of famous writers and musicians. The literary figures, including Alexandre Dumas, Victor Hugo, and George Sand, have all interrupted their reading to listen to Liszt play. This group portrait idealizes the power of music—it could be more important than drama, poetry, and fiction. Even the great writers of the era stop reading to listen to the music!

The Italian composer and violin virtuoso **Nicolò Paganini** (1782-1840). He is to the violin what Liszt is to the piano. Paganini is widely rumored to have made a pact with the devil in exchange for his talent; he does nothing to dispel the story.

Victor Hugo (1802-1885), the greatest literary figure in nineteenth-century France. He is famous for his poetry, dramas, criticism, and above all his novels, which include *Les Misérables* and *The Hunchback of Notre Dame.*

Alexandre Dumas *père* (1802-1870), author of *The Count of Monte Cristo* and *The Three Musketeers.*

The novelist **George Sand** (1804-1876), whose real name is Amandine-Aurore-Lucile Dudevant. She wrote under a man's name, dressed in men's clothes, and smoked in public. In the 1830s she was Chopin's lover.

Gioacchino Rossini (1792-1868), the enormously successful and beloved composer of Italian opera. He stands arm-in-arm with Paganini listening to Liszt.

A portrait of the English poet **George Gordon, Lord Byron** (1788-1824). Byron had died fighting for Greece's independence from the Ottoman Empire and was beloved in death both as a poet and as a fighter for freedom.

A bust of the composer **Ludwig van Beethoven** (1770-1827). Beethoven cast a long shadow over musicians in the nineteenth century and is accorded pride of place here. While others contemplate Liszt, Liszt contemplates Beethoven.

Franz Liszt (1811-1886), virtuoso pianist and composer.

Marie d'Agoult (1805-1876), French author who writes under the pen name "Daniel Stern." She lived with Liszt in the late 1830s and bore him three children. One of their children, Cosima, eventually marries the composer Richard Wagner (see Chapter 37).

▲ Josef Danhauser, *Franz Liszt at the Piano*, 1840.
Juergen Liepe/Art Resource/Bildarchiv Preussischer Kulturbesitz

Music proved an important vehicle for expressing political sentiment throughout the nineteenth century. The numerous choral societies that sprang up across the continent were as much political as artistic. Much of the repertory of these groups, like Clara Schumann's "Forward!," gave voice to aspirations for political freedoms.

Nationalism

Another political impulse that developed over the course of the nineteenth century was nationalism. More and more peoples began to perceive their social identities on the basis of a shared language and cultural practices in a community that extended far beyond any one locale or region. The idea of the nation as the focal point of social identity became a powerful social and political force. The U.S. Civil War (1861–1865) helped change the United States from a plural noun to a singular. Government documents that had once read "The United States *are* determined to . . ." now read "The United States *is* determined to. . . ."

But not all groups united by language and culture had their own nation-states. Many ethnic Czechs and Hungarians, for example, were subjects of the Austrian Empire, whose capital (Vienna) and official language (German) were foreign to them. Poles, in turn, fell under the rule of the Prussian or Russian Empires at various times and places. Music proved a powerful outlet for the expression of nationalistic feelings. Without recourse to language, and without the incrimination specific words might bring, composers could express in sound their sense of national pride by using the characteristic melodic and rhythmic elements of their peoples. Chopin, living in Paris, felt deep sympathy for the plight of his native Poland. His Mazurka in B-flat Major, op. 7, no. 1 (chapter 33), was one of numerous pieces he wrote using elements of Polish folk music. Chopin's Polonaises, in particular—piano works based on the proud national dance of Poland—were described by a contemporary as "cannons wrapped in flowers."

▲ *The End of Poland (Finis Poloniae)* shows a Polish officer comforting two disconsolate soldiers after the Battle of Ostrolenka (1830), in which the Russian army defeated Polish forces. Polish nationalism was a driving force behind the uprising.
Ruth Schacht/Art Resource/Bildarchiv Preussischer Kulturbesitz

The Revolution in Transportation

Increased mobility on both land and sea in the nineteenth century fostered commercial and cultural connections that would have been unthinkable only a few generations before. In the summer of 1893, Antonín Dvořák was able to travel from New York City to the Czech-American community of Spillville in northeastern Iowa in less than three days, where he would compose a string quartet he called "The American" (chapter 39). Music publishers could distribute their music on a global basis for the first time. European musicians could tour the United States and American musicians could tour Europe with ease.

Populations increased dramatically in the nineteenth century: from 1800 to 1900, the world's major powers grew 150 percent. At the same time, technological innovations including the telegraph, telephone, railroads, and steamships made the world a smaller place. The completion of the transcontinental railroad in 1869 reduced the six-month travel time from New York to San Francisco to one week. On the water, steam-powered engines replaced sails, cutting the ocean voyage from Europe to the United States to as little as six days.

▲ This hand-colored photograph shows the ceremony marking the completion of the Transcontinental Railroad in 1869, linking the eastern and western United States by rail for the first time.
The Granger Collection

The Nineteenth Century CHAPTERS AT A GLANCE

chapter 27
p. 240

1770–1827
Ludwig van Beethoven
Symphony no. 5 in
C Minor, op. 67
Composed: 1808

GENRE
Symphony

KEY CONCEPTS
Orchestral timbre, rhythmic-motivic development, dynamics, sonata form, alternating theme and variations, scherzo, cyclic form.

CHAPTER HIGHLIGHT
Nineteenth-century Symphony
The Fifth Symphony helped redefine the symphony as a genre that carried a meaning beyond the notes themselves. Its four movements trace a path from struggle to triumph.
EXPAND YOUR PLAYLIST: Beethoven's Symphonies

chapter 28
p. 248

1797–1828
Franz Schubert
"Erlkönig," D. 328
Composed: 1815

GENRE
Song

KEY CONCEPTS
Modified strophic form, ballad.

CHAPTER HIGHLIGHT
Ballad
Schubert's song for voice and piano is a setting of a ballad, a poem that tells a story. The music enhances the twists and turns of the plot and calls for the singer to serve not only as a narrator but also to portray the story's three very different characters.
EXPAND YOUR PLAYLIST: Schubert's Songs

chapter 29
p. 255

1809–1847
Felix Mendelssohn
Overture to
A Midsummer Night's Dream
Composed: 1826

GENRE
Concert overture

KEY CONCEPTS
Program music, relationship of drama and purely instrumental music, sonata form without exposition repeat.

CHAPTER HIGHLIGHT
Programmatic Orchestral Music
Mendelssohn's instrumental music presents a wordless rendition of Shakespeare's drama, or at the very least, of its principal characters.
EXPAND YOUR PLAYLIST: Shakespeare in Music

chapter 30
p. 261

1803–1869
Hector Berlioz
Symphonie fantastique, fourth movement ("March to the Scaffold")
Composed: 1830

GENRE
Programmatic symphony

KEY CONCEPTS
The modern orchestra, program music, major vs. minor mode.

CHAPTER HIGHLIGHT
Program Music
Program music became increasingly important during the nineteenth century as many composers sought to integrate purely instrumental music with ideas by providing verbal clues about the "content" of the music.
EXPAND YOUR PLAYLIST: The Music of Dreams

chapter 34
p. 285

1829–1869
Louis Moreau Gottschalk
Union: Concert Paraphrase on National Airs
Composed: 1862

GENRE
Solo piano

KEY CONCEPTS
Virtuosity, nationalistic melodies, homophonic vs. polyphonic texture.

CHAPTER HIGHLIGHT
Virtuosity
While a great deal of music was written for amateur performance, some composers wrote music that lay well beyond the reach of any but the most accomplished musicians. Nineteenth-century composers like Gottschalk toured with their own compositions and were accorded near-divine status.
EXPAND YOUR PLAYLIST: The Nineteenth-Century Virtuoso

GLOBAL CONNECTION
KEY CONCEPT
Virtuosity

chapter 35
p. 292

Global Connection: Virtuosity
b. 1920
Ravi Shankar
Raga Sindhi-Bhairavi
Recorded: 1968

GENRE
Indian Music

KEY CONCEPTS
Virtuosity, sitar, tonal pattern and mood, pulse cycles, metered vs. unmetered rhythm, improvisation.

CHAPTER HIGHLIGHT
Indian Music
Perhaps the most highly developed classical music in the world, the concert music of India features a complex set of scale and rhythms. The raga is a multi-movement composition comparable to a Western concerto.
EXPAND YOUR PLAYLIST: Raga: Ravi Shankar, Anoushka Shankar, Ali Akbar Khan, George Harrison

chapter 36
p. 300

1813–1901
Giuseppe Verdi
La Traviata, Act I, selection
Composed: 1853

GENRE
Opera

KEY CONCEPTS
Integration of recitative and aria, vocal virtuosity, word-music relationships.

CHAPTER HIGHLIGHT
Vocal Virtuosity
Opera had long provided a venue for singers to demonstrate their technical prowess, and this tradition continued into the nineteenth century. This excerpt from Verdi's *La Traviata* places extraordinary technical demands on the soprano, even while incorporating her emotions into a dramatic situation that is highly realistic.
EXPAND YOUR PLAYLIST: The Art of the Diva: Renata Tebaldi, Joan Sutherland, Kiri Te Kanawa, Anna Netrebko

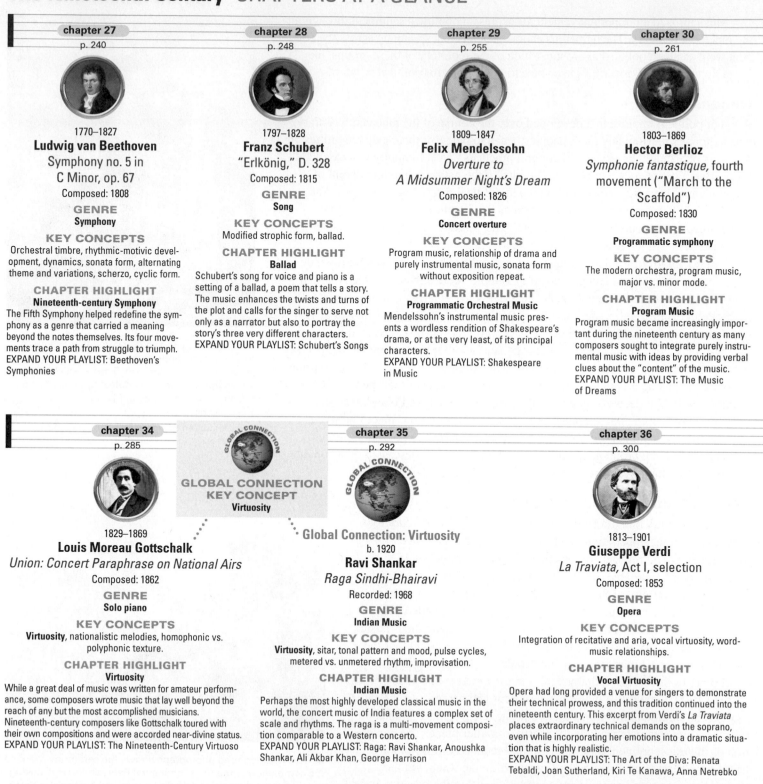

27

Ludwig van Beethoven
Symphony no. 5 in C Minor, op. 67
Composed: 1808

Beethoven's Fifth Symphony is one of the most famous works of music ever written, and with good reason: its energy and drive have proven irresistible to generations of listeners. This chapter's Listening Guide covers the symphony's opening movement. Listening guides for all four movements are available on MyMusicLab.

Listen to this first

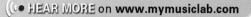
HEAR MORE on www.mymusiclab.com

Rhythm

Dynamics

Timbre

Form

Rhythm	Dynamics	Timbre	Form
You may already know the opening motif: "short-short-short-LONG." Listen for how this basic rhythmic idea is varied not only in the first movement, but in all four movements.	Notice the repeated and sudden contrasts between loud and soft.	Listen to the how Beethoven varies the sound of the full orchestra by using all of it at times and only a small portion of it at others (just strings, or just winds). Be ready for the addition of new instruments (especially trombones) at the beginning of the finale.	Listen for the variety of forms among the four movements: • First movement: This is in sonata form. • Second movement: This is a set of variations on two different themes, one soft and one loud. • Third movement: Listen for the ternary form (**ABA'**), with the return of **A** varied. This movement leads without a break into the next one. • Fourth movement: This is in sonata form. Listen for the surprise return of material from the third movement just before the beginning of the recapitulation.

LEARN MORE on
www.mymusiclab.com
Chapter Objectives

The opening of Beethoven's Fifth Symphony is quite possibly both the briefest and best-known theme in all of music: it is instantly recognizable. Generations of listeners around the world have heard this theme as an aural symbol of strength and resolve precisely because it is so simple and straightforward. Like an acorn that grows into a giant oak tree, this theme provides the basic rhythmic motif for almost every theme in the work. Even though Beethoven gave no indication in the score of an extramusical meaning of this work, critics from his time onward have interpreted it as a progression from struggle (in the first movement) to triumph (in the finale), from the darkness of C minor to the brightness of C major.

Beethoven never wrote a program for the work, but when asked the meaning of this opening idea, he is said to have grumbled in response: "Thus Fate pounds at the portal." Whether the report is true or not—it was first published long after the composer's death by a notoriously unreliable witness (see "Fate?" page 243)—it has been repeated many times over. This symphony does indeed seem to "describe" a process that moves from struggle (in the first movement) to triumph (in the finale).

Beethoven's symphonies—he wrote nine altogether—helped establish his reputation as the greatest instrumental composer of his time. Works like the Fifth Symphony helped redefine the symphony as a genre that carried meaning beyond the notes themselves, without the aid of a sung text or program. Beethoven's last symphony, the Ninth, includes voices and a text in its finale, and his Sixth Symphony ("Pastoral") is programmatic. But in the Fifth Symphony, Beethoven created a work that challenged listeners to create their own sense of meaning.

Rhythm: A Germinal Cell

The Fifth Symphony opens with a distinctive but deceptively simple theme. It consists of only four notes and two different pitches. The texture is monophonic: the instruments play in unison, and we hear no harmony of any kind. The rhythm is what gives this idea its real identity: short-short-short-LONG—that is, three notes of equal length followed by one longer note. One of the things that make this symphony so remarkable is the fact that Beethoven transforms this simple musical idea in so many different ways.

In the first movement, the process of transformation begins almost instantly:

1. 0:00 Opening statement of the *s-s-s-L* figure, with last note held out long (unison texture).

2. 0:03 Restatement of the *s-s-s-L* figure, moved down a step. The texture is still unison, and the rhythm is still the same, but the notes are different.

3. 0:06 Restatement of the *s-s-s-L* figure in different voices in succession (polyphonic texture) and on different pitches. Now the texture *and* the notes are different; only the rhythm remains the same.

This transformation continues throughout all the movements that follow (see the Listening Guide for the first movement in this chapter; Listening Guides for the remaining movements are online). The pitches, harmonies, and textures are constantly shifting, but the same basic rhythmic idea—short-short-short-LONG—remains recognizable from the beginning of the symphony to the very end. Only occasionally does it leave the stage, and when it does, it always comes back.

Dynamics: Loud vs. Soft

One of the more striking features of the Fifth Symphony is its treatment of dynamics. The music repeatedly moves without warning from extremely loud to extremely soft and vice versa. The very opening establishes this contrast: the loud unison is immediately followed by

1770–1827
Ludwig van Beethoven
Symphony no. 5 in
C Minor, op. 67
Composed: 1808
GENRE
Symphony

KEY CONCEPTS
Orchestral timbre, rhythmic-motivic development, dynamics, sonata form, alternating theme and variations, scherzo, cyclic form.

CHAPTER HIGHLIGHT
Nineteenth-century Symphony
The Fifth Symphony helped redefine the symphony as a genre that carried a meaning beyond the notes themselves. Its four movements trace a path from struggle to triumph.

CONNECT YOUR PLAYLIST

Unison Opening

Find a work that opens with a statement in unison Texture.

Example: Pink, "So What" (2008) One critic described the opening of this song as ideal for "massive car singalongs."

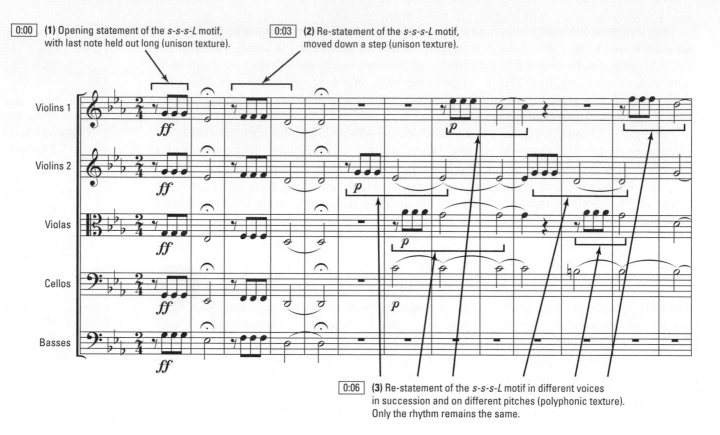

0:00 **(1)** Opening statement of the *s-s-s-L* motif, with last note held out long (unison texture).

0:03 **(2)** Re-statement of the *s-s-s-L* motif, moved down a step (unison texture).

0:06 **(3)** Re-statement of the *s-s-s-L* motif in different voices in succession and on different pitches (polyphonic texture). Only the rhythm remains the same.

a soft passage. These dynamic contrasts are especially prominent at the end of the third movement, where the music remains extremely quiet for a very long time before moving without a break into the finale, which erupts in an explosion of sound. Composers had exploited dynamic contrasts long before the early nineteenth century, but the number of sudden changes, their rapidity, and, above all, the wide extremes of volume in this work were unprecedented.

Timbre: The Orchestra Grows

The contrast in dynamics between the end of the third movement and the beginning of the finale is reinforced by the addition of new instruments at that point. The piccolo and contrabassoon enrich the upper and lower ranges of the orchestra, respectively, and the trombones help create an even fuller sound in the middle ranges.

Already, in the first movement, Beethoven repeatedly contrasts wind instruments (flute, clarinet, oboe, bassoon, horns, and trumpets) against the stringed instruments (violins, violas, cellos, and double basses). The oboe has an unusual and wholly unexpected solo in the recapitulation of the first movement. The double basses have an unusually prominent and difficult passage in the middle (**B**) section of the ternary-form third movement. By using these instruments in such distinctive ways, Beethoven creates an enormous sense of breadth within a small space: the Fifth is among the shortest symphonies he wrote. Later composers of the nineteenth century would extend the range of orchestral timbre still further.

Cyclic Form

When the individual movements of a work are linked in some tangible and distinctive way (usually through the use of a common musical idea) we say that the work as a whole is **cyclic**. In his Fifth Symphony, Beethoven links all four movements through various permutations of the *short-short-short-LONG* figure and by repeating an extended passage of the third movement during the course of the fourth. These devices contribute to the sense of growth across the work as a whole. Other composers of the nineteenth century would follow Beethoven's lead.

With these points in mind, listen again to the entire work, using the Listening Guide in this chapter for the first movement and the Automated Listening Guides online for the last three movements.

LEARN MORE on
www.mymusiclab.com
MyMusicLibrary:
"E. T. A. Hoffman's Review of Beethoven's Fifth"

HISTORICAL CONTEXT Fate?

According to one story, Beethoven claimed that the powerful opening theme of the Fifth Symphony—the short-short-short-LONG motif—represented "Fate pounding at the portal." But did he really say this?

Over the last decade of his life, Beethoven employed a personal assistant to help him with various chores. One of these assistants was Anton Schindler (1794–1864), who published a lengthy biography of the composer in 1840, 13 years after Beethoven's death. Given Schindler's close contact with Beethoven, this book was long accepted as an authoritative, eyewitness account of the composer's later years. In the last 30 years, however, scholars have discovered that Schindler fabricated evidence on many occasions, so it is not always easy to know which of his stories are true. Schindler is the source of the story about Beethoven's alleged explanation of the Fifth Symphony.

Even if Beethoven really said it, how are we to interpret it? Was he serious? Or was he just trying to get Schindler off his back? Does the statement apply only to the opening of the symphony, the first movement, or the entire work? And can a musical idea really "mean" anything at all?

Winston Churchill, prime minister of Great Britain during World War II, flashes the "V for Victory" sign to a jubilant crowd celebrating the end of the war in Europe in May 1945. The short-short-short-LONG figure that opens the Fifth Symphony happens to correspond to the letter "V" in Morse code (dot-dot-dot-DASH). For the Allies in World War II, "V" was shorthand for "Victory." The opening motif of Beethoven's Fifth soon became an audible icon for the resolve of the allies to achieve victory in Europe: the British Broadcasting Corporation opened its European broadcasts each night with this stirring theme.

Topham/The Image Works

Listening Guide

GO TO www.mymusiclab.com
for the Automated Listening Guide
CD III • Tracks 4–7/Download
Tracks 52–55

Ludwig van Beethoven Composed: ca. 1808 Symphony no. 5 in C Minor, op. 67, first movement (7:32)

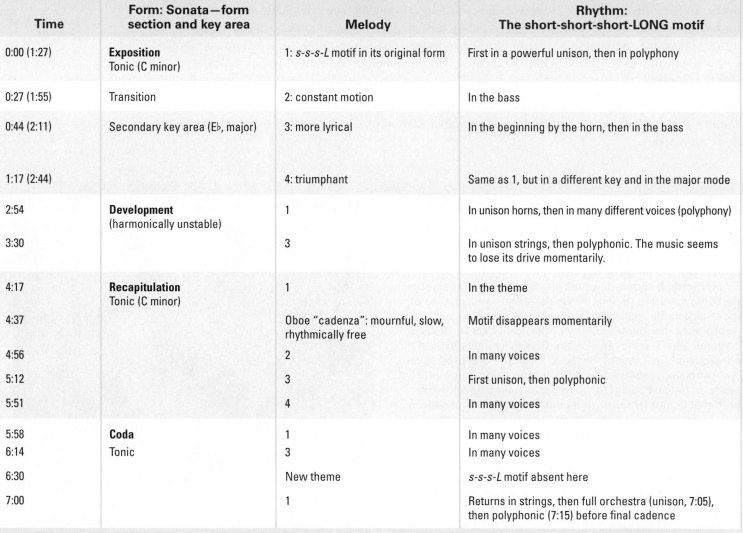

Time	Form: Sonata—form section and key area	Melody	Rhythm: The short-short-short-LONG motif
0:00 (1:27)	**Exposition** Tonic (C minor)	1: *s-s-s-L* motif in its original form	First in a powerful unison, then in polyphony
0:27 (1:55)	Transition	2: constant motion	In the bass
0:44 (2:11)	Secondary key area (E♭, major)	3: more lyrical	In the beginning by the horn, then in the bass
1:17 (2:44)		4: triumphant	Same as 1, but in a different key and in the major mode
2:54	**Development** (harmonically unstable)	1	In unison horns, then in many different voices (polyphony)
3:30		3	In unison strings, then polyphonic. The music seems to lose its drive momentarily.
4:17	**Recapitulation** Tonic (C minor)	1	In the theme
4:37		Oboe "cadenza": mournful, slow, rhythmically free	Motif disappears momentarily
4:56		2	In many voices
5:12		3	First unison, then polyphonic
5:51		4	In many voices
5:58	**Coda**	1	In many voices
6:14	Tonic	3	In many voices
6:30		New theme	*s-s-s-L* motif absent here
7:00		1	Returns in strings, then full orchestra (unison, 7:05), then polyphonic (7:15) before final cadence

Second timing in parentheses = exposition repeat

Timbre

Strings alone at first, alternating with
full orchestra

Full orchestra

Starts with horns; strings and other winds
enter gradually; a sense of relative rest after
the turmoil of the opening

Full orchestra; a sense of triumph

Full orchestra; a sense of quiet
desperation returns

Strings alternate against winds

Full orchestra in unison; even louder and
more powerful than the opening

Solo oboe, a complete surprise

Full orchestra

Starts with bassoons, then full orchestra

Full orchestra

Full orchestra

Photos.com

Student FAQs

*Why isn't the short-short-short-LONG motif
present in every theme?*

It is rarely absent for very long, but Beethoven
no doubt wanted to avoid having the theme over-
stay its welcome. He created sufficient variety by
transforming the motif both within and across
movements,
and also by
providing
some con-
trast in the
form of
themes that
don't use the
motif at all.

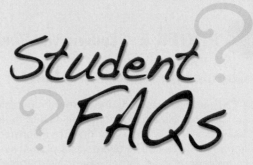

*What do the extra musicians
who come in at the
beginning of the finale
do during the first
three movements?*

Nothing. They must sit
quietly and wait their
turn. They are neverthe-
less paid at the same rate
as the musicians who
have been playing
throughout.

Tim Ridley ©
Dorling Kindersley

245

PROFILE   Ludwig van Beethoven (1770–1827)

Composing Through Deafness

Deafness was only one of many obstacles Beethoven faced as a composer. He was exploited as a child by his father, a court musician in Bonn (in present-day northern Germany), who lied about his son's age to make the boy's talents as a pianist seem even more remarkable. More seriously, his father's alcoholism forced the young Beethoven to become the principal breadwinner for his family while still in his mid-teens. But a grant from the elector of Bonn allowed him to travel to Vienna to study composition with Joseph Haydn (among others), and Beethoven quickly established a reputation there both as a piano virtuoso and as a composer. He would spend the rest of his life in Vienna.

When Beethoven began to go deaf in his late 20s, he became increasingly withdrawn from society. It is unclear exactly what caused this deafness, but we know from his letters that it caused him great psychological pain. He eventually had to stop performing in public altogether, and his despair at one point drove him to contemplate suicide. "It was only *my art* that held me back," he confessed to a friend in 1802. "Ah, it seemed to me impossible to leave the world until I had brought forth all that I felt was within me."

Beethoven's contemporaries found his music demanding. Still, he was widely recognized at the time as the greatest living composer of instrumental music, and he enjoyed the financial support of an important group of aristocratic patrons in Vienna. The last 15 years of his life were nevertheless filled with difficulties. He suffered from chronic poor health, his deafness grew even worse, and he became embroiled in a bitter custody battle with his sister-in-law over her son, Karl. Beethoven held his sister-in-law in low regard—as did the courts, who awarded him custody of the boy in 1816. But Beethoven was ill-prepared to become the single parent of a teenager, and constant struggles over the next decade, both in and out of court, took their toll both emotionally and financially.

When he died in 1827, Beethoven was hailed as a national hero. His funeral was attended by throngs of spectators who wanted to catch a last glimpse of the great composer who called himself a "tone poet," a poet who created with musical sounds rather than words.

◉➜ **EXPLORE MORE** on www.mymusiclab.com

Beethoven, ca. 1804–1805, as depicted by his friend, the painter J. W. Mähler. Beethoven's pose is similar to that of the Greek character Orpheus (see chapter 10): he holds a lyre in his hand and beckons from the darkness and turmoil behind him to the light and order ahead of him.

Willibrord Joseph Mähler, (1778–1860), "Ludvig van Beethoven", 1804, oil on canvas/Historisches Museum der Stadt, Vienna, Austria/The Bridgeman Art Library

---

⏮ EXPAND YOUR PLAYLIST: BEETHOVEN ⏭

- **Piano Sonata in C# Minor, op. 27, no. 2** ("Moonlight")

- **Piano Sonata in D Minor, op. 31, no. 2** ("Tempest")

- **Piano Sonata in F Minor, op. 57** ("Appassionata")

- **String Quartet in F Major, op. 59, no. 1** ("Razumofsky")

- **Violin Concerto in D Major, op. 61**

- **Piano Concerto in E-flat Major, op. 73** ("Emperor")

((•● **HEAR SAMPLES** on www.mymusiclab.com

EXPAND YOUR PLAYLIST

Beethoven's Symphonies

- **Symphony no. 1 in C Major, op. 21**
- **Symphony no. 2 in D Major, op. 36**
  Beethoven's first two symphonies are similar in format and scope to Haydn's late symphonies.

- **Symphony no. 3 in E-flat Major, op. 55**
  Called the "Eroica" ("Heroic") Symphony by Beethoven himself, this is widely viewed as Beethoven's breakthrough symphony, a work almost twice as long as any previous symphony by any other composer. Beethoven originally intended to dedicate the work to Napoleon but became disillusioned when Napoleon crowned himself Emperor of France. He finally issued it instead "In memory of a great man."

- **Symphony no. 4 in B-flat Major, op. 60**
  An energetic work in four movements.

- **Symphony no. 6 in F Major, op. 68**
  Called the "Pastoral" by Beethoven, this is the most programmatic of his symphonies.

- **Symphony no. 7 in A Major, op. 92**
  A large work in four movements, one of the most popular of all the symphonies. Sarah Brightman's 2000 hit "Figlio Perduto" ("Lost Son") is based on the music of this symphony's second movement.

- **Symphony no. 8 in F Major, op. 93**
  A relatively small-scale work and more playful than Beethoven's other symphonies.

- **Symphony no. 9 in D Minor, op. 125**
  The finale incorporates vocal soloists and a chorus singing Schiller's "Ode to Joy." This is the symphony that was performed in celebration of the fall of the Berlin Wall in 1989.

SEE MORE on www.mymusiclab.com   Inside the Orchestra, "The Orchestra through History": Beethoven's Sixth Symphony, first movement

HEAR SAMPLES on www.mymusiclab.com

TEST YOURSELF on www.mymusiclab.com   Flashcards and chapter tests

28

Franz Schubert
"Erlkönig," D. 328
Composed: 1815

Schubert's song "Erlkönig" presents a drama in miniature, the story of a father riding on horseback through the night, holding his ill child. The song uses only one singer and a pianist to portray a narrator, three different characters, and one highly emotional series of events.

Listen to this first

((● HEAR MORE on www.mymusiclab.com

Form

Listen for the way in which the same basic musical idea is presented in each strophe of the text, but in a new guise each time.

Word-Music Relationships

Listen to how the song captures the rhythms of the horse's hooves beating along the road. Notice the way in which this conveys the perspectives of four different characters—the narrator, the father, the child, and the Erlking—by changes in register (high vs. low), dynamics (loud vs. soft), and harmony (minor vs. major).

⚙ LEARN MORE on
www.mymusiclab.com
Chapter Objectives

CONNECT YOUR PLAYLIST

The Ballad

Find an example of a musical ballad.

Example: Simon & Garfunkel, "The Boxer" (1969)
Like many musical ballads, this song tells its story in strophic form, with the same music used for each strophe.

Schubert's song opens with a loud, fast, repetitive figure that evokes the sound of a galloping horse. The narrator tells us about the father and child on horseback. We hear a dialogue between father and son: the feverish boy imagines that he hears and sees the malicious Erlking, a shadowy figure from the land of the spirits, who has come to take him away from the land of the living; the father tries to comfort the child, telling him that his visions come from the wind and from wisps of cloud. And then we hear the voice of the Erlking himself, who at first tries to attract the child with promises of a wonderful realm of games, dance, and beautiful clothing, but who eventually tires of this and resorts to force to carry the child away. At the end, the narrator returns to tell us the grim conclusion.

The text of Schubert's song is a poem written in the 1780s by the celebrated German poet Johann Wolfgang Goethe (1749–1832). Goethe's "Erlkönig" is a **ballad**, a poem that tells a story, and Schubert's setting of it, also known as a ballad, makes the poetry even more intense. Just as a speaker giving a dramatic reading can shape a poem's sound and meaning by emphasizing certain words, varying the speed of delivery, or altering the register and volume of the voice, so can a composer shape the sound and meaning of the text by manipulating these same elements—rhythm, tempo, register, dynamics—and by incorporating other elements unique to music, such as melody and harmony. Schubert's setting is longer and more musically varied than any of the many earlier settings of the poem: the piano part is more important and technically demanding, and the voice part covers a wider range than ever before.

Songs for voice and piano were so widespread and popular in Germany from the late eighteenth century onward that we often use the German term today to identify this genre: ***Lied*** (pronounced "leet") is the German word for "song" (the plural, *Lieder*, is pronounced like "leader"). Schubert wrote hundreds of *Lieder* for voice and piano during his short life. "Erlkönig" is one of his earliest: he wrote it when he was only 18.

Modified Strophic Form

Almost every composer who writes a song begins with the text. In this case, Schubert began with Goethe's poem of eight strophes (also known as stanzas). He could have set each strophe to the same music, creating a song in simple strophic form. Or he could have written entirely new music for each strophe. In the end, he chose a middle path: he set each strophe to the same basic melody and rhythms presented in the first strophe, but he varied the music with every subsequent strophe. If there were no words to this song, we would hear, in effect, a set of variations (strophes 2–8) on a theme (strophe 1). But because there are words, we call the form of this song **modified strophic form**. Each strophe, as we shall see, is varied (modified) to fit the text in a particular way.

Word-Music Relationships: Creating Characters

Like any good song composer, Schubert studied the content, meter, and rhyme scheme of the poem very carefully before deciding on an appropriate musical setting, and he used these musical elements to connect the music with the words:

- **Rhythm:** Schubert uses a repetitive rhythmic figure at the very beginning of his setting to capture the constant forward movement of the pair on horseback and the thundering of the horse's hooves.

- **Register:** There are three characters and a narrator in this dramatic poem, all of them sung by a single voice. Schubert differentiates among them by placing each in a particular range or register of the voice. The narrator occupies a neutral space in the middle, the father's words are always sung in the lowest register, and the words of the child and the Erlking both sound in the highest range.

- **Dynamics:** Schubert indicates gradations of volume with great care in this song. The father is unchanging: he always sings forte (loud). The child starts softly but grows louder and louder. The Erlking starts softly and grows even softer before erupting at the end, when he loses patience and finally seizes the child.

- **Harmony:** Schubert begins and ends in the key of G minor but moves through several different keys in between to provide harmonic variety. He even shifts to the major mode when the voice of the Erlking enters.

Now listen to the piece again, using the Listening Guide.

1797–1828
Franz Schubert
"Erlkönig," D. 328
Composed: 1815
GENRE
Song
KEY CONCEPTS
Modified strophic form, ballad.
CHAPTER HIGHLIGHT
Ballad
Schubert's song for voice and piano is a setting of a ballad, a poem that tells a story. The music enhances the twists and turns of the plot and calls for the singer to serve not only as a narrator but also to portray the story's three very different characters.

⚙ **LEARN MORE** on
www.mymusiclab.com
MyMusicLibrary:
"The Salon"

Listening Guide

GO TO www.mymusiclab.com
for the Automated Listening Guide
CD III • Track 8/Download Track 56

Franz Schubert Composed: 1815 "Erlkönig," D. 328 (4:00)

Time	Strophe	Character	Melody: Register	German Original	English Translation
0:00	1	Narrator	Middle	Wer reitet so spät durch Nacht und Wind? Es ist der Vater mit seinem Kind; er hat den Knaben wohl in dem Arm, er fasst ihn sicher, er hält ihn warm.	Who rides so late through night and wind? It is the father with his child; He holds the boy fast in his arms He holds him tightly, he keeps him warm.
0:50	2	Father	Low	Mein Sohn, was birgst du so bang dein Gesicht?	My son, why do you hide your face so anxiously?
1:03		Son	High	Siehst, Vater, du den Erlkönig nicht? den Erlkönig mit Kron und Schweif?	Do you not see, father, the Erlking? The Erlking with crown and train?
1:20		Father	Low	Mein Sohn, es ist ein Nebelstreif.	My son, it is a streak of clouds.
1:29	3	The Erlking	High	"Du liebes Kind, komm, geh mit mir! gar schöne Spiele spiel' ich mit dir; manch bunte Blumen sind an dem Strand, meine Mutter hat manch gülden Gewand."	"You dear child, come with me! Such wonderful games I will play with you; So many beautiful flowers are on the shore, My mother has many a golden robe."
1:50	4	Son	High	Mein Vater, mein Vater, und hörest du nicht, was Erlenkönig mir leise verspricht?	My father, my father, do you not yet hear, What the Erlking softly promises me?
2:04		Father	Low	Sei ruhig, bleibe ruhig, mein Kind: in dürren Blättern säuselt der Wind.	Be calm, stay calm, my child: Through the dry leaves rustles the wind.
2:13	5	The Erlking	High	"Willst, feiner Knabe, du mit mir gehen? meine Töchter sollen dich warten schön; meine Töchter führen den nächtlichen Reihn und wiegen und tanzen und singen dich ein."	"Will you, dear child, come with me? My daughters shall wait on you well; my daughters dance at night and will cradle and dance and sing to you."

Dynamics	Rhythm	Harmony: Key area
Forte (loud)	Driving, repetitive triplets	G minor
Forte		
Piano (soft)		
Forte		
Pianissimo (very soft)	Lilting triplets	B-flat major
Forte	Driving, repetitive triplets	Unstable
Pianississimo (extremely soft)	Flowing triplets	C major

Student FAQs

Could this song be performed by a female singer?

Yes. This song has been performed and recorded many times by men and women alike. Songs are often transposed—re-set in a different key—to fit the range of the singer.

JAN PERSSON/Lebrecht
Music & Arts Photo Library

What do singers do with their bodies while singing? Do they act out the drama of these songs?

This is always a challenge. Singers can't (and don't) remain completely motionless: such woodenness would distract from the emotional content of the song. At the same time, overly emphatic gesturing with the hands and arms might be even more distracting to an audience. So singers generally try for something in between: subtle gestures, changes of pose, slight movement of the body and expressions of the face, but nothing excessive.

Chris Christodoulou/Lebrecht
Music & Arts Photo Library

What does "Erlkönig" mean?

In German, "König" means "king" and "Erl" means "alder," a type of birch tree. But the legend of the Erlking, a figure visible only to those who are about to die, originated in Denmark as *ellerkonge*, which means "elf king." At some point in the eighteenth century *ellerkonge* became "Erlkönig" in German.

Time	Strophe	Character	Melody: Register	German Original	English Translation
2:30	6	Son	High	Mein Vater, mein Vater, und siehst du nicht dort Erlkönigs Töchter am düstren Ort?	My father, my father, do you not see there Erlking's daughters in the desolate place?
2:44		Father	Low	Mein Sohn, mein Sohn, ich seh es genau, es scheinen die alten Weiden so grau.	My son, my son, I see it clearly, The old fields appear so gray.
2:55	7	The Erlking	High	"Ich liebe dich, mir reizt deine schöne Gestalt, und bist du nicht willig, so brauch ich Gewalt."	"I love you, your lovely form charms me, and if you're unwilling, then I'll use force."
3:11		Son	High	"Mein Vater, mein Vater, jetzt fasst er mich an! Erlkönig hat mir ein Leids getan!"	"My father, my father, now he seizes me! Erlking has done me harm!"
3:25	8	Narrator	Middle	Dem Vater grauset's, er reitet geschwind, er hält in Armen das ächzende Kind, erreicht den Hof mit Müh und Not; in seinen Armen das Kind war tot.	The father, filled with horror, rides fast, He holds in his arms the groaning child, Reaches the courtyard with toil and trouble, In his arms the child was dead.

The first edition of Schubert's "Erlkönig," billed as a "Ballad by Goethe, set to music for a solo voice with piano accompaniment . . . by Franz Schubert." The name of the dedicatee, Count Moriz von Dietrichstein (one of Schubert's patrons), is considerably larger than the composer's name. The vignette illustration shows the Erlking hovering over the father and the son on horseback.
Lebrecht Music & Arts/Lebrecht Music & Arts Photo Library

Dynamics	Rhythm	Harmony: Key area
Forte	Driving, repetitive triplets	Unstable
Pianissimo		D minor
Fortississimo (extremely loud)		
Forte		G minor

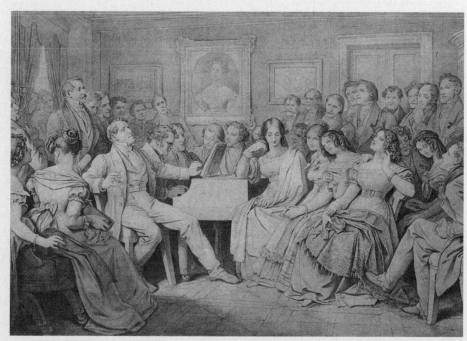

Moritz von Schwind, *A Schubert Evening with Joseph von Spaun*. In this scene from a Viennese salon, Schubert plays the piano while the singer sits beside him. The salon was a gathering in a home, where guests conversed, ate, drank, and entertained one another with song, poetry readings, or reenactments of scenes from dramas. During Schubert's lifetime, the *Lied* was a distinctly domestic genre. Only later did it move into the concert hall.
Dagli Orti (A)/Picture Desk, Inc./Kobal Collection

PROFILE   Franz Schubert (1797–1828)

Turning Poetry into Music

Franz Schubert was an astonishingly prolific composer of songs for voice and piano. The most recent recording of all his songs fills no fewer than 37 compact discs—quite an accomplishment for a composer who died so young, at the age of 31. In the year 1815 alone, when he was 18, he composed 144 songs, including "Erlkönig." Even more remarkably, each song is distinct.

Schubert was constantly looking for poetry to set to music. Some of his *Lieder* are settings of verse by the greatest writers of the day; others draw on works by poets who are largely forgotten today. He approached each new text on its own terms, trying to interpret, through music, the words he had chosen to set. As if his song output alone were not impressive enough, Schubert composed many other works: nine symphonies, dozens of piano sonatas, and dozens of works for various chamber ensembles. He never achieved widespread fame during his life, however. He enjoyed a devoted following in Vienna and probably would have attracted a wider audience had he not died so young (five years younger than Mozart at the time of his death).

Franz Schubert, ca. 1825, by W. A. Rieder. As in many portraits of composers from this time, he sits near a piano, quill pen in hand.
Lebrecht Music & Arts/Lebrecht Music & Arts Photo Library

◉➔ **EXPLORE MORE** on **www.mymusiclab.com**

⏪ **EXPAND YOUR PLAYLIST: SCHUBERT** ⏩

- **"The Trout"** ("Die Forelle"), D. 550. A strophic song about the brevity of all forms of life, not just that of fishes.

- **Piano Quintet in A Major** ("The Trout"), D. 667. For violin, viola, cello, double bass, and piano; the nickname comes from Schubert's song "The Trout," whose melody is the basis for the theme-and-variations fourth movement.

- **"Death and the Maiden"** ("Der Tod und das Mädchen"), D. 531. A brief song song about Death's visit to a young woman.

- **String Quartet in D Minor, D. 810** ("Death and the Maiden")

- **Symphony no. 8 in B Minor, D. 759** ("Unfinished")

- **Symphony no. 9 in C Major, D. 944**

((• **HEAR SAMPLES** on **www.mymusiclab.com**

⏪ **EXPAND YOUR PLAYLIST** ⏩

Schubert's Songs

"Erlkönig" is only one of many hundreds of songs written by Schubert. Some others worth exploring include the following:

- **"Gretchen am Spinnrade"** ("Gretchen at the Spinning Wheel"). The song is taken from Goethe's drama *Faust*. Gretchen muses over her agitated state (she is in love), and the music of the piano imitates the motion of her spinning wheel.

- **"Prometheus."** A stirring song set to another text by Goethe, narrated by Prometheus, the god who gave fire to mortals and was punished for his deed.

- **"Ständchen"** ("Serenade"). One of Schubert's best-known melodies, a song from a lover to his beloved.

((• **HEAR SAMPLES** on **www.mymusiclab.com**

✓ **TEST YOURSELF** on **www.mymusiclab.com**   Flashcards and chapter tests

Felix Mendelssohn
Overture to A Midsummer Night's Dream
Composed: 1826

Mendelssohn's music is an overture to Shakespeare's play *A Midsummer Night's Dream*. It reflects through music alone many of the leading characters in that comedy.

Listen to this first

((•● HEAR MORE on www.mymusiclab.com

Word-Music Relationships

As you listen for the first time, try to identify which passages might be associated with fairies, kings and queens, lovers, and a donkey. (The last one is particularly obvious!)

Form

This one-movement work is in sonata form, but without a repeat of the exposition. Listen for those elements of the form that you have learned to expect: a modulation to a new key early on, a development section, and a return to the tonic key and opening idea in the recapitulation, about two-thirds of the way through.

Mendelssohn's overture to Shakespeare's play *A Midsummer Night's Dream*, **written when he was just 17**, captures the chaotic, magical spirit of an enchanted forest. Shakespeare's play is about the collision between the world of fantasy and the world of reality. Mendelssohn translates these two worlds into music by using melodies that can be readily associated with the play's principal characters, which range from the real (two pairs of human lovers) to the unreal (fairies) to the real transformed into the unreal (a workman whose head is changed into that of a donkey). The title alone supplies the verbal cue to these links, for in this composition Mendelssohn creates a purely instrumental work that embodies the spirit of the play, its main characters, and its overall dramatic shape.

This kind of music—a purely instrumental work openly linked in some way to an object, story, or idea outside of the music—is a good example of **program music**. Program music was not new in the nineteenth century (see chapter 15), but it became increasingly important during the nineteenth century as artists sought to integrate purely instrumental music with ideas.

⚙ **LEARN MORE** on
www.mymusiclab.com
Chapter Objectives

Word-Music Relationships: Creating Characters Through Sound

All the principal thematic ideas in this piece can be linked to characters in Shakespeare's play. The number identifying each of the following themes is the same as that used in the Listening Guide.

1. **Theme 1.** The opening five measures, given entirely to the winds, draw us into the enchanted forest that is the setting for much of the play.

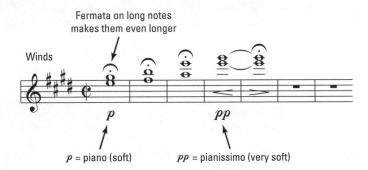

2. **Theme 2.** The scurrying, high-pitched figure in the strings that begins at 0:21 conjures up the kingdom of the fairies, led by Oberon and Titania.

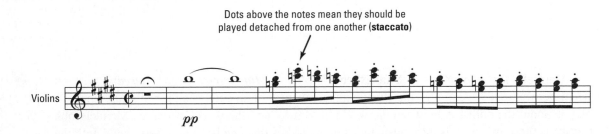

3. **Theme 3.** This loud, pompous theme (beginning at 1:05) reflects the heavier world of the humans and its ruler, Theseus.

4. **Theme 4.** The first theme in the secondary key area (beginning at 2:01) corresponds to the two pairs of human lovers who over the course of the play, through magic, fall in and out of love with one another and in various combinations.

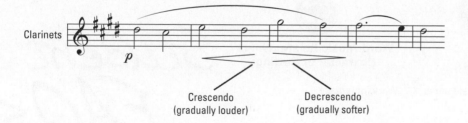

Clarinets

Crescendo
(gradually louder)

Decrescendo
(gradually softer)

5. **Theme 5.** The loud, braying theme at 2:54 is clearly associated with Bottom, the weaver, who figures prominently in Shakespeare's play-within-the-play, when he appears on stage with the head of a donkey.

Accent marks

Hee-haw   Hee-haw

The Drama of Sonata Form

This one-movement work follows the basic conventions of sonata form. Mendelssohn introduces all the principal characters to us in the exposition. In the development section (beginning at 3:42; the exposition does not repeat), the scurrying theme associated with fairies predominates. Mendelssohn captures the sometimes chaotic magical spirit of the midsummer night's forest by having different sections of the orchestra play in simultaneously contrasting dynamics. At 4:17, for example, he brings in the horns fortissimo, "with all force"—even as the strings and high winds maintain their elfin pianissimo—extremely quiet—figure. The recapitulation brings all the main themes back in the tonic, and the coda ends the work as it began, with the sound of long-held notes high in the winds.

With this framework in mind, listen to this piece again, using the Listening Guide.

1809–1847
Felix Mendelssohn
*Overture to
A Midsummer Night's
Dream*
Composed: 1826
GENRE
Concert overture

KEY CONCEPTS
Program music, relationship of drama and purely instrumental music, sonata form without exposition repeat.

CHAPTER HIGHLIGHT
Programmatic Orchestral Music
Mendelssohn's instrumental music presents a wordless rendition of Shakespeare's drama, or at the very least, of its principal characters.

CONNECT YOUR PLAYLIST

Dynamics

Find a work that makes effective use of contrasting dynamics (loud vs. soft).

Example: The Isley Brothers, "Shout" (1959)
This song, which features a progression from loud to soft and back to loud again, figures prominently in one of the dance scenes in the movie *Animal House* (1978).

Listening Guide

GO TO www.mymusiclab.com
for the Automated Listening Guide
CD III • Track 9/Download Track 57

Felix Mendelssohn Composed: 1826 *Overture to A Midsummer Night's Dream* (11:29)

Time	Form: Sonata form section	Melody	Word-Music Relationships Character or Setting
0:00	**Exposition** (tonic)	Theme 1 (long-held notes in winds only)	World of fantasy
0:21		Theme 2 (scurrying figure in strings)	Fairies
1:05	Tonic, with modulation beginning around 1:33	Theme 3 (full orchestra, loud)	Theseus, the ruler of the humans: a loud, pompous theme
2:00	Secondary key area	Theme 4 (lyrical, first in clarinet, then in strings)	The two pairs of human lovers
2:54		Theme 5 (loud, braying sound: full orchestra)	Bottom, the weaver dressed as a donkey
3:25		Theme 3 again, but now in new key area (full orchestra)	Theseus's theme, varied
3:42	**Development** (unstable harmony)	2 (scurrying figure)	Confusion in the dark woods
5:24		4 (lyrical)	Lovers' theme, now in minor; the pairs of lovers become separated.
5:53	**Recapitulation** (tonic)	1 (long-held notes in winds)	Return of the opening theme and key
6:18		2 (scurrying theme)	Fairies again, but now with added winds and timpani
6:53		4 (lyrical)	Lovers' theme, now in the tonic
7:47		5 (braying)	Bottom's theme (the donkey)
8:48		3 (pompous)	Theseus's theme
9:17	**Coda** (tonic)	2 (scurrying)	Fairies
10:06		4 (lyrical)	Lovers' theme, now in major mode and much slower
11:00		1 (long-held notes)	Opening phrase closes the work

Student FAQs

I don't know Shakespeare's play. Can the music still make sense?

Yes. Composers can never really be certain that their listeners will have a program in hand, or in their heads, and so they generally try to write music that can function on its own, in purely musical terms. Mendelssohn's overture is no exception to this pattern. While our understanding of it can be enriched through knowledge of Shakespeare's play, we can enjoy the work even without being aware of its connections to the drama.

Photos.com

Why is there no repeat of the exposition?

By the end of the eighteenth century, it had become common to omit the exposition repetition in opera overtures, and Mendelssohn continues that tradition with this overture to a spoken play.

Photos.com

PROFILE   Felix Mendelssohn (1809–1847)

The Cosmopolitan Composer

Perhaps the most cosmopolitan composer who ever lived, Mendelssohn spoke fluent English, French, and Italian—in addition to his native German—and he could read ancient Greek and Latin with ease. He was as much at home in England as he was in Germany. He even excelled at painting and created a number of watercolors of very high quality.

Mendelssohn was born into a prominent family whose fame was based not on music, but on philosophy and finance. His grandfather, Moses Mendelssohn, was one of the leading philosophers of his day, and his father, Abraham Mendelssohn, was one of Berlin's most successful bankers.

Felix was the greatest child prodigy of his age, both as a composer and as a pianist. As a young child, he traveled across Europe in much the same manner Mozart had half a century before. By the time he was 17, he had already written the Octet for Strings, op. 20, and the *Overture to A Midsummer Night's Dream*, op. 21. He also excelled as a conductor. In 1828, on the hundredth anniversary of its premiere, he led a hugely successful performance of J. S. Bach's *Saint Matthew Passion*, a then-forgotten work he had helped rediscover.

Mendelssohn on one of his many trips to England, painted by James Warren Childe. Mendelssohn was a particular favorite of Queen Victoria.
Ruth Schacht/Art Resource/Bildarchiv Preussischer Kulturbesitz

A 19th-century depiction of Felix Mendelssohn's workroom in Leipzig. In the foreground, a square piano is covered with a cloth; by the window, a writing desk is visible where the composer could work on scores.
Abigail Lebrecht/Lebrecht Music & Arts Photo Library

⚙ **LEARN MORE** on **www.mymusiclab.com**
MyMusicLibrary: Mendelssohn in London

⊙ **EXPLORE MORE** on **www.mymusiclab.com**

⏪ EXPAND YOUR PLAYLIST: MENDELSSOHN ⏩

- **Complete Incidental Music to *A Midsummer Night's Dream.*** Sixteen years after writing this stand-alone overture to Shakespeare's play, Mendelssohn composed music for all the songs in Shakespeare's play (Shakespeare had provided only the poetry, not the music), along with other incidental music—marches, dances, intermezzos, and the like—including the celebrated "Wedding March."

- **Symphony no. 3 in A Minor** ("Scottish")

- **Symphony no. 4 in A Major** ("Italian")

- **Violin Concerto in E Minor**

- ***Elijah.*** An oratorio for soloists, chorus, and orchestra, written for the Birmingham Festival of 1846 during one of the composer's many visits to England.

((• **HEAR SAMPLES** on **www.mymusiclab.com**

Mendelssohn never issued a program to accompany this work, but in a letter to his publisher, he explained the relationship between the musical elements of the overture and the drama on the stage. He acknowledged broad parallels between his overture and Shakespeare's play, but he stopped short of drawing direct equivalencies between the two. This reflects the feelings of many composers about attaching specific meanings to their music. Clearly, Mendelssohn wanted his listeners to associate his overture with Shakespeare's play—otherwise, he would not have given it the title that he did—but he also wanted listeners to accept the work on its own terms, as music.

In the 1999 film version of *A Midsummer Night's Dream* directed by Michael Hoffman, Kevin Kline (Nick Bottom) and Michelle Pfeiffer (Titania) spin out love's sweet dream. The soundtrack uses Mendelssohn's overture and some of the additional incidental music he wrote for the play much later, in 1842. The music Mendelssohn added later includes the celebrated "Wedding March."
20TH CENTURY FOX/THE KOBAL COLLECTION/TURSI, MARIO

The piece is . . . closely associated with the play, and thus it might perhaps be quite appropriate to indicate to the public the main events of the drama. . . . I believe it would suffice to recall how the elf-royalty, Oberon and Titania, appear with all their train throughout the play, at one moment here, at another there; then comes Duke Theseus of Athens, who goes hunting in the forest with his bride-to-be; then the two pairs of tender lovers, who lose and find one another; and finally the troop of clumsy, coarse tradesmen, who pursue their heavy-handed amusements; then the elves once again, who tease all of them—it is precisely out of all this that the work is constructed. When at the end everything is resolved and the main characters depart fortunate and happy, the elves follow them, bless the house, and disappear as the morning dawns. So ends the play, and my overture too. I would prefer it if on the printed program you would summarize only this content and say nothing further about my music, so that it can simply speak for itself, if it is good; and if it is not good, then no explanation will help at all.

Felix Mendelssohn, *Briefe an deutsche Verleger* (Berlin: de Gruyter, 1968) pp. 25–26.

◀◀   **EXPAND YOUR PLAYLIST**   ▶▶

Shakespeare in Music

Many of Shakespeare's plays call for moments of instrumental music, song, or both. A good anthology of settings by Shakespeare's contemporaries is available in *Shakespeare's Songbook*, ed. Ross Duffin (New York: Norton, 2004).

- **Hector Berlioz**, *Roméo et Juliette*. A symphony consisting of both instrumental and vocal movements for soloists, chorus, and orchestra.
- **Franz Liszt**, *Hamlet*. An orchestral work loosely based on Shakespeare's play.
- **Giuseppe Verdi**, *Macbeth* (1847), *Otello* (1887), and *Falstaff* (1893). All three are operas. The last of these draws on *The Merry Wives of Windsor* and the *Henry IV* plays for its libretto.

- **Pyotr Ilich Tchaikovsky**, *Romeo and Juliet, Fantasy-Overture*. A work for orchestra.
- **Sergei Prokofiev**, *Romeo and Juliet*. A ballet.
- **Cole Porter**, *Kiss Me, Kate*. A Broadway adaptation of *The Taming of the Shrew*.
- **Leonard Bernstein**, *West Side Story*. A Broadway adaptation of *Romeo and Juliet* (see chapter 54).

((• HEAR SAMPLES on **www.mymusiclab.com**

✔ **TEST YOURSELF** on **www.mymusiclab.com**   Flashcards and chapter tests

Hector Berlioz

Symphonie fantastique, fourth movement ("March to the Scaffold")

Composed: 1830

The fourth movement of this symphony depicts a nightmare through music alone. A sensitive young artist dreams that he has killed his unfaithful lover and that he is now being led away to the scaffold, where he will be executed by guillotine.

 Listen to this first

((• HEAR MORE on www.mymusiclab.com

Timbre

Listen for the massive sound of the orchestra, especially in the brass (trumpets, horns, trombones, and tubas) and percussion (timpani, snare drum, cymbals, and bass drum).

Word-Music Relationships

Berlioz's *Symphonie fantastique* is a work of program music. How does the music reflect the scenario outlined here?

Form

Listen for the alternation between large sections of music in the minor mode and large sections in major mode. What happens at the very end of the movement?

This "Fantasy-Symphony" re-creates, in music, the thoughts, dreams, and nightmares of an artist. Originally entitled *Episode in the Life of the Artist: Symphonie fantastique*, this work is one of the most celebrated instances of program music in the entire concert repertory. Berlioz himself wrote a detailed prose narrative to be distributed at performances. It is the story of a dream (the "fantasy" in the title) that moves from blissful reverie (in the opening movement) to nightmare (in the fourth and fifth movements). The artist dreams about his beloved and her eventual rejection of him. In the fourth movement, the "March to the Scaffold," (presented here) the artist dreams that, having killed his beloved, he

⚙ **LEARN MORE** on
www.mymusiclab.com
Chapter Objectives

"Before" and "After" views of the guillotine at work. The basket used to catch the severed head is clearly visible in front of both machines. At the time of the French Revolution, the guillotine was hailed as a humane form of execution because of its swiftness. The guillotine remained the only legal means of execution in France until the abolition of the death penalty there in 1981. Public executions ended in 1939.

Getty Images, Inc.

is being led up to a large platform (the scaffold), where he is beheaded by a guillotine. The music is so detailed that we even hear his head plop into the basket placed below and slightly in front of the blade.

The *Symphonie fantastique* captures Romanticism's fascination with the world of the gothic and the grotesque. The artist who "dreams" this symphony dreams not of glory, but of his own downfall and death. In this work, Berlioz paints a musical picture of darkness and despair, and he uses the full resources of the orchestra to portray this nightmare in sound.

The Modern Orchestra

Berlioz is widely acknowledged as the first great master of **orchestration**, the art of arranging music for the instruments of the orchestra. He came of age at a time when concert halls—and thus orchestras—were becoming larger and larger, and he incorporated a wider variety of instruments into his compositions than anyone before. Berlioz achieved novel and spectacular orchestral effects, and even his detractors praised his ability to draw new sounds out of the orchestra by combining individual instruments or groups of instruments to create timbres that had never been heard before. The brass section in this particular movement is unusually prominent, and the percussion section (timpani, bass drum, and snare drum) comes to the fore in ways that no one had ever imagined. Berlioz would go on to write an important treatise on orchestration. Then, as now, any composer who wanted to write a work of music for orchestra must know the particular characteristics of every instrument, starting with its range (what notes are within its reach) and extending to what kinds of melodies or figures work best for it.

Word-Music Relationships: The Program

LEARN MORE on
www.mymusiclab.com
MyMusicLibrary:
Berlioz's Program for the
Symphonie fantastique

Berlioz wrote a detailed program for his *Symphonie fantastique* and gave each of its five movements a distinctive title. "A young musician of morbidly sensitive temperament and fiery imagination poisons himself with opium in a fit of lovesick despair," he explains in the introduction to his program. "The dose of the narcotic, too weak to kill him, plunges him into a deep slumber accompanied by the strangest visions, during which his sensations, his emotions, his memories are transformed in his sick mind into musical thoughts and images. The loved one herself has become a melody to him, an *idée fixe* as it were, that he encounters and hears everywhere."

This *idée fixe* is a melody whose form changes from movement to movement but that appears at some point in all five, transformed to fit the emotion of the moment. In the fourth movement, presented here, the *idée fixe* is heard only once, just before the end (at 4:14). Its appearance marks the last thought of the artist, a split second before the blade of the guillotine chops off his head.

Here are the titles of all five movements and a summary of the program of each:

1. "Dreams—Passions." The artist fixates on his beloved and imagines her in the form of a melody, the *idée fixe* or "obsessive idea" heard in every movement in one guise or another.
2. "A Ball." The artist imagines he sees his beloved at a ball, during a waltz.

3. "Scene in the Countryside." A slow movement in which the artist dreams he is in the countryside. The scene begins peacefully, but he is soon seized by panic, thinking that his beloved has been unfaithful to him.

4. "March to the Scaffold." Having murdered his beloved for her unfaithfulness, the artist is led to the scaffold, a large elevated platform supporting a guillotine. There, he dreams of her one last time, but her musical image—the *idée fixe*—is interrupted by the fall of the guillotine's blade. The artist dies, at least in his dream.

5. "Dream of a Witches' Sabbath." In this dream within a dream, the artist finds himself "in the midst of a frightful troop of ghosts, sorcerers, and monsters of every kind, gathered for his funeral." The beloved, in the form of her melody, the *idée fixe*, now appears in grotesque form, for in the artist's nightmare, she has become a witch. In the end, evil triumphs over good.

Musical Form, Programmatic Form

The form of this movement is fairly straightforward. It consists of two contrasting sections based on two contrasting themes—the opening **A** section is in the minor mode, the contrasting **B** section is in the major mode. The movement as a whole is framed by an introduction and coda. Graphically, the form of this movement can be represented as

Introduction A / B / A / B / A Coda

But this tells only half the story of the music's form, which would seem to be dictated every bit as much by the prose of Berlioz's program:

> He [the artist] dreams he has killed his beloved, and that he is condemned to death and led to the scaffold. The procession moves forward to the sounds of a march that is at times gloomy and ferocious, at times solemn and brilliant. Noisy outbursts are followed without pause by the heavy sound of measured footsteps. At the end, the *idée fixe* appears for a moment, like a last thought of love broken off by the fatal blow [of the guillotine's blade].

"At times gloomy and ferocious, at times solemn and brilliant": this description is reflected directly in the form of the music in the alternation between the minor-mode **A** section ("gloomy and ferocious") and the major-mode **B** section ("solemn and brilliant"). The ending is particularly graphic, because the *idée fixe*, the musical image of the beloved, is interrupted—almost literally "cut off"—with the sudden fall of the guillotine's blade represented by a thundering chord played by the entire orchestra.

The guillotine's blade falls here in the "March to the Scaffold," interrupting the *idée fixe*

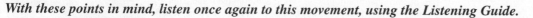

With these points in mind, listen once again to this movement, using the Listening Guide.

1803–1869
Hector Berlioz
Symphonie fantastique,
fourth movement ("March to the Scaffold")
Composed: 1830
GENRE
Programmatic symphony

KEY CONCEPTS
The modern orchestra, program music, major vs. minor mode.

CHAPTER HIGHLIGHT
Program Music
Program music became increasingly important during the nineteenth century as many composers sought to integrate purely instrumental music with ideas by providing verbal clues about the "content" of the music.

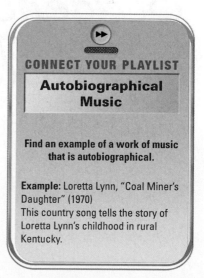
CONNECT YOUR PLAYLIST
Autobiographical Music

Find an example of a work of music that is autobiographical.

Example: Loretta Lynn, "Coal Miner's Daughter" (1970)
This country song tells the story of Loretta Lynn's childhood in rural Kentucky.

Listening Guide

GO TO www.mymusiclab.com
for the Automated Listening Guide
CD III • Track 10/Download Track 58

Hector Berlioz Composed: 1830 *Symphonie fantastique*, fourth movement ("March to the Scaffold") (4:47)

Time	Form: Section	Harmony: Mode	Word-Music Relationships: Berlioz's Program	Timbre
0:00	Introduction	Minor	He [the artist] dreams he has killed his beloved, and that he is condemned to death and led to his execution. The procession moves forward to the sound of...	Rumblings in the low strings, low winds, and low brass
0:27	A	Minor	...a march, at times gloomy and ferocious...	March-like theme in low strings, descending by step
1:39	B	Major	...at times solemn and brilliant. Noisy outbursts...	Brass and winds predominate.
2:11	A	Minor	...are followed without pause by the heavy sound of measured footsteps.	March-like theme, descending by step
2:22	B	Major		Brass and winds predominate.
2:53	A	Minor		March-like theme, descending by step
4:14	Coda	Major	At the end, the *idée fixe* appears for a moment [4:14, on the clarinet], like a last thought of love broken off by the fatal blow [of the guillotine's blade, at 4:24].	The severed head falls into the bucket (pizzicato figure at 4:25) and the crowd (the full orchestra) roars its approval (4:27).

Student FAQs

Did audiences in Berlioz's time know about the program?

Sometimes yes, sometimes no. Berlioz once wrote that "at concerts where this symphony is to be performed, it is essential that this program be distributed in advance in order to provide an overview of the dramatic structure of this work." Later in life, however, he felt that the program was actually drawing attention *away* from the music, and he declared that the names of the individual movements would suffice.

Does the program account for everything in the music?

No. As is almost always the case with program music, many details are left to the listener's imagination. As Berlioz himself noted, the purpose of the program was to give listeners "an overview of the dramatic structure of the work," not an explanation of its every detail.

Reduce model of a guillotine (wood & metal) (see also 216411), French School, (18th century)/Musee de la Ville de Paris, Musee Carnavalet, Paris, France, Giraudon/Bridgeman Art Library

PROFILE   Hector Berlioz (1803–1869)

Music as Autobiography

Berlioz wrote his personal life into his music. The *Symphonie fantastique* mirrors his obsession with Harriet Smithson. He wrote his second symphony, *Harold en Italie* (*Harold in Italy*), which was loosely based on Byron's epic poem *Childe Harold*, after a two-year stay in Italy. His sequel to the *Symphonie fantastique*, entitled *Lelio; or, The Return to Life*, has often been seen as a thinly veiled marriage proposal to Harriet Smithson.

Berlioz had to struggle to establish himself in music. His father wanted his son to follow in his footsteps and become a doctor, so he sent the young Hector off to Paris to study medicine. But the younger Berlioz was more interested in music: he stopped attending medical classes and began spending more and more time at the national conservatory of music, where he eventually enrolled as a student. His teachers thought him talented but undisciplined. He had to supplement his income for some time by writing music criticism, and only late in life did he enjoy the accolades of a public that for decades had not quite known what to make of his music.

⚙ **LEARN MORE** on **www.mymusiclab.com**
MyMusicLibrary: Heine on Berlioz, Harriet Smithson, and the Symphonie fantastique

◉➤ **EXPLORE MORE** on **www.mymusiclab.com**

Hector Berlioz in a portrait from 1832, two years after the premiere of the *Symphonie fantastique*. Caricatures invariably exaggerated the composer's dramatic hairstyle (see the image on page 266). One contemporary compared Berlioz's hair to a "forest growing on the edge of a steep cliff."
Scala/Art Resource, NY.

EXPAND YOUR PLAYLIST: BERLIOZ

- *Symphonie fantastique (complete).*

- *Harold in Italy (Harold en Italie).* A symphony loosely based on Byron's epic poem *Harold in Italy*, with a prominent part for solo viola.

- *Roméo et Juliette.* A symphony based on Shakespeare's play, for soloists, chorus, and orchestra.

- *Requiem.* A mammoth setting of the Catholic service for the dead, requiring multiple choruses and instrumental ensembles.

- *The Infancy of Christ* (*L'enfance du Christ*). An oratorio for soloists, chorus, and orchestra.

((•● **HEAR SAMPLES** on **www.mymusiclab.com**

PERFORMANCE   How Loud Is Too Loud?

Volume is relative: what is unbearably loud to some seems perfectly acceptable to others. And perceptions of volume have changed over time. In an era before amplified sound, few things were louder than a large orchestra playing with full force. Berlioz's contemporaries were quick to point out the physical pain associated with the volume of sound he could elicit from a large ensemble of instruments.

Berlioz conducts. This caricature reflects the reactions of contemporaries to the sheer level of sound called for in certain passages in Berlioz's music, including the "March to the Scaffold" from the *Symphonie fantastique*. While clearly exaggerated—a cannon spews notes and giant hammers strike the timpani—the reactions of Berlioz's contemporaries are not without foundation.

"Caricature of Hector Berlioz Leading an Orchestra in 1846." Color engraving. The Pierpont Morgan Library, New York, N.Y., U.S.A. The Pierpont Morgan Library/Art Resource, NY.

The decibel is the standard measurement of sound volume: the higher the decibel level, the louder the sound. Most experts consider prolonged exposure to anything over 80 dB as potentially dangerous. Decibels increase logarithmically: an increase of 10 dB, for example, means that a sound becomes 10 times louder. A large orchestra playing at peak volume can reach potentially painful levels, as high as 110 decibels (dB). Ear-buds for portable listening equipment often produce decibel levels of over 120 dB. Hearing damage is a function not only of the decibel level but also of the duration of exposure to that level. As little as 15 minutes of exposure to 100 dB can cause permanent hearing damage.

Decibels	Sound Source	Relative Musical Dynamic
150	Jet engine (at 1,000 ft.)	
130	Jackhammer	
120	Rock concert	
110	Large orchestra (full volume)	
100	Piano (loudest peak)	fff
90	Shouting voice	ff
80	Busy street noise	f
60	Speaking voice	mp
50		p
40		pp
30	Whispering voice	ppp

Source: http://sonomatics.com/usf/acoustics/CommonDBLevels.pdf

◀◀   **EXPAND YOUR PLAYLIST**   ▶▶

The Music of Dreams

Berlioz's *Symphonie fantastique* is only one of many musical compositions that deal with dreams.
- **Vincenzo Bellini**, *La Sonnambula* (*The Sleepwalker*; 1831). An opera whose plot turns on the heroine's walking in her sleep (she sings, too).
- **Felix Mendelssohn**, *Overture to A Midsummer Night's Dream* (see chapter 29).
- **Robert Schumann**, "Träumerei" ("Dreaming"; 1838) is one of a group of short pieces for solo piano in a collection called "Scenes from Childhood."

- **Edward Elgar**, *The Dream of Gerontius* (1900). An oratorio for soloists, chorus, and orchestra that traces the fate of a soul from death through purgatory.
- **Thelonious Monk**, *Monk's Dream* (1963). A work created and performed by the jazz pianist.
- **Elvis Costello**, *Il Sogno* (2004). Costello's ballet, based on Shakespeare's *Midsummer Night's Dream*, combines classical and jazz idioms in a work for large orchestra.

((•● **HEAR SAMPLES** on **www.mymusiclab.com**

31

Fanny Mendelssohn Hensel

Piano Trio in D Minor, op. 11, third movement
Composed: 1846

The third movement of Hensel's Piano Trio in D Minor, op. 11, is a song that has no words. The composer specifically labeled this movement a **Lied** ("Song"), suggesting that it might have a hidden text behind it, even though it is for instruments alone.

((● **HEAR MORE** on www.mymusiclab.com

Timbre	**Word-Music Relationships**	**Melody**
Listen to the interplay of the three instruments: piano, violin, and cello. How would you describe their relationship? Is any one instrument more important than the others?	Why might the composer have called this movement a "Song"? What kind of poetic text would fit the mood of this movement?	There is only one melody in this entire movement, but it returns repeatedly in a varied form. Listen for these differences across the course of the movement.

In an era before recorded sound, people who wanted to hear music at home had to play it themselves. Pieces for solo piano and songs formed a major part of the domestic repertory. No medium proved as versatile and wide-ranging as the **piano trio**, an ensemble consisting of piano, violin, and cello. The third movement of Fanny Mendelssohn Hensel's Piano Trio in D Minor, op. 11, offers an excellent example of the genre and invites us to imagine what it must have been like to make music in a nineteenth-century parlor. Because so many homes had pianos, the piano trio lent itself particularly well to music making in the home. We can hear the intimacy of the setting in the intimacy of the music, which presents a single melody in ever-changing guises.

 LEARN MORE on www.mymusiclab.com
Chapter Objectives

The Timbre of the Piano Trio

The piano trio had been a popular medium ever since the middle of the eighteenth century: Haydn, Mozart, Beethoven, Schubert, and Felix Mendelssohn (Fanny's brother) had all written piano trios. Part of the appeal of this ensemble was the breadth of sound available from only three instruments: the violin and cello are melodic instruments in the high and low ranges,

 SEE MORE on www.mymusiclab.com
Inside the Orchestra: The Piano

267

PROFILE   Fanny Mendelssohn Hensel (1805–1847)

Overcoming Obstacles

Fanny Mendelssohn Hensel.
ColouiserAL/Lebrecht Music & Arts Photo Library

As a composer, Fanny Mendelssohn faced two major obstacles. The first was the immense fame of her younger brother Felix, who was an international celebrity as both a performer and composer while still in his teens. In spite of her own accomplishments as a pianist and composer, Fanny was inevitably known as "Felix's sister." Only recently have critics and historians begun to discover the full range of her talents as a composer of more than 200 songs, more than 100 works for piano, and more than 24 works for chorus, as well as various works for chamber ensembles.

The second obstacle was her gender. Fanny grew up in an era when musical composition was not considered an appropriate profession for women, and she grew up in a family in which women were not expected to pursue a vocation of any kind. Her father, Abraham Mendelssohn, wrote to her in 1820—she was 15 at the time—that while Felix might pursue a musical career, music "for you will always remain but an ornament; never can or should it become the foundation of your existence." This helps explain why for most of her life, Fanny published her music under her brother's name. Only later—just a year before her death, as it turned out—did she begin issuing compositions under her own name.

Felix and Fanny were extremely close not only in childhood but in their adult years as well, even after Fanny married the painter Wilhelm Hensel in 1829. She shared her brother's interest in the music of J. S. Bach and remained his closest musical confidante until her sudden death at the age of 41. Felix himself died only six months later.

👁 **SEE MORE** on **www.mymusiclab.com**
Documentary: Music and the Middle Class

⊙→ **EXPLORE MORE** on **www.mymusiclab.com**

⏪   **EXPAND YOUR PLAYLIST: FANNY MENDELSSOHN HENSEL**   ⏩

- *Gartenlieder*, Six Songs for Soprano, Alto, Tenor, and Bass, op. 3
- **Six Songs, op. 9**
- **Four Songs (Without Words) for Piano, op. 2 op. 6.** Two sets of Songs Without Words—that is, short, lyrical works for solo piano.
- **Prelude in F Major, for organ**
- *Das Jahr (The Year).* A cycle of 12 pieces for piano, each a portrait of a month of the year.

((⏺ **HEAR SAMPLES** on **www.mymusiclab.com**

respectively, while the piano can play chords as well as melodies in all registers. Because so many amateur musicians owned and played at least one of these instruments, piano trios enjoyed special popularity in the nineteenth century. Indeed, many musicians and listeners of the time heard the symphonies of Haydn, Mozart, and Beethoven performed more often in the home in arrangements for piano trio than in their original orchestral setting in the concert hall.

In this particular movement, the piano takes the lead from the very beginning, introducing the melody in an extended solo passage and then playing continuously throughout. The violin and cello each has its turn of presenting the melody as well. In the end, the three instruments blend to create a full, rich sound.

A Song Without Words

Fanny Mendelssohn Hensel placed the word "Lied"—"Song"—at the head of this movement. It is a provocative title, for the music has no words. How can a song not have words? Fanny and her brother Felix had in fact already written a number of piano pieces with precisely this title: *Songs Without Words*. These are short, lyrical works that imitate songs, both in their form and in their texture, with a clear melodic line throughout. In this movement, Fanny Mendelssohn Hensel creates a song without words for piano, violin, and cello.

What are we, as listeners, to make of this wordless song? The title serves as an invitation to us to create our own lyrics. What kind of text would best fit the music? Is this song lyrical (describing an emotional state) or is it a ballad (narrating a story)? Are there points at which the "voice" drops out?

This meter is called *trochaic tetrameter*. Trochaic indicates that the basic unit is LONG-short (or TUM-ta); tetrameter means that each line consists of four basic units ("tetra" = "four"). Henry Wadsworth Longfellow's *Song of Hiawatha* is written in this meter, and the words in fact fit the opening theme of this piano trio's movement quite well:

> **By** the **shores** of **Git**che **Gu**mee,
> **By** the **shi**ning **Big**-Sea-**Wa**ter,
> **Stood** the **wig**wam **of** Nokomis,
> **Daughter of** the **Moon**, Nokomis.

Can you think of other texts in this meter that might fit this music, or create your own?

Melodic Metamorphosis

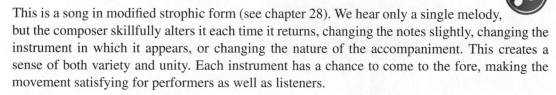

This is a song in modified strophic form (see chapter 28). We hear only a single melody, but the composer skillfully alters it each time it returns, changing the notes slightly, changing the instrument in which it appears, or changing the nature of the accompaniment. This creates a sense of both variety and unity. Each instrument has a chance to come to the fore, making the movement satisfying for performers as well as listeners.

Now listen to this movement again, using the Listening Guide.

1805–1847
Fanny Mendelssohn Hensel
Piano Trio in D Minor, op. 11, third movement
Composed: 1846
GENRE
Piano trio

KEY CONCEPTS
Chamber music, song without words, modified strophic form.

CHAPTER HIGHLIGHT
Songs without Words
Conveying ideas through instrumental music was so powerful in the nineteenth century that Mendelssohn Hensel called the third movement of this work a *Lied* or "Song." The title suggests that even though this music has no words, there is a hidden text behind the regular metric pattern of the music.

CONNECT YOUR PLAYLIST

Trochaic Meter

Find a work, either vocal or instrumental, whose underlying rhythm is based on trochaic meter (LONG-short).

Example: Britney Spears, "Womanizer" (2008)
This song highlights a rhythm that reflects the LONG-short-LONG-short pattern of the title's lone word.

Listening Guide

GO TO www.mymusiclab.com
for the Automated Listening Guide
CD III •Track 11/Download Track 59

Fanny Mendelssohn Hensel Composed: 1846 Piano Trio, op. 11, third movement (1:56)

Time	Melody	Timbre	Word-Music Relationships
0:00	**A**	Piano alone; violin joins in at 0:14, cello at 0:16.	The imagined text is presented in its original form.
0:23	**A1**, more somber, with minor mode inflections	Piano alone at first; cello joins in at 0:30, violin at 0:33.	The "text" begins similarly but takes a darker and more circuitous turn.
0:50	**A2**	Violin has the melody.	The "text" reappears closer to its original form in the violin and reaches its most intense point toward the end of this section.
1:18	**A3**	Cello has the melody at first, then all three instruments (1:33).	The "text" reappears in its original form, now in the cello, with a confident and affirmative ending.

Student FAQs

Does the piano always have the leading role in piano trios?

The piano is the biggest, loudest, and widest-ranging of the three instruments, and so in fact it usually does play more often than either of the other two. The violin and cello might occasionally have a passage to themselves as soloists or as a duet, but the piano is rarely out of the spotlight for long in a piano trio.

Photos.com

Not all songs have words. What makes the lack of a text here significant?

In English, many people tend to use the word "song" rather loosely to mean any work of music. Technically, however, a song is a piece of music that has a text to be sung. Particularly in German, the word placed at the head of this movement by Fanny Mendelssohn Hensel—"Lied"—strongly suggests the presence of a text, which makes the absence of one here all the more surprising.

Clipart.com

HISTORICAL CONTEXT   Women Composers of the Nineteenth Century

Fanny Mendelssohn Hensel was one of a growing number of women in the nineteenth century who won fame through their compositions. Like women in many other professions of the time, most of these composers struggled to win recognition in a sphere dominated and controlled by men. Women were widely encouraged to sing or play the piano, but rarely encouraged to pursue a career in composition.

Maria Szymanowska (1789–1831), born in Warsaw (Poland), toured extensively as a piano virtuoso throughout Europe before settling in St. Petersburg (Russia) in 1827. She wrote primarily for her own instrument, the piano, and was an important precursor of Chopin (also a native Pole), writing mazurkas and nocturnes (see chapter 33).

Louise Farrenc (1804–1875) wrote three symphonies, a piano concerto, four piano trios, and many other chamber works, in addition to a large number of works for piano. She was the only woman in the nineteenth century to hold a permanent chair at the Paris Conservatory, where she taught piano.

Clara Wieck Schumann (1819–1896). See chapter 32.

Augusta Holmès (1847–1903) was born in France of Irish parents and added the accent to her last name when she became a French citizen in 1871. Her *Triumphant Ode* was commissioned as the musical centerpiece of the 1889 World's Fair, which gave us the Eiffel Tower. It is an enormous work for soloists, chorus, and orchestra, requiring more than 1,000 musicians to perform.

Cecile Chaminade (1857–1944), a native of Paris, achieved both critical and commercial success through her compositions for solo piano, as well as larger-scale compositions like her

Concertstück for piano and orchestra and her Concertino for flute and orchestra. The French government awarded her the prestigious Order of the Legion of Honor in 1913 for her achievements in music.

Teresa Carreño (1853–1917), born in Venezuela, studied piano with Louis Moreau Gottschalk (see chapter 34). Her piano technique was so powerful that she was known as the "Valkyrie of the Piano." She played in the White House for both Abraham Lincoln (in 1863) and Woodrow Wilson (in 1916); she also sang in and conducted operas. Carreño composed almost exclusively for solo piano.

Amy Marcy Cheney Beach (1867–1944) was born in New Hampshire but spent most of her life in Boston. She performed as a piano soloist several times with the Boston Symphony Orchestra, beginning in 1885. After marrying that year, she turned her attention away from performance and toward composition. She wrote in many genres, from chamber music to orchestral music to choral music, and her output includes such works as a piano concerto and a Mass. Her "Gaelic" Symphony (1897) shows the influence of Dvořák and was the first symphony written by an American woman.

Amy Marcy Cheney Beach, ca. 1900.

Milne Special Collections and Archives, University of New Hampshire Library

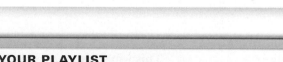

◄◄   **EXPAND YOUR PLAYLIST**   ►►

Chamber Music of the Nineteenth Century

Chamber music enjoyed great prestige throughout the nineteenth century. Composers, performers, and listeners all approached it as a serious and demanding category of music. It also became increasingly public over time, moving more and more into the concert hall, even as it continued to be cultivated in the home.

- **Ludwig van Beethoven: Piano Trio in B-flat Major, op. 97 ("Archduke").**
  The most famous of Beethoven's six piano trios, so named because he dedicated it to one of his composition pupils, Archduke Rudolph of Austria.

- **Ludwig van Beethoven: String Quartet in A Minor, op. 132.**
  One of Beethoven's "late" quartets, written in the last years of his life. The slow movement is labeled "Song of Holy Thanksgiving from a Convalescent to the Almighty."

- **Franz Schubert: Piano Trio in B-flat Major, D. 898.**
  One of two lengthy piano trios by Schubert, as long as many symphonies of the time.

- **Felix Mendelssohn: Piano Trio in C Minor, op. 66.**
  One of two piano trios by Fanny's brother Felix. The finale incorporates a sacred chorale (hymn tune).

- **Johannes Brahms: Piano Quintet in F Minor, op. 35.**
  Densely textured but richly melodic, this quintet resembles a symphony in its scope and tone.

- **Johannes Brahms: Clarinet Quintet in B Minor, op. 115.**
  Brahms became attracted to the clarinet as a solo instrument relatively late in life; this work is one of the few of its kind in the repertory.

((● **HEAR SAMPLES** on **www.mymusiclab.com**

✓ **TEST YOURSELF** on **www.mymusiclab.com**   Flashcards and chapter tests

32

Clara Wieck Schumann
"Forward!"
Composed: 1848

"Forward!" is an overtly political work, written during the heat of the uprisings throughout continental Europe in 1848–1849. It is for chorus without instrumental accompaniment of any kind.

((• HEAR MORE on www.mymusiclab.com

Timbre

Listen for the range of voices from highest (soprano) to lowest (bass).

Melody

Listen for the return of the opening melody at later points in the work, and listen for the way it is varied each time. Also listen for the contrasting melody between these returns of the opening theme.

Word-Music Relationships

Listen for the ways in which the melodic contour or texture of the music emphasizes certain words in the text. Which words—even if on first hearing you do not understand their meaning—*sound* the most important?

LEARN MORE on www.mymusiclab.com
Chapter Objectives

This work began as a birthday present. Clara Schumann wrote it as a gift to her husband, Robert Schumann, on his 38th birthday, on June 8, 1848. She even arranged a performance of it on that day in their home, engaging members of the Dresden Choral Society, a group her husband had founded earlier that same year.

But the text of "Forward!" ("Vorwärts!") is political, not personal. The poem was written in 1840 by the poet Emanuel Geibel, and its title was a slogan for those who believed in a united and democratic Germany. What we now think of as Germany was at the time divided into a myriad of large and small states including Prussia, Swabia, Baden, Saxony, and others. Each state had its own monarch, laws, and currency. The idea of unifying these various states into a single nation (Germany) with provisions for representative government was the chief goal of the revolutionaries who fought in the streets during the uprisings of 1848 and 1849. These outbreaks of violence were scattered and sporadic and ultimately failed. Not until 1871 did Germany emerge as a united country under the leadership of the former king of Prussia, with a limited form of representative government.

272

When Clara Schumann wrote this work, in the early summer of 1848, revolution was in the air, and she was well aware of the political implications of Geibel's text. Her husband did not participate actively when revolution broke out in Dresden a year later, but he did follow the events closely in the newspapers and even wrote to a colleague in 1849 that he felt a responsibility "to tell, in music, of the sorrows and joys that motivate the times." In "Forward!," Clara Schumann had beaten him to the punch.

A Cappella Timbre

A group of unaccompanied voices is called an **a capella** chorus. The voices in this particular work are "mixed," consisting of both women (sopranos, altos) and men (tenors, basses). The practice of a cappella singing goes back to the Middle Ages and Renaissance, so the timbre itself was not new in the nineteenth century, even if the harmonies now moved in a wider range, the rhythms were more jagged and irregular, and the dynamic contrasts were more pronounced. But performances of choral music took on special social significance in German-speaking lands in the nineteenth century, where laws of association strictly regulated and limited large social gatherings of any kind. Choruses of all varieties were permitted on the grounds that they were artistic and not political. In reality, everyone knew that these groups were to some extent political organizations giving voice to what they could otherwise not say in public.

Contrasting Melodies

Clara Schumann's setting of the text follows the form of the poem's five strophes, three of which (1, 3, and 5) begin with or culminate in the word *Vorwärts* ("Forward"). She sets these three strophes to a loud, rhythmically energetic melody, varying it with each strophe. The other two strophes (2 and 4), which speak to the temptations of complacency and fatigue, are set to a very different melody that is softer and more rhythmically smooth. Here, too, the melody is varied when it returns. The contrasting melodies become the basis of contrasting sections, creating a form that approximates that of a rondo (**A B A' B' A"**).

Painting Revolutionary Words

The key word of the text, *Vorwärts* ("Forward"), is a charged one. The composer goes to great lengths to emphasize it at its first appearance, at the end of the first strophe, where it stands out by virtue of its unison texture and trumpet-like melodic line. Passages that speak of calm and peace—the contrasting strophes 2 and 4—are set to a low dynamic (piano), and the music hits its registral high point on the word *Himmel* ("heaven") just before the very end. All of these are good examples of **word-painting**, in which individual words are "painted" with music that matches their meanings.

Now listen to this work again, using the Listening Guide.

1819–1896
Clara Wieck Schumann
"Forward!"
Composed: 1848

GENRE
A cappella choral music

KEY CONCEPTS
Political music, word-painting, timbre of the a cappella chorus.

CHAPTER HIGHLIGHT
Political Music
The public uprisings that began with the French Revolution of 1789 opened up new ways of connecting music and politics. Every mass political movement since then has had its songs. This song for a cappella chorus captures the progressive spirit of its time and place.

CONNECT YOUR PLAYLIST

A Cappella Timbre

Find an example of work that includes at least one extended passage performed *a cappella*.

Example: Kansas, "Carry On Wayward Son" (1976)
This song begins with an *a cappella* introduction, creating a sense of dramatic contrast when the instruments enter.

GO TO www.mymusiclab.com
for the Automated Listening Guide
CD III • Track 13/Download Track 61

Listening Guide

Clara Wieck Schumann Composed: 1848 "Forward!" (1:20)

Time	Original German Text	English Translation	Melody
0:00	1. Lass das Träumen, lass das Zagen, Unermüdet wandre fort! Will die Kraft dir schier versagen, "Vorwärts!" ist das rechte Wort.	Leave the dreaming and hesitation behind, Without fatigue, go forward! If you simply run out of energy, "Forward!" is the right word.	1 = rising figure, dotted rhythms
0:15	2. Darfst nicht weilen, wenn die Stunde Rosen dir entgegenbringt, Wenn dir aus des Meeres Grunde Die Sirene lockend singt.	You may not dally, if the day Brings you roses, Or if from the depths of the ocean The siren sings seductively to you.	2 = higher register, leaps up, then moves down
0:28	3. Vorwärts, vorwärts! Im Gesange Ringe mit dem Schmerz der Welt, Bis auf deine heisse Wange Goldner Strahl von oben fällt,	Forward, forward! In song Wrestle with the suffering of the world, Until on your hot cheek A golden ray from above should fall,	1 (varied)
0:41	4. Bis der Kranz, der dichtbelaubte, Schattig deine Stirn umwebt, Bis verklärend überm Haupte Dir des Geistes Flamme schwebt.	Until the crown, thickly woven, wraps itself with shadows around your head, Until above your head transfigured The flame of the spirit hovers before you.	2 (varied)
0:55	5. Vorwärts drum durch Feindes Zinnen, Vorwärts durch des Todes Pein, Wer den Himmel will gewinnen, Muss ein rechter Kämpfer sein!	Forward, then, through the enemy's lines, Forward through the pain of death, Whoever would gain entry to heaven Must be a true fighter!	1 (varied)

Form: Section	Word-Music Relationships
A	Unison trumpet-like figure on the word *Vorwärts!* ("Forward!") (0:09)
B	Soft dynamics for passage of text describing a lack of conflict in life.
A′	*Goldner Strahl von oben* ("Golden ray from above") moves from high to low.
B′	Soft dynamics describing the transport of the soul to heaven.
A″	Highest note of the entire work on the word *Himmel* ("heaven") at 1:02.

How many singers are in an a cappella chorus?

The number can vary. Some a cappella groups, like the one pictured here, have only one or two singers on each part (thus, 4 to 8 singers in total), while others might have as many as 8 or 10 to a part. In the recording here, we hear a group of about two dozen singers.

Abigail Lebrecht/ Lebrecht Music & Arts Photo Library

Whatever happened to the tradition of a cappella singing?

It continues to this day. Many colleges in the United States feature a cappella groups (men, women, or mixed). The Fisk Jubilee Singers, of Fisk University in Nashville, Tennessee, is one of the oldest groups of this kind. The original members consisted of emancipated slaves, and they broke racial barriers when they began touring with their repertory of spirituals and "slave music" in 1871. Today, it is estimated that there are more that 1,500 a cappella ensembles on U.S. college campuses. Many of these groups specialize in a particular repertory of music, such as classical, popular, gospel, or jazz.

The Fisk Jubilee Singers of Fisk University, ca. 1880. This a cappella ensemble was one of the first of many such groups established at American colleges in the nineteenth century. Its repertory included many songs with political implications.
CORBIS—NY

PROFILE   Clara Wieck Schumann (1819–1896)

Independent Spirit

Clara Wieck's father, Friedrich Wieck, was adamantly opposed to the idea of his daughter marrying a musician, particularly a composer of such limited means as Robert Schumann. The situation was complicated by the fact that Wieck was Robert Schumann's piano teacher. The young couple eventually eloped without her father's approval. Clara and her father were estranged for many years, and at one point she had to go to court to recover her piano from him.

Schumann's independence of spirit grew even stronger after her husband's death. Finding herself a young widow in her mid-thirties, she went on to pursue a highly successful career as a soloist and teacher. Her performances of Beethoven's sonatas and concertos, Chopin's piano pieces, and her husband's compositions were legendary in their time. Critics hailed her as one of the great piano virtuosos of her generation. Her compositional output includes a piano concerto, a piano trio, and many short piano works and songs for voice and piano. Later in life, she edited the first complete edition of her husband's musical works.

⚙ **LEARN MORE** on **www.mymusiclab.com**
MyMusicLibrary: From the Common Diary of Robert and Clara Schumann

◉➔ **EXPLORE MORE** on **www.mymusiclab.com**

Clara Wieck, ca. 1840, around the time of her marriage to Robert Schumann.

Clara Schumann, photo by Dagli Orti, courtesy of Picture DeskInc./Kobal Collection

---

EXPAND YOUR PLAYLIST: CLARA WIECK SCHUMANN

- *Three Songs on Texts by Rückert*

- *Variations on a Theme by Robert Schumann.* A set of variations on a theme by her husband.

- **Piano Trio in G Minor, Op. 17**

- **Piano Concerto in A Minor, Op. 7.** An early work written to showcase her talents both as a performer and composer.

((•● **HEAR SAMPLES** on **www.mymusiclab.com**

HISTORICAL CONTEXT Music, Patronage, and Politics

Rulers from all periods and all corners of the world have competed for musical talent in order to demonstrate their cultural power. In the early nineteenth century, when Beethoven was at one point considering leaving Vienna for good, the city's nobility and aristocracy considered it a point of national pride to keep him there, so they raised sufficient funds to persuade him to stay. Beethoven responded by writing a number of works on overtly political texts that glorified Austria. For many composers before the nineteenth century, having a patron, an influential person who supported them, was the only way they could earn a living in music.

The public uprisings that began with the French Revolution of 1789 opened up new ways of connecting music and politics. Communal singing became an important means of fostering solidarity among a large and diverse population, and the idea that every nation should have its own national song or anthem took root around this time. Every mass political movement since then has had its songs. In the twentieth century, protesters for and against many different causes used music to galvanize support. Labor unions, supporters of the civil rights movement, and opponents of the Vietnam War all developed extensive repertories of songs.

Politicians have also perceived certain kinds of music as threats at various times. Some types of jazz were prohibited in Nazi Germany and the Soviet Union. Even in the United States there have been movements to ban types of rock, rap, and hip-hop music or at least give them ratings so people are aware of the "dangerous" content.

Martin Luther King Jr. addresses the Civil Rights March on Washington on August 28, 1963. Musical performers at the event included Marian Anderson, Joan Baez, Bob Dylan, Mahalia Jackson (see Web Bonus Chapter 5), and Peter, Paul, and Mary. But the most moving performance, by all accounts, was by the assembled crowd itself singing "We Shall Overcome."

AP Wide World Photos

⏪ **EXPAND YOUR PLAYLIST** ⏩

Political Music

Music has a long history of being used to promote political causes. Some examples follow:

The French Revolution
• "La Marseilles"
• "Ça ira"

The Civil War
• "The Battle Hymn of the Republic"

The Civil Rights Movement
• "The Battle Hymn of the Republic"
• "If I Had a Hammer"
• "We Shall Overcome"

The Vietnam War
• Country Joe and the Fish, "I-Feel-Like-I'm-Fixin'-to-Die Rag" (1965)
• Creedence Clearwater Revival, "Fortunate Son" (1969)

((•● HEAR SAMPLES on www.mymusiclab.com

 TEST YOURSELF on www.mymusiclab.com   Flashcards and chapter tests

33

Frédéric Chopin
Mazurka in B-flat, op. 7, no. 1
Composed: 1830s

Politics can play a role in purely instrumental music. This mazurka by Chopin uses the characteristic rhythms of a Polish folk dance. In the context of its time and place—Paris in the 1830s—listeners would have recognized at once its political implications, for Chopin's native Poland had recently ceased to exist.

Listen to this first

((●● HEAR MORE on www.mymusiclab.com

Texture	**Melody**	**Rhythm**	**Form**
Notice how clearly the melody stands out in the uppermost voice. The lower voices play a strictly supporting role. This piece is thoroughly **homophonic**.	Listen for a direct upward path through a series of steps (punctuated by jagged dotted rhythms), which then lead to three leaps downward (also in dotted rhythms). In the quiet, mysterious middle section, do you notice that the melody now moves *downward*, primarily by steps?	Listen carefully to the opening rhythm, which repeats itself many times, and then see if you can tap it out yourself afterward.	In this work, Chopin uses just a few brief melodic ideas to create a larger whole, through repetition, variation, and contrast. Listen for the return of the opening idea and the way in which themes introduced later contrast with the opening.

 LEARN MORE on
www.mymusiclab.com
Chapter Objectives

SEE MORE on
www.mymusiclab.com
Documentary:
Romanticism

For many, Frédéric Chopin epitomizes Romanticism. His piano music is passionate and direct. A renowned piano virtuoso, he was able to evoke a wide range of emotions in the works he composed for his instrument. Without recourse to words, he created poetry for the keyboard that still speaks in a profound way to pianists and audiences today. His repertory consists mainly of what are called **character pieces**, relatively short works that capture a particular character—not in the sense of a character in a story, but in the sense of a mood. The titles of these works always provide a clue to the character they seek to establish.

A **mazurka** is a Polish folk dance in triple meter, often with a heavy accent on the second or third beat of each measure (1-**2**-3 | 1-**2**-3 or 1-2-**3** | 1-2-**3**) instead of the usual accent on the first beat (**1**-2-3 | **1**-2-3). Chopin, who was born in Poland but later moved to France, wrote many mazurkas and other types of Polish dances as an expression of his intense national pride for his native land, using the rhythms of folk dances as the basis for miniature works of art. This work is thus an example of musical **nationalism**. Chopin was neither the first nor the last composer to draw on folk music for inspiration, but the particular context of a work like the mazurka—Poland was under Russian occupation at the time—gave this music a sense of political meaning that was quite obvious to his contemporaries, regardless of their nationality.

Texture: The Singing Piano

Chopin advised young pianists to listen carefully and often to great singers and to imitate at the keyboard their manner of projecting the voice. In composing, he put this advice into practice. He endowed one part with a beautiful melody—as though giving a line to a singer—and created other parts to support and enhance the melody—as though giving the singer a truly inspired and creative accompanist or backup. This homophonic texture worked particularly well on the piano because it is an instrument that can play both lyrical melodies and accompaniment at the same time. In this piece, the right hand carries the melody, in a higher register, while the left hand provides the accompaniment.

About two-thirds of the way through (at "C" in the Listening Guide), the accompaniment changes markedly. It moves from a series of varied chords to a **drone bass**, a single pair of notes repeated over and over, rather like the sound of a bagpipe. This static harmony creates a strong sense of contrast between this section and those before and after. It also reinforces the folk-like origins of the mazurka as a genre, for the bagpipe is an instrument associated almost exclusively with the music of the countryside.

Melody: Scales Going Up, Scales Going Down

If you ever learned to play an instrument or sang in a choir, you probably learned to play or sing scales (or "Do-Re-Mi's"). Maybe you even wondered why you were asked to spend time practicing something other than actual songs. If you have not played or sung much music yourself, you have probably still heard of scales as a building block of music, and wondered what they actually have to do with the music itself. This mazurka is an example of how scales can form important parts of melodies, and also how different scales can create completely different-sounding music.

This mazurka, a very popular one with pianists, opens with a theme that consists quite simply of an ascending scale—a series of steps up. Pianists who have practiced their scales conscientiously will have an easier time playing this scalar melody. Because it is a major scale, it sounds bright and optimistic. (You may come up with slightly different terms, because the quality of a sound remains subjective.) The top note of this scale is marked by a trill (two notes a step apart played in alternation so rapidly it can be difficult for the listener to separate them).

1809—1848
Frédéric Chopin
Mazurka in B-flat,
op. 7, no. 1
Composed: 1830s

GENRE
Character piece for piano

KEY CONCEPTS
Homophonic texture, drone base, scalar melodies, song-like texture, "vocal" melody.

CHAPTER HIGHLIGHT
Nineteenth-Century Piano Music
This short character piece uses the rhythms of a Polish folk dance, and in the context of its time and place—Paris in the 1830s—audiences would have grasped its political implications, for Chopin's native Poland had recently ceased to exist. The homophonic texture of the music allows the piano to "sing."

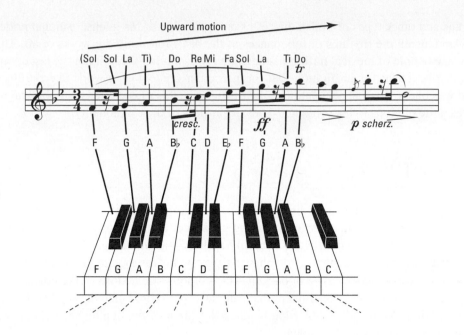

Later, at 1:05, the mood changes to one of perhaps mystery or contemplation, and we hear a scale going downward. But it is not the downward motion that creates this unusual sound with a completely different feel. It is the kind of scale that it is: a variation on a minor scale—which, as we have already heard, imparts a sadder or more somber quality to music. You hear that the dynamics are suddenly very quiet, which enhances the minor mood or mystery.

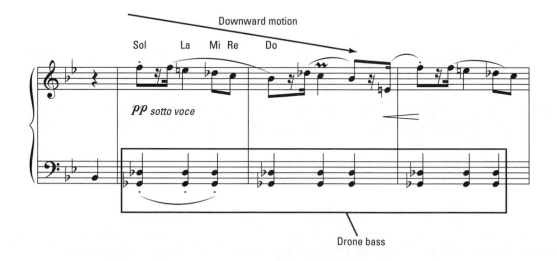

Between these two melodies, at 0:34, we hear a gentler melody that has neither a long trajectory upward or downward nor wide leaps. It moves within a limited range of notes.

Undulating motion, narrow range

p *legato*

Form: Repetition, Variation, Contrast

Chopin uses just a few brief melodic ideas to create a larger whole. Here, the various sections (**A, B, C**) are restated without significant variation to create a rondo-like pattern, in which **A** returns repeatedly after the interjection of contrasting ideas (**B** and **C**):

A   A   B   A   B   A   C   A   C   A

Rhythm: The Pride of Poland

The rhythm that you hear at the beginning is found in some guise in every mazurka Chopin wrote—and he wrote at least 57, all in triple meter. They encompass many different moods, from melancholy to exuberant, but all contain this rhythm typical of Polish folk dance, with an accent on the second beat of a three-beat measure ("2") rather than on the downbeat ("1"):

1   **2**   3 | 1   **2**   3

Now listen to the Mazurka again, using the Listening Guide.

CONNECT YOUR PLAYLIST

Nationalism

Find a piece that expresses nationalism in music.

Example: Brooks & Dunn, "Only in America" (2001)
This song by the country duo Brooks & Dunn offers a strongly pro-American message.

Listening Guide

GO TO www.mymusiclab.com
for the Automated Listening Guide
CD III • Track 14/Download Track 62

Frédéric Chopin, Composed: 1830s Mazurka in B-flat, op. 7, no. 1 (2:10)

Time	Form/Melody	Texture
0:00	A (= a long ascending scale with sudden downward leaps; major mode)	Homophonic throughout
0:17	A	
0:34	B (= a much narrower range; major mode)	
0:46	A	
1:05	C (= a downward trajectory; minor mode)	With drone bass
1:18	A	
1:37	C	With drone bass
1:50	A	

Student FAQs

How is the mazurka actually danced?

As a folk dance, the mazurka emphasizes the off-beat accents (on "2" of each measure) by calling on the dancers to click their heels or stamp their feet. More stylized forms of the dance emerged later, allowing the dancers relatively great freedom to improvise steps and gestures of the hands.

Would anyone have actually danced to Chopin's mazurkas?

Probably not, at least not in public. Even though this is dance music, with a steady beat, it was meant to be heard rather than serve as the accompaniment to an actual dance.

This 1844 Polish drawing shows two enthusiasts dancing the Mazurka.
Abigail Lebrecht/Lebrecht Music & Arts Photo Library

PROFILE Frédéric Chopin (1809–1848)

A Polish Composer in France

The son of a French father and a Polish mother, Chopin never felt quite at home in either land. After early training in his native Poland, he set out on an extended tour of Western Europe and never returned. But Poland was never far from his mind. When Russia annexed all but a tiny portion of the country in 1831, the cause of Polish nationalism burned even brighter in the nation's exile community. Chopin's cultivation of such national dances as the polonaise and mazurka manifests his deep feelings toward his native land.

Thanks in part to the large number of Polish expatriates in Paris, Chopin was able to circulate in the highest levels of society. He made a good living from his teaching and sales of his own music, along with the occasional public concert, though he avoided these as much as he could, especially in his later years. In 1837, he began a decade-long liaison with the novelist Amandine Lucile Aurore Dudevant (1804–1876), better known by her pen name, George Sand. In 1838–1839, the two wintered on the island of Majorca, off the Spanish coast in the Mediterranean. There, local doctors diagnosed Chopin's growing illness as tuberculosis. In spite of his poor health, Chopin continued to compose steadily until the last few months of his life.

Most of Chopin's music is for solo piano, and even the small number of works that are not—such as songs, concertos, and a piano trio—include the piano.

Chopin was one of the first composers to have been photographed. This daguerreotype was taken only a few months before his death.

Getty Images/De Agostini Editore Picture Library

◉➤ **EXPLORE MORE** on **www.mymusiclab.com**

EXPAND YOUR PLAYLIST: CHOPIN

- **Preludes, op. 24.** A collection of 24 short pieces for solo piano in each of the major- and minor-mode keys.

- **Etudes, op. 10 and op. 25.** Two sets of "studies" for solo piano, each of which emphasizes a particular technical skill, such as playing in octaves or in contrasting rhythms in the two hands.

- **Ballade no. 1 in G Minor, op. 25.** A wordless "story" for solo piano.

- **Berceuse in D-flat Major, op. 57.** A "cradle song" for solo piano that features a constant rocking rhythm.

- **Polonaise in A Major, op. 40, no. 1 ("Military").** One of Chopin's most famous polonaises, another stylized Polish dance for solo piano.

- **Piano Concerto no. 1 in F Minor, op. 21.** The more popular of Chopin's two concertos for piano and orchestra, a highly dramatic work.

((•● **HEAR SAMPLES** on **www.mymusiclab.com**

PERFORMANCE   Speeding Up and Slowing Down: Robbed Time

Listen carefully to almost any recording of Chopin's solo piano music and you will notice that the performer does not always maintain a strict tempo but instead speeds up and slows down. The changes are not dramatic, but they are noticeable and effective. These subtle changes of tempo applied by the performer are known as **tempo rubato**—literally "robbed time"—or simply **rubato**.

Many accounts of Chopin's piano playing mention his use of rubato. One particularly intriguing account has come down to us from one of his students:

> In keeping time Chopin was inexorable, and . . . the metronome never left his piano. Even in his much maligned *tempo rubato*, the hand responsible for the accompaniment would keep strict time while the other hand, singing the melody, would free the essence of the musical thought from all rhythmic fetters, either by lingering hesitantly or by eagerly anticipating the movement with a certain impatient vehemence akin to passionate speech.

The key phrase here is "akin to passionate speech." Music that imitates singing must capture the flexible delivery so characteristic of singers. Just as we speak with varying speeds—speeding up here, slowing down there for emphasis—so, too, do operatic performers vary the pace of their delivery, altering the rhythm of their words to match the emotion. Pianists imitating singers have a corresponding obligation to play this kind of music with a sense of expression, as "passionate speech."

Source: Carl Mikuli, Preface to his edition of *Chopin's Pianoforte-Werke*. (Leizpig: Kistner, 1880), quoted in Jean-Jacques Eigeldinger, *Chopin: Pianist and Teacher as Seen by his Pupils*, ed. Roy Howat, trans. Krysia Osotowicz and Maomi Shohet. (Cambridge: Cambridge University Press, 1987), p. 276.

The metronome is a mechanical device developed in the early 19th century for measuring musical time more precisely. By raising or lowering the weight on the stick, the user can decrease or increase the pace of the clicking sound produced by the back-and-forth motion of the pendulum.

© Dorling Kindersley

EXPAND YOUR PLAYLIST

Piano Music of the Nineteenth Century

Many of the nineteenth century's leading composers were themselves pianists, and they wrote extensively for the instrument.

Ludwig van Beethoven
Beethoven's 32 piano sonatas, of which these are only a few, remain a staple of the repertory and cover an enormous range of styles and moods. Some of his more famous sonatas include the following:
• Piano Sonata in C-sharp Minor, op. 27, no. 2 ("Moonlight")
• Piano Sonata in F Minor, op. 57 ("Appassionata")
• Piano Sonata in B-flat Major, op. 106 ("Hammerklavier")
• Piano Sonata in E Major, op. 109

Robert Schumann
• *Carnaval*, op. 9
  A cycle of small works based on the theme of Carnival, in which party-goers wear masks and behave in unusual ways.

• *Fantasia*, op. 17
  A three-movement work comparable to a sonata.

Franz Liszt
• Sonata in B Minor
  A central idea is transformed across the entire work.
• *Etudes d'execution transcendentale*
  A set of studies or exercises of transcendental difficulty.

Johannes Brahms
• Intermezzo, op. 118, no. 2
  One of Brahms's most beloved piano miniatures, it is deceptively simple.

((• HEAR SAMPLES on **www.mymusiclab.com**

✓ **TEST YOURSELF** on **www.mymusiclab.com**   Flashcards and chapter tests

Louis Moreau Gottschalk

Union: Concert Paraphrase on National Airs
Composed: 1862

Gottschalk wrote *Union* in response to the outbreak of the American Civil War. Although born and raised in New Orleans, Gottschalke was an ardent Unionist who opposed slavery and secession. To express his political convictions, he composed a work that incorporated three well-known patriotic tunes: "Yankee Doodle," "Hail, Columbia," and "The Star-Spangled Banner."

Listen to this first

((• HEAR MORE on www.mymusiclab.com

Melody

Listen for the three well-known patriotic tunes. Listen, too, for the way in which Gottschalk has the piano imitate the sound of distant and approaching drums.

Texture

Listen for differences in texture in the way these melodies are presented. "The Star-Spangled Banner" and "Hail, Columbia" are homophonic (melody with accompaniment). But when "Yankee Doodle" is introduced toward the end, it is combined with "Hail, Columbia" to produce a polyphonic texture, two independent melodies played at the same time.

***Union* did more than help galvanize Northern sentiment in support of the war**: it gave Gottschalk a vehicle by which to display his talents both as a composer and (in performance of the work) as a piano virtuoso. Gottschalk was the first American-born piano virtuoso to achieve international fame. His solo recitals were legendary, and his repertory consisted almost entirely of music he had written himself, because it allowed him to display his technical abilities to greatest effect. He performed *Union* to great acclaim throughout the United States—at least in the North—and in Latin America. Gottschalk noted in his diary that a performance of *Union* in Philadelphia during the Civil War elicited "unheard-of enthusiasm. . . . Recalls, encores, hurrahs, etc.!"[1]

⚙ LEARN MORE on
www.mymusiclab.com
Chapter Objectives

[1]Louis Moreau Gottschalk, *Notes of a Pianist*, ed. Clara Gottschalk, trans. Robert E. Peterson (Philadelphia: Lippincott, 1881), p. 81.

HISTORICAL CONTEXT   Music in the Civil War

Works like Gottschalk's *Union* remind us of the power of music to arouse intense feelings of community spirit, whether for a school, a faith, or a nation. When giving a concert in Maryland—a slave state that had not seceded and whose citizens' loyalties were deeply divided between North and South—Gottschalk realized that he could not play both *Union* and "Dixie" on the same program without risking a riot, so fierce were the sentiments that could be aroused by certain works of music.

Some songs had more universal appeal. "All Quiet Along the Potomac Tonight," for example, was sung on both sides of the conflict. The words had been written as a poem in 1861 by Ethel Lynn Beers, a New Yorker. Two years later, South Carolinian John Hill Hewitt set them to music while living in Georgia. The song speaks to the quiet fate of an enlisted soldier killed by a sniper; the newspapers the following day report no action along the Potomac River—the river separating Virginia from Maryland, South from North—but the soldier's family knows better.

With the advent of war, old tunes received new texts: a newly minted Confederate version of "Yankee Doodle," issued early in the Civil War, begins,

Yankee Doodle had a mind
To whip the Southern "traitors,"

Because they didn't choose to live
On codfish and potaters.

Several Northern poets, in turn, penned new words to the melody of "Dixie," including these:

Away down South in the land of traitors,
Rattlesnakes and alligators,
Right away, come away, right away, come away.
Where cotton's king and men are chattels,
Union boys will win the battles,
Right away, come away, right away, come away.

Music provided a source of comfort and inspiration to both soldiers in the field and their families back home. And for the soldiers, music was more than entertainment: every unit had its allotted number of musicians, who conveyed orders across wide distances (through musical signals), mustering the troops, and moving them into position for both drill and battle.

Band of the 107th U.S. Colored Infantry at Fort Corcoran, Arlington, Virginia, in 1865. The most common band instruments of the Civil War were trumpets, fifes (a small, high flute, similar to the piccolo), and many different kinds of drums. The large instruments in the front row are saxhorns, a brass instrument named after Adolphe Sax, who also invented the saxophone. Players carried the instrument over their shoulders, with the bell pointing backward, which allowed troops in the rear to hear their music.
Courtesy of the Library of Congress.

Many of Gottschalk's works incorporate national or ethnic elements. His piano piece *The Banjo*, for example, imitates the sound of that quintessentially American instrument and includes a reference to Stephen Foster's beloved song "Camptown Races." Another of Gottschalk's piano works, *Bamboula*, incorporates the rhythms of African American dances of the mid-nineteenth century.

Patriotic Melodies Made Virtuosic

The "national airs" that Gottschalk incorporates in this piece—"The Star-Spangled Banner," "Hail, Columbia," and "Yankee Doodle"—were all closely identified with the Union cause. The work presents no original melodies of its own but offers instead, as its title promises, a "paraphrase" on these "national airs." The patriotic melodies themselves are fairly simple, but Gottschalk embellished them in ways that allowed him to demonstrate his abilities as a piano virtuoso. This work is fiendishly difficult to play, and contemporary audiences were probably responding not only to the **nationalism** inherent in the music, but also to the sheer skill it took to perform it. With its rapid runs, large leaps, and complicated rhythms, all played for the most part at a very rapid speed, *Union* is the kind of work that only the most technically skilled pianists can perform convincingly. The virtuosity demanded in this work is in many respects physical, similar in kind to that required by a figure skater to execute a difficult maneuver.

Same Melodies, Different Textures

The texture of this work builds from homophonic at the beginning to polyphonic at the end. The harmonization of "The Star-Spangled Banner" is unusual, but the texture is clearly homophonic: melody above, accompaniment below. When "Yankee Doodle" enters clearly for the first time, however, it is combined not with a simple accompaniment underneath, but with another well-known melody, "Hail, Columbia." Both melodies are clearly audible at the same time. Even more remarkably, Gottschalk proceeds to reverse the relative position of these two "national airs," moving "Hail, Columbia" to the uppermost voice and placing "Yankee Doodle" underneath it. Writing two different melodies that work together is difficult enough; writing two melodies whose positions can be reversed is even harder. (The technical term for this kind of polyphony is "invertible counterpoint.") Even though Gottschalk wrote neither of these melodies, he recognized their compatibility and was thus able to demonstrate his skills as a composer and performer at the same time.

Now listen to this piece again, using the Listening Guide.

1829–1869
Louis Moreau Gottschalk
Union: Concert Paraphrase on National Airs
Composed: 1862
GENRE
Solo piano
KEY CONCEPTS
Virtuosity, nationalistic melodies, homophonic vs. polyphonic texture.
CHAPTER HIGHLIGHT
Virtuosity
While a great deal of music was written for amateur performance, some composers wrote music that lay well beyond the reach of any but the most accomplished musicians. Nineteenth-century composers like Gottschalk toured with their own compositions and were accorded near-divine status.

CONNECT YOUR PLAYLIST

Virtuosity

Find a work that places extreme demands of virtuosity on its instrumentalists.

Example: DragonForce, "Through the Fire and Flames" (2006)
This song is known for its extremely difficult instrumental solos. That's why it's featured in the final challenge of the popular video game *Guitar Hero III: Legends of Rock* (2007).

Listening Guide

GO TO www.mymusiclab.com
for the Automated Listening Guide
CD III •Track 15/Download Track 63

Louis Moreau Gottschalk Composed: 1862 *Union* (7:24)

Time	Section	Melody	Texture	Rhythm: Meter
0:00	A	Fragments of "Yankee Doodle" (in minor mode), beginning at 0:24	Homophonic	Duple
1:36	B	"The Star-Spangled Banner" ("with melancholy")		Triple
3:22	A	Fragments of "Yankee Doodle" in minor mode		Duple
3:39	C	Imitation of trumpets (3:39), followed by "Hail, Columbia." This section begins softly, grows in volume, and recedes—as if played by a band approaching, marching by, and departing. The "drums" become more audible at 5:00, then recede, as if into the distance.		
6:06	D	"Yankee Doodle" (upper voice) and "Hail, Columbia" (lower voice); voices switch positions at 6:22. "Yankee Doodle" returns to its usual major mode in this section.	Polyphonic	
6:29	A	Fanfare-like figure from the beginning	Homophonic	
6:43	D	"Yankee Doodle" (upper voice) and "Hail, Columbia" (lower voice); voices switch positions at 6:58.	Polyphonic	

Student FAQs

Why is "The Star-Spangled Banner" section marked "With melancholy"?

We can't know for certain what Gottschalk had in mind here, but the melody does gradually grow more resolute. Perhaps this reflects the dissolution of the Union at the beginning of the Civil War (April 1861) and the subsequent resolve to preserve it.

I've never heard of "Hail, Columbia" before. Was it well known in Gottschalk's time?

"Hail, Columbia" was widely known in the nineteenth century and served as a kind of unofficial national anthem, along with "The Star-Spangled Banner." For reasons that remain unclear, the tune fell out of use sometime after World War I.

A CLOSER LOOK   Gottschalk's 1862 Concerts

⊙➤ **EXPLORE MORE** on www.mymusiclab.com

In 1862 during the Civil War and after almost six years in Latin America, Louis Moreau Gottschalk returned to the United States. He concertized extensively throughout the North, including one tour of some 15,000 miles by train in which he gave 85 concerts over the course of 18 weeks. Some of his concert stops are presented here with excerpts from his diary.

1. February 22. Gottschalk premieres *Union* in New York City to great acclaim on Washington's birthday.

2. Spring. In St. Louis, Gottschalk writes, "The Germans (they are numerous here, as throughout the West) have organized a Philharmonic Society, which performs the works of Beethoven, Mendelssohn, Schumann, and Wagner."

3. April 18. On his way east from Chicago, Gottschalk witnesses a convoy of wounded soliders recently arrived from the Battle of Shiloh in Tennessee. "I have never in my life seen a more heart-rending sight than the spectacle of these heroic victims of our monstrous war," he writes.

4. June 6. In Portland, Maine, Gottschalk observes, "The hall contains twenty-five hundred persons, and is one of the finest in the world for its acoustic properties. The public are desirous that I should return and give another concert. Extraordinary enthusiasm."

5. June 28. In Springfield, Massachusetts, Gottschalk "visited a large manufactory of guns belonging to the government, where as many as twelve hundred rifles are made daily by a machine. Three thousand workmen are employed here."

6. November 26. Gottschalk is not impressed by Toledo: "Nothing interesting. Audience stupid. In the Artist's Room there was a bill attached to the wall: 'If, before commencing the concert, the performers do not pay the rent of the hall, the porter has orders from the proprietors to turn off the gas.'"

7. Early December. In Madison, Wisconsin, Gottschalk writes, "This town is hardly more than twelve years old, and nevertheless is already remarkable. The cathedral (Catholic) and the marble capitol are superb."

8. December 15. Indianapolis according to Gottschalk: "Whistling is here applause carried to its highest point... Another annoyance is the people who arrive late at the concert, and who traverse the hall in the middle of a piece, marching as if they were marking time for a battalion of raw recruits."

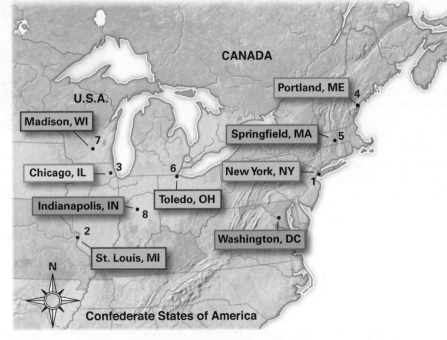

CANADA

U.S.A.

Madison, WI   7

Chicago, IL   3

Indianapolis, IN   8

2

St. Louis, MI

Toledo, OH   6

Portland, ME   4

Springfield, MA   5

New York, NY   1

Washington, DC

N

Confederate States of America

PROFILE   Louis Moreau Gottschalk (1829–1869)

The Musician as Showman

Wherever he performed, Gottschalk won over audiences with a combination of superb piano technique, good looks, and showmanship. He always made a ceremony of taking off his white gloves before performing at the piano, and critics raved about his ability to play even the most difficult passages with ease.

Orchestras around the country featured Gottschalk as a soloist in showpieces he wrote to display his own talents, like the *Grand fantasie triomphale*, a series of brilliant variations on the Brazilian national anthem, or the *Grande tarentelle* for piano and orchestra, based on the traditional Italian dance said to cure the bite of a tarantula. Other nineteenth-century musicians took full advantage of the concerto as a vehicle for showing off their talents as both composers and performers. Franz Liszt wrote two fiendishly difficult piano concertos—he was one of the few musicians of his time who could do justice to them—and Felix Mendelssohn, Frédéric Chopin, and Johannes Brahms also wrote piano concertos in addition to solo piano pieces (see Expand Your Playlist).

A native of New Orleans, Gottschalk studied piano in Paris, where his playing was praised by Chopin, Berlioz, and other leading European musicians. He returned to the United States in 1853 and soon became one of the nation's most popular soloists, touring the country extensively and playing almost entirely works he had composed himself (see A Closer Look: Gottschalk's 1862 Concerts, page 289). He died of yellow fever in Rio de Janeiro, Brazil, during an extended tour of Latin America.

⊙➜ **EXPLORE MORE** on **www.mymusiclab.com**

Louis Moreau Gottschalk, ca. 1860. He had a long-standing business relationship with Chickering, a major piano manufacturer, endorsing their instruments and performing on them whenever possible. Notice the bust of Beethoven in the background, much like the bust of Beethoven in the group portrait with Liszt at the piano (see page 236).

Art Resource/The New York Public Library

EXPAND YOUR PLAYLIST: GOTTSCHALK

- *The Banjo.* This work for solo piano imitates the strumming and plucking sound of the title instrument.

- *Bamboula.* For solo piano; the bass line imitates the bamboo drum of African American musical traditions.

- *Souvenir de Puerto Rico.* A work for solo piano that captures the characteristic rhythms of the Caribbean island.

- **Symphony no. 1** ("A Night in the Tropics"). The finale incorporates a Latin-inspired dance melody.

- *Grande Tarentelle.* A concerto-like work for piano and orchestra. Its central theme uses the rhythm the tarantella, a traditional Italian dance.

((•● **HEAR SAMPLES** on **www.mymusiclab.com**

◀◀   ▶▶

EXPAND YOUR PLAYLIST

The Nineteenth-Century Virtuoso

Audiences throughout Europe and the United States paid big money to hear the great virtuosos of their time perform, either in one-person recitals or as soloists with an orchestra, in concertos. Virtuosos were part musician, part showman. Many of these individuals, like Gottschalk, wrote and performed their own music.

Niccolò Paganini (1782–1840) was the greatest violin virtuoso of the nineteenth century. He did nothing to dispel rumors that he had made a pact with the devil to achieve his mastery of the instrument.

- *Caprices,* op. 1, no. 24. This is a fiendishly difficult set of variations on a short theme.
- Violin Concerto no. 2 in B Minor, op. 7, finale. The main theme of this rondo sounds like the ringing of bells.

Franz Liszt (1811–1886) was the greatest piano virtuoso of the nineteenth century. As a child, he met Beethoven, one of his daughters married the composer Richard Wagner, and he almost single-handedly created the public solo piano recital.

- Hungarian Rhapsody no. 2. This is the most famous of the 19 solo piano works Liszt wrote in a quasi-Hungarian style. Although Liszt was born in present-day Hungary, his native language was German, and he started to learn Hungarian only later in his life.

- Piano Concerto no. 2 in A Major. This is one of two concertos Liszt wrote to perform himself.
- *Grandes etudes de Paganini*, no. 3 in G-sharp Minor ("La Campanella"). Liszt's reworking of the finale of Paganini's Violin Concerto no. 2 (see earlier), for piano, adds extra lines to make the music even more difficult.

Ignacy Jan Paderewski (1860–1941) was famous as a piano performer, composer, and statesman. In later life, he served briefly as prime minister of his native Poland and was active in the Polish government-in-exile during World War II.

- *Humoresques de concert*: Minuet in G Major. The most famous of Paderewski's many works for solo piano.

(((• HEAR SAMPLES on **www.mymusiclab.com**

⟳ **TEST YOURSELF** on **www.mymusiclab.com**   Flashcards and chapter tests

35

Ravi Shankar
Raga Sindhi-Bhairavi
Recorded: 1968

Instrumental virtuosity plays a role in the music of many cultures around the world. In this work for solo sitar—an Indian plucked-string instrument—the famed Indian sitarist Ravi Shankar demonstrates his musicianship through music that is extremely difficult to play.

 Listen to this first

 HEAR MORE on www.mymusiclab.com

Timbre	**Melody**	**Texture**	**Form**	**Rhythm**
The sitar includes strings that are plucked and produce pitches and also strings that simply resonate when other pitches sound. Listen for the difference between these two kinds of sounds. Also listen for other instruments as well. How many and what kind of instruments do you hear?	Listen to the melodies produced on the sitar. Do some notes sound more important than others?	Is the texture homophonic or polyphonic? How many instruments do you hear? How does the texture change throughout the piece?	Listen for four different sections and the way each section changes in texture and rhythm.	Listen to how the rhythm begins freely but becomes more established throughout.

 LEARN MORE on
www.mymusiclab.com
Chapter Objectives

During India's Mughal Period—which lasted from the early sixteenth to the mid-nineteenth centuries—the musician Tansen (1500–1589) was brought to the court of Emperor Akbar in Delhi. Tansen introduced the *raga* as a genre of North Indian music. ***Raga***, which means "mood," "color," or "musical scale," is also the term that refers to an instrumental performance featuring a soloist who played to color the emperor's mood or day. Although this was a century before the Baroque Era in Europe, Tansen developed a solo instrumental genre prior to the solo violin sonatas of Arcangelo Corelli, the Italian composer and violin virtuoso (see Expand Your Playlist, chapter 13). The dissolution of the Mughal court after 1720 led to the dispersal of Hindustani musicians and *raga* performance throughout northern India at about the same time the *sonata* spread throughout Europe.

Timbre: The Sound of the Sitar

The **sitar** is a plucked-stringed instrument that usually has 18 strings ("tar" is the Indian word for "string"). The strings are arranged in three sets: the playing strings, the drone strings, and the sympathetic strings. The playing strings are fretted and produce the melody. (Frets are made of a thick twine that is wrapped around the neck of the instrument. They determine the pitch of a note when the non-plucking hand presses down against the top of the fret.) The main melody string is played by bending it far across the frets to produce a wide range of pitches. One of the drone strings is struck periodically to resonate with an important tone in the melody. The sympathetic strings are located under the frets and resonate or are played during the melody; they vibrate when a corresponding pitch is sounded (but typically a soloist often strums down across the sympathetic strings at the very beginning and very end of a piece, which can be heard in the accompanying listening example).

The strings are fastened to a wooden neck with pegs. The base of the neck of the sitar is attached to a large gourd resonator, and at the top of the neck is often attached a smaller gourd resonator. For plucking, the player wears a wire plectrum around the index finger of the right-hand. Players perform seated.

Global Connection: Virtuosity

b. 1920
Raga Sindhi-Bhairavi
Recorded: 1968
Ravi Shankar

GENRE
Indian Music

KEY CONCEPTS
Virtuosity, sitar, tonal pattern and mood, pulse cycles, metered vs. unmetered rhythm, improvisation.

CHAPTER HIGHLIGHT
Indian Music
Perhaps the most highly developed classical music in the world, the concert music of India features a complex set of scale and rhythms. The raga is a multi-movement composition comparable to a Western concerto.

👁 **SEE MORE** on
www.mymusiclab.com
Video: "Raga Kirwani"

Ravi Shankar is considered to be one of the finest sitarists in the world. He is certainly the most famous sitarist in the Western Hemisphere. George Harrison of the Beatles, one of his best-known pupils, learned the sitar and performed on it on the Beatles' albums *Rubber Soul* and *Revolver*. Schools for *raga* performance exist throughout the world today.
David Farrell/Lebrecht Music & Arts Photo Library

HISTORICAL CONTEXT   The Sitar in Popular Music

Ravi Shankar, who was born in Benares, India, in 1920, was already well known in Western classical and jazz circles when George Harrison first heard his playing in the mid-1960s. The lead guitarist for the Beatles—the most popular group of the day—Harrison first played sitar on their recording of the song "Norwegian Wood." Soon after, Brian Jones of the Rolling Stones played a sitar part on that group's hit single "Paint It Black." Harrison remained deeply devoted to Indian music and philosophy, studying with Shankar and also incorporating Indian tonalities and instruments into several of his songs, most notably "Within You, Without You" on *Sgt. Pepper's Lonely Heart's Club Band.*

Shankar's fame in rock circles grew after he appeared at several major festivals in the late 1960s, including the Monterey International Pop Music Festival in 1967 and the famous Woodstock festival in 1969. His best-known appearance was at the Concert for Bangladesh at New York's Madison Square Garden in 1971. Shankar had approached Harrison after hearing of the devastating floods in the Bangladesh region, situated between India and Pakistan. Harrison enlisted other rock artists—including Bob Dylan, Eric Clapton, and Ringo Starr—to perform at the concert. The concert opened—as did the later three-album record set—with a half-hour performance by Shankar on sitar.

Benares, on the Ganges River, is one of the world's oldest cities still inhabited today.

Shankar has continued to perform a mix of traditional *ragas* with his own compositions and to cross genres to work with classical orchestras and jazz and pop ensembles. His daughter, Anoushka, is also a noted sitar artist; another daughter, Norah Jones, is well known as a pop singer, songwriter, and pianist.

British pop musician George Harrison, right, of the Beatles, with seven top Indian instrumentalists, singers, and dancers. Ravi Shankar is third from the right.

Getty Images Inc.—Hulton Archive Photos

Melody of the Sunrise

Raga (also the plural form of the word) are scalar patterns with distinct melodic shapes and are derived from numerous tones. Each combination of tones has a certain character, or mood, that is believed to affect the universe. North Indian classical music uses far more tones than European classical music does. Theoretically, thousands of *raga* exist; however, 72 *raga* are known and performed today. Based on the larger vocabulary of available tones, new *raga* may still be invented.

Raga Sindhi-Bhairavi is a morning *raga*. It was created by Shankar, who is also a composer and improvisor. From the sixteenth through mid-nineteenth centuries, a morning *raga* could be performed at the court only at sunrise to regulate the sun's movement over the horizon. A different type of *raga* performed at that time of day, or a morning *raga* played with mistakes, was believed to throw off the entire day because the musical vibrations would be "out of synch" with the vibrations of the universe at that moment. Today, any *raga* can be performed at any time of day because they have become concert pieces. Many European composers have depicted the sunrise in their works as well, and those pieces, too, may be performed in the evening.

At the opening of this performance, Ravi Shankar demonstrates the ascending and descending scales that form the basis of this *raga*. Note that these scales are not identical; the descending scale has more notes than the ascending one and also more up-and-down motion. Note also the small bends and ornaments that he applies to certain notes to give them a distinct flavor; these also help give each raga scale its distinctive sound.

A *raga* solo always begins with the sounding of the tones of the *raga* scale in descending motion. Then, throughout the first three unmetered sections, the soloist freely improvises themes using the tones of this particular *raga*. Each *raga* has scale tones that are more important than others; you can hear during the improvisations that Shankar lingers on certain tones longer (for example from 0:36 to 0:54), or decorates them with brief upward or downward movements in pitch while basically remaining on the same note (for example from approximately 1:29 to 1:35). These key notes are the ones that will be used to build the principal melody of the *raga*, known as a *gat* (see the following discussion).

A performance of a *raga* features improvisation. Improvisation was also a typical practice in nineteenth-century Europe among virtuoso instrumentalists and composers, such as Frédéric Chopin, Franz Liszt, and the American artist Louis Moreau Gottschalk (see chapters 33 and 34). The *raga* improvisations gain in intensity throughout and culminate in the statement of the principal theme of the melody (at 5:48).

A Triple Texture

In addition to the texture created by the sitar's numerous strings, Indian music requires three players to produce the layers of musical activity: a melodic soloist (sitar or other instrument), a separate drone instrument, and an accompanying drummer. *Raga* performance by a sitarist is always accompanied by two instruments: the *tambura* and the *tabla*. The **tambura** is a plucked stringed instrument like the sitar, but it has four to six strings and is used only to provide a drone.

The **tabla** is a set of two drums struck with the fingertips. The *tabla* enters in the fourth and final section of the *raga*, when the meter becomes established. The *tabla* player is able to vary the pitch of each drum by pressing his or her hand against the drum head, creating a sliding sound something like the bending of the melody string on the sitar. So the *tabla* part can combine rhythm and melody, and can "answer" the melodies stated by the sitar.

Ravi Shankar and his daughter, Anoushka.
Mladen Peric/Lebrecht Music & Arts Photo Library

Form by Four Sections

The improvisation of the *raga* takes place over four sections of music:

1. The *alap* is the introductory section. The soloist is accompanied only by the *tambura*. The *alap* section allows a free-ranging exploration of the *raga* without a regular meter or pulse. It starts out in free rhythm and increases through a series of plateaux until the listener has a sense of a regular rhythmic pulse.
2. The *jor* is the section of the pulsed improvisation that develops from the *alap*. The *jor* tempo is faster than the *alap*, and the density of the rhythm increases.
3. The *jhala* section, the second type of pulsed improvisation, involves repeatedly striking a *jhala* (drone) string on the sitar.
4. The *gat tora* section introduces the meter set by the *tabla* drums. The *gat*, as mentioned previously, is a short composed melody, and the primary theme of the song. *Tora* are the alternated, improvised passages between the *gat* statements.

Rhythm from Free to Established

Tala are fixed, repeated cycles of pulses. Certain pulses receive accents and are thus more important than the others. *Tala* is absent from *alap*, *jor*, and *jhala* sections, because these sections build from free rhythm to a constant unmetered pulse. The *tala* always is established at the *gat tora* section of a *raga*. As Shankar says in his introduction, the basic rhythm can be played at various speeds, in this case at a medium and fast tempo.

CONNECT YOUR PLAYLIST

Instrumental Virtuosity

Find a recording that showcases a performer's virtuosity on an instrument.

Example: Charlie Daniels, "The Devil Went Down to Georgia" (1979) The song, about a fiddling contest between the devil and a boy named Johnny, features two extended instrumental sections in which each character displays his talents.

There are many *tala* patterns. In *Raga Sindhi-Bhairavi*, the *tala* is *tintál*, a 16-beat cycle. The 16 beats are further broken down into groups of 4, with the first beat of each grouping receiving extra emphasis: **1**-2-3-4 **5**-6-7-8 **9**-10-11-12 **13**-14-15-16. In the *gat tora* the soloist and *tabla* player can exchange roles, one improvising for a rhythmic cycle or two, while the other plays the fixed melody or rhythmic pattern.

Virtuosic Performance

As ragas have become popular on the concert stage, they have become showcases for individual musicians to show off their virtuosity.

Now listen to this piece again, using the Listening Guide.

EXPAND YOUR PLAYLIST

Raga

Ravi Shankar
- *Three Ragas*, Angel 67310.
  First issued in 1956, this recording captures Shankar at his youthful prime playing three traditional ragas.
- *At Woodstock*, BGO 117.
  Three ragas recorded live at the famous 1969 rock festival.
- *Improvisations*, Angel 67049.
  Originally released in 1961, this album features Shankar playing with two American jazz musicians, Bud Shank on saxophone and Gary Peacock on bass. It represents an early attempt at "fusion" of North Indian *raga* and American jazz music.

Anoushka Shankar
- *Anoushka*, Angel 53729.
  The 2000 debut album by Ravi's talented daughter is a program of original compositions in the style and spirit of classical *raga*.

Ali Akbar Khan
- Khan is a master of the *sarod*, a 25-string fretless lute that features a skin head stretched over the gourd-shaped body. The use of metal strings and neck and the skin head produce a much sharper and louder sound than is heard on the sitar.
- *Signature Series No. 1: Three Ragas*, Aamp 7500.
  The "Signature Series" brings onto CD classic recordings by Khan and represents some of his best works. This CD includes the night *raga* "Chandranandan."

George Harrison, Ravi Shankar, and Others
- *The Concert for Bangladesh*, Sony 4688352.
  The famous live concert from 1971, featuring a wonderful traditional performance by Ravi Shankar.

((•● HEAR SAMPLES on **www.mymusiclab.com**

Listening Guide

GO TO www.mymusiclab.com
for the Automated Listening Guide
CD IV • Track 1/Download Track 64

Ravi Shankar Recorded: 1968 *Raga Sindhi-Bhairavi* (14:59)

Time	Melody	Texture	Form
0:00	Shankar demonstrates the *raga*'s tones and tells the rhythmic pattern of the piece. In his narration, Shankar refers to "two pieces" of the *raga*: the first piece includes the *alap*, *jor*, and *jhala*, played in medium tempo; and the second piece is the *gat*, played quickly.		
0:28	After an opening strum down across the sympathetic strings, which are individually tuned to the tones of the *raga*, the piece begins with freely improvised short melodic phrases on the playing strings. Listen to how some phrases lead up to the highest tone of the *raga* while other phrases feature lower tones of the *raga*. Bending of the strings is used in an expressive and decorative style.	Drone harmony. The *tambura* continues providing a soft drone to the freely improvised introduction of the *raga* scale.	*Alap*
4:26	The soloist strikes a string to create a pulse and continues improvising now with a rhythmic pulsation.		*Jor*
4:54	The soloist features a repeatedly struck *jhala* string to build the first part of the piece to a climax.		*Jhala*
5:48	The *gat* theme begins with a brief flourish by the sitar, which is answered by the entrance of the *tabla*.	The drone continues; the introduction of the *tabla* drums creates a homophonic texture when the *tabla* supports the sitar's melodies	*Gat tora*
7:28	More improvisation is featured during this section. Listen to how the melody of the *gat* features more improvised variations as this section continues.	Homophonic	
11:26	Second, faster gat and final section of the raga. Improvisation is more quickly employed in this final section. The faster tempo helps build the performance to a climactic finish.	Homophonic	

Rhythm

Free rhythm

Rhythm established but in unmetered pulsations.

Rhythm continues in unmetered pulsations.

Tintál begins on the first tone of the *gat*. It is a 16-beat cycle. The *tabla* drums enter midway through the rhythm cycle.

Tintál rhythm cycle continues.

Tintál rhythm cycle continues with the final note struck by both the sitar and *tabla* on the first note of the *raga* and beat one of the rhythm cycle. The sitar concludes with a strum down across the sympathetic strings.

Dorling Kindersley
Media Library

Student FAQs

What are sympathetic strings? How do they work?

A sound wave creates physical movement in the air around it. When a string is plucked, its vibrations move through the air; if another string is nearby, even if it is not touched by a pick or finger, it is set into vibration by the original sound. This is described as a "sympathetic vibration," although of course the second string doesn't feel any sympathy for the first!

© Dorling Kindersley

How are drone strings different from sympathetic strings?

Both sympathetic and drone strings play only one note and are not "fretted" by the sitar player. However, the drone strings are regularly played with the pick to sound throughout the piece. Sympathetic strings are never struck; rather, they simply vibrate on their own when the sound of another string sets them into motion.

How does a sitar player play different ragas if each raga has a different set of scale notes?

The sitar player can adapt his or her instrument to different scales by moving the frets on the fingerboard. Unlike a guitar, which has frets permanently placed into the neck, the sitar's frets are arched metal pieces attached to the back of the neck by thick twine to stay in place. To play a different scale, it is easy to slide the frets into different positions.

36

Giuseppe Verdi
La Traviata, Act I, selection
Composed: 1853

In Verdi's *La Traviata*, Violetta, a high-class prostitute, thinks she may be falling in love with Alfredo, a young gentleman she has just met at a party. Alone back in her apartment, she moves from recitative at the beginning—simple, declamatory, syllabic—to a virtuosic aria at the end. Her singing is interrupted by Alfredo, whom she hears but does not see, singing his own aria to her from the street. At the end of this excerpt, we hear two separate melodies—two separate arias—being performed simultaneously

Listen to this first

((•● HEAR MORE on www.mymusiclab.com

Melody

Listen to the contrast between the melodic styles of Violetta's recitative, the aria, and the purely lyrical nature of Alfredo's singing.

Word-Music Relationships

Listen to the contrast between the introspective nature of the opening recitative and the growing exuberance of the music that leads into the aria. Note in particular Verdi's setting of the key word "*gioir*" ("enjoy"), set melismatically and in an extremely high register. Listen for the changes in tempo and melody later in the aria that reflect Violetta's attraction to Alfredo.

⚙ LEARN MORE on
www.mymusiclab.com
Chapter Objectives

This scene takes us on an emotional roller coaster. Violetta and Alfredo, a young gentleman, have fallen in love. But Violetta is already suffering from the consumption (tuberculosis) that will eventually kill her. She senses that her days are numbered, and she must decide whether to keep her freedom or commit to one man alone (Alfredo). The music she sings here ranges from uncertainty and fear of abandonment to the ecstasy of freedom to the crippling pain of love.

Verdi projects these profoundly contrasting emotions through a variety of singing styles. In this scene, we hear passages of declamatory, syllabic recitative flowing in and out of more lyrical, aria-like sections. We hear spectacularly virtuosic singing and extremely high notes—the kind that can sometimes break glass—and a moment later, simple, declamatory song. By writing long units of music that encompass both lyrical and declamatory moments, Verdi is able to move the plot forward (through recitative) and at the same time provide plenty of space for both the lyrical and virtuosic singing that opera audiences love so dearly. In this scene, in fact, Violetta's aria becomes a duet, for about halfway through this scene, Alfredo joins in. We do not see him onstage—he is singing his serenade of love to her from the street up to her balcony. This is a melody Alfredo had sung to her earlier in Act 1, and the combined sound of Alfredo's voice and this hauntingly lyrical melody causes Violetta to doubt her own resolve to live freely, alone and independent of anyone else's demands.

Verdi's *La Traviata* exemplifies the best elements of nineteenth-century Italian opera. It showcases the voice and uses the orchestra sparingly but effectively. Above all, it is dramatically realistic—who has not been torn between the desire for freedom and the pull of love?—and musically satisfying. Even if we do not understand the words, we can hear the sound of the emotions expressed by the singers.

Melody: Declamatory, Lyrical, Virtuosic

Verdi uses three distinct types of melody in this brief scene:

- **Declamatory.** Violetta begins her monologue by singing in the declamatory style of accompanied recitative. The melody is syllabic, making the text easy to understand. The melody is quite simple: at one point, Violetta sings the same note repeatedly, as if talking to herself—which, in fact, she is. The focus here is on the text.

- **Virtuosic.** At the exclamation *"Gioir!"* ("Enjoy!"), the music suddenly becomes melismatic. The text is not so easy to understand at this point, for intelligibility has taken a back seat to virtuosic display. Violetta hits some extremely high notes (at 0:36 and 0:56) and navigates through difficult runs at a rapid pace. When the aria begins (at 1:07), the orchestra introduces the principal melody but then gives way to Violetta, who continues to sing in a highly virtuosic style throughout the aria portion of the scene. When a soprano sings this role well, few things can be more thrilling in the world of opera.

- **Lyrical.** When Alfredo (or to be more precise, Alfredo's voice) enters the scene, we hear a very different kind of singing. The tempo is slower, the notes are longer and smoother, and the declamation is for the most part syllabic. There are no enormous leaps to the extreme end of the tenor's vocal range, no breathtaking runs. The music is sustained and lyrical.

The Russian-born soprano Anna Netrebko as Violetta in a production of *La Traviata* at the Salzburg Festival in 2005. New opera productions often update the scenery and staging of the original.

1813–1901

Giuseppe Verdi
La Traviata, Act I, selection
Composed: 1853

GENRE
Opera

KEY CONCEPTS
Integration of recitative and aria, vocal virtuosity, word-music relationships.

CHAPTER HIGHLIGHT
Vocal Virtuosity
Opera had long provided a venue for singers to demonstrate their technical prowess, and this tradition continued into the nineteenth century. This excerpt from Verdi's *La Traviata* places extraordinary technical demands on the soprano, even while incorporating her emotions into a dramatic situation that is highly realistic.

PROFILE   Giuseppe Verdi (1813–1901)

The Composer as Social Reformer

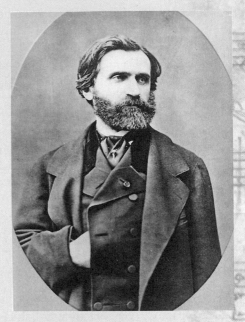

The story of *La Traviata* mirrors Giuseppe Verdi's own life in certain respects. Audiences were scandalized by the portrayal of an unwed couple living together, but this is exactly the situation in which Verdi found himself while composing *La Traviata*. He and Giuseppina Strepponi, a soprano, had been living together openly since 1848; they eventually married (in 1859), but Verdi experienced first-hand the same kind of scorn cast at those who, like his operatic characters Violetta and Alfredo, defy social conventions.

Through his art, Verdi sought to reform political conventions as well. Several of his operas incorporate thinly veiled appeals for the unification of Italy, which at the time was still a loose confederation of small states, many of them under the domination of the Austrian Empire. The chorus of captive Israelites in ancient Babylon in Verdi's *Nabucco* (1842) became the unofficial anthem of the simmering Italian uprising that would eventually liberate and unify Italy. Verdi himself was elected to the newly constituted Italian parliament in 1860, though by his own admission he spent little time there. He was too busy fulfilling commissions for new operas from around Europe, including France, Russia, and even Egypt. His *Aïda* (1871), set in ancient Egypt, was written to celebrate the opening of the Suez Canal.

For all his accomplishments, Verdi remained a private and modest individual, spending most of his life in Italy (see A Closer Look: Verdi's World, page 306). A few years before his death, he established a home for retired musicians unable to support themselves, and he consigned all royalties for the 30 years after his death to this institution.

Giuseppe Verdi.

Giuseppe Verdi (1813–1901) (b/w photo), French School, (19th century). Archives Larousse, Paris, France/The Bridgeman Art Library

Julia Roberts and Richard Gere at the opera house in the 1990 film *Pretty Woman*. They are watching Verdi's *La Traviata*, which provides the basis for much of the plotline of *Pretty Woman*.

Everett Collection

⚙ **LEARN MORE** on **www.mymusiclab.com**
MyMusicLibrary: Verdi Reacts to the Censors

◉ **EXPLORE MORE** on **www.mymusiclab.com**

◀◀   **EXPAND YOUR PLAYLIST: VERDI**   ▶▶

- *Il Trovatore* ("The Troubadour"). An opera about a series of loves and rivalries among a group of gypsies.

- *Rigoletto*. An opera about a hunchback court jester (Rigoletto) and a lascivious duke.

- *Aïda*. An opera commissioned to celebrate the opening of the Suez Canal; the story takes place in ancient Egypt.

- *Requiem*. A Mass for the dead, composed in honor of the Italian writer Alessandro Manzoni, this work is for chorus, soloists, and orchestra. It is quite operatic in its style, despite its being written for the church.

((• **HEAR SAMPLES** on **www.mymusiclab.com**

Word-Music Relationships:
Signs of Contemplation, Ecstasy, Love

Like every good opera composer, Verdi captures the drama of the text through music. The contrasting styles of singing noted earlier—declamatory, virtuosic, and lyrical—correspond to the emotional states of the characters singing them. When Violetta is unsure of what to do, she sings in recitative. But at the moment when she decides to devote herself to a life of pleasure, her whole manner shifts quite suddenly. When she sings *"gioir"* ("enjoy"), we can almost feel with her the bodily pleasure she takes in singing the word, lingering over it, repeating it, hitting the highest range of her register. Even if we do not understand the word itself, we know that her emotion is one of ecstasy. She reinforces this sense with the way she goes on to sing the word *"vortici"* ("vortices," in the phrase: "Perish in the vortices of pleasure!"), spiraling downward from a high note to a low one.

Love—emotional love, as opposed to merely physical love—appears in the guise of Alfredo's lyrical melody. Dramatically, the sound of Alfredo's voice derails Violetta's ecstatic singing. She suddenly shifts to her original mood of contemplation and sings in the manner of recitative once again, punctuating the phrases of Alfredo's melody. When she once again rejects the path of emotional commitment and returns to her ecstatic, virtuosic style of singing (2:43), she sings a variation of the aria's opening text and music that is even more spectacular than before. This highly virtuosic moment of intensification is motivated by the drama itself, for Violetta has contemplated her choices (as heard in the sections of accompanied recitative) and opted for pleasure (as heard in her virtuosic singing).

With these points in mind, listen to this scene once again, using the Listening Guide.

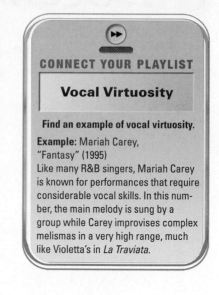

CONNECT YOUR PLAYLIST

Vocal Virtuosity

Find an example of vocal virtuosity.

Example: Mariah Carey, "Fantasy" (1995) Like many R&B singers, Mariah Carey is known for performances that require considerable vocal skills. In this number, the main melody is sung by a group while Carey improvises complex melismas in a very high range, much like Violetta's in *La Traviata*.

SEE MORE on **www.mymusiclab.com** Video: "La Traviata"

EXPAND YOUR PLAYLIST

The Art of the Diva

A comparison of different artists performing the same work—here, the excerpt from Verdi's *La Traviata*—quickly reveals the enormous difference singers can make in bringing a work to life. Listen for dif- ferences in interpretation—tempo, rhythm, articulation, dynamics— and above all, the quality of the voice itself.

- **Renata Tebaldi** (1922–2004) was widely perceived as the greatest rival of Maria Callas. Like Callas and Sutherland, she excelled in Italian opera. Opera d'Oro 1276.
- **Joan Sutherland** (b. 1926) was one of the great sopranos of her generation until her retirement from the stage in 1990. Born in Australia, she established her reputation singing Italian opera of the nineteenth century. The Italians dubbed her "La stupenda" ("The stupendous one"). Decca 430491.

- **Kiri Te Kanawa** (b. 1944) began her career in her native New Zealand singing in clubs. She is of both Maori and European descent and was made Dame Commander of The Order of the British Empire in 1982. Philips 464982.
- **Anna Netrebko** (b. 1971) was born in St. Petersburg, Russia, and became an Austrian citizen in 2006. She has entranced audiences around the world with both her voice and striking physical appearance. DG 000692209.

HEAR SAMPLES on **www.mymusiclab.com**

GO TO www.mymusiclab.com
for the Automated Listening Guide
CD IV • Track 2/Download Track 65

Giuseppe Verdi Composed: 1853 *La Traviata*, Act I, selection (4:49)

Time	Character	Original Italian Text	English Translation
0:00	Violetta	Follie! Delirio vano è questo! Povera donna, sola, abbandonata In questo popoloso deserto Che appellano Parigi, Che spero or più? Che far degg'io?	It's madness! Empty delirium! A poor woman, alone, abandoned In this populated wasteland They call Paris; What can I now hope? What should I do?
0:26		Gioir! Di voluttà ne' vortici perir!	Take delight! Perish in the vortices of pleasure!
0:49		Gioir!	Take delight!
1:07		Sempre libera degg'io Folleggiare di gioia in gioia, Vo' che scorra il viver mio Dei sentieri del piacer.	Always free I must Frolic from pleasure to pleasure, I want to glide through my life Along the paths of pleasure.
1:31		Nasca il giorno, oil giorno muoia, Sempre lieta ne' ritrovi,	As each day dawns, or as each day dies,
1:44		A diletti sempre nuovi Dee volare il mio pensier.	I shall always be joyful in discovering Constantly new pleasures that make my spirit soar.
2:06	Alfredo [underneath the balcony]	Amor è palpito ...	Love is the pulse
2:14	Violetta	Oh!	Oh!
2:15	Alfredo	... dell'universo intero ...	... of the entire universe ...
2:22	Violetta	L'amore!	Love!
2:24	Alfredo	Misterioso, altero, Croce e delizia al cor.	Mysterious, proud, The torment and delight of the heart.
2:43	Violetta	Follie!	It's madness!
2:58		Gioir!	Take delight!
3:14		Sempre libera degg'io Folleggiare di gioia in gioia, Vo' che scorra il viver mio Dei Sentieri del piacer.	Always free I must Frolic from pleasure to pleasure, I want to glide through my life Along the paths of pleasure...
3:26		Nasca il giorno, oil giorno muoia, Sempre lieta ne' ritrovi,	As each day dawns, as each day dies, I shall always be joyful in discovering
3:40		A diletti sempre nuovi Dee volare il mio pensier	Constantly new pleasures That make my spirit soar.
4:02	Alfredo	Amor è palpito ... dell'universo intero...	Love is the pulse ... of the entire universe... [transl. MEB]

Melody	Word-Music Relationships
Accompanied recitative (syllabic, many repeated notes)	Violetta contemplates and sings in declamatory manner.
Virtuosic	Resolved to dedicate herself to pleasure, she begins to sing virtuosically.
Aria	Continues to sing in a virtuosic fashion
Aria (to words and a melody Alfredo had sung to Violetta earlier in the opera).	Lyrical melody: long, sustained notes, no high leaps or rapid runs
Accompanied recitative	Violtetta contemplates her options once again, and she returns to a more declamatory style of singing.
Aria	
Accompanied recitative	
Aria	
Accompanied recitative (resumes)	Once again, Violettta rejects emotional love and returns to a virtuosic style of singing.
Virtuosic	
Aria	
	We briefly hear both voices at the same time, each singing in its own way.
Aria	

Student FAQs

Can high notes like the one in this aria really break glass?

Yes, although crystal is easier to break than glass. If you tap a fine crystal wineglass, you will hear a tone: this is the pitch that corresponds to the structures of the crystals that make up the glass. If a singer hits precisely this pitch and sings loudly enough, the glass can break. The crystals in a normal pane of glass, or in a beer bottle, are irregular enough to resist this kind of breakage.

Deborah Davis/PhotoEdit Inc.

Are operas amplified with microphones and speakers when they are performed?

Sometimes they are, especially if they're being performed outside or in an extremely large arena. But for the most part, opera companies tend to avoid amplified sound. Opera singers are trained to fill large spaces with their voices, and most opera lovers want to hear voices in their purest form. Even the very best amplification systems distort sound in subtle ways.

Laurie Lewis/Lebrecht Music & Arts Photo Library

A CLOSER LOOK   Verdi's World

EXPLORE MORE on www.mymusiclab.com

Except for a few years in Paris and occasional extended visits to London and Vienna, Giuseppe Verdi spent most of his life on the Italian peninsula. His professional career was closely linked to the major opera houses of the region, and most of his stage works received their premieres in Italy.

Many of Verdi's operas premiere in **Milan** at the Teatro alla Scala, one of the world's leading opera houses. These include *Otello* (1887) and *Falstaff* (1893), the last operas Verdi composes. He dies in Milan January 27, 1901.

Verdi is born in Roncole, a small village near **Busseto**, in 1813, the son of an innkeeper and small landowner. In the 1840s Verdi acquires a house (known today as the "Villa Verdi") in nearby Sant' Agata and lives here off and on throughout his life.

Macbeth, based on Shakespeare's drama, premieres in **Florence** in 1847.

In 1850 *Stiffelio* premieres in **Trieste**. The plot, centering on adultery, creates a furor with the censors.

In **Venice**, several of Verdi's operas premiere, including *Rigoletto* (1851) and *La Traviata* (1853) at the Teatro La Fenice. True to its name, the "Phoenix Theater" has twice been rebuilt after serious fires, the most recent of which occurred in 1996.

Several of Verdi's operas, including *Il Trovatore* (1853), one of his most popular, premiere in **Rome** at the Teatro dell' Opera di Roma.

In 1849 *Luisa Miller,* an early work based on a drama by Friedrich Schiller, opens in **Naples** at the Teatro San Carlo.

Milan

Busseto

Venice   Trieste

Florence

ITALY

Corsica

Rome

Naples

Sardinia

N

Sicily

HISTORICAL CONTEXT   The Diva

"Diva" is an Italian word that means "goddess" and in the world of opera, it is used to describe that small handful of singers in each generation whose voices and personalities together capture the imagination of opera lovers. Some of the great divas of the last 50 years include Maria Callas, Joan Sutherland, Marilyn Horne, and Leontyne Price.

The diva is more than just a singer: she is a phenomenon, a force whose life story fascinates as much as her artistic accomplishments. The soprano Maria Callas (1923–1977) attracted an enormous following during her lifetime, and through her recordings, her reputation has grown still greater. She remains one of the top-selling operatic vocalists to this day, more than 30 years after her death.

Callas's voice was spectacular, with an enormous range, a huge variety of colors, and an unmistakable sound that belonged to her and to no other soprano. Her personal life was equally distinctive. She was notoriously temperamental and demanding, and she was romantically linked for many years to Aristotle Onassis, a Greek shipping magnate. But when Onassis abandoned Callas in 1968 to marry Jacqueline Kennedy, widow of the late U.S. president, the diva was once again in the news, even though she had retired from the stage three years before.

There is a male counterpart to the diva—the divo—but the image has not sparked nearly the same response in audiences. The idea of the diva, however, has extended itself beyond the opera house to include any female entertainer whose off-stage persona is as eagerly followed as her on-stage presence and who can be difficult or demanding. One might call these entertainers modern divas: Liza Minnelli, Barbra Streisand, Diana Ross, Whitney Houston, Mariah Carey, and Lady GaGa.

CORBIS—NY
Getty Images
Maria Callas (left) and Lady GaGa (right). Every true diva knows how to strike a meaningful pose.

⏱ **TEST YOURSELF** on **www.mymusiclab.com**   Flashcards and chapter tests

Richard Wagner
The Valkyrie, Act III, selection ("Wotan's Farewell")
Composed: 1856

The excerpt here is the closing scene of *The Valkyrie (Die Walküre)*, the second opera in a cycle of four operas known as *The Ring of the Nibelungs (Der Ring des Nibelungen)*. Wotan, the chief of all gods, is bidding farewell to his daughter, Brünnhilde, who as punishment for disobeying him has been deprived of her supernatural powers and is now being put into a deep sleep, surrounded by a ring of fire.

Listen to this first

((•· HEAR MORE on www.mymusiclab.com

Texture

Listen to the relationship between the voices and the orchestra. In traditional opera, the orchestra supports the voice; in Wagner's operas, the two blend into a single unit.

Word-Music Relationships

Listen for the return of certain musical themes or fragments of themes and their relationship to what is being sung or acted on the stage.

⚙ LEARN MORE on
www.mymusiclab.com
Chapter Objectives

Richard Wagner's Ring of the Nibelungs traces the fate of a magic ring that has supreme powers of both good and evil. The libretto, by Wagner himself, draws heavily on northern European mythology, including many of the same sources used by J. R. R. Tolkien in his *Lord of the Rings* (see "Wagner and Tolkien: A Tale of Two Rings," page 316). There are many strands running through the plot. In *The Valkyrie*, the principal characters are Wotan, the supreme god of Norse mythology, and his daughter Brünnhilde, a warrior-like Valkyrie. Against Wotan's explicit command, Brünnhilde has interceded on behalf of a human couple (Siegmund and Sieglinde). Enraged, Wotan condemns his daughter to death. But she pleads for a lesser sentence, and because she is his favorite offspring, Wotan relents. He strips Brünnhilde of her godlike powers, encloses her in a deep sleep, and surrounds her with a ring of fire that can be crossed only by an individual who has no fear of Wotan's spear, an object that represents his authority over the universe. As it turns out, in the next opera of the *Ring* cycle, Brünnhilde will be awakened by Siegfried, who in the meantime has in fact shattered Wotan's spear. For the moment, though, all this still lies in the future. In the scene here, a Wotan full of mixed emotions bids farewell to his beloved Brünnhilde, puts her into a deep sleep, and then summons Loge, a shifty, firelike figure, to create the circle of magic fire that will protect her from ordinary mortals, who would fear the fire.

Texture: The Relationship of Voice and Orchestra

Wagner and Verdi were contemporaries, but the styles of singing in their operas are very different. In Verdi's *La Traviata*, the voices predominate over the orchestra and dazzle with their virtuosic runs, elaborate melismas, and spectacular high notes. Wagner felt that this kind of singing sacrificed the intelligibility of the text (the libretto) for the sake of musical effect. In fact, he considered conventional opera—by Mozart, Verdi, and others—to be based on a fundamentally false premise: that the words being sung constituted little more than an excuse for virtuosic singing. The "error of opera," Wagner declared, was that "a means of expression"—the music—had become an end in its own right while the goal of that expression—the drama—"had been made a means." Wagner wanted to restore dramatic integrity to opera by creating a style of singing that was at once musically satisfying and readily intelligible. Thus in Wagnerian opera, the vocal writing tends to be more syllabic—one note per syllable of text—and not nearly so virtuosic. There is also very little repetition of text: just as actors in a spoken drama rarely repeat their lines, singers typically sing their words only once. The melodies also tend to be more rhythmically fluid, avoiding any strong sense of periodic phrase structure.

In a particularly memorable turn of phrase Wagner called the drama—the events transpiring on the stage—"deeds of music made visible." What happens on the stage, in other words, is a tangible reflection of what is going on in the orchestra pit. Ideally, then, one should be able to follow the course of a Wagnerian music drama through the music alone, without the aid of words, by tracing the fate of its various musical ideas. These musical ideas would eventually come to be known as *Leitmotifs* (see the following discussion).

1813–1883

Richard Wagner
The Valkyrie, Act III, selection ("Wotan's Farewell")
Composed: 1856

GENRE
Opera

KEY CONCEPTS
Relationship of voices to orchestra, relationship of thematic ideas to the drama (the *Leitmotif*).

CHAPTER HIGHLIGHT
Wagnerian "Music-Drama"
This excerpt illustrates the principles behind the Wagnerian music-drama: voices and instruments are placed on an equal footing, the declamation is largely syllabic, and events on the stage are reflected in the music through a network of *Leitmotifs*.

Word-Music Relationships: The Themes and the Drama

Minimizing virtuosity and projecting the text more clearly were only two of Wagner's strategies for integrating text, voices, and instruments. Another important element of Wagnerian opera is the technique of *Leitmotif*, a brief musical phrase or idea connected dramatically to some person, event, or idea in the drama. These "leading motifs" are meant to lead—direct—our minds in such a way as to help us understand what we see happening onstage. A modern example of this technique is found in the *Star Wars* movies: every time Darth Vader appears on screen we hear the theme associated specifically with him. In the excerpt here, the bright but constantly shifting music heard at 0:09, 0:31, 1:00, etc., is consistently associated with the character of Loge, who in the world of northern European mythology is half-creature, half-flame, a cunning figure who resists taking on solid shape. The musical *Leitmotif* for Loge reflects this unstable

The Valkyrie, Act III: Wotan puts Brünnhilde into a deep sleep within a ring of magic fire; only a hero with no fear of Wotan's spear will brave the flames to awaken her.

Bayreuther Festspiele, Jochen Quast/AP Wide World Photos

nature: the theme, like the character himself, darts around and avoids any clearly defined shape. Thus, whenever we hear Loge's *Leitmotif*—his "signature tune," as it were—we know that Loge or fire (or both) are about to figure in the plot.

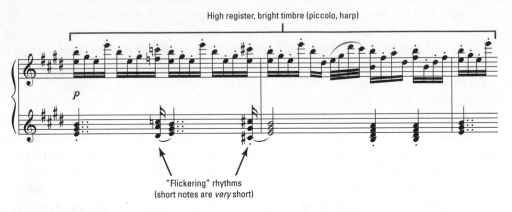

High register, bright timbre (piccolo, harp)

"Flickering" rhythms
(short notes are *very* short)

The other *Leitmotifs* heard in this excerpt are the following:

1. **Wotan's spear** (0:00–0:07, 0:27–0:31). This is a steady, confident, downward-striding figure in the brass. The character of this theme captures the solidity and confidence of Wotan's authority, in contrast to the flitting, ever-changing form of Loge's fire-music. All the laws of the world are carved on Wotan's spear; in the excerpt here, it represents Wotan's duty to punish Brünnhilde, who has broken one of these laws.

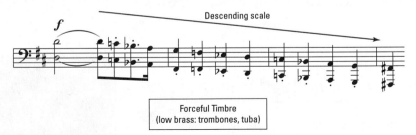

Descending scale

Forceful Timbre
(low brass: trombones, tuba)

2. **Sleep** (1:37–1:51). Also a descending line, but this time it is played softly by winds and high strings (as opposed to the loud brass of Wotan's spear). The sleep *Leitmotif* is also highly **chromatic**. This means that it contains many notes that do not naturally occur in the scale or key area on which it is based. These extra notes undermine the sense of a harmonic center or goal. This motif thus gives the impression of gentle falling, as in falling asleep. Even if you don't play the piano, you can produce a chromatic line by simply playing any series of adjacent notes—both black keys and white keys—in succession. You'll notice that no matter where you stop, there is no sense of closure, no center of melodic or harmonic gravity. This is the essence of chromaticism.

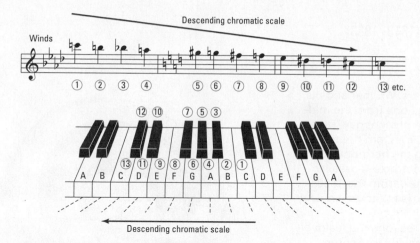

3. The Sword (2:01–2:29, 2:32–2:58). The sword is the magic talisman that Siegfried will eventually use to shatter Wotan's spear. The theme is loud, bright, and confident, rather like a fanfare. Wotan sings it to the words "Whoever fears the point of my spear shall never pass through the fire!" Siegfried, brandishing the magic sword, is the one mortal who has no fear of Wotan's spear; thus when Wotan sings this *Leitmotif*, he is (consciously? unconsciously?) anticipating the future. The words do not tell us this, but the music does.

4. Fate (3:49–3:55, 3:56–4:02). A brief, open-ended, rather questioning phrase associated throughout the *Ring* with the idea of destiny, of what must be.

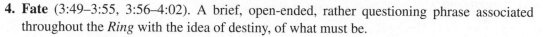

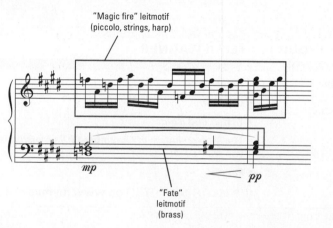

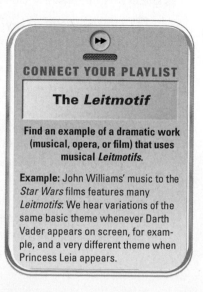

CONNECT YOUR PLAYLIST

The *Leitmotif*

Find an example of a dramatic work (musical, opera, or film) that uses musical *Leitmotifs*.

Example: John Williams' music to the *Star Wars* films features many *Leitmotifs*. We hear variations of the same basic theme whenever Darth Vader appears on screen, for example, and a very different theme when Princess Leia appears.

PROFILE   Richard Wagner (1813–1883)

The Composer as Radical

Worshipped by some, reviled by others, Wagner and his music have provoked extreme reactions from the middle of the nineteenth century to the present day. Those who admired him during his lifetime considered him the most progressive composer of his day, advancing the harmonic idiom of music into new and exciting realms. His detractors assailed his music as ear-splitting noise. One caricature from the 1860s captures this sense of pain quite graphically (see the accompanying image).

Wagner's influence, moreover, went well beyond the realm of music. His operas are full of social and political ideas. George Bernard Shaw, for one, interpreted the massive *Ring of the Nibelungs* as an allegory on capitalism and communism. *Tristan and Isolde* was seen by many as an impassioned plea for free love, an assault on the institution of marriage. And *Die Meistersinger von Nürnberg* has long been viewed as a monument to German political and cultural nationalism. Drawing on Wagner's well-documented anti-Semitism, the Nazis would later use his music to promote their own racial and social agendas.

Born in Leipzig, Wagner immersed himself in the music of Beethoven and secured a series of increasingly prestigious appointments as a conductor. His participation in the uprisings of 1848, however (see chapter 32) forced him to flee to Switzerland to avoid arrest. After a decade of exile, he won the support of King Ludwig II of Bavaria, who spared no expense to support the composer and his art. The final phase of Wagner's life centered around Bayreuth, a small city about halfway between Munich and Berlin, the respective capitals of Bavaria and Prussia, where he built an opera house that is still in operation (see A Closer Look: Wagner's World, page 313).

For many of Wagner's contemporaries, the composer's chromatic harmonies were literally painful. In this French caricature from 1869, Wagner hammers away at the modern ear, using a quarter note as a chisel.

Leonard de Selva/CORBIS—NY

⚙ **LEARN MORE** on **www.mymusiclab.com**
  MyMusicLibrary: Shaw on Wagner

◉→ **EXPLORE MORE** on **www.mymusiclab.com**

⏮   **EXPAND YOUR PLAYLIST: WAGNER**   ⏭

- *The Ring of the Niebelungs* (*Der Ring des Nibelungen*)
- *The Rhine Gold* (*Das Rheingold*)
- *The Valkyrie* (*Die Walküre*)
- *Siegfried*
- *Twilight of the Gods* (*Götterdämmerung*)
- *The Flying Dutchman* (*Der fliegende Holländer*)

- *Tannhäuser*
- *Lohengrin*
- *Tristan und Isolde*
- *The Mastersingers of Nuremberg* (*Die Meistersinger von Nürnberg*)
- *Parsifal*

((•● **HEAR SAMPLES** on **www.mymusiclab.com**

A CLOSER LOOK   Wagner's World

EXPLORE MORE on www.mymusiclab.com

In 1872, when Wagner moved to Bayreuth, a city between Munich and Berlin, Germany had just become a unified nation. It was Wagner's aim to build a *Festspielhaus*—a "festival drama house"—that would unify Germany culturally as well. He oversaw every detail of the building and the performances to be held within it. Thus, when the *Ring* received its premiere there in 1876, Wagner could legitimately claim not only to have written the libretto and the music, but also to have built the opera house. Wagner's descendants still control the *Festspielhaus* in Bayreuth. Here is a look into Wagner's world.

1. Leipzig. Wagner is born here in 1813, the son of a police clerk.

2. Riga, 1837-1839. Wagner works as musical director of the theater in Riga (now the capital of Latvia). He eventually must flee to escape his creditors.

3. Paris, 1839-1842. By making arrangements of works by others and writing music criticism, Wagner ekes out a living. He fails to get any of his own works performed in Paris at this time.

4. Dresden, 1842-1849. Wagner is court conductor at one of Europe's leading theaters. His fame spreads but his career in Dresden is cut short by his revolutionary activities in 1848-1849. He flees to Switzerland after a warrant is issued for his arrest.

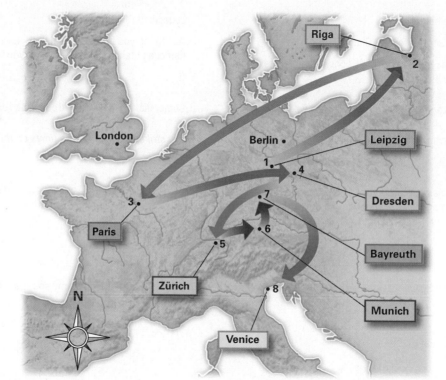

5. Zürich, 1849-1863. Wagner continues to compose and also writes many of his most important treatises on music, society, and the nature of opera.

6. Munich, 1864-1872. Wagner comes under the protection and patronage of Ludwig II of Bavaria, who pays off the composer's debts and finances the production of his stage works.

7. Bayreuth, 1872-1883. Wagner designs and builds a "festival drama house" for the production of his works. The first Bayreuth Festival takes place in 1876. It eventually becomes a yearly event that continues to the present.

8. Venice. Wagner dies on February 13, 1883.

Of particular importance is the way in which these *Leitmotifs* transform themselves and combine with one another. These are not inert themes, but flexible ideas that are developed in much the same way that themes in the development section of a sonata-form movement are developed. *Now listen to this selection again, using the Listening Guide.*

SEE MORE on www.mymusiclab.com Video: Wotan's Farewell

Listening Guide

GO TO **www.mymusiclab.com**
for the Automated Listening Guide
CD IV •Track 3/Download Track 66

Richard Wagner Composed: 1856 *The Valkyrie*, Act III, selection ("Wotan's Farewell") (4:34)

Time	Original German text	English translation
0:00	*Wotan, having put Brünnhilde into a deep sleep, kisses her on her closed eyes and turns away from her slowly. Then he strides with solemn resolution to the middle of the stage and points his spear toward a massive, rocky cliff.*	
0:09	Loge, hör'! Lausche hieher! Wie zuerst ich dich fand, als feurige Glut, wie dann einst du mir schwandest, als schweifende Lohe; wie ich dich band, bann ich dich heut'!	Loge, listen! Listen here! As I found you first, a fiery ember, as you once fled from me, a flitting flame; as I tamed you, so I call on you today!
0:33	Herauf, wabernde Loge, umlodre mir feurig den Fels!	Come, flickering glow, Surround the rock for me with flames!
0:48	*(He strikes his spear three times on the rock.)* Loge! Loge! Hieher!	*(He strikes his spear three times on the rock.)* Loge! Loge! Come!
1:00	*A flash of flame comes out of the rock and gradually swells into a glowing fire. Bright flickering erupts. Wotan directs the flame to form a circle around the sleeping figure of Brünnhilde. He then recedes into the background, even as the flames continue to glow.*	
2:01	Wer meines Speeres Spitze fürchtet, durchschreite das Feuer nie!	Whoever fears the tip of my spear shall never pass through the fire!
2:01	*He stretches out his spear as if to cast a spell, then looks with pain back upon the figure of Brünnhilde (2:57) and turns slowly to depart (3:25). He looks back once again (3:46), before disappearing through the fire (4:00). The curtain drops.*	

Word-Music Relationships
Musical Leitmotifs

- Spear (= Wotan's authority) at 0:00

- Loge (= fire) at 0:07

- Loge (= fire) at 0:09

- Spear (= Wotan's authority) at 0:27 on Wotan's command that Loge appear.

- Loge (= fire) at 0:31

- Loge (= fire) at 0:49

- Magic fire music at 1:00, a variant of Loge's Leitmotif, but much brighter and in a higher register, representing the flames that rise up to surround Brünnhilde.

- Sleep at 1:37, representing Brünnhilde's sleep within the circle of fire.

- The sword at 2:01, again at 2:32. The music tells us that a sword will in fact eventually destroy Wotan's spear, and that Siegfried will awaken Brünnhilde from her sleep.

- Magic fire music throughout. This Leitmotif, in the high register, plays simultaneously with the one above and throughout this entire section.

- Magic fire music throughout.

- Fate at 3:49, 3:56. Wotan knows what must happen (fate), but it pains him nevertheless.

Student FAQs

How did Wagner's original audience know the meaning of the Leitmotifs when this work was first performed?

Wagner believed that anyone following the plot would associate the music they heard with the action on the stage. Whether they made these associations consciously or unconsciously did not matter to him. He was in fact quite reluctant to attach names to specific musical motifs, and only later did critics begin to compile guides to the *Leitmotifs* in *The Ring*.

Lebrecht Music & Arts/Lebrecht Music & Arts Photo Library

Is it true that Brünnhilde is the Fat Lady in the saying "It ain't over 'til the Fat Lady sings"?

Yes. After Siegfried slays the dragon guarding the ring, he awakens Brünnhilde and gives her the ring as a token of his love, not understanding its full power. When Siegfried is killed in the last opera of *The Ring of the Nibelungs*, Brünnhilde sings an enormously long passage, at the end of which she throws the ring back into the Rhine, where it came from in the first place. When she finishes singing, *The Ring*—all four nights of it—is over.

Lebrecht Music & Arts/ Lebrecht Music & Arts Photo Library

HISTORICAL CONTEXT   Wagner and Tolkien: A Tale of Two Rings

J. R. R. Tolkien vehemently denied any connection between his *Lord of the Rings* and Wagner's *Ring of the Nibelungs*. "Both rings were round, and there the resemblance ceases," he once declared. But the parallels are too strong for us to accept this assertion at face value. We know, in fact, that Tolkien collaborated on a translation of *The Valkyrie* with his friend C. S. Lewis (author of *The Chronicles of Narnia*); unfortunately, the translation was never finished.

Tolkien may or may not have borrowed directly from Wagner, but both artists drew on the same Nordic myths for their subject matter. Thus the characters, events, and themes of the two works exhibit striking similarities. See the following examples:

1. Each cycle consists of four works, the first of which (Wagner's *Das Rheingold*, Tolkien's *The Hobbit*) serves as a prelude to the central sequence of three.
2. In both cycles, the ring holds great power but also brings grief to any owner who covets that power.
3. The plots center on efforts to own and control the ring.
4. Both cycles begin in a state of innocence (the Rhine; the Shire) that is corrupted and then ultimately restored.
5. Both cycles feature giants, dragons, dwarves who are great metalworkers, a riddling match, and a shattered sword recast into one even more powerful.

Nikolai Putilin performs as Alberich with the Kirov Opera. Alberich, the dwarf in Wagner's *Ring of the Nibelungs*, owns the magic ring for a brief time; he wins it by renouncing love, but it is later stolen from him.
Photo by Brian Ach/ WireImage/Getty Images, Inc.

Gollum (Andy Serkis) holds the Ring in Peter Jackson's film adaptation of Tolkien's *Lord of the Rings*.
© New Line/Everett Collection

EXPAND YOUR PLAYLIST

Opera in the Nineteenth Century

Operas written in the nineteenth century form the core repertory of most opera houses. Italian opera (by Rossini, Bellini, Verdi, and Puccini, among others) dominated the stage across all of Europe, but operas in French (by Bizet) and German (by Weber, Wagner, and others) had strong followings as well.

Italian Opera
- Gioacchino Rossini: *The Barber of Seville* (*Il Barbiere di Siviglia*). Like Mozart's *Marriage of Figaro*, this opera is based on a play by Beaumarchais and even includes many of the same characters (Figaro, the Count, the Countess).
- Vincenzo Bellini: *Norma*. A Romeo-and-Juliet-style story set in ancient Gaul. Norma is a Druid, her lover a Roman.
- Giuseppe Verdi: *La Traviata*. See chapter 36.
- Giacomo Puccini: *La Bohème*. The story of struggling young artists, set in late nineteenth-century Paris. The Broadway musical *Rent* draws on the plotline of this opera.
- Giaccomo Puccini: *Madama Butterfly*. The story of the relationship between a young American naval officer and the Japanese woman he marries and then abandons.

French Opera
- Georges Bizet: *Carmen*. The story of an enchantress (Carmen) and her ill-fated lover (Don José), who is torn between love and duty.

German Opera
- Carl Maria von Weber: *The Free Shooter* (*Der Freischütz*). A hunter makes a pact with the devil to win a shooting competition, and with it, the hand of the woman he loves.

English Opera
- Arthur Sullivan: *The Pirates of Penzance*. The most successful operas in English in the nineteenth century were the operettas (literally, "little operas") by Arthur Sullivan and his librettist, W. S. Gilbert. Together, Gilbert and Sullivan created a long series of what we today call musicals: spoken dialogue interspersed with musical numbers (arias, duets, choruses, etc.).

((•● HEAR SAMPLES on **www.mymusiclab.com**

☑ **TEST YOURSELF** on **www.mymusiclab.com**   Flashcards and chapter tests

Johannes Brahms
Symphony no. 4 in E Minor, op. 98, finale
Composed: 1885

The finale of Brahms's Fourth Symphony is a kaleidoscope of emotions: the 30 short variations on a very short theme present a series of constantly shifting moods. Each group of instruments—strings, winds, brass, and percussion—comes to the fore at various points.

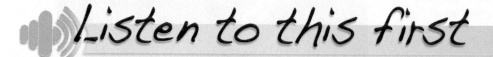 Listen to this first

((• HEAR MORE on www.mymusiclab.com

Form

Listen for the succession of varied restatements of the central melodic idea. This movement is in the form of **theme and variations**. Also listen for the change in tempo (to slow) and mode (to major) in the middle of the movement.

Timbre

Each variation has its own distinctive sound, depending on which instrument or group of instruments predominates. The textures created by these groupings are sometimes quite thick, and sometimes quite transparent.

The changes in Brahm's Fourth Symphony from one variation to the next are at times subtle, at times sudden. The theme makes its first appearance in a majestic, grandiose fashion in the brass. The first variation is subdued and reticent, played by the timpani and low brass. The winds create a new, more wistful mood when they join in for the second variation. The third variation is more rhythmically lively, and the violins take over with a lyrical counter-melody in the fourth variation. The shifting moods continue as each variation establishes its own sound world.

Brahms wrote only four symphonies, but all four are mainstays of today's concert repertory. His Fourth Symphony calls for a large orchestra to match the growing size of concert halls in the last decades of the nineteenth century. It also synthesizes the old and new in ingenious ways. Brahms takes both the form and theme of this movement from the Baroque Era. Theme and variations form had been popular in Bach's time, and the theme itself is in fact derived from a work by Bach (see the following discussion). But Brahms creates harmonies, textures, and timbres that were novel in their day. The harmonies are often highly chromatic, and the textures tend to be richly layered and dense. The timbres range from the bright to the dark, but in this movement, more often than not, they veer toward a somber, serious kind of sound that many listeners find lush and—to use a metaphor drawn from the world of food—ripe. Brahms demands our attention when we listen, and his music repays the effort.

⚙ LEARN MORE on
www.mymusiclab.com
Chapter Objectives

PERFORMANCE   The Conductor

Exactly what does a conductor do? It's a good question, and the answer is not so obvious, particularly because most concertgoers tend to see only the conductor's back during performances.

Even from the back, however, conductors' styles can vary enormously. Some are like gymnasts on the podium: they jump, twist, crouch. Others are more reserved and seem to move scarcely at all. Some use a baton, others use only their hands.

For all these outward differences, all conductors have a basic responsibility of keeping performers playing together, in time. They do this by beating the basic meter of the music during performance: every player can see the conductor, so all the performers can follow the same beat together. The more rhythmically complicated the work at hand, the greater the need for a conductor. In the finale of Brahms's Fourth Symphony, for example, Brahms calls on the orchestra to change to a slow tempo at Variation 12. But how slow? That is up to the conductor to decide, and the players follow the conductor's lead.

At a deeper level, conductors also shape the interpretation of the work at hand through such elements as dynamics, rhythm, texture, and timbre. Are the trumpets playing too loud? Are the flutes too soft? Are the violins entering sharply enough? These are just a few of the many questions conductors have to answer when rehearsing with an orchestra. Even in performance, there is room for spur-of-the-moment changes: holding a long note just a fraction of a second longer, slowing down just a little more, or making a loud passage even louder.

No two performers play the same music exactly the same way: each has an individual style. This is true for conductors as

Like all conductors, Marin Alsop uses her hands, her eyes, and her entire body to communicate with the musicians in her orchestra. Like most but not all conductors, she also uses a baton; many orchestral musicians say that this small stick helps them see the conductor's beat out of the corner of their eyes, which are largely focused on the notated music on their stands.
Toby WALES/Lebrecht Music & Arts Photo Library

well, whose instrument is in effect the orchestra. Listen to multiple recordings of the finale of Brahms's Fourth Symphony—or of any other work in this book, for that matter—and you will immediately realize the enormous freedom performers have in bringing a work of music to life.

Form: Theme and Variations Plus

The theme consists of only eight notes. This type of form—many variations on a very short theme—was tremendously popular during the Baroque Era. Purcell had used it in the ostinato bass of Dido's aria in Act I of *Dido and Aeneas* in the late seventeenth century (see chapter 11), and Johann Sebastian Bach had used this kind of structure in a number of works.

Brahms borrowed the theme from Bach's Cantata no. 150, and it is extremely simple. Notes 1–6 move up, step by step, then drop down (note 7), only to end up (note 8) exactly where the theme had begun. This simplicity works to the listener's advantage because Brahms subjects the theme to an increasingly complex series of variations. But because the theme itself is so simple, listeners can hear it more easily. This movement represents what might be called compositional virtuosity, for Brahms demonstrates his ability to construct a great deal out of very little.

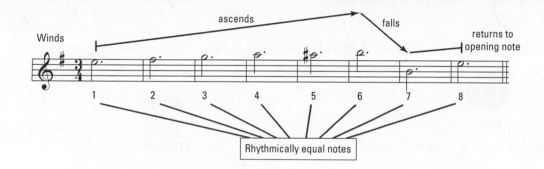

1833–1897
Johannes Brahms
Symphony no. 4 in E Minor,
op. 98, finale
Composed: 1885

GENRE
Symphony

KEY CONCEPTS
Theme and variations and ABA
form, orchestral timbre.

CHAPTER HIGHLIGHT
Blending Old and New
This finale of this symphony incorporates an old form—theme and variations—into a movement scored for a large orchestra, using advanced chromatic harmonies. Brahms's theme is a simple eight-note melody, but the 30 variations exploit the full resources of the late nineteenth-century orchestra.

There is no end of melodic richness in this movement. Each variation uses the eight notes of the theme as a framework for its own counter-themes. The texture throughout is strongly polyphonic, for in many variations we hear the original theme played against a new and different counter-melody. At other times, Brahms adds many additional notes around the theme, so that it is in effect embedded within a new and different theme (as in Variation 12). In still other variations, Brahms distributes the notes of the theme across different instruments.

On a larger scale, Brahms creates a **ternary form (ABA)** by making the middle variations (10–15) markedly different from the others. They are all slower, and the first three of them (13–15) are in E major rather than E minor. This creates a strong sense of contrast in the middle of the movement (the **B** section of the **ABA** form). The sense of a ternary form superimposed on a set of theme and variations is reinforced by the clear return of the opening theme of the movement in variation no. 16 (the second **A** in the **ABA** form).

Timbre: The Drama of Orchestration

Brahms also used orchestration to create a sense of forward movement and contrast among the 30 different variations. The winds and brass announce the theme together at the very beginning with great force. The focus then moves to the timpani and the plucked low strings (Variation 1), after which the winds join in (Variation 2), followed by the full orchestra (Variation 3). At times, a pair of variations share the same basic orchestration (Variations 5 and 6, Variations 8 and 9), but more often than not each new variation differentiates itself from the one before through its timbre. The theme itself appears in all the different instruments (except timpani) at one point or another.

This movement is remarkable in its emotional sweep. It embraces an ever-changing series of moods that might be described as extending from angry at first, to brooding, energetic, melancholic, docile, pleading, devotional, anxious, and in the end triumphant: each listener will find slightly different adjectives. The last movement of Brahms's last symphony sums up an entire century of symphonic composition: its orchestration is rich, its textures varied, its harmonies advanced.

Now listen to this symphony finale again, using the Listening Guide.

CONNECT YOUR PLAYLIST

Same Theme, Different Timbres

Find a work that presents the same theme in two different timbres.

Example: Louis Armstrong, "Ain't Misbehavin'" (1929)
In this classic recording of a jazz standard, Armstrong first plays the melody on the trumpet and then immediately afterward sings it.

Listening Guide

➤ GO TO www.mymusiclab.com
for the Automated Listening Guide
CD IV • Track 4/Download Track 67

Johannes Brahms Composed: 1885 Symphony no. 4 in E Minor, op. 98, finale (10:36)

Time	Theme and Variations	Ternary Form	Timbre
0:00	Theme	**A** (E minor)	Winds and brass
0:15	Variation 1		Pizzicato (plucked) strings, with percussion and low brass
0:30	Variation 2		Winds join in
0:46	Variation 3		Full orchestra
1:01	Variation 4		Strings
1:18	Variation 5		Strings and winds
1:32	Variation 6		
1:48	Variation 7		High strings and winds
2:04	Variation 8		Strings and winds
2:20	Variation 9		
2:36	Variation 10		Strings and winds
2:53	Variation 11		Strings, winds, horns
3:14	Variation 12		Flutes, horn, and strings
3:57	Variation 13	**B** (E major)	Winds and strings in dialogue
4:37	Variation 14		Brass enter with hymn-like sound, all parts moving together in a slow, stately rhythm
5:17	Variation 15		Winds join in
6:03	Variation 16	**A'** (E minor)	Return to opening theme: winds and brass, then strings join in
6:16	Variation 17		Strings (tremolo) and high winds in dialogue

Melody

Theme in high winds; long note values

Theme in pizzicato (plucked) strings

Theme stays in pizzicato (plucked) strings

Theme in violins

Theme in low strings; counter-melody in violins

Theme in low strings; counter-melody in high strings and winds

↓

Theme in low strings; counter-melody of dotted rhythms (short-LONG-short-LONG, etc.) in high strings and winds

Theme in low strings; rapid figure in violins

Theme in strings; longer note values give the impression of slowing down

Theme in low strings; syncopated figure in high strings (off the beat)

Theme embedded within flute's counter-melody

Theme distributed among various instruments

Theme distributed among trombones

↓

Theme in high winds; new counter-melody in violins

Theme in syncopated high winds

Form

Timbre

Time	Theme and Variations	Ternary Form	Timbre
6:28	Variation 18		Full orchestra
6:40	Variation 19		
6:53	Variation 20		
7:05	Variation 21		
7:19	Variation 22		High winds and low strings
7:31	Variation 23		Full orchestra
7:44	Variation 24		
7:57	Variation 25		Full orchestra, strings tremolo
8:11	Variation 26		Full orchestra
8:26	Variation 27		Winds and strings in dialogue
8:40	Variation 28		
8:54	Variation 29		
9:08	Variation 30		Full orchestra
9:29	**Coda**	Coda (E minor)	Full orchestra

Melody

Theme distributed among high winds

Theme distributed among various instruments; strings with fast triplet figure (*1-2-3-1-2-3-1-2-3*)

Theme distributed among various instruments

Theme distributed among various instruments

Theme clearly presented in horns

Theme in high strings

Theme distributed among various instruments

Theme distributed among horns and winds; somewhat calmer

Theme embedded in counter-melody in strings

Theme embedded in counter-melody in winds

Theme embedded in pizzicato strings in syncopation

Theme distributed among various instruments; counter-melodies in both strings and winds

Theme clearly stated in brass and winds at the beginning of this section, but the music continues beyond this in a free fashion for the first and only time in the movement.

Student FAQs

I can't always hear the theme. Is that a problem?

No. Brahms's self-imposed challenge was to say the same thing in a different way 30 times in a row. For this reason, he wanted to mask the theme often enough so that it would not become tiresome. Some of the variations in the **B** section (Variations 13–15) hide the theme so well it becomes very difficult to hear. As you become more familiar with the movement, you will probably hear the theme more clearly in most variations with each new listening.

Is there any consistent meter in this movement?

The theme and every variation are always in triple meter, though Brahms creates a good deal of variety by skillfully varying the underlying rhythms and (in the middle of the movement) the tempo.

Vicky Alhadeff/Lebrecht Music & Arts Photo Library

PROFILE   Johannes Brahms (1833–1897)

The Composer as Hedgehog

In an age of flamboyant composer-celebrities who wrote and talked endlessly about themselves and their own music, Johannes Brahms was by comparison a recluse. He preferred to let his works speak for themselves and remained an intensely private individual to the end of his life. One particularly revealing caricature of him done during his lifetime shows him walking next to a hedgehog: the prickly composer and prickly animal bear a striking resemblance.

Perhaps Brahms became a bit prickly because of the criticism he received during his lifetime. Part of this can be traced to the unrealistic expectations projected on him by no less a figure than Robert Schumann, editor of one of the leading music journals of the day (the nineteenth-century equivalent of *Rolling Stone* or *Spin*). Brahms was a virtually unknown 20-year-old when Schumann introduced him as the savior of music, a messiah who had arrived on the scene "fully developed," ready to assume the mantel of the deceased Beethoven. This publicity cut both ways for Brahms: he was an instant celebrity, but the public expected more than he was prepared to offer, at least at that point in his career. As in the musical world of today, the best artists can withstand criticism, and Brahms eventually proved that Schumann was right in the end. By the time he died in 1897, Brahms had become the last of the "three Bs" of German music—Bach, Beethoven, Brahms—and he would be buried next to Beethoven in Vienna's Central Cemetery.

Brahms's links to Bach and Beethoven rest on more than mere alliteration. He was deeply interested in the music of the past, and in the music of the two other "Bs" in particular. He helped edit works by Bach and zealously collected sketches by Beethoven. The finale of the Fourth Symphony, in a sense, represents Brahms's synthesis of the two: he presents Bach's technique of varying a brief theme within Beethoven's most challenging genre, the symphony. Brahms uses this traditional form and genre to create what is nevertheless a thoroughly modern work.

Brahms (right) and Johann Strauss Jr. (1894). Brahms deeply admired Strauss. The difference in appearance of the two composers is striking, especially when we realize the grandfatherly Brahms was almost eight years younger than the dapper Strauss. Brahms was 61 and Strauss was 69.
CORBIS—NY

⚙ **LEARN MORE** on **www.mymusiclab.com**
    MyMusicLibrary: Schumann Proclaims the Young Brahms a Musical Messiah

◉➜ **EXPLORE MORE** on **www.mymusiclab.com**

⏮ EXPAND YOUR PLAYLIST: BRAHMS ⏭

- **Symphony no. 1 in C Minor, op. 68**

- **Symphony no. 2 in D Major, op. 73**

- **Symphony no. 3 in F Major, op. 90.** A dramatic and emotionally wide-ranging work.

- **Piano Concerto no. 2 in B-flat Major, op. 83**

- **Violin Concerto in D Major, op. 77**

- ***A German Requiem,* op. 45** (for chorus, orchestra, and soloists). A setting of German-language biblical texts relating to death and resurrection, written after the death of the composer's mother.

((•● **HEAR SAMPLES** on **www.mymusiclab.com**

Brahms and the hedgehog.
A contemporary caricature
by Otto Bohler.
Lebrecht Music & Arts/Lebrecht
Music & Arts Photo Library

EXPAND YOUR PLAYLIST

The Art of the Conductor

You can learn more about what goes into leading an orchestra by listening to recordings of the same work by different conductors. Here are some alternative performances of the finale of Brahms's Fourth Symphony. Listen carefully for different approaches to tempo, dynamics, phrasing, and balance among the instruments.

- **Felix Weingartner** (1863–1942) was one of the leading conductors of his day. His style, in a recording made with the London Symphony Orchestra in 1938, reflects a more flexible approach to rhythm and phrasing than would be fashionable later in the century. Centaur 2128.

- **Arturo Toscanini** (1867–1957) was born in Italy but immigrated to the United States in the late 1930s to escape the Fascist government. In New York, NBC created an orchestra expressly for Toscanini, and he made many recordings and radio broadcasts with it. His style of conducting attracted an almost cult-like following. RCA Red Seal 55838.

- **Leonard Bernstein** (1918–1990) was the first American-born conductor to lead the New York Philharmonic, one of the premier orchestras in the nation. A composer as well as a conductor, he was known for promoting modern music and the music of other American composers. Sony 61846.

- **Marin Alsop** (b. 1956) is one of a growing number of female conductors who have enjoyed both artistic and commercial success. She is currently director of the Baltimore Symphony Orchestra. Her performance, recorded with the London Philharmonic Orchestra in 2007, combines both flexibility and drive. Naxos 8570233.

((•● **HEAR SAMPLES** on **www.mymusiclab.com**

Ⓥ **TEST YOURSELF** on **www.mymusiclab.com**   Flashcards and chapter tests

39

Antonín Dvořák
String Quartet in F Major, op. 96 ("American"), third movement
Composed: 1893

Antonín Dvořák tried to create a distinctively national sound in several of the works he wrote during his three-year stay in the United States in the mid-1890s. He called one of the quartets from this period his "American" String Quartet.

Listen to this first

((• HEAR MORE on **www.mymusiclab.com**

Timbre

Listen to the call-and-response of various combinations of the four instruments—two violins (high register), a viola (medium), and cello (low)—at the very beginning of the movement and at later points as well. Listen, too, for extended passages in which only the two highest or the two lowest of the four instruments are playing.

Melody

Listen for the folk-like sound of the various melodies of this movement. What makes this music sound like folk music?

Form

Consider all three principles of form—repetition, variation, and contrast—as you listen for the musical elements listed earlier. Can you identify the sections of the piece?

Originally from Prague, Dvořák crossed the Atlantic to spend two years in the United States.

Antonín Dvořák wrote his String Quartet in F Major, op. 96, in Iowa, more than 5,000 miles from his native Prague. In the United States on a two-year contract as director of the National Conservatory of Music in New York City, Dvořák welcomed the opportunity for a change of scenery. He spent the summer of 1893 in Spillville, a small town recommended by his personal assistant who had grown up there. Most of Spillville's approximately 350 inhabitants were immigrants or the children of immigrants from Dvořák's native Bohemia.

Shortly after arriving in Iowa, Dvořák set out, by his own account, "to write something really melodious and simple." Of course, writing good melodies is not easy, and what seems simple is often difficult to craft. But he must have been inspired by his new surroundings, for in just a little over two weeks, he completed a four-movement string quartet he called the "American." The selection here is the third movement of this quartet.

Timbre: Call-and-Response Between Strings

Dvořák had been a professional violist earlier in his career, and he knew the instruments of the string quartet from the inside out. In the very opening of this movement, he creates a kind of call-and-response pattern that begins with two instruments (second violin and cello, 0:00) answered by the full ensemble (0:04). The music continues with the upper three instruments (0:07) punctuated by the lowest, the cello (0:08). This kind of back-and-forth between individual instruments or groups of instruments continues throughout the movement and creates timbral variety. Call-and-response is a basic element of many kinds of folk music, particularly in African music (see chapter 12) and music cultivated by the descendants of Africans in the Americas, such as the blues (see chapter 46). In emphasizing this kind of pattern, Dvořák was at the same time emphasizing the folk-like nature of his quartet.

Folk-Like Melodies

The movement features two principal melodies, each of which is based on a limited number of notes. The opening phrases of both melodies use only four different notes, and the consequent phrases introduce only two new ones. Although not based on a strictly **pentatonic scale** (see Web Bonus chapter 3), these melodies convey a feeling of simplicity because they use fewer than the standard seven notes in the diatonic scale that is so common in Western music. In this way, Dvořák creates a folk-like sound. The clarity of the antecedent-consequent phrase structure (see chapter 20) also contributes to the apparent simplicity of the melodies.

1841–1904
Antonín Dvořák
String Quartet in F Major,
op. 96 ("American"),
third movement
Composed: 1893

GENRE
String quartet

KEY CONCEPTS
Call-and-response texture, pentatonic melody, folk-like rhythms, nationalism.

CHAPTER HIGHLIGHT
Nationalism
In the nineteenth century composers began to write works for the concert hall that incorporated musical devices associated with folk music. When he lived in the United States, the Czech composer Antonín Dvořák wrote a string quartet he called "American." The third-movement scherzo of this quartet uses a number of folk-like elements.

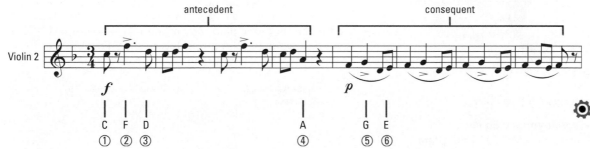

LEARN MORE on
www.mymusiclab.com
Chapter Objectives

The first part of the second principal theme consists of only *four* notes:

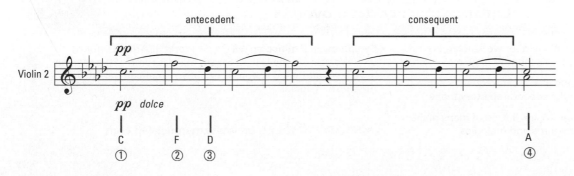

PROFILE   Antonín Dvořák (1841–1904)

In Search of National Sounds

Even before he arrived in the United States in 1892, Antonín Dvořák was known as a composer who drew widely on the folk music of his native Bohemia (a region corresponding roughly to today's Czech Republic). As director of the (now defunct) National Conservatory of Music in New York City, he felt a responsibility to show American composers how to incorporate the characteristic sounds and

Dvořák (right) and his family shortly after their arrival in the United States in 1892.

Lebrecht Music & Arts/Lebrecht Music & Arts Photo Library

⚙ **LEARN MORE** on **www.mymusiclab.com**
    MyMusicLibrary: Dvořák on Music and the State

◉➜ **EXPLORE MORE** on **www.mymusiclab.com**

inflections of the folk music of their own country. He studied with interest the melodies of African Americans—freed slaves and their first-generation descendants—and of Native Americans and discovered that pentatonicism figured prominently in both repertoires. He wrote pentatonic melodies into his next symphony, which quickly became known as the "New World" Symphony. Composers, critics, and audiences took note, for all were eager to find a way by which the United States could establish its own musical sound, distinct from the traditions of European music.

Dvořák was less interested in borrowing from specific African American or Native American songs than he was in seeking an idiom based in the spirit of all those who made music outside the concert hall, outside the traditions of "learned" music. He seems to have been seeking a kind of nationalism that would speak to the varied ethnic backgrounds of the American people, no matter what the color of their skin (see "The Composer Speaks," page 331). In the end, though, in spite of being so closely associated with American music, Dvořák remained true to his roots. His personal assistant, Josef Kovařík, the man of Czech descent who took him to Iowa, reports Dvořák saying,

> So I am an American composer, am I? I was, I am, and I remain a Czech composer. I have only showed them the path they might take—how they should work. But I'm through with that! From this day forward I will write the way I wrote before.

Source: Beckerman, Michael. 2003. *New worlds of Dvořák*, 16. New York: Norton.

EXPAND YOUR PLAYLIST: DVOŘÁK

- **Piano Quintet in A Major, op. 81.** A chamber work of large dimension, particularly notable for its lengthy, slow movement.

- **Cello Concerto in B Minor, op. 104.** The most frequently performed of all cello concertos in the concert repertory today.

- **Slavonic Dance for Orchestra, op. 46, no. 8.** One of many orchestral dances inspired by ethnic rhythms and melodies.

- **Symphony in E Minor, op. 96** ("New World"). Written during Dvořák's years in the United States, at least some of the themes have been attributed variously to Native American or African American melodies.

((•• **HEAR SAMPLES** on **www.mymusiclab.com**

But what is the "folk" in question here? Like other composers of his time, Dvořák felt that composers should draw on the folk or indigenous music of their countries, and he wrote the "New World" Symphony and "American" String Quartet to provide examples for composers of the United States (see "The Composer Speaks," page 331), using pentatonic melodies in both. Dvořák himself once observed that pentatonic melodies were common to music of African Americans, Native Americans, and (remarkably enough) "the music of Scotland." Pentatonic or quasi-pentatonic melodies also figure in the folk music of Dvořák's native Bohemia, so it is hard to say clearly which tradition this quartet represents. In any case, its unmistakably folk-like feel contrasts with the more formal sound of Haydn's string quartet from more than 100 years before.

Scherzo Form: Repetition, Variation, Contrast

This third movement is a **scherzo**. "Scherzo" is the Italian word for "joke," and a musical scherzo is a light-hearted movement in a fast tempo and in triple meter. Over the course of the nineteenth century, the scherzo gradually replaced the minuet (see chapter 22) as one of the internal movements of a four-movement cycle in a symphony, sonata, string quartet, or other similar instrumental work. The scherzo retained the basic **ABA** form of the minuet, but often with the addition of an extra trio section (**ABABA**), as in this particular movement. The overall form can be represented graphically in this way:

A	B	A′	B′	A
Scherzo	Trio I	Scherzo	Trio II (varied)	Scherzo
Proper		Proper (varied)		Proper (literal repetition of A)

Dvořák uses all three principles of form in this movement:

- **Repetition.** The scherzo proper is repeated literally ("da capo") at the end of the movement. The movement thus ends with exactly the same section of music with which it began.

- **Variation.** Both the scherzo proper and the trio are subject to variation: **A** becomes **A′**, and **B** becomes **B′**.

- **Contrast.** **A** and **B** differ markedly in their melodies, harmonies (modes), and timbres. The differences in the melodies of **A** and **B** have already been noted earlier. The two sections are also in contrasting modes: **A** is consistently in F major, while **B** is consistently in F minor. The timbres of the two sections also contrast markedly: the **A** section is quite expansive, covering a wide register, while **B** tends to move in a more narrow range, with the instruments closer together.

Now listen to this movement once again, using the Listening Guide.

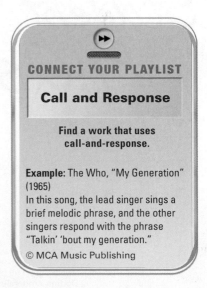

CONNECT YOUR PLAYLIST

Call and Response

Find a work that uses call-and-response.

Example: The Who, "My Generation" (1965)
In this song, the lead singer sings a brief melodic phrase, and the other singers respond with the phrase "Talkin' 'bout my generation."
© MCA Music Publishing

Listening Guide

GO TO www.mymusiclab.com
for the Automated Listening Guide
CD IV • Track 5/Download Track 68

Antonín Dvořák Composed: 1893 String Quartet in F Major, op. 96 ("American"), third movement (3:46)

Time	Melody	Form: Section	Timbre
0:00	Theme 1 = disjunct, clear antecedent/consequent phrase structure	**A** = Scherzo proper (F major)	Call-and-response interplay between individual instruments and groups of instruments
0:46	Theme 2 = narrow range, begins with only four notes; clear antecedent/consequent phrase structure	**B** = Trio I (F minor)	Passages for two instruments (0:46–0:52; 1:06–1:12) contrast with passages for all four instruments
1:26	Theme 1, but this time it begins quietly, with the themes in different instruments from the first time around	**A'** = Variation of Scherzo proper: (F major)	
2:15	Theme 2, but this time it begins quietly and in a much higher register than before	**B'** = Trio II (in fact a variation of Trio I) (F minor)	Higher register than before. All four instruments together throughout
2:57	Theme 1	**A** = Literal repeat of Scherzo proper (F major)	

Student FAQs

Did Dvořák ever actually hear any music performed by Native Americans?

He did when he was in Iowa, although it's not entirely clear just what kind of Native Americans were performing, and we should remember that musical styles vary widely from tribe to tribe. We also know that Dvořák read at least one account of Native American music.

Why does the movement end so softly? It doesn't sound like a real ending.

Quiet endings are not all that uncommon, actually. Keep in mind that this is the third movement of a four-movement string quartet, and that a very lively finale begins shortly after this movement ends. By not ending this movement with a bang Dvořák is able to start the next movement with one.

© Dorling Kindersley, Courtesy of the Junior Department, Royal College of Music, London

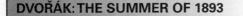

DVOŘÁK: THE SUMMER OF 1893

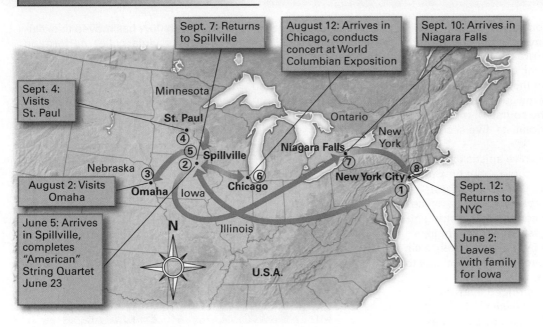

Sept. 7: Returns to Spillville

August 12: Arrives in Chicago, conducts concert at World Columbian Exposition

Sept. 10: Arrives in Niagara Falls

Sept. 4: Visits St. Paul

Minnesota

St. Paul

Ontario

New York

Nebraska

Niagara Falls

New York City

August 2: Visits Omaha

Omaha   Iowa   Chicago

Sept. 12: Returns to NYC

June 5: Arrives in Spillville, completes "American" String Quartet June 23

Illinois

U.S.A.

June 2: Leaves with family for Iowa

Dvořák's travels in America, Summer 1893.

THE COMPOSER SPEAKS   The Sources of an American Musical Style

On his arrival in America, Dvořák was impressed by the "native" music that he heard, particularly the music of Native Americans and African Americans. Two years after writing his "American" Quartet, Dvořák wrote an essay entitled "Music in America," published in *Harper's New Monthly Magazine*.

A while ago I suggested that inspiration for truly national music might be derived from the Negro melodies or Indian chants. I was led to take this view partly by the fact that the so-called plantation songs are indeed the most striking and appealing melodies that have yet been found on this side of the water, but largely by the observation that this seems to be recognized, though often unconsciously, by most Americans. All races have their distinctively national songs, which they at once recognize as their own, even if they have never heard them before. When a Tcech [Czech], a Pole, or a Magyar [Hungarian] in this country suddenly hears one of his folk-songs or dances, no matter if it is for the first time in his life, his eyes light up at once, and his heart within him responds, and claims that music as his own. So it is with those of Teutonic or Celtic blood, or any other men, indeed, whose first lullaby mayhap [perhaps] was a song wrung from the heart of the people. . . .

It matters little whether the inspiration for the coming folk songs of America is derived from the Negro melodies, the songs of the creoles, the red man's chant, or the plaintive ditties of the homesick German or Norwegian. Undoubtedly the germs for the best in music lie hidden among all the races that are commingled in this great country. The music of the people is like a rare and lovely flower growing amidst encroaching weeds. Thousands pass it, while others trample it under foot, and thus the chances are that it will perish before it is seen by the one discriminating spirit who will prize it above all else. The fact that no one has as yet arisen to make the most of it does not prove that nothing is there.

Source: Antonin Dvořák. "Music in America," *Harper's New Monthly Magazine*, February 1895, pp. 433–434.

PERFORMANCE   How to Make a Quartet

Forming a string quartet is really no different from putting together a rock band. Two or more players know one another well and look for others to fill out the group, musicians who can bring their own creative ideas to the table. And like rock bands, string quartets often transform themselves over time. The Juilliard String Quartet, based at the Juilliard Conservatory of Music in New York City, has over the course of more than 60 years featured two different first violinists, five second violinists, two violists, and three cellists.

Artistic collaborations invariably involve artistic differences: quartet members can (and often do) disagree about how to perform a particular work or a passage in a work, but the best groups work through these differences to create performances that are fresh and exciting. There is no conductor in a string quartet: the four players have to agree on just about everything, including where and what to perform. By the same token, a single player who has fundamentally different ideas about how to make music likely will not last very long in a quartet.

Not all quartets play the standard stringed instruments. The Kronos Quartet, formed in 1973 and based in San Francisco, was one of the first to use electronic as well as acoustical instruments and incorporated many special lighting and stage effects into their concerts. In 1991 the group started taking "roadies" on its tours to handle this end of its performances. More recently, bond (the group uses a lower-case "b"

to avoid copyright infringements with 007) has moved to exclusively electronic instruments (violins, viola, cello), performing a repertory that ranges from classical to pop to New Age. The group's first album sold more than two million copies. In 2001 bond performed with the tenor Luciano Pavarotti at his annual all-star charity concert and collaborated with the Royal Philharmonic Orchestra on their 2003 album *Classified*.

The group bond performing at the Classical Brit Awards, 2005. The instruments of this string quartet are electric, its repertory eclectic.

C. Christodoulou/Lebrecht Music & Arts

EXPAND YOUR PLAYLIST

Nationalism in Nineteenth-Century Music

Dvořák was one of many composers working in the late nineteenth century who sought to infuse at least some of his works with nationalistic elements, though not necessarily from his own country. Just as Dvořák (a Czech) wrote at times in an "American" style, Brahms (a German) sometimes wrote in a "Hungarian" style, and Chabrier (a Frenchman) wrote in a "Spanish" style.

- **Bedřich Smetana** (1824–1884), *The Moldau*. This symphonic poem paints a picture of the most important river in Smetana's native Bohemia (present-day Czech Republic).
- **Louis Moreau Gottschalk**: *Union*. See chapter 34.
- **Johannes Brahms**: *Hungarian Dances*. These piano pieces (later orchestrated by the composer) incorporate characteristic Hungarian rhythms and melodic turns of phrase. Brahms lived most of his life in Vienna, not far from present-day Hungary.
- **Alexander Borodin** (1833–1887): *Polovtzian Dances* from the opera *Prince Igor*. Borodin's native Russia extended eastward into Asia, and these dances capture its flavor.

- **Emmanuel Chabrier** (1841–1894): *Espana*. This single-movement work for large orchestra reflects the Frenchman Chabrier's fascination with Spain.
- **Nikolai Rimsky-Korsakov** (1844–1908): *Scheherazade*. This suite for orchestra narrates, without words, episodes from a series of stories originating in ancient Persia, *The Book of One Thousand and One Nights*. Rimsky-Korsakov's music evokes many effects associated with music of the Near East.

((• **HEAR SAMPLES** on **www.mymusiclab.com**

 TEST YOURSELF on **www.mymusiclab.com**   Flashcards and chapter tests

PART 5 Summary

	Classical Era	Nineteenth Century
Texture	Both polyphonic and homophonic, but on the whole more homophonic.	Both homophonic and polyphonic.
Melody	Growing importance of periodic phrase structure in all genres of music, not just in dance.	Periodic phrase structure continues, but also more fragmented thematic ideas; some use of pentatonic scales. Growing tendency toward virtuosic writing for both voices and instruments.
Rhythm	More smoothly flowing melodies.	Highly varied, from simple to complex.
Timbre	Establishment of the modern orchestra (strings, winds, percussion).	Orchestra continues to grow, with addition of trombones, tubas, piccolos, contrabassoon, and more percussion instruments.
Harmony	Harmony becomes increasingly important as a large-scale structural element (tonic/not-tonic/tonic).	Harmony becomes increasingly chromatic.
Form	Theme and variations, minuet (**ABA**), rondo, sonata form, double-exposition concerto form.	Sonata form, ternary forms, theme and variations, modified strophic form.
Word-music relationships	Word painting still present, but not as prevalent and often more subtle.	Greater importance of program music.

IN REVIEW: Nineteenth-Century Style

Program music Although not new in the nineteenth century, program music took on increasing importance as composers attempted to connect purely instrumental music with the wider world of events and ideas.

- Mendelssohn, *Overture to A Midsummer Night's Dream* (Chapter 29)
- Berlioz, *Symphonie fantastique* (Chapter 30)
- Gottschalk, *Union* (Chapter 34)

Virtuosity While most composers continued to write for amateur performers in many instances, at least some devoted their energies to writing for performers of exceptional talent, creating music that was notoriously difficult to perform.

- Gottschalk, *Union* (Chapter 34)
- Verdi, *La Traviata* (Chapter 36)

Nationalism At least some nineteenth-century music expresses the aspirations of national groups united either politically or ethnically.

- C. Schumann, "Forward!" (Chapter 32)
- Chopin, Mazurka in B-flat, op. 7, no. 1 (Chapter 33)
- Gottschalk, *Union* (Chapter 34)
- Dvořák, String Quartet in F Major, op. 96 (Chapter 39)

Song The song (German: *Lied*) became an important domestic genre, noted for its lyricism and intimacy of tone. These works were mostly for voice and piano, but the style could be applied in almost any medium, including solo piano music or the piano trio.

- Schubert, "Erlkönig" (Chapter 28)
- Hensel, Piano Trio, op. 11 (Chapter 31)
- R. Schumann, "Dedication" (Web Bonus Chapter 4)

The Growth of the Orchestra The orchestra continued to expand throughout the nineteenth century, growing in both the number and variety of instruments.

- Beethoven, Symphony no. 5 (Chapter 27)
- Mendelssohn, *Overture to A Midsummer Night's Dream* (Chapter 29)
- Berlioz, *Symphonie fantastique* (Chapter 30)
- Brahms, Symphony no. 4 (Chapter 38)

Opera as a Fusion of Music and Drama Leading composers used different means to integrate music and drama. Verdi created large-scale units that move fluidly between declamatory and lyrical singing; Wagner created even larger units in which the voice and orchestra present ideas on an equal footing.

- Verdi, *La Traviata* (Chapter 36)
- Wagner, *The Valkyrie* (Chapter 37)

TEST YOURSELF on www.mymusiclab.com   Part Exam

PART 6 The Twentieth Century

1901–2000

The pace of musical change—like the pace of life itself—increased dramatically in the twentieth century. Thanks to advances in technology—sound recordings, radio, film, television, and the computer, to name only a few—listeners had greater access to more diverse kinds of music than ever before. Musical styles were changing just as rapidly. By the 1930s, listeners could choose to listen to music that went beyond long-standing principles of harmony, melody, rhythm, and timbre. Many composers created entirely novel approaches to music by writing works without a tonal center and without a clear sense of meter or regular rhythm. Others incorporated sounds from the music of non-Western cultures. Still others opened up the realm of timbre by using the wealth of electronically generated sounds that had only recently become available. And some composers wrote works that called into question the nature of music itself.

But novelty did not always mean a rejection of the past. Twentieth-century listeners could also choose from a wide variety of fresh and innovative music that remained tonally based and rhythmically regular, from the concert hall to the jazz club. Ragtime, jazz, and the blues developed novel ways of applying tonal harmonies and metered rhythms. Indeed, music became such a lucrative business in the twentieth century that many talented composers and musicians earned fortunes writing for a mass-market audience These new genres of popular music both appealed to and reflected the tastes of a musical public that was now broader and more diverse than ever. The influence of African American and

▲ For some audiences, the pace of musical change in the 20th century was a bit too fast. This cartoon is based on an actual scuffle that occurred at one of Arnold Schoenberg's concerts in 1913 (see chapter 43). Schoenberg continues to conduct, apparently perceiving the noise of the riot as music. The musicians use their instruments as weapons with which to assault listeners. A figure resembling Franz Schubert (see chapter 28) lies sprawled in the foreground.
Phaidon Press Limited/Mark Evan Bonds

Latin composers and musicians became particularly pronounced in all realms of music, recorded and live, popular and classical.

Modernism

Paris, May 1913: The composer Igor Stravinsky sits expectantly in the auditorium at the premiere of his ballet *The Rite of Spring* (see chapter 44). After the first few bars, some audience members begin to laugh derisively. Stravinsky slips out into the backstage wings and listens with astonishment. Before long, the dancers can hardly hear the irregular beats of the music, and they begin to dance out of step with each other. General chaos in the audience ensues, and the press reports a "riot" at the performance.

◄ Pablo Picasso, *Violin and Grapes* (1912), retains elements of representation—one can recognize certain aspects of both a violin and some grapes—but the sense of perspective is heavily distorted: we see the violin from several different angles all at once. This style of painting is known as cubism.

Pablo Picasso (1881–1973), "Violin and Grapes. Ceret and Sorgues, Spring-Summer" 1912. Oil on Canvas, 20 x 24". Mrs. David M. Levy Bequest. The Museum of Modern Art, New York, NY, U.S.A. Digital Image ©The Museum of Modern Art/Licensed by SCALA/Art Resource, NY. © 2010 Estate of Pablo Picasso/ARS Artists Rights Society, NY

Twentieth Century ⊙→ EXPLORE MORE on www.mymusiclab.com

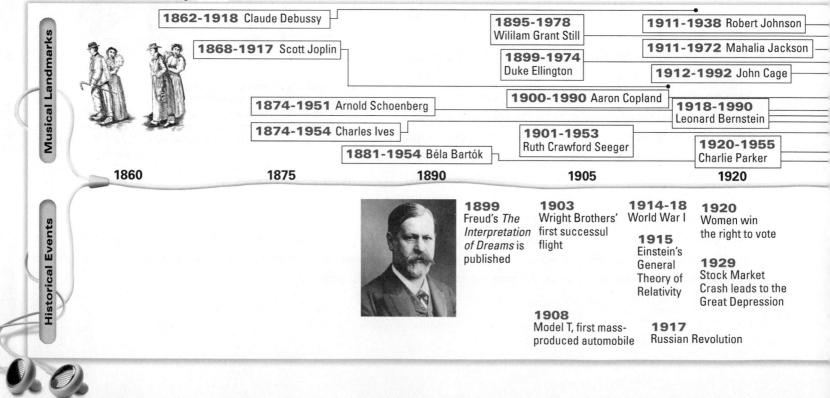

Musical Landmarks

1862-1918 Claude Debussy

1868-1917 Scott Joplin

1895-1978 Wililam Grant Still

1899-1974 Duke Ellington

1911-1938 Robert Johnson

1911-1972 Mahalia Jackson

1912-1992 John Cage

1900-1990 Aaron Copland

1874-1951 Arnold Schoenberg

1918-1990 Leonard Bernstein

1874-1954 Charles Ives

1901-1953 Ruth Crawford Seeger

1881-1954 Béla Bartók

1920-1955 Charlie Parker

1860   1875   1890   1905   1920

Historical Events

1899 Freud's *The Interpretation of Dreams* is published

1903 Wright Brothers' first successul flight

1908 Model T, first mass-produced automobile

1914-18 World War I

1915 Einstein's General Theory of Relativity

1917 Russian Revolution

1920 Women win the right to vote

1929 Stock Market Crash leads to the Great Depression

This scene exemplifies the relationship between many artists and the public in the early decades of the twentieth century. Stravinsky was writing in a new—and to many listeners, shocking—manner. A new spirit, known as modernism, had taken hold in all the arts, and it represented a disregard for tradition and a quest for novelty that far exceeded any such drive in the past.

Ironically, the work that unleashed a riot at its premiere is now one of the most popular works in today's concert halls, a staple of the orchestral repertory. A similar pattern of shock followed by acceptance can be seen in the other arts as well. Many modernist painters rejected the time-honored idea that a painting had to represent a particular object exactly; abstract art, based on color and form, became a touchstone of modernism. Even artists who created representational images began to do away with the illusion of perspective (depth) in their paintings. Viewers were scandalized at first, but eventually they came to accept and even embrace such new approaches. In architecture, modernists advocated a style of design based on the spirit of contemporary times. Modernist architects eliminated elements of ornamentation and focused on smooth, clean lines. Novelists experimented with such techniques as writing in an unbroken "stream of consciousness," in which readers were often at a loss to decipher any clear story line. While these approaches no longer seem unusual to us today, they were unsettling in their time.

▲ Wassily Kandinsky, *Improvisation No. 7 (Storm)*, 1910. The Russian modernist Kandinsky was among the first painters to abandon the idea of representation, preferring instead to create images based on forms and colors.

Wassily Kandinsky (1866–1944) "Improvisation No. 7 (Storm)". 1910. Oil on pasteboard. 70 x 48.7 cm (27 9/16 x 19 3/16 in.). Gift of Collection Société Anonyme. 1941.527 Location: Yale University Art Gallery, New Haven, Connecticut, U.S.A./Art Resource, NY. ©2010 Estate of Wassily Kandinsky/ARS Artists Rights Society, NY

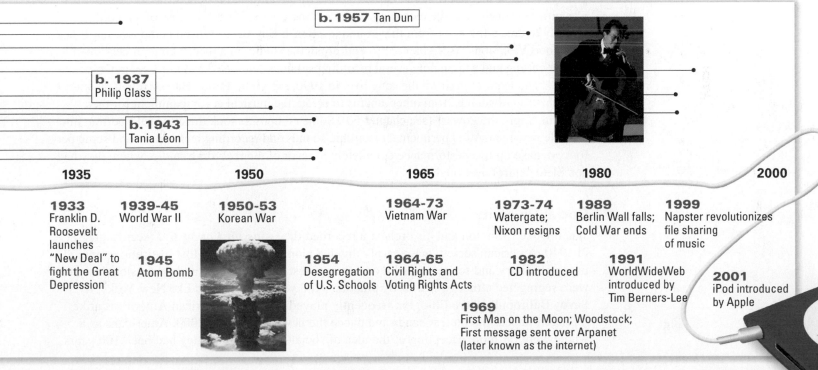

b. 1957 Tan Dun

b. 1937 Philip Glass

b. 1943 Tania Léon

1935   1950   1965   1980   2000

1933 Franklin D. Roosevelt launches "New Deal" to fight the Great Depression

1939-45 World War II

1945 Atom Bomb

1950-53 Korean War

1954 Desegregation of U.S. Schools

1964-73 Vietnam War

1964-65 Civil Rights and Voting Rights Acts

1969 First Man on the Moon; Woodstock; First message sent over Arpanet (later known as the internet)

1973-74 Watergate; Nixon resigns

1982 CD introduced

1989 Berlin Wall falls; Cold War ends

1991 WorldWideWeb introduced by Tim Berners-Lee

1999 Napster revolutionizes file sharing of music

2001 iPod introduced by Apple

▲ "Little Nipper" listens to "His Master's Voice." This 1899 painting by the English artist Francis Barraud served as the logo for the HMV record label (and later RCA and JVC) for most of the 20th century. The gramophone is playing a 78 rpm shellac disk that contains only about three minutes' worth of music. The machine operated on a windup hand crank; speakers and electrical wiring came only later.

CORBIS—NY

Audio Technology

Perhaps the single most remarkable aspect of music in the twentieth century is that for the first time listeners could hear music when and where they wanted to. We take the portability of music—on radio, CDs, and iPods—for granted nowadays, but being able to hear music without the physical presence of performing musicians marked a radical change in the history of music. In theory at least, anyone could hear anything at any time, anywhere.

Thomas Edison invented the cylinder disk in 1877, but the earliest recordings were poor and served only to emphasize the gulf between live and recorded sound. With the advent of 78 rpm (revolutions per minute) disks in 1897, the availability and quality of recorded music began to expand exponentially. For the first time, listeners could hear the same performance more than once, and they could listen to music without any performers present. Radio stations, which first appeared in the early 1920s, radically changed the music industry by broadcasting everything from grand opera to hillbilly music to audiences who had never had the chance to hear those performances live. Eventually, film, television, and the Internet gave listeners even more choices and easier access to music.

This revolution in listening changed the way music was produced. Traditional written notation became irrelevant in many musical styles. With the ready availability of audiotape beginning in the 1940s, composers could for the first time manipulate sound by splicing and re-recording taped sounds. It was now possible to use the recording studio not merely to refine the sound of a recording, but actually to create the work from the ground up. Beach Boy Brian Wilson composed his 1960s hit "Good Vibrations" (see chapter 59) entirely in the studio, in a painstaking process involving the cutting and splicing of several recording sessions into one 3.5-minute song. Only later did the band learn to perform the song live. In 1990, rap group Public Enemy relied on studio manipulation of sounds from other albums to create the musical accompaniment for their lyrics in "Fight the Power" (see chapter 60). Some composers took the classical tradition into a whole new realm of experimental electronic sounds and recording techniques, and some performers gave up live performance completely in favor of the recording studio, where they had complete control over quality.

Social Diversity

When Duke Ellington and his orchestra recorded the swing hit *Cotton Tail* (see chapter 47) in 1940, American society was sharply divided along racial lines. Most institutions, including the military and schools as well as housing, restaurants, hotels, and professional sports, were segregated either by law or by practice. And yet in dance halls like New York City's Savoy Ballroom, where Ellington frequently played, whites and African Americans alike thronged to hear the hottest bands and dance the newest steps. By 2000, Americans as a whole were far more accepting of the idea of social diversity than they had been 100 years before. Over the course of the twentieth century, the image of a social melting pot had given way to the idea of society as a mosaic of different cultures and traditions, each contributing in its own distinctive way toward the larger whole.

Music played an important role in this change. Styles with roots in the traditions of African American culture in particular helped bridge the divide between the races. As early as the 1930s, whites and blacks were playing together in instrumental ensembles. Ragtime, jazz, rock, and hip-hop all became a part of mainstream American culture. But the move across racial and social divides was never easy. At different times, every one of these very same kinds of music erupted as a flashpoint of social conflict. In the 1920s, many white parents expressed open opposition to the sexual overtones in ragtime and jazz. Many of their children, in turn, were shocked in the 1950s when white teenagers began listening (and worse, dancing) to music written in a style traditionally associated with the music of African Americans. Throughout the twentieth century, pop music has been an integral part of social change and protest—gospel in the civil rights movement of the 1950s and 1960s, psychedelia in the antiwar movement of the 1960s and 1970s, punk as an outcry against economic repression in the 1970s and 1980s, and hip-hop as a statement on racism and discrimination at the end of the century and beyond.

▲ More than any other kind of music, jazz promoted racial integration for audiences and performers alike. Here, the celebrated clarinetist Artie Shaw jams with Duke Ellington and drummer Chick Webb in 1937 while a racially mixed audience listens with obvious pleasure.

Photograph by Charles Peterson, courtesy of Don Peterson

Globalization

It was a revelation for the French composer Claude Debussy when, in 1889, he heard the Javanese musical ensemble known as the gamelan play at Paris's International Exposition (the same event that gave us the Eiffel Tower). A gamelan includes many percussion instruments—drums, gongs, and xylophones, among others—and its music has what Western ears often perceive as a floating, nondirectional quality that operates outside the conventions of Western harmony (see chapter 41). Debussy was so impressed by this kind of sound that he incorporated elements of it into his *Voiles*, for piano, in 1910 (see chapter 40). In an age before recordings, such cross-cultural musical encounters were rare. Few gamelan ensembles had ever performed outside of what is now Indonesia, and if Debussy had wanted to travel there it would have taken him several weeks by steamship. Thanks to air travel, gamelan ensembles perform all over the world today, and recordings make their music even more widely available. Indeed, more than 100 gamelan ensembles are now based in the United States alone.

The growing ease of telecommunications and transportation made the world of 2000 a far smaller place than it had been in 1900. Telephones, fax machines, video transmissions, and the Internet made it possible to communicate from almost any point on the globe to almost any other. National economies grew increasingly dependent on one another. Disparate cultures mingled even within individual composers and performers, who often rebelled against the notion that they or their music belonged strictly to one tradition or another. Whether in the concert hall, the jazz club, or on the dance floor, music had become a global phenomenon.

The Twentieth Century CHAPTERS AT A GLANCE

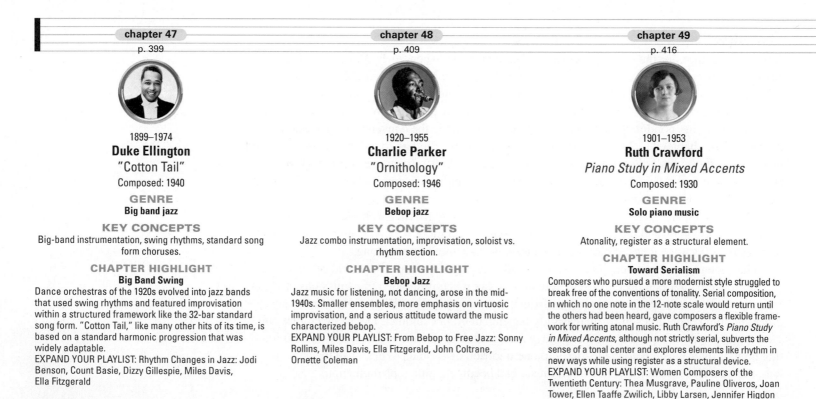

GENRE
Song cycle for voice and chamber ensemble

KEY CONCEPTS
Atonality, *sprechstimme*.

CHAPTER HIGHLIGHT
Expressionism
Expressionism gave priority to truth over beauty, including the sometimes less-than-beautiful workings of the human psyche. In grappling with raw human emotions, expressionist works like Schoenberg's *Pierrot lunaire* could be grotesque and surreal.
EXPAND YOUR PLAYLIST: Expressionism: Anton Webern, Alban Berg, Ernst Křenek

GENRE
Ballet

KEY CONCEPTS
Polytonality, metrical irregularity, pentatonic melodies, instruments of the modern orchestra.

CHAPTER HIGHLIGHT
Modernism
Stravinsky's ballet caused a riot on its opening night, in part because of the unconventional harmonies, its angular, irregular rhythms, and the unconventional style of dance on the stage itself.
EXPAND YOUR PLAYLIST: Ballet Music: Adolph Adam, Leo Delibes, Pyotr Illich Tchaikovsky, Francis Poulenc, Sergei Prokofiev

GENRE
Ragtime

KEY CONCEPTS
Syncopation, sectional form, compound melodies.

CHAPTER HIGHLIGHT
Ragtime
Ragtime, with its syncopated rhythms, laid the groundwork for early jazz.
EXPAND YOUR PLAYLIST: Rooted in Ragtime: James P. Johnson, Zez Confrey, Jelly Roll Morton, Meade "Lux" Lewis, Marcus Roberts

GENRE
Downhome blues

KEY CONCEPTS
Twelve-bar blues, blue notes, timbre of vocal blues.

CHAPTER HIGHLIGHT
Blues
Early blues recordings captured an oral tradition with deep roots in the Mississippi Delta region. The characteristic "blue note" and the 12-bar blues form would go on to have influence in music of many different kinds.
EXPAND YOUR PLAYLIST: The Blues in Different Styles: Bessie Smith, Cream, Rolling Stones, Fleetwood Mac

GENRE
Neoclassicism

KEY CONCEPTS
Periodic phrase structure, transparency of texture, rondo form.

CHAPTER HIGHLIGHT
Neoclassicism
Neoclassicism was a response to modernism. Neoclassical works draw on the idioms of earlier eras even while incorporating at least some modern elements as well. No one would mistake Tailleferre's Concertino for Harp and Orchestra for an eighteenth-century work, even though it is deeply indebted to the idioms of the Classical style.
EXPAND YOUR PLAYLIST: Neoclassicism: Igor Stravinsky, Sergei Prokofiev, Maurice Ravel, Darius Milhaud, Paul Hindemith

GENRE
Art song

KEY CONCEPTS
Blues inflections, chromatic harmony, through-composed form.

CHAPTER HIGHLIGHT
Art Song
The art song in the twentieth century took on the inflections of many different styles. Still's setting of a text by Langston Hughes blends a highly chromatic idiom with elements of the blues.
EXPAND YOUR PLAYLIST: Twentieth-Century African American Composers in the Western Classical Tradition: Florence Beatrice Price, Henry T. Burleigh, Margaret Bonds, George Walker, Keith Jarrett

GENRE
Ballet

KEY CONCEPTS
Populist modernism, traditional folk tunes, "open" orchestration and texture, rondo form.

CHAPTER HIGHLIGHT
Nationalism
Copland pioneered a sound that evoked the open spaces of the western United States. In the ballet *Rodeo*, wide spacing of instruments, bright timbres, and energetic rhythms contribute to a distinctively American sound.
EXPAND YOUR PLAYLIST: The Sound of the American West: Aaron Copland, Ferde Grofé, Dmitri Tiomkin, Elmer Bernstein, Enrico Morricone

The Twentieth Century CHAPTERS AT A GLANCE

chapter 53
p. 440

1881–1945
Béla Bartók
Concerto for Orchestra, second
movement ("Game of Pairs")
Composed: 1943

GENRE
Concerto

KEY CONCEPTS
Orchestration, instruments of the orchestra, symmetrical form, folk
melodies, ethnomusicology.

CHAPTER HIGHLIGHT
Orchestral Virtuosity
Bartók collected folk melodies not only from his native Hungary, but
from other regions of Europe and the world as well, and the
melodies of his own compositions, as in this movement from the
Concerto for Orchestra, reflect these unusual melodies in their
inflections and harmonizations. This work allows individual instruments of the orchestra, especially the winds in this movement, to
come to the fore.
EXPAND YOUR PLAYLIST: Orchestral Music of the Twentieth Century:
Dmitri Shostakovich, Krzysztof Penderecki, Ellen Taaffe Zwilich

chapter 54
p. 446

1918–1990
Leonard Bernstein
"Tonight" from *West Side Story*
Composed: 1957

GENRE
Musical

KEY CONCEPTS
Additive form, ensembles.

CHAPTER HIGHLIGHT
The Broadway Musical
The Broadway musical is a direct descendent of
European operetta, a spoken play with ample quantities
of sung music. While often lighter in tone than standard
opera, many musicals, including Bernstein's *West Side
Story,* have carried with them messages of social signif-
icance. The ensemble "Tonight" is particularly elabo-
rate in its formal structure.
EXPAND YOUR PLAYLIST: Broadway's Social Conscience:
Kern/Hammerstein, Rodgers/Hammerstein, Lerner/Loewe,
Schönberg/Boublil, Schönberg/Maltby, Larson

chapter 55
p. 455

1912–1992
John Cage
Indeterminacy (excerpt)
Composed: 1959

GENRE
Aleatory music

KEY CONCEPTS
Aleatory music, *musique concrète,* electronic music.

CHAPTER HIGHLIGHT
Experimental Music
This work, like many of Cage's compositions, compels
listeners to confront basic questions about the very
nature of music. *Indeterminacy* is highly aleatoric, relying on chance to create connections (or not) between
text and music. It uses a combination of a speaking
voice, standard instruments, and recorded sounds from
everyday life that are electronically amplified and
manipulated.
EXPAND YOUR PLAYLIST: Experimental Composers of
the Twentieth Century: Henry Cowell, Harry Partch,
Moondog, Lejaren Hiller

chapter 58
p. 475

The Marvelettes
"Please, Mr. Postman"
Composed: 1961

GENRE
Motown

KEY CONCEPTS
Close vocal harmonies, doo-wop chord progression,
verse-chorus form.

CHAPTER HIGHLIGHT
Motown
The "Mowtown Sound" relies on close vocal harmony
from backup singers behind a feature lead singer and
sophisticated studio production.
EXPAND YOUR PLAYLIST: Close Harmony in Different
Styles: The Chords, The Coasters, The Beatles,
Manhattan Transfer, Dolly Parton, *NSYNC

chapter 59
p. 483

The Beach Boys
"Good Vibrations"
Composed: 1966

GENRE
Psychedelia

KEY CONCEPTS
Composition in the studio, psychedelic sound effects,
verse-chorus form with extensions.

CHAPTER HIGHLIGHT
Sixties Rock
In the mid-sixties, rock music entered a period of great
creative innovation. Even the Beach Boys, previously
known for their light surf music, experimented with "psychedelic" sounds, using such exotic instruments as the
theremin and incorporating sophisticated textures and
forms into their music.
EXPAND YOUR PLAYLIST: Psychedelia: The Byrds, The
Beatles, Jefferson Airplane, Pink Floyd, Brian Wilson

WEB BONUS chapter 6

The Sex Pistols
"God Save the Queen"
Composed: 1977

GENRE
Punk

KEY CONCEPTS
Irony, distorted rock timbre, extreme vocal techniques.

CHAPTER HIGHLIGHT
Rebellious Rock
Punk revived earlier rock traditions of immediacy and
directness and combined them with biting social com-
mentary. The do-it-yourself attitude is audible in the Sex
Pistol's "anthem," which features distorted timbres and
straightforward forms.
EXPAND YOUR PLAYLIST: Punk and New Wave: The
Ramones, Dead Kennedys, Elvis Costello, The Cars,
Blondie

40

Claude Debussy
Voiles
Composed: 1910

Debussy's *Voiles,* a short piece for solo piano, represents a major shift in musical styles. Many of the nineteenth century's standard elements of music are used in new ways to create a distinctively modern sound for the twentieth century.

Listen to this first

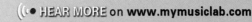
HEAR MORE on www.mymusiclab.com

Timbre	**Melody**	**Dynamics**	**Rhythm**	**Harmony**	**Form**
How would you describe the sound of the piano in this work? How is it different from the sound of other works for piano (for example, the Mazurka by Chopin discussed in chapter 33)?	How many distinct themes can you identify?	What is the predominant volume of this work? Does it change at any point?	Is the basic meter of this work duple or triple?	Listen for a sense of a harmonic center. Can you hum a note that sounds like home base, or *do* (as in do-re-mi)? Does the music feel at rest anywhere, as though it has arrived?	Listen for the return of the opening idea toward the end of the work.

LEARN MORE on
www.mymusiclab.com
Chapter Objectives

Debussy's title is deliberately ambiguous: the French word *voiles* (pronounced like "wall" with a "v" immediately before the "w") can mean either "sails" (as in the sails on a boat) or "veils." Thus, even though the work has a programmatic title, we cannot be sure of the exact sense of that title. Interestingly, Debussy placed this title at the end of the written score rather than at the beginning. The music, too, suggests rather than states: the timbre is muted, melodies appear and disappear without development or conclusion, harmonies remain unresolved, and the rhythm never establishes any strong sense of meter. In this sense, it fits both meanings of the word *voiles*, for both sails and veils are light and fluttering and constantly in motion.

This quality of suggesting rather than stating is basic to an artistic movement known as **impressionism**. Impressionism was particularly important in the realm of painting (see "Impressionism," page 351), where artists focused more on sensations, perceptions, and light than on the direct representation of objects. Although paintings by Monet and Renoir are among the most familiar and treasured images in art museums today, at the time of their creation, they met with considerable skepticism and at times outright derision. Were the paintings even finished? Critics and viewers of the time wondered. Similarly, the music of Debussy confronted listeners with an entirely new sound that ignored conventions and defied expectations. In this way,

Debussy's music was an early manifestation of the modernist impulse, and critics and audiences were often at a loss to understand it.

In literature, a group of French poets known as symbolists (including Stéphane Mallarmé, Arthur Rimbaud, and Paul Verlaine) used comparable techniques with words, avoiding clear syntax and using symbols to suggest rather than articulate ideas. Debussy was drawn to their texts, setting some of them as songs, and he regularly attended readings by his friend Mallarmé.

Timbre: A Nonpercussive Sound

It may surprise some people to learn that the piano is a percussion instrument, but consider its action: the performer strikes a key, which in turn activates a hammer that strikes metal strings, which vibrate and produce sound. When pianists play a melodic line, they must work to make this sound as lyrical and nonpercussive as they can. But Debussy asks performers to go even further here, to play the piano as if it were (in his own words) an "instrument without hammers." The ultra-smooth lines and the persistently soft volume create a timbre that is more intimate and more inward than the often bold, crisp sound of the piano.

Where did Debussy come up with such an unusual idea? Debussy heard a Javanese ensemble known as the **gamelan**, a large collection of drums, gongs, xylophones, and plucked string instruments (see chapter 41) at the International Exposition in Paris in 1889. He was fascinated by the gentle, floating timbres of what is essentially a percussion ensemble. The gongs in a gamelan, in particular, can be set in motion by the softest of touches, and it would seem that Debussy was trying to recreate this kind of sound on the piano. A French composer absorbs and reinterprets the sound of Javanese music: *Voiles* thus reflects the growing globalization of music in the twentieth century.

We also know that Debussy was intent on exploring musical timbre in much the same way that the French symbolist poets—all of them his contemporaries, some of them his friends—explored sound for sound's sake, unconstrained by logic or syntax. Debussy's rich sonic palette particularly inspires performers to listen and make careful choices regarding touch and pedaling, so that the exploration continues with each new performance.

Melody: Fragments

Instead of clear themes, Debussy presents what sound more like fragments of themes than actual self-sufficient melodies:

1 = a downward contour, ending with a leap upward (first presented at 0:00)

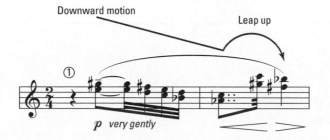

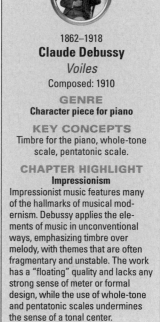

1862–1918
Claude Debussy
Voiles
Composed: 1910
GENRE
Character piece for piano
KEY CONCEPTS
Timbre for the piano, whole-tone scale, pentatonic scale.
CHAPTER HIGHLIGHT
Impressionism
Impressionist music features many of the hallmarks of musical modernism. Debussy applies the elements of music in unconventional ways, emphasizing timbre over melody, with themes that are often fragmentary and unstable. The work has a "floating" quality and lacks any strong sense of meter or formal design, while the use of whole-tone and pentatonic scales undermines the sense of a tonal center.

SEE MORE on
www.mymusiclab.com
Video of "Jagul Bebarongan" by Gamelan Dharma Swara

2 = a single repeated note in the bass (first presented at 0:10)

3 = a slow, rising three-note figure (first presented at 0:15)

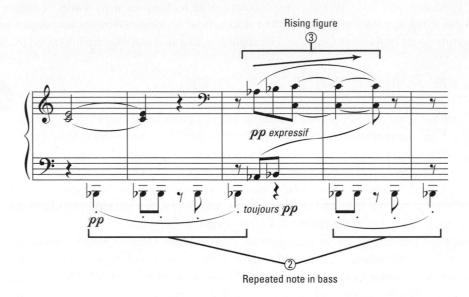

4 = a turning figure (first presented at 1:01)

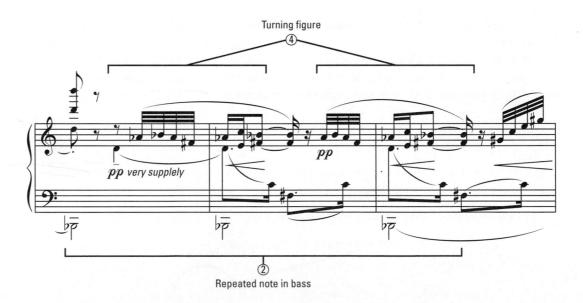

5 = a harp-like glissando figure (first presented at 2:08)

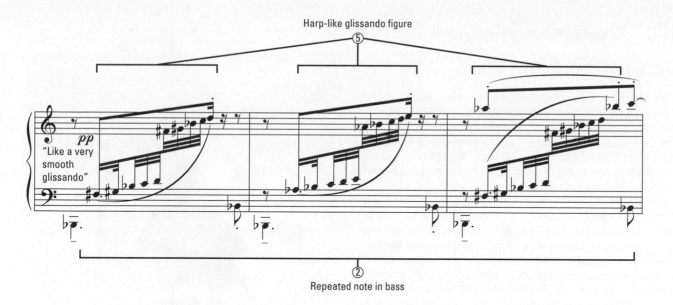

Harp-like glissando figure

⑤

pp
"Like a very smooth glissando"

②
Repeated note in bass

None of these themes has a particularly sharp profile: each is as fluid as a sail or veil, altered slightly every time it returns. The music as a whole avoids any sense of strong direction: we do not feel at any point as if it is moving toward a goal or climax. Instead of a kind of musical narrative, Debussy is presenting something more like a succession of slowly changing images.

Dynamics: Whispering, Hinting

Except for one very brief passage in the middle (2:08–2:20), the entire work is written at the level of *piano* (soft) or *pianissimo* (very soft). This extremely low dynamic reinforces the nonpercussive timbre of the instrument, as the pianist touches the keys lightly, even wiping or caressing them rather than striking them. It also allows the one *forte* (loud) moment to stand out all the more markedly. In this manner, dynamics assume a kind of structural importance, providing a point of contrast against an otherwise unchanging plane of softness

Rhythm: Where's the Downbeat?

Although notated in duple meter, *Voiles* provides the listener with almost no sense of a fixed metrical pattern. Most music in duple meter would follow a pattern of **1**-2 **1**-2 **1**-2, with a strong accent on the downbeat, but Debussy's music resists any such pattern. Instead, the music seems to float or drift, again evoking the images suggested by the work's title.

The repeated B-flats in the lower register help obscure the meter of the work even more. At times they fall on the beat, at times off it. This repeated note seems to operate in its own little world and never quite synchronizes with the upper voices. It disappears, returns, and then disappears again. It is as unpredictable as a flowing veil or as a sail flapping in a light breeze.

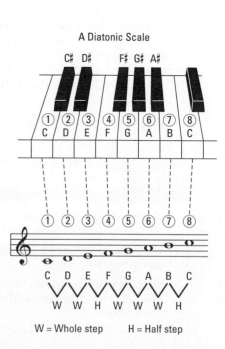

A Diatonic Scale

C♯ D♯   F♯ G♯ A♯

① ② ③ ④ ⑤ ⑥ ⑦ ⑧
C D E F G A B C

① ② ③ ④ ⑤ ⑥ ⑦ ⑧

C D E F G A B C
∨ ∨ ∨ ∨ ∨ ∨ ∨
W W H W W W H

W = Whole step   H = Half step

PROFILE   Claude Debussy (1862–1918)

The Path Less Taken

Debussy's life straddled two centuries—he was born during the U.S. Civil War and died a few months before the end of World War I— yet he is widely regarded as the first great composer of the twentieth century. The inevitable association of his style with the label of impressionism tends to obscure the wide-ranging novelties of his music: no other single figure of his era did more to expand the possibilities of form, harmony, and timbre.

Debussy was born on the outskirts of Paris and studied piano and composition at the renowned Conservatory of Paris, where he won a prestigious prize in composition. But from that point on, Debussy pursued a highly unconventional career as a composer. He never held a public post, accepted no students on any regular basis, and rarely appeared in public as a pianist or conductor. Instead, he pushed the boundaries of composition with increasing intensity, exploring new ways of applying the basic elements of music to his works. He rejected many of the conventions of composition and sought to create sounds that had never before been heard. He was a master of orchestration and drew sounds from the orchestra that had never been heard before. Like the impressionist artists and symbolist poets who were his contemporaries, Debussy often worked in obscurity. Works that are now recognized as masterpieces, like *The Afternoon of a Faun*, were initially greeted with indifference and occasionally scorn.

Ultimately, Debussy was vindicated in his drive to extend the boundaries of music. He had many imitators (*Debussyistes*, as they were known), and his death was widely mourned throughout the musical world. In 1920, a group of prominent composers—Igor Stravinsky, Béla Bartók, Paul Dukas, Manuel de Falla, Maurice Ravel, and Erik Satie—honored his memory with a series of short piano pieces issued in a commemorative volume called *Le tombeau de Claude Debussy* ("The Tomb of Claude Debussy").

Claude Debussy on vacation, 1911
Lebrecht Music & Arts/Lebrecht Music & Arts Photo Library

⊙→ EXPLORE MORE on www.mymusiclab.com

⏪   EXPAND YOUR PLAYLIST: DEBUSSY   ⏩

- *Suite bergamasque.* A series of movements for piano, including the famous *Clair de lune.*

- *Préludes,* Books 1 and 2. Two collections of works for solo piano, including *Voiles.*

- *Children's Corner.* A suite of dances about childhood, for piano, including the famous *Golliwogg's Cake-Walk*, a quasi-ragtime piece.

- *Prélude à l'après-midi d'un faune* ("**Prelude to the Afternoon of a Faun**"). A ballet later made famous by Nijinsky and the Ballets Russes (see chapter 44).

- *Pelléas et Melisande.* Debussy's only completed opera, based on a drama by Maurice Maeterlink about a doomed love affair in legendary times.

((•● HEAR SAMPLES on www.mymusiclab.com

Harmony: A Centerless Center

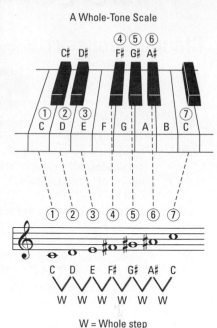

A Whole-Tone Scale

W = Whole step

The piece opens in a relatively high register, but at 0:10, a single, low note—the note B♭;—enters in the bass. This B♭; is repeated in various rhythms throughout the entire work until just before the very end (it drops out at 3:29). Yet the constant presence of this one note actually *reduces* the sense of any harmonic center. Because it is always there, it recedes into the background and contributes still further to the sense of floating or drifting created by the timbre, dynamics, and rhythm. It is a little like the sound of wind flapping against a sail: we hear these sounds if we listen for them, but after a while, we stop hearing them precisely because they never stop.

Another element that undermines any sense of a harmonic center is the use of the **whole-tone scale**. A scale, as we have seen (see "The Elements of Music," as well as chapter 33), is an ordered arrangement of notes that together make up a kind of palette for melodies. The standard Western-music scale, known as the **diatonic scale**, consists of a combination of whole steps and half steps. To recap:

- A **half step** is the smallest distance between two adjacent notes on a piano (white or black), such as C-C#; it is also the smallest distance you can comfortably sing.

- A **whole step** is a little bigger. An example on the keyboard is C-D, which skips C#. In other words, one whole step equals two half steps.

- The standard diatonic scale uses a combination of whole and half steps to emphasize the tonal center of any given key. The placement of those half steps tells your ear which note is home base, or the **tonic**.

But a whole-tone scale has no half steps, and this eliminates a sense of a tonal center.

Debussy's use of the whole-tone scale in *Voiles* helps give the music the sense that it has no tonic, that all notes are equally important. In this way, too, the music may offer an impression of a drifting cloud or a billowing sail. Western listeners tend to associate the whole-tone scale with the music of East Asia. And as noted earlier, Debussy was in fact influenced by certain repertories from this part of the world, particularly the gamelan from Indonesia (see chapter 41).

Debussy was one of several composers working in the early twentieth century who was questioning **tonality**, which for many centuries had been the primary system of organizing pitch. Other composers would take the challenge still further, until it became possible to compose using an entirely nontonal or "atonal" style altogether (see chapters 43 and 49).

Form: Nondirectional

All the elements discussed to this point—timbre, dynamics, rhythm, harmony—combine to create a sense of nondirectional form. The music never seems to be moving toward a particular goal. There is a climax of sorts in the middle, when the music becomes rhythmically more animated and loud for a brief moment before returning to its original tempo and dynamic. This creates a vague sense of an overall **ABA′** form. But even this change in the middle comes as something of a surprise: it simply arrives, one more event in a series of seemingly random events. And thanks to the whole-tone scale, we do not have a sense that the music is moving away from or back toward a tonic key at any point. Even the ending seems inconclusive. The music stops, but it does not convey any strong sense of closure.

With these points in mind, listen to the work again, using the Listening Guide.

CONNECT YOUR PLAYLIST

Dynamics

Find a work that uses soft dynamics either exclusively or almost exclusively.

Example: Eric Clapton, "Tears in Heaven" (*Unplugged* version, 1992) This acoustic performance maintains soft dynamics throughout.

Listening Guide

GO TO www.mymusiclab.com
for the Automated Listening Guide
CD IV • Track 6/Download Track 69

Claude Debussy Composed: 1910 *Voiles* (3:55)

Time	Melody	Rhythm	Harmony	Dynamics	Form
0:00	1 (descending line, ending with leap up). Debussy's instructions to the pianist: "Moderately, in a rhythm without rigor and caressingly"	Begins with dotted rhythms	Whole-tone scale is established by the first five notes.	p (*piano*, soft)	**A**
0:10	2 (single low note repeated in bass)	Slow, irregular	Low note is disconnected from harmonies above.	pp (*pianissimo*, very soft)	
0:15	3 (rising three-note figure)	Slow, regular	Octaves imply no harmony at all.		
0:26	1 and 2 and 3 simultaneously, in various combinations.		The three voices are seemingly unconnected.		
1:01	4 (turning figure), to be played "very supply." Combined with 2 (repeated bass note), which continues throughout	Moderately fast, regular	Based on whole-tone scale		
1:38	3 (rising three-note figure) added to 4 and 2				
2:08	5 (harplike glissando figure). "Becoming more animated." Combined with 3 underneath	Fast, regular	Based on pentatonic scale (five notes: see chapter 39)	p growing to f (*forte*, loud)	**B**
2:44	5 and 2 and 3. "As at the beginning of the work."			**pp**	**A'**
3:15	1 returns. "Very calmly and growing increasingly faint from here to the end." Combined with 5; 3 (repeated bass note) drops out for first time.				

Student FAQs

Debussy stands to the pianist's left while judging a piano trio contest with other composers and musicians in 1903.
Lebrecht Music & Arts/Lebrecht Music & Arts Photo Library

Is this music difficult to play?

Yes and no. It's not difficult to hit the right notes, but it is very difficult to sustain such a quiet sound for this length of time. It's a little like holding one's hand still in midair: it's easy to do it for a short time, but after a while it becomes a challenge. The performer has to pay attention to every subtle nuance in this work, and that requires a high degree of musicianship.

I can't really hear the difference between "piano (soft)" and "pianissimo (very soft)." Is that a problem?

Not all pianists bring out the difference clearly, but most do, and given the limited range of dynamics in this work, it's a difference worth listening for. You should be able to hear the one "*forte* (loud)" moment as quite clearly different, though.

HISTORICAL CONTEXT Impressionism

Debussy's music is often associated with **impressionism**, an artistic movement spearheaded by French painters like Claude Monet, Pierre Auguste Renoir, and Edgar Degas in the late 1860s. These artists used an accumulation of short, visible brush strokes instead of a continuous line to produce not so much a representation of an object as the sensation—the impression—produced by it. They were particularly interested in the effects of light on our perception of an object. Color took precedence over line. Because the idea was to capture a moment in time, impressionists worked quickly to reproduce on canvas the fleeting appearance of a scene, and then moved on to the next painting, leading some critics to call their works unfinished.

In music, the impressionist style is similarly based on a blurring of harmonies, rhythms, and forms. It tends to avoid clear cadences and rhythmic patterns, and the music often seems to ebb and flow with a fluid sense of motion. Above all, impressionist composers placed great emphasis on the color (timbre) of sound. Debussy, the leading composer in this style, brought new sounds out of the orchestra and piano alike. Early critics were not so enthralled. One took the composer to task for writing "unprecise harmonies and fleeting phrases." Another said of his opera *Pelléas et Melisande* that "Debussy has definitely discounted all melody. . . . He lets us hear only chords. . . . The score resembles a curiosity shop of tangled harmonies . . . which makes a less disagreeable impression only because it falls on our ears in soft and discreet half fading tones."

Debussy himself intensely disliked the term "impressionism," especially if it was applied to music. He insisted he was more concerned with making "something new—realities—as it were." An impression, he maintained, was reality reconstructed in the mind from our sensory perceptions of the world. These mental reconstructions offered, in effect, an alternative reality of ideas to the reality of the physical world.

Claude Monet's painting *Impression: Sunrise* (1872) supplied the name of the movement that would later be known as "impressionism." Though a few objects in this painting—two boats and the sun, for instance—are recognizable, Monet's emphasis is on capturing the mood of early morning on the water.

Monet, Claude (1840–1926)—"Impression, Sunrise". 1872. Oil on canvas, 48 x 63 cm. Painted in Le Havre, France. © Estate of Claude Monet/ARS Artists Rights Society, NY

EXPAND YOUR PLAYLIST

Impressionism

Debussy is regarded as the great master of impressionism, but other composers wrote in this style as well.

Maurice Ravel
• "Mirrors" (*Miroirs*). A suite of movements for piano, including "Sad Birds" and "Valley of the Bells."

Frederick Delius
• *Appalachia*. This "American Rhapsody," for orchestra, records the impressions of an English composer who spent considerable amounts of time in the southern United States.

Charles Griffes
• *The White Peacock*. This "tone poem" for orchestra is by the leading American composer associated with the impressionist movement.

Manuel de Falla
• "Nights in the Gardens of Spain" (*Noches en los jardines de España*). Though often categorized as a composer who expressed nationalist sentiments through his music for his native Spain, de Falla was also influenced in at least some of his compositions by the impressionist idiom, including this work for piano and orchestra.

 HEAR SAMPLES on **www.mymusiclab.com**

 TEST YOURSELF on **www.mymusiclab.com**   Flashcards and chapter tests

41

Gamelan Gong Kebyar of Belaluan
Kebyar Ding III, "Oncang-oncangan"
Recorded: 1928

Gamelan means "musical ensemble." It is played in Indonesia and consists of a number of instruments, typically a variety of bells, gongs, drums, and xylophone-like instruments.

Listen to this first

(((• HEAR MORE on www.mymusiclab.com

Timbre	**Melody**	**Dynamics**	**Form**
How do the tones of the instruments sound? Why do they sound that way?	What do you notice about the way the melody is put together? Can you identify the individual parts?	When and how does the volume level change?	How are sections marked off? When and why does the speed of the music change? How are the rhythmic pulses marked by the instruments?

LEARN MORE on
www.mymusiclab.com
Chapter Objectives

SEE MORE on
www.mymusiclab.com
Gamelan Dharma
Swara performs
"Jagul Bebarongan"

The gamelan consists of melody and rhythm instruments and originated at the courts on the islands of Java and Bali, in what is now Indonesia. The primary melody instruments of the gamelan are the *gender*, a bronze-keyed **vibraphons**, and the *trompong*, horizontally mounted, bowl-shaped gongs. These instruments are played in pairs, with one set tuned slightly apart from the other, creating a shimmering sound. The rhythm section consists of vertically hung gongs, which are struck to mark off fixed beats within the metric structure of the piece. Each section of the performance has its own specific rhythmic pattern played by these gongs. They are joined by a number of drums and smaller percussion instruments (see A Closer Look: The Gamelan, page 354).

Gamelan music traditionally was not notated, and the players learned their parts by rote. Today, the music is taught using a numerical notation, with each number representing a corresponding scale step. Gamelans of all types are found in the music departments of many American, Canadian, and British universities.

Gamelan gong kebyar is easily distinguished from the older Javanese gamelan, which was sedate, elegant, and performed for princes. The Balinese style is energetic, with many abrupt changes of tempo and dynamics. The word *kebyar* means "explosive." Compositions are built of series of **ostinatos**— repeated musical patterns—and each has a different length and is set in a

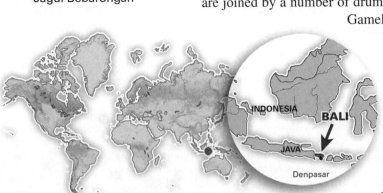

Gamelan music comes from the Indonesian islands of Bali and Java.

INDONESIA
BALI
JAVA
Denpasar

GLOBAL CONNECTION

different tempo. The technique of Balinese ostinato composition later influenced American minimalist composers (see Philip Glass's "Knee Play 1," chapter 56).

This recording of *gamelan gong kebyar* comes from the first historic set of Balinese music recordings made in 1928. It is the third part of a longer composition, so it is called *Kebyar Ding III: Oncang-oncangan.* We already know that the term *kebyar* means "explosive"; *ding* means "first tone," referring to the tone that forms the central focus of the piece. The term *oncang-oncangan* imitates the sound of the pounding of rice mortars as grain is husked; in the section from approximately 1:22 and 1:38 you will hear a rhythm that is meant to evoke the sound of this physical activity.

Shimmering Timbre

The shimmering sound of gamelan music is the first thing that listeners often notice. This effect is intentionally produced by the paired melody instruments being tuned to tones very slightly apart. One instrument might be pitched slightly higher than the other; when they are played in unison, this creates a shimmering effect.

A Textured Melody

The melody is played on a group of high-pitched *gender.* You may notice that the melody is often played at breathtaking speeds. How do the musicians do this? Instead of all of the gender playing every note, each pair of musicians plays a single note. Imagine a melody consisting of three notes, C-D-E; in the gamelan, C might be played by one pair of gender players, D played by another, and E by a third set. (Eventually you would return to the first pair of players, as there is in any one ensemble a finite number of lead instruments.) Each pair only has to play one note, in rapid succession. This speed would be impossible to achieve if all three notes were played by a single pair of instruments. In this way, the parts are said to "interlock" to form the melody. These melodies are then repeated to form an ostinato. *Trompong* (or bowl-shaped gongs) enter at points with their own repeated melodic patterns that run counter to the *gender* melodies. Drumming and gongs marking pulsations add to the textural coloration.

Dynamics and Tempo

Dynamics vary widely in *gamelan gong kebyar* pieces, and they change along with tempo to create different sections. More abrupt changes in tempo occur to mark the end of a section and the start of a new one. This involves loud *kebyar*: striking of all the instruments in the ensemble together. Sometimes the loud *kebyar* is just one struck sound, and sometimes the *kebyar* proceeds briefly in an ensemble interlude in which all the instruments are playing in the same rhythm. Listen for these distinctive sections while you study this piece.

A *gender* (metal-keyed xylophone) player.
William Waterfall/PacificStock.com

A CLOSER LOOK   The Gamelan

⊙ EXPLORE MORE on www.mymusiclab.com
◉ SEE MORE Video: The Gamelan

Gamelan music originated in Indonesia in South East Asia. Centuries old, gamelan was largely a ceremonial type of music used in rituals and religious gatherings. The gamelan, like the Western orchestra, includes a variety of instruments: drums and other percussion instruments, gender (a kind of vibraphone), and trompong which are gongs.

Double-headed drums: A pair of double headed drums, one characterized as "male" and the other as "female," establish the rhythmic underpinning for the gamelan. Because the drummers also signal transitions from one section of the composition to another, they have sometimes been compared to Western orchestra conductors.

Trompong: These bowl-shaped brass gongs play one of the lead melody parts of the composition. In this ensemble, there is a single musician assigned to playing this part.

NOT SHOWN: Large suspended gongs. Large gongs suspended in wooden frames are typically included in the Balinese gamelan. These are used to mark off longer rhythmic units.

Steve Vidler/eStock Photography LLC

Gender: Along with the trompong, the gender—brass-keyed xylophones—are the primary lead instruments in the gamelan. The instruments are paired, with one tuned slightly higher than the other, which gives the characteristic "shimmering" sound to gamelan music.

Small percussion instruments: Depending on the individual gamelan, smaller percussion instruments may "fill out" the rhythmic part. Also, some gamelan feature flutes or stringed instruments to augment the melody line.

Gamelan music has had a deep influence on twentieth-century composers in the Western classical tradition, from Debussy's encounter with a gamelan at the famous Paris International Exposition; through composers like Henry Cowell, John Cage, and Lou Harrison, all of whom tried to emulate the percussive sound of gamelan in their compositions; to the minimalists of the 1960s and 1970s, notably Philip Glass (see chapter 56) and Terry Riley. Minimalists were interested in the hypnotic quality of the repeated melodic fragments and interlocking patterns that are created by the gamelan.

In 1975, filmmaker Geoffrey Reggio began working on a film drawing together images of contemporary American life. Using techniques of speeding up and slowing down film, rapid cuts, and unusual camera angles and edits, he wanted to create a kind of montage of what life was like in a highly industrialized society. The result was the film *Koyaanisqatsi*, taken from the Hopi Indian term that means "crazy life" or "life out of balance." Because of the many hypnotic, repetitive images in the film, it seemed natural to invite composer Philip Glass—known for his minimalist scores—to contribute to the work. Glass and Reggio worked an additional three years after the film was completed to carefully fit the music to the imagery. The result was finally issued in 1982, and the film quickly became a favorite on college campuses and in alternative cinemas.

The powerful visual impact of the film is matched by Glass's adventurous score. Although it sounds like an electronic composition, the work is actually scored for conventional brass instruments, strings, organ, and six vocalists. Like many of Glass's works of the period, it consists of short, repeated parts that are layered on top of each other in interlocking patterns, much in the way a gamelan composition is created. The "Vessels" section of the score is sometimes performed separately by small choral ensembles.

Philip Glass at the keyboard, 2003.
Toby WALES/Lebrecht Music & Arts Photo Library

Form

The *gamelan gong kebyar* is structured in different sections with varied tempo and dynamics. In this example there are six sections. The fifth section—occurring between 1:22 and 1:38—features two distinctive rhythmic patterns played in succession that are meant to imitate the sound of rice being pounded in a mortar-and-pestle. *Kebyar* explosions and sections where the ensemble plays in a unified rhythm mark off the sections, and a new section may be recognized by its tempo change.

Unlike traditional Western classical music, the piece seems to have no "direction." The sections simply follow one after the other (something like the Western **suite** structure (see chapter 17). The overall effect is not a dramatic story, with melodies moving forward towards a stunning climax, but rather a static, almost meditative sound. This was highly influential on Western composers of the turn of the twentieth century like Debussy, whose *Voiles*, which we studied in chapter 40, has a similar directionless feeling.

Now listen to this piece again, using the Listening Guide.

CONNECT YOUR PLAYLIST

Ostinato

Find a piece that contains a repeated melodic part.

Example: The extended coda to the Beatles' "Hey Jude" consists of an (seemingly) endless repetition of a simple melody sung as "lah-lah-lah/lah-lah-lah-lah/lah-lah-lah-lah/Hey Jude."

Listening Guide

GO TO www.mymusiclab.com
for the Automated Listening Guide
CD IV • Track 7/Download Track 70

Gamelan Gong Kebyar of Belaluan Recorded: 1928 *Kebyar Ding III,* "Oncang-oncangan" (2:56)

Time	Melodic Texture	Tempo	Dynamics
0:00	The *gender* state an introductory melodic figure.	Moderate	Soft
0:03	The entire *gamelan* strikes simultaneously.		Very loud
0:05	*Gender* play high-pitched rapid melody.	Moderate pulse, rapid ostinato	Medium
0:17	*Gender* and drums abruptly play in unison.	Rapid	Soft to loud (crescendo)
0:20	New section with a slower ostinato.	Slow	Soft
0:32	*Trompong* gongs are struck to mark a strong point in the structure.		Medium
0:40	Drumming begins and accelerates.		Soft
0:42	Higher gongs on the *trompong* enter in an interlocking ostinato.		
0:44	A short rhythmic break and unison pattern.	Stopping	
0:46	Continued *gender* interlock now with *trompong* part added.	Resumption of tempo	
1:07	Drumming again begins and accelerates.		
1:10	Another unison break of the ensemble.		Very loud
1:12	Continuation of interlocking melodic ostinato at a much faster tempo.	Fast	Loud
1:22	Ensemble begins a prolonged unison passage; rhythm becomes grouped around three quick pulses.		

Form

Introduction

Kebyar, or "explosion"

First section. The lowest gong marks the beat (0:05, 0:10) while a higher set of gongs mark other pulses occurring more frequently between the low gong strokes.

Low gong marks last tone of this section.

The second section; the sound of a higher gong marks the rhythmic structure.

Lull in activity

Third section.

Resumption of rhythmic pulses.

Lowest gong strikes pulse (0:52; 1:01).

Kebyar

Fourth section.

Colot

Fifth section.

Student FAQs

How hard is it to play this music?

While the overall piece is complex, each individual part is not that hard to learn. Each player, like the young girl pictured here, has to play a short pattern that is usually repeated many times through a composition. Most Balinese gamelan musicians are not professional and perform in this kind of ensemble only on specific holidays.

Kate MOUNT/Lebrecht Music & Arts Photo Library

Who organizes a gamelan?

Originally, gamelans were sponsored by the Javanese courts and were heard only by the nobility. However, in this century, local villages and clubs have taken over the sponsorship of these ensembles.

Time	Melodic Texture	Tempo	Dynamics
1:34	A counter rhythm (LONG-short-short) begins to be played, set against the main rhythm of three quick pulses. This "rubbing" sound imitates the sound of rice being pounded in order to remove its outer husk.		
1:38	Drum roll	Break	Soft
1:40	The *gender* start a new, slow melody over a slow drum accompaniment. The *gender* are struck by one mallet per tone together.	Slow	Soft
1:58	*Trompong* enter in interlocked ostinato softer than the *gender* melody.		
2:02	*Trompong* discontinue. *Gender* continue the slow melody.		
2:18	*Trompong* again enter in ostinato.		
2:21	*Trompong* discontinue. *Gender* continue the slow melody.		
2:31	*Gender* begin to accelerate the melody.	Beginning to get quicker	Beginning to get louder
2:38			
2:41	*Gender* interlocking becomes more rapid.	Getting faster	Getting louder
2:43	Drumming enters and accelerates. The *gender* accelerate to the end.	Faster to the end	Louder to the end
2:53	Ensemble marks the end of the piece in a *kebyar* unison rhythm.		
2:54	Final drum strike marks the end.		

Form

Lull in activity

Sixth section.

Lowest gong again marks the structure.

Lowest gong tone

Lowest gong tone

Lowest gong tone

Trompong begin marking the rhythm structure in the background.

Low gong begins to strike more regularly.

Trompong join the low gongs to emphasize basic rhythmic structure.

Rhythmic structure increase in tempo.

42

Charles Ives
The Unanswered Question
Composed: 1908

Ives, like other modernists working in the early twentieth century, was trying to find new means of musical expression that went beyond standard conventions of harmony and melody. Nowhere is this struggle between old and new styles more evident than in *The Unanswered Question*.

 *Listen to this first*

((• HEAR MORE on www.mymusiclab.com

Timbre

Listen for the distinctive sound of three different groups of instruments: strings, solo trumpet, and a quartet of wind instruments (two flutes and two clarinets).

Texture

Listen for the layered texture of these instruments. Notice that the strings play continuously, while the trumpet and the quartet of winds come and go.

Harmony

Which group plays the most conventional-sounding musical harmonies? Which plays the most unconventional musical harmonies?

⚙ **LEARN MORE** on
www.mymusiclab.com
Chapter Objectives

Ives both absorbed and rebelled against almost every musical tradition of his time. "Please don't try to make things nice. All the wrong notes are right," he once implored a scribe he had hired to copy some of his music. But what makes notes "wrong" or "right"? Ives, along with many other modernists working in the early twentieth century, was trying to change conventional notions of musical correctness.

Contrasting Timbres

The music is performed by three contrasting groups of instruments:

- **Strings:**   A small string orchestra of violins, violas, cellos, and double basses plays throughout the entire work from beginning to end, without pause.

- **Solo trumpet:**   A single trumpet interjects what Ives called "The Unanswered Question" at five different points over the course of the piece.

- **Wind quartet:**   An ensemble of four wind instruments (two flutes and two clarinets) responds to the trumpet's "question," each time with a different "answer."

Layered Texture

Many composers had used contrasting groups of instruments before—think of Vivaldi's "Winter" from *The Four Seasons* (violin vs. string orchestra, chapter 15) or Mozart's Piano Concerto in A Major, K. 488 (piano vs. full orchestra, chapter 24)—so the idea of having two groups of instruments in dialogue with one another was certainly not new. What is unusual here is the manner in which the strings seem utterly oblivious to the dialogue taking place between the two groups of wind instruments (the solo trumpet and the flute quartet). The result is a kind of layered texture in which three blocks of sound—the strings, the solo trumpet, and the winds—are moving completely independently of one another.

Atonal vs. Tonal Harmony

Ives uses these contrasting timbres and textures to highlight, in microcosm, the conflict between two very different harmonic languages: **tonal** and **atonal**.

- Tonal music establishes a harmonic center of gravity, a central note (the tonic) that provides a strong sense of resolution and closure. We have talked about the role of the tonic in chapters 15 and 40, for example. There is an experiment that you can use to help clarify the significance of the tonic. When we sing the end of "The Star-Spangled Banner" ("... home of the *brave*"), the note for "brave" is the tonic, also known as the "tonal center," of the melody. Try singing the last phrase but not the last note ("O'er the land of the free, and the home of the ...": if you end on the word "the," you will immediately sense the strength and pull of the tonic note in tonal music. You want to go there!

- Atonal music, by contrast, has no harmonic center of gravity. No single note exerts the kind of force, the attraction, that we find in the tonic note in tonal music. Or, to put it more positively, all notes in atonal music are of equal weight: no particular note is more important than any other. Without a tonal center, everything our ears have come to expect notes to do, in the music we have listened to so far in this book and in the music we hear most often in the world around us, simply does not happen. Not only do notes not follow other notes the way we expect, but notes do not line up together the way we expect to hear them, and often they sound like they clash—like they are wrong. This sound is called a **dissonance**. (The opposite sound, the one our ear finds naturally right, is called a **consonance**.) A dissonance gives us the sense that something has not quite been finished or resolved.

In *The Unanswered Question*, the strings play in a decidedly tonal fashion, moving in a slow, measured pace, almost as if playing a very slow hymn. What little dissonance we hear is carefully resolved afterward: nothing is left open-ended or unresolved.

The solo trumpet, by contrast, repeatedly poses a five-note figure that implies no harmonic center at all. The instruments of the wind quartet are even more tonally diffuse and grow rhythmically more independent as the work progresses. The music of all these instruments is atonal.

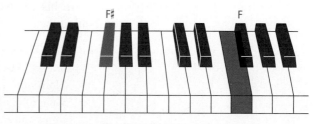

(1874–1954)
Charles Ives
The Unanswered Question
Composed: 1908

GENRE
Programmatic work for chamber orchestra

KEY CONCEPTS
Consonance, dissonance, layered texture.

CHAPTER HIGHLIGHT
Tonality vs. Atonality
Ives's work for string orchestra, wind quartet, and solo trumpet, is in a way music about music, pitting the tonal and rhythmically regular strings against the atonal and rhythmically irregular wind quartet. The trumpet stands somewhere between these two extremes, posing "the unanswered question" as if to ask, "Where is music going?"

Dissonance: Play these two notes at the same time

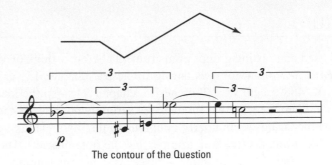

The contour of the Question

Rhythmically uneven

In his foreword to the score of *The Unanswered Question*, Ives hinted at the symbolism behind these contrasting elements of tonal (strings) and atonal (trumpet, wind quartet) writing:

The strings play *ppp* [*pianississimo*—extremely quietly] throughout with no change in tempo. They are to represent "The Silence of the Druids—Who Know, See and Hear Nothing." The trumpet intones "The Perennial Question of Existence," and states it in the same tone of voice each time. But the hunt for "The Invisible Answer" undertaken by the flutes and other human beings, becomes gradually more active, faster and louder through [a section marked] *animando* [animatedly] to [one marked] *con fuoco* [with fire]. This part need not be played in the exact time position indicated. It is played in somewhat of an impromptu way; if there be no conductor, one of the flute players may direct their playing. "The Fighting Answerers,". . . after a "secret conference," seem to realize a futility, and begin to mock "The Question"—the strife is over for the moment. After they disappear, "The Question" is asked for the last time, and "The Silences" are heard beyond in "Undisturbed Solitude."[1]

It is revealing that Ives should choose to represent this metaphysical debate through a simultaneous contrast of the musical old (conventional harmony and regular rhythms within a single tempo) and the musical new (unconventional harmony and irregular rhythms across shifting tempos). Like other modernist composers of the early twentieth century, Ives was trying to shock listeners out of what he perceived to be their all-too-comfortable habit of listening to "beautiful" music—listeners who, like the Druids of *The Unanswered Question*, are content within themselves and oblivious to all that is around them. Ives elsewhere wrote that

> . . . beauty in music is too often confused with something that lets the ear lie back in an easy chair. Many sounds that we are used to do not bother us, and for that reason we are inclined to call them beautiful. Frequently—possibly almost invariably—analytical and impersonal tests will show, we believe, that when a new or unfamiliar work is accepted as beautiful on its first hearing, its fundamental quality is one that tends to put the mind to sleep. A narcotic is not always unnecessary, but it is seldom a basis of progress—that is, wholesome evolution in any creative experience.[2]

Now listen to this work once again, using the Listening Guide.

[1]Foreword by Charles Ives to the score of the *Unanswered Question*. Published by Peer International Corporation. International Copyright secured. Used by permission. All rights reserved.

[2]From ESSAYS BEFORE A SONATA, THE MAJORITY AND OTHER WRITINGS BY CHARLES IVES by Charles Ives, edited by Howard Boatwright. Copyright © 1961, 1962 by W. W. Norton & Company, Inc., renewed 1990. Used by permission of W. W. Norton & Company, Inc. This selection may not be reproduced, stored in a retrieval system, or transmitted in any form or by any means without the prior written permission of the publisher. Book available at www.amazon.com/Essays-Before-Sonata-Majority-Writings.

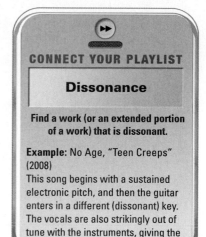

CONNECT YOUR PLAYLIST

Dissonance

Find a work (or an extended portion of a work) that is dissonant.

Example: No Age, "Teen Creeps" (2008)
This song begins with a sustained electronic pitch, and then the guitar enters in a different (dissonant) key. The vocals are also strikingly out of tune with the instruments, giving the song an overall disturbing feeling.

EXPAND YOUR PLAYLIST

Tonal versus Atonal

Ives was not the only composer of his generation to write music that openly contrasts tonal and atonal blocks of sound.

Arnold Schoenberg
- *Pierrot lunaire*, op. 21, no. 1, "O alter Duft." The music of the finale of this song cycle (see chapter 43), which has been entirely atonal to this point, becomes surprisingly tonal.
- String Quartet no. 2, op. 10. The third movement includes a distorted version of the children's folksong "O du lieber Augustin" (known in English as "The More We Get Together" or "Did You Ever See a Lassie?").

Alban Berg
- Violin Concerto, finale. Berg quotes a well-known chorale melody "Es ist genug" ("It is enough") in the finale, along with J.S. Bach's harmonization of it, in an otherwise atonal work.

Béla Bartók
- String Quartet no. 5, third movement. This Scherzo "Alla bulgarese" ("In the Bulgarian Style") juxtaposes an intentionally cheap-sounding tonal melody against music that, while not atonal, is not clearly tonal either.

((•• HEAR SAMPLES on **www.mymusiclab.com**

Listening Guide

GO TO www.mymusiclab.com
for the Automated Listening Guide
CD IV • Track 8/Download Track 71

Charles Ives Composed: 1908 *The Unanswered Question* (4:34)

Time	Timbre	Texture	Harmony
0:00	Strings	Homophonic throughout by themselves	Strings tonal throughout
1:08	Trumpet	Monophonic by itself; polyphonic when heard against strings throughout	Trumpet atonal throughout
1:27	Wind quartet	Polyphonic by itself; more densely polyphonic when heard against strings	Wind quartet atonal throughout
1:42	Trumpet		
1:54	Wind quartet		
2:14	Trumpet		
2:26	Wind quartet		
2:46	Trumpet		
2:56	Wind quartet		
3:15	Trumpet		
3:27	Wind quartet		
3:39	Trumpet		
3:47	Wind quartet		Strings land on final (tonic) chord at 4:10 and sustain to the end.
4:14	Trumpet		

Student FAQs

What does Ives mean by the strings representing "The Silence of the Druids"?

Druids were Celtic priests in pre-Christian Britain and Ireland. It's not entirely clear what Ives meant by this remark, but the Druids are (or were) mystical figures of the distant past who practiced ancient rituals—which seems consistent with the role Ives assigns to the strings in this work: tonal, brooding, slow-moving, unchanging.

How did early critics respond to this work?

Remarkably, *The Unanswered Question* did not receive its first performance until 1946, almost 40 years after it was written. By that point, critics had begun to realize just how far ahead of his time Ives really was, and they responded positively. Had it been performed at the time of its composition, the work would probably not have been received nearly as well.

PROFILE   **Charles Ives** (1874–1954)

Against the Grain

I ves both absorbed and rebelled against almost every musical tradition of his time. The son of a Civil War bandmaster, he grew up in Danbury, Connecticut, where he learned many different kinds of music: the orchestral repertory of the concert hall, church hymns, band music, and popular songs in the parlors of the town's homes. Ives worked all of these idioms into his own music, often in the same work.

As a composer, Ives's career path also went against the grain. If a composer "has a nice wife and some nice children," he once asked, "how can he let them starve on his dissonances?" His "day job" was in insurance, and as it turned out, Ives did quite well for himself. He composed in his spare time, but his music was rarely performed or published during his lifetime. Declining health forced him to more or less give up composition after 1918. Only toward the end of his life did critics and performers begin to take note of his music. By the time he died, he was recognized as a pioneer who had challenged convention and gone against the grain well before other American composers would take up the cause of modernism.

Charles Ives in his study, ca. 1947.
CORBIS—NY

◉➜ **EXPLORE MORE** on **www.mymusiclab.com**

◀◀   EXPAND YOUR PLAYLIST: IVES   ▶▶

- ***Piano Sonata no. 2: Concord, Mass., 1840–60.*** A solo sonata with movements devoted individually to Emerson, Hawthorne, the Alcotts, and Thoreau.

- **String Quartet no. 2**. In Ives's own words, this work depicts "four men who converse, discuss, argue . . . fight, shake hands, shut up—then walk up the mountainside to view the firmament."

- ***Three Places in New England.*** A series of orchestral movements based on specific locales. The second is "Putnam's Camp," about

the dream of a small boy who falls asleep during a Fourth of July celebration at the site of a Revolutionary War camp.

- **Symphony no. 2.** This piece uses thematic material derived from patriotic tunes, Stephen Foster melodies, gospel hymns, and a college song.

((◉ **HEAR SAMPLES** on **www.mymusiclab.com**

⊘ **TEST YOURSELF** on **www.mymusiclab.com**   Flashcards and chapter tests

43

Arnold Schoenberg
"Columbine" from *Pierrot lunaire*
Composed: 1912

Can anguished thoughts be expressed through beautiful music? "Columbine," one of a set of 21 songs for soprano and a small ensemble of instruments from Arnold Schoenberg's *Pierrot lunaire*, offers one answer.

Listen to this first

((• HEAR MORE on www.mymusiclab.com

Timbre

How would you describe the vocalist's sound? Is it singing? Speech?

Harmony

Does the music feel at rest anywhere, or as though it finds resolution in a certain place? In other words, do you hear a tonal center?

Word-Music Relationships

The text being sung here expresses the despair of a spurned lover. How does the music capture this feeling?

LEARN MORE on
www.mymusiclab.com
Chapter Objectives

LEARN MORE on
www.mymusiclab.com
MyMusicLibrary: "The Last Word in Musical Anarchy"

"Columbine" is not beautiful in any conventional sense. Schoenberg purposely set this anguished text to music that is equally tormented. He saw no point in trying to project pain through beauty. Instead, his music captures pain itself.

Schoenberg's *Pierrot lunaire* represents **expressionism**, a broad artistic movement that flourished in music, painting, and literature in the early decades of the twentieth century. Expressionist painters used exaggerated imagery and sometimes garish colors to create art that was not so much beautiful as probing. Their concern was not with the representation of external objects, but rather with the expression of inner moods and thoughts. Expressionism sought to give voice (expression) to the unconscious, to make apparent humanity's deepest and often darkest emotions. In Freudian terms, expressionist art bypasses the ego—the conscious self—and aims straight for the id, the unconscious bank of basic instincts and drives. Expressionist art rejects conventional techniques of representation, favoring instead devices that exaggerate and distort. Psychological truth comes before beauty, and inner emotion comes before any sense of external reality. Widely dismissed by more conservative critics in its time, expressionist art has since come to be recognized as one of the most important outcomes of modernism in the twentieth century.

Pierrot is the pale, moonstruck clown of the *commedia dell'arte*, a type of improvisational theater that originated during the Renaissance in Italy but eventually spread across Europe. Its stock characters include such figures as Harlequin and Punch and Judy. These figures always behave according to type: the cunning Harlequin is constantly playing tricks; the anarchic Punch is constantly swinging at other characters with his stick; and the lovesick Pierrot is forever pining away, unduly influenced by beams of moonlight ("lunaire" = "lunar"). Pierrot's view of life is darkly tragic yet at the same time laughable: he can scarcely control his own emotions and takes himself so seriously that we alternately sympathize with and scorn him.

Pierrot was in this sense the perfect vehicle for expressionist art, which sought to remove all inhibitions on personal expression. Schoenberg was drawn to the surreal, violent, and eerie imagery in Albert Giraud's *Pierrot lunaire*, a cycle of poems that had recently been translated from their original French into German. The text of the selection here, the second of the 21 songs in Schoenberg's cycle, concerns Columbine or Columbina, another character from the commedia dell'arte. She is a sharp-witted maidservant and is usually linked romantically to Harlequin. Here, Pierrot laments that Columbine has rebuffed him; he sings the lament of a rejected lover.

Timbre: The *Sprechstimme*

Throughout *Pierrot lunaire*, Schoenberg calls on the soprano to sing in a manner that is halfway between speech and song. He called this device ***Sprechstimme***, which means literally "Speech-Voice," with "voice" understood here in the sense of "singing voice." Everyday speech has its own notes, but we do not sustain those notes. In *Sprechstimme*, Schoenberg calls for the singer to hit—but not sustain—precise pitches. Thus when the singer hits the note, she drops her voice. This creates an eerie, disassociated sort of sound that fits well with the eerie, disassociated texts of *Pierrot lunaire*.

Sprechstimme is similar to the recitative of earlier eras (see chapters 10, 11, 25, and 36) in some respects but different in important ways. Like conventional recitative, it is syllabic, which makes it more like speech and less like lyrical song. But in *Sprechstimme*, the notes are delivered slowly enough so that the sound of the voice actually tails off at the end of each word, creating something that sounds like someone talking in an exaggeratedly slow fashion. The vocalist has to sustain the tone to connect the words, but the tone is not sustained as it would be in conventional singing: the vocalist hits the specified pitch but then releases it almost at once. The effect is eerie and somehow surreal.

Harmony: Atonality

Debussy had used the whole-tone scale in *Voiles* (see chapter 40) to create a harmonic idiom in which all notes are of equal weight and no single note forms a center of attraction (a "tonic"). Ives, similarly, had explored the possibility of writing melodies or melodic fragments also lacking a tonal center. Yet both composers had kept one foot squarely in the tonal universe: Debussy by using a single tone underneath the entire work to ground it all, and Ives by playing off the atonal trumpet and wind instruments against the thoroughly tonal strings. In *Pierrot lunaire*, Schoenberg breaks all ties with the tonal tradition to create a work that is thoroughly **atonal**, without any sense of a tonal center or resolution or harmonic closure. From its

1874–1951
Arnold Schoenberg
"Columbine" from
Pierrot lunaire
Composed: 1912

GENRE
Song cycle for voice and chamber ensemble

KEY CONCEPTS
Atonality, *sprechstimme*.

CHAPTER HIGHLIGHT
Expressionism
Expressionism gave priority to truth over beauty, including the sometimes less-than-beautiful workings of the human psyche. In grappling with raw human emotions, expressionist works like Schoenberg's *Pierrot lunaire* could be grotesque and surreal.

A recent Pierrot. The facial expression captures the character's sense of longing and anxiety. Pierrot's mood is subject to sudden and unpredictable changes—exuberant one moment, lugubrious the next. Like a true expressionist, he wears his heart on his sleeve.

Darren Matthews/Alamy Images

CONNECT YOUR PLAYLIST

Sprechstimme

Find a work that incorporates the technique of *Sprechstimme*.

Example: "Your Love is My Drum" by Ke$ha (2010)
In the verses of this song, Ke$ha uses *Sprechstimme* consistently (in contrast to the harmonized singing on the chorus).

first performance until today, many listeners have found this kind of composition jarring and unpleasant, while others have found in it a powerful means of expression. What better way to convey the agony of rejection and Pierrot's overwhelming sense of alienation from the world than by ignoring the tonal tradition?

Word-Music Relationships: Expressing Anguish

Pierrot is suffering from an inability to express his emotions through action. He wants to scatter white rose petals on Columbine's hair but lacks the courage to pluck even a single rose. He sings in mostly very short notes, often broken by short pauses, creating a sense of breathlessness. One repeated phrase comes in for special treatment: whenever he sings of the "miraculous white roses," the music makes large leaps or descends to the very lowest range of the singer's register, or both.

When Pierrot begins to describe the way in which he would pluck the petals off the roses and strew them in Columbine's hair, the music makes a sudden shift: the flute and clarinet, silent up until this point, enter with a repeated three-note figure that seems to mimic the sound of petals dropping. The music is as quietly desperate as Pierrot himself.

With these points in mind, listen again to this selection, using the Listening Guide.

HISTORICAL CONTEXT   Expressionist Film

Expressionism came of age in the years just after World War I, when filmmaking was becoming a serious art form. A number of prominent directors around this time, especially in Germany, made movies that reflect the expressionist outlook. These films tend to be dark, severe, and highly stylized. They are often gruesome and surreal. The plots of these movies rarely involve action and revolve instead around issues of insanity and the psychologically abnormal.

Fritz Lang (1890–1976) is widely regarded as the greatest of all expressionistic directors. Like Schoenberg, he immigrated to the United States because of his Jewish ancestry. Lang's most famous films, *Metropolis* (1927) and *M* (1931), won international acclaim and still hold their own in movie houses today. The tradition of expressionist film lives on in the work of such modern-day directors as Tim Burton (*Batman Returns, Edward Scissorhands*) and David Lynch (*Eraserhead, Lost Highway*).

A still from *The Cabinet of Dr. Caligari*, an early (1920) German expressionist film about the head of an insane asylum who is himself a serial murderer. Notice the distorted use of perspective, the grotesque costumes and makeup, and the stylized decor of the room.
The Museum of Modern Art/Film Stills Archive

Listening Guide

GO TO www.mymusiclab.com
for the Automated Listening Guide
CD IV • Track 9/Download Track 72

Arnold Schoenberg Composed: 1912 "Columbine" from *Pierrot lunaire* (1:44)

Time	Original German Text	English Translation	Timbre	Word-Music Relationships
0:00	Des Mondlichts bleiche Blüten, Die weißen Wunderrosen, Blühn in den Julinächten— O bräch ich eine nur!	Moonlight's pale blossoms, The miraculous white roses, Blossom in the nights of July Oh, if I could pluck just one!	Vocal soloist (*Sprechstime*), piano, and violin, which alternates between bowed and plucked (pizzicato) passages	Conjunct motion for most words except those describing the "miraculous white roses," which are set to large leaps. Notes are short, broken, breathless.
0:27	Mein banges Leid zu lindern, Such ich am dunklen Strome Des Mondlichts bleiche Blüten, Die weißen Wunderrosen.	To still my anxious suffering, I seek alongside the dark stream Moonlight's pale blossoms, The miraculous white roses.		The notes of "the miraculous white roses" go extremely deep in the singer's range.
0:52	Gestillt wär all mein Sehnen, Dürft ich so märchenheimlich, So selig leis —entblättern Auf deine braunen Haare Des Mondlichts bleiche Blüten!	All my longing would be stilled If I could, in fairy-tale fashion, Secretly and softly—pluck onto your brown tresses Moonlight's pale blossoms!	Vocal soloist (*Sprechstime*), flute and clarinet enter for the first time at 1:13, on the word *entblättern* ("pluck").	Repetitive three-note pattern in the wind instruments, beginning at 1:13, reflects the image of Pierrot dropping the white rose petals onto Columbine's brown hair.

Student FAQs

Why would anyone want to listen to such ugly music?

"Ugly" is in the ear of the listener. Besides, works of art don't always have to be beautiful to be moving. For many listeners, a work like Schoenberg's is appealing not because it is beautiful, but because it is true, because it confronts the reality of the mind and doesn't try to sugarcoat things.

Why Sprechstimme?

Schoenberg probably felt that normal singing would sound too, well, normal. So he settled on a technique that would make the voice seem stylized and distorted, the sonic counterpart of expressionist painting and (later) expressionist film (see Historical Context, "Expressionist Film").

Schoenberg (third from left) with the ensemble of musicians who performed *Pierrot lunaire* for the first time (Berlin, 1912).
© Arnold Schoenberg Center, Vienna

PROFILE   Arnold Schoenberg (1874–1951)

The Composer as Outsider

Schoenberg was a tortured soul, an outsider who longed to be accepted yet never felt comfortable regardless of his place in the world. Widely perceived as a musical radical, he considered himself a traditionalist who was extending the heritage of Bach, Beethoven, and Brahms. Born Jewish, he converted to Christianity but later went back to Judaism. An Austrian by birth, he moved back and forth between Vienna and Berlin, finally immigrating to the United States when the Nazis assumed power in Germany. (It was in the United States that he changed the spelling of his name from Schönberg to Schoenberg.) He eventually moved to Los Angeles and bought a home in Brentwood, across the street from Shirley Temple and only a few doors down from what would become O. J. Simpson's house.

As composers challenged tonality and then finally pushed beyond it entirely, Schoenberg began a relentless search for a new system for organizing music. What he came up with, in the 1920s, completely altered the way composers thought about their craft. Twelve-tone composition, as his system was called, organized pitches into rows of 12 different notes. Each of the 12 tones had equal weight, and none was repeated before all the others had been played. We will take a closer look at the principles of 12-tone composition when we look at the work of Ruth Crawford (chapter 49).

In 1935 Schoenberg was appointed to the faculty of the University of Southern California; he later taught at UCLA, and he became an American citizen in 1941. He had many

Arnold Schoenberg, ca. 1920. Notice the similarity of this photographic portrait by Man Ray with Schoenberg's painting "The Gaze."

Man Ray (1874–1951) "Arnold Schoenberg". 1930 AKG Images. © 2010 Estate of Man Ray/Artists Rights Society (ARS), NY

"The Gaze" by Arnold Schoenberg, 1910.

Arnold Schoenberg, "Gaze". Oil on Cardboard, 32.2 x 24.5 cm. Signed and dated (b.r.): Arnold Schoenberg May 1910 Catalogue raisonne 61. © Belmont Music Publishers, Los Angeles, © VBK, Vienna

pupils in the United States and exerted a powerful influence. Every subsequent generation of composers has studied Schoenberg's music carefully, and in this sense he stands as one of the most influential composers of the entire century—maybe *the* most influential.

⊙➤ EXPLORE MORE on www.mymusiclab.com

👁 SEE MORE on www.mymusiclab.com
Watch the Documentary "A Brand New Day"

◀◀   EXPAND YOUR PLAYLIST: SCHOENBERG   ▶▶

- *Chamber Symphony no. 1 in E Major, op. 9.* One of Schoenberg's last works to bear a key designation ("E Major").

- *Variations for Orchestra.* A 12-tone work that is a series of variations on a 12-tone theme.

- *Erwartung.* A "monodrama" for soprano and orchestra, a stream-of-consciousness monologue from a woman who discovers the corpse of her lover in the woods.

- *A Survivor from Warsaw.* A cantata for narrator, male chorus, and orchestra, based on a report of Jews being shipped to the gas chambers in World War II bursting into the *Shema Yisrael*, a sung prayer.

- *Moses und Aron.* An opera based on Moses and the Israelites in the wilderness.

((•) HEAR SAMPLES on www.mymusiclab.com

EXPAND YOUR PLAYLIST

Expressionism

Schoenberg was the leading composer of the expressionist movement, but others followed his lead and developed their own personal varieties of expressionism.

Anton Webern
- Six Bagatelles, op. 9. These aphoristic works for string quartet, by an Austrian protégé of Schoenberg, are highly atonal and intense. The title ("Little Trifles") is ironic. These works are anything but trifles, in spite of their size.
- *Five Pieces for Orchestra*, op. 10. Like all Webern's works, these are brief but concentrated. Webern's music does not "scream" in the same way that some of Schoenberg's does, but it can be quietly desperate.

Alban Berg
- *Wozzeck*. This expressionist opera, by another Austrian disciple of Schoenberg, is a mainstay of the operatic repertory today; its story, about the fate of a poor soldier, still exerts a powerful effect on audiences around the world.
- *Lulu*. Another highly successful expressionist opera, this one about the rise and fall of a *femme fatale*.

Ernst Křenek
- *Jonny spielt auf!* (*Johnny Strikes Up the Band*). This opera, by an Austrian composer of Czech ancestry, mixes jazz idioms with atonal expressionism.

HEAR SAMPLES on **www.mymusiclab.com**

TEST YOURSELF on **www.mymusiclab.com**   Flashcards and chapter tests

44

Igor Stravinsky
The Rite of Spring, Part One
Composed: 1913

Stravinsky's ballet *The Rite of Spring* (*Le Sacre du printemps*) was so new and different that the audience at its premiere in Paris in 1913 rioted. Many found the harmonies, melodies, and rhythms to be beyond the limits of the acceptable, and they let their feelings be known. Yet within a few years it became an audience favorite around the world and remains so today.

Listen to this first

((• HEAR MORE on www.mymusiclab.com

Harmony

Are the harmonies here tonal or atonal? Do you hear a harmonic center of gravity?

Melody

Listen for the fragmentary nature of the melodies, which seem to start and stop suddenly, without warning.

Rhythm

What is the meter of this work? Can you tap a regular pattern of beats? Are some sections more regular than others?

Timbre

The enormous size of the orchestra for this ballet was virtually without precedent. Listen for the variety of sounds in all families of instruments: woodwinds, brass, strings, and percussion.

Word-Music Relationships

The dancers present through movement and gesture the storyline of the ballet. What images, events, or moods come to mind as you listen to this music?

⚙ LEARN MORE on
www.mymusiclab.com
Chapter Objectives

In ballet, music tells a story through movement. The idea of interpreting sound through gesture on stage has a long history, dating back to ancient times. Many operas, from the Baroque Era onward, have incorporated dance scenes. But the ballet as an independent genre—the focus of an evening's entertainment—did not come into its own until the nineteenth century. It has flourished since that time, however, thanks to works like Stravinksy's *The Rite of Spring*.

Stravinsky's *Rite* was commissioned by Sergei Diaghilev for his Ballets Russes (The Russian Ballet), a company of largely Russian dancers whose home base was in Paris (see "The Business of Dance," page 375). The score follows the scenario of a ballet Stravinsky himself recalls as having first conceived in "a fleeting vision which came to me as a complete surprise. . . . I saw in my imagination a solemn pagan rite. Sage elders, seated in a circle, watched a young girl dance herself to death. They were sacrificing her to propitiate the God of Spring. I heard and I wrote what I heard. I am the vessel through which *Le Sacre* passed." In the end, the scenario for the ballet was drawn up by Stravinsky and Nikolai Roerich, a leading expert in Russian folklore and ancient ritual. Originally called *The Great Sacrifice*, the ballet was eventually divided into two parts: (1) The Adoration of the Earth, and (2) The Sacrifice.

Polytonal Harmonies

Does Stravinsky's *The Rite of Spring* lack a tonal center, as Schoenberg's *Pierrot lunaire* and parts of Ives's *Unanswered Question* do? Is this atonal music? No, it is not. The reason the harmonies of *The Rite of Spring* sound different, and the reason the tonal center is hard to find, is not because there isn't one, but because at any given moment there is often *more* than one. The repetitive chords at 3:36, for example, juxtapose two conventional harmonies in a way that creates a new dissonance of its own. Each of the two chords is tonal in its own right, but when combined, they clash. This kind of harmony is called **polytonal**.

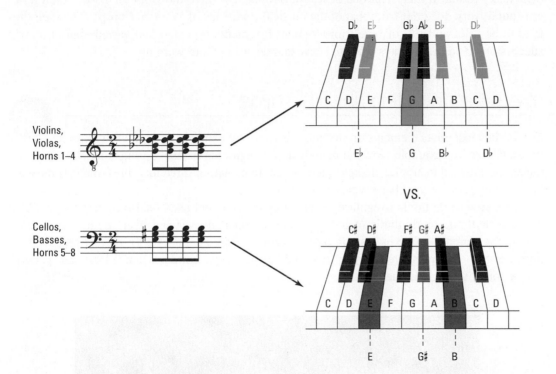

To hear this clash of tonalities, ask someone who knows how to play the piano to play an E-major chord with the left hand. Then ask that person to play an E-flat seventh chord with the right hand. Separately, the two chords sound perfectly consonant. Finally, ask the person to play the two chords together. Simultaneously, they sound dissonant. This is an example of **polytonality**.

Pentatonic Melodies

Many of the melodies in *The Rite of Spring* are built on the **pentatonic scale**. As its name implies ("pent" = "five," as in the word "pentagon"), this scale consists of five notes instead of the conventional seven. An example of a melody based on a pentatonic scale may be found at the beginning of the "Spring Round Dance" (8:22).

Like Dvořák before him (see chapter 39), Stravinsky was trying to capture a folk-like sound. The setting of this ballet, after all, is "Pagan Russia," before the arrival of Christianity there in the tenth century. In the context of this ballet, the pentatonic melodies—some of which Stravinsky found in transcriptions of Russian folksong—give the work an exotic, even modern sound, very different from that of the musical traditions of Western Europe. The melodies tend to be brief and full of repetitions—small fragments repeated and varied many times in succession—and they always seem to arrive and depart without warning.

Irregular and Regular Rhythms

One of the most novel elements of this music is its use of extremely irregular rhythms at times. Notice, for example, how the melody at the beginning of the "Spring Round Dance" (see the earlier musical example) changes meter three times within three measures: the first measure has five beats, the second has seven, and the third has six.

This kind of rhythmic irregularity is offset by the frequent use of **ostinato** figures, in which a single rhythmic or rhythmic-melodic gesture is repeated over and over again, many times. Listen, for example, to the ostinato in the low strings beginning at 8:48. This figure repeats itself no fewer than 32 times over the next two-and-half minutes. Similar extended ostinato patterns can be found throughout the work.

A recent production of *The Rite of Spring*, performed by the Kirov Ballet, using recreations of the original 1913 costuming and choreography.

Laurie Lewis/Lebrecht Music & Arts Photo Library

HISTORICAL CONTEXT   The Business of Dance

Sergei Diaghilev (1872–1929) had a great eye for talent. As director of the Ballets Russes in Paris, he encouraged the still relatively unknown Igor Stravinsky to write music for his company. In addition to Stravinsky, he engaged groundbreaking composers such as Claude Debussy, Maurice Ravel, Erik Satie, Richard Strauss, Sergei Prokofiev, and Francis Poulenc. And he worked with an equally impressive array of artists on set designs, including Pablo Picasso, Leon Bakst, and Juan Gris. Many of the dancers and choreographers in his company became legends in their own right, including Vaslav Nijinsky (chief choreographer for *The Rite of Spring*), Anna Pavlova, and Georges Balanchine (1904–1983), the last of whom became a leading force in the world of American ballet.

Diaghilev combined his sense of taste with the skills of a businessman. The early years of the Ballets Russes, from its founding in 1909 until the outbreak of World War I in 1914, were the most financially successful. The musical repertory consistently included new works by promising young composers, which were always a topic of conversation among the Parisian elite. Even the riot at the premiere of *The Rite of Spring* produced excellent press for the company (see "The Audience Riots," page 382).

The years after the war were less rewarding. Cultural life did not return to its earlier level for several years, and Diaghilev had to use great ingenuity to keep his company afloat. The revival of *The Rite of Spring* in 1920 offers a case in point. The work was in great demand—audiences *wanted* to hear the work

Sergei Diaghilev, the Russian impresario who found great success in Paris through his collaborations with Stravinsky, Picasso, and others.
Lebrecht Music & Arts/Lebrecht Music & Arts Photo Library

now, not shout it down—but the orchestra demanded by the score was enormous, almost twice the size of the company's normal ensemble, and all 97 musicians had to be paid. Diaghilev turned to the fashion designer Gabrielle ("Coco") Chanel for help, and she contributed a large sum of money that made the production possible. After Diaghilev's death, the Ballets Russes struggled, changing its name and locale at various times but never recreating its earlier success.

"The Elect" from Stravinsky's *Rite of Spring* in the original 1913 production. The innovative costumes and masks were by Russian designer N. K. Roerich and were part of what made the original production so shocking to audiences.
Lebrecht Music & Arts/Lebrecht Music & Arts Photo Library

Timbre and The Mega-Orchestra

The orchestra for Brahms's Fourth Symphony (1885) seems like a chamber ensemble by comparison to the orchestra of Stravinsky's *The Rite of Spring*, which calls for an ensemble consisting of the following:

Woodwinds:
1 piccolo
3 flutes, 1 doubling on second piccolo
1 alto flute
1 English horn
4 oboes, 1 doubling on second English horn
1 E♭ clarinet
3 clarinets, 1 doubling on second bass clarinet
1 bass clarinet
4 bassoons, 1 doubling on second contrabassoon
1 contrabassoon

Brass:
8 French horns, 2 doubling on tenor tubas
1 high trumpet (D trumpet)
4 trumpets
1 bass trumpet
3 trombones
2 tubas

Percussion: Timpani, bass drum, cymbals, gong, guero ("scraper"), tambourine, triangle

Strings: Violins 1 & 2, violas, cellos, double basses

See A Closer Look: The Mega-Orchestra, pages 380–381.

Unsung Words: The Scenario

In ballet, the dancers present, through their movement, a story line known as the **scenario**. The words of the scenario are not sung, but they shape the form of the music directly. In the fall of 1913, a few months after the work's premiere, Stravinsky drew up the following description of the ballet's scenario:

> *The Rite of Spring* is a musical choreographic work. It represents pagan Russia and is unified by a single idea: the mystery and great surge of creative power of Spring. The piece has no plot, but the choreographic sequence is as follows:
>
> **Part One: The Adoration of the Earth**
> The Spring celebration. The pipers pipe and young men tell fortunes. The old woman enters. She knows the mystery of nature and how to predict the future. Young girls with painted faces come in from the river in single file. They dance the Spring dances. Games start. The Spring *Khorovod* [a stately dance]. The people divide into two opposed groups. The holy procession of the wise old men. The oldest and wisest interrupts the Spring games, which come to a stop. The people pause trembling before the Great Action. The old men bless the earth. The Kiss of the Earth. The people dance passionately on the earth, sanctifying it and becoming one with it.
>
> **Part Two: The Great Sacrifice**
> At night the virgins hold mysterious games, walking in circles. One of the virgins is consecrated as the victim and is twice pointed to by fate, being caught twice in the perpetual circle of walking-in-rounds. The virgins honor her, the Chosen One, with a marital dance. They invoke the ancestors and entrust the Chosen One to the old wise men. She sacrifices herself in the presence of the old men in the Great Sacred Dance, THE GREAT SACRIFICE.[1]

[1]From Vera Stravinsky and Robert Craft, *Stravinsky in Pictures and Documents* (New York: Simon & Schuster, 1978), p. 75. Reprinted by permission of Robert Craft and Frankfurt, Garbus, Klein & Selz.

CONNECT YOUR PLAYLIST

Ostinato

Find a piece that uses an ostinato at some point.

Example: Jonathan Larson, "Seasons of Love" from *Rent* (1993)
This song from the musical *Rent* begins with an ostinato figure in the piano, which continues unchanged through much of the song.

PROFILE   **Igor Stravinsky** (1882–1971)

"Modernsky"

Like many of today's pop artists—Bob Dylan, David Bowie, Madonna—Stravinsky was constantly reinventing himself. The son of a famous Russian operatic bass singer, many of Stravinsky's early works, including *The Rite of Spring*, reflect his Russian ancestry. By 1917 he was at the forefront of a new movement, Neoclassicism, which turned its back on the huge orchestras and complex textures of his own earlier music. In this period, Stravinsky wrote music that was more clearly tonal, using forms and rhythmic patterns that owed much to the music of the eighteenth century. Many other composers followed his lead.

With the advent of World War II, Stravinsky continued his travels settling in Los Angeles and becoming a U.S. citizen in 1945 (see Stations in Stravinsky's Life, page 379). Late in life, to everyone's astonishment, he began writing 12-tone music, the most intellectually rigorous and severe form of atonal music. Even at an advanced age, the old composer could learn new tricks.

From the 1920s onward, Stravinsky was widely regarded as one of the century's two greatest composers, together with Arnold Schoenberg (see chapter 43). Unlike Schoenberg, however, Stravinsky was able to connect with audiences so that he had quite a following despite his modernism (one clever critic dubbed him "Modernsky"). He had no direct students, but his influence on subsequent generations of composers has been profound.

⊙➤ **EXPLORE MORE** on www.mymusiclab.com

⚙ **LEARN MORE** on www.mymusiclab.com
Stravinsky on Musical "Objectivity"

Stravinsky (seated) visiting Claude Debussy, a composer whose works he admired enormously, ca. 1912. Like Debussy, Stravinsky sought to expand the vocabulary of music.
CORBIS—NY

⏪ EXPAND YOUR PLAYLIST: STRAVINSKY ⏩

- *Petrouchka*. A ballet written for Diaghilev shortly before *The Rite of Spring*, also based on Russian themes.

- *Pulcinella*. A ballet in the Neoclassical style, again for Diaghilev, based in part on actual melodies from the eighteenth century.

- *Symphony in Three Movements*. Another Neoclassical work that includes a fugue.

- *The Rake's Progress*. An English-language opera set to a libretto by the English poet W.H. Auden, tracing the decline and fall of a libertine.

- *Canticum sacrum*. A late, 12-tone work for tenor, baritone, chorus, and orchestra.

((• **HEAR SAMPLES** on www.mymusiclab.com

In writing *The Rite of Spring*, Stravinsky gave each of these scenes its own distinctive music. The form of the work is **through-composed**. There is very little repetition of music between individual sections.

With these points in mind, listen once again to Part One of Stravinsky's The Rite of Spring, using the Listening Guide.

Listening Guide

GO TO www.mymusiclab.com
for the Automated Listening Guide
CD IV • Track 10/Download Track 73

Igor Stravinsky Composed: 1913 *Rite of Spring,* Part One (excerpt) (16:40)

Time	Word-Music Relationships The Scenario	Timbre	Rhythm
0:00	**Introduction** (the curtain remains down). Stravinsky later said that this introduction "should represent the awakening of nature" after a long Russian winter, "the scratching, gnawing, and wiggling of birds and beasts."	Wind instruments predominate. Each instrument seems to function independently of the others, from the solo on the bassoon at the opening through the gradual addition of horns, clarinets, English horn, oboes, and flutes.	Free
3:14	*The Spring celebration. The pipers pipe and young men tell fortunes. The old woman enters. She knows the mystery of nature and how to predict the future.*	The entrance of the fortuneteller (3:14) is signaled by the appearance of an ostinato motif in the violins (pizzicato).	
3:36	**The Harbingers of Spring; Dances of the Adolescents.** *Young girls with painted faces come in from the river in single file. They dance the Spring dances.*	Full orchestra. Strings enter in force for the first time.	Same chord repeated many times, but with no predictable pattern of accent
6:56	**Game of Abduction.** *The games start.*	Full orchestra, including heavy beating of timpani and bass drum.	Frenzied pace, fast rhythm
8:22	**Spring Round Dance.** *The Spring Khorovod (a traditional Russian circle dance).*	High winds introduce the main melody, played on clarinets.	A slow, stately dance, which transforms the preceding mood of frenzy into one of calm. Ostinato bass begins at 8:48.
12:16	**Games of Rival Tribes.** *The people divide into two opposed groups.*	Percussion and low brass open this section.	Another energetic section based on a succession of ostinato patterns.
14:16	**Procession of the Sage.** *The holy procession of the wise old men. The oldest and wisest interrupts the Spring games, which come to a stop.*	Steady drum beat, with prominent brass parts	Another section based on a slow, steady, ostinato pattern. Comes to a sudden and extremely abrupt stop.
14:58	**Adoration of the Earth.** *The people pause trembling before the Great Action. The old men bless the earth. The Kiss of the Earth.*	Sustained low winds, with high notes on double bass, punctuated by timpani	For the first time, the forward momentum of the music stops.
15:20	**The Dance of the Earth.** *The people dance passionately on the earth, sanctifying it and becoming one with it.*	Full orchestra	Ostinato pattern in bass.

Melody

Fragments are mostly based on a pentatonic scale. Several of the melodies are based on Russian folk tunes that Stravinsky knew from a published source.

The ostinato figure that occurs here will come back later.

Ostinato figure throughout (3:46, 4:01, 5:02, etc.); melodic fragments above and below

Short fragment running up and down, repeated many times

Pentatonic melody at 8:22. The theme sounds extremely simple at first but becomes more complicated as it progresses.

Many thematic fragments simultaneously, in layers of the orchestra

Again, many fragments in layers of the orchestra

The "kiss" is an eerily quiet chord played on a group of 14 solo string instruments (violins, violas, cellos, double basses).

The "kiss" unleashes a frenzy of motion. Once again, the music builds over a sustained ostinato pattern. And once again, the music comes to an abrupt halt.

Student FAQs

Is this work always performed as a ballet?

No. In fact, ballet performances of it are fairly rare. Stravinsky's *The Rite of Spring* has become a staple of the concert hall, where it is enjoyed without the added dimension of dance.

Why did the first audience riot?

Some were offended by the music's unconventional nature. Others found the choreography preposterous: ballet dancers had always emphasized grace, but Nijinsky's choreography called for the dancers to do many ungraceful moves, like a rapid series of standing vertical leaps. And there is speculation that Diaghilev, dance company director, may have encouraged a scandal at the opening. A scandal meant publicity, and publicity meant ticket sales, not only for this ballet, but for others produced by the Ballets Russes.

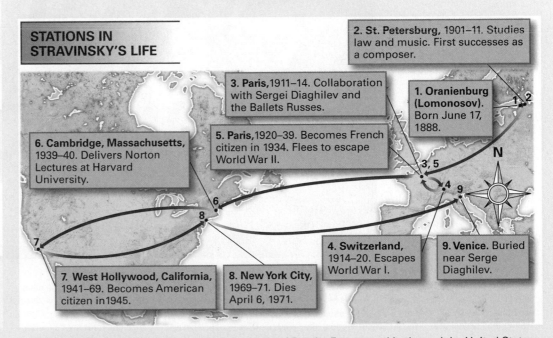

STATIONS IN STRAVINSKY'S LIFE

2. St. Petersburg, 1901–11. Studies law and music. First successes as a composer.

3. Paris, 1911–14. Collaboration with Sergei Diaghilev and the Ballets Russes.

1. Oranienburg (Lomonosov). Born June 17, 1888.

6. Cambridge, Massachusetts, 1939–40. Delivers Norton Lectures at Harvard University.

5. Paris, 1920–39. Becomes French citizen in 1934. Flees to escape World War II.

4. Switzerland, 1914–20. Escapes World War I.

9. Venice. Buried near Serge Diaghilev.

7. West Hollywood, California, 1941–69. Becomes American citizen in 1945.

8. New York City, 1969–71. Dies April 6, 1971.

Stravinsky was at various stages in his life a citizen of Russia, France, and in the end the United States.

379

A CLOSER LOOK   The Mega-Orchestra

By the early twentieth century, the size of orchestras had grown considerably compared to those in use during Haydn's lifetime (see page 188). The image here shows a large orchestra similar (but not identical) to that called for in Stravinsky's *Rite of Spring*.

Horns. Sometimes called "French horns," this versatile member of the brass family covers a wide range of both pitches and timbres, from bold to mellow.

Percussion. Works that call for percussion typically require only a fraction of the large number of instruments in this family. Seen here, from left to right, are a gong, a snare drum, cymbals, a bass drum (set upright), and timpani (four "kettle drums").

Woodwinds. These instruments include (from highest range to lowest) piccolo, flute, oboe, English horn, clarinet, bassoon, contrabassoon, and bass clarinet.

Chris Zuidyk/Bournemouth Symphony Orchestra

Harp. This is another stringed instrument but one that is plucked rather than played with a bow.

Second violins. In an orchestra, playing "second fiddle" is by no means a secondary task. This group, about equal in number to the first violin section, often plays its own independent line.

First violins. Although the seating of the other stringed instruments can vary, the first violins are always found on the left side of the stage. The violinist closest to the conductor is the concertmaster, the orchestra's equivalent of a team captain.

Conductor. The conductor holds everything together. All eyes are on her—or at least should be!—as she controls tempo, phrasing, and the overall balance of sound among the many instruments and instrument groups.

⊙➤ **EXPLORE MORE** on www.mymusiclab.com

👁 **SEE MORE** Inside the Orchestra: The 20th Century

Trumpets. Trumpets come in different sizes and ranges but typically produce a bright, piercing sound.

Trombones. These often operate in groups of three, corresponding to the alto, tenor, and bass ranges of the voice. The sliding mechanism allows trombones to "slide" into and out of pitches quite easily.

Tuba. The lowest-sounding of the family of brass instruments.

Violas. Slightly lower in range than the violins but much higher than the cellos, the violas often provide the harmonies of the inner voices between high and low. They can carry the principal melodic line at times as well.

Cellos. These instruments are, in effect, very large violins—so large, in fact, that they must be played upright, held between the legs. Because a cello produces a much larger volume of sound than a violin, an orchestra requires far fewer cellos. In this ensemble, there are only 8, as opposed to the 14 first and 14 second violins.

Double basses. This instrument is even larger (and louder) than the cello. In this ensemble, only five double basses are required to balance the sound of the other stringed instruments.

PERFORMANCE   The Audience Riots

The audience at the premiere of *The Rite of Spring* in Paris in May 1913 was scandalized by the music and the dancing, which by the composer's own account was seriously out of step with the music. As Stravinsky later recalled:

> The complexity of my score had demanded a great number of rehearsals, which [Pierre] Monteux had conducted with his usual skill and attention. . . . During the whole performance I was at [the choreographer Vaslav] Nijinsky's side in the wings. He was standing on a chair, screaming "sixteen, seventeen, eighteen" — they had their own method of counting to keep time. Naturally, the poor dancers could hear nothing by reason of the row in the auditorium and the sound of their own dance steps. I had to hold Nijinsky by his clothes, for he was furious, and ready to dash on to the stage at any moment and create a scandal. [The impresario Sergei] Diaghilev kept ordering the electricians to turn the lights on or off, hoping in that way to put a stop to the noise. That is all I can remember about that first performance. Oddly enough, at the dress rehearsal . . . everything had gone off peacefully, and I was very far from expecting such an outburst.[1]

[1]Igor Stravinsky, *Stravinsky: An Autobiography* (New York: Simon and Schuster, 1936), 72–73.

The noted Parisian critic Pierre Lalo spoke for many of his contemporaries when he characterized the work in these terms:

> *Le Sacre du Printemps* is . . . the most dissonant and the most discordant composition that has ever been written. . . . Never before has the system and cult of the wrong note been applied with such industry, zeal, and obstinacy. From the first measure of the work to the last, whatever note one expects is never the note that follows. . . . Whatever the previous chord, the chord one actually hears, and this chord and this note are used expressly to produce the impression of falseness that is acute and almost excruciating. When two themes are superimposed, the composer scarcely uses themes that might work together; quite to the contrary, he chooses themes whose superimposition produces the most irritating friction and grating that can be imagined.[2]

But the riot soon turned to Stravinsky's advantage. Within a few short months, audiences across Europe were greeting *The Rite of Spring* with great enthusiasm, and the initial rejection of the work served to rally all artists of modernist tendencies.

[2]*Le Temps*, Paris, June 3, 1913.

EXPAND YOUR PLAYLIST

Ballet Music

Ballet can be danced to almost any kind of music, but from the middle of the nineteenth century onward, a number of prominent composers have written works expressly to be danced onstage.

Adolph Adam
- *Giselle*. One of the earliest (1841) full-length ballets to establish itself in the repertory. A love story, full of intrigues and disguises.

Leo Delibes
- *Coppélia*. An intricate plot centered around a pair of lovers. It premiered in 1870 at the Paris Opera.

Pyotr Ilich Tchaikovsky
- *The Nutcracker, Swan Lake, Sleeping Beauty*. Tchaikovsky's three ballets, are standards of the repertory today.

Francis Poulenc
- *Les biches*. Commissioned by Diaghilev and the Ballets Russes in 1922, the scenario of this ballet (whose title translates awkwardly as "The Female Deer") takes place at a fashionable party in contemporary Paris. Poulenc was a member of the French group of composers who called themselves "Les Six" (see Chapter 50).

Sergei Prokofiev
- *Romeo and Juliet*. This 1935 score, commissioned by the Kirov Theater of Leningrad (St. Petersburg), follows the basic outline of Shakespeare's tragedy.

 **HEAR SAMPLES** on **www.mymusiclab.com**

⊘ **TEST YOURSELF** on **www.mymusiclab.com**   Flashcards and chapter tests

Scott Joplin
Maple Leaf Rag
Composed: 1899

45

When Scott Joplin published *Maple Leaf Rag* in 1899, the piece became an enormous hit, selling half a million copies over the next 10 years and inspiring countless musicians to perform it, create new arrangements of it, and imitate it. Joplin and other composers were discovering that there was an enormous public appetite for works inspired by the traditions of African American music making, including the musical style known as ragtime.

 **Listen to this first**

((• HEAR MORE on www.mymusiclab.com

Rhythm

Find the basic beat of the piece, and then listen for rhythmic accents. Do they occur on the beat or off the beat? Are some sections of the recording more rhythmically active than others?

Melody

Can you identify any melodies that contain wide leaps? If you were asked to sing back the melody of the piece, what would you sing? Are there ever multiple melodies audible at the same time?

Form

Do you hear discrete musical sections? Do any of them repeat or return later in the recording? How long are the sections?

Ragtime is a style of music that emphasized rhythmic syncopation (regularly spaced musical accents that occur off the beat) while continuing many of the characteristics of marches, cakewalks, two-steps, and popular songs from the late nineteenth century. Ragtime music during the first decade of the twentieth century included solo piano pieces, songs (with lyrics), and pieces for small dance ensembles, but most listeners today know the piano solos best.

The style originated in the Midwest when musicians improvised catchy rhythmic variations of popular songs, a technique known as "ragging" a tune. In 1893, Chicago hosted the World's Columbian Exposition, which drew musicians and performers from around the country. African American musicians excluded from the official entertainment performed outside the exposition in countless venues, exchanging musical ideas and learning each other's styles. Musical developments at these and similar gatherings brought ragtime into existence. The first pieces titled "Ragtime" or "Rag" appeared in 1897 in Chicago, and the style spread rapidly across the country.

In the first years of the twentieth century, ragtime was perceived as a threat to the "moral, spiritual, mental, and even physical well being" of the nation (as historian Edward Berlin explained).[1] One reason was that the music was associated with saloons, brothels, and illicit establishments, all of which frequently hired ragtime pianists to entertain customers. Furthermore, the music used

⚙ **LEARN MORE** on
www.mymusiclab.com
Chapter Objectives

[1]Edward A. Berlin, *King of Ragtime: Scott Joplin and His Era* (New York: Oxford University Press, 1994), 87.

rhythmic patterns that were associated with African American musical traditions. During those years, racist perceptions of African American musical practices in many communities meant that ragtime was seen as undermining the more genteel, socially appropriate, and proper (i.e., white) cultural forms. Finally, ragtime was dance music, and dance music invoked sexual interpretations that again threatened the social decorum of the era. Although older generations mostly disapproved of the music, ragtime became immensely popular with the young people. Its rhythms, melodies, and performance traditions provided one of the foundations of jazz, and it became known as a quintessentially American musical style.

Rhythmic Syncopation

The piece is in duple meter, and one can easily count "one-and-two-and-one-and-two-and" along with the music. Notice that every other high note in the opening few measures falls between those counted moments.

While it is easy to hear the beat in *Maple Leaf Rag* and tap along with it, many of the rhythmic accents, such as those high notes in the first few measures, do not fall on the beat. Instead, they occur at regularly spaced intervals that oppose the underlying beat. This rhythmic technique is called **syncopation**. It occurs in Western classical music as well as in many other traditions around the world, but its pervasive use in ragtime makes it a primary identifier of the style.

The syncopation in *Maple Leaf Rag* occurs because the music's accompaniment consists of notes that are evenly spaced two rhythmic pulses apart, while the melody uses patterns that are three rhythmic pulses long. (In music notation, these rhythmic pulses are sixteenth notes; see the following example). The rhythmic relationship between the melody and accompaniment creates the following pattern, where "x's" represent rhythmic accents:

Melody:	X O O X O O X O O X O O...
Accompaniment:	X O X O X O X O X O X O...

To hear this pattern of syncopation, tap your foot in a steady beat of one tap for every "x" or "o" in the chart. Have one person clap on the "x's" in the accompaniment pattern, while a classmate claps on the "x's" in the melody pattern.

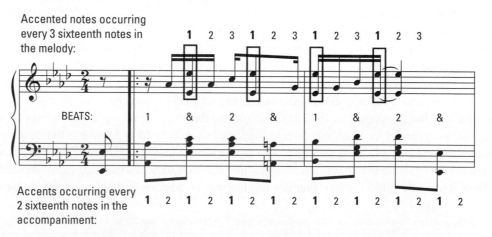

This particular type of syncopation, where patterns of "2s" occur at the same time as patterns of "3s," is identified as **hemiola**. Hemiola is a more complex type of syncopation than what is found in many other ragtime compositions. Its use in *Maple Leaf Rag* helps the piece stand out from the hundreds of other ragtime publications from the same time period.

Another type of syncopation in the piece occurs when the melody sounds like it jumps in "early" in relation to the accompaniment. Listen to the repeated notes in the melody at 0:16–0:18. The first and the last of the melody's repeated notes come in before the metric downbeat, and sooner than the steady pulse of the pattern would indicate.

Joplin also writes rhythmically straight passages so that the syncopated patterns sound fresh in contrast. Like most effective rhythmic techniques, if syncopation were used continuously, it would lose its magic.

Hidden Melodies and Stride Bass

Listen to the melody that begins at 0:44. If you focus on all the notes that the pianist is playing in the higher register, the melody sounds jumpy and disjointed.

The red line on this score excerpt shows the leapy contour of the melody.

However, the notes that form the peaks of this contour are all close in pitch. This passage uses a technique known as "compound melody," in which a single melody has additional pitches from other melodies woven between its notes. We can hear the main melodic line by focusing only on the notes that move down by half steps. The performer's task is to differentiate these notes from those of the other melody lines.

The connected melodic line is marked with circles and a red line:

1868–1917
Scott Joplin
Maple Leaf Rag
Composed: 1899
GENRE
Ragtime
KEY CONCEPTS
Syncopation, sectional form, compound melodies.
CHAPTER HIGHLIGHT
Ragtime
Ragtime, with its syncopated rhythms, laid the groundwork for early jazz.

PROFILE   Scott Joplin (1868–1917)

The King of Ragtime

Scott Joplin is widely known as the King of Ragtime, but he always wanted to be respected as a classical composer. During his lifetime there was a wide gulf between the two musical worlds, and in spite of his best efforts, Joplin never succeeded in obtaining recognition for his classical works.

Little is known for sure about the first decades of Joplin's life. He learned to play the piano, violin, guitar, and mandolin in his early teens. Shortly thereafter, he left his family's home in Texarkana, Arkansas, for St. Louis to pursue a musical career. In 1894, he moved to Sedalia, Missouri, and built a career as a pianist at local social clubs. These performances gave Joplin ample opportunity to hone his ragtime skills. Five years later, he began a long-term business association with John Stark, an ambitious businessman who agreed to publish *Maple Leaf Rag* in spite of his reservations that the piece was too difficult for amateur pianists. Sales were slow at first, but after a decade, the piece was selling approximately 15,000 copies a year, turning a healthy profit for both Stark and Joplin.

Joplin and Stark called his pieces "classic rags" in an attempt to make them sound more sophisticated, refined, and cultured than other ragtime pieces. While he made most of his money from ragtime hits, Joplin spent much of his life seeking critical acceptance as a composer of art music. He published a theater tableau piece for narrator and dancers, "The Ragtime Dance," and an opera, *Tremonisha*. Joplin spent his last years in New York composing prolifically and trying desperately to get a full production of *Tremonisha*

Scott Joplin
Art Resource/The New York Public Library for the Performing Arts

staged. Sadly, he never succeeded in getting the opera produced during his lifetime, and modern audiences still know him best for his ragtime compositions.

⊙➔ **EXPLORE MORE** on www.mymusiclab.com

EXPAND YOUR PLAYLIST: JOPLIN

Over the span of his career, Joplin published approximately 80 pieces. His best-known ragtime works include four that were featured (in instrumental arrangements by Marvin Hamlisch) in the 1973 movie *The Sting*, starring Paul Newman and Robert Redford (all for piano solo):

- **"The Easy Winners"**
- **"The Entertainer"**
- **"Pine Apple Rag"**
- **"Solace"**

⸜⸜⸟ **HEAR SAMPLES** on www.mymusiclab.com

At 1:48, we can identify three distinct registers in the music: a high melody, a low bass line that is played in octaves, and some chords in the middle register. There is a significant distance between the lowest notes and the chords in the middle of the piano. If we could watch the pianist play this passage, we would see his left hand jump from the bottom section of the piano keyboard for the bass notes to the middle section for the chords, and back again in rapid motion. This physical movement of the hand "striding" up and down the keyboard led to the term "stride bass." The stride bass pattern occurs throughout most of *Maple Leaf Rag* and was extremely common in ragtime piano compositions.

Here is the stride bass:

The stride bass pattern from ragtime became the foundation for an entirely new style of music known as stride piano. Stride piano developed in Harlem after World War I, and combined a stride bass pattern with an increasingly virtuosic and blues-influenced set of melodies and flourishes for the pianist's right hand. It was one of the ways in which ragtime contributed significantly to later jazz styles.

Sectional Form

There are four distinct musical sections in *Maple Leaf Rag*. The juxtaposition of discrete units of music to create the complete piece is known as sectional form, and in this book we have also encountered it in William Byrd's "Sing Joyfully" (see chapter 8). Every section in *Maple Leaf Rag* is 16 measures long, which is standard for ragtime compositions, and every section is composed of phrases and subphrases in 2-, 4-, or 8-measure lengths.

TIME:	0:00	0:44	1:26	1:48	2:31
	0:21 (repeat)	1:06 (repeat)		2:09 (repeat)	2:52 (repeat)
FORM:	‖: A :‖:	B :‖	A	‖: C :‖:	D :‖
KEY:	A♭			D♭	A♭

The complete form is represented graphically above. The third section ("C") is known as the "Trio," an idea borrowed from ternary forms in the Western classical tradition (see chapter 22). It features a change of key and a change of texture.

Now listen to this piece again, using the Listening Guide.

CONNECT YOUR PLAYLIST

Syncopation

Find a work in which syncopation plays a prominent role.

Example: Stevie Wonder, "Superstition" (1972) Like much funk music, "Superstition" makes extensive use of accents that fall off the beat. The recurring guitar line is highly syncopated, as is the brass countermelody later in the song.

Listening Guide

GO TO www.mymusiclab.com
for the Automated Listening Guide
CD V • Track 1/Download Track 74

Scott Joplin Composed: 1899 *Maple Leaf Rag* (3:12)

Time	Form	Rhythm	Melody
0:00	**A**	Syncopation, with the hemiola pattern at the beginning	Static, with emphasis on the same pitches and attention focused more on rhythm than on melody
0:21	**A** repeats.		
0:44	**B**	Syncopation continues.	Compound melody, with a chromatic descending line
1:06	**B** repeats.		
1:26	**A** returns again.		
1:48	**C**, in a new key (D♭ major). Also known as the Trio section.		High melody uses more chords (a different texture) than the previous sections. Clear stride bass in the accompaniment.
2:09	**C** repeats.		
2:31	**D**, in the original key (A♭ major)	Simplicity and straight (nonsyncopated) rhythms at the beginning of this section	Complex interactions between inner voice melodies and bass-line melodies at the end of this section
2:52	**D** repeats.		

Student FAQs

Why does this piece remind me of Charlie Chaplin?

During the era of silent films, theater orchestras, organists, or pianists performed live music to accompany movies, an old-fashioned version of today's soundtracks. Ragtime was frequently used, partly because theater pianists knew the songs and audiences liked them. *Maple Leaf Rag* was certainly one of most popular. Chaplin chose to include it in the music to accompany his 1928 film *The Circus*.

Is there anything in the music that unites the A, B, C, and D sections?

There are some abstract motivic relationships between the sections, but basically the melodies are different—that's what makes it sectional form.

© Dorling Kindersley

PERFORMANCE   How did Joplin Play This Piece?

The recording used for the Listening Guide is the only evidence we have of how Joplin himself might have played *Maple Leaf Rag*. In 1916 the composer recorded it on a piano roll (a long strip of paper) designed to be played on a player piano (see the image). In the years before record players were commonly available, families purchased player pianos as a means of hearing the latest hits. The piano roll had holes punched in it to represent each note in the performance. The paper was placed in the player piano, where a mechanized device translated the holes in the paper back into sounds. The keys moved, the hammers struck strings, and it looked as though the piano was playing itself. On the piano roll he cut for *Maple Leaf Rag*, Joplin adds extra bass, arpeggios, and flourishes throughout the piece that are not in the notated score. He also plays the melody in some sections an octave higher than it is written in the score. These types of alterations are typical for a musician who is used to improvising and is not concerned with strict adherence to the score.

Whether Joplin actually played all the notes on the piano roll is subject to debate. Many piano rolls were edited after they were recorded, and additional embellishments were added simply by punching holes in the correct places on the paper. By this technique, elaborate performances were created, sometimes with so many additional notes that it would have been physically impossible for a live pianist to play them all.

Still, the existence of Joplin's piano-roll performance of *Maple Leaf Rag* hints that indeed the ragtime pianists of his day did not adhere strictly to the score. Furthermore, many of the most famous ragtime pianists from Joplin's era could not read music and learned the tunes by ear before recreating them in personalized versions. One of the traditions during that time was "cutting" contests, in which two ragtime pianists attempted to outplay each other by adding virtuosic embellishments. Furthermore, in the 1920s and 1930s, jazz musicians frequently used ragtime melodies as the starting point for entirely new, improvised performances (such as Jelly Roll Morton's and Marcus Roberts's versions of *Maple Leaf Rag*—see "Expand Your Playlist"). In subsequent decades, attitudes toward the importance of the score in ragtime have varied. Thus, a performer today might stick to the score or embellish it in any number of ways, and either approach is historically justified.

An Aeolian player piano, c. 1925. The piano roll (with the holes cut out for each note in the piece) sits in the front panel area, and the "performer" pumps the pedals to power the pneumatic mechanisms in the instrument.

Richard Booth/Lebrecht Music & Arts Photo Library

HISTORICAL CONTEXT   Making Money on a Hit

John Stark, publisher of *Maple Leaf Rag*, was continually look-ing for new pieces. Sheet music was one of the most lucrative parts of the music business at the end of the nineteenth cen-tury. Long before most households owned a record player, live musical performance was the primary way most Americans enjoyed their entertainment. Touring musicians and theater performers presented new songs to their audiences, and ama-teur enthusiasts then purchased the sheet music, usually for a few cents, to perform those songs at home.

Songwriters and composers of popular music often sold their music to publishing firms for a flat fee of $25 or $50. The publisher registered the copyright for the piece and then retained all the profits on the sales. A popular song might sell several thousand copies a year, netting a handsome sum for the publisher. The composer, on the other hand, not only received no royalties but might not even have his or her name appear on the published sheet music.

Joplin signed a very different contract when he agreed to publish *Maple Leaf Rag* with Stark's firm. Their contract speci-fied that Joplin's name would appear as the composer. It also guaranteed the minimum retail price for the music ($.25) and assigned to Joplin a royalty of $.01 per copy sold—a reason-able rate for 1899. A decade after the piece's initial publication, those royalties had netted Joplin approximately $600 per year, according to biographer Edward Berlin, which was enough to easily cover most of Joplin's basic living expenses.

With the rise of recordings and the popularity of new styles of music that were not as easily notated, sheet music sales plum-meted after World War II. Songwriters and composers today still

The cover for the first printing of *Maple Leaf Rag*.
Courtesy of David A. Jasen

sign contracts with publishing firms, however, and they receive royalties required by copyright law. The contract between the songwriter and publisher determines how much of that money goes to the songwriter and how much to the publisher. Another source of royalties is the fee that businesses pay for the right to play recorded music in their establishments. Performance rights organizations collect these fees and distribute them to the pub-lishers. The two major performance rights organizations are the American Society of Composers, Authors, and Publishers (ASCAP, founded in 1914) and Broadcast Music Incorporated (BMI, founded in 1939). When you go to a restaurant or nightclub, or listen to a radio station that plays recorded music, look at the business's window: you will likely see stickers confirming that the business has licenses with both ASCAP and BMI.

EXPAND YOUR PLAYLIST

Rooted in Ragtime

These pieces illustrate various piano styles that had their roots in ragtime.

James P. Johnson
- "Carolina Shout" (1921). Johnson's recording transformed basic musi-cal ideas from ragtime into the style known as Harlem Stride Piano.

Zez Confrey
- "Kitten on the Keys" (1921). Confrey's composition was one of the most successful "Novelty Piano Pieces," which followed after rag-time faded from popularity. Novelty pieces were showy bits of entertainment that featured stride bass patterns under lengthy scalar passages and glitzy arpeggios.

Jelly Roll Morton
- "Maple Leaf Rag" (1938). Morton played the piece at the Library of Congress for collector Alan Lomax, and his version was heavily improvised and different from the published version of the piece.

Meade "Lux" Lewis
- "Honky Tonk Train Blues" (1938). One of the next virtuosic styles of piano jazz to emerge was the boogie woogie style of Lewis, best demonstrated on his biggest hit.

Marcus Roberts
- *Maple Leaf Rag* (1998). This is a contemporary jazz pianist's improvi-sation derived from Joplin's classic and shows the incredible diver-sity of musical styles the piece can support.

((•● HEAR SAMPLES on **www.mymusiclab.com**

✓ **TEST YOURSELF** on **www.mymusiclab.com**   Flashcards and chapter tests

46

Robert Johnson
"Terraplane Blues"
Composed: 1936

Like ragtime, the blues owe much to the traditions of African American music making. The Mississippi blues musician Robert Johnson made this recording in 1936, only a few years before his death at the age of 27.

Listen to this first

((• HEAR MORE on www.mymusiclab.com

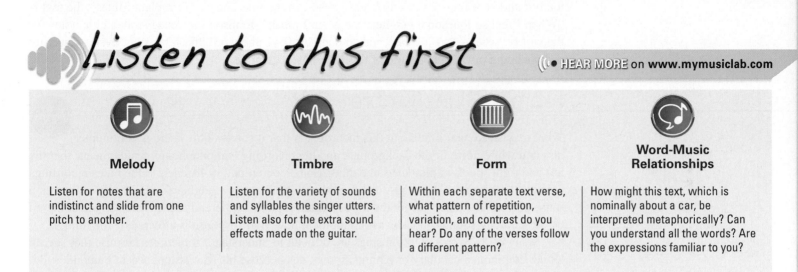

Melody	Timbre	Form	Word-Music Relationships
Listen for notes that are indistinct and slide from one pitch to another.	Listen for the variety of sounds and syllables the singer utters. Listen also for the extra sound effects made on the guitar.	Within each separate text verse, what pattern of repetition, variation, and contrast do you hear? Do any of the verses follow a different pattern?	How might this text, which is nominally about a car, be interpreted metaphorically? Can you understand all the words? Are the expressions familiar to you?

Derived from African American performance traditions, the blues is a musical genre that uses "blue notes" in its melodies and tells first-person stories of hard knocks and love gone wrong. It was originally transmitted orally, without any formal notation. The earliest recordings of **blues** were made in 1920, when record companies began sending producers and recording teams to different cities to capture folk traditions and local styles that they had previously ignored. These "city blues" or "vaudeville blues" usually featured a female singer with a small instrumental ensemble including a piano and sometimes a trumpet, cornet, clarinet, or saxophone. The first female singer to have a major hit was Gertrude "Ma" Rainey, but the most popular of these singers was Bessie Smith, who recorded prolifically through the 1920s.

About three years later, record companies began to send producers and small teams of sound engineers with portable equipment to more rural regions. Many of the most successful trips were to the Deep South, where a very different style of blues records were made. These recordings, often called "country blues," "delta blues," or "downhome blues," featured solo male singers accompanying themselves on guitar. Throughout the 1920s and 1930s, the Mississippi Delta and Texas in particular produced many of the most famous blues musicians. Robert Johnson recorded 29 blues tunes including "Terraplane Blues" in the 1930s. His recordings include some of the most influential examples of early "downhome blues" recordings ever made. "Terraplane Blues" was Johnson's only hit during his lifetime.

LEARN MORE on
www.mymusiclab.com
Chapter Objectives

391

A Blue-Note Melody

One of the most significant musical features of downhome blues recordings is the use of **blue notes**, particularly in the melody. Blue notes are pitches that are performed flatter (lower) than the standard major scale; usually these notes occur as substitutes for the third and seventh (and occasionally the fifth) notes of the scale. These blue notes are not necessarily exactly a half step lower. Instead, a singer or instrumentalist lowers the note as much as the mood and emotional inflection indicates. An extension of this style is the incorporation of notes that are indistinct or slide between several different pitches. In the first line of "Terraplane Blues," the text is "When I feel so lonesome you hear me when I moan." Johnson uses exaggerated blue notes for the words "when," "so," "hear," and "moan." At 0:42, the word "flash" is sung over a wavering and changing pitch, another use of this blue-note technique.

Historic Blues Timbre

What may strike you first about this recording is that it sounds old. There is continuous hiss and white noise in the background, and the recording is monophonic, which means that the left and right speakers play the same thing. Some contemporary listeners value blues recordings more if they sound old because the recording's timbre—raw, authentic, and noisy—invokes a sense of time and place before the music became fully commercial. Other listeners are bothered by the scratchy sounds. Consider for a moment how your response is affected by the timbre.

Many of the words Johnson sings are difficult to understand, sometimes because they are no longer common vocabulary or phrases, sometimes because his Mississippi accent blurs the syllables, and sometimes because of the poor quality of the recording. For instance, at 0:57, Johnson sings "I'm going to hoist your hood, mama . . . ," but many of the individual syllables are missing, merged together, or altered with different vowel sounds. Johnson's vocal style encompasses a variety of techniques that convey the song's emotional meaning even when the individual words are hard to understand: he sings some words in his regular voice, but he also speaks some words, sings other words in a high, hollow falsetto tone, adds a growl to his voice at times, and occasionally utters generic syllables instead of words. Note, for instance, the spoken interjection at 0:37, "Somebody's been running my batteries down on this machine." Here, Johnson takes on the role of commenting on his own song. The falsetto high notes, such as those heard when Johnson is "crying" at 1:30–1:32, convey the emotion of the text. At 1:46, he adds a vocal growl to the word "Highway" that evokes the gritty realism of the blues. When Johnson half-sings and half-speaks "and I'm booked and I got to go" at 2:05, the change in vocal timbre conveys both the casual nature of the performance and the sense that the singer is revealing his most sincere thoughts to the listener.

His guitar also offers a range of timbres that are as varied and expressive as those Johnson provides with his voice. At key moments, Johnson presses a short bar against the strings on the instrument to produce a wavering tone (a technique known as slide guitar), always on a long note in the middle of the guitar's pitch register. Listen for this at 0:26, 0:51, 1:14, 1:40, and several times later in the song.

U.S.A.

Mississippi

Texas

Most early blues players came from and performed in southern states such as Texas and Mississippi.

12-Bar Blues Form

Each verse of "Terraplane Blues" contains three vocal phrases:

- The first line of text
- The first line repeated, sometimes with slight variation or additional commentary
- The second line of text, often a response or reaction to the situation described in the first line

The first verse begins at 0:06 and ends at 0:31, with the following text in the three-line pattern:

> And I feel so lonesome, you hear me when I moan.
> When I feel so lonesome, you hear me when I moan.
> Who been drivin' my Terraplane for you since I been gone?*

This text pattern is typical of verses in the **12-bar blues**, the best-known and most commonly used model for blues songs. The model is not strict; instead, it describes the underlying patterns from which individual songs and performers frequently deviate. Each three-line unit forms one verse of the song, and the overall form of the 12-bar blues is strophic, which means that it consists of a series of verses (strophes), each set to essentially the same music.

Although there are some typical text patterns, the 12-bar blues is first and foremost a musical form, not a textual one. Each verse consists of just that: 12 bars (measures) of music—although in many instances, musicians either stretch or compress the basic pattern a bit. The three lines of text each receive four measures of music. The singer typically finishes singing the words in the beginning of the third measure, leaving time for the guitar or other accompaniment to add a **fill**, or short, instrumental response that occupies the time between the singer's phrases. Each musical phrase has a predetermined chord progression, or pattern of harmonies, although musicians frequently add variations or substitutions. The three chords used in the 12-bar blues pattern are built on the first, fourth, and fifth scale degrees, represented in the following chart as roman numerals (I, IV, and V).

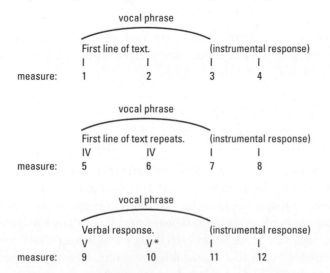

	vocal phrase			
	First line of text.		(instrumental response)	
	I	I	I	I
measure:	1	2	3	4

	vocal phrase			
	First line of text repeats.		(instrumental response)	
	IV	IV	I	I
measure:	5	6	7	8

	vocal phrase			
	Verbal response.		(instrumental response)	
	V	V*	I	I
measure:	9	10	11	12

*Some blues songs substitute a IV chord here.

1911–1938
Robert Johnson
"Terraplane Blues"
Composed: 1936
GENRE
Downhome blues
KEY CONCEPTS
Twelve-bar blues, blue notes, timbre of vocal blues.
CHAPTER HIGHLIGHT
Blues
Early blues recordings captured an oral tradition with deep roots in the Mississippi Delta region. The characteristic "blue note" and the 12-bar blues form would go on to have influence in music of many different kinds.

Like most downhome blues artists, Robert Johnson seldom sings a verse that follows the 12-bar blues pattern exactly. His most common variation is to shorten the third phrase to less than four full measures of music. In the first verse, for instance, "Who's been drivin' my Terraplane since I been gone?" is three beats shorter than the 12-bar blues model predicts.

In the fourth verse, Johnson uses a different text pattern that became important to later generations of musicians. Instead of the usual three lines of text, he sings four lines, or a quatrain consisting of a pair of rhymed couplets:

> Now, you know the coils ain't even buzzin', little generator won't get that spark;
> Motor's in a bad condition, you gotta have these batteries charged;
> But I'm cryin', plee-ease, plee-ease don't do me wrong.
> Who been drivin' my Terraplane now for you since I been gone?*

The musical pattern of chords (harmonies) and musical phrases remains the same as in the other verses. Two of the lines of text are sung rapidly during the first four-measure musical phrase, with the other two lines of text placed over the second and third musical phrases as follows:

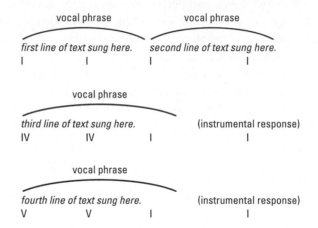

This four-line text pattern is only one of many used with the 12-bar blues (see chapter 57 for a different text pattern). It also is a common pattern in the blues-based recordings from the 1950s that were made by rockabilly artists in Memphis.

Word-Music Relationships: Metaphors and the Vernacular

"Terraplane Blues" is ostensibly about a car—the Terraplane was an affordable automobile built by the Hudson Motor Company in the 1930s—but in the vernacular tradition of the blues, the car is merely a risqué metaphor for sexual troubles and an unfaithful woman.

Blues performances, particularly in the types of road houses and bars where Johnson played, were often lively events where audiences responded to the singer's tales of romantic woe not with depressed sympathy but with a humor-filled empathy. Blues lyrics occasionally relate to social protest, personal misery, depression, or discrimination; the vast majority of downhome

*Excerpt from lyrics to "Terraplane Blues" by Robert Johnson. Reprinted by permission of MCPA.

PERFORMANCE   Who Wrote the Blues?

With "Terraplane Blues," we regard Robert Johnson as both composer and performer. As a composer he created the words, melody and chords. As a performer, he also created a unique way to perform them. When other musicians played "Terraplane Blues" they used much of Johnson's original piece, and then in the downhome blues tradition they added their own nuances. This practice was not always welcome. Robert Johnson sometimes refused to play facing his audience, not due to shyness but because he didn't want other guitarists to figure out the fingerings for his signature motives and styles. Even in songs as unique in their use of images and metaphors as "Terraplane Blues," stock phrases appear that are common to many downhome blues songs. For instance, one can find variations on the phrases "since I been gone" and "I got a woman" in countless other blues songs. These common phrases tie together the many different songs and performers into a single tradition.

The blues tradition was one in which music was both shared broadly and occasionally protected as personal. Thus, while we talk about Robert Johnson as both composer and performer—and he certainly put his own signature on his songs—it is essential to bear in mind that blues, and, indeed, most oral musical traditions, are also the product of many different musicians.

Son House, a blues performer who knew Robert Johnson, in 1960.

Photo by Estate of Raeburn Flerlage/ Michael Ochs Archives/ Getty Images

EXPAND YOUR PLAYLIST

The Blues in Different Styles

Once you learn to recognize the 12-bar blues form, it is easy to spot it in many different recordings.

Bessie Smith
- "St. Louis Blues" (1925). This classic blues written by W.C. Handy in 1912 is one of the most popular of all blues styles and illustrates the 12-bar blues form. Smith's recording is considered the classic version. During the 1920s and early 1930s, female blues singers like Bessie Smith and "Ma" Rainey were far more popular than country blues singers like Johnson.

Since the 1960s, many British and American rock musicians drew inspiration from Robert Johnson's recordings and covered his songs.

Listen to some of the cover versions to see how his blues tunes sound in different musical styles:

Cream
- "Crossroads" (1968). This live performance features Eric Clapton.

Rolling Stones
- "Love In Vain" (1969).

Fleetwood Mac
- "Hellhound on My Trail" (1971).

John Mayer
- "Crossroads" (2009).

((•● HEAR SAMPLES on **www.mymusiclab.com**

blues songs, however, address romantic relationships, almost always with some sexual undertones and usually where love has gone wrong. Listeners familiar with the blues anticipated these topics and had no trouble hearing the wry humor and double meanings in these lyrics.

Now listen to this song again, using the Listening Guide.

Listening Guide

GO TO www.mymusiclab.com
for the Automated Listening Guide
CD V • Track 2/Download Track 75

Robert Johnson Composed: 1936 "Terraplane Blues" (2:59)

Time	Text	Form	Melody
0:00		Introduction	
0:06	And I feel so lonesome . . . . . . since I been gone?	Verse 1: three lines of text in a 12-bar blues form, with the length of the last phrase altered	Basic melody for the blues tune is introduced. Blue notes on "when," "so," and "hear."
0:32	I'd said I flash your lights, mama . . . . . . it's way down below.	Verse 2.	Melody is similar to the one used in Verse 1, but slightly varied. Wavering blue-note tone on "flash." Johnson's voice trails off to indistinct low notes at the end of the verse.
0:57	I'm gon' h'ist your hood, mama . . . . . . down in Arkansas.	Verse 3: the metaphoric interpretation of the text becomes more explicit.	
1:20	Now, you know the coils ain't even buzzin . . . . . . since I been gone?	Verse 4: the form of the text changes to a four-line (quatrain) structure. This verse is a point of contrast in the middle of the recording.	Vocal melody changes to a very repetitive pattern that emphasizes just two notes.
1:45	Mr. Highway Man . . . . . . I'm booked and I got to go.	Verse 5: the form of the text returns to the standard three-line pattern.	Vocal melody is a new variation on the first melody.
2:11	Mmm . . . . . . since I been gone?	Verse 6.	Vocal melody is quite similar to Verse 1.
2:35	I'm gon' get deep down in this connection . . . . . . your spark plug will give me fire.	Verse 7.	Vocal melody is quite similar to Verse 3.

Robert Johnson had unusually large fingers, which helped him play more complex guitar parts.

Timbre

Solo guitar, playing in a Delta, Mississippi, downhome blues style

Johnson's voice slides between several notes, matching the sound of the slide used on the guitar (at 0:26).

At 0:37, spoken comment interjected.
Johnson introduces a brief falsetto exclamation at 0:52, and there is a guitar slide.

Johnson uses the wooden body of the guitar to add percussive sounds. At 1:14, there is a guitar slide.

Johnson's falsetto expression on "Plea—, please" matches the meaning of the words. Guitar slide at 1:40.

Vocal growl on the word "Highway." At the end of this verse, Johnson adopts a speechlike pattern for the last few words.

At 2:46, Johnson uses a long falsetto utterance that mimics a pattern earlier blues artists used.

Student FAQs

Were all blues singers black?

There were plenty of white blues musicians during Johnson's time. Record companies, however, kept two separate catalogs of recordings, sorted by the race of the performer, because the white musicians' recordings were not marketed the same way. Many early country musicians, including Jimmie Rodgers (shown here), recorded lots of blues tunes.

Courtesy BenCar Archives

Did the blues musicians know about the 12-bar blues model?

They learned the style from other performers. Although they intuitively knew what patterns did and did not work in the style, they were not consciously trying to use a particular formal model, nor were they concerned with how many measures each phrase lasted. We use models like the 12-bar blues as analytical tools to help understand musical developments and styles.

What are the percussive noises at 1:08?

Johnson is tapping the wooden body of his guitar to add rhythmic energy to the performance.

PROFILE   Robert Johnson (1911–1938)

A Deal with the Devil

For many modern listeners, the legend of Robert Johnson making a deal with the devil is the most famous aspect of Johnson's entire career. According to the story, Johnson traveled at midnight to a deserted crossroads, where he met with the devil and traded his soul for the ability to play blues guitar. One of Johnson's blues recordings was titled "Cross Road Blues," and became associated with the legend.

The story first appeared in print in 1966 (nearly three decades after Johnson's death), based on a vague recollection from one of Johnson's contemporaries. The same year, a southern preacher gave an interview in which he described a bluesman's fateful deal with the devil, but this interview was about a musician named Tommy Johnson, not Robert. In subsequent years, the story gained credence merely through the telling, and in 1986, it appeared in a popular movie called *Crossroads*. By the 1990s, when Johnson's complete recordings were reissued on CD, the legend was inextricably linked to him in spite of the tale's sketchy sources. Part of its appeal is the story's similarities to the tale of Faust, a character in German legend who made a deal with the devil in exchange for knowledge, power, or happiness (in various versions of the tale). Faust has been a popular theme for many literary, musical, and artistic works.

Relatively little is known about Robert Johnson. He was born in Hazlehurst, Mississippi, and became interested in music at a young age. He traveled throughout Arkansas, Mississippi, and Tennessee, learning from and playing with the best blues musicians he could find. In 1936, Johnson started working with Don Law, a well-known producer, who arranged two recording sessions for him in San Antonio and Dallas. Several of his recordings including "Terraplane Blues" were released, but only "Terraplane Blues" was a hit.

Robert Johnson

In 1938, Johnson booked two performances in Greenwood, Mississippi, at a jook joint, a roadside tavern that featured rowdy carousing and dancing (the term "jukebox" derives from the fact that coin-operated phonographs were installed in jook joints). He took up with a local woman, who—as misfortune would have it—was married to the owner of the joint. How exactly Johnson died has never been conclusively determined, but most evidence indicates that he was poisoned at his second performance, possibly by a bottle of tainted whiskey supplied by the cuckolded owner. Johnson died a few days later.

◉➔ **EXPLORE MORE** on www.mymusiclab.com

⏮   EXPAND YOUR PLAYLIST: JOHNSON   ⏭

Johnson made most of his recordings in the last three years of his short life. "Terraplane Blues" was Johnson's only real hit during his lifetime. It took decades for his other recordings to become popular.

• **"Cross Road Blues"**

• **"I Believe I'll Dust My Broom"**

• **"Sweet Home Chicago"**

• **"Hellhound on My Trail"**

• **"Love in Vain"**

((•● **HEAR SAMPLES** on www.mymusiclab.com

⊘ **TEST YOURSELF** on www.mymusiclab.com   Flashcards and chapter tests

Duke Ellington
"Cotton Tail"
Composed: 1940

Swing was a highly danceable style of jazz that emerged in the early 1930s. It featured large ensembles known as big bands. Duke Ellington recorded "Cotton Tail" in 1940 with a band of 15 stellar players on trumpets, conrnet, trombones, saxophones, clarinet, guitar, bass, and drums, with the composer leading from the piano.

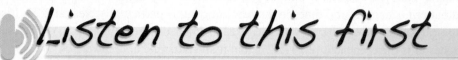 **Listen to this first**   ((•• HEAR MORE on www.mymusiclab.com

Harmony	**Texture**	**Rhythm**	**Form**
Listen for patterns of chords (harmonies) that repeat frequently in the piece. Listen also for chords that consist of many notes and are sonically dense.	Notice how the different instrumental groups fill different roles of melody and accompaniment as the piece unfolds. Listen, too, for sections where groups of instruments engage in musical dialogue with each other.	The tempo of this piece is extremely fast. See if you can also hear the uneven (long-short-long-short) rhythmic quality in the quick notes played by the lead instruments. What is it that gives this piece its momentum, or "swing" quality?	Try to identify the beginning of each new section. How does the ending of the piece relate to the opening?

Jazz is a musical genre that evolved out of many styles of music, including ragtime and the blues. Its earliest practitioners were mostly black, and its earliest forms did not rely on musical notation. **Jazz** made heavy use of rhythmic innovations like syncopation (a major characteristic of ragtime) and swing rhythms, which are discussed later. Improvisation, in which a performer makes up the melody while playing it, is another key feature of most styles of jazz. Improvisation also alters the concept of the "composer." In the case of "Cotton Tail," Ellington wrote the main melody and many of the detailed instrumental sections, but the bulk of this recording is a solo improvised by the saxophonist Ben Webster. Thus, while we talk about Ellington as the composer, in a certain way the soloist "composed" many of the notes we hear on this recording.

 LEARN MORE on
www.mymusiclab.com
Chapter Objectives

Harmony: Rhythm Changes

The harmonic progression used in "Cotton Tail" was written by American composer George Gershwin for his song "I Got Rhythm," which he used in his 1930 Broadway musical *Girl Crazy*. "Cotton Tail" is only one of dozens of jazz numbers that have borrowed Gershwin's

LEARN MORE on
www.mymusiclab.com
MyMusicLibrary:
"Jazz and Sytlistic Purity"

pattern. The pattern is so common, in fact, that it has come to be known by the term **rhythm changes**. There are three characteristic features of rhythm changes:

- A "circle-of-fifths" progression, a series of chords whose roots are all five notes below the previous chord. This chord progression is one of the most common chord patterns in big band jazz. The progression moves at a quick speed, with only two beats per chord. We hear the pattern twice in the first four seconds (0:00–0:02 and 0:03–0:04), then again at 0:08–0:10 and 0:10–0:12.

- A bass line that steps down chromatically (by half steps) from the first degree of the scale. You can hear this beginning at 0:04.

- A **sequence**, a short musical motif that repeats at successively higher or lower pitches. The sequential pattern occurs several times in the recording but is particularly clear at 2:20. Listen to the musical pattern when the saxophones ascend, then descend (2:20–2:23). That same musical material is then repeated (2:24–2:27), but it all starts one note lower.

Unlike classical music, in which the harmony is based mainly on three-note chords, jazz often uses "stacked" chords of many more than three pitches. Listen, for example, to the dense harmonies in the brass section at 1:32. Ellington makes frequent use of multinote chords like these, and in this arrangement he uses what are known as close, tight **voicings**. The term "voicing" refers to the spacing of the individual notes in a chord, and a close voicing is one in which as many individual notes of a chord as possible are played within the same octave. The result of a close, or "tight," voicing is a dense, colorful, and bright sound, which is heard again at 2:04 in the saxophone section and at 2:50 from the whole band.

Contrasting Textures

When we refer to a **section** of an orchestra, choir, or band, we are referring to a group of instruments or voices with similar timbres or the same role within the ensemble.

Ellington generates variety and excitement throughout the recording by using the different sections of his band to create striking contrasts in texture, in part by letting them trade roles in melody and accompaniment. At 0:45, the trumpets and tenor saxophone set up a **call-and-response** texture, in which the brass instruments offer a short musical motif and the saxophone improvises an answer. Within big band arrangements, call-and-response textures act as a form of musical conversation, moving the focal point of the music back and forth. The call-and-response at 2:35 is known as a "shout" chorus, because the trumpets are playing long, attention-getting harmonies in an extremely high register. In many jazz pieces, the last section is a shout chorus because that brings the piece to an exciting conclusion.

Swing Rhythms

The fast notes throughout the recording alternate between slightly longer and slightly shorter durations, creating a rhythmic **groove** known as **swing**. Swing rhythms generate internal momentum because the shorter notes continually propel the music toward the longer ones. Musicians resist attempts to define the rhythmic pattern according to any fixed ratio; however, in most instances it approximates 2:1. Notated jazz music uses regular "straight," or even, notes on the page, and musicians intuitively know how to alter them to produce the effect of swing.

Durations as notated:
(Straight)

Durations as played:
(Swing)

A major component of the swing groove is Jimmy Blanton's "walking bass" line, which connects one chord to the next smoothly by moving stepwise, one note per beat. Ellington uses contrast between heavily syncopated rhythms played by some instruments, and "square" rhythms played on the beat by other instruments, to give his arrangement of "Cotton Tail" its energized, swing character.

32-Bar Standard Song Form

Composers of Broadway show tunes and popular songs from the Tin Pan Alley era through the 1930s wrote many of their songs in the same musical form: a short verse that set up the characters and the scene, followed by a 32-measure "chorus" that followed a predictable form. The 32 measures were divided into four phrases as follows:

Section	Duration	Melody
A	Eight measures	First melody
A	Eight measures	First melody, with slight variation
B	Eight measures	New melody that used a musical sequence
A	Eight measures	Return of the first melody, with slight variation

This pattern of **AABA** is known as "Standard Song Form" because it was so pervasive among the "standards" or popular hits of the 1920s and 1930s. When jazz musicians borrowed the harmonic progressions (or sometimes even the melodies themselves) from these songs, they discarded the comparatively forgettable opening verse and simply repeated the more memorable 32-bar chorus several times. In "I Got Rhythm," the chorus is the part most people have heard, beginning with the title of the song, whereas the verse is seldom performed today at all.

"Cotton Tail" uses six iterations of the chorus, and the first chorus presents the main tune, which is called the **head**. However, Ellington subtly manipulates this structure. In the opening chorus, we expect to hear 32 measures that follow the form **AABA**. However, the fourth unit (starting at 0:25) is shortened to only half its expected length, and instead of the opening melody, we hear a bold passage played by the trumpets. The sixth chorus (2:35) begins as a bold shout chorus, and we expect it to finish with the same high-energy, high-volume style with which it begins. However, its final **A** section reverts to the opening texture and timbre and presents the first melody exactly as we had anticipated at 0:25. Ellington delays the sense of closure through the recording by moving the first chorus's expected conclusion to the very end of the whole piece!

Now listen to this song again, using the Listening Guide.

1899–1974
Duke Ellington
"Cotton Tail"
Composed: 1940
GENRE
Big band jazz
KEY CONCEPTS
Big-band instrumentation, swing rhythms, standard song form choruses.
CHAPTER HIGHLIGHT
Big Band Swing
Dance orchestras of the 1920s evolved into jazz bands that used swing rhythms and featured improvisation within a structured framework like the 32-bar standard song form. "Cotton Tail," like many other hits of its time, is based on a standard harmonic progression that was widely adaptable.

CONNECT YOUR PLAYLIST
Close-Voiced Harmony
Find a song that uses close harmony to emphasize the beat.
Example: Beyoncé and Sean Paul, "Bad Boy" (2003)
Listen to how closely voiced chords are played on the beat while the vocals by Beyoncé and Sean Paul are highly syncopated. Ellington uses a similar affect in his arrangement of "Cotton Tail" at several places (notably 0:08–0:17 and again at 1:16–1:24).

Listening Guide

GO TO www.mymusiclab.com
for the Automated Listening Guide
CD V • Track 3/Download Track 76

Duke Ellington Composed: 1940 "Cotton Tail" (3:10)

Time	Form	Harmony	Texture
0:00	First Chorus: **A** section (head)	Characteristic descent of the rhythm changes are audible at 0:04 in the upright bass.	The head (main melody) is introduced by trumpet and tenor saxophone, accompanied by the rhythm section.
0:08	**A** section		Opening melody repeats, accompanied by both rhythm section and trombones.
0:17	**B** section		Improvised trumpet solo over thick saxophone accompaniment
0:25	**A** section (shortened to half its typical length, and featuring loud trumpets)		Full ensemble plays the melody; saxophone solo provides a countermelody.
0:29	Second Chorus: **A** section (improvised solo begins)	Harmonies are *implied*, mainly by the walking bass line, with only occasional chords from guitar and piano supporting them.	Thin texture of solo (tenor saxophone) accompanied by bass and drums, with occasional piano and guitar chords added
0:37	**A** section		
0:45	**B** section	Solo incorporates a bit of the Gershwin song "I Got Rhythm."	High trumpets create a call-and-response texture with the tenor saxophone solo.
0:53	**A** section		Solo accompanied by rhythm section
1:01	Third Chorus: **A** section	The piano interrupts the expected harmonic progression and plays a single chord as a means of building dramatic tension.	
1:09	**A** section	Expected chord progression returns.	
1:16	**B** section	Chord sequence is punctuated by band.	
1:24	**A** section		

Rhythm

Swing groove is established at the beginning of the tune.

Contrast between melody's rhythms (heavily syncopated) and trombone chords (on the beat)

Long, sustained chords in the saxophone

Exaggerated off-beat rhythms in trumpets

Long, sustained note in the saxophone solo at the beginning of this section adds rhythmic drama. Staccato trumpets at 0:58 punctuate the end of this chorus.

Trumpets' chords on the beat contrast with the off-beat and syncopated solo.

Student FAQs

Why does the trumpet have a strange timbre in its solo at 0:17?

© Dorling Kindersley

Cootie Williams played this trumpet solo with a plunger mute—literally the rubber end of a bathroom plunger —which he held near the bell opening of the trumpet. By adjusting the angle and the distance between the mute and the trumpet, he was able to add "wah-wah" effects that imitate speech.

What instrument is playing the opening melody?

The head is played by both a trumpet and tenor saxophone at the same time, and this combination of instruments creates a unique timbre. Ellington enjoyed a well-deserved reputation for his innovative jazz orchestrations.

Cootie Williams playing trumpet with Duke Ellington's band.
CORBIS—NY

Time	Form	Harmony	Texture
1:32	Fourth Chorus: **A** section (new melodic material features the brass instruments)	Tight, close voicings in the trumpets emphasize jazz harmonies.	Homophonic section with brass instruments playing a new melody in close harmony
1:41	**A** section		
1:48	**B** section	Baritone saxophone solo, accompanied by prominent, sustained piano chords	
1:56	**A** section		Piano solo in a stride style, accompanied by the rhythm section
2:04	Fifth Chorus: **A** section (new melodic material features the saxophones)	Tight, close voicings in the saxophone chords	Homophonic section with saxophones playing a new melody.
2:11	**A** section		
2:20	**B** section	Sequence is clearly audible.	
2:27	**A** section		
2:35	Sixth Chorus: **A** section (shout chorus)		Call-and-response between "shout" trumpets and saxophone section, which plays a variation of the original melody
2:43	**A** section	Horn harmonies	
2:50	**B** section	Close jazz voicings create a harmonic climax for the tune.	Homophonic brass section creates a thick texture.
2:59	**A** section (return of the head)		Tenor saxophone plus trumpet play the opening melody again.

Rhythm

Piano solo emphasizes the downbeats, rather than off-beats.

Long, sustained trumpet chords contrast rhythmically with the active melody from the saxophones.

◀◀ **EXPAND YOUR PLAYLIST** ▶▶

Rhythm Changes in Jazz

Jodi Benson

- "I Got Rhythm" (1992). This track from the original Broadway cast recording of *Crazy for You* features a lively version of Gershwin's song in a contemporary recording. *Crazy for You* was a reworked revival of Gershwin's original musical, *Girl Crazy* (1930), and Benson performs it in a traditional Broadway style.

Count Basie

- "Lester Leaps In" (1939). Saxophonist Lester Young played with the famous, hard-swinging Count Basie Orchestra from 1936 until 1940. This recording, which is set to the rhythm changes, features one of his most famous solos.

Dizzy Gillespie Sextet

- "Dizzy Atmosphere" (1945). Gillespie's group (including saxophonist Charlie Parker [chapter 48]) was a significant force in the birth of bebop, audible in the style of the solos here. This tune uses rhythm changes at a slightly faster tempo than "Cotton Tail."

Miles Davis Quintet

- "Oleo" (1956). This tune, by saxophone legend Sonny Rollins, follows rhythm changes with understated, cool-jazz soloing from trumpeter Miles Davis.

Ella Fitzgerald

- "Cotton Tail" (1957). Fitzgerald recorded this version with Duke Ellington's band. It features vocal scat (nonsense syllables) on the melody, as well as memorable improvised jazz solos on violin and guitar.

((• HEAR SAMPLES on
www.mymusiclab.com

PROFILE   Duke Ellington (1899–1974)

Composing Jazz and Beyond

Edward Kennedy "Duke" Ellington is widely revered as the greatest American jazz composer, but his musical ambitions reached far beyond any one genre. He was a major bandleader in the swing era of the 1930s and the big band era of the 1940s, and he wrote hundreds of tunes that have become jazz standards. Yet he also wrote film scores for Hollywood, concertos and concert pieces, and works for theater, which influenced the development of many young jazz artists. His greatest compositional innovations include his use of unusual combinations of instruments and careful control of timbre in his orchestrations. He was also intimately aware of the strengths and styles of his individual band members and exploited those personal abilities to great effect.

Born and raised in Washington, D.C., Ellington found his big break as house bandleader at New York City's Cotton Club, an upscale nightclub in Harlem where celebrities, tourists, and New York's high society went to hear the hottest music and see a spectacular stage show (see "The Swing Revival," page 408). Working with stage performers, he gained crucial experience that served him well when he began to compose for film.

Ellington never left behind his love of jazz, but he appropriated musical forms of Baroque suites, classical concertos,

Duke Ellington
CORBIS—NY

and other larger concert works for his own compositions. Public reception of these works never rivaled that of his shorter big-band tunes, but those compositions challenged the idea that jazz and classical music should be perceived and treated as two different types of art.

⊙➜ **EXPLORE MORE** on **www.mymusiclab.com**

◉ **SEE MORE** on **www.mymusiclab.com**
Documentary on Duke Ellington

⏪   **EXPAND YOUR PLAYLIST: ELLINGTON**   ⏩

- "It Don't Mean a Thing (If It Ain't Got That Swing)"
- "Satin Doll"
- "Take the 'A' Train"

- "Mood Indigo"
- *Black, Brown, and Beige*

((⦁ **HEAR SAMPLES** on **www.mymusiclab.com**

A CLOSER LOOK Duke Ellington

◉➔ **EXPLORE MORE** on **www.mymusiclab.com**
◉ **SEE MORE** Documentary on Duke Ellington

Duke Ellington was an extremely influential and prolific composer and arranger, as well as a gifted soloist and pianist, whose creative life spanned five decades. Even though the main traits of Swing era dance music are present in his work, there is great variety and depth in his music. He went beyond the confines of Swing style by exploring innovative orchestration and extended compositional forms. This photo shows Ellington's band in the mid-to-late 1930s. Many of his musicians worked with him for two or three decades, and he made a point of showcasing their unique talents in his compositions.

Juan Tizol, Joe Nanton, Lawrence Brown (l. to r.) – Trombones The trombone section of Swing era big bands contained usually two to three musicians. Trombone and trumpet players formed the brass section. Typical big band arrangements used the sax and brass sections as the two main melodic voices. These two groups were used prominently in call-and-response sections.

Sonny Greer – Drums Drums in Swing era big bands were mostly timekeepers so that the beat could be better communicated to dancers. The use of high-hat cymbals was introduced during this period. Drummer Sonny Greer worked with Duke Ellington for 32 years!

Johnny Hodges, Ben Webster, Otto Hardwick, Harry Carney (l. to r.) – Alto, Baritone, Tenor Saxes The sax section contained three to five reed players, some often doubling on clarinet. Individual players would also be featured soloists.

Wallace Jones, Cootie Williams – Trumpets The trumpet section of Swing era big bands contained two to five musicians, usually three.

Michael Ochs Archives/Getty Images Inc. — Michael Ochs Archives

Barney Bigard – Clarinet One of Ellington's best-known long-time collaborators, Barney Bigard also doubled on sax, the instrument he's holding here. However, his best solo work was as a clarinetist.

Duke Ellington – Piano Pianists in Swing era big bands were not limited to playing chords and embellishments, but could also play melody. The rhythmic style of accompaniment included stride and occasionally "comping," a way of playing chords in improvised, flexible syncopated rhythms that complement and interact with the soloist. Ellington used stride-style in his early years, but thereafter developed his own, sometimes percussive, original style.

Fred Guy, Jimmy Blanton – Guitar, Bass Guitarists and bassists in this era were primarily timekeepers. They mostly played a "two-feel" (playing on the first and third beat of bar) or a "walking" baseline (playing on all four beats).

Rex Stewart – Cornet The cornet, an instrument that was losing its popularity during the Swing era, is pretty much indistinguishable to the ear when compared to a trumpet.

HISTORICAL CONTEXT The Swing Revival

In the 1920s and 1930s, New York's Harlem was home to a new movement in art, literature, and music, known as the Harlem Renaissance. New Yorkers, both white and black, were captivated by the new jazz sounds emanating from New York's nightclubs. The Cotton Club featured some of the greatest bands of the swing era, and the Savoy Ballroom hosted the best dancing.

Unlike the Cotton Club, which only allowed whites as customers (the musicians and waiters were black), the Savoy Ballroom opened its doors in the 1930s to white and black patrons alike, who came to hear hot swing bands engage in battles of musicianship and showmanship. On the floor, a group of young, black dancers began to improvise a new social dance that borrowed from the Charleston, and other popular dances of the day. The new dance, called the Lindy hop in celebration of Charles Lindbergh's heroic solo flight or "hop" over the Atlantic, matched the high-energy swing rhythms of the bands with its footwork, including "breakaways," in which one partner flings the other out for a few solo steps, along with acrobatic jumps, throws, and kicks.

Herbert "Whitey" White, who worked as a bouncer at the Savoy, recognized the commercial potential in the new dance and assembled a performance troupe of the best Lindy hoppers. White's group, known as Whitey's Lindy Hoppers, was hired to dance not only in stage shows but in Hollywood films. African American and white dancers alike took up the Lindy hop during the 1940s, with new variations evolving on the West Coast. By the end of the decade, the Lindy hop began to fade from popularity.

In the 1980s, a new generation discovered the Lindy hop. Several of Whitey's Lindy Hoppers were still alive, and they began to teach their old footwork to young fans. In 1992,

director Spike Lee featured an extensive Lindy hop scene in his biographical film *Malcolm X*. By the mid-1990s, the dance fad had grown into a full revival, which renewed interest not only in the dancers but also in the old bands, clothes, styles, and slang expressions from the 1930s and 1940s.

Dancers from the "Burn the Floor," a dance extravaganza. This group of 44 of the world's most talented dancers from 11 countries performs a mix of styles, including the Lindy hop.

Gerry Penny/Agence France Presse/Getty Images

✓ TEST YOURSELF on **www.mymusiclab.com**   Flashcards and chapter tests

Charlie Parker
"Ornithology"
Composed: 1946

Saxophonist Charlie Parker's recording of "Ornithology" captures the jazz style known as bebop, which emerged in the years just after World War II.

 Listen to this first

(((•● HEAR MORE on www.mymusiclab.com

 | |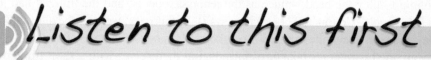

Timbre	**Melody**	**Texture**	**Form**
Listen as the instruments blend to play the opening melody and then introduce themselves separately with short solos. Notice the different sounds the drums make in different sections of the piece.	Listen for melodies that rise and fall rapidly, for sustained dissonant pitches, and for short motifs that repeat.	Notice the clear melodic line throughout, and its rhythmic accompaniment.	Listen for timbre changes that mark the beginning of new sections. Listen also for repeating chord progressions.

The instrumentalists who created bebop wanted jazz to be treated as serious music for listening. Unlike swing, **bebop** was too rhythmically and formally irregular to lend itself to dance. It emerged from the work of a group of young jazz musicians working in New York nightclubs in the period just after the end of World War II. They played in small groups that typically consisted of five to seven players, called "jazz combos." This, too, was a major move away from the big band ensembles that had been so popular in the 1930s and that still played the big dance halls. Bebop was considered the new, modern jazz, and the attitude of its proponents matched the serious, postwar developments in other arts as well.

The main emphasis of bebop was improvisation: spontaneously created solos. While improvisation had played a role in swing jazz, bebop called for a style that was even more free, individualized, and extravagant. Improvisation, the musicians believed, was the ultimate means of self-expression that reflected an individual's experience in the moment. The musicians devised a new approach to improvisation that emphasized fast, virtuosic playing. Bebop soloists used more dissonant notes, more extreme highs and lows, and a tone quality that was more intense and less sweet than their swing predecessors. They also developed a simple approach to musical form: they composed new melodies that were angular, dissonant, and challenging to the performer. These melodies, or "heads," were the core of a piece. The lead instruments (usually trumpet and saxophone) played the head through once and then took turns soloing. The piece ended with another rendition of the head. All of these features are evident in this 1946 recording by the saxophonist Charlie Parker, the trumpet player Miles Davis, and a group of backup musicians.

⚙ **LEARN MORE** on
www.mymusiclab.com
Chapter Objectives

👁 **SEE MORE** on
www.mymusiclab.com
"Masters of Bebop"
documentary

Fans who were accustomed to big band swing music found bebop difficult to listen to. The music was strikingly dissonant, favored very fast tempos, and used radical new harmonies that added more notes to each chord. Drummers frequently played with irregularly spaced accents, while pianists inserted chords in rhythmically sporadic patterns.

Jazz Combo Timbre

The recording opens with an attention-grabbing drum solo. The lead instruments then fuse into a single timbre to play the head—much as the tenor saxophone and the trumpet had joined their sounds in Ellington's "Cotton Tail" (see chapter 47). In this case, we hear the alto saxophone and trumpet play a unison line while the tenor saxophone plays the same notes an octave lower.

After the head, the instruments take turns introducing themselves with a short triplet motif, while the drums and bass remain in a supporting role. At the end of the song (2:50–2:57), each instrument plays the triplet motif alone once again, in a parting musical comment.

The extended solos feature some unique timbres that give the recording personality and intimacy. For example,

- at 1:13–1:46, the trumpet plays with more buzz than a typical trumpet. Davis used a mute, which changed the timbre of his instrument.
- at 2:10–2:14, as the tenor sax concludes its solo by moving into its upper register; it is possible to hear a faint whistling-wind sound above the notes.

Timbral changes, particularly in the drums, also mark new sections of the piece. In choruses 2 and 4 (0:39–1:12 and 1:47–2:20), we hear a high-frequency shimmer. The drummer is using his ride cymbal extensively. In chorus 3 (1:13–1:46), we hear a distinct change. The drummer has switched to more hi-hat and less cymbal.

From Improvisation to Melody

The head for "Ornithology" has three different melodic segments, each with different basic contours:

- First segment (0:04–0:09): alternates rising and falling lines and presents the basic melodic idea for the tune
- Second segment (0:10–0:13): a short, descending fragment that is then **sequenced**, or repeated, starting on a different note
- Third segment (0:14–0:17): an ending or **cadential** motif, followed by a triplet motif that repeats the same notes over and over (0:15–0:17)

All three of those segments then repeat for the second half of the head (0:21–0:38), with only slight variations in the exact pitches.

The head of "Ornithology" comes from a famous solo that Parker had improvised four years earlier, on a recording called "The Jumpin' Blues." For the harmony, Parker borrowed the chord progression from a popular song called "How High the Moon." Borrowing the chord progressions, or "changes," from popular songs was common practice in bebop and other styles of jazz (see also chapter 47). "How High the Moon," shares not only its chord progression but also its opening melodic motif with the new composition.

Each new instrumental solo begins with a melodic fragment that loosely echoes the music preceding it. In this way, the soloists more easily transfer the focus of the song from one player to the next. The solos reveal some signature features of the bebop style:

- Angular melodic lines, from high to low and with jagged motion
- A squeezed, forced sound as players reach the highest ranges of their instruments
- Prolonged dissonant notes (notes outside the prevailing harmony)

Texture: Rhythm Section Plus Soloist

The rhythm section, comprising bass, drums, and piano, creates a steady foundation and groove for the tune. Together, the piano and bass articulate the chords of the song, over which the other instruments solo. The texture features a single-line melody even at the beginning when all the instruments are playing, because the head is presented in unison and octaves. The only instrument that moves between the roles of soloist and accompanist is the piano, which emerges briefly to provide **fills**, or very brief solos that occupy musical gaps between sections (2:35–2:38, for instance).

Sectional Form

In "Ornithology," the lead instrument changes with each of the five major sections, or choruses (0:04, 0:39, 1:13, 1:47, 2:21). Each is different except the last, which is a repetition of the opening chorus. Bebop compositions typically use this sectional form, with the head providing the first and last chorus and the number of iterations dependent on the number of soloists and how many choruses each soloist wishes to play.

Each chorus, is 32 measures long—the typical length for early twentieth-century popular songs. Unlike many others, however, including "I Got Rhythm" (see chapter 47), "How High the Moon" does not follow the "Standard Song Form" of **AABA**. Instead, it uses a two-part form, **A A′**. The tick-mark next to the second **A** means it is a variant of the first **A**: it has a slightly different ending. Each section is divided into two phrases, "a" and "b."

"Ornithology" retains the **A A′** form of "How High the Moon," but the two-part division (a–b) within each section becomes a three-part division, as we saw earlier under "From Improvisation to Melody." The head's second melodic segment begins during the chords from the first phrase of the original tune and continues over part of the second phrase.

Melodic Segments and Chord Progression			
Melodic segments in "Ornithology"	First segment (0:04–0:09)	Second segment (0:10–0:13)	Third segment (0:14–0:17)
Chord progression from "How High the Moon"	"a" phrase		"b" phrase

The five choruses of this recording are vaguely similar in concept to a theme and variations movement (see chapters 20 and 21). However, because a different individual shapes each improvised solo, there is no large-scale plan or progression of the "variations." Furthermore, in the bebop performance practice, unlike in classical themes and variations, the last section revisits the opening melody in its original form.

Now listen to this piece again, using the Listening Guide.

1920–1955
Charlie Parker
"Ornithology"
Composed: 1946

GENRE
Bebop jazz

KEY CONCEPTS
Jazz combo instrumentation, improvisation, soloist vs. rhythm section.

CHAPTER HIGHLIGHT
Bebop Jazz
Jazz music for listening, not dancing, arose in the mid-1940s. Smaller ensembles, more emphasis on virtuosic improvisation, and a serious attitude toward the music characterized bebop.

CONNECT YOUR PLAYLIST

Improvisation

Find a recording that incorporates improvisation
Example: "Empire State of Mind," Jay-Z and Alicia Keys (2009) Jay-Z improvises his rapped lyrics, varying the number of syllables he chants against the unchanging accompaniment. He repeats words (like "Yankees" in the second verse) but varies where he places them against the beat.

Listening Guide

GO TO www.mymusiclab.com
for the **Automated Listening Guide**
CD V • Track 4/Download Track 77

Charlie Parker Composed: 1946 "Ornithology" (2:59)

Time	Form	Timbre	Melody
0:00	Introduction	Drum solo	
0:04	First Chorus (Head): **A** section.	Trumpet and alto sax playing in unison, with the tenor sax one octave below	First segment of the head
0:10			Second segment of the head
0:15			Third segment of the head. During the piano's fill (0:17–0:21), the pianist arpeggiates the chords, alternating ascending and descending runs.
0:21	First Chorus: **A'** section.		First segment
0:27			Second segment
0:33			Third segment
0:39	Second Chorus	The drummer uses lots of ride cymbal, which adds a high-frequency shimmer to this section.	The first three notes of the alto sax solo are the same triplet figure that ended the previous section. Note the emphasized dissonance (0:53). The contour of his improvised melody spans extreme highs and lows in almost every measure (especially 1:08–1:13).
1:13	Third Chorus	Trumpet player uses a mute, which adds additional complexity to the timbre of the trumpet. Drummer shifts to more hi-hat.	This solo emphasizes repeated notes and pairs of notes (e.g., 1:32–1:33, 1:35–1:37). The climax of the solo is one high registral section (1:38). The trumpet player emphasizes dissonant pitches at several places (e.g., 1:48).
1:47	Fourth Chorus	Drummer switches back to heavy use of the ride cymbal. When the tenor saxophone is playing in the highest register (2:10–2:14), the instrument makes faint but audible whistling-wind sounds.	Tenor sax uses his highest register, allowing the melody to become pinched (2:01, 2:03, 2:06). At the end of the solo, the sax player arpeggiates the chords, alternating ascending and descending lines (2:16–2:19).
2:21	Fifth Chorus (repeats the head): **A** section		
2:38	**A'** section	All instruments except bass and drums play the final triplet motif in turn (trumpet, alto, tenor, guitar, and piano).	

Texture

Melody plus accompaniment (homophony), separating the rhythm section from the lead instruments

The lead instruments pause, allowing the piano to provide the fill.

Each lead instrument repeats the same triplet motif: trumpet, then alto sax, then tenor sax, then guitar, with a piano fill afterward.

Alto sax solo. Notice the piano plays chords in a free and asymmetric rhythmic pattern in the rhythm section.

Trumpet solo

Tenor sax solo

The head is played in unison. At 2:33–2:34, the trumpet plays the triplet motif as a solo, and the pianist fills the remainder of that phrase (2:35–2:38) with a short solo.

Piano becomes more active within the rhythm section (2:46–2:50).

Student FAQs

Where did the term "bebop" come from?

The term "bebop" came from the nonsense syllables that jazz vocalists used in their solos. The singers strung together syllables in interesting phonetic patterns that helped them sing the elaborate, improvised melodies.

Dave King
© Dorling Kindersley

© Dorling Kindersley

What is the difference between a tenor and an alto saxophone?

A tenor saxophone is larger and plays lower notes than an alto sax. Saxophones are transposing instruments, which means that the notes we hear a saxophone play are different than the pitches notated on a saxophone player's music. The pitch C written on a piece of music would sound as an E♭ on an alto saxophone and a B♭ on a tenor saxophone. Although this may seem unnecessarily confusing, it allows performers to switch more easily between playing instruments in the same family.

Odile Noel/
Lebrecht Music &
Arts Photo Library

I found another recording of "Ornithology" by Charlie Parker, but it sounds completely different. Is it still the same piece?

Jazz musicians play a piece differently almost every time they perform it, sometimes transforming even the head itself. Every recorded version of the piece captures a specific time, place, and moment in musical history, and jazz fans frequently talk not about a song (i.e., "Ornithology"), but instead about a specific recording, simply because they're all so different.

413

PROFILE   Charlie Parker (1920–1955)

The Self-Destructive Artist

Charlie "Yardbird" Parker left behind a legacy as a jazz innovator of profound musical genius troubled by a lifetime of drug addiction, a series of failed relationships, and a frustrating inability to control his professional life. He was raised in Kansas City, Missouri, when that city's nightlife was hopping with innovative jazz musicians who gathered in open jam sessions. Parker honed his craft by sitting in with those local bands and practicing obsessively. In 1939 he moved to New York City and sought out the best jam sessions in Harlem. In the jazz clubs there, Parker developed a style of virtuosic soloing that used complex harmonies, lightning-fast technique, and dissonance. With those innovations, bebop was born.

At the same time he was crafting new styles of jazz, Parker was sinking deeper into his drug addiction and either failing to turn up at performances or showing up in such a state that he could barely play. As Parker's career progressed, it was pockmarked with arrests, emotional breakdowns, the failure of four relationships, and declining health. He lost his license to perform in New York City nightclubs because of his arrest record and, by 1955, was at a state of physical collapse and entertaining thoughts of suicide. He passed away a recluse, living alone at the apartment of a jazz patron. Unlike his collaborator Miles Davis, Parker never shook off the demons of his addiction. But the music he created astounded listeners. Parker's name, his solos, his compositions, and his recordings are revered among jazz fans, who sometimes wonder if they came to fruition only through the same destructive yet mind-altering forces that ultimately cost him his life.

How he acquired his nickname of "Yardbird" is hotly debated. The Birdland jazz club in New York opened in 1949 as a tribute to him, and even the title "Ornithology" paid homage.

Charlie Parker in 1947.
Frank Driggs Collection

EXPLORE MORE on www.mymusiclab.com

EXPAND YOUR PLAYLIST: PARKER

- "Shaw 'Nuff"
- "Ko Ko"
- "Scrapple from the Apple"

- "Night in Tunisia"
- "Embraceable You"

HEAR SAMPLES on www.mymusiclab.com

PERFORMANCE   Improvisation

When Charlie Parker improvised, his musical decisions were informed both by the chord progression of the song and by an extensive catalog of musical formulas he spent a lifetime collecting. In some styles of improvisation, the solo is essentially a variation on the song's main melody. In bebop, however, only occasionally did the musicians quote from the original melody. Instead, they devised a system in which certain scales were determined to match certain chords. When those chords appeared in the song, the musicians used fragments of the matching scale, along with arpeggiations of the chord itself, to build a new melody. The musicians also spent hours working on short motifs that they could play rapidly starting on successive pitches to create a melodic sequence. They even borrowed short motifs from books on technique for violinists, pianists, and clarinetists.

Once the musicians had a catalog of motifs, scales, and arpeggios that they could play fluently in any key, they used this musical vocabulary to construct their new improvised solos. Thus, one can find the same motifs and musical fragments in many different Charlie Parker tunes.

In the decade after Parker's best known bebop recordings, jazz musicians pushed the concept of improvisation to the point where it became the very structure of the music itself. This style came to be known as free jazz.

Tommy Potter, Charlie Parker, Dizzy Gillespie, and John Coltrane in 1951 at the New York City club Birdland, which was named for Parker.
Frank Driggs Collection

EXPAND YOUR PLAYLIST

From Bebop to Free Jazz

Sonny Rollins
- "Strode Rode" (1956). This bebop recording mixes variety in the rhythm section's playing with Rollins's tenor saxophone solo. Note the extended section where the saxophone plays just with the bass.

Miles Davis
- "So What" (1959). Davis's solo is an example of modal jazz, in which melodic development becomes more important than adhering to tonal chord changes.

Ella Fitzgerald
- "How High the Moon" (1960). Fitzgerald uses vocal "scat" in one of her most memorable solos. Notice that she quotes Parker's "Ornithology" in her solo.

John Coltrane
- "Giant Steps" (1960). Coltrane's famous tune demonstrates the furthest reaches of bebop.

Ornette Coleman
- "Free Jazz" (1960). Coleman's recording is nearly 40 minutes long and illustrates simultaneous improvisation in the absence of a predetermined form or chord progression.

((•● HEAR SAMPLES on **www.mymusiclab.com**

✓ **TEST YOURSELF** on **www.mymusiclab.com**   Flashcards and chapter tests

49

Ruth Crawford
Piano Study in Mixed Accents
Composed: 1930

Writing in a new style means avoiding old styles, and in her *Piano Study in Mixed Accents*, Ruth Crawford made a conscious effort to avoid using some of the most basic elements of music in any conventional sort of way. Instead, she used a new, modern idiom in music, freed from the constraints of conventional harmony, melody, and rhythm.

 Listen to this first

((• HEAR MORE on www.mymusiclab.com

Rhythm

Texture

Harmony

Melody

Form

Rhythm	Texture	Harmony	Melody	Form
What is the meter of this piece? Can you tap the beats? Are some notes long and some short, or are they all even?	Do you hear one melodic line played at a time, or more than one? Do you hear a melody plus accompaniment?	Can you hear a tonal center? What helps establish one, or what prevents one from being established?	How would you describe the contours of the melody?	How is this piece divided into sections? Can you identify what makes sections similar or different? Can you identify an overall shape to the piece?

⚙ **LEARN MORE** on
www.mymusiclab.com
Chapter Objectives

Ruth Crawford blazed new ground for American women composers in the first half of the twentieth century. In 1930 she became the first woman ever to be awarded a prestigious Guggenheim Fellowship in composition. She used the funds to travel to Europe, where she spent most of her time in Berlin, one of the liveliest cultural cities in the world and a hotbed of modernism. For a brief time in the 1920s and early 1930s, there was an "anything goes" mentality in the arts there: painters, playwrights, poets, and musicians were all exploring new ways of expressing themselves. Crawford did not study with Arnold Schoenberg or any of the other modernist composers in Berlin at the time; instead, she forged her own brand of modernism by working under a series of self-imposed limitations that helped her avoid such basic elements as meter, tonality, and patterned rhythms. The result is like no work of music ever heard before: its forward drive is relentless, and the absence of a tonal center has the effect of liberating the entire spectrum of notes.

Mixed Rhythms

These notes go by very fast, so it may be hard to tell at first, but they are all of equal value. Is the meter duple or triple? The answer is neither. The music establishes absolutely no sense of meter or fixed pattern of rhythms. Instead, we hear a series of small units. The music is organized into groupings of anywhere between two and eight notes, with the first note of each unit accented. The very opening of the work, for example, consists of a series of units made up of 6, 5, 5, 5, 3, 6, and 4 notes:

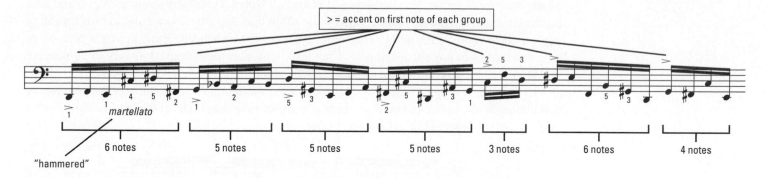

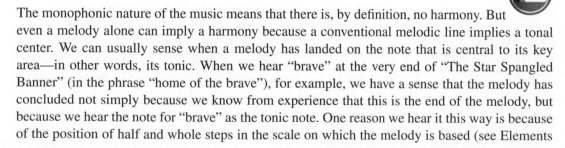

| 6 notes | 5 notes | 5 notes | 5 notes | 3 notes | 6 notes | 4 notes |

These irregular groupings create a series of what Crawford called "mixed accents." As you listen, there is no way of knowing in advance how many notes will be in any given unit. This unpredictability of rhythmic organization helps distance this work from the fixed metrical and rhythmic patterns that characterize more conventional music.

Monophonic Texture

Again, it may be difficult to tell at first because of the rapidity of the notes, which linger in our ear and mind even as the next ones are being played, but there is in fact only one melodic line. Texture is thus another way in which Crawford succeeded in separating this work from more conventional approaches to music: we haven't heard much monophony since the Middle Ages. Here, the pianist plays the same melodic line simultaneously in the right and left hands: only the register differs. The first three notes of the work in the right hand, for example, are D-F-E. The first three notes in the left hand are also D-F-E, played at exactly the same time and in the same rhythm, but an octave lower on the keyboard. (An octave is the distance between two different notes with the same name, like D and D, one higher than the other.) There is no accompaniment (as in homophony), and there is no interplay of equal melodic lines (as in polyphony).

An Absence of Harmony

The monophonic nature of the music means that there is, by definition, no harmony. But even a melody alone can imply a harmony because a conventional melodic line implies a tonal center. We can usually sense when a melody has landed on the note that is central to its key area—in other words, its tonic. When we hear "brave" at the very end of "The Star Spangled Banner" (in the phrase "home of the brave"), for example, we have a sense that the melody has concluded not simply because we know from experience that this is the end of the melody, but because we hear the note for "brave" as the tonic note. One reason we hear it this way is because of the position of half and whole steps in the scale on which the melody is based (see Elements

1901–1953
Ruth Crawford
Piano Study in Mixed Accents
Composed: 1930

GENRE
Solo piano music

KEY CONCEPTS
Atonality, register as a structural element.

CHAPTER HIGHLIGHT
Toward Serialism
Composers who pursued a more modernist style struggled to break free of the conventions of tonality. Serial composition, in which no one note in the 12-note scale would return until the others had been heard, gave composers a flexible framework for writing atonal music. Ruth Crawford's *Piano Study in Mixed Accents*, although not strictly serial, subverts the sense of a tonal center and explores elements like rhythm in new ways while using register as a structural device.

and chapters 40 and 42). Another reason we hear this particular note as the central one is that we have heard it early and often: "Oh, <u>say</u> . . ." "twilight's last glea<u>ming</u>" "Whose broad <u>stripes</u> . . ." "gallantly strea<u>ming</u>" "O'er the <u>land</u> of the free <u>and</u> the home of the <u>brave</u>."

The melodic line in Crawford's *Piano Study in Mixed Accents*, by contrast, projects no sense of any such tonal center. In other words, it is **atonal**. Notes do not play specific roles based on a particular scale, and no one note returns more often than any other. Crawford avoids repeating any one note until 9, 10, or 11 other different notes have sounded. By avoiding repetition or repeated returns to any particular note, Crawford reinforces the essential equality of all notes in this work. In this way, she creates a very modern sound.

Let's look once again at the very opening of the *Piano Study in Mixed Accents*: we can see that although "D" is the first pitch we hear, we do not hear it again until we have heard 11 other pitches—every other pitch, in fact, except one (G#).

HISTORICAL CONTEXT   *Twelve-Tone Composition*

Ruth Crawford's efforts to avoid giving prominence to any one particular note in a melodic line is typical of those modernist composers determined to cut all ties to conventional notions of tonality. The most widely used means for avoiding such repetition was developed in the 1920s by Arnold Schoenberg (see chapter 43). He called this system "12-tone composition" because its fundamental basis is a series ("row") of the 12 notes in the chromatic scale (A-A#-B-C-C#-D, etc., up through G#). Here is the row for one of Schoenberg's early 12-tone works, the Suite for Piano, op. 25:

Rows could be written forward or backward, or even inverted (a sort of "mirror" image of the row) or inverted *and* backwards. Rows could also be transposed to start on different pitches. All these variables allowed the composer considerable freedom but helped ensure that the music written in this system would not betray any unintentional vestiges of tonality.

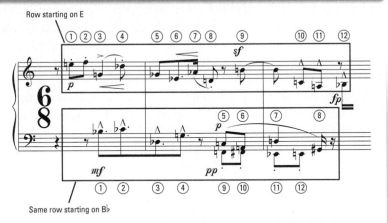

Row starting on E

Same row starting on B♭

Twelve-tone composition (or serial composition, as it is sometimes called) was at the cutting edge of Western art music for the middle decades of the twentieth century. Even composers who did not write in this system experimented with it at times. By the 1970s, however, the system had begun to lose its grip on compositional thought, though all student composers continue to learn it as one of many different approaches to writing music.

🔘 **LEARN MORE** on **www.mymusiclab.com**
MyMusicLibrary: "Schoenberg on the 12-Tone Row"

Registers of Melody

Without certain notes being more important than others or having roles to play based on a tonal scale, it is difficult to create a melody that is easy for a listener to follow, remember, or understand in the usual ways. Crawford creates interest and variety by giving unusual prominence to the melodic element of **register**, the range in which the music is presented. The melodic line never makes very large leaps, but it does move gradually from its opening low range to a very high register in the middle of the work and then back down again at the end, finishing very close to where it had begun. This attention to register helps give the work a strong sense of shape, with a beginning,

PROFILE   Ruth Crawford (1901–1953)

Modernist Composer and Folksong Arranger

Ruth Crawford is known today in two fields of music that might at first seem wholly incompatible. She was an uncompromisingly modernist composer (as is evident in her *Piano Study in Mixed Accents*), and she was also an important collector and arranger of American folksongs. Her early career focused on composition. Born in Ohio (East Liverpool) and raised in Indiana (Muncie) and Florida (Jacksonville), she studied composition with Charles Seeger, whom she married in 1932. From that point onward she published her work under the name Ruth Crawford Seeger. While studying musical modernism in Europe, she continued her search for a new idiom different from that of the musical past.

After her return to the United States, Crawford continued to compose, but she began to devote more and more of her attention to collecting, editing, and arranging American folksongs. Part of the drive behind this was musical: folksongs have captured the imagination of composers and music lovers in many countries for generations. But another element behind her interest in this repertory was social and political. Folk music, as she observed in 1948, "knows and tells what people have thought about the ways of living. It bears many fingermarks. It has been handled roughly and gently. It has been used. . . . It is not 'finished' or crystallized—it invites improvisation and creative aliveness. . . . It invites participation." Her children, Mike Seeger and Peggy Seeger, along with her stepson Pete Seeger, would later become major recording artists of folksong.

Ruth Crawford, ca. 1930.
Fernand de Guidre/Judith Tick

⊙➤ EXPLORE MORE on **www.mymusiclab.com**

◀◀   EXPAND YOUR PLAYLIST: CRAWFORD   ▶▶

- *Five Songs to Poems by Carl Sandburg.* Settings of verse by one of America's most beloved poets.

- **String Quartet.** A modernist work based in part on the principles of 12-tone composition.

- *Rissolty Rossolty.* An "American Fantasia" for orchestra, based on folk tunes.

 HEAR SAMPLES on **www.mymusiclab.com**

a middle, and an end. It also draws attention to the differing sounds of the piano in its low, middle, and high ranges. The growling rumble of the low bass gives way to the more delicate sounds of the upper range in the middle of the work, but the journey ends back where it began, in the bass.

Sectional Form

The music is punctuated by a few brief but important moments of silence—musical rests—that help divide the work into five large-scale sections. The proportions of these sections combine with the rise and fall of the melodic register to create a strong sense of symmetry. The following musical timeline represents visually what you heard. Notice how the work begins by setting out two relatively short sections of eight and nine seconds each, then expands into a large section in the middle (which is almost as long as the other four combined), then shrinks back down into two very brief sections (nine and six seconds) on the other side. There is a kind of rough formal symmetry to the architecture of this work.

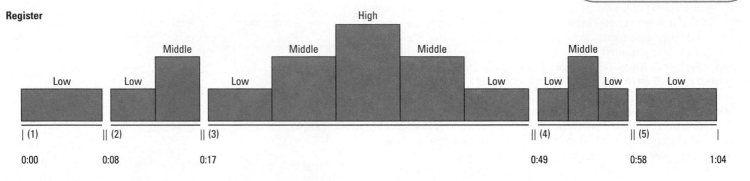

Register

With these points in mind, listen to the work once again, using the Listening Guide.

CONNECT YOUR PLAYLIST

Atonality

Find a work or extended passage of music that is atonal.

Example: Jerry Goldsmith, soundtrack to the original *Planet of the Apes* (1968) As in many science-fiction movies, Goldsmith's score relies heavily on atonal music to create a sensation of disorientation and distance.

◄◄　EXPAND YOUR PLAYLIST　►►

Women Composers of the Twentieth Century

The opportunities for women composers expanded enormously over the course of the twentieth century. In addition to Ruth Crawford, Germaine Tailleferre (chapter 50), and Tania León (chapter 61), these women composers achieved renown:

- **Thea Musgrave** (b. 1928), born in Scotland, has lived in the United States since the 1970s. Some of her best-known works are the operas *Mary, Queen of Scots* and *Pontalba*.
- **Pauline Oliveros** (b. 1932), a native of Houston, has been at the forefront of American experimental music. Her *Sound Patterns*, for a cappella chorus, uses phonetic sounds rather than words.
- **Joan Tower** (b. 1938) teaches composition at Bard College in her native New York. Her *Fanfares for the Uncommon Woman* is a response to Aaron Copland's *Fanfare for the Common Man*.

- **Ellen Taaffe Zwilich** (b. 1939), born in Miami, was the first woman composer to win the Pulitzer Prize in music (in 1983), which she received for her *Three Movements for Orchestra (Symphony No. 1)*.
- **Libby Larsen** (b. 1950) was the first woman to serve as resident composer with a major orchestra (the Minnesota Orchestra). She has written in many genres, including opera (*Frankenstein*) and song (*Songs from Letters: Calamity Jane to Her Daughter Jamey*).
- **Jennifer Higdon** (b. 1962) teaches composition at the Curtis Institute of Music, in Philadelphia. Her *Blue Cathedral*, a one-movement work for orchestra, has won wide praise from critics.

((•● **HEAR SAMPLES** on **www.mymusiclab.com**

Listening Guide

GO TO www.mymusiclab.com
for the Automated Listening Guide
CD V • Track 5/Download Track 78

Ruth Crawford Composed: 1930 *Piano Study in Mixed Accents* (1:07)

Time	Form: Section	Melody: Register	Texture
0:00	1	Low	Monophonic
0:08	2	Low → Middle	
0:17	3	Low → High → Low	
0:49	4	Low → Middle → Low	
0:58	5	Low	

Student FAQs

Is there any way to slow this piece down? It's almost too fast to hear what's going on.
The speed is part of what makes this piece so challenging and exciting. Don't fight it: accept it on its own terms and let it carry you along. It might help to think of this work as a piece that travels through the dimension of space, starting low, moving upward, and returning back to where it started. Multiple listenings will help, too.

Is it all right to think up a storyline to go with this music? It almost sounds like the soundtrack to a scene in a movie.
Absolutely. You're free to associate whatever you hear with whatever you wish at any time, keeping in mind that the associations will be more meaningful if they relate in some concrete way with the musical elements of the work itself.

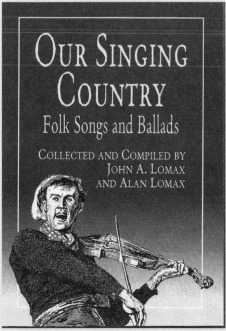

The cover of a recent re-issue of *Our Singing Country*, a collection of American folk songs originally published in 1941. Although not named on the cover, Ruth Crawford Seeger made the musical transcriptions from the field recordings done by John and Alan Lomax. A few years later, the composer Aaron Copland would find the fiddle tune "Bonaparte's Retreat" in this volume and use it in his ballet *Rodeo* (see Chapter 52).

Dover Publications/Dover Publications, Inc.

TEST YOURSELF on www.mymusiclab.com Flashcards and chapter tests

421

50

Germaine Tailleferre
Concertino for Harp and Orchestra, finale
Composed: 1927

Not all new music in the early twentieth century rejected the past. Germaine Tailleferre's Concertino for Harp and Orchestra was one of many new works that sought to synthesize traditional applications of harmony, melody, and form with an idiom that was distinctively modern. This chapter presents the last of the work's three movements.

Listen to this first

((•● HEAR MORE on www.mymusiclab.com

Melody

How would you characterize the opening melody? Does it seem balanced or unbalanced? Is it regular or irregular in its meter and the length of its phrases? Do the melodies in this piece seem to express intense emotion?

Harmony

Do you feel points of musical arrival and resolution? Does this piece have a harmonic center? In other words, is it tonal or atonal?

Timbre

Listen carefully to the variety of timbres throughout the piece. Consider how the differing timbres emerge clearly even when groups of instruments are playing together.

Form

Listen for the repeated return of the opening idea in this movement, which is structured as a rondo.

 **LEARN MORE** on **www.mymusiclab.com**
Chapter Objectives

Modernism had barely established itself in the early twentieth century before it inspired a counter-reaction. While many composers wanted to write in a new and contemporary style, they were reluctant to discard traditional applications of the elements of music altogether. In the years after World War I, these composers began to develop a style of writing that, although distinctly modern, drew on older uses of melody, harmony, rhythm, and form. They incorporated more traditional ("classical") approaches to their music even while maintaining a modern edge. Rather than look to the nineteenth century for their inspiration—a century that had only recently passed—they turned back to the eighteenth century. This style is known as **Neoclassicism**. The "classic" in "Neoclassical" refers not to the music of the Classical Era specifically, but rather to the eighteenth century in general, including Bach and Handel as well as Haydn and Mozart. Neoclassical composers were not attempting to recreate or imitate past styles, but to incorporate past styles into a contemporary idiom (hence *Neo*classicism).

Germaine Tailleferre's Concertino for Harp and Orchestra, commissioned and premiered by the Boston Symphony Orchestra in 1927, reflects this new–old style quite well. Its finale reveals the basic characteristics of musical Neoclassicism. While clearly a work of the twentieth century, it draws on older conventions of melody built on the basis of periodic phrase structure (see chapter 20), tonal harmony, and a clearly audible conventional form. It even includes a fugue (in the contrasting **C** section of the Listening Guide), but in keeping with Neoclassical principles, it is a witty, almost light-hearted fugue, not heavy or particularly serious.

Melody: A Return to Tradition

The structure of the principal melody is quite traditional. It feels very balanced, with clear antecedent and consequent phrases, and it focuses on a clear tonal center.

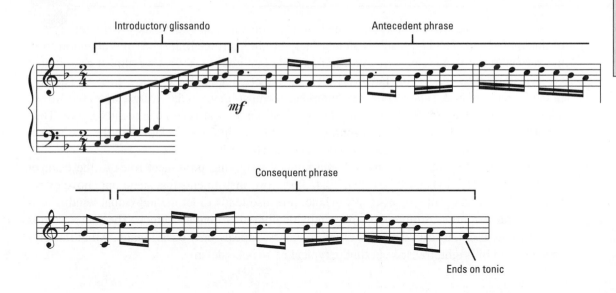

For the sake of contrast, the second melody (**B**) is less symmetrical in its structure, yet we can still hear how it divides into distinct phrases. The third melody (**C**) does not divide into distinct subunits, but that is because it is the subject of a fugue (see the Clarity of Form section), a decidedly traditional way of writing. Even though this work was written in the 1920s, Haydn or Mozart would have felt quite at home with the general shape of all these themes, even if some of the notes would have sounded slightly "off" to them. The dissonance, compared to modernist works of the early twentieth century, is minimal. What stands out here is the structural clarity of the melodies and their goal-oriented sense of direction toward a tonal center. These characteristics are basic to Neoclassical melodies.

1892–1982
Germaine Tailleferre
Concertino for Harp and Orchestra, finale
Composed: 1927

GENRE
Neoclassicism

KEY CONCEPTS
Periodic phrase structure, transparency of texture, rondo form.

CHAPTER HIGHLIGHT
Neoclassicism
Neoclassicism was a response to modernism. Neoclassical works draw on the idioms of earlier eras even while incorporating at least some modern elements as well. No one would mistake Tailleferre's Concertino for Harp and Orchestra as an eighteenth-century work, even though it is deeply indebted to the idioms of the Classical style.

Tonal Harmony with Modern Inflections

While Haydn or Mozart would have recognized the shape and tonal grounding of Tailleferre's melodies, they would not have written them in exactly the same way. We can hear that this is a twentieth-century piece by its chromatic inflections. The ending of the main melody (1), for example (see the previous notated example), flows into a wind fanfare (0:21–0:24) that sounds tonal but ever so slightly "off." The dissonant harmonies at 0:44–0:55, in turn, sound decidedly "modern," even while remaining within the bounds of tonality. These are small but telling moments: in both instances we hear the tonic, and there is never any real doubt about where we are tonally. But the tonic is inflected. It's a little like hearing someone speak a language with an accent: we understand perfectly well what the person is saying, but we also hear that this is not the standard, "classical" way of speaking. This kind of subtle harmonic inflection helps give the piece its twentieth-century sound, even while keeping it grounded in tradition.

Transparent Timbre

Neoclassical music strives for lightness and clarity, words that aptly describe the timbre of this movement. The harp itself is an unusually bright instrument: it seizes our attention from the very start with a long upward **glissando**, a scale that goes by so fast we almost cannot hear the individual notes. It is a blur, but a very pleasant and bright blur. The opening melody (Theme 1 in the Listening Guide) stands out over minimal accompaniment in the strings; when the strings take over the melody (at 0:24), the harp begins to strum a rapid accompanimental figure. Thus when the orchestra steps to the forefront, the harp recedes into the background: the two instruments share the music's sonic space and do not compete for it.

Tailleferre also creates a sense of transparency by giving prominent roles to the trumpet (0:34, 0:48, 0:56, 1:19) and flute (1:09, 2:24, 3:39), two instruments that stand out above or cut through the sound of the orchestra as a whole. She also tends to let the individual wind instruments—clarinet, horns, trombones—play individually rather than as a block. The snare drum is the only percussion instrument in the orchestra, and it appears only occasionally. All of this creates the kind of bright, transparent timbre typical of Neoclassicism.

Clarity of Form

The distinctive opening theme returns at regular intervals throughout the movement, separated by a series of contrasting musical ideas. The rondo form of the movement is easy to hear, and it evokes a type of finale common to concertos of the late eighteenth century. The themes of the contrasting sections (**B** and **C** in the Listening Guide) are markedly different from each other and from the principal opening idea, making the rondo structure particularly transparent.

With these points in mind, listen to the finale of this work once again, using the Listening Guide.

CONNECT YOUR PLAYLIST

Glissando

Find a piece that makes use of a glissando.

Example: Jerry Lee Lewis, "Great Balls of Fire" (1957)
In this rock 'n' roll classic, Jerry Lee Lewis makes frequent use of the glissando.

Listening Guide

GO TO www.mymusiclab.com
for the Automated Listening Guide
CD V • Track 6/Download Track 79

Germaine Tailleferre Composed: 1927 Concertino for Harp and Orchestra, finale (5:03)

Time	Form Rondo Section	Melody	Timbre	Harmony
0:00	A	1 = conjunct, moving down and then up; clear antecedent-consequent structure	Harp solo at first with minimal orchestral accompaniment; full orchestra joins in at 0:21	Strongly tonal, slightly inflected at cadences (0:10) and in wind fanfares.
0:44	B	2 = fragmented, slightly more agitated theme	Harp solo, trumpets interject	Trumpet interjections are harmonically "off."
1:00	A′	1 returns	Harp carries the main theme.	
1:50	C	3 = fugue theme, disjunct, moves upward	Theme enters in the low strings, other instruments join in gradually from bottom to top.	Harmonies in entering voices do not always match perfectly with each other, though we never lose a sense of the tonic.
3:15	A″	1 returns	Harp takes the lead, then the orchestra carries the theme.	
3:57	B′	2 returns	Harp predominates; trumpets interject.	
4:12	A‴	1 returns	Flutes reintroduce the theme; harp and other instruments follow.	Strong tonic ending

Student FAQs

Does a soloist always memorize his or her part and perform in public without music?

Getty Images, Inc.—
Altrendo Images

Usually, but not always. At a professional level, every soloist has internalized the work he or she is playing, but some musicians prefer to have the notated part in front of them, even if they are playing essentially from memory.

Why aren't there more harp concertos?

There should be, but there aren't nearly as many harpists as there are pianists, violinist, clarinetists, or performers of other instruments in the standard orchestra, and so composers have traditionally been less inclined to write for harp and orchestra. The harp is an ancient instrument—it appears repeatedly in the Bible—but it has never figured prominently in the concerto repertory. However, the harp concerto by Alberto Ginastera (a twentieth-century Argentinian composer) is well worth exploring, as is Mozart's Concerto for Flute and Harp, K. 299.

PROFILE   Germaine Tailleferre (1892–1983)

One of Six

Germaine Tailleferre was the only woman in a group of young French composers of the 1920s who called themselves *Les six* ("The Six"). The six knew each other personally—Tailleferre, Georges Auric, Arthur Honegger, and Darius Milhaud had all studied counterpoint in the same class at the Paris Conservatory in 1917—but the music they wrote differed widely in style. What united them was their youth and their devotion to the idea of continuing a tradition of writing music that was distinctively French. This was particularly important in the wake of World War I, when French composers were anxious to establish a style free from German influence. In the case of "The Six," this meant writing music that was, among other things, lighter, more transparent, and less emotionally charged. For Tailleferre and others of the group, works like Schoenberg's *Pierrot lunaire* stood for everything music should not be.

Tailleferre first came to promise as a pianist, and her music (including the Concertino for Harp) reflects her understanding of the illustrious tradition of French composers who had written for the harpsichord in the seventeenth and eighteenth centuries. Much of Tailleferre's music from the 1920s incorporates the same sense of clarity and playfulness so typical of this earlier repertory. She later went on

"The Six" plus one. Jean Cocteau, the celebrated poet, novelist, and playwright, is seated at the piano: he was not a member of the group but helped publicize their cause. Standing are (from left to right) Darius Milhaud, Georges Auric, Arthur Honegger, Germaine Tailleferre, Francis Poulenc, and Louis Durey.
CORBIS—NY

to write operas, ballets, incidental music to plays, film scores, choral music, songs, and a large quantity of music for solo piano.

◉→ **EXPLORE MORE** on **www.mymusiclab.com**

⏪ **EXPAND YOUR PLAYLIST: TAILLEFERRE** ⏩

- **Harp Sonata.** For solo harp, also in a Neoclassical style.

- *Partita.* A three-movement work for chamber ensemble, a haunting mixture of Baroque and modern styles.

- *Chansons populaires françaises.* "French Popular Songs" for voice and chamber ensemble.

- **Piano Concerto no. 1.** A Neoclassical concerto for orchestra and piano.

- **Concerto Grosso for 2 pianos, female vocal quartet, male vocal quartet, saxophone quartet, and orchestra.** A work with a Baroque-sounding title for an unusual combination of forces.

(((• **HEAR SAMPLES** on **www.mymusiclab.com**

HISTORICAL CONTEXT   Using the Past to Send a Message

Art is almost always a mixture of old and new. Few works of art ignore the past entirely, and few are entirely novel. But some works rely more openly on past traditions than others, and often for a reason. The Supreme Court building in Washington, D.C., for example, openly evokes the architectural style of ancient Greece because the style of the architecture is meant to create an implicit link to ancient Athens, the first great democracy in the Western world. Yet the building was not completed until 1935. Architects at the time could just as easily have designed something in a more contemporary style. The Empire State Building, a sleek, thoroughly modernist building, had opened its doors for business four years earlier. But this is not the message the government wanted to send. The law is based on principles of consistency, and the government wanted a building that would convey these ideals. A modernist Supreme Court might have conveyed the impression that the institution was heading in a new direction. So the Supreme Court today works in a building that from the outside, at least, looks like it might have been built some 2,500 years ago.

Music operates along much the same lines. What message would a modernist national anthem send? Could a large public

The U.S. Supreme Court building. Its Neoclassical architecture evokes the democratic ideals of ancient Greece.
Ted Russell/Creative Eye/MIRA.com

gathering be expected to sing an atonal melody? Why are national anthems invariably tonal and metrically regular? The same questions could be asked about college fight songs and alma maters, hymns, or love songs.

◀◀   EXPAND YOUR PLAYLIST   ▶▶

Neoclassicism

Germaine Tailleferre belonged to a generation of composers who came of age during and after World War I, a war of unprecedented horror that included chemical warfare and widespread destruction. Many artists and audiences alike sought a return to what they called a more "civilized" kind of art, one that did not turn its back on the best traditions of the past. Some composers, like Stravinsky, could write in both modernist and Neoclassical styles. Indeed, Stravinsky is widely considered the key figure in the emergence of Neoclassicism in music.

Igor Stravinsky
- *L'Histoire du soldat*. "The Soldier's Tale" is a theater piece for three characters (who recite but do not sing), a small instrumental ensemble, and a dancer. It tells the story of a soldier returning from war and trading his violin with the devil for a magic book.

Sergei Prokofiev
- *Classical Symphony*. Openly indebted to the style of Haydn and Mozart, even in its title, this is a symphony that follows the standard pattern of four movements. It is squarely tonal yet at the same time decidedly a work of the early twentieth century.

Maurice Ravel
- *Le tombeau de Couperin*. "The Tomb of Couperin" is a piano suite in homage to—and somewhat in the style of—François Couperin, a French composer of keyboard music in the early eighteenth century.

Darius Milhaud
- *Scaramouche*. This suite for two pianos exemplifies Milhaud's own estimation of his musical style as one of "clarity, soberness, lightness . . . [a] sense for the proportions of the outlines, and aspiration to express oneself clearly, simply, and succinctly."

Paul Hindemith
- *Kleine Kammermusik*. The German composer Paul Hindemith's "Little Chamber Music" is a concerto for small wind ensemble that uses the melodic and rhythmic structures of Baroque music, but with twentieth-century harmonies.

(((• HEAR SAMPLES on **www.mymusiclab.com**

✅ **TEST YOURSELF** on **www.mymusiclab.com**   Flashcards and chapter tests

51

William Grant Still
"A Black Pierrot" from *Songs of Separation*
Composed: 1949

The text of this song takes up the same imagery Arnold Schoenberg used in *Pierrot lunaire* (see chapter 43), but with a twist. In this text by the African American poet Langston Hughes (1902–1967), the quintessentially pale-white figure of Pierrot is black. As in Schoenberg's "Columbine," Pierrot has again been rejected, but instead of seeking more whiteness, he creeps away into the night ("and the night was black, too") to "seek a new brown love."

Listen to this first

((• HEAR MORE on www.mymusiclab.com

Harmony

Does the music sound tonal, atonal, or somewhere in between?

Melody

Listen for the changes in register throughout. Where is the highest note of the vocal line? What passages in the song suggest the style of the blues?

Form

Does the same music appear with each strophe, or is there new music for each strophe?

LEARN MORE on
www.mymusiclab.com
Chapter Objectives

Like Schoenberg's Pierrot, Still's lovelorn clown is never successful in his amorous pursuits. But Still's Pierrot conveys the same profound sense of insecurity and quiet desperation in a very different musical style: the musical language is tonal, with melodic inflections borrowed from the blues. This "Black Pierrot" expresses himself in an idiom that at once mixes traditions of the **art song** used by composers such as Schubert and Schumann (see chapter 28 and web bonus chapter 4) with traditions more closely associated with African American music (for example, Robert Johnson—see chapter 46).

Chromatic Harmony

From the very first puzzling, unsettled chord in the piano, we suspect this piece won't offer much comfort in the way of a home key. The octave notes that follow do little more to establish a tonic. When the voice enters, it starts in a low register with a simple statement ("I am a black Pierrot"), but it moves in wholly unpredictable directions. It wavers between major and minor and seems to change its mood constantly. And yet interspersed throughout this first, searching strophe we do hear sounds that we recognize and chords that give us moments of harmonic stability, even if they are only brief ones.

The style of harmony Still employs here is called **chromatic**: it is tonal, but it has strong inflections that make the tonic less powerful (see also chapter 37). A chromatic scale consists entirely of half steps.

1895–1978
William Grant Still
"A Black Pierrot" from
Songs of Separation
Composed: 1949
GENRE
Art song
KEY CONCEPTS
Blues inflections, chromatic harmony, through-composed form.
CHAPTER HIGHLIGHT
Art Song
The art song in the twentieth century took on the inflections of many different styles. Still's setting of a text by Langston Hughes blends a highly chromatic idiom with elements of the blues.

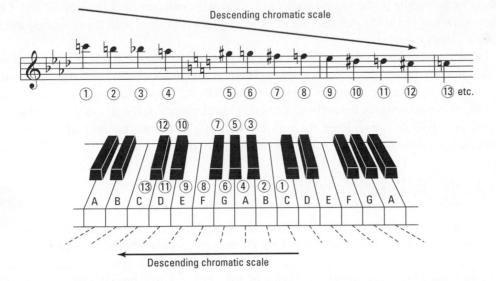

Descending chromatic scale

Descending chromatic scale

HISTORICAL CONTEXT The Harlem Renaissance

William Grant Still and the poet Langston Hughes are only two of the many African American artists associated with a movement known as the "Harlem Renaissance." During the 1920s, Harlem—in upper Manhattan, in New York City—emerged as a kind of cultural capital of African American arts, including literature, painting, and music. Other artists associated with the Harlem Renaissance include the writers Zora Neale Hurston and Wallace Thurman, the entertainers Josephine Baker and Paul Robeson, and the composer-musician Duke Ellington (see chapter 47). Many works by these artists, including Langston Hughes's poem "A Black Pierrot," openly celebrated African American identity. In many ways, the Harlem Renaissance brought African American art into the American mainstream.

Culture and politics, never too distant from one another, were closely allied in the Harlem Renaissance. Artists and the public alike recognized that the production of art by African American artists could help promote the struggle for racial equality. The poet James Weldon Johnson (author of the lyrics to "Lift Ev'ry Voice and Sing") was a longtime activist in the National Association for the Advancement of Colored People (NAACP); the singer Paul Robeson would later become an important leader in the civil rights movement.

The poet Langston Hughes in front of his house in Harlem, New York City.
Robert W. Kelley/Getty Images/Time Life Pictures

It therefore implies no tonal center. (In the same way, a scale consisting entirely of whole steps implies no tonal center—see chapter 40.) To create a tonic sound, a scale must contain both half and whole steps—as, for example, the familiar major and minor scales do. Still bases this song on a major scale, but he uses extra half steps from the chromatic scale to obscure the tonic and continually move the music away from it.

We hear the tonic center infrequently enough in this song for it to stand out. It appears most strongly in the middle of the second stanza and again at the end (see the Listening Guide). Listen to the contrasting sense of tonal stability in these passages compared with the chromatic instability of the others.

The harmonizations at the end of the song are particularly intense when the last two lines of text are presented three times in succession. The first two times (1:42–1:59) the voice and the piano harmonize the tonic together. The third time (2:00–2:23), only the voice stays in the tonic, while the piano harmonizes the melodic line in highly chromatic fashion, using lots of half steps to pointedly avoid the tonic. Even the very last harmony of the work—normally a tonic—is a chromatic inflection of the tonic, not a pure resolution to the home key.

Melody: A Touch of Blue

The melody, always in the voice, is chromatic throughout, wandering and weaving around the notes of the chromatic scale. Like the harmony, it rarely establishes a firm sense of arrival, and when it does land on a point of stability, it does not stay there very long. Only at the end of the song do we hear an extended point of arrival ("... a new brown love").

The melody also shows certain affinities at points to the blues; this is, after all, the song of a rejected lover. When the music finally lands squarely on the tonic for the first time, for example (on the word "black" in "black Pierrot" at 0:40), we hear what sounds rather like a "blue note," a note that is slightly lower than its given pitch in a standard scale; see page 392). The accompanimental figures at several subsequent points (0:48, 1:11) aid the melody in evoking the spirit of the blues, at least indirectly, with the walking bass line and the off-beat chords in the piano.

Still also uses changes of register in the vocal line to emphasize important moments in the text. The first strophe moves gradually from a low to a high register, the second occupies a middle range, and the third moves from high to low and back to high again, hitting the highest note of the entire song at the very end, by the musical and emotional climax of the song.

Through-Composed Form

CONNECT YOUR PLAYLIST

Through-Composed Form

Find a work in through-composed form.

Example: Queen, "Bohemian Rhapsody" (1975)
This song by Queen does not use a typical verse-chorus format, but instead has very different sections of music that proceed one after another.

In spite of a good deal of textual repetition between strophes—each strophe begins with the same two lines, and the first word of the third line ("So") is also the same—there is very little repetition or even variation of musical ideas in this song. Instead, each strophe receives its own musical setting. This type of form is called **through-composed**, in which the composer uses distinctly new music from beginning to end. Through-composed form differs from strophic form (same music for each strophe) and modified strophic form (a variation of the same music for each strophe—see chapter 28).

PROFILE   **William Grant Still** (1895–1978)

A Career of Firsts

In an age when the world of the American concert hall was still largely closed to African American composers and musicians, William Grant Still compiled a remarkable record of "firsts." He was the first African American composer to have a symphony performed by a major orchestra (*Afro-American Symphony*, Rochester Philharmonic, 1931), the first to conduct a major American orchestra (the Los Angeles Philharmonic, in 1936), and the first to have an opera performed by a major American opera company (*Troubled Island*, New York City Opera, 1949).

Born in Woodville, Mississippi, Still was raised in Little Rock, Arkansas. After attending Wilberforce University, he studied composition at Oberlin Conservatory and the New England Conservatory of Music. (This was not a first: these schools, and others like them north of the Mason-Dixon line, had been accepting African American students for many decades, even if not in great numbers.) Still worked in New York City throughout the 1920s, arranging music for jazz bands and dance orchestra while launching his career as a composer. He moved to Los Angeles in the early 1930s and spent the rest of his life there, composing and arranging music for films and writing works for the stage and concert hall. In many of his works he sought to create an idiom that blended such African American idioms as spirituals or the blues into more traditionally European genres like the symphony, the opera, and the ballet.

William Grant Still, ca. 1930.
Lebrecht Music & Arts/Lebrecht Music & Arts
Photo Library

◉➔ **EXPLORE MORE** on **www.mymusiclab.com**

◀◀   **EXPAND YOUR PLAYLIST: STILL**   ▶▶

- *Songs of Separation.* The complete cycle of songs for voice and piano.

- *Africa.* For piano.

- **Symphony no. 1** (*Afro-American Symphony*). Uses blues progressions.

- *Troubled Island.* An opera.

- *And They Lynched Him on a Tree.* For chorus.

(((• **HEAR SAMPLES** on **www.mymusiclab.com**

Through-composed form was not new in the twentieth century: composers had been using this approach to setting texts for centuries. But it is one of the devices that tends to distinguish the art song repertory from that of popular song, which tends to use strophic or modified strophic form.

With these points in mind, listen to this song once again, using the Listening Guide.

Listening Guide

GO TO www.mymusiclab.com for the Automated Listening Guide
CD V • Track 7/Download Track 80

William Grant Still Composed: 1949 "A Black Pierrot" from *Songs of Separation* (2:26)

Time	Text	Form	Harmony	Melody
0:00	I am a black Pierrot: / She did not love me, / So I crept away into the night / And the night was black, too.	A	Avoids landing on the tonic clearly.	Voice line moves from a low to high register.
0:37	I am a black Pierrot: / She did not love me, / So I wept until the dawn / Dripped blood over the eastern hills / And my heart was bleeding, too.	B	Establishes tonic clearly finally at 0:48, but then starts moving away from it again after 0:58.	The voice line stays in the middle register.
1:16	I am a black Pierrot: / She did not love me, / So with my once gay-colored soul / Shrunken like a balloon without air, / I went forth in the morning / To seek a new brown love.	C	The last two lines are repeated three times, with the voice and piano both in the tonic the first two times, but only the voice in the tonic the third time (from 2:00 onward), with the piano harmonizing against and not with the tonic key.	Moves from high to low and back to high again, reaching the highest note of the entire song at the very end

"A Black Pierrot," from THE COLLECTED POEMS OF LANGSTON HUGHES by Langston Hughes, edited by Arnold Rampersad with David Roessel, Associate Editor, copyright © 1994 by The Estate of Langston Hughes. Used by permission of Alfred A. Knopf, a division of Random House, Inc. and by permission of Harold Ober Associates Incorporated.

Student FAQs

Schoenberg's Pierrot is sung by a female, Still's by a male. Why is that?

Still's setting preserves the male persona of Pierrot. Schoenberg's creates an even greater sense of distance between the character (Pierrot, a male) and the singer (a female). Which approach is more effective in setting texts like these? That is a matter of debate.

"Zora and Langston" by Phoebe Beasley depicts African American authors Zora Neale Hurston and Langston Hughes

Phoebe Beasley, "Zora and Langston", 1988, Mixed Media Collage, 36 x 36. From the collection of: Ron and Charlayne Hunter-Gault

Did Langston Hughes and William Grant Still collaborate on these settings?

No. While the two were acquainted, Still set a text that Hughes had written more than 20 years before. It is also worth remembering that Still had to pay royalties to Hughes for using his texts in these new songs.

Langston Hughes
Getty Images

◀◀   **EXPAND YOUR PLAYLIST**   ▶▶

Twentieth-Century African American Composers in the Western Classical Tradition

In addition to William Grant Still, Scott Joplin (see chapter 45), Duke Ellington (see chapter 47), and Tania León (see chapter 61), many African American composers have established their place in the concert hall, writing in genres and idioms associated with the Western classical tradition.

Florence Beatrice Price (1887–1953)
• was born in Little Rock, Arkansas, and studied at the New England Conservatory. A number of her works incorporate Negro spirituals, including her *Mississippi River Suite*.

Henry T. Burleigh (1866–1949)
• was born in Erie, Pennsylvania. He taught the Czech composer Antonín Dvořák about the music of African Americans during Dvořák's years in the United States (see Chapter 39). He wrote many art songs that use melodies from Negro spirituals, including *Deep River*.

Margaret Bonds (1913–1972)
• although born in Chicago, spent most of her life in New York City. She was a friend of Langston Hughes and set many of his texts to music, including *Three Dream Portraits*.

George Walker (b. 1922)
• born in Washington, D.C., studied composition at Oberlin College and the Eastman School of Music. He was the first African American composer to win the Pulitzer Prize in music (in 1996), for his *Lilacs*, a work for voice and orchestra.

Keith Jarrett (b. 1945)
• born in Allentown, Pennsylvania, performs and composes in many different styles, including jazz, gospel, and classical. His *Elegy for Violin and Strings*, written for his Hungarian grandmother, uses idioms often associated with gypsy music.

((•● HEAR SAMPLES on **www.mymusiclab.com**

 TEST YOURSELF on **www.mymusiclab.com**   Flashcards and chapter tests

52

Aaron Copland
"Hoe-Down" from *Rodeo* (3:05)
Composed: 1942

How do you create the sense of a place through music alone, without words or images? Aaron Copland did just that in his *Rodeo* (pronounced "ro-DAY-oh") when he captured the sound of the American West in a ballet. "Hoe-Down" is a scene from that ballet.

 Listen to this first

((• HEAR MORE on www.mymusiclab.com

Melody	**Timbre**	**Rhythm**	**Form**
How long before you hear something in this work that actually sounds like a real melody? And when it finally arrives, what is it like? Is it conjunct or disjunct—that is, does it move by steps or by leaps? What about other melodies that come in later on?	This work is for a large orchestra, but how often do you actually hear all the instruments playing? Listen for long passages with smaller groupings of instruments within the orchestra.	Listen to the way the meter is simple at times, complex at others. Some sections are in straightforward duple meter, while others are full of syncopation (off-beat accents).	Listen for the repeated return of the opening section's main idea and the contrast with sections based on other melodies. This movement is a rondo.

⚙ LEARN MORE on
www.mymusiclab.com
Chapter Objectives

Copland composed *Rodeo* at the request of the dancer Agnes de Mille, who choreographed the work and danced the lead role. The story takes place somewhere in the American West and centers on the Cowgirl, who is determined to win the heart of the Head Wrangler. The Head Wrangler is unimpressed with the Cowgirl's prowess with ropes and horses. Not until the concluding Hoe-down—the big Saturday night dance—does she succeed in catching his eye (and his heart), having traded her cowboy outfit for a dress. De Mille once jokingly described the scenario as "The Taming of the Shrew—cowboy style." Shortly after completing the ballet, Copland extracted four scenes to be played in concert settings, of which "Hoe-Down" is the last.

Copland creates an identifiably American sound in this movement by using actual folk tunes that are rhythmically vigorous and cover a wide range. He also orchestrates his music in an extremely open fashion—that is, he uses the full range of registers from highest to lowest and leaves as much space as possible between groups of instruments. This "open scoring," as musicians refer to it, creates a kind of sonic counterpart to the open spaces of the American West.

Folk Melodies

The opening melody—and the one that keeps returning in this movement—is a traditional fiddle tune called "Bonaparte's Retreat." Alan Lomax, a folklorist, recorded a version of it by "Fiddler Bill" Stepp (1875–1957) in eastern Kentucky in 1937. Ruth Crawford Seeger (see chapter 49) transcribed the recording for Alan and John Lomax's anthology *Our Singing Country* (1941). Copland found the melody in this collection (called "Bonyparte" there), orchestrated it, and incorporated it into the larger movement he called "Hoe-Down." He introduces the theme gradually by first presenting only a small portion of it at the very beginning, followed by the sounds of a square-dance band tuning up. Only later do we hear the main melody in its full form. The music stays squarely in the tonic in this opening section, in keeping with the mood of a folk dance.

The jaunty, disjunct melody in the middle of the movement (**C** in the Listening Guide) is also based on a traditional fiddling tune. Copland found this melody, called "McLeod's Reel," in another published anthology of American folk tunes. Like "Bonaparte's Retreat," it contributes to the identifiably American sound of "Hoe-Down."

Timbre: Smaller Ensembles Within the Orchestra

Copland creates variety within this movement by varying the orchestration throughout. At times we hear the full ensemble—a big orchestra, with a large percussion section of timpani, piano, xylophone, snare drum, bass drum, cymbal, and wood block— and at other times we hear a reduced ensemble of only a few instruments. The piano is a relative newcomer to the orchestra; Copland uses it sparingly but to good effect by imitating the sound of a piano one would typically hear in a Western dance-hall.

The timbres are noticeably bright and transparent. Even though Copland is writing for a large orchestra, he allows the individual instruments or groups of instruments to come through clearly because he writes in what might be called sonic layers, with each instrumental grouping projecting its own identity. Listen to the groups of sounds at the very opening: the strings are clearly divided into low and high groupings that are distinct from each other and distinct yet again from the brass instruments, which themselves are clearly divided into high and low groupings. This kind of writing helps reinforce the contrast of sound between these layers. And like many twentieth-century composers writing for orchestra, Copland also gives unusual prominence to the percussion instruments. The notion of giving a fiddle tune to a xylophone (at 0:34, for example) creates a particularly penetrating sound.

1900–1990
Aaron Copland
"Hoe-Down" from *Rodeo*
Composed: 1942
GENRE
Ballet
KEY CONCEPTS
Populist modernism, traditional folk tunes, "open" orchestration and texture, rondo form.
CHAPTER HIGHLIGHT
Nationalism
Copland pioneered a sound that evoked the open spaces of the western United States. In the ballet *Rodeo*, wide spacing of instruments, bright timbres, and energetic rhythms contribute to a distinctively American sound.

The American dancer Agnes de Mille in the role of the Cowgirl in the premiere of Copland's *Rodeo* (1942). De Mille also choreographed this production, which blended modern ballet with square dancing. She later choreographed a number of Broadway musicals, including *Oklahoma!* (1943), *Carousel* (1945), *Brigadoon* (1947), and *Paint Your Wagon* (1951).
© 2008 Ronald Seymour, Inc. Photo: Maurice Seymour

Dance Rhythms

A hoe-down is an energetic, duple-meter dance that has come to be associated particularly with the tradition of Western square-dancing, and Copland maintains duple meter throughout. But he varies the beat by presenting some sections in clearly demarcated duple meter while introducing a high degree of syncopation into other sections. Consider the opening melody ("Bonaparte's Retreat"): Copland accents the highest notes of the tune whenever it leaps upward. Or listen to the main melody when first presented by the full orchestra: the brass instruments come in consistently off the beat, and this creates a sense of forward momentum that would otherwise be lacking.

Rondo Form

Copland constructs this dance in the form of a **rondo**. The main theme (**A**), or at least parts of it, alternates with contrasting melodic ideas. The opening is particularly clever: Copland captures the spirit and even the sequence of events in a Western-style dance by having the orchestra "tune up" early on, and by presenting accompanimental patterns but no real melodies until about half a minute into the piece: the ensemble is getting ready, but it takes a little while for it to get into the full swing of things. Only with the first return of the **A** section do we hear the main theme in its entirety for the first time. We've been anticipating it, and the orchestra has been hinting at it, but only now do we actually hear it.

Now listen to this music again, using the Listening Guide.

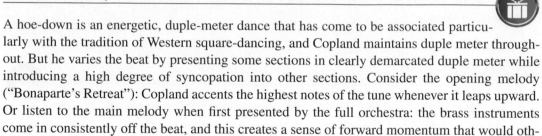

HISTORICAL CONTEXT   Using "Hoe-Down"

Copland's re-working of a traditional fiddle tune in "Hoe-Down" has been used in a number of very different ways, from movie soundtracks to TV ads to the Olympics:

1. The British rock group Emerson, Lake, and Palmer recorded their version of the tune, called "Hoedown," on the 1972 album *Trilogy.* The album reached number 5 on Billboard's chart at one point.

2. In the early 1990s, the National Cattlemen's Beef Association and Beef Board began using Copland's version of the tune as the musical backdrop for a series of television commercials with the tagline "Beef: It's What's for Dinner."

3. The director Spike Lee used Copland's version in the soundtrack to the 1998 film *He Got Game.* Actually, Lee used several of Copland's works in the soundtrack. "When I listen to Copland's music," Lee explained, "I hear America, and basketball is America. It's like he wrote the score for this film."

4. In 2000, the bluegrass-jazz group Béla Fleck and the Flecktones recorded their own version of the tune on *Outbound.*

5. The opening ceremony of the 2002 Winter Olympics, in Salt Lake City, used Copland's version from *Rodeo* as a backdrop to an enormous hoe-down with hundreds of dancers.

6. In 2006, Bob Dylan used a recording of Copland's "Hoe-Down" for his stage entrance at live performances.

Listening Guide

GO TO www.mymusiclab.com
for the Automated Listening Guide
CD V • Track 8/Download Track 81

Aaron Copland Composed: 1942 "Hoe-Down" from *Rodeo* (3:05)

Time	Form: Section	Melody	Timbre	Rhythm
0:00	A	Fanfare-like figure in the brass, swirling figures in the strings; then (0:04) an imitation of instruments being tuned in the strings, but no real melody yet	Full orchestra	No clear sense of meter, much syncopation
0:15	B	Dancelike accompaniment, but still no clear melody	Piano bass line, wood blocks, imitation of a dance-hall double bass in the lower strings	Clear duple meter
0:34	A′	Same swirling figure as in **A**, but now it continues to present the main melody of the movement, a rapid, energetic theme that swoops down and then up.	Violins play the melody as if it were being played on a country fiddle (0:42). Prominent parts for oboe (0:58) and xylophone (throughout).	Duple meter, but with syncopation in some voices
1:25	C	Jaunty, disjunct melody with large upward leap	Solo trumpet (1:25), solo oboe (1:33), solo violin (1:36), then the full orchestra (1:40)	Duple meter, no syncopation at first; then increasing syncopation as brass enter (1:47) and grow stronger
2:07	B′	Dancelike accompaniment, again without any clear melody	Piano bass line, wood blocks (2:09); trombone (2:15); strings and celesta (2:30)	Duple meter, no syncopation. Tempo gradually slows down, as if the music is running out of energy
2:32	A″	Main melody returns	Full orchestra	Tempo returns to its original fast pace. Duple meter with much syncopation.

Student FAQs

What was Agnes de Mille's choreography of Rodeo like?

From still pictures, her notes, and eyewitness accounts, we know that de Mille's choreography combined the free movements of modern dance with more traditional elements of folk dancing and square-dancing. Unfortunately, we have no film version of how she and her troupe performed this ballet.

This music is used so often and in so many places (see "Using Hoe-Down," page 436). Who gets the royalties today?

The royalties go to Aaron Copland's estate, which funds a program that allows individual composers to spend six weeks in residence at the house in which Copland lived for the last 30 years of his life, in Cortlandt, New York, in Westchester County, just north of New York City.

Rodgers & Hammerstein Organization/
Lebrecht Music & Arts Photo Library

PROFILE   Aaron Copland (1900–1990)

Populist Modernist

Born in Brooklyn, Aaron Copland came of age in the 1920s and 1930s. He was consumed with the idea of writing "American music." Like so many of his contemporaries, he was trained in the European tradition, and he could write in the style of cutting-edge modernists when he wanted to. Yet he was politically and emotionally a populist at heart. He never lost touch with his American roots, using actual folk tunes in such works as *Rodeo* and *Appalachian Spring*. He also wrote music for a number of Hollywood films, including *Our Town*, *Of Mice and Men*, and *The Heiress*, for which he won an Oscar.

In addition to his work as a composer, Copland was also a superb lecturer and writer on music. His *What to Listen for in Music* remains a model of its kind.

Aaron Copland and Nadia Boulanger, 1972. In the 1920s, Copland studied composition with Boulanger (1887–1979) in her native France. Her later pupils included such prominent American composers as Roy Harris, Walter Piston, Virgil Thomson, and Elliott Carter.

Douglas Lyttle

⊙➔ **EXPLORE MORE** on **www.mymusiclab.com**

EXPAND YOUR PLAYLIST: COPLAND

- *Fanfare for the Common Man.* A short but memorable work, often used (like "Hoe-Down") in commercials.

- *Appalachian Spring.* A ballet written for Martha Graham, celebrating the virtues of frontier life.

- *Lincoln Portrait.* For narrator and orchestra, using Lincoln's own words as a spoken text.

- *Twelve Poems of Emily Dickinson.* For solo voice and piano.

((•• **HEAR SAMPLES** on **www.mymusiclab.com**

HISTORICAL CONTEXT   "Are You Now or Have You Ever Been . . .?"

It is ironic that Aaron Copland, whose music has been so strongly identified with America, was the most prominent composer brought before Congress to testify in the McCarthy hearings of the early 1950s. Sen. Joseph McCarthy was convinced that Communists and Communist sympathizers had infiltrated the U.S. government. The arts of all kinds, including music, were part of the Cold War effort to fight the influence of the Soviet Union, and Copland was an ideal ambassador for American culture. But he had also belonged to several musical groups that fostered contacts between American and Soviet composers, and this brought him—and many other artists—under the suspicion of being a "Communist sympathizer."

Copland protested strenuously that participation in such groups was based entirely on his concern with cultural and musical affairs. But the taint of association lingered, and Copland had trouble securing a passport to travel abroad for several years. When his *Lincoln Portrait* was performed on television's *Ed Sullivan Show* in 1956, Ed Sullivan pointedly failed to identify the composer of the work. With time, however, Copland regained his status as an iconic American composer. In 1986, the same Congress that had investigated him 30 years earlier awarded him the Congressional Gold Medal, its highest civilian honor.

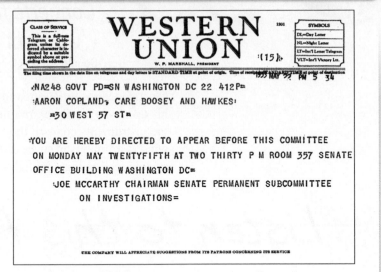

Copland's subpoena to testify before Congress on May 25, 1953. He received this telegram on May 22.

Reprinted by permission of the Aaron Copland Fund for Music, Inc., copyright owner.

EXPAND YOUR PLAYLIST

The Sound of the American West

Rodeo was one of several works by Copland to evoke the American West, and other composers were quick to follow his lead in using sonic layers to create an open sound reflecting the open spaces of the region.

Aaron Copland
- *Billy the Kid*. A ballet commissioned by the choreographer Lincoln Kirsten in 1938.
- *The Red Pony*. A film score to the 1949 movie, starring Robert Mitchum and Myrna Loy, based on the short story by John Steinbeck.

Ferde Grofé
- *Grand Canyon Suite*. A suite for orchestra, composed in 1931. Each of the five movements paints in sound a scene from the Grand Canyon.

Dmitri Tiomkin
- *High Noon*. The film score won an Academy Award both for best song ("Do Not Forsake Me, Oh My Darlin'") and for best soundtrack.

Tiomkin was a Ukrainian who did not arrive in the United States until the age of 31.

Elmer Bernstein
- *The Magnificent Seven*. The main title theme has been used in innumerable commercials and is instantly recognizable as a sonic icon of the Old West.

Enrico Morricone
- *The Good, the Bad, and the Ugly*. One of the Italian composer's many scores for "spaghetti Westerns," so called because the films were produced and often directed by Italian artists (in this case, Sergio Leone). Morricone received a Lifetime Achievement Award at the 2007 Oscars ceremony for his film scores.

((•● HEAR SAMPLES on **www.mymusiclab.com**

✓ TEST YOURSELF on **www.mymusiclab.com**   Flashcards and chapter tests

53

Béla Bartók
Concerto for Orchestra, second movement ("Game of Pairs")
Composed: 1943

Most concertos are written to showcase the abilities of a soloist or a small group of soloists. In his *Concerto for Orchestra*, the Hungarian composer Béla Bartók created a work in which *all* of the instruments come to the fore at different times. The second movement features each of the wind instruments in succession including woodwinds (bassoons, oboes, clarinets, flutes), with a middle section that highlights the brass instruments (trumpets, trombones, tuba, horns).

 Listen to this first

((•● HEAR MORE on www.mymusiclab.com

Timbre	**Melody**	**Form**
Listen for the variety of instrumental sounds, beginning with a succession of prominent passages by the woodwinds (first bassoons, then oboes, clarinets, and flutes), and then brass instruments (trumpets, trombones, horns, tuba). A small side drum introduces and ends the movement.	Listen for phrases and cadences within each melody. Also listen for a tonal center in each: do these melodies have a tonal center, or are they atonal?	Listen for the large-scale A-B-A' form: the opening section with the woodwinds returns in varied form about two-thirds of the way through the movement. Where does the "B" section begin? How is A' different from the original A?

⚙ LEARN MORE on
www.mymusiclab.com
Chapter Objectives

Bartók's *Concerto for Orchestra* is one the most frequently performed of all twentieth-century orchestral works. Popular with audiences and performers alike, it gives every instrument a chance to shine. Bartók's style of writing reflects his fascination with the melodies and rhythms characteristic of eastern European folk music idioms.

Wind Timbres

The second movement, entitled *Giuoco delle coppie* ("Game of Pairs") features a series of wind instruments introduced mostly in pairs. The "game" element stems from the playful nature of the music: there is a loose, almost carefree feeling to the way each pair of instruments steps up to the spotlight and then gives way to the next pair. One might almost imagine this movement as a series of paired dancers who emerge out of a crowd to take center stage for a brief time and then recede back into the crowd.

Listen for the contrast of timbres among these instruments:

- **Bassoons** (0:12). A double-reed instrument in the lower register, with a gruff, slightly raspy sound.

Bassoons

- **Oboes** (0:36). Another double-reed instrument, in a higher range, with a somewhat more piercing, nasal sound.

Oboes

- **Clarinets** (1:05). A single-reed instrument with a wide range and a resonant timbre.

Clarinets

- **Flutes** (1:27). A woodwind instrument (though nowadays mostly made of metal) without a reed. The flute features a delicate, "breathy" sound in a relatively high register.

Flutes

- **Trumpets** (2:12). A brass instrument with a high register and a sharp sound. At first, each trumpet here plays with a mute, a "stopper" placed in the bell of the instrument, which creates a softer, more subdued timbre. At (3:12) the trumpets remove the mutes.

Trumpets

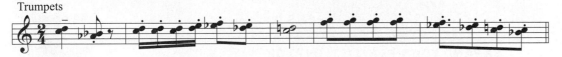

- **Trombones and Tuba** (3:12). These low brass instruments join the trumpets and play quietly here, producing a rounded, mellow tone.

Trumpets, Trombones, Tuba

- **Horns** (3:48). Also a member of the brass family, the horns (also known as "French horns") play here in a higher range, quietly.

1881–1945
Béla Bartók
Concerto for Orchestra,
second movement
("Game of Pairs")
Composed: 1943

GENRE
Concerto

KEY CONCEPTS
Orchestration, instruments of the orchestra, symmetrical form, folk melodies, ethnomusicology.

CHAPTER HIGHLIGHT
Orchestral Virtuosity
Bartók collected folk melodies not only from his native Hungary, but from other regions of Europe and the world as well, and the melodies of his own compositions, as in this movement from the *Concerto for Orchestra*, reflect these unusual melodies in their inflections and harmonizations. This work allows individual instruments of the orchestra, especially the winds in this movement, to come to the fore.

PROFILE   **Béla Bartók** (1881–1945)

Scholar-Composer-Performer

Although remembered today primarily as a composer, Bartók was active throughout his life as a scholar and performer as well. He devoted much of his early career to collecting, recording, and transcribing the music of various ethnic groups throughout central and eastern Europe (see "Bartók the Ethnomusicologist," page 445). He also concertized widely as a pianist, performing his own works as well as those by other composers. In 1940 he emigrated from Hungary to the United States, where he worked for a time at Columbia University in New York City, editing collections of eastern European folk music. Aside from a devoted but relatively small group of enthusiasts, however, his music did not generate much interest in the United States. His *Concerto for Orchestra* (1943), commissioned by Serge Koussevitsky, the conductor of the Boston Symphony Orchestra, soon attracted a wide following and established itself as one of the most popular of all twentieth-century orchestral works. Already ill, the composer died of leukemia less than a year after its premiere.

Bartók transcribing his field recordings of traditional music.
Sovfoto/Sovfoto/Eastfoto

⊙➔ **EXPLORE MORE** on **www.mymusiclab.com**

◄◄   EXPAND YOUR PLAYLIST: BARTÓK   ►►

- *Music for Strings, Percussion, and Celesta*. A work that features an orchestra without winds, and with the addition of a celesta, a keyboard instrument that creates a bell-like sound.

- *Piano Concerto No. 3*. The most popular of the composer's solo concertos, this work reflects Bartók's talents as a pianist.

- **String Quartet No. 4**. One of six Bartók wrote in this genre.

- *Mikrokosmos*, **for piano**. A large collection of mostly short works for piano, many of them inflected with folk-inspired elements.

((•● HEAR SAMPLES on **www.mymusiclab.com**

From 4:18 onward, the same instruments return in varied form but now in groups of three (three bassoons) or in combination with one another (two oboes and two clarinets together at 4:42; then two flutes and two clarinets together at 5:17). Listen for the combinations of timbres throughout. Two harps join in for the first time, discreetly, at 5:53.

Folk-Inflected Melodies

Throughout his life, Bartók collected and sometimes used in his works melodies played and sung by folk musicians from his native Hungary, eastern Europe, and even as far away as northern Africa and the Middle East. Although the *Concerto for Orchestra* does not use any specific melodies collected by the composer, its thematic ideas, rhythmic patterns, and harmonies are shaped by sounds that clearly derive from sources outside the tradition of Western art music. The opening theme on the bassoons (0:12), according to one scholar familiar with this repertory of folk music, imitates a round dance melody popular in the Balkans. The slightly menacing-sounding melody played by the muted trumpets (2:12) is harmonized largely in seconds (think of the opening of "Chopsticks") rather than the more conventional thirds (think of the first change in harmony just after the opening of "Chopsticks"). This kind of harmonization in seconds is common among certain ethnic repertories of eastern Europe. The resulting idiom is tonal, but not in a conventional way: while there is a tonal center, the melodies and the associated harmonies do not follow the practices of "standard" repertory by composers like Beethoven, Schumann, or Brahms.

Asymmetrical-Symmetrical Form

The second movement is in ternary form (ABA') and in many respects resembles a minuet from a classical symphony (see, for example, Haydn's Symphony no. 102, chapter 22), with a sharply contrasting middle section. But here, the return of the "A" section is far from literal: while the themes are recognizably the same as those heard before, they are altered in subtle ways and presented with new combinations of instruments.

The resulting form is basically symmetrical. Bartók held a lifelong fascination with the idea of musical symmetry at many levels: he liked melodies that balanced on a central axis, moving toward and away from a central point. He also frequently constructed entire movements—including this one—around a central point, with a beginning and ending that "mirror" each other. The solo side drum opens and closes the movement, and the woodwind sections (A and A') surround the central brass section (B):

Introduction	Coda	A	B	A'
Side drum	Woodwinds	Brass	Woodwinds	Side drum
0:00	0:12	3:12	4:18	6:42

Within this basic framework of symmetry, Bartók varies the return of the A' by changing both the instrumentation and the manipulation of the thematic ideas heard earlier in the movement. The result is a movement that is both symmetrical and asymmetrical at one and the same time.

Now listen to this music again, using the Listening Guide.

CONNECT YOUR PLAYLIST

Symmetrical Form

Find a work whose ending is either very similar or identical to its beginning.

Example: Béla Fleck, "Crossfire" (1982) The rolling melodic figure played by the banjo (0:00–0:15) that opens the piece is repeated, with a syncopated guitar accompaniment, to close the piece (3:05–3:20).

Listening Guide

GO TO www.mymusiclab.com
for the Automated Listening Guide
CD V •Track 9 /Download Track 82

Béla Bartók Composed: 1943 *Concerto for Orchestra,* second movement ("Game of Pairs") (6:47)

Time	Melody	Timbre: Solo Instruments	Timbre: Supporting Instruments	Form
0:00		Side drum	none	Introduction
0:12	1	Bassoons (2)	Strings, pizzicato (plucked)	A
0:36	2	Oboes (2)	Strings, both pizzicato and bowed	
1:05	3	Clarinets (2)		
1:27	4	Flutes (2)		
2:12	5	Trumpets (2)		
2:57		Side drum		Transition
3:02	6	Brass choir: Trumpets with mutes (2), trombones (2), tuba	Side drum	B
3:48		Brass choir: Horns (4), tuba		
4:09	1	Woodwinds return one by one		Transition
4:18	1	Bassoons (3)	Strings, pizzicato (plucked)	A'
4:42	3	Oboes (2), clarinets (2)	Strings, both pizzicato and bowed	
5:07	4	Flutes (2), clarinets (2), bassoons (2)		
5:53	5	Trumpets (2), clarinets (2)	Strings (with mutes) and harps (2)	
6:42		Side drum	none	Coda

Student FAQs

Don't the harps enter in the first section of the movement, when the trumpets come in?

Bartók creates a harp-like sound at this point (2:12) by asking some of the violins to play a series of glissandi or "gliding" figures in which the player moves a finger up and down the fingerboard continuously, creating a kind of sound similar to what harps produce. But the harps themselves enter the movement only at 5:53. This is a good example of Bartók's ability to create asymmetrical symmetry through timbre.

Is the side drum the same as a snare drum?

The "snares" on a drum are heavy strings or wires that, when engaged, vibrate against the drum-head, creating a sort of "rattling" sound. In this movement, Bartók calls for a side drum, which is, in effect, a drum without snares, or with the snares disengaged.

© Dorling Kindersley

HISTORICAL CONTEXT   Bartók the Ethnomusicologist

Ethnomusicology is a field of musicology—the scholarly study of music—that focuses on the social dimension of the art and the ways in which music is used within and between cultures. Although ethnomusicologists today study music of all kinds from all times and places, the origins of the discipline began in the late nineteenth century with the study of non-Western and vernacular ("folk") repertories, many of which had been transmitted orally from one generation to the next, without the use of musical notation.

Béla Bartók was among the first generation of scholars who did ethnomusicological field work, traveling not only across his native Hungary but throughout eastern Europe and as far afield as the Middle East and northern Africa to record the music of communities whose music had never been documented. Like many other early ethnomusicologists, Bartók used a combination of musical notation and mechanical recording devices (including early phonographs) to capture and preserve a repertory that might otherwise have been lost in the coming advance of radio, television, and other mass media. At the time Bartók was doing his field work, many of these communities were largely isolated and self-contained. When he visited an area of Transylvania (in a region that is now part of Romania) in 1909, he observed that "for miles on end, in these parts, there are entire villages with illiterate inhabitants, communities which are not linked by any railways or roads. . . . When one comes into such a region one has the feeling of a return to the Middle Ages."[1] Such isolation meant that the melodies of the people were (to use Bartók's own terms) "pure" and "uncontaminated" by the outside elements. In this "uncontaminated" music,

Bartók (fourth from left) records folksongs in a village located in what is now the Czech Republic. Before the advent of microphones and tape recorders, early recordings were made directly onto a disc or wire cylinder. In this photograph from 1908, Bartók assists a villager who is singing directly into the recording device.
CORBIS—NY

Bartók found inspiration for his own compositions destined for the concert hall, a fresh source of material that was at once both very old and very new.

[1]Bartók, Béla. *Essays*, ed. Benjamin Suchoff (London: Faber & Faber, 1976), 119–120.

◀◀   **EXPAND YOUR PLAYLIST**   ▶▶

Orchestral Music of the Twentieth Century

Debussy, Ives, Schoenberg, Stravinsky, Copland, and Bartók are only a few of the twentieth-century composers who wrote works in many genres for the orchestra. Some others include the following:

Dmitri Shostakovich
• Symphony No. 7 (1942). Inspired by the Siege of Leningrad (St. Petersburg) during World War II.

Krzysztof Penderecki
• *Threnody for the Victims of Hiroshima* (1960). A work for large string orchestra that calls for performers to play their instruments in unusual ways. A "threnody" is a lament for the dead, in this case the victims of the first atomic bomb dropped on Japan in 1945.

Ellen Taaffe Zwilich
• *Three Movements for Orchestra (Symphony No. 1)*. Winner of the Pulitzer Prize for Music in 1983.

((•● HEAR SAMPLES on **www.mymusiclab.com**

 TEST YOURSELF on **www.mymusiclab.com**   Flashcards and chapter tests

54

Leonard Bernstein
"Tonight" from *West Side Story*
Composed: 1957

Leonard Bernstein's *West Side Story* is a modern-day retelling of the story of Romeo and Juliet. The feuding "families" in this case are urban gangs: the Jets (whites) and Sharks (Puerto Ricans). When Tony, a Jet, falls in love with Maria, whose brother Bernardo is leader of the Sharks, the stage is set for a tragic ending.

Listen to this first

(((● HEAR MORE on www.mymusiclab.com

Melody	**Texture**	**Form**	**Word-Music Relationships**
Listen for the two contrasting melodies in this scene. How are they different? Who sings which?	Listen for the growing complexity of texture, from the homophonic beginning (one singer with accompaniment) to the polyphonic ending (five different vocal lines).	Listen for the way in which the scene grows from a series of sections sung by individual singers (solos) to a trio (three different singers) to a quintet. Also listen for the way in which the two main themes are varied and eventually combined.	The key word in this scene is "tonight." Listen for the way in which it is sung consistently (but very differently) in each of the two melodies. Notice, too, how all the singers arrive at this one word together from different routes at the very end of the scene.

⚙ **LEARN MORE** on
www.mymusiclab.com
Chapter Objectives

Unlike opera, which is sung from beginning to end, the **musical** is a spoken drama with substantial amounts of singing. The idea of working songs into spoken plays goes back to Shakespeare and even before. During the eighteenth century, however, the music in some of these plays became more extensive and important than the spoken parts. Mozart even wrote a few works like this (the German term is *Singspiel*, or "song-play"), and this new genre of **operetta**—literally "small opera"—flourished in the nineteenth century, particularly in the works of Johann Strauss (*Die Fledermaus*) and Gilbert and Sullivan (*Pirates of Penzance*, *H.M.S. Pinafore*, *The Mikado*). These works were typically comic and lighthearted, often sentimental. They were also enormously popular and profitable. Transplanted to the United States, the operetta reached new heights, becoming known as the musical or the "Broadway musical," in honor of the street in New York City with the greatest concentration of musical theaters. In the hands of such American composers as Jerome Kern (*Show Boat*), Richard Rodgers (*Oklahoma!*), and Allen Jay Lerner (*My Fair Lady*), the Broadway musical soon developed into an institution that would be exported throughout the world.

The musical *West Side Story* was an instant hit when it premiered in 1957. Bernstein's music uses elements of jazz, both in its orchestration and in its syncopated rhythms. The characters in the scene here are as follows:

- Riff, leader of the Jets
- Bernardo, leader of the Sharks
- Chorus of Jets
- Chorus of Sharks
- Anita, a Puerto Rican, the girlfriend of Bernardo
- Tony, a Jet in love with Maria
- Maria, the sister of Bernardo, in love with Tony

All of them have big plans for "tonight." The Jets and Sharks are planning a rumble (fight). Anita readies herself for a night of passion with Bernardo. And Tony and Maria plan to see each other when it is dark, for they cannot carry on their romance in the light of day.

Representative Melodies

There are two opposing emotions in this scene: hate (between the Jets and the Sharks) and love (between Tony and Maria). Bernstein gives each a representative melody. The opening of the scene sets out a choppy, fast-paced melody over an ostinato bass (marked as "1" in the Listening Guide) with strong syncopations. Though they are rival gangs, the Jets and Sharks both want the same thing, a fight, and we hear this in their music: their words are different, but both gangs sing the same melody. Tony and Maria also want the same thing—to be together— and we hear this in the very different music the two of them sing ("2," in the Listening Guide), a soaring, lyrical melody. This melody ("Tonight") is one they had sung earlier in the show in the "balcony scene." (The balcony in this urban setting was a fire escape.)

Anita occupies an interesting position here. She is more worldly than Maria, and her interest in Bernardo seems largely physical ("Anita's gonna get her kicks tonight"). She sings words of passion ("Don't matter if he's tired, As long as he's here") to the same melody sung by the Jets and Sharks in anticipation of their rumble.

Additive Form

The scene introduces the characters one by one and brings them all together (musically, at least) in the following order. The principal themes (1 and 2) are shown in parentheses.

1. Chorus: The Jets (led by Riff) and Sharks (led by Bernardo) each lay out their grievances with the other group. The two gangs occupy opposite ends of the stage and do not interact, even though they are singing the same music together and at times even the same words (1).
2. Solo (Anita). Anita sings the same melody in anticipation of her evening with Bernardo, after the fight (1).
3. Solo (Tony). Tony sings a new melody in anticipation of his evening with Maria (2).
4. Solo (Maria). Maria sings the same melody as Tony, anticipating her evening with him (2).
5. Chorus (Jets). The Jets approach Tony (1).

Bernardo (George Charkiris) leads two of his Sharks down the street. Jerome Robbins's choreography, both for the 1957 Broadway production and for the 1961 film, was widely acclaimed.

Mirisch-7 Arts/United Artists/The Kobal Collection

6. Trio (Maria, Tony, Riff). Maria continues Tony's lyrical melody (2). But instead of echoing her, Tony agrees to Riff's demands (1). We hear both themes simultaneously.

7. Quintet (Maria, Tony, Anita, Jets, Sharks). All the characters sing at once: Tony and Maria sing their melody (2) while all the others sing theirs (1). Everyone lands on the same word—"tonight"—at the very end.

By using just two basic melodies and distributing them among different characters, Bernstein is able to create a kind of **additive form** in which nothing disappears, but new layers are constantly added. This is a technique Bernstein had learned from the world of opera, in which the music in a given scene often becomes more layered—and the stage more populated—as the action progresses.

Increasingly Complex Textures

Closely related to the scene's additive form are its increasingly complex textures, which move from homophonic at the beginning (one melodic line with accompaniment), to a trio (three voices), to a quintet (five voices). What we hear at the end is, in effect, five monologues performed simultaneously. This reveals one of the advantages of sung drama over spoken drama. If these same characters were merely speaking their parts, we would comprehend none of them, and it would all sound like mere babble. Because we hear the characters singing their parts, we can differentiate among the contrasting melodies and emotions and experience them simultaneously.

Word-Music Relationships: "Tonight," Two Ways

The contrasts in the setting of this one word capture the basic conflict between the world of Tony and Maria and the world of the Jets and Sharks. Those anticipating the physical side of things—Riff and the Jets, Bernardo and the Sharks, and Anita—sing the word to a menacing-sounding figure that sounds impatient and pressed (Theme 1), while Tony and Maria sing the same word very differently, leaping up or down to a long, sustained note (Theme 2).

We would, of course, expect lovers to be singing the same melody to each other: in opera, this is one sure-fire indication that a couple is really in love, and it often marks a major moment in an onstage relationship. Bernstein plays off this convention by having the two lovers sing separately, in simultaneous monologues. He applies the same device to the two warring gangs: they are not singing to each other, either, and the fact that they share a common melody makes the whole situation that much more ironic, for in the end, the two gangs are not really all that different on a personal, human level. It is only their races that separate them.

With these points in mind, listen to this scene again, using the Listening Guide.

CONNECT YOUR PLAYLIST

Additive Form

Find a work in additive form.

Example: The Postal Service, "Nothing Better" (2003)
This song begins softly with only electronic sounds, and gradually adds musical layers, including bass, drums, and voice.

PROFILE   Leonard Bernstein (1918–1990)

Four Lives in One

Shortly after Leonard Bernstein died in 1990, the composer Ned Rorem observed that he had not died at the age of 72, but 288. Why? Because "Lenny led four lives in one." And indeed, Bernstein achieved what for many musicians would amount to four lifetimes' worth of accomplishments:

- As a conductor, he was the first American-born musician to lead a major symphony orchestra, the New York Philharmonic. He made his debut with the group in 1943 and served as its music director from 1958 to 1969. He was chosen to conduct the performance of Beethoven's Ninth Symphony in Berlin in 1989 that celebrated the fall of the Berlin Wall.

- As a composer, Bernstein wrote for the stage (*West Side Story*, *Candide*), the concert hall (three symphonies), the screen (*On the Waterfront*), and the ballet (*Fancy Free*).

- As a pianist, he collaborated with such prestigious groups as the Juilliard String Quartet, the Vienna Philharmonic, and the New York Philharmonic.

- As an educator, Bernstein worked tirelessly to expand audiences for classical music. His "Young People's Concerts," televised nationwide between 1958 and 1972, exposed millions to a repertory they might otherwise never have heard.

Bernstein in rehearsal in 1947 with the American soprano Marian Anderson (1897–1993).

Ruth Orkin/Estate of Ruth Orkin Photo Archive

◉➤ **EXPLORE MORE** on www.mymusiclab.com

EXPAND YOUR PLAYLIST: BERNSTEIN

- *On the Town.* Bernstein's first Broadway hit (1944).

- *Candide.* Another musical, based on Voltaire's satirical novel.

- *Chichester Psalms.* A setting of Psalms for chorus and orchestra, commissioned by the dean of Chichester Cathedral, England.

- *Mass.* A "theater piece" for dancers, singers, and orchestra, commissioned to inaugurate the opening of the Kennedy Center, Washington, D.C. (1971).

((•● HEAR SAMPLES on www.mymusiclab.com

Listening Guide

GO TO www.mymusiclab.com
for the Automated Listening Guide
CD V • Track 10/Download Track 83

Leonard Bernstein Composed: 1957 "Tonight" from *West Side Story*

Time	Form	Character(s)	Text	Melody
0:00	Orchestral Introduction			Agitated fanfare
0:07	Chorus	**JETS**	The Jets are gonna have their day—Tonight. The Jets are gonna have their way—Tonight. The Puerto Ricans grumble: "Fair fight." But if they start a rumble, We'll rumble them right.	1 = choppy melody with ostinato bass
0:22		**SHARKS**	We're gonna hand 'em a surprise—Tonight. We're gonna cut 'em down to size—Tonight We said, "O.K., no rumpus, No tricks." But just in case they jump us, we're ready to mix—Tonight.	
0:40		**JETS**	We're gonna rock it tonight, We're gonna jazz it up and have us a ball!	
0:46		**SHARKS**	They're gonna get it tonight; The more they turn it on the harder they'll fall!	
0:52		**JETS/SHARKS**	Well, they began it! Well, they began it!	
0:54		**ALL**	And we're the ones to stop 'em once and for all—Tonight!	
0:58	Orchestral Interlude			As in Intro
1:02	Solo	**ANITA**	Anita's gonna get her kicks—Tonight. We'll have our private little mix—Tonight. He'll walk in hot and tired, poor dear! Don't matter if he's tired, as long as he's here—tonight.	1 = variant of same melody
1:18	Solo	**TONY**	Tonight, tonight, won't be just any night, Tonight there will be no morning star. Tonight, tonight, I'll see my love tonight. And for us, stars will stop where they are.	2 = lyrical melody
1:42	Solo	**MARIA**	Today, the minutes seem like hours, the hours go so slowly, And still the sky is light. Oh moon, grow bright, And make this endless day endless night!	
2:05	Orchestral Interlude			Repeated fanfare

 Texture	Word-Music Relationships
Prominent brass with accompanying strings	
Homophonic	The word "tonight" stands out because it is sung smoothly to the same upward-moving figure each time. The Jets and Sharks are leaders of opposing gangs, but they have the same ideas (and music) about what will happen "tonight."
	Both gangs sing in unison; they have agreed that there will be a fight tonight.
As in Intro, with added clarinet figure	
	Anita is also singing of her (very different) plans for what will happen "tonight," using a variant of the same melody sung by the gangs.
Homophonic	A new melody, lyrical rather than choppy. The ostinato bass gives way to a flowing accompaniment. This is the return of a melody sung by Tony and Maria earlier in the show in their "balcony scene."
Full orchestra	

Time	Form	Character(s)	Text	Melody
2:12	Group	**JETS**	The Jets are comin' out on top—Tonight. We're gonna watch Bernardo drop—Tonight. That Puerto Rican punk'll go down. And when he's hollered "Uncle," we'll tear up the town!	1 = choppy melody
2:27	Trio	**MARIA**	Tonight, tonight, won't be just any night, Tonight there will be no morning star . . .	2
		RIFF	We'll be in back of you, boy?	1
		TONY	All right.	
		RIFF	We're gonna flatten him good.	
		TONY	All right.	
		RIFF (spoken)	One, two, three!	
		TONY (spoken)	One, two, three!	
		RIFF	And then we'll have us a ball:	
		TONY	Tonight . . .	
2:40	Quintet	**MARIA**	Tonight, tonight, I'll see my love tonight. And for us, stars will stop where they are.	2
		JETS/SHARKS	We're gonna rock it tonight! We're gonna jazz it tonight! They're gonna get it tonight.	1
		MARIA AND TONY	Today the minutes seem like hours. The hours go so slowly, And still the sky is light. Oh moon, grow bright, And make this endless day endless night,	2
		ANITA	Tonight, late tonight We're gonna mix it tonight. Anita's gonna have her day, Bernardo's gonna have his way, tonight.	
		JETS/SHARKS	They began it, they began it, they will watch. We'll stop 'em once and for all. The Sharks are gonna have their way, the Sharks are gonna have their day, We're gonna rock it tonight. Tonight!	
3:12		**ALL**	Tonight!	

Texture	Word-Music Relationships
Homophonic	
Polyphonic: both (1) and (2) at the same time	Maria sings Tony's melody (2) while Riff reminds Tony that he has to be at the fight tonight (1); Tony agrees (1).
Polyphonic	The climax of the scene, presenting the emotions of all the characters at once.
Maria and Tony sing the same music together for the first time in this scene	

What's the difference between music that is sung in an opera and music that is sung in a musical?

The two styles of writing overlap considerably—both genres have their arias, ensembles, choruses—so it's impossible to make hard-and-fast distinctions between the styles of the two. In general, the vocal parts in musicals tend to be somewhat less demanding from a technical point of view, though there are plenty of musically challenging roles on Broadway. There is perhaps more of a difference in styles of singing. Singers with a "Broadway voice" often project with a bigger, brassier kind of voice and in a manner that is more declamatory; they certainly have to be better actors than singers in a standard operatic production.

Harry Redl/Camera Press London/Retna Ltd.

Why are the lyrics in the stage version slightly different?

The 1961 movie version "cleaned up" the lyrics at several points to conform to the standards for Hollywood productions of the time. In the original stage production, for example, Anita sings: "He'll walk in hot and tired / So what? / Don't matter if he's tired / As long as he's hot."

What happens in the fight?

That would be a plot-spoiler. The movie version of *West Side Story* won many Academy Awards and is well worth seeing in its entirety.

Getty Images Inc.—Hulton Archive Photos

The costumes have been updated but the music and the story endure. This scene from the high school dance in *West Side Story* is taken from the recent Broadway revival, whose soundtrack won a Grammy award.

Getty Images, Inc.

◄◄ EXPAND YOUR PLAYLIST ►►

Broadway's Social Conscience

West Side Story stands in a long tradition of musicals that combine entertainment with social commentary.

Show Boat
• (1927, music by Jerome Kern, lyrics by Oscar Hammerstein II). The first major musical to tackle the issue of racial bigotry.

South Pacific
• (1948, music by Richard Rodgers, lyrics by Oscar Hammerstein II). One of the plot strands deals with prevailing prejudices against interracial love; the story is set against the backdrop of World War II.

My Fair Lady
• (1956, music by Frederick Loewe, lyrics by Alan Jay Lerner). Based on George Bernard Shaw's play *Pygmalion*, this musical tackles serious issues—poverty and social mobility—in a humorous but moving manner, focusing on language and speech as weapons of class warfare.

Les Misérables
• (1980, music by Claude-Michel Schönberg, lyrics by Alain Boublil). An adaptation of Victor Hugo's novel of the same name, this French musical (translated into English in 1982) explores the nature of poverty.

Miss Saigon
• (1989, music by Claude-Michel Schönberg, lyrics by Richard Maltby, Jr., and Alain Boublil). Based loosely on Puccini's *Madame Butterfly*, this musical considers the aftermath of the U.S. military involvement in Vietnam.

Rent
• (1996, music and lyrics by Jonathan Larson). A reinterpretation of Puccini's opera *La Bohème* (1897), *Rent* confronts issues of sexual orientation, drug addiction, and AIDS.

((•● HEAR SAMPLES on **www.mymusiclab.com**

✓ **TEST YOURSELF** on **www.mymusiclab.com** Flashcards and chapter tests

John Cage

Indeterminacy (excerpt)

Composed: 1959

Indeterminacy is a work of music in which many basic elements are left to chance. The excerpt here consists of two selections—each one a minute long—from a much larger work. In this performance, John Cage reads the text while David Tudor creates the musical accompaniment.

Listen to this first

((• HEAR MORE on www.mymusiclab.com

Word-Music Relationships

How does the music relate to the text being recited?

Timbre

Aside from the voice, what kinds of sounds do you hear? How do you think they are made?

The subtitle John Cage gave this work is *New Aspect of Form in Instrumental and Electronic Music*. The linguistic awkwardness of the wording ("Aspect"?) is the first clue that this composition is not going to follow standard conventions of music or musical form. The text consists of 90 brief stories written by Cage himself. As the composer later recalled,

⚙ LEARN MORE on www.mymusiclab.com Chapter Objectives

> Most of the stories are things that happened that stuck in my mind. . . . The continuity of the 90 stories was not planned. I simply made a list of all the stories I could think of and checked them off as I wrote them. . . . Whenever I have given the talk, someone comes up afterwards and insists that the continuity was a planned one, in spite of the ideas that are expressed regarding purposelessness, emptiness, chaos, etc. One lady, at Columbia, asked, during the discussion following the talk, "What, then, is your final goal?" I remarked that her question was that of the John Simon Guggenheim Memorial Foundation to applicants for fellowships, and that it had irritated artists for decades. Then I said that I did not see that we were going to a goal, but that we were living in process, and that that process is eternal. My intention in putting 90 stories together in an unplanned way is to suggest that all things, sounds, stories (and, by extension, beings) *are* related, and that this complexity is more evident when it is not oversimplified by an idea of relationship in one person's mind.

Source: From Program notes to *Indeterminacy: New Aspect of Form in Instrumental and Electronic Music* (Folkways FT 3704), republished in *John Cage: Writer*, ed. Richard Kostelanetz (New York: Limelight Editions, 1993), p. 78. Reprinted by permission of Folkways Music.

Cage's approach to setting these stories to music was, to say the least, unconventional.

Word-Music Relationships: Chance Meetings

Performers always have a large degree of control over what they are playing or singing. This is more obvious in certain types of music than in others. Jazz, for example, not only allows for improvisation but encourages it: performers are expected to make up things on the spot. But even a pianist playing a sonata by Beethoven makes countless decisions—some of them spontaneous—about exactly *how* to play a work of music, and no two performers will play it exactly alike. In fact, no one performer will (or even *can*) play the same piece exactly the same way twice. What's the tempo? How much should the music slow down in approaching the final cadence? How loud should the last chord be? The notated music is a starting point for performance. A musical score—the notes on the page—is like the script of a play: actors must bring it to life, and they have considerable leeway in deciding just how to do this. A great deal depends on how they happen to feel at the moment of performance.

In many of his works, Cage gave musicians a combination of detailed instructions and an unprecedented degree of freedom in performance. His *Indeterminacy* is to be read out loud in such a way that each story lasts exactly one minute. The spoken text is accompanied by a musician situated in a different room, far enough away so as not to hear what the reciter is saying. Within a series of one-minute units, the musician creates whatever sounds he or she wishes to create: this is where the element of chance comes into play.

We call music like this, in which chance plays a basic role, **aleatory music**. The word comes from the Latin word *alea* meaning "die," the singular of the more common word "dice." Just as the roll of dice necessarily involves chance—no one can know what numbers will come up in any given roll—so does aleatory music leave basic elements up to chance. Here, the musician does not know exactly what words are being spoken within any one-minute unit, and the reciter does not know what sounds the musician is performing.

Cage and Tudor, by Cage's own account, did not rehearse their performance of *Indeterminacy* in any way when they entered the recording studio. Cage read each selection in such a way that his recitation would fill exactly one minute. This meant that he had to read texts with more words more quickly than texts with fewer words. Both Cage and Tudor used stopwatches to monitor the length of each unit. Thus even in this work that leaves so much up to chance, certain parameters—the texts and the length of each unit—are defined quite precisely.

Timbre: *Musique concrète* and Electronic Music

In the performance recorded here, John Tudor accompanies Cage's recitations by using sounds from three kinds of sources:

1. Pre-recorded tapes of excerpts from a different work by Cage (his *Fontana Mix*, composed in 1958–1959)
2. Musical instruments: a piano and a whistle
3. An amplified slinky. This child's toy provides the basis for what is known as **musique concrète**.

The "concrete" in this French term for "concrete music" refers to music created by real—that is, concrete or everyday—objects that are not normally regarded as musical instruments. The sounds produced by these objects are in turn recorded and are then usually modified in some way.

In the 1950s and 1960s, before the advent of digital technology, this usually meant recording a sound on reel-to-reel tape and then manipulating the tape by speeding it up, slowing it down, looping it, splicing it, or by applying some combination of these techniques to create new sounds derived from everyday ("concrete") sounds. *Musique concrète* had been fundamental to *Fontana Mix*, which is itself a collage of other works by Cage whose realization depends heavily on elements of chance. Thus an aleatory work (*Fontana Mix*) is applied in aleatory fashion to yet another aleatory work (*Indeterminacy*). The amplified slinky, heard quite distinctly at the beginning of the first text excerpted here ("One evening I was walking along Hollywood Boulevard. . . .") provides yet another layer of *musique concrète* that is applied in an aleatory fashion.

    Musique concrète and electronic music in general opened up enormous new realms of timbre in the middle decades of the twentieth century. It was now possible to create sounds that could not be produced by merely acoustical (non-electrical) means. **Electronic music**—that is, music using sounds generated either in whole or in part by electronic means—created timbres that had quite literally never been heard before. Today, we are surrounded by electronic music and are quite used to such sounds as those created by midi files or by electronically manipulated wavelengths. In the 1950s, this was all still quite novel.

    Is *Indeterminacy* really art, or is it just a prank? Cage himself would probably be delighted with questions like this that cause us to think about the nature of art and its relationship to life. Can a slinky really be considered a musical instrument? What's the difference between a musical instrument and an object that produces sound? Can music have any relationship to a text if the music is produced without any knowledge of what words are being declaimed or even what they simply sound like, quite apart from their meaning? Some critics have praised Cage as a genius, while others have condemned him as a charlatan. His most celebrated composition, *4'33"* is one of the most controversial works in the entire history of music. (See *4'33"*: The Music (?) of Silence (?), page 460).

Now listen to this music again, using the Listening Guide.

1912–1992
John Cage
Indeterminacy (excerpt)
Composed: 1959
GENRE
Aleatory music
KEY CONCEPTS
Aleatory music, *musique concrète*, electronic music.
CHAPTER HIGHLIGHT
Experimental Music
This work, like many of Cage's compositions, compels listeners to confront basic questions about the very nature of music. *Indeterminacy* is highly aleatoric, relying on chance to create connections (or not) between text and music. It uses a combination of a speaking voice, standard instruments, and recorded sounds from everyday life that are electronically amplified and manipulated.

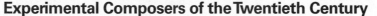

EXPAND YOUR PLAYLIST

Experimental Composers of the Twentieth Century

A number of important twentieth-century composers confronted audiences with basic questions about the nature of music. John Cage is the most famous, but he was by no means alone.

Henry Cowell (1897–1965), a native of California, was one of John Cage's teachers. *The Banshee* calls for the performer to manipulate the strings inside the piano, which creates an eerie, otherworldly sound.

Harry Partch (1901–1974), a native Californian who sometimes wrote under the name "Paul Pirate," designed and constructed his own new instruments capable of playing music based on unusual tuning systems, with as many as 55 notes in the span of conventional octave. *O Frabjous Day!* is a setting of the poem from Lewis Carroll's *Alice in Wonderland* for voice and an ensemble of original instruments.

Moondog was the pseudonym of **Louis Thomas Hardin** (1916–1999), a blind American composer and musician who by his own choice lived on the streets of New York City for almost 20 years. *Bird's Lament*, written in memory of the saxophonist Charlie Parker, was later sampled by the deejay Mr. Scruff for "Get a Move On" and eventually reused in a television commercial for the Lincoln Navigator SUV.

Lejaren Hiller (1924–1994) taught at the University of Illinois, where he wrote the *Illiac Suite* in 1957, the first work of music composed by means of a programmed computer.

((•● HEAR SAMPLES on **www.mymusiclab.com**

GO TO www.mymusiclab.com
for the Automated Listening Guide
CD V • Track 11/Download Track 84

Listening Guide

John Cage Composed: 1959 *Indeterminacy* (excerpt) **(1:59)**

Time	Text	Timbre
0:00	One evening I was walking along Hollywood Boulevard, nothing much to do. I stopped and looked in the window of a stationary shop. A mechanized pen was suspended in space in such a way that, as a mechanized roll of paper passed by it, the pen went through the motions of the same penmanship exercises I had learned as a child in the third grade. Centrally placed in the window was an advertisement explaining the mechanical reasons for the perfection of the operation of the suspended mechanical pen. I was fascinated, for everything was going wrong. The pen was tearing the paper to shreds and splattering ink all over the window and on the advertisement, which, nevertheless, remained legible.	0:00–0:24: Amplified slinky (an example of *musique concrète*) 0:13: Piano enters 0:39: Pre-recorded sounds manipulated on tape (an example of electronic music), excerpts from Cage's earlier composition *Fontana Mix*
1:00	It was after I got to Boston that I went into the anechoic chamber at Harvard University. Anybody who knows me knows this story. I am constantly telling it. Anyway, in that silent room, I heard two sounds, one high and one low. Afterward I asked the engineer in charge why, if the room was so silent, I had heard two sounds. He said, "Describe them." I did. He said, "The high one was your nervous system in operation. The low one was your blood in circulation."	1:00: Pre-recorded sounds manipulated on tape (an example of electronic music), excerpts from Cage's earlier composition *Fontana Mix* 1:41: Piano

From Indeterminacy by John Cage. Reprinted by permission of Folkways Music.

Student FAQs

Is all musique concrète electronic?

Yes. Although the original sound source (here, a slinky) is not electronic, it is recorded and manipulated in some way to produce *musique concrète*. The broader category of electronic music includes not only pre-recorded sounds but also any sound generated electronically. These, too, can be subjected to an infinite degree of manipulation.

If the text is read and not sung, is this really a song?

Cage would probably answer this question with other questions: What is the difference between singing and speaking? Where does one end and one begin? Can we really make a clear distinction between the two?

If so much chance is involved, is this really music?

Good question. It's one of the ones Cage would certainly have wanted us to ask about this and many of his other works. What makes music music?

PROFILE   John Cage (1912–1992)

What Is a Composer?

"Everything we do is music," Cage once declared. He did not see himself as a high priest of art but rather as a facilitator between listeners and sounds. Profoundly influenced by Zen Buddhism and its renunciation of striving and the will, Cage maintained that his "purpose is to eliminate purpose," and many of his works from the late 1940s on seem to avoid or challenge the traditional stance of the composer as an omnipotent creator of a small musical world.

Born in Los Angeles, Cage studied composition with Arnold Schoenberg but soon moved on to composing in a manner even more radically modern than that of his teacher. In the 1940s, Cage began writing a series of works for "prepared piano," a piano whose strings were outfitted with such everyday objects as screws, rubber bands, and coins, producing a range of timbres as oddly familiar as they are strange. In the 1950s, he became interested in the possibilities of electronic music and multimedia art that combined word, music, and movement and often mixed live and recorded sounds and images.

Cage and his music consistently polarized listeners. Most of the audience at New York's Lincoln Center walked out of his *Atlas eclipticalis* (whose notated score superimposes transparent staff paper on star charts to determine pitches) when it was first presented by the New York Philharmonic in 1964; even members of the orchestra hissed the composer. But Cage's provocative music and writings remained fresh over time, and toward the end of his life he was showered with honors. He delivered the prestigious Charles Eliot Norton lectures at Harvard University in 1988, continuing in the tradition of other composers before him, including Igor Stravinsky, Aaron Copland, and Leonard Bernstein. Some saw genius in his works, others charlatanism, but all were provoked by them to rethink the nature of music and its relationship to the world around us.

⊙➤ **EXPLORE MORE** on **www.mymusiclab.com**

John Cage gathering wild greens in Rockland County, New York, May 1971. He was an acknowledged authority on mushrooms and won a large cash prize on an Italian television quiz show in 1958 for answering a series of questions about these plants.

James Klosty

◀◀   **EXPAND YOUR PLAYLIST: CAGE**   ▶▶

- *Sonata and Interludes*. A series of pieces for what Cage called "prepared piano," a piano with various screws, bolts, and pieces of felt placed strategically on the strings inside, thereby creating a radically different sound from the instrument.

- *Fontana Mix*. A work for magnetic tape.

- *Roaratorio: An Irish Circus on Finnegans Wake*. For magnetic tape and live performers, based on James Joyce's novel.

- *0' 00"*. The performer is instructed to perform "a disciplined action," sonically amplified to the greatest possible degree.

((•● **HEAR SAMPLES** on **www.mymusiclab.com**

PERFORMANCE *4'33"*: The Music (?) of Silence (?)

John Cage's *4'33"* has polarized listeners ever since its first performance in 1952. Its admirers find it endlessly fascinating, while its detractors dismiss it as a mere gimmick. Cage's score calls for the piece to "be performed by any instrumentalist or combination of instrumentalists and last any length of time," and it consists of three movements, each of which is marked "Tacet," the traditional indication for a musician not to play his or her instrument at all over a specified length of time.

4'33" is often said to consist of four minutes and thirty-three seconds of silence. This is not quite true. Neither the length of the work nor the "silence" is quite so straightforward. Cage's score contains the comment that when it was premiered by the pianist John Tudor on August 29, 1952, the performance on that occasion lasted for four minutes and thirty-three seconds. The real title of the work, Cage notes in his score, "is the total length in minutes and seconds of its performance," which can vary from performance to performance. The "silence,"

moreover, is an illusion. Even when musicians are not playing, we hear sounds. Cage's experience in an anechoic chamber, which he describes in one of the movements in *Indeterminacy*, reminds us that there is no such thing as true silence.

According to Cage, *4'33"* was inspired by the "white paintings" created by one of his friends, the artist Robert Rauschenberg (1925–2008). These "blank" canvases are never truly blank: each one has its own unique color and textures even before any paint is applied, and each canvas is constantly changing because of the way it reflects the light of its surroundings. But as viewers, we have been conditioned not to notice such details and to mentally compensate for them. In much the same way, Cage's *4'33"* challenges the idea that music can exist in sonic isolation, that some sounds are music while other are not. Sounds, as Cage reminds us, are always present. Whether we choose to hear them or not and treat them as part of the music is up to us.

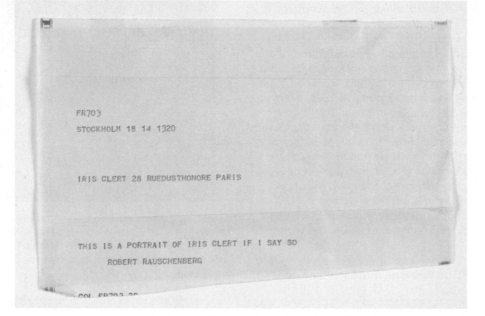

Robert Rauschenberg's "Portrait of Iris Clert" (1961). Just because an artist calls something "a work of art," does that mean it is art?

Robert Rauschenberg, "This is a portrait of Iris Clert if I say so". 1961. Photo: Jurg Dontasch/Robert Rauschenberg Studio/Untitled Press Inc. Art © Robert Rauschenberg/Licensed by VAGA, New York, NY

⚙ **LEARN MORE** on **www.mymusiclab.com**   MyMusicLibrary: John Cage on *4'33"*

✓ **TEST YOURSELF** on **www.mymusiclab.com**   Flashcards and chapter tests

Philip Glass
"Knee Play 1" from *Einstein on the Beach*
Composed: 1976

56

An opera with very little singing and no plot: this is the world of Philip Glass's *Einstein on the Beach*. The four acts, performed without intermission, are introduced and connected by a series of "Knee Plays," a term Glass adapted from the joining function of the human knee. *"Knee Play 1"* is the opening number of the opera. Only small portions of the text are sung: most of it is recited, and the text that is sung is limited to the counting of numbers ("One, two, three," etc.) or solfege syllables (do-re-mi-fa-so-la-ti).

 Listen to this first

(((• HEAR MORE on www.mymusiclab.com

Timbre

Listen for three layers of sound: (1) the bass line (the organ), (2) the chorus of voices that sing above it, and (3) the two speaking parts that operate seemingly independently of the music.

Harmony

Listen for the simple and strongly tonal harmonic progression that is repeated over and over in this scene.

Form

Listen for the repeated pattern in the bass line (the organ) that continues from beginning to end. Try to identify variations in the basic rhythmic and melodic patterns of the voices. Finally, be aware of the added elements (new voices, both singing and speaking) that emerge over the course of the scene as a whole.

Glass's opera has no plot in the conventional sense. Instead, it is built around a series of recurring images: a train, a trial, a spaceship in a field. A character resembling Einstein appears at several points playing the violin (the real Einstein was in fact an amateur violinist).

Glass worked closely with the director and playwright Robert Wilson (b. 1941) to develop this radical new form of opera. "It never occurred to us that *Einstein on the Beach* would have a story or contain anything like a plot," Glass would later explain. "The title merely provided an occasion for which a theatrical/visual work could be constructed. . . . In a sense, we didn't need to tell an Einstein story because everyone who eventually saw our *Einstein* brought their own story with them." The work premiered in France in July 1976. "In the four months that we toured *Einstein* in Europe," Glass noted, "we had many occasions to meet with our audiences, and people occasionally would ask us what it 'meant.' But far more often people told us what it meant to

 LEARN MORE on
www.mymusiclab.com
Chapter Objectives

them. . . . The point about *Einstein* was clearly not what it 'meant' but that it was *meaningful* as generally experienced by the people who saw it."[1]

Glass's music for *Einstein on the Beach* is written in a style known as **minimalism**, in which a brief musical idea or group of ideas is repeated and varied incrementally over a long span of time, with a relatively slow rate of change. Minimalist music, in spite of its name, tends to unfold across long periods and relies on the passage of time to create an almost trance-like state in the mind of the listener. Indeed, there is so much repetition that as listeners, our scale of perception changes, so that even a slight variation in the rhythm becomes a major event. "Knee Play 1" is typical of minimalist music in its use of fairly simple melodic, harmonic, and rhythmic building blocks.

Layered Timbres

The musical forces performing in this opening scene are quite modest: an electronic organ, a small chorus of mixed voices (soprano, alto, tenor, bass), and two speakers (both women). The organ and chorus move in close coordination, while the spoken voices enter and drop out in a manner that seems to be random. Glass allows for considerable latitude in the score, leaving it up to performers how many times they will repeat a certain section or exactly when the spoken texts will be recited and at what speed.

Simple Harmony

The organ and chorus outline a standard harmonic progression, one often heard in cadences in tonal music. The chords used are those built on the fourth, fifth, and first scale degrees (IV, V, and then I, in musical terms). The 12-bar blues chord progression, for example, makes exclusive use of these three chords (see chapters 46 and 57), and these are the same three chords that, according to some learn-how-to-play-music advertisements, will allow you to perform a thousand songs. By making the harmony so simple and by repeating it so often, Glass is able to draw our attention toward other elements of change, such as the varied rhythms of the melody and the gradual addition of new performing forces.

Variation Form

The form of this scene is actually quite simple: it is a series of variations on a series of short melodic fragments, with the music unfolding over a constantly repeated bass, an **ostinato** (see chapters 11, 41, and 44). The rhythm of the theme and each of its variations remains essentially constant from beginning to end, with the singers counting the beats they sing out loud to some variation of this basic pattern:

1 2 3 4 | 1 2 3 4 5 6 | 1 2 3 4 5 6 7 8 |

[1]Glass quote on *Einstein on the Beach*, page 32, from MUSIC BY PHILIP GLASS by PHILIP GLASS. Copyright © 1987 by Dunvagen Music Publishers, Inc. Reprinted by permission of HarperCollins Publishers.

Glass repeats this basic unit, with its three subunits of four, six, and eight beats, many times, but often with subtle variations. He creates variety in three ways:

1. **Altered rhythms.** Certain beats at the beginning of each subunit drop out in no predictable pattern. For example, at 1:03 we hear

1 2 3 4 | [pause] 2 3 4 5 6 | 1 2 3 4 5 6 7 8 |

and at 1:45 we hear

[pause] 2 3 4 | 1 2 3 4 5 6 | [pause] 2 3 4 5 6 7 8 |

Glass uses these and other rhythmic permutations throughout, eliminating the "1" beat in one or more of the three subunits of four, six, and eight that make up the basic rhythmic unit.

2. **Divided voices.** At 2:06, the two vocal lines we have heard up to this point—sopranos and altos singing the upper line together, tenors and basses singing the lower line—split into four parts. Sopranos now sing "do-re-mi" to the same notes as the altos, who continue to sing as before, but the sopranos sing these syllables at a much slower rhythm. The tenors do the same (on the syllables "la-so-do") with the basses underneath.

3. **Added spoken voices.** Glass makes no distinction between speech or song: all become a part of the sonic landscape. At 1:03, we hear the first of two women's voices recite (in speech) some of the numbers being sung by the chorus. At 1:24, these voices begin to recite their own independent texts. This text (by the poet Christopher Knowles) is itself full of internal repetitions and is not meant to make sense syntactically. Here, for example, is the opening (beginning at 1:03):

> Will it get some wind for the sailboat. And it could get for it is.
> It could get the railroad for these workers. And it could be were it is.
> It could Franky it could be Franky it could be very fresh and clean.
> It could be a balloon.
> Oh these are the days my friends and these are the days my friends.
> It could get some wind for the sailboat. And it could get for it is.
> It could get the railroad for these workers. It could get for it is were.
> It could be a balloon. It could be Franky. It could be very fresh and clean.
> All these are the days my friends and these are the days my friends.
> It could be those ways.[2]

With these points in mind, listen to the scene once again, using the Listening Guide.

[2]Excerpt of lyrics from *Einstein on the Beach*, music by Philip Glass, lyrics by Christopher Knowles. Reprinted by permission of Dunvagen Music Publishers.

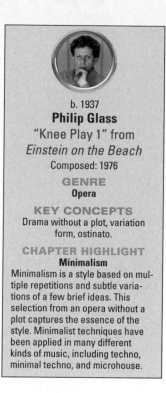

b. 1937
Philip Glass
"Knee Play 1" from
Einstein on the Beach
Composed: 1976

GENRE
Opera

KEY CONCEPTS
Drama without a plot, variation form, ostinato.

CHAPTER HIGHLIGHT
Minimalism
Minimalism is a style based on multiple repetitions and subtle variations of a few brief ideas. This selection from an opera without a plot captures the essence of the style. Minimalist techniques have been applied in many different kinds of music, including techno, minimal techno, and microhouse.

CONNECT YOUR PLAYLIST

Minimalism

Find a work whose formal structure is based on the principles of minimalism.

Example: The Postal Service, "Nothing Better" (2003)
This song by the two-man indie band the Postal Service features a number of small repeating musical lines, which combine in different ways throughout.

GO TO www.mymusiclab.com
for the Automated Listening Guide
CD V • Track 12/Download Track 85

Listening Guide

Philip Glass Composed: 1976 "Knee Play 1" from *Einstein on the Beach* (3:52)

Time	Form: Section (each section is stated twice)	Timbre	Rhythm	Spoken Text
0:00	1	Organ only	Ostinato figure: long, slow notes	
0:21	2	Sopranos and altos sing the upper line; tenors and basses sing the lower line.	1 2 3 4 1 2 3 4 5 6 1 2 3 4 5 6 7 8	
0:42	3		1 2 3 4 1 2 3 4 5 6 [pause] 2 3 4 5 6 7 8	
1:03	4		1 2 3 4 [pause] 2 3 4 5 6 1 2 3 4 5 6 7 8	First voice enters, speaking numbers with the sung chorus, seemingly at random.
1:24	5		[pause] 2 3 4 1 2 3 4 5 6 1 2 3 4 5 6 7 8	First voice begins to recite the text ("Will it get some wind for the sailboat," etc.).
1:45	6		[pause] 2 3 4 1 2 3 4 5 6 [pause] 2 3 4 5 6 7 8	Second voice enters to join in reciting the text.
2:06	7	Two lines in chorus divide to become four. The sopranos now sing the same pitches in longer notes to "do-re-mi," and the tenors sing the same pitches in longer notes to "la-so-do."	1 2 3 4 1 2 3 4 5 6 [pause] 2 3 4 5 6 7 8	
2:27	8		1 2 3 4 [pause] 2 3 4 5 6 [pause] 2 3 4 5 6 7 8	
2:48	9		[pause] 2 3 4 [pause] 2 3 4 5 6 [pause] 2 3 4 5 6 7 8	
3:09	10		1 2 3 4 [pause] 2 3 4 5 6 1 2 3 4 5 6 7 8	
3:30	11		[pause] 2 3 4 1 2 3 4 5 6 [pause] 2 3 4 5 6 7 8	

Student FAQs

Don't people get tired of so much repetition?

Some do, but to call this music repetitious reminds us that the term is relative. Like John Cage before him (see chapter 55), Glass challenges listeners to reconsider the basic premises of how they listen. Listening to a minimalist work is a little like looking at something under the microscope: we begin to see (hear) things that we sometimes take for granted.

The spoken text makes no sense. What does it add?

As Glass suggests (see his comments earlier), the point is not so much what the opera "means" as what listeners hear in it. The text means whatever listeners think it means.

PROFILE Philip Glass (b. 1937)

Prolific Minimalist

Philip Glass stands out among contemporary composers for having become so famous that he is mentioned in no fewer than three episodes of *The Simpsons* and is satirized in an episode of *South Park*. He was born and raised in Baltimore, where he studied flute at the Peabody Conservatory of Music. He went on to study composition at the Juilliard School of Music in New York City, after which he worked in Paris with Nadia Boulanger, who 40 years before had been Aaron Copland's teacher (see page 438). He traveled widely in Asia as well, studying Indian music with the legendary sitar player Ravi Shankar (chapter 35). Glass returned to New York in the mid-1960s, convinced that modern music needed to reach out to audiences more directly, and so he established the Philip Glass Ensemble, a group of musicians who still tour the country on a regular basis and draw consistently large audiences to concerts of new music.

Glass is an astonishingly prolific composer. In addition to 10 operas, he has written large quantities of vocal and instrumental music, as well as soundtracks for a number of mainstream films, including *The Illusionist*, *The Secret Garden*, *The Truman Show*, and *Candyman*.

Philip Glass at the electronic organ, ca. 1976.
Richard Pasley Photography

⊙➜ **EXPLORE MORE** on **www.mymusiclab.com**

EXPAND YOUR PLAYLIST: GLASS

- *Etudes.* A series of technical studies for piano.

- *Violin Concerto.* A work written for violin and orchestra, in three movements.

- *The Hours.* Film score, one of three for which Glass was nominated for an Academy Award, along with his music for *Notes on a Scandal* and *Kundun*.

- *A Descent into the Maelstrom.* A dance theater piece inspired by Edgar Allen's Poe short story of the same name.

- *Akhnaten.* An opera set in ancient Egypt.

((•) **HEAR SAMPLES** on **www.mymusiclab.com**

Lucinda Childs (left) and Sheryl Sutton in "Knee Play 1" from *Einstein on the Beach*, at the Brooklyn Academy of Music Opera House, New York.

◀◀   EXPAND YOUR PLAYLIST   ▶▶

Minimalism

Terry Riley

• *In C*. A series of 53 brief thematic fragments that can be played "by any number of instruments of any kind." Each performer plays all 53 fragments but may repeat each as often as he or she likes, so the length of the work can vary enormously in performance. One recent recording runs for 43 minutes, another for 76 minutes.

Steve Reich

• *Three Tales*. A video opera made in collaboration with Beryl Korot, the composer's wife. The first of the three scenes revolves around the crash of the dirigible *Hindenburg* in Lakehurst, New Jersey, in 1937; the second centers on the testing of an atomic bomb in the South Pacific in 1946; and the third focuses on the sheep named Dolly, who in 1996 became the world's first successfully cloned mammal.

John Adams

• *Short Ride in a Fast Machine*. A brief work for orchestra that has proven extremely popular with concert audiences. The composer has said of the title: "You know how it is when someone asks you to ride in a terrific sports car, and then you wish you hadn't?"

The Beatles

• "Tomorrow Never Knows." A drone-based composition influenced by Indian raga. The backdrop changes only minimally through the piece.

Peter Gabriel

• "This Is the Picture." A synthesized backdrop repeats a simple melodic figure, very much in the style of African traditional music, as Gabriel sings the lyric above it.

 **HEAR SAMPLES** on **www.mymusiclab.com**

⊘ **TEST YOURSELF** on **www.mymusiclab.com**   Flashcards and chapter tests

Chuck Berry
"School Day"
Composed: 1957

Rock music has become such a standard part of the musical scene today that we rarely stop to think about its musical elements and how they work together. Chuck Berry's rock 'n' roll hit "School Day" illustrates the basic building blocks of this quintessentially American art form.

 Listen to this first

((• HEAR MORE on www.mymusiclab.com

 Rhythm

Tap along with the beat and try to identify the rhythmic patterns that appear most frequently. Listen for the moments when the entire band stops together.

 Timbre

Notice the aggressive tones of the guitar that cut through the sound of the rest of the instruments. Listen for the high notes in the piano that are present throughout almost all the recording.

 Form

Listen for individual verses. Try to identify the length (number of measures) and harmonic pattern of each verse.

During the mid-1950s, Chuck Berry, along with Elvis Presley, Little Richard, Buddy Holly, Fats Domino, and Jerry Lee Lewis blended the musical styles of jump blues and honky-tonk with an edgy attitude to create a new genre known as rock 'n' roll. It was music aimed at a teenage audience, produced mainly by independent record labels and marketed by hip deejays to youngsters, both white and black. Among those six musicians, Berry stands out because he not only sang but also played the guitar in a unique style and wrote the majority of his hits.

Rock 'n' roll capitalized on the youth culture of the baby boom generation, who had more disposable income, more free time, and more technological access to entertainment than any previous generation. The 1950s were a time of social contradictions for American youth. The idyllic domestic life portrayed on television shows like *Leave It to Beaver* and the relative prosperity of the middle class provided unprecedented material wealth and freedom to teenagers. Yet at the same time, the burgeoning civil rights movement brought change and even violence to many regions of the country. Tensions of the Cold War and McCarthy-era communist paranoia further fueled social unrest. Rock 'n' roll music offered escape from adult concerns and serious issues. It provided teenagers with music that openly defied their parents' artistic sensibilities. And it blended white and black art forms with dancing, partying, and barely disguised metaphors for sex: deejay Alan Freed co-opted the phrase "rock 'n' roll" from a black slang phrase for sex.

⚙ **LEARN MORE** on
www.mymusiclab.com
Chapter Objectives

Two years before "School Day" was released, the movie *Blackboard Jungle* portrayed high school students as rebels obsessed with sex and delinquent behavior of all sorts, set to the rock 'n' roll sounds of "(We're Gonna) Rock Around the Clock" (see Expand Your Playlist). One scene in the film depicted teens breaking treasured old jazz records, and the theme song was reputed to have sparked riots and hoodlum behavior. The same year *Blackboard Jungle* appeared, James Dean brought the angst-ridden world of teen pop culture to the silver screen in *Rebel Without a Cause*. Although Chuck Berry was 30 years old when he recorded "School Day," his lyrics captured the attitude of his young fans perfectly.

Shuffle Rhythm and Stop Time

The rhythmic elements of this song provide the core of its appeal. At several points the melody consists of a single note or chord repeated many times, and here it is the rhythm that creates a sense of excitement. At other points, the rhythmic patterns come to a sudden and dramatic stop, leaving a wide open space for the singer or soloist to enter.

The introduction (0:00–0:02) mimics the ringing of a school bell with 13 attacks on the same guitar chord. With these 13 chords, Berry establishes what is known as a **shuffle groove**, a mid-tempo rhythmic pattern, typically in quadruple meter, in which each beat is subdivided into three pulses. The shuffle groove for "School Day" is based on four beats per measure, as follows:

```
Beats:            1     2     3     4
Guitar chords:  x x x  x x x  x x x  x x x
```

The shuffle groove was used frequently in earlier rhythm and blues (R&B) recordings by artists like Fats Domino (see Expand Your Playlist). In most shuffle grooves, the bass player and drummer do not play all three subdivisions of the beat. Instead, they play only the first and the third. The first note occupies two-thirds of the beat, and the second note occupies the last third of the beat, forming a LONG-short-LONG-short rhythmic pattern similar to swing rhythms (see chapter 47). You can hear this pattern in the bass when it first enters (0:04).

The poetic meter of the lyrics follows the pattern of the shuffle groove. For instance, "Workin' your fingers right down to the bone" (0:17) places accented syllables on the beats, and three syllables in each beat:

Syllables:	*Work*-in' your	*fin*-gers right	*down* to the	*bone*
Beats:	X	X	X	X

Six times in the song, the shuffle rhythm comes to an abrupt halt. The instruments that provide the basic accompaniment strike a single note on a downbeat of a measure together and then

Chuck Berry on electric guitar.
Frank Driggs Collection

remain silent for the rest of the measure. This is known as **stop time**. These moments punctuate the end of individual sections, simultaneously opening up rhythmic space for the singer or soloist to launch a new section. Once one has gotten a sense of how the verses flow, it is relatively easy to anticipate where these moments of stop time will occur.

During each stop-time moment, Berry enters with lyrics for the next verse. The beginning vocal phrase of each verse corresponds to beats 2, 3, and 4, and then concludes on the downbeat:

Time:	2:14				
Beats:	1	2	3	4	1
	(stop time)				(band enters)
Lyrics:		Hail,	hail	Rock 'n'	**roll**
		(pick-up notes, or anacrusis)			
	(downbeat)				

Notes that begin a phrase before the downbeat are known as an **anacrusis**, or "pick-up notes." Anacrusis is a significant rhythmic feature of "School Day."

b. 1926
Chuck Berry
"School Day"
Composed: 1957

GENRE
Rock 'n' roll

KEY CONCEPTS
Shuffle rhythm, electric guitar solos, 12-bar blues.

CHAPTER HIGHLIGHT
Rock 'n' Roll
A distinctive timbre and rhythm, fused with the 12-bar blues form, helped create the genre of rock 'n' roll. More than any other individual, Chuck Berry helped bring these elements together.

Rock 'n' Roll Timbre

Chuck Berry's recordings highlighted his electric lead guitar. "School Day" features Fred Below on drums and Willie Dixon on bass. Guitarist Hubert Sumlin recalls playing on the recording as well, although his name is not listed in the session's paperwork. Although he is difficult to hear on this particular recording, pianist Johnnie Johnson, Berry's musical partner since 1952, added a signature sound to the band that was particularly important in live performances and that helped the whole band come together in the tight rhythmic grooves his audiences loved. On "School Day," Johnson's left hand plays boogie-shuffle patterns in the lower notes of the piano and his right hand plays continuous fills, featuring melodic counterpoint and decorations. You can hear him particularly well during the guitar solo at 1:32, after the words "days of old . . ." at 2:20, and while Berry sings "the beat of the drum . . ." at 2:25.

Fans can recognize most of Chuck Berry's hit records from just their short guitar introductions. The most famous of these is the introduction to "Johnny B. Goode" (see "Musical Recipe for Rock 'n' Roll," page 470). Although Berry's brief introductions are indelibly linked to him, he often borrowed or adapted them from other artists and earlier recordings. The opening of "Johnny B. Goode," for instance, is almost identical to the introduction Carl Hogan played on Louis Jordan's recording "Ain't That Just Like a Woman." Pianist Johnnie Johnson came up with the introduction for "School Day," which he borrowed from a piano-boogie recording of "Honky-tonk Train Blues" by Meade "Lux" Lewis. With these short introductions, Berry's recordings pay tribute to his musical influences and connect his rock 'n' roll recordings to the traditions that came before him.

PROFILE   Chuck Berry (b. 1926)

Musical Recipe for Rock 'n' Roll

Chuck Berry grew up on a blend of blues, hillbilly, and western swing tunes in his native St. Louis. As a high school student, Berry borrowed a four-string guitar and cultivated his musical ambitions. Those plans were derailed, however, when in 1944 Berry and a few friends were involved in an automobile theft. The accompanying shenanigans landed him in prison for three years. He was released on his 21st birthday and bounced from odd job to odd job for a few years before rekindling his interest in performing. In 1950, Berry purchased an electric guitar and a reel-to-reel recorder and began to pursue music with a new sense of purpose.

Berry quickly established himself as a multitalented musician whose guitar work was unforgettable and whose songwriting ability connected with youth culture. On stage, Berry's charisma won over teen audiences, and he developed a distinctive performance gimmick known as the "duck walk," in which he crouched on one leg, stuck the other out in front of him, and scooted across the stage, pecking his head back and forth at the same time.

The heyday of rock 'n' roll was short-lived, from Elvis Presley's first rockabilly recordings in 1954 to the "day the music died" (a fateful plan crash that claimed the lives of Buddy Holly, Ritchie Valens, and the Big Bopper) in 1959. By the end of the decade, troubles plagued many of the first stars of the genre. Elvis had been drafted, Jerry Lee Lewis married his 13-year-old cousin in a scandal that sank his reputation, and Chuck Berry was convicted of transporting a minor across state lines for immoral purposes and began another prison sentence. Berry later recorded more hits (including the novelty number "My Ding-a-Ling") and toured successfully for many decades, but the rock 'n' roll craze was over.

Chuck Berry performs his signature "duck walk" on stage, ca. 1958.

Michael Ochs Archives Ltd./Getty Images Inc.—Los Angeles

⊙➔ EXPLORE MORE on www.mymusiclab.com

EXPAND YOUR PLAYLIST: BERRY

The Rock and Roll Hall of Fame and Museum's website sums up Chuck Berry's accomplishments with these words: "While no individual can be said to have invented rock and roll, Chuck Berry comes the closest of any single figure to being the one who put all the essential pieces together." His biggest hits include the following:

- "Johnny B. Goode"
- "Memphis"

- "Sweet Little Sixteen"
- "Roll Over Beethoven"
- "Maybelline"
- "No Particular Place to Go"
- "You Never Can Tell"

((• HEAR SAMPLES on www.mymusiclab.com

12-Bar Blues Form

"School Day" is a strophic song (see also chapter 46). The recording consists of a short introduction, followed by six verses and a guitar solo that follows the same musical form as the verses. There is no separate chorus or bridge. Each verse consists of the same 12-measure chord progression, known as the 12-bar blues (see chapter 46 for another example). The 12-bar blues uses just three different chords, built on the first, fourth, and fifth scale degrees. Unlike down-home blues performers like Robert Johnson, rock 'n' roll performers tended to use the 12-bar blues without any variations. To follow the 12-bar blues progression, count four beats per measure, starting at where the bass enters, and listen for when the bass player changes notes: these moments represent changes to a new chord. Timings and reference points in the text for the first verse are shown here:

Time:	0:04			
Lyrics:	... *school*		... *rule*	
Chords:	I	I	I	I
Time:	0:11		0:15	
Lyrics:	... *math*		... *pass*	
Chords:	IV	IV	I	I
Time:	0:19		0:22	
Lyrics:	... *bone*		... *alone*	
Chords:	V	V	I	I

The guitar solo is one of the most exciting moments in the recording. Berry begins a repetitive guitar pattern at the end of the fourth verse (1:29). Other verses conclude with a stop-time moment and a break in the music. Here, however, the guitar pattern continues right into the guitar-solo section—also a 12-bar blues chord progression (beginning at 1:32)—building momentum and dramatic tension by bridging the gap between verse and instrumental solo.

Now listen to this song again, using the Listening Guide.

CONNECT YOUR PLAYLIST

Guitar Riff

Find a song that has a distinctive opening guitar part.

Example: Guns N' Roses: "Sweet Child o' Mine" (1987)
Like "School Day," "Sweet Child o' Mine" opens with a distinctive part played by Guns N' Roses' lead guitarist Slash. This short repeated melody helps us immediately recognize the song.

Listening Guide

GO TO www.mymusiclab.com
for the Automated Listening Guide
CD V • Track 13/Download Track 86

Chuck Berry Composed: 1957 "School Day" (2:36)

Time	Text	Form	Rhythm
0:00		Introduction	The repeated chords establish the shuffle groove.
0:02	Up in the mornin'...	Verse 1: the vocal phrase begins as the anacrusis to the 12-bar blues section.	Stop time. Poetic meter of the text matches the shuffle groove.
0:04	... school ...	The 12-bar blues pattern for Verse 1 begins.	Bass enters, with LONG-short-LONG-short rhythm.
0:24	Ring, ring goes the ...	Verse 2: the vocal phrase begins.	Stop time.
0:26	... bell ...	The 12-bar blues pattern for Verse 2	
0:46	Soon as three o'clock rolls ... *The text's narrative continues chronologically through the day.*	Verse 3: vocal phrase begins.	Stop time
0:48	... around ...	The 12-bar blues pattern for Verse 3	
1:08	Drop the quarter right into the ...	Verse 4: vocal phrase begins.	Stop time
1:10	... slot ...	The 12-bar blues pattern for Verse 4	
1:29		End of the 12-bar blues pattern for Verse 4	Repeated guitar chords are the final phrase of Verse 4, but continue into the next section of the recording. No stop time at the end of Verse 4.
1:32	(guitar solo)	The 12-bar blues pattern under the guitar solo	While the guitar continues the same chords as the end of Verse 4, a new 12-bar section begins as the piano enters.
1:52	Drop the quarter right into the ...	Verse 5 (repeating the lyrics of Verse 4): vocal phrase begins.	Stop time
1:54	... slot ...	Twelve-bar blues pattern for Verse 5	
2:14	Hail, hail rock 'n'...	Verse 6: vocal phrase begins.	Stop time
2:16	... roll ...	The 12-bar blues pattern for Verse 6	

Timbre

Solo electric guitar

Call-and-response: the vocalist sings his phrases before the downbeat of each section, and the guitar echoes the singer.

Call-and-response

Call-and-response continues.

Call-and-response continues.

Guitar solo with full accompaniment

Call-and-response pattern between guitar and vocals resumes

Call-and-response

Student FAQs

How does Berry get his unique guitar sound?

The unique timbre of Berry's solos is characteristic of the specific electric guitar he played (a Gibson ES350TN for the first several years of his career), combined with the type of amplifiers used in 1956. The specific R&B motives he borrowed from earlier styles also contributed, but his equipment was the primary determinant of his sound.

© Dorling Kindersley

If the chord progression is the same throughout this song, why doesn't the music sound boring?

There are many styles of music, both classical and popular, that rely on repeated chord progressions. In these styles, listeners focus on the melodic variations, the lyrics (if there are words), the embellishments, and the rhythmic groove. Listeners also generally like some aspect of their music to include repetition because that sets up subconscious expectations for what is coming next, and then the music can either reward or surprise.

HISTORICAL CONTEXT   Television and the Rise of Rock 'n' Roll

In the 1940s, televisions were a novelty item that few Americans had seen. By 1954, more than 55 percent of all American households had a television, and the major broadcasting networks were vying to create the most successful programs. Variety shows hosted by established stars were common. Steve Allen, Milton Berle, Arthur Godfrey, and Ed Sullivan were a few of the entertainers who had their own shows.

Television also captured the inherent tensions between the conservative older generation and their children. Adults were outraged when Elvis Presley gyrated his hips during his televised performances, while the younger generation swooned over the hot, young star. In 1956, a reported 60 million viewers saw Presley's famous debut on the Ed Sullivan Show. At the end of his third performance, Sullivan offered, "This is a real decent, fine boy." With this endorsement from the show's famous host, Presley began his transformation from short-lived teen star to lasting cultural icon.

In 1952, a Philadelphia television station launched a staged version of the type of Saturday-night dance most teenagers regularly attended in their hometowns. The show's host introduced hit musicians and showed youngsters dancing in the most popular styles. In 1956, Dick Clark was invited to host the show, which was picked up for national distribution and christened *American Bandstand* in 1957. The show spread new records, new artists, and new dance styles across the country.

Dick Clark, at the podium in the upper left, surrounded by teenage fans on his nationally televised dance show *American Bandstand* in 1958.
AP Wide World Photos

◄◄   EXPAND YOUR PLAYLIST   ►►

Styles of Early Rock 'n' Roll

While there are many commonalities in early rock 'n' roll recordings, the first generation of musicians all had distinctive individual styles. The musicians listed here include both black and white performers who drew equally frequently from R&B and honky-tonk musical sources.

Elvis Presley
- "Blue Moon of Kentucky" (1954). Bluegrass pioneer and mandolinist Bill Monroe wrote and recorded this song in 1946. When Presley covered it, he changed its style from a moderate waltz to a hard-driving rockabilly number, using only the minimalist instrumentation of electric guitar, acoustic guitar, and bass.

Bill Haley and His Comets
- "(We're Gonna) Rock Around the Clock" (1954). This song's appearance in the soundtrack to *Blackboard Jungle* brought the new sound of rock 'n' roll to an enormous audience.

Buddy Holly
- "That'll Be the Day" (1957). Holly combined rockabilly sounds with Texas swing in many of his hits, including this one. Holly's distinctive voice is the central focus of this recording.

Jerry Lee Lewis
- "Great Balls of Fire" (1957). This recording uses 12-bar blues and features Lewis's distinctive piano style and flourishes, along with lots of reverb and echo effects, in an eight-to-the-bar boogie groove.

Fats Domino
- "Ain't It a Shame" (1955). Frequently mislabeled by the song's lyrics, "Ain't *that* a shame," this recording features a shuffle groove and a saxophone solo that illustrates one of the more mid-tempo, mellow sides of early rock 'n' roll.

Little Richard
- "Tutti Frutti" (1955). Named for the nonsense-syllable introduction to the stop-time moments at the end of each chorus, this recording mixes blues lyric couplets with heavy drums, twelve-bar blues progressions under the chorus, and a raging saxophone solo.

꒰•● HEAR SAMPLES on **www.mymusiclab.com**

⊘ **TEST YOURSELF** on **www.mymusiclab.com**   Flashcards and chapter tests

The Marvelettes
"Please, Mr. Postman"
Composed: 1961

What makes the sound of a musical style so immediately recognizable? The sound known as "Motown" is built on the basic elements of timbre, harmony, and texture.

 Listen to this first

((•● HEAR MORE on www.mymusiclab.com

Timbre	**Harmony**	**Form**
Listen for hand-claps. Pay attention to the tone quality of the backup vocal quartet. How does the rhythm section contribute to the overall sound?	Do you recognize the basic, repeating chord progression?	Do any sections repeat? Do you hear slight variations in those sections? How does the song end?

In 1961, the rhythm and blues label Tamla Motown badly needed a new hit. Nearly a year had passed since Smokey Robinson and the Miracles' "Shop Around" had reached number one on the R&B charts, which tracked music played on black radio stations for a mostly black audience. And then five high-school girls from Inkster, a suburb of Detroit—Gladys Horton, Katherine Anderson, Juanita Cowart, Georgeanna Tillman, and Wanda Young—recorded "Please, Mr. Postman" and provided that hit. Calling themselves the Marvelettes, their single reached the top of both the R&B charts and the pop charts (tracking a mostly white audience), a response that indicated success that crossed conventional boundaries of race and audience. The song's gold-record sales assured the continuation of "Motown," as the label was more commonly known, and established the Marvelettes among its early stars.

"Please, Mr. Postman" was released during a period in music history caught between the early rock 'n' roll innovations of the mid-1950s and the popular-music revolution of 1964 brought about by four young men from Liverpool. In the years before this "British Invasion," as the Beatles' success in America became known, black rhythm and blues ensembles such as the Coasters and the Shirelles reached new audiences by melding rhythmically innovative pop songs with blues idioms. Motown took advantage of the burgeoning popularity of R&B, cultivating its danceable grooves into an instantly recognizable musical style. By the mid-1960s, the Motown sound had evolved into the mature, pop sounds of groups like Diana Ross and the Supremes, and the Temptations (see "The Making of 'Please, Mr. Postman,'" page 478), and Motown had become a major contributor to American popular music.

⚙ **LEARN MORE** on
www.mymusiclab.com
Chapter Objectives

Timbre: The "Motown Sound"

Recordings made for the Motown label had an instantly recognizable, highly polished sound. The way the instruments were played and mixed in the studio produced a timbral sheen far different than the grittier, rougher sounds coming out of other R&B labels at the time. By the mid-1960s, Motown had made solid inroads into popular music, and its musical arrangements routinely featured strings and horns (especially extended saxophone solos); lots of rhythmic sound effects from claps, snaps, and tambourines; and a tight rhythmic groove from the bass and drums. Motown vocals used close harmony from backup singers behind a featured lead singer, and the musical arrangements often used sophisticated techniques like modulation (changing keys) and phrase expansions to make the titles of the songs more memorable. "Please, Mr. Postman" was recorded before that formula was fully established, and so while it contains only some of these devices, it is still recognizably the Motown sound:

- **Hand-claps.** These set up a **hook**, or a short, catchy motif that forms the memorable core of the song, right at the beginning. Hand-claps were common throughout the R&B hits of the 1950s like The Coasters' "Smokin' Joe's Cafe" (see Expand Your Playlist). They mark "Please, Mr. Postman" as a recording in the up-tempo R&B tradition.

Rhythmic pattern for the hand-claps.

Songs like "My Guy" (Mary Wells), "The Way You Do the Things You Do" (The Temptations), or "Baby Love" (The Supremes) also use hand-claps.

- **Close, female vocal harmony.** Close harmony from female voices was a common R&B formula that launched a new style of music in the late 1950s and early 1960s featuring "girl groups," such as the Chantelles and Shirelles. Throughout "Please, Mr. Postman," the backup singers provide a full, brassy layer of sound that supports the lead singer. What makes this sound so clear and penetrating is the tight spacing of pitches within chords, combined with generally stepwise motion from chord to chord. The chords are arranged in brief, repetitive and memorable fragments ("wait, wait for you")—like the hand-claps, generating another musical hook for the song.

- **A tight, rehearsed groove.** The Funk Brothers were the house band at Motown studios, and it was their perfectly coordinated rhythm section that compelled Motown fans to move. The rhythmic groove emphasized the back beats (1 **2** 3 **4**) and combined rhythmic patterns with strong ties to dance traditions.

Harmony: Descending Thirds

The basic progression of chords in "Please, Mr. Postman" may sound familiar to you. These four chords were used in countless popular songs during the 1950s and 1960s, like "Blue Moon," "Earth Angel," "Johnny Angel," "Duke of Earl," and "Those Magic Changes" (from the musical *Grease*). They are the progression for "Heart and Soul," which children often like to play as a duet on the piano. The progression and its variants also show up in classical music quite frequently—even Pachelbel's famous *Canon in D* uses something closely related.

The four chords are sometimes called the "doo-wop" chord progression. Doo-wop was a style of R&B and precursor of Motown, popular in the 1950s, that relied heavily on nonsense syllables (including the syllables "doo-wop"), sung by backup vocalists to accompany the lead singer. The doo-wop chord progression is also called a "descending thirds" progression because for the first few chords, the bass moves down three notes (a distance of a third) from one chord to the next. The last chord in the pattern carries with it a strong sense of tension requiring resolution: after hearing it, the listener naturally would like to hear the first chord again. The progression therefore creates the sense of an endless loop.

Chord progression: I   vi   IV   V

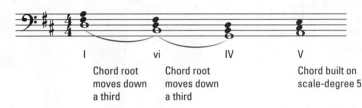

Chord numbers are represented in roman numerals; the vi is lowercase because it is a minor chord.

Verse-Chorus Form with a Twist

"Please, Mr. Postman" opens with a chorus, a savvy move for a song that was marketed toward a radio audience because it puts the catchiest and most memorable part at the very beginning. The song's core structure is

Chorus-Verse-Verse-Chorus-Verse-Chorus.

Verse-chorus is one of the simplest models of form in popular music. The chorus contains the main idea of the song, usually incorporating the title as well. When the chorus returns, it keeps the same text and music. The verses, on the other hand, advance the plot. Each different verse uses the same music but different texts, as building blocks in the story. Verse-chorus form can use any combination of verses and choruses, although the last unit will always be a chorus.

Verse-chorus form relies on repetition, and the chord progression is repetitious as well. The piece nevertheless builds in excitement and variety as the basic form is augmented by a few subtle yet important features:

- **A vamp section at the end.** After the last chorus, the singers and band **vamp**, or repeat a basic section of the music, while the lead singer improvises on a single motif ("wait a minute, wait a minute"). A vamp section builds energy and allows a song an infinitely expandable length. In this case, the producers kept three of the vamp sections at the end of the song, although more were recorded in the studio.

The Marvelettes
"Please, Mr. Postman"
Composed: 1961
GENRE
Motown
KEY CONCEPTS
Close vocal harmonies, doo-wop chord progression, verse-chorus form.
CHAPTER HIGHLIGHT
Motown
The "Mowtown Sound" relies on close vocal harmony from backup singers behind a feature lead singer and sophisticated studio production.

CONNECT YOUR PLAYLIST

Girl Groups

Find a song performed by an all-girl vocal group.

Example: Destiny's Child "Survivor" (2001) Destiny's Child is modeled on the Motown groups of the '60s, like the Marvelettes, featuring a lead singer (Beyonce Knowles) who is accompanied, vocally and visually, by two backup vocalists.

PERFORMANCE The Making of "Please, Mr. Postman"

The question of who wrote "Please, Mr. Postman" is not a simple one. Five people are credited with writing the song, but their work does not account for all we hear on the record. The creative contributions for any recording include the work of each arranger, each musician who played or sang, and each producer and sound engineer who worked on the mix.

When the teenage quintet who became the Marvelettes auditioned for Motown's record label, they sang hit songs by the Chantels and the Shirelles, both famous girl groups. Motown signed the Marvelettes but asked them to come back with original songs. Georgia Dobbins, at that time a member of the group, asked William Garrett, a local pianist and friend, for help. He gave her a blues number he had written, which Dobbins then reworked into an R&B girl-group piece. The Marvelettes took it to Motown, where staff songwriters Brian Holland and Robert Bateman, plus singer Freddie Gorman, edited it further. "Please, Mr. Postman" then went back to the Marvelettes, who recorded it with the record label's house band. In the studio, the musicians worked out the final details of the arrangement themselves.

The piece was then turned over to the producers and sound engineers, who mixed the various tracks from the recording session into the final 45 revolution-per-minute (rpm) vinyl single. They determined the balance between the instruments, background vocals, and lead singer; when to fade out the recording; and even how many of the verses in the extended vamp at the end to include. "Please, Mr. Postman" was co-produced by Holland and Bateman, working under the name "Brianbert."

Motown released a new version of "Please, Mr. Postman" in 2005 that illustrates the impact producers and sound engineers have on the music we hear. For the new release, a different team of sound engineers and producers remixed the original recording session. The new track is longer, in stereo, and balanced differently so that the listener hears different fragments of melody, different parts of the rhythm section, and even an extra verse (with different lyrics) that had been cut out of the extended vamp.

The Marvelettes, ca. 1963. From left: Gladys Horton, Wanda Young, Georgeanna Tillman, and Katherine Anderson. Juanita Cowart had left the group by the time this photo was taken.

Michael Ochs Archives/Getty Images, Inc.

👁 **SEE MORE** on
www.mymusiclab.com
Motown Documentary

⏪   EXPAND YOUR PLAYLIST: MOTOWN   ⏩

- **"Shop Around,"** Smokey Robinson and the Miracles (1960)

- **"(Love Is Like a) Heat Wave,"** Martha & The Vandellas (1963)

- **"The Way You Do the Things You Do,"** The Temptations (1964)

- **"Baby I Need Your Loving,"** Four Tops (1964)

- **"Baby Love,"** The Supremes (1964)

- **"Ain't No Mountain High Enough,"** Marvin Gaye and Tammi Terrell (1967)

((• HEAR SAMPLES on **www.mymusiclab.com**

- **Best for last.** The lead singer does not sing the main text of the chorus until its third appearance, and the audience subconsciously waits for this last, most exciting iteration.

- **Intensifying hooks.** The backup singers intensify their contributions to each verse, as the song progresses, with more elaborate parts. The hooks become successively longer.

Backup singers, verse 1:	You, for you.
Backup singers, verse 2:	You, wait, wait for you.
Backup singers, verse 3:	You, wait Mr. Postman.

Listen for the expanded verse-chorus structure as you follow the Listening Guide.

HISTORICAL CONTEXT Reading Labels

When listeners in the 1960s picked up a record with the Motown label, they had a pretty good idea what they would be getting.

Motown was the brainchild of Berry Gordy, a Detroit native who, in 1959, founded Tamla Motown Records to produce black R&B musicians from the area. His "assembly-line" style of musical production has led to comparisons with the auto industry, quite apropos given that the label's name, "Motown," derives from "Motor Town," a reference to Detroit's main business. Gordy's methods also guaranteed that the records shared certain sonic qualities (a "Motown" sound), and that the artists shared aspects of image and style.

Gordy sought widespread distribution for his singers in an era when many black artists had a difficult time obtaining a fair record deal or getting sufficient promotion to place their songs on the pop charts. To compete, Gordy assembled a stable of the best songwriters and session musicians and used them to create almost all the hits that Motown enjoyed in the 1960s. He also invested in a professional choreographer and an "artist development department," responsible for teaching the young artists how to comport themselves, give interviews, and present a polished social image.

Gordy's approach was extremely successful: not only did his artists top the R&B charts, but they also regularly scored number one hits on the pop charts. By the early 1970s, Motown Records was the largest African American–owned business in the United States.

Other record labels also have cultivated an easily recognizable sound. For instance, producer Sam Phillips started

Motown's headquarters, ca. 1964. Smokey Robinson is standing on the right.
Michael Ochs Archives/Stringer/Getty Images

Sun Records in Memphis in the 1950s, which developed the raw rockabilly sound that Elvis Presley and Johnny Cash used on their first recordings. Also located in Memphis, Stax Records used in-house musicians to create the Southern soul sounds of Otis Redding in the 1950s and 1960s. Other artists who recorded in the Stax studios, including Wilson Pickett, ended up with the same, readily identifiable "Stax Sound" on their records.

GO TO www.mymusiclab.com
for the Automated Listening Guide
CD V • Track 15/Download Track 88

Listening Guide

The Marvelettes Composed: 1961 "Please, Mr. Postman" (2:28)

Time	Text	Form	Harmony
0:00	*Wait** Woh yes, wait a minute . . .	Introduction	The close vocal harmony of the background singers appears right at the beginning (after a single drum-hit).
0:09	*Please Mr. Postman . . . /Woh yeah* *Is there a letter . . . /Please, please* Mr. Postman . . .	First chorus	One complete "doo-wop" (descending thirds) progression accompanies each verse.
0:25	*You . . . /There must be . . .* *For you . . . /From my boyfriend . . .*	First verse: backup singers use their shortest phrase, "for you," between the lead's lines.	Complete descending thirds chord progression
0:40	*You . . . /I've been standin' . . .* *Wait, wait for you . . .*	Second verse: backup singers use a longer, syncopated phrase, "wait, wait for you."	Etc.
0:56	Please . . . /*Please . . .* Oh yeah/*Is there a letter . . . (1:04)* Mr. Po-wo-wo-wostman . . .	Second chorus	
1:12	*You . . . /So many days . . .* *Wait, Mr. Postman, you/*You saw the tears . . .	Third verse: backup singers use longest phrase of any verse, "wait, Mr. Postman, you."	
1:28	Please Mister Postman, . . ./ *Postman, postman* Is there a letter . . . *Postman, postman . . . /*You know it's . . . *Postman, postman . . . /* Yeah, since I heard . . .	Third chorus: lead singer sings complete chorus for the first time.	
1:43	You better wait . . . *Wait, wait a minute . . .* . . .Please check and see . . .	Extended vamp 1: repetitive pattern builds energy, prolongs the song, and creates space for vocal improvisation.	
1:59	You better wait . . . *Wait, wait . . .* . . . Deliver dee letter . . .	Extended vamp 2	
2:15	You better wait . . . *Wait, wait. . . .*	Extended vamp 3 to a fade-out	

*The backup vocalists' text is shown in italics

Timbre

Rhythmic hand-claps, the loud presence of the drums, the R&B-style bass and piano, and the close vocal harmony

Brassy, high sounds from the backup singers contrast sharply with the bluesy lead singer.

The lead singer's voice incorporates a bluesy growl (0:50–0:55).

Hand-claps return, but not in a regular pattern yet (1:55).

Hand-claps are still present, now in their regular rhythmic pattern.

Student FAQs

Why doesn't this recording sound as slick as the Motown recordings that are more famous?

Keep in mind that this was done very early in Motown's timeline, and the label's fully mature sound had not yet been established. Also, even though three Motown staff musicians worked on the song, it was the product of amateur songwriters in the first place, so its basic musical structure was less sophisticated than later Motown songs.

What can I do to hear the doo-wop chord progression more clearly?

Listen to some of the other songs mentioned in this chapter that use the progression. If you hear it in different contexts, it will likely become easier to recognize.

The Jackson 5 perform on television, Septebmer 1973. The group's style owed much to the Motown Sound. From left to right: Tito, Marlon, Jackie, Michael, and Jermaine Jackson.
Michael Ochs Archives/Getty Images

◄◄   **EXPAND YOUR PLAYLIST**   ►►

Close Harmony in Different Styles

Close vocal harmony was the hallmark of the 1960s girl groups, but it is an important feature of many other styles of popular music. Here is a sampling from five different decades:

The Chords
- "Sh'Boom" (1954). This doo-wop classic predates the girl groups and Motown songs that were popular in the 1960s. The Chords' recording features the best of close vocal harmony, clearly displayed in the introduction.

The Coasters
- "Smokin' Joe's Cafe" (1955). Often called "Smokey Joe's Cafe," this recording features the hand-claps popular in R&B hits and close vocal harmony using similar chord structures to the Marvelettes. The chord progression, though, uses the 12-bar blues pattern for the song's main sections.

The Beatles
- "Please, Mr. Postman" (1963). Prior to their arrival in the United States, the Beatles covered many U.S. artists' songs, including this Marvelettes' recording for their album *With the Beatles*. The primary differences are the timbre of the ensemble, which lacks Motown's bluesy blend of instruments, including the piano; the gendered elements of the lyrics, which are changed from female to male; and the groove, which lacks the emphasis on rhythmic hooks.

Manhattan Transfer
- "Java Jive" (1975). The sweet jazz harmonies of this song are presented in tight, close vocal harmony, but in a style very different from that of the girl groups that topped the pop charts the previous decade.

Dolly Parton
- Emmylou Harris, and Linda Ronstadt, "Wildflowers" (1987). These three country superstars collaborated on an album with acoustic, old-time influences. This recording highlights their close vocal harmony on the chorus.

*NSYNC
- "God Must Have Spent A Little More Time on You" (1998). The boy bands of the 1990s, of which *NSYNC was one of the best known, brought close vocal harmony and R&B grooves to the top of the pop charts. Listen to the close harmony in the chorus, in particular, where the lead vocal is blended into the background vocals.

((• **HEAR SAMPLES** on **www.mymusiclab.com**

 TEST YOURSELF on **www.mymusiclab.com**   Flashcards and chapter tests

The Beach Boys
"Good Vibrations"
Composed: 1966

Beginning around the middle of the 1960s, many popular music groups, including the Beatles and the Rolling Stones, started to incorporate increasingly sophisticated elements of harmony, timbre, texture, and form into their music. The Beach Boys' "Good Vibrations" illustrates these trends.

 ## Listen to this first

((• HEAR MORE on www.mymusiclab.com

Harmony	**Texture**	**Timbre**	**Form**
Listen to the minor quality of the first chord. Notice the sections where the same music is played at successively higher or lower pitches.	Listen for the addition and subtraction of polyphonic layers.	Listen for unusual instruments and sound effects. Pay attention to the close vocal harmony and the sound of the individual vocal lines.	Listen for three sections in the second half of the recording that interrupt the standard verse-chorus form and introduce very different material.

"Good Vibrations" was part of the psychedelic movement in rock music, which emerged in the mid-1960s on the West Coast of the United States and in London. Psychedelia began with the idea that music could create a hallucinogenic trip for the listener, transporting the mind to a freer, higher consciousness. Many of the musicians in this scene became interested in Eastern philosophies and meditation (see chapter 35). They experimented with instruments that had not been used in rock music before, and their lyrics were increasingly abstract and cryptic. Although psychedelic music originated in conjunction with the hippie movement, which denounced established middle-class society, the music itself became widely accepted in mainstream culture.

In a songwriting process that was essentially backwards—normally, live performance precedes recording—Beach Boy Brian Wilson created "Good Vibrations" during seven separate recording sessions held in four studios over several months. Wilson recorded individual sections of the song as separate modules. After the instrumental sections were complete, Wilson and fellow Beach Boy Mike Love wrote the lyrics.

"Good Vibrations" was unusually long for a single record in 1966. Three minutes was the industry standard. However, Wilson crafted a longer, more formally complex song that

⚙ **LEARN MORE** on **www.mymusiclab.com** Chapter Objectives

encapsulated a mind-expanding journey for its listeners. His project was successful: when it was released in October 1966, "Good Vibrations" quickly topped both the U.S. and U.K. charts and became one of the most discussed rock singles ever.

Minor Chords and a Shaped Harmonic Progression

The first chord progression establishes the key as minor—uncommon in rock music at the time. The minor mode in this section adds to the exotic and unusual quality of the recording and ties it to the sonic world of psychedelia.

The bass guitar, foundation of the harmony, gives us an immediate taste of the kind of harmonic motion we will hear throughout the song. From 0:00 to 0:12, we hear the same motif four

---

HISTORICAL CONTEXT   The Summer of Love

"Good Vibrations" helped launch a wave of unprecedented musical development and hippie celebration known as the Summer of Love. In January 1967, the first "Human Be-In" took place in San Francisco's Golden Gate Park, when 20,000 hippies gathered to revel in their outlook on life. The following summer, a musician from San Francisco's psychedelic scene collaborated with a number of businessmen to host the Monterey International Pop Festival, a three-day outdoor celebration of rock's newest musical styles. Historians estimate that well over 50,000 people came to hear the biggest bands of the day as well as up-and-coming stars, all of whom agreed to perform for free. The Beach Boys had been invited to headline the Monterey festival, but at the last minute they withdrew. Although their hit single "Good Vibrations" had been a major factor in mainstream acceptance of psychedelic music, they feared the band's image and the rest of their set list was far too straitlaced and old-fashioned for the new generation of fans.

Just a few weeks before the festival, the Beatles' concept album *Sgt. Pepper's Lonely Hearts Club Band* was released to wild critical acclaim. The Grateful Dead, Jefferson Airplane, and the Byrds also supplied their fans with new musical highs that summer. Jimi Hendrix, who first caught fans' attention when he set his guitar ablaze after a stunning performance at Monterey, ushered in a new era of virtuosic rock guitar. From the United Kingdom, bands from London's psychedelic underground scene (including Pink Floyd) added their hits to the U.S. charts. *Rolling Stone* published its first issue in late 1967, and in several cities, FM radio stations began to program more experimental styles of rock music.

The Summer of Love cultural movement culminated in August 1969, when nearly half a million hippies gathered in Bethel, New York, for Woodstock, unquestionably the most

Members of the audience during the Woodstock festival in 1969.

John Dominis/The Image Works

famous of the outdoor music festivals. By then, however, the dark realities of Vietnam had shaken the optimism of the hippie movement's "flower power." Later that year, at a music festival at Altamont Speedway in California, the era of the idealistic rock festival came to a sudden end when a fan was tragically killed.

times, on successively lower pitches. This chord progression is called a "descending tetrachord," which means the chords move down successively by steps on four different pitches. It was used extensively in Western classical music, beginning in the seventeenth century, and shows up in other pop music as well.

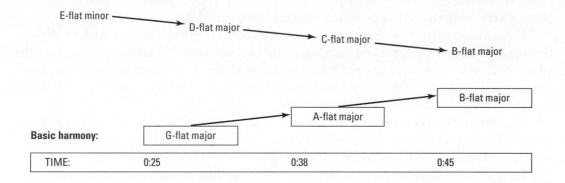

The Beach Boys
"Good Vibrations"
Composed: 1966

GENRE
Psychedelia

KEY CONCEPTS
Composition in the studio, psychedelic sound effects, verse-chorus form with extensions.

CHAPTER HIGHLIGHT
Sixties Rock
In the mid-sixties, rock music entered a period of great creative innovation. Even the Beach Boys, previously known for their light surf music, experimented with "psychedelic" sounds, using such exotic instruments as the theremin and incorporating sophisticated textures and forms into their music.

By contrast, in the chorus that follows the music hoists itself twice to a higher set of pitches, increasing the musical tension and excitement. At 0:38 and 0:45, Brian Wilson repeats the same musical motif but sets it one chord higher, creating this underlying harmonic shape. The second chorus follows the same pattern. The third time the chorus appears, however, the progression is reversed so that the music's harmonic shape descends:

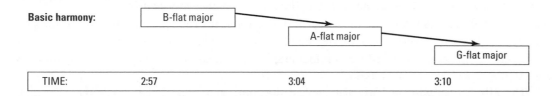

The harmonic ascent in the first two choruses builds up the energy in the piece, while the descent in the third chorus helps bring the piece toward its conclusion.

In the final section (3:13–3:36), the music ascends and then descends, creating a miniature version of the shape that governs the entire rest of the piece:

The climax occurs immediately before the third chorus, in one of the most recognizable moments in the entire recording. The vocal lines blend into a single, thick-textured chord, sung on "Ah" (2:54), which is held for a full measure and then continues ringing through the rest of the band's silence.

A Layered, Polyphonic Texture

When the chorus begins (0:25), there is only one vocal line ("I'm pickin' up good vibrations . . ."), sung by the bass in a low register. A new vocal layer, consisting of two voices in harmony, is added at 0:32 ("ooh, bop-bop . . ."). A third vocal layer is added at 0:38 ("good, good, good, good vibrations . . ."). Instrumental melodies contribute more layers to the texture.

This additive polyphonic technique appears elsewhere in the piece as well. At 2:14, the section opens with only an organ and maracas. Every two measures, the pattern repeats, with the addition of a new polyphonic layer: at 2:21, a vocal line is added, followed by the bass and a new line of vocal harmony (2:28), and a high-pitched motif (2:36). The vocals then fade out of the texture, leaving only the instrumental polyphony.

The reverse process occurs at 2:57: the section starts with three layers of vocal polyphony over a full instrumental texture. The voices then fade out, beginning at 3:08, and the last motivic statement in this section is reduced to just a few distinct instrumental layers.

There are also abrupt changes in texture. Two of the most striking occur at 0:51, when the piece moves from the full polyphony of the chorus back to a single vocal line over accompaniment, and at 2:57, when the full ensemble comes in suddenly.

The Russian-born inventor Leon Theremin (1896–1993) demonstrates the original version of the instrument he named after himself. The box includes oscillators that produce an electronic pulse. The player never actually touches the instrument but instead controls frequency (pitch) with one hand, volume with the other. The Beach Boys' "Good Vibrations" uses a later version of the instrument with a slide that allows the performer to manipulate pitches with greater precision.

Courtesy Bob Moog, Big Briar, Inc., Asheville NC

Psychedelic Timbres

The high, ghostly, howling sound in the choruses and at the very end is an electro-theremin. The theremin was one of the earliest electronic instruments, and it allowed the performer to slide from one pitch to the next, creating eerie and other-worldly tones. The electro-theremin was a modified version that employed a small slider, making it comparatively easy to play specific melodic motifs.

The electro-theremin in particular evoked the topic and title of the song—the vibrations Wilson imagined exist around all of us in an extradimensional plane. But other unusual instruments also connected powerfully to the ideology of musical psychedelia and fueled the imaginations of listeners in the late 1960s: a tack piano, whose tinny sound is created by adding metal tacks to the hammers; a buzzing jews harp; and sleigh bells.

A number of timbres and musical fragments reveal Brian Wilson's influences:

- **Phil Spector's "wall of sound."** Producer Phil Spector, who produced hits such as the Ronettes' "Be My Baby" and the Righteous Brothers' "You've Lost That Lovin' Feeling" in the 1960s, was famous for bringing huge ensembles into his studio to create one dense timbre for his monophonic recordings. Wilson borrowed heavily from this production style.

- **George Gershwin's *Rhapsody in Blue*.** Wilson was fascinated with the hybrid blend of classical and jazz elements in this famous work from 1924. The orchestration he used for "Good Vibrations" was inspired by the concept of bridging boundaries between a rock band and a classical orchestra.

- **Rhythm and blues.** This style is particularly evident in the bass line at 2:28.

- **Doo-wop.** The close vocal harmony on nonsense syllables at the end of the piece (3:13) reflects the 1950s doo-wop tradition, as does the "Ah" chord at 2:54.
- **Motown.** The chorus, with its layered vocals, could easily have been a Motown recording (see chapter 58). Brian Wilson was also very much attuned to the rhythmic grooves that characterized Motown's biggest hits.

Verse-Chorus Plus Sectional Form

CONNECT YOUR PLAYLIST

Layered Texture

Find an example of a recording that has a layered texture.

Example: The Eurythmics: "Sweet Dreams (Are Made of This)" (1983) In "Sweet Dreams," The Eurythmics created a densely layered song in the studio using a variety of synthesizers and tape loops as an accompaniment to the multiple vocal parts.

The first half of the song consists of a typical alternation between verses and choruses. The second half incorporates three unique musical extensions—the product of Brian Wilson's modular compositional method. Where Wilson spliced together individual modules, we hear noticeable shifts in texture, timbre, and even tempo, similar to the contrasts that characterize multi-movement works in the Western classical tradition. Wilson described "Good Vibrations" as a "pocket symphony," a term that captures its condensation of different moods, themes, tempos, and orchestrations in a single piece.

Now listen to this song again, using the Listening Guide.

EXPAND YOUR PLAYLIST

Psychedelia

The late 1960s spawned some of the most influential rock recordings of any decade. After the Beach Boys' album *Pet Sounds* paved the way, the Beatles released *Sgt. Pepper's Lonely Hearts Club Band*, a concept album that allowed the Beatles to recreate themselves as this fictional performing group.

The Byrds
- "Eight Miles High" (1966). The timbres in this recording, especially the 12-string guitar and the haunting, open-fifth harmonies in the vocals, have led historians to identify it as one of the earliest fully psychedelic recordings.

The Beatles
- "Tomorrow Never Knows" (1966). The song features a sitar (see chapter 35), as well as processed sound effects on the vocals and tape effects created by reversing (running the tape backwards), particularly on the guitar solo.

Jefferson Airplane
- "White Rabbit" (1967). The lyrics on this San Francisco band's recording borrow heavily from drug culture. Notice the echoing reverb on the vocals and the intensification of the dynamics and texture as the song reaches its climax.

Pink Floyd
- "Flaming" (1967). British groups began experimenting with psychedelic music in an underground scene several years before it became part of the mainstream American sound.

The Beatles
- "Lucy in the Sky with Diamonds" (1967). Notice the dramatic differences in timbre, tempo, groove, and texture in the individual sections of this recording.

Brian Wilson
- "Good Vibrations" (2004). When Wilson rerecorded the song for his *Smile* album, he used the original lyrics he had commissioned from collaborator Tony Asher but then discarded for the 1966 version. Wilson also inserted an additional section and mixed the recording in stereophonic sound.

((•· HEAR SAMPLES on **www.mymusiclab.com**

Listening Guide

GO TO www.mymusiclab.com
for the Automated Listening Guide
CD V • Track 16/Download Track 89

Beach Boys Composed: 1966 "Good Vibrations" (3:55)

Time	Text	Form	Harmony
0:00	I, I love the colorful clothes she wears . . .	Verse 1	First harmony is minor. Chord progression descends through four different harmonies (0:00–0:12), then repeats.
0:25	I'm pickin' up good vibrations . . .	Chorus	The chorus's main motif appears twice on one chord, then moves up a step (0:38), and finally up another step (0:45).
0:51	Close my eyes . . .	Verse 2	Repetition of the chord progression from verse 1
1:16	I'm pickin' up good vibrations . . .	Chorus	Same chord progression as in first appearance of the chorus
1:42	. . . ta-tions . . . I don't know where but she sends me there . . .	Extension 1. There is a sense of time slowing down because the bass plays longer notes, but the tempo does not change.	Very static chord progression
2:14	Gotta keep those lovin' good vibrations a happenin' with her . . .	Extension 2. The tempo is noticeably slower in this section.	Chords change more rapidly than in Extension 1. Harmonic climax at 2:54.
2:57	Good, good, good, good vibrations . . .	Chorus. Tempo is the same as in the previous choruses (noticeably faster than in Extension 2).	The chorus's main motif appears twice on one chord, then moves *down* a step to a lower chord (3:04), and finally down another step (3:10).
3:13	Na na na . . .	Extension 3.	The chord progression here moves up twice (3:17 and 3:20), then back down (3:23).

Texture	 **Timbre**
Vocal solo over instrumental accompaniment	Lead vocal line is multi-tracked with lots of reverb.
Complex polyphony begins with a bass vocal motif (0:25), on top of which background harmonies are layered (0:32—"ooh, bop-bop . . ."), and finally a third vocal layer (0:38—"good, good, good, good vibrations . . .").	The cellos play a rapidly repeating note in the low register; the tambourine adds shimmer, and the electro-theremin adds the ghostly howling sound in the high register.
Instant change in texture back to the original vocal line plus accompaniment.	
	The splice at 1:16 is audible as a fraction of a second of silence before the chorus begins.
Extremely thick instrumental texture under layered vocals	Tack piano plus jews harp, bass harmonica, and rhythm section create an unusual timbre. The vocal harmony enters on "ah . . ." (1:55), followed by sleigh bells and new, abstract lyrics (2:01).
Texture starts very simply, builds up through the gradual addition of new layers, and then reverses the process as the vocals fade out.	Organ plus maracas (shakers) open the section. Bass enters at 2:28, using an R&B style.
Texture moves from many layers to only a few.	Full ensemble gradually reduces to just cellos, bass, drums, and tambourine.
The first part of this section (3:13–3:27) is complex vocal polyphony with many different lines.	The first part of this section (3:13–3:27) borrows close vocal harmony on nonsense syllables.

Jimi Hendrix, another legendary rock star of the 1960s, listens to a playback in the studio and consults with the engineer (left) on how the final product will sound.

Jay Good

Student FAQs

Why does the lead singer's voice sound thicker and more resonant than most vocals?

Carl Wilson sang the same melody more than once in the recording studio, and those "takes" were layered together in a technique known as "multitracking." When two recordings of the same melody are combined, the two sets of sound waves exhibit tiny differences, which give the final version a more robust timbre. Multitracking occurs through most of "Good Vibrations."

How did Brian Wilson combine different recordings to make this song?

Before digital technology was available in the recording studio, producers used razor blades and tape to cut and splice the magnetic recording tape from different takes. Different splicing techniques created different effects; for instance, cross-fading could be done by slicing the tape at an angle.

PROFILE   The Beach Boys

Making the Album that Never Was

The Beach Boys began in 1961 as a surf-rock band with brothers Brian, Carl, and Dennis Wilson plus the boys' cousin Mike Love and their friend Al Jardine. Brian (b. 1942), the group's most prolific composer, combined the basic style of rock 'n' roll, the ensemble's remarkable vocal abilities, and lighthearted lyrics to create early hits for the quintet, including "Surfer Girl," "Surfin' U.S.A.," "Fun, Fun, Fun," and "409." Good Vibrations" was slated to be part of a Beach Boys album called *Smile*, Brian's intended masterpiece.

In the mid-1960s, while the rest of the Beach Boys embarked on live concert tours, Brian Wilson stayed home to cultivate his ambitions as a composer and producer. The money he earned from the band's "surf rock" hits allowed him unprecedented freedom in the recording studio. Wilson's extensive drug use and mental illness contributed to occasional wild eccentricities. He once had a full symphony orchestra wear plastic fireman's hats and sit around a burning bucket of kindling to inspire their recording of a musical "Fire" module. He had a sandbox built around the piano in his home so he could simultaneously compose and experience the beach. Such creative compositional approaches laced his vision for a radical new album called *Smile* that he hoped would revolutionize popular music.

Unfortunately, the rest of the band did not like the music as much, neither Brian's record company nor his fans shared his vision, and the project stalled. In place of *Smile*, the band released a haphazardly recorded substitute version called *Smiley Smile*. Nothing the group did after that attained the same recognition as their earlier work. Eventually, the Beach Boys returned to playing their original surf rock hits.

For decades, fans speculated about the sound of the original *Smile* album. In 2004, Brian Wilson finally reentered

The Beach Boys pose around a dragster in London's West End. From left: Carl Wilson, Brian Wilson, Dennis Wilson, Mike Love, and Al Jardine.
Getty Images Inc.— Hulton Archive Photos

the recording studio to finish the project, but by that time, both Carl and Dennis had passed away, and the other band members had splintered into separate groups. None of them was involved in the album's completion. Thus, though Brian released *Smile* to critical acclaim, the album never came to light in the way it was originally conceived. It was intended to stand on equal footing with the Beatles' *Sgt. Pepper's Lonely Hearts Club Band*, revolutionize American rock, and declare unconditionally that rock was serious art music. Instead, it became the most famous album in rock history that very few heard.

◉▸ **EXPLORE MORE** on www.mymusiclab.com

Public Enemy
"Fight the Power"
Composed: 1990

60

By the end of the twentieth century, digital technology made it easier than ever to manipulate recorded sound. The results have been many and varied. Public Enemy's "Fight the Power" offers one example of how musicians have used technology to create new sounds.

Listen to this first

((•) HEAR MORE on www.mymusiclab.com

Timbre

Listen for many different layers of sound and for fragments taken from other recordings. Notice the reverberation on the low bass and drums.

Form

Listen for obvious changes in timbre, rhythm, and lyrics that divide the song into sections. Notice that some sections repeat with slight variations.

Rhythm

Be aware of repetition in the rhythmic groove. Feel the steady pulse. Listen to the rhythmic pattern of the lyrics and how it creates tension against the accompaniment's meter.

Word-Music Relationships

Notice references to other artists, historical figures, and songs.

Public Enemy recorded "Fight the Power" for film director Spike Lee, who used it as the theme song for *Do the Right Thing* (1989). The movie's plot centers on racial tension in a Brooklyn neighborhood, and Public Enemy's abrasive rap recording vividly conveyed the film's sentiments. Publicity from the movie helped the recording reach number one on *Billboard*'s rap chart. Public Enemy also released it as the last track on their 1990 album *Fear of a Black Planet*, which is the version discussed here. (Several different versions of the song were released at the time.)

Rap music is an art form that combines rhymed speech patterns with hip-hop beats. Within hip-hop culture, "beat" refers not to a simple pulse but to a complete rhythmic groove constructed from many different sounds repeated in complex patterns. When Public Enemy were recording in the late 1980s, the sounds used to create hip-hop beats were **sampled**, or recorded from existing albums—often funk and soul albums from the 1960s and 1970s. Rap musicians took short excerpts—sometimes only a fraction of a second of sound—then programmed their drum machines and synthesizers to play the sounds back in various repetitive patterns, while manipulating their pitch, duration, and timbre. Those patterns provided the rhythmic and musical accompaniment for the rapper's lyrics.

⚙ **LEARN MORE** on
www.mymusiclab.com
Chapter Objectives

A Layered, Sampled Timbre

The lengthy sample from Dr. King's speech sets the political tone for the song. The speaker's pitch and dynamic levels build up for the first few seconds, then drop off with the phrase "refuse to fight." This pattern of rise and fall creates a wave of rhetorical energy and is often used when delivering sermons.

An opening gesture, which catches the listener's attention but does not start the song's rhythmic groove, follows at 0:16. We hear faint vocals repeating the words "pump it" in a syncopated rhythmic pattern. This short fragment of text is taken from a band called Trouble Funk. It is layered densely with other samples, including a harsh snare drum that defines the pulse of the song. Most significantly, these samples contain audible fuzz and distortion because the sampling process then in use reduced the fidelity of the original recording. The resulting timbre evokes the sound of a boom box playing cassette tapes, obscures the origins of the samples, and makes the rap vocals stand out more because of their relative clarity.

The timbre most strongly identified with hip-hop beats is "scratching." Listen for the high-pitched sounds that appear at 2:26, 2:29, 2:31, and 2:33. This scratch technique, originally developed by Grandwizard Theodore (Theodore Livingston), Grandmaster Flash (Joseph Saddler), and Kool Herc (Clive Campbell) in the early 1980s, involves rapidly rotating a vinyl record on a turntable (record player) back and forth while the record is playing. The sound of the scratch is determined by the music on the record at that particular place, as well as the techniques used by the deejay (see "Hip-Hop's Elements," page 495).

Verse-Chorus Form

"Fight the Power" uses a verse-chorus form found in many different genres of popular music, but it also features a lengthy opening section, verses and choruses that vary, instrumental sections, and an epilogue.

- **Extensive opening section.** This consists of the spoken prologue, the musical gesture with "pump it," and the more typical introduction, where the rhythmic groove begins.

- **Expanding verses.** The three verses in this song are different lengths, which is unusual in popular music. The first verse is 12 measures long, the second is 16 measures long, and the third is 18. Listeners are probably not consciously aware that each verse is a bit longer than the previous one, but the tension builds as the listener waits longer and longer for the climax of each verse and the arrival of the chorus.

- **Repeating hook in a chorus.** At 1:13 there is a noticeable change in the song's rhythmic groove, which signals the beginning of the chorus. That chorus occurs five times, but the last two appearances omit some lines and alter the rhythmic groove slightly, preventing monotony.

- **Instrumental breaks.** There are two long "breaks," in which the singers are silent while the rhythmic groove takes the stage. The break at 2:25 features scratching as an instrumental solo. The other break, at 4:00, is where other mixes feature Branford Marsalis's solo. This version continues instead with many of the samples from the chorus's accompaniment. At 4:10, a segment of the rhythmic groove repeats in short, syncopated rhythmic patterns, building up the energy level right before the final chorus begins.

- **Epilogue.** At the end of the recording, we hear fragments of an interview asking the band about the future of Public Enemy. These short excerpts are cut off before we hear the band's answer, which suggests that the band's future was uncertain. Indeed, this album appeared during a media firestorm over a band member's apparently anti-Semitic comments, and this epilogue provides a cryptic response to both fans and detractors.

A Repetitive Rhythmic Groove with Syncopated Lyrics

The rhythmic character of "Fight the Power," like most rap recordings, consists of three elements:

- A steady, throbbing pulse that does not change during the song
- A complicated set of rhythmic patterns that repeat to create a unique groove, or hip-hop beat
- Syncopated lyrics that create tension in relation to the accompanying groove

The basic pulse of this rap recording is 106 beats per minute, and the tempo does not change during the song. Listen carefully to the groove that is established at 0:23. There is a high-pitched, ringing, electronic sound in the left channel of the stereophonic recording that occurs at the beginning of each four-beat measure. However, the sound is not placed exactly on the downbeat. Instead, it occurs a fraction of a second after the downbeat. The exact placement of each sample in relation to the music's meter gives a particular groove its character. If the samples in this groove were shifted even a fraction of an instant in relation to the meter, the hip-hop beat would have a fundamentally different musical flavor.

Syncopation plays a significant role in the rhythmic profile of rap music, particularly when conflicting accents occur between the text and the accompanying groove's meter. Another important layer of syncopation occurs when a rhythmic phrase is repeated, but the second time it occurs, it lines up differently with the underlying pulse. The technique generates conflicting accents in the music: the accents from the metric downbeats, and the accents at the beginning of repeated text phrases. The phrase "Fight the power," which is the hook of the song, starts on the downbeat at the beginning of the chorus (1:13). When it repeats two seconds later, the rhythm of the phrase is the same, but its relationship with the meter has shifted so it starts on the second beat of the measure. The text's phrases repeat after five beats, but the song is clearly in quadruple meter, creating a large-scale syncopation:

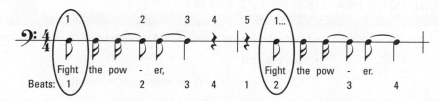

PROFILE   **Public Enemy**

Politics and Music

When Public Enemy began to make records, they brought a powerful, abrasive, and unapologetically radical social agenda to hip-hop on the East Coast. In contrast to popular mid-1980s artists who rapped about partying and romance, Public Enemy incited controversy with their politicized lyrics and outspoken commentary on such topics as racism, civil rights, and AIDS. They found a welcome audience for their messages and emerged as major stars during the genre's explosive growth period.

Chuck D (Carlton Douglas Ridenhour) entered the world of hip-hop as a graphic artist who designed flyers for parties. There, he met musicians in Long Island's growing rap scene and began to hone his skills as an MC—a hip-hop "Master of Ceremonies" (see "Hip-Hop's Elements," page 495). In 1984, he and collaborator Flavor Flav (William Jonathan Drayton Jr.) made a tape called "Public Enemy #1" to answer a challenge from a local rapper, and that tape found its way into the hands of producer Rick Rubin, who founded Def Jam Records with Russell Simmons. Rubin heard tremendous commercial potential in Chuck D's tape and immediately wanted to sign the artist to Def Jam, which was growing into the most significant record label in hip-hop. In June 1986, Chuck D finally agreed to a record contract under the name Public Enemy.

As a condition of the contract, Chuck D insisted that he be allowed to assemble an ensemble in the style of hip-hop's earliest crews like Grandmaster Flash and the Furious Five, rather than sign as a solo artist. Public Enemy became a self-contained production and entertainment unit. It consisted of Flavor Flav, DJ Terminator X (Norman Rogers), Professor Griff (Richard Griffin) in the role of "minister of information" (essentially a sidekick member of the entourage), an onstage security team known as S1W, plus the "Bomb Squad" production team: Hank Shocklee, his brother Keith Shocklee, and Eric "Vietnam" Sadler. Public Enemy's success had much to

Public Enemy
Michael Ochs
Archives Ltd./
Getty Images
Inc.—Los Angeles

do with their production team's talent. The Bomb Squad had a unique ability to create hip-hop beats that were sonically dense, heavily layered, and musically chaotic. These timbres and grooves reinforced the serious themes of Public Enemy's lyrics with a musical aggression that cut through the waves of hip-hop recordings during that era.

Public Enemy was not the only hip-hop ensemble to write politically charged lyrics laced with expressions of black nationalism. During the same era, West Coast rap artists were lashing out with raps about race, poverty, and oppression, most notably N.W.A.'s *Straight Outta Compton* (1988). The media's attention to West Coast rap and the ensuing rise of gangsta rap threatened to overshadow Public Enemy's role in transforming rap into a politically charged musical genre. However, their first three albums were seminal in that process and are widely regarded as groundbreaking by hip-hop fans.

⊙➤ **EXPLORE MORE** on **www.mymusiclab.com**

⏮   **EXPAND YOUR PLAYLIST: PUBLIC ENEMY**   ⏭

- **"Public Enemy #1"**
- **"Don't Believe the Hype"**
- **"911 Is a Joke"**

- **"Fight the Power"**—Soundtrack version from *Do the Right Thing*
- **"Can't Truss It"**

((• **HEAR SAMPLES** on **www.mymusiclab.com**

Word-Music Relationships: Politically Charged Hip-Hop Rhymes and References

"Fight the Power" used quotations and references from late 1980s hip-hop culture to connect with its audience. In the first verse, for instance, the singer says, "funky drummer" and "I know you got soul," both of which are titles of songs that are sampled in the accompaniment, and both of which were popular with other deejays who were laying down hip-hop beats during those years. The song cites Bobby McFerrin's hit "Don't Worry Be Happy" in a derogatory statement on the quality of contemporary black music. Both Elvis Presley and John Wayne, entertainers from earlier decades, are mentioned as tokens of white culture and, according to the rap lyrics, its disregard for black role models. At 1:58, Public Enemy also includes a reference to their own first album to compel their audience to join their political crusade for black nationalism. "Yo! bum rush the show," in hip-hop slang, means to run full speed ahead into something with reckless abandon.

Now listen to this song again, using the Listening Guide.

HISTORICAL CONTEXT   Hip-Hop's Elements

Hip-hop music grew out of an environment in which graffiti, deejaying, emceeing, and break dancing were equally significant forms of cultural expression. In predominantly black neighborhoods of New York City, graffiti was a visual art that let the individual lay claim to space, property, and a public identity through his or her "tags," or graffiti signatures. Deejaying involved manipulating vinyl records on turntables to mix and repeat sections of songs, usually drum breaks or solos, in innovative ways, and emceeing involved calling out improvised rhymes to entertain a crowd and keep a party lively; this became rap. Break dancers, known as b-boys and b-girls, responded to the deejay's selection of drum breaks with acrobatic moves. Aspects of fashion and rhetoric were also woven into hip-hop culture.

Harsh economic conditions, gang violence, and a sense of despair motivated the first generation of hip-hop artists to find a creative outlet through their music, but record executives quickly saw the potential to transform this culture of self-expression into a highly commercial genre that, in its early days, did not espouse strongly politicized messages. With records, radio shows, and growing media coverage, hip-hop quickly spread beyond its original neighborhoods. And yet despite many pockets of interest, mainstream acceptance of hip-hop was slow in coming. The day before Def Jam Recordings released *Fear of a Black Planet*, *Newsweek* published a scathing critique of hip-hop culture that described its music as a "thumping, clattering, scratching assault." Accusations abounded that the music was merely noise and that the artists were not really musicians, given that they did not play instruments and rapping

Public Enemy's *Fear of a Black Planet* album cover.
© Dorling Kindersley

was different than singing. The artists also faced harsh criticism and the occasional lawsuit for their sampling practices. Over time, however, those controversies faded as new, legal accountability became the norm, and as fans and writers alike acknowledged that the manipulation of pre-recorded sound was also a form of musical composition.

Permission could not be obtained to reproduce this recording from the copyright owner.

Public Enemy Composed: 1990 "Fight the Power" (4:42)

Time	Text	Form	Timbre
0:00	Yet our best-trained . . .	Prologue	Male voice preaching. Audience noise; monophonic, low fidelity recording
0:16		Opening gesture	Sampled sounds, overlaid at 0:18 with a sampled snare drum
0:23	Get it, get, get . . .	Introduction	Amplified bass frequencies, ringing high frequencies, sampled fragments of text
0:45	1989 . . . Sound of the . . . I know . . .	Verse 1	Male rapping, with second voice adding commentary
1:13	(Lemme hear you say. . .) Fight the power . . .	Chorus	Additional reverberation on low bass and drum sounds; new collection of samples create a deeper resonance.
1:31	As the rhythm's designed . . . Yo! Bum rush the show. . .	Verse 2	Return to the first verse's hip-hop beat.
2:07	Fight the power: fight the power . . .	Chorus	Same accompaniment as the first chorus.
2:25		Break	Scratching featured throughout the solo; heavy-metal guitar sample at 2:41.
2:43	Fight the power . . .	Chorus	Same accompaniment as the first chorus
3:01	Elvis was a . . . Nothing but rednecks . . . 'Don't worry, be happy' was a . . .	Verse 3	Guttural vocal insertions punctuate the rap ("huh" at 3:03; "yeah" at 3:05; "huh" at 3:08).
3:42	Fight the power . . .	Chorus (variant)	New accompaniment under this chorus
4:00		Break	Break extracts parts of the groove from the first chorus but omits some of the samples.
4:19	What we got to say, yeah, fight the power . . .	Chorus (second variant)	Samples and rhythmic grooves from the first verse are combined with vocals from the chorus.
4:37		Epilogue	Three distinct male voices, separated in the stereo mix

Rhythm

Tension is built through the pace of the text's delivery.

Harsh articulation of the beat at 0:18

Text fragments are repeated to create syncopated rhythmic patterns.

Regular, steady pulse under a repetitive four-bar rhythmic pattern. Vocals create syncopated patterns against the underlying groove.

Changing metric placement of the hook phrase generates large-scale syncopation.

This verse is four bars longer than the first verse.

Constantly changing rhythmic patterns in the scratching

Rhythmic repetition of opening phrase emphasizes lyrics. Verse is two bars longer than the second verse.

Sampled vocal becomes rhythmic focal point.

First half of the break preserves the rhythmic patterns from the first chorus. Then, at 4:10, a tiny fragment from 4:00 is recast in a more intense and active rhythmic pattern.

Vocals and accompaniment are rhythmically in sync.

Groove ends abruptly; dialogue uses the free rhythms of casual speech.

Student FAQs

Is there a list somewhere of all the samples used in this recording?

There are partial lists (including the one at the end of this chapter: see Expand Your Playlist), but in interviews, Public Enemy has explained that they aren't even sure exactly what they used. Unlike today, in the first decade of rap recordings artists frequently used samples without documenting their original sources and with little regard for copyright issues. The original sounds were also often altered beyond recognition. Thus, it is sometimes impossible to identify all sources of this work's samples.

Chen Chao © Dorling Kindersley

With so many different mixes of this song available, which is the official version?

With a song like this one, there isn't any one version that is considered either original or official. Each mix was done for a specific purpose, and so the more revealing question to ask would be "How does each version fit its purpose?"

Bobby McFerrin, whose music Public Enemy criticizes in "Fight the Power."
Getty Images, Inc.

EXPAND YOUR PLAYLIST

Musical References in "Fight the Power"

The lyrics to "Fight the Power" quote phrases and titles from several different songs and refer to historical figures both directly and through the use of samples.

Elvis Presley
• "Hound Dog" (1956). Recorded by black blues legend Big Mama Thornton three years before Presley, this song is often cited by critics who accuse Presley of appropriating black music. However, this overlooks the fact that the song was written for Thornton by the white songwriting team of Lieber and Stoller.

Sly and the Family Stone
• "Sing a Simple Song" (1968). The line "Lemme hear you say" comes from this funk song. It brings an authentic funk voice into the text of "Fight the Power."

James Brown
• "Funky Drummer" (1969). Listen to Brown's lyrics that give the instrumentalists instructions. The drum solo toward the end of the recording has been sampled and used in countless hip-hop recordings, especially in the late 1980s.

Bobby Byrd
• "I Know You Got Soul," (1971). Byrd worked as James Brown's second vocalist for many years, and this song was a favorite source for hip-hop samples. Listen to the growls and gravelly quality in Byrd's voice that support the emotional tenor of Public Enemy's message.

Public Enemy
• "Yo! Bum Rush the Show" (1987). The phrase "bum rush" is part of hip-hop slang; it is also the title of the band's first album and one of its tracks. By using this phrase again in "Fight the Power," Public Enemy invoked their own pioneering role in bringing political messages into rap albums.

Bobby McFerrin
• "Don't Worry Be Happy" (1988). This song won the Grammy for Best Song of the Year right before "Fight the Power" was released. The recording uses vocal *a cappella* techniques to create all the rhythmic sounds.

 **HEAR SAMPLES** on **www.mymusiclab.com**

TEST YOURSELF on **www.mymusiclab.com**   Flashcards and chapter tests

Tania León
A la Par, second movement (*Guaguancó*)
Composed: 1986

What happens when modernism confronts popular music in the same work? Leon's *A la par* offers one possible scenario, for it mixes the rhythms of a Cuban popular dance with atonal harmonies.

 **Listen to this first** ((• HEAR MORE on www.mymusiclab.com

Timbre	**Rhythm**	**Harmony**	**Form**
Listen for the contrast between those percussion instruments that play specific pitches (like the piano, the vibraphone, and the bongo drums) and those that make only percussive sounds that cannot be tied to any specific pitch (like the cowbell, the cymbals, and the snare drum).	Listen for the repeated melodic and rhythmic figure in the lower register of the piano. This kind of figure is typical of the Afro-Cuban dance known as the *guaguancó*.	Listen for the mixture of tonal and atonal harmonies in this work.	The movement divides into two very different sections. Where does the change occur?

The Spanish title *A la par* translates loosely as "at the same time as" or "on the same level as," and it is a fitting description of the relationship between popular and modernist styles. The repeated melodic-rhythmic figure in the bass line derives from the vernacular idioms of Cuban dance, while the other instrumental lines reflect the principles of European modernism. Even though they are often quite distinct—each goes its own way—they nevertheless complement one another to create a whole larger than the sum of its parts. Every instrument seems to occupy its own space, yet in the end everything is indeed *a la par*. The composer herself has said that this work reflects her own attempt "to express the dichotomy between the folk-music traditions of my native Cuba and the Classical European training I received at the Havana Conservatory."

This musical style in which modern and traditional elements are combined is often called **postmodernism**. Postmodernism is a style of modernism—no one would think of León's music as old-fashioned—but it embraces tonality as well as atonality, rhythmic predictability as well as unpredictability. Postmodern works are often playful in spirit, a reaction against the unrelenting seriousness of much modernist art. As a work of postmodernism, León's *A la par* is both tonal and atonal, rhythmically regular and irregular, serious and playful.

⚙ **LEARN MORE** on
www.mymusiclab.com
Chapter Objectives

Percussion Timbres

A percussion instrument is one that produces sound by being struck or shaken, and all the instruments in this work belong to the percussion family, including even the piano (a finger strikes the key, which activates a hammer, which strikes a string). Some percussion instruments (like the piano or certain kinds of drums) produce specific pitches, while others do not. In the second movement of *A la par*, León uses both kinds of instruments. The timings in the following list indicate examples of when you can hear these individual instruments. Notice that not all the instruments are played the same way all the time. The player striking the timbales (a pair of small drums), for example, sometimes hits the side of the instrument with a stick and sometimes hits the membrane surface on the top. The conga player sometimes uses the hand, sometimes a stick.

Pitched Instruments

- **Piano**: 0:00 and throughout.
- **Timbales** (a small drum): 0:06 and throughout. In this particular movement, the player most often uses a stick to strike the side of the instrument, but at other times strikes the membrane on top of the drum (as at 0:28–0:30), which is the more standard way of playing the instrument.
- **Tom-toms** (a pair of large drums): 0:35–0:40.
- **Bongos** (a pair of very small hand drums): 0:50–0:52.
- **Snare drum** (a medium-sized drum): 0:23–0:25.
- **Marimba** (a xylophone-like instrument with tubular resonators under each bar): 1:55–end.
- **Vibraphone** (an electrified marimba with motorized controls that can produce different degrees of vibrato, a wavering-like sound, for each pitch): 1:50–end.

Non-Pitched Instruments

- **Conga** (a long, narrow drum): 0:05, very briefly, then again at 0:12–0:15, played first with the hand and then with the stick
- **Cowbell** (struck with a stick): 0:43–0:45.
- **Suspended cymbal** (a single cymbal, struck with a stick): 0:34.
- **Cachiche** (a maraca-like "shaker"): 1:02–1:08.

Male and Female Rhythmic Lines

In the lower register of the piano, we hear a syncopated figure over and over, the kind of rhythmic pattern to which Cuban dancers could dance the *guaguancó*. The central element of this rumba-style dance is the *vacuno*, a pelvic thrust by the man toward the woman, who both encourages and avoids these thrusts. Listen to the way in which the repeated figure in the bass suggests a physical thrust and how the voices around it—all the other percussion instruments, including the piano in its middle and upper ranges—seem to both encourage and resist this repeated thrusting figure.

Parallel (Non-) Harmonies

The repeated figure in the lower register of the piano is chromatically inflected but squarely tonal: it keeps landing over and over on the same note, so we feel that the music—or at least this portion of the music—has a tonal center. It has some notes that sound slightly dissonant (because they are chromatic), but the repeated note is so prominent that our ear hears this note as a harmonic foundation. Everything else—all the pitches around this bass line—is less centered, including even the higher notes on the piano. The other pitched instruments are insistently atonal. (The non-pitched percussion instruments cannot play a role in the harmony, and function in a purely rhythmic fashion.) This movement thus combines elements of both tonality (the repeated *guanguacó* figure) and atonality.

A couple in Havana dances the *guaguancó*; drummers are visible in the background.
Rebecca Bodenheimer, PhD

Sectional Form

The contrast between the last third of the movement and all that has gone before is sudden and obvious: the steady rhythmic figure disappears, the tempo shifts suddenly from fast to slow, almost all the percussion instruments drop out, and two new instruments, the marimba and the vibraphone, enter for the first time. On closer listening, we realize that the first quarter or so of this movement is an introduction of sorts, for while it presents the basic *guanguacó* figure, it does so only sporadically. Only after a short break in the music (at 0:39) does this figure become an ostinato. The movement thus divides into three sections: an introduction, the central *guanguacó*, and a coda. The first two sections are closely related, while the third is quite different.

With these points in mind, listen to the second movement of this work again, using the Listening Guide.

b. 1943
Tania León
A la Par, second movement (*Guaguancó*)
Composed: 1986
GENRE
Music for percussion ensemble
KEY CONCEPTS
Tonal vs. atonal elements, percussion instruments.
CHAPTER HIGHLIGHT
Postmodernism
Postmodernism integrates modern idioms with more traditional ones. Postmodern works are often playful in spirit, a reaction against the unrelenting seriousness of much modernist art. Tania León's *A la Par* combines traditional Cuban dance rhythms with atonal harmonies.

CONNECT YOUR PLAYLIST
Repeated Melodic-Rhythmic Figure

Find an example of a piece that contains a repeated melodic-rhythmic figure.

Example: Paul Simon, "You Can Call Me Al" (1986)
In this song, the prominent, repeated bass line establishes both a melodic pattern and rhythmic support for the vocal.

Listening Guide

Tania León Composed: 1986 *A la Par,* second movement (*Guaguancó*) (2:27)

Time	Form: Section	Rhythm	Timbre	Harmony
0:00	(1) Introduction (fast)	*Guaguancó* rhythm in lower register of piano, but not continuously. The upper register of the piano and all the other instruments weave around this recurring figure.	Piano, percussion instruments	No sense of tonality at first, but the melodic figure in the bass (starting at 0:11) establishes its lowest note as the central tone.
0:39	(2) Ostinato (fast)	The rhythmic figure now becomes an ostinato in the bass, repeated without a pause.		Non-ostinato pitches are atonal; ostinato figure centers on its lowest note.
1:33	(2) Coda (slow)	*Guaguancó* rhythm drops out for the first time. Piano plays a disjunct, atonal line its place.	Reduced instrumentation and new instruments: Piano, cowbell (briefly), then the vibraphone and marimba enter for the first time.	Wholly atonal; no sense of a tonal center at all.

Student FAQs

How many musicians does it take to perform this work?

In a percussion ensemble, one player usually covers multiple instruments, switching from, say, marimba to vibraphone to claves (wooden sticks) as the score demands. The number of performers is optional, but the score determines how many are needed at a minimum. The excerpt given here would require at least four percussionists.

What's the difference between postmodernism and neoclassicism?

The two are related but not the same. Both make reference to earlier idioms, though neoclassicism is generally associated with the 1920s and 1930s, whereas postmodernism is a phenomenon of the late twentieth century. Postmodern music, unlike neoclassicism, embraces modernism as one of many legitimate approaches to artistic expressions, whereas neoclassicism rejects the extremes of modernism. In the end, the terms are labels whose applicability to any given work or artist can be debated.

A Marimba.
© Dorling Kindersley

GO TO www.mymusiclab.com
for the Automated Listening Guide
CD V • Track 17/Download Track 90

HISTORICAL CONTEXT   Postmodern Architecture

The spirit of postmodernism is perhaps most readily apparent in the field of architecture. For many decades in the middle of the twentieth century, modernist architecture dominated the scene. The typical modernist building favored clean, straight lines with little or no hint of ornamentation.

Advocates of modernist architecture praised its emphasis on functionality and its break with traditions of the past. But in the second half of the twentieth century, more and more critics came to see this style as cold and impersonal. Postmodern architects began adding elements to building that were not driven entirely by function. The curved walls of the Walt Disney Theater in Los Angeles (2004) capture the more playful spirit of postmodernism.

With its symmetrical design and clean, straight lines, the John F. Kennedy Center for the Performing Arts in Washington, D. C. (1971), exemplifies modernist architecture.

Bill Helsel/Alamy Images

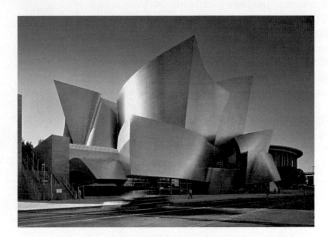

The fanciful, irregular shape of the Walt Disney Concert Hall in Los Angeles (2004) reflects the more recent style of postmodern architecture.

© Lara Swimmer/Esto

◀◀   EXPAND YOUR PLAYLIST   ▶▶

Postmodern Music

The postmodern idiom has attracted a number of leading composers in recent decades, including the following:

George Rochberg (1918–2005)
• *String Quartet no. 6.* A postmodern work by a composer who was an avowed modernist in his early career. The slow movement is a set of variations on Pachelbel's celebrated Canon.

William Bolcom (b. 1938)
• *Songs of Innocence and Experience.* A setting of texts by William Blake, this cycle of songs juxtaposes a wide range of musical idioms, including atonal and tonal, jazz, gospel, blues, ragtime, and rock.

Luciano Berio (1925–2003)
• *Sinfonia.* The second movement of this work for orchestra and eight amplified voices uses the second movement of Gustav Mahler's Second Symphony as its basis, with samplings from works by many other composers superimposed on it, along with a text by Samuel Beckett.

Alfred Schnittke (1934–1998)
• *Carmen Suite.* This is a reworking of themes from Georges Bizet's well-known *Carmen* (1875), rewritten and reorchestrated in such a way as to create an arresting mixture of nineteenth- and twentieth-century idioms.

John Zorn (b. 1953)
• *The Big Gundown: John Zorn Plays the Music of Ennio Morricone.* This album, released in 1985, superimposes idioms of jazz, soul, and other genres on the film scores of a composer who specialized in creating soundtracks for films set in the American West (*A Fistful of Dollars, Once Upon a Time in the West*).

((|• **HEAR SAMPLES** on **www.mymusiclab.com**

PROFILE   Tania León (b. 1943)

Resisting Labels

"I have a lot of trouble with labels," the composer Tania León recently confessed. "I'm totally anti-label. . . . Everybody has called me so many things. . . . How do they see me? Do they see me? Do they hear me? Do they watch me? Every time I read a different article, I have a different category. Now, the latest thing is Afro-Cuban. The first time that I heard that term, I was announced to an audience by a colleague of mine. I was totally surprised that this colleague of mine chose to say something like that. What is this all about?"

León's music indeed defies easy categorization: it synthesizes a great many traditions, from Cuban dance to atonality and many other styles in between. In this respect, it reflects León's exposure to a great many musical traditions, not only in her native Cuba, where she studied to become a pianist, but also in the United States, where she turned her attention more and more toward composing and conducting. Shortly after immigrating to the United States in 1967, she became the first music director of the Dance Theater of Harlem in 1969 and has taught composition at Brooklyn College since 1985. She has received commissions from throughout the world for works in a variety of genres, including operas and several works for orchestra. As a

Cuban-born composer Tania León in 1996, conducting one of her compositions in a concert at the New School, in New York City.

Jack Vartoogian/Front Row Photos

conductor, she has performed with such prestigious ensembles as the Gewandhaus Orchestra of Leipzig and the New York Philharmonic.

⊙→ EXPLORE MORE on **www.mymusiclab.com**

EXPAND YOUR PLAYLIST: LEÓN

- *Rituál.* A modernist work for piano.

- *Pueblo mulato.* Three songs to texts by the Cuban poet Nicolás Guillén, for soprano, oboe, guitar, double bass, percussion, and piano.

- *Indigena.* A work for chamber orchestra that draws on the composer's Cuban roots.

- *Scourge of Hyacinths.* An opera based on a radio play by the Nobel Prize–winning Nigerian author Wole Soyinka.

- *Momentum.* A work for piano, with an energetic rhythm, as its title suggests.

⦅•● HEAR SAMPLES on **www.mymusiclab.com**

⊘ TEST YOURSELF on **www.mymusiclab.com**   Flashcards and chapter tests

62

Tan Dun

"Farewell" from *Crouching Tiger, Hidden Dragon*

Composed: 2000

The music for the 2000 film *Crouching Tiger, Hidden Dragon* unites Western and non-Western timbres and melodic styles to create a soundscape that seems to transcend both time and place.

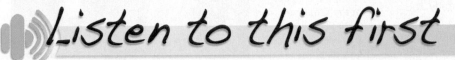

Listen to this first

HEAR MORE on www.mymusiclab.com

Timbre

Listen for the complementary sounds of the deeply resonant cello and the eerily human Chinese erhu, both string instruments. Listen for additional layers of sound from the hand drums and from the Western-style string orchestra.

Melody

The principal melody, in the cello, is presented eight times, each time in a slightly different form. Listen to the cello and the erhu "slide" into and around their notes. Also listen for the way in which the cello ends each statement of the melody on the same note until the very last time, when the ending is not so clear.

Texture

The texture is polyphonic throughout, with three independent lines: the cello, the erhu, and the orchestra, which plays quietly throughout in the background. Notice the way the melody in the erhu weaves around the melody in the cello.

LEARN MORE on **www.mymusiclab.com** Chapter Objectives

***Crouching Tiger, Hidden Dragon*, directed by Ang Lee,** is set in eighteenth-century China and tells the story of two couples whose lives are overshadowed by fate. The plot revolves around a legendary sword known as the Green Destiny, and the film includes spectacular fight scenes. The film's music, composed by Tan Dun, won the Academy Award in 2001 for Best Music in an Original Score, as well as a Grammy Award in 2002 for Best Score Soundtrack Album. The selection here comes after the bittersweet end of the action, during the credits. Its central theme is one that has been associated with the two love stories throughout the movie. Tan Dun's score at this point is a purely musical commentary on the sweetness and brevity of love and life.

Eastern and Western Timbres

When Ang Lee first approached Tan Dun about writing the score to this film, the composer recalls, "We started to talk about the high and low cultures, east and west, world instruments and the western symphony orchestras, all those types of things we wanted to use in the score."[1] In the end, it was agreed that the music would draw on both European and Chinese

[1] "Tan Dun, His music, *Crouching Tiger, Hidden Dragon* and collaboration with Ang Lee. A conversation between Tan Dun and writer Rudy Koppl about the nature of scoring." Excerpted from *Music from the Movies* magazine, issue #31/32, Winter 2001.

PERFORMANCE   Matching Images with Sound

In the era of silent films—before 1927—the only way to provide a musical soundtrack was to have live musicians perform at every showing of a film. The organ was the favorite instrument for providing such music, in part because it is so versatile and can produce so many different timbres; some older theaters today have preserved or reconstructed their organs from days of silent film.

In 1927, Warner Brothers released *The Jazz Singer*, the first feature film with synchronized sound. Not coincidentally, the main character in the film—played by Al Jolson—is a singer who has the opportunity to sing several songs. From that point onward, synchronized sound became the standard in Hollywood. The technology has grown increasingly sophisticated over the years, but the basic process has remained unchanged:

The noted film composer Hans Zimmer scoring a sequence for *Spirit: Stallion of the Cimarron* in 2002.
© DreamWorks/Everett Collection

1. The composer develops ideas based on the general outline of the story and genre: a science-fiction film will have a different kind of sound from a Western, which in turn will be different from a romantic comedy, and so on. Using these basic ideas, the composer refines them and develops them into a score based on the edited film, giving close attention to exactly how much time is needed for any given action in any given scene. For example, a composer will know in advance that a scene requires "10.4 seconds of music to accompany a chase," followed by "3.5 seconds of music to accompany a close-up of a character out of breath."

2. The orchestra rehearses the score.

3. The orchestra records the score. The conductor and the performers all have visual access to some projection of the scene they are recording in order to ensure precision of timing. Performers often wear earpieces that provide "click tracks," low clicking noises that help players make shifts from one tempo to another with maximum precision. Audio engineers play a vital role in determining the placement of microphones, the balance of the instruments, and the overall shape of the final sound.

4. The music editor superimposes the recorded soundtrack onto the film.

5. The editor makes final adjustments based on the final cut of the film.

instruments. The Chinese-American cellist Yo-Yo Ma (b. 1955) proved to be the bridge between these worlds of sound. In "Farewell," the solo cello is matched with the erhu, a traditional Chinese instrument with two strings (made of silk) and a small, octagonal sound box covered with snakeskin. For two instruments that produce sound in such a similar fashion—a bow drawn across strings—the timbres are strikingly different. The cello plays in a lower register and owes its deep sound to the resonance of wood in a large instrument, while the erhu plays in a higher register, produces a smaller sound (because the resonating surface of the instrument is so small), and creates a tone remarkably like the human voice. Further layers of sound can be heard in the string orchestra (a Western ensemble) and the more Eastern-sounding group of hand drums.

Fluid Melody

Stringed instruments like the cello and the erhu can produce sounds that are far more flexible and fluid than those of instruments that can play only fixed pitches, like the piano. On a piano, one key can produce only one note. The cello and erhu, played by fingers moving along strings, can "bend" their notes, sliding up or down in fluid fashion, like a voice. Indeed, both instruments in this selection, particularly the erhu, have a strongly vocal quality. Tan Dun himself has acknowledged that the style of playing he calls for from these instruments was influenced by styles of singing in Chinese opera, in which singers frequently slide into and out of pitches (see web bonus chapter 3). This style of playing helps give the music a distinctively non-Western sound, even when played on a Western instrument like the cello. Yet the melody itself is not pentatonic (that is, based on five notes), which is the kind of melody often associated with music of the Far East. It begins as a pentatonic melody, but the dramatic leap upward introduces a sixth note that gives the line a more Western sound.

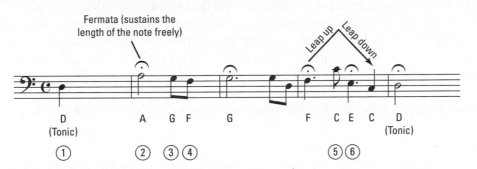

The repeated return to the tonic note demarcates the end of each statement of the brief melody. This might seem like a recipe for a choppy, fragmented work, but the composer skillfully uses the erhu to bridge the gaps between each of the cello's statements of the theme. Thus the melody is both clearly demarcated (by the repeated return to the tonic, in the cello) and constantly in motion (thanks to the erhu).

b. 1957
Tan Dun
"Farewell" from *Crouching Tiger, Hidden Dragon*
Composed: 2000
GENRE
Film music

KEY CONCEPTS
Western and Eastern instruments juxtaposed, quasi-pentatonic melodies.

CHAPTER HIGHLIGHT
Global Music
Tan Dun's score synthesizes elements of traditional Chinese music with the idioms of European-American music. The texture created by the two solo instruments, one Western and low in register (a cello) and one Eastern and high in register (the erhu), resonates with the plot of the film for which the soundtrack was written.

Xiaohui Ma plays the erhu. A graduate of the Shanghai Conservatory of Music, Xiaohui Ma has concertized throughout the world and recorded more than 40 albums, including the soundtrack for *Crouching Tiger, Hidden Dragon* with the cellist Yo-Yo Ma.

Courtesy of Chia-Chi Charlie Chang and Burnett Thompson Music

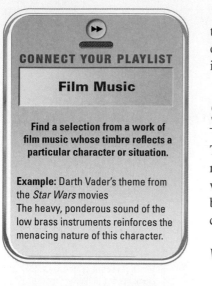

At the very end of this selection—the last statement of the melody—the cello lands on the tonic but does not stop there. Instead, it wavers between two notes, the tonic and the note immediately below it. The music does not resolve to the tonic. Instead, it simply fades away, suggesting that the love of the two couples never ceases.

Symbolic Texture

The registers of the two principal instruments here, the cello and the erhu, correspond roughly to the registers of the voices of a man and a woman. The way the two lines differ yet wrap themselves around each other wistfully can be heard as representing the relationship between both pairs of lovers at the end of the movie. This "Farewell," after all, is a purely musical commentary on the loves of two couples, both of which have ended in sorrow.

With these points in mind, listen to this selection again, using the Listening Guide.

EXPAND YOUR PLAYLIST

Film Music

Film music was an entirely new genre in the twentieth century, and many composers were drawn to Hollywood.

Max Steiner
* *Gone with the Wind*. Steiner (1888–1971) wrote operettas in his native Austria before immigrating to the United States in 1914. His soundtrack for *Gone with the Wind* (1939) captured the sound of the antebellum American South.

Erich Wolfgang Korngold
* *The Adventures of Robin Hood*. Korngold (1897–1957) was a successful composer of operas before moving to the United States in 1934. He won an opera Academy Award for this 1938 score.

Bernard Hermann
* *Psycho, North by Northwest, Taxi Driver*. Hermann (1911–1975), a native New Yorker, collaborated with Alfred Hitchcock on some of the director's greatest movies. He also supervised the eerie avian sound effects in Hitchcock's *The Birds*.

John Williams
* *E.T., Star Wars, Jurassic Park*, and the first two *Harry Potter* films. The most successful and prolific of all film music composers, John Williams has an uncanny ability to alter his style to capture the mood of many different kinds of films.

Jerry Goldsmith
* *Planet of the Apes, The Omen, Patton, Hoosiers*. Goldsmith (1929–2004) was born in Los Angeles and became one of the most productive film composers of his generation.

Howard Shore
* *Lord of the Rings*. This Canadian composer (b. 1946) won Academy Awards in 2002 and 2004 for his music to different installments of *Lord of the Rings*.

((•• HEAR SAMPLES on **www.mymusiclab.com**

Listening Guide

GO TO www.mymusiclab.com
for the Automated Listening Guide
CD V • Track 18/Download Track 91

Tan Dun Composed: 2000 "Farewell" from *Crouching Tiger, Hidden Dragon* (2:25)

Time	Timbre	Melody	Texture
0:00	Cello, orchestra, drums; erhu joins in at 0:12 and continues throughout; the instruments all gradually grow louder until the very end, when they fade out.	1. Cello lands on tonic at 0:16. The erhu bridges the gap to the next statement of the theme, here and at the end of all subsequent statements of the theme.	Polyphonic throughout, first between the cello and the orchestra, then additionally with the erhu.
0:18		2. Cello lands on tonic at 0:30.	
0:34		3. Cello lands on tonic at 0:46.	
0:50		4. Cello lands on tonic at 1:02.	
1:05		5. Cello lands on tonic at 1:18.	
1:21		6. Cello lands on tonic at 1:34.	
1:38		7. Cello lands on tonic at 1:50.	
1:53		8. Cello lands on tonic at 2:07 but then wavers back and forth between tonic and the note below it, fading into unresolved silence.	

Student? ?FAQs

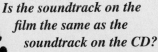

Is the soundtrack on the film the same as the soundtrack on the CD?

Not in the case of *Crouching Tiger, Hidden Dragon*, and usually not with other films, either. Almost invariably, the two are different. Take any movie you know very well and watch it sometime, paying attention only to the music. You'll probably be amazed at how often music is present, and you may discover that the CD of the soundtrack is actually quite selective.

Cellist Yo Yo Ma, one of the musicians on this recording.
© Reuters/Gary Hershorn/ CORBIS. All Rights Reserved.

How does a composer get commissioned to write a soundtrack?

Getting a commission to compose a soundtrack is like getting any other kind of commission. People go on the basis of what you've already written. So a well-known film composer like John Williams can pick and choose his commissions, while an aspiring young composer will feel fortunate to get a request from a low-budget film. But even John Williams had to start out by writing music for a late-1950s television series called *Playhouse 90*.

Tan Dun conducting.
Chris Christodoulou/Lebrecht Music & Arts Photo Library

PROFILE   Tan Dun (b. 1957)

Composer in Two Worlds

Born in Hunan Province, in southern China, Tan Dun was forced to work on a commune during the Great Cultural Revolution of the 1970s, planting and harvesting rice. It was during this time that he began to collect folksongs and other music of the Chinese countryside and, though he was only a teenager, to organize his coworkers into musical ensembles. When Beijing's Central Conservatory of Music reopened in the late 1970s, Tan Dun began his formal studies in composition. But a second wave of cultural repression banned performances of his music, and he eventually immigrated to the United States, where he continued his studies, receiving a doctor of musical arts degree from Columbia University in 1993.

As a composer, Tan Dun has always drawn inspiration from the music of his Chinese ancestry, combining it with the traditions of Western classical music. He was 20 years old before he heard a note of Bach, and he was overwhelmed. "You are standing on the ruins," he recently recalled of growing up during the Great Cultural Revolution. "Everything's been destroyed. Family's been destroyed, culture [has] been destroyed. And nobody [was] allowed to touch anything Western or ancient. And suddenly you heard Bach. It's like a medicine curing everything you were suffering."

"An artist's creation more or less always comes from his life experiences, his imagination comes out this way. My imagination always comes out from my experiences in life. I've been living in the United States for fifteen years, but I was living in China for more than twenty years. All

Director Ang Lee (left), cellist Yo-Yo Ma (center), and composer Tan Dun (right) during the recording of the soundtrack to *Crouching Tiger, Hidden Dragon.*

Sam Mircovitch/Reuters Limited

those experiences crossing together is what comes out of my music. So of course yes, in all my early experiences I was trained in Chinese theatre and music, this has somehow become very interesting because it comes out of my music today."

Source: Adapted from "Tan Dun's Cultural Evolution," *National Public Radio Morning Edition,* June 15, 2006.

 EXPLORE MORE on www.mymusiclab.com

EXPAND YOUR PLAYLIST: TAN DUN

- *The First Emperor.* An opera, premiered by the Metropolitan Opera of New York City in December 2006; the tenor Plácido Domingo sang the title role.

- *The Banquet.* Another film score, this one for a re-interpretation of Shakespeare's *Hamlet.*

- *The Map.* A work for cello, orchestra, and video recording, based on the composer's return to China to record folk music of his native land.

- *Symphony 1997.* A large-scale work for orchestra, cello soloist, bells, and children's choir, commissioned to celebrate the transfer of Hong Kong from British to Chinese sovereignty.

- *Hero.* A film score for the 2002 film starring Jet Li and directed by Yimou Zhang.

((•● HEAR SAMPLES on www.mymusiclab.com

TEST YOURSELF on www.mymusiclab.com   Flashcards and chapter tests

PART 6 Summary

	Nineteenth Century	Twentieth Century
Texture	Full spectrum between homophonic and polyphonic	Same
Melody	Longer, more complex melodies, often with wider range, often quite technically demanding	Both tonal and atonal, with or without metrical structure
Rhythm	Wider range of extremes, from balanced to irregular; use of folk rhythms occasionally	Full range of possibilities, from regular to irregular, predictable to unpredictable
Timbre	Emergence of the modern orchestra with large brass and percussion sections	Even greater possibilities of sound from new techniques for playing old instruments, increased use of percussion instruments, and audio technology
Harmony	Increasingly chromatic, undermining a sense of a tonal center	Tonal and atonal, both with and without a sense of a harmonic center
Form	Earlier forms, plus new emphasis on cyclic form (in instrumental music) and larger basic units of construction (in opera)	All earlier forms continue; emergence of aleatory music based on chance
Word-music relationships	Greater use of program music; intense cultivation of the song as a genre	Continued use of program music; new techniques of singing (*Sprechstimme*)

IN REVIEW: The Twentieth Century

Genres

Ballet A staged work that presents a drama through dance.
• Stravinsky, *The Rite of Spring* (Chapter 44)
• Copland, *Rodeo* (Chapter 52)

Song A relatively short work for a singer and accompanying instruments.
• Still, "A Black Pierrot" from *Songs of Separation* (Chapter 51)
• Johnson, "Terraplane Blues" (Chapter 46)
• Jackson, "It Don't Cost Very Much" (Web Bonus Chapter 5)

Aleatory music A work whose structure is determined to some degree by chance.
• Cage, *Indeterminacy* (Chapter 55)

Minimalist music Music based on the frequent repetition (with slight variations) of a small musical idea.
• Glass, *Einstein on the Beach* (Chapter 56)

Musical A spoken play with ample sung numbers (arias, ensembles, choruses).
• Bernstein, *West Side Story* (Chapter 54)

Film music Music written expressly for a film.
• Tan Dun, "Farewell" (Chapter 62)

Jazz Popular music style that weds African American rhythms with European influences.
• Ellington, "Cotton Tail" (Chapter 47)
• Parker, "Ornithology" (Chapter 48)

Rock and Roll Dominant popular music of the second half of the twentieth century.
• Berry, "School Day" (Chapter 57)
• Marvelettes, "Please, Mr. Postman" (Chapter 58)
• Beach Boys, "Good Vibrations" (Chapter 59)
• Sex Pistols, "God Save the Queen" (Web Bonus Chapter 6)

Rap African American popular music style, combining rhymed recitations with complex recorded accompaniments.
• Public Enemy, "Fight the Power" (Chapter 60)

Stylistic Developments

Impressionism Music that emphasizes timbre (color) at the expense of line (melody).
• Debussy, *Voiles* (Chapter 40)

Atonality A style of writing without a tonal center.
• Ives, *The Unanswered Question* (Chapter 42)
• Schoenberg, "Columbine" from *Pierrot lunaire* (Chapter 43)

Polytonality The simultaneous sounding of two different harmonies.
• Stravinsky, *The Rite of Spring* (Chapter 44)
• Crawford, *Piano Study in Mixed Accents* (Chapter 49)

Neo-classicism A style of writing that embraces the harmonic, rhythmic, and formal styles of the past (specifically, those of the eighteenth century), with limited modernist inflections.
• Tailleferre, Concertino for Harp and Orchestra, finale (Chapter 50)

Postmodernism A style of writing that integrates modernism with more traditional idioms.
• León, *A la Par* (Chapter 61)

Syncopation A rhythmic style that emphasizes the off-beat.
• Joplin, *Maple Leaf Rag* (Chapter 45)

⌖ **TEST YOURSELF** on **www.mymusiclab.com**   Part Exam

PART 7 Music Today

Who knows the music of today better than the students of today? You will be the author of this book's final section and create your own Listening Guide for a work of music of your choice. This exercise will allow you to apply the listening skills, terminology, and musical knowledge you have acquired over the course of the past semester to a specific work of music, one that *you* enjoy. And when you have finished this project, you may well have broadened the musical horizons of your instructor.

Step 1: Choose Your Work

Choose a work of music you like or you'd like to know more about (or better still, both). Your instructor may have specific guidelines about such things as when your work of music was written or how long it lasts. He or she will probably also have specific instructions about the format in which to turn in your recording (burned CD, mp3, etc.). Follow your instructor's guidelines as you complete this section.

Step 2: Listen

You will have almost certainly listened to your chosen work before, but this time, listen to the elements: melody, rhythm, harmony, texture, timbre, dynamics, form, and word–music relationships. It will help to focus on only one or two elements at a time. Listen once, for example, for changes in timbre, listen another time for changes in rhythm, and so on.

Step 3: Identify the Central Elements

Decide which three or four elements are central to this work. If an element does not change at any point—for example, if your work is loud from beginning to end—this will not be a particularly meaningful basis on which to break down the music. If on the other hand the dynamics keep moving between loud and soft, that may well be a useful parameter to explain how the work is constructed. Make special note of the timing of important changes in the music. When the words begin a new section, does the music change as well? Do you hear a modulation at some point? Does the timbre shift at some point? Does the texture change markedly anywhere?

Step 4: Construct a Grid

Following the pattern of the Listening Guides in this book, construct a grid with the timings of key points in the work in the far left column and the three or four central elements you have identified to the right. If there is a text that is sung, reproduce the text within the grid in a way that reflects its musical setting. Gradually fill in the grid. Apply the terminology and concepts used in the Listening Guides throughout this book.

⊙→ EXPLORE MORE on www.mymusiclab.com
Create your own Listening Guide using the sample grid on MyMusicLab.

Step 5: Review Your Work

Have you identified the key elements in your work? Have you charted their progression through the work thoroughly and accurately? Listen again, following your own grid, and imagine that you have never heard the work before. Does your grid show its essential features? Are the timings accurate? Have you followed your professor's instructions? Remember to proofread your work. You might also ask a friend to follow your Listening Guide as a further way to proof your work.

If you have carried out this assignment carefully, you will almost certainly gain added appreciation of how music works. What might seem like a "simple" song is often far more intricate than it appears on the surface. Most important of all, you will have learned valuable skills that will help you listen to any kind of music, from any time or place, with greater understanding.

Happy listening!

Glossary

A cappella   Sung without instrumental accompaniment of any kind.

Accompanied recitative   Recitative accompanied by the orchestra, as opposed to by basso continuo alone.

Acoustics   The science of sound: how it is produced, transmitted, and received.

Additive form   A compositional technique in which nothing disappears, but new layers are constantly added.

Aleatory music   Music composed using elements of chance.

Amplitude   The size of a sound wave; determines volume.

Anacrusis   A starting note that falls on a beat before the downbeat. Also called a pickup beat or an upbeat.

Anapestic   A poetic meter of short-short-LONG.

Antecedent phrase   In periodic phrase structure, an opening phrase, which sets up the consequent phrase to follow.

Anthem   An English sacred choral work.

Aria   Italian for "air" or "melody"; any lyrical movement or piece for solo voice, usually with some kind of instrumental accompaniment.

Art song   A song set to serious poetry, usually for solo voice and piano, in the tradition of the German Lied.

Atonal   A style of writing that establishes no harmonic or melodic center of gravity; without a tonic, all notes are of equal weight and significance.

Ballad   A poem or song that tells a story.

Bar form   A melodic form in which the opening phrase is sung twice and a contrasting phrase follows (**AAB**). Also called song form.

Basso continuo   "Continuous bass"; a small ensemble, widely used in music of the Baroque, that plays throughout a work and provides an underlying bass line and harmonies. It consists of two instruments: one that can sustain long notes (such as a bass viol, a cello, or a bassoon), and one that can play chords (such as a lute or a harpsichord).

Bebop   New jazz style of the late 1940s/early 1950s that developed in response to the popularity of big band music. Bebop is characterized by fast tempos, short bursts of melodic phrases, heavy and unexpected rhythmic accents, and virtuosic soloing.

Big band music   A style of jazz popular in the 1930s and 1940s in which instruments were grouped into sections by function, with carefully constructed arrangements. Many of these arrangements featured call-and-response between the sections, often based on repeated, short melodic riffs.

Binary form   A musical structure consisting of two repeated halves (**AABB**).

Binary song form   A form common in popular song in the early twentieth century. The basic pattern (**AABB**) is 32 bars long, with each of the four sections occupying 8 bars of music.

Blue note   A pitch performed flatter (lower) than the standard major scale would indicate; usually blue notes occur as substitutes for the third and seventh (and occasionally the fifth) notes of the standard major scale.

Blues   A musical genre derived from African American performance traditions that uses blue notes (flattened pitches) in its melodies and tells first-person stories of hard knocks and love gone wrong.

Cadence   A point of arrival signaling the end of a musical unit.

Cadenza   In a concerto, an elaborate improvisation by the soloist on themes heard earlier in the movement, with no accompaniment from the orchestra. It occurs near the end of the recapitulation.

Call-and-response   A technique in which one musician or group sings or plays an opening motive, and another musician or group sings or plays an answer.

Cantata   A type of vocal genre typically sung during a service of worship. In Italian: "that which is sung," as opposed to *sonata,* "that which is played."

Chamber music   Instrumental music for a small ensemble, with only one player to each part.

Character piece   A relatively short work, usually for piano solo, that captures a particular mood ("character").

Choral music   Vocal music with more than one singer to a part.

Chorale   A hymn tune.

Chord   Three or more notes played or sung at the same moment.

Chorus   An ensemble with multiple singers to a part; "chorus" is also the name for the musical number or movement sung by this ensemble. In Baroque opera, the chorus comments on the action and emotions unfolding onstage.

Chromatic   A type of harmony or melody that incorporates many more notes than occur naturally in the scale or key area on which a work is based. A chromatic scale is produced by playing all half steps. On the piano, this would mean all adjacent keys—black or white.

Coda   Italian for "tail." A section at the end of a musical work or movement that stands outside any formal structure and brings the whole to a close.

Comic opera   In Italian, *opera buffa.* A genre that uses many of the same conventions as serious opera—arias, recitatives, ensembles, choruses—but with plots revolving around believable, everyday characters rather than mythical or historical figures.

Concerto   An instrumental genre for a soloist (or sometimes more than one soloist) and a larger ensemble.

Concerto grosso   Italian for "big concerto"; a concerto with multiple soloists.

Conjunct motion   Melodic motion of pitches by step.

Consequent phrase   In periodic phrase structure, a closing phrase that follows an antecedent phrase and creates a sense of musical completion.

Consonance   The sound of notes together that our ear finds naturally right. Like dissonance, consonance is a relative concept that can change over long periods of time.

Contrafactum   A work setting new words to an established melody.

Cornetto   A wind instrument of the Middle Ages and Reinassance, a forerunner of the trumpet.

Counterpoint   A style of writing in which every voice is a melody and all voices work together; from the Latin word *contrapunctum,* or "note-against-note." Counterpoint is basic to polyphonic texture.

Courtly love   A code of behavior in medieval courts in which the knight worshipped a lady from afar.

Cyclic form   A form in which individual movements are linked in some tangible and distinctive way, usually through the use of a common musical idea.

Da capo   Italian for "from the head"; a direction to go back and play from the very beginning of the piece.

Da capo aria   An aria that opens with two contrasting sections, **A** and **B**; at the end of the **B** section, the singer and orchestra return to the beginning of the **A** section, following the direction in the score of "da capo"—literally, "from the head." When the singer performs this **A** section a second time, he or she embellishes it heavily.

Development   The section within a sonata-form movement that thematically and harmonically manipulates ("develops") the movement's themes most intensively.

Diatonic scale   A scale consisting of whole and half steps.

Disjunct motion   Melodic motion of pitches by leap.

Dissonance   The sound of notes that clash, either harmonically or melodically, and do not seem to belong together. Dissonance is a relative concept: what was dissonant in one era is later perceived as consonant.

Dotted rhythm   Consistent alternation between long and short notes.

Double   To play or sing the same musical line in multiple voices or on multiple instruments; most often used to describe an instrument playing the same line being sung by a voice.

Double-exposition concerto form   A structure based on sonata form but with two expositions, one for the orchestra alone and one for the soloist and orchestra together. It also includes, near the end of the recapitulation, a cadenza for the soloist.

Drone bass   A single long note held underneath the melodic line.

Drone harmony   A texture in which a melodic instrument plays over a constant repeated pattern of only a few tones.

Duple meter   An underlying pattern of rhythm in which each unit (measure) consists of one accented (strong) beat followed by one unaccented (weak) beat (**1**-2 | (**1**-2 | (**1**-2 | etc.) or some multiple of two (such as four or eight). A unit of four beats per measure, for example, in which the first is the strongest and the third is the next-strongest (**1**-2-**3**-4, **1**-2-**3**-4, **1**-2-**3**-4, etc.), is a type of duple meter.

Dynamics   The volume of sound, determined by the size (amplitude) of each sound wave.

Electronic music   Music using sounds generated (and not merely amplified) either in whole or in part by electronic means.

Elide   To begin a new line of text and music before the previous one has come to a complete stop.

Episode   In a fugue, a passage in which the subject is not present.

Exposition   The section within a sonata-form movement that introduces ("exposes") all of the movement's themes.

Expressionism   A broad artistic movement that flourished in music, painting, and literature in the early decades of the twentieth century, in which psychological truth took precedence over beauty, and inner emotion took precedence over any sense of external reality.

Extramusical   Referring to an idea outside the sound. This term is used by ethnomusicologists to describe the equivalent of program music, in Western music.

Fill   In jazz and popular styles, a short, instrumental response between a singer's phrases, or a brief solo occupying a musical gap between sections of a piece.

Finale   A last movement of a multimovement work.

Form   The structure of a musical work; the way in which its individual units are put together.

French overture   An overture common in French Baroque opera, usually consisting of a slow introduction with dotted rhythms, followed by a fast section frequently employing imitation.

Frequency   The number of sound-wavelengths in one second.

Fugal exposition   The opening section of a fugue, in which all the voices enter with the main subject.

Fugue   A polyphonic work based on a central theme and employing imitation.

Full cadence   A musical point of arrival that creates a strong sense of closure.

Gamelan   An Indonesian musical ensemble consisting primarily of a variety of pitched gongs and xylophones. The conductor or leader of the ensemble often plays a double-headed drum.

Genre   The category of a work, determined by a combination of its performance medium and its social function.

Glissando   A continuous ("gliding") melodic motion up or down that goes by so fast we almost cannot hear the individual notes.

Gospel music   Religious-themed music that borrows from R&B, blues, and other popular styles in its vocal and instrumental styles.

Gregorian chant   Monophonic vocal music in the medieval church, designed to project religious texts. So called because it was alleged to have been written mostly by Pope Gregory I, in the late sixth century.

Groove   In popular and jazz styles, the underlying rhythmic pattern of a song.

Ground   See ground bass.

Ground bass   Another name for an ostinato in the bass part.

Half cadence   A point of musical arrival that is not yet closure. If thought of as punctuation, a half cadence is like a comma, whereas a full cadence is like a period.

Half step   The smallest distance between two adjacent notes on a piano (white or black), such as C-C#.

Harmonics   Further subdivisions of the primary vibration producing a sound, resulting in additional faintly heard pitches.

Harmony   The sound created by multiple voices playing or singing together.

Head   In jazz, the main melody of the song.

Hemiola   A type of syncopation in which patterns of twos occur at the same time as patterns of threes.

Heterophonic texture (heterophony)   The simultaneous playing or singing of two or more versions of a melody.

Hip hop   A cultural movement of the late 1970s through the turn of the century that included fashion, dance (break dancing), art (graffiti), and music (rap). Hip hop music is characterized by semi-spoken lyrics that are recited against an accompaniment often consisting of short, repeated melodic fragments set against a heavily rhythmic beat.

Hocket   A form of polyphony consisting of two or more rhythmically interlocking voices.

Homophonic texture (homophony)   A musical texture in which a melody is performed with a supporting accompaniment.

Homorhythm   All instruments playing in the same rhythm.

Honky tonk music   A country style of the late 1940s/early 1950s that originally developed in the small bars (known as honky tonks) that catered to rural and working-class audiences. Honky tonk is characterized by a small ensemble, usually featuring a vocalist-guitarist, fiddler, steel guitarist, bass player, and sometimes drums. Themes of lost love and the effects of heavy drinking predominate.

Hook   A short, catchy motive that forms the memorable core of the song.

Humanism   An early-Renaissance intellectual and cultural movement that explored human interests and values through the pursuit of science, philosophy, literature, painting, sculpture, and music, particularly vocal music.

Iambic   A poetic meter of short-LONG, short-LONG, short-LONG, short-LONG.

Imitation   A shortened form of the term "imitative counterpoint": the same theme introduced by different instruments or voices in succession.

Imitative counterpoint   A particular type of counterpoint in which one voice introduces a new theme and is answered ("imitated") by other voices that enter in succession shortly afterward, even as the first voice continues to sing or play.

Impressionism   An artistic movement focused more on sensations, perceptions, and light than on the direct representation of objects. In music, the term was used by critics of the early twentieth century to describe harmonies, melodies, and forms they considered indistinct.

Interlock   A technique in which one voice fills the spaces left by another's rests to complete a melodic unit.

Interval   The distance between two pitches.

Intonation   In Bahamian rhyme singing, as well as in other African-influenced musical cultures: a melody line consisting of words spoken in tones.

jingju   In Chinese, "capital theater." The principal form of opera in China today. Characters are stock types distinguished by singing style, costume, makeup, and role. On stage, there is no scenery, and the action usually takes place in front of a curtain.

Key   The central note and mode on which a melody or piece is based.

Leitmotif   A brief musical phrase or idea connected dramatically to some person, event, or idea in the drama.

Lied (plural *Lieder*)   German for "song." A genre for voice and piano, popular from the late eighteenth century onward, particularly in Germany but in many other countries as well.

Madrigal   A musical setting of a text in a single strophe (stanza).

Major mode   A type of scale produced by singing "do-re-mi-fa-so-la-ti-do," or by playing the white keys of the piano between C and C, in which half steps occur between notes 3 and 4 and notes 7 and 8. The sound of the major mode is often described as "bright" or "happy," in contrast to the minor mode.

Manual   The keyboard of an organ or harpsichord. These instruments often have more than one manual.

Mazurka   A polish folk dance in triple meter, often with a heavy accent on the second or third beat of each measure.

Measure   A rhythmic unit, indicated by bar lines in notated music, that presents one complete statement of the meter.

Melisma   A syllable of text sung to many notes.

Melismatic   A style of setting a text to music so that there is more than one note per syllable.

Melodic motion   The movement of pitches within a melody up or down, either by step (conjunct motion) or by leap (disjunct motion).

Melody   A single line of notes heard in succession as a coherent unit.

Metabole   A change of pitch level.

Meter (of music)   An underlying pattern of beats that maintains itself consistently throughout a work. See also "duple meter"; "triple meter."

Meter (of poetry)   A poem's basic rhythmic unit.

Middle entries   In a fugue, later entries of the subject, after the exposition.

Minimalism   In music, a style in which a brief musical idea or group of ideas is repeated and varied incrementally over a long span of time, with a relatively slow rate of change.

Minor mode   A type of scale produced by playing the white keys on the piano between A and A, in which half steps occur between notes 2 and 3 and notes 5 and 6, but often with the seventh note raised so that a half step also occurs between notes 7 and 8. The sound of the minor mode is often described as "dark" or "sad," in contrast to the major mode.

Minuet form   A ternary form (**ABA**) in which the opening section, known as the minuet proper (**A**), is followed by a contrasting trio (**B**), which is followed by a repeat of the minuet proper. The minuet is always in triple meter and its individual units—the minuet proper and the trio—are each in binary form.

Modernism   A spirit that took hold in all the arts, in the early twentieth century, representing a quest for novelty that far exceeded any such drive in the past.

Modified strophic form   A form in which each strophe is modified musically to fit the text in a particular way.

Modulate   To move to a different key area. (Noun: "modulation.")

Monophonic texture (monophony)   A musical texture consisting of a single melodic line.

Motet   In the Renaissance, a sacred choral work for the Roman Catholic Church.

Musical   A spoken drama with a substantial amount of singing.

Musical appropriation   The use or adaptation of a work to serve something other than its original purpose.

Musique concrète   French for "concrete music." Music using sounds generated by everyday, real ("concrete") objects not normally thought of as musical instruments and then manipulated electronically.

Nationalism   In music, the use of melodies, rhythms, harmonies, or instruments that reflect the musical practices of a particular nation.

Neoclassicism   A style of composition in the years after World War I that, although distinctly modern, drew on older (particularly eighteenth-century) uses of melody, harmony, rhythm, and form.

Nocturne   "Night piece." Originally a vocal serenade from lover to beloved. Later, an instrumental work that imitates, though its homophonic texture, such a song.

Octave   The interval between two pitches of the same name (C to C, G to G, etc.). The frequency of the higher pitch is twice that of the lower pitch.

Opera   A drama sung from beginning to end.

Opera buffa   Italian for "comic opera"; a genre that uses many of the same conventions as serious opera—arias, recitatives, ensembles, choruses—but with plots revolving around believable, everyday characters rather than mythical or historical figures.

Opera seria   Italian for "serious opera"; Italian Baroque opera on a serious subject, typically consisting of alternating recitatives and da capo arias.

Operetta   Italian for "small opera." A nineteenth-century stage work that incorporated both singing and spoken dialogue, typically on a comic, lighthearted, or sentimental subject. A precursor to the American musical.

Oral tradition   One passed down without the aid of written words or notated music.

Oratorio   A work musically similar to an opera but not staged, and usually on a sacred topic.

Orchestration   The manner in which various instruments are assigned to the musical lines.

Ostinato   A short pattern of notes repeated over and over.

Overture   A purely instrumental opening movement that introduces a longer work, often for voices (as an opera).

Pentatonic scale   A scale consisting of five tones.

Percussion instrument   An instrument that produces sound when it is struck.

Periodic phrase structure   A musical structure in which antecedent and consequent phrase units make up a larger whole.

Phrase   A brief musical statement.

Piano trio   A work written for an ensemble of piano, violin, and cello. The term is also used for the ensemble itself.

Pitch   The position of a sound on a range from very low to very high, determined by the frequency of its sound waves.

Plainchant   Monophonic vocal music in the medieval church designed to project religious texts.

Polyphonic texture (polyphony)   A musical texture consisting of multiple lines of equal importance.

Polytonal   See polytonality.

Polytonality   The juxtaposition of two conventional harmonies in a way that creates a new dissonance.

Postmodernism   A style in music and the other arts, beginning in the mid-twentieth century, in which modern and traditional elements are combined.

Powwow   An intertribal gathering where Native Americans of mixed tribes express their mutual bond and identity.

Program music   An instrumental work that is in some way associated with a story, event, or idea.

Psychedelia   Music influenced by the hippie movement of the late 1960s/early 1970s, with its emphasis on mind-expanding drugs, brightly colored fashions, and spiritual and social freedom.

Punk   Popular music of the mid-1970s that originally arose in reaction to the increasingly commercial and corporate rock of the era. Punk emphasized a do-it-yourself (DIY) attitude. Musical or vocal skills were downplayed; lyrics expressed anger at the failings of the economic and social systems. Fashions included torn T-shirts, body piercings, brightly dyed hair, and other "anti-fashion" looks.

Raga   In the music of India, a mood, color, or musical scale that forms the basis of a musical composition.

Ragtime   A style of music from the early twentieth century that emphasizes rhythmic syncopation while continuing many of the characteristics of marches, cakewalks, two-steps, and popular songs from the late nineteenth century.

Recapitulation   The third and final section within a sonata-form movement, in which all the themes presented in the exposition return, all in the tonic key.

Recitative   A style of singing that lies somewhere between lyrical song and speech; also, the operatic number that is sung in this style.

Recorder   A wind instrument widely used until ca. 1750, similar to a flute but blown into from one end rather than from the side.

Refrain   The same words with the same basic melody recurring at regular intervals over the course of a work.

Register   The range of a pitch or series of pitches, usually described as high, middle, or low.

Responsorial chant   A type of plainchant in which a soloist's passage is followed by a response from the chorus.

Rhyme   In a Bahamian rhyme singing group, the lead singer.

Rhythm   The ordering of music through time.

Ritornello   Italian for "little return"; name for the statement and return of the full ensemble, in a work alternating between the orchestra and soloist or soloists.

Ritornello principle   The formal design of alternating ritornello and solo sections.

Rock 'n' roll   A style of music that evolved in the mid-1950s out of R&B and country styles. Rock 'n' roll is teenage music, expressing the concerns of mid-century young people (romance, cars, dancing). The typical rock group consisted of electric guitar, bass, and drums, with the occasional addition of piano or saxophone.

Rondo form   A form in which an opening theme (**A**) returns repeatedly over the course of the movement, interspersed with contrasting ideas (**B**, **C**, etc.). An example of the resulting pattern would be **ABACA**.

Rounded binary form   A binary form in which the opening idea returns in the tonic key about halfway through the second section, "rounding out" the form.

Rubato   See tempo rubato.

Sackbut   A wind instrument of the Renaissance, a forerunner of the modern trombone.

Sample   To record music or sound from an existing album.

Scale   A series of notes that provide the essential pitch building blocks of a melody.

Scenario   The story line of a ballet.

Scherzo   In Italian, "joke." A musical scherzo is a lighthearted movement in a fast tempo and in triple meter, similar in form to the minuet.

Section   In a musical ensemble, a group of instruments or voices with similar timbres or roles.

Sectional form   A form in which each verse or half verse receives its own material (for example, **ABCD**).

Sequence   A short musical motive that repeats at successively higher or lower pitches.

Serialism   A style of writing in which notes are drawn not from a scale, but from a predetermined series of notes. Serial composition flourished between ca. 1920 and 1980. See also "twelve-tone composition."

Shuffle groove (or, shuffle rhythm)   A mid-tempo rhythmic pattern, typically in quadruple meter, in which each beat is subdivided into three pulses.

Sitar   A plucked stringed instrument widely used on the Indian subcontinent.

Sonata   A type of instrumental genre; literally, a work that is played, as opposed to sung ("cantata").

Sonata da camera   In the Baroque period, a "chamber" sonata, to be performed for entertainment in the home.

Sonata da chiesa   In the Baroque period, a "church" sonata, to be performed during sacred services to provide devotional music.

Sonata form   A musical structure consisting of an exposition, development, and recapitulation, allowing for the presentation, development, and resolution of multiple themes within a single movement. Sonata form was widely used throughout the Classical Era and the nineteenth century.

Sound wave   The vibration through air that produces sound.

Sprechstimme   In German, "speech-voice." A style of singing halfway between speech and lyrical song, in which the singer hits precise pitches and then allows them to tail off, rather than sustaining them, as in lyrical singing.

Standard song form   A common form for the choruses of "standards" or popular hits of the 1920s, 1930s, and 1940s. It consists of 32 measures divided into four phrases in the pattern **AABA**.

Stanza   A verse of poetry, or the music corresponding to that verse (see also "strophe").

Stop time   A kind of musical punctuation between sections, in which the instruments that provide the basic accompaniment strike a single note on a downbeat of a measure together, then remain silent for the rest of the measure.

String instrument   An instrument that produces sound when a taut string is plucked or stroked with a bow.

Strophe   A verse of poetry, or the music corresponding to that verse (see also "stanza").

Subject   The central theme of a fugue.

Suite   A series of individual dance movements, typically in a variety of types such as minuets, gavottes, and gigues, and a variety of characters such as fast vs. slow, lively vs. stately, duple vs. triple.

Surrogate speech   The use of musical tones as a replacement for words.

Swing   A rhythmic pattern of long and short notes approximating a two-to-one ratio, but varying from piece to piece and performer to performer.

Swing music   The name given generally to the popular jazz of the 1930s and 1940s that prominently featured a swing rhythm.

Syllabic   A style of setting a text to music so that there is one note per syllable.

Syncopation   A type of rhythm in which the notes run against the regular pulse of the musical meter, with accents on beats other than the ones usually accented.

Syncretism   The combination of different forms of belief and practice.

Tabla   A set of two drums, struck with the fingertips, widely used in music of the Indian subcontinent.

Tag   In popular styles, a closing section that relies on extensive repetition of a short motive.

Tala   Fixed, repeated cycles of pulses widely used in music of the Indian subcontinent.

Tambura   A plucked stringed instrument similar to the sitar, used only to provide a drone in music of the Indian subcontinent.

Tempo rubato   In Italian, "robbed time." Subtle changes of tempo (speeding up and slowing down) applied by the performer, with expressive intent.

Ternary form   A form consisting of three parts, labeled **ABA**.

Terraced   Having a melody that moves up or down through a series of stages, remaining in one general area a while before moving to the next.

Texture   The number and general relationship of musical lines or voices to one another.

Theme and variations form   A form in which a theme is presented and then altered in some way—through harmony, melody, texture, dynamics, or some combination of these—in a succession of individual variations.

Through-composed   A form in which each section has its own music, with very little or no repetition between sections.

Timbre   The character or quality of a sound.

Tonal   A style of writing that establishes a central note (the tonic) as a harmonic and melodic center of gravity, which in turn creates the potential for a strong sense of resolution and closure.

Tonality   A system of organizing pitches (both melodies and harmonies) around a central note, as opposed to atonality, a system with no tonal center. See also "tonal" and "atonal."

Tonic   The note that establishes a key, based on its distinctive relationship with a particular set of harmonies or other notes in the underlying scale. Also, the chord based on the first scale degree.

Tremolo   Rapid repeated notes that produce a shivering or trembling sound.

Trio sonata   A work for two high-ranged instruments (such as two violins, or two oboes, or two flutes) and basso continuo.

Trio-sonata texture   A texture consisting of three main voices: two in the soprano range and one in the bass (the basso continuo).

Triple meter   An underlying pattern of rhythm in which each unit (measure) consists of one accented (strong) beat followed by two unaccented (weak) beats (**1**-2-3, **1**-2-3, **1**-2-3, etc.).

Trochaic   A poetic meter of LONG-short, LONG-short, etc.

Tutti   Italian for "all": the full ensemble (as opposed to a soloist).

Twelve-bar blues   A common model for blues songs, in which each verse consists of three lines of text over twelve measures of music. Each line receives four measures in a predetermined harmonic pattern using chords built on the first, fourth, and fifth scale degrees.

Twelve-tone composition   A type of serial composition in which twentieth-century composers manipulated a series ("row") consisting of all twelve notes of the chromatic scale, not repeating any one of these notes until all other eleven had been sounded, thereby effectively avoiding any sense of tonality.

Unison   More than one performer playing or singing the same pitch or pitches at the same time.

Vamp   To repeat a basic section of the music in order to fill time or provide a basis for improvisation.

Verse-chorus form   One of the simplest models in popular music. The chorus contains the main idea of the song, usually incorporating the title as well. When the chorus returns, it keeps the same text and music. Verses advance the plot, using the same music each time but different texts. Verse-chorus form can use any combination of verses and choruses, although the last unit will always be a chorus.

Vibraphone   A percussion instrument similar to the xylophone, with resonators that cause the pitches to vibrate.

Vocables   Meaningless sung syllables that take the place of song lyrics.

Voicing   The spacing of the individual notes in a chord.

Wavelength   The distance between peaks of sound waves.

Waza   An ensemble performed by the Berta people of the Blue Nile Province in southern Sudan, consisting of twelve trumpets made from gourds.

Whole step   Two half steps. On the piano, a whole step skips exactly one key, white or black.

Whole-tone scale   A scale with only whole steps, no half steps; this eliminates any sense of a tonal center.

Wind instrument   An instrument that produces sound when air passes through it.

Word painting   Music that imitates, describes, or conjures images of the text being sung.

Word-music relationships   The way a text influences our hearing of the music, and the way music affects our perception of the words.

Index